Into the Heart of the Fire

THE BRITISH IN
THE SPANISH CIVIL WAR

JAMES K. HOPKINS

Into the Heart of the Fire

THE BRITISH IN
THE SPANISH CIVIL WAR

STANFORD UNIVERSITY PRESS
STANFORD, CALIFORNIA
1998

Stanford University Press
Stanford, California

© 1998 by the Board of Trustees of the
Leland Stanford Junior University

Publication of this book is supported by a grant from
the Fund for Faculty Excellence of Dedman College,
Southern Methodist University

Printed in the United States of America

CIP data are at the end of the book

Last date below indicates year of this printing:
06 05 04 03 02 01 00 99 98

To Patti

Preface

The years reveal successively the true
Significance of all the casual shapes
Shown by the atlas.
The pages char and turn. Our memories
Fail. What emotions shook us in our youth
Are unimaginable as the truth
Our middle years pursue. And only pain
Of some disquieting vague variety gnaws,
Seeing a boy trace out a map of Spain.

— Roy Fuller

I

The lives of historians are necessarily complicit at some level in the history they choose to write. The existence of this book would be highly unlikely if I had not spent a number of months in El Salvador and Nicaragua from 1984 to 1990, where I had contact with the FMLN (Farabundo Martí Frente de Liberación Nacional) and the FSLN (Frente Sandinista de Liberación Nacional) revolutionary movements. During those years, I saw the tortuous dilemma faced by Central American intellectuals, particularly members of the clergy. Should they take up arms and join the conflict against those they judged to be oppressive? Or must they use their abilities in some alternative way to work toward social and economic justice for their people? In short, what kind of relationship should be struck between the intellectual life and moral and political engagement? Not least of all, could intellectuals genuinely "connect" with the illiterate, sub-literate, or newly literate poor who became the objects of their political devotions? And, conversely, could the poor discover new capacities for leadership and intellectual expression in this revolutionary world, which put them into startling and sympathetic new conjunctions with those of other classes?

I also came to know a number of the hundreds and then thousands of volunteers from a score of countries, including workers, intellectuals, students, and members of the professions, who in sometimes perilous circumstances organized work brigades in Nicaragua. Their purpose was to free governmental forces during the harvest season to fight in the war against the U.S.-backed *contras*. I particularly recall one night in the mountains outside of Matagalpa when a young North American volunteer improbably began singing the *Jarama*, the song most closely identified with the English-speaking XVth Brigade in the Spanish Civil War. More significantly, many of the intellectual and moral issues that emerged in my research on Spain possessed a haunting similarity to those I had encountered in Central America. In ways both explicit and implicit, "Spain" served as a "text" that gave an illumination to the shape and densities of my own experiences in a world whose architecture was inspired by an ardent social hope—but which at the same time was endangered not only by armed enemies from without but ideological ones from within. As a result, many determined their actions by the standards of revolutionary "necessity."

As I think back over those years in Central America, I remember Northrop Frye's remark that historical study can lead to a "recognition scene, a discovery in which we see, not our own past lives, but the total cultural form of our present life."[1] This study of the British in the Spanish Civil War has provided me with a number of such "recognition scenes," as well as an abundance of reflections on "present" life.

II

In their pioneering examination of the interwar period, *The Long Week-End*, Robert Graves and Alan Hodge agreed that the Spanish Civil War deeply affected "all intelligent people in Britain."[2] This book principally concerns middle-class and proletarian "thinkers" for whom the choice of Spain reflected a world of ideas, class, and politics that was intimately connected but has yet to be fully explored.

Against the backdrop of the Depression and the rise of fascism, the manner in which militants understood and responded to the political choices that lay before them became an issue of crucial importance. Because virtually all on the left, including proletarian intellectuals, were at least "vaguely Marxist," their vision of the "just" society was one in which class would be abolished and genuine egalitarianism achieved. A large radical intelligentsia emerged in the 1930s that made this vision fundamental to its politics.[3] My study will examine the particular forms this vision assumed and the strategies developed to realize them.

The second emphasis will be on class. In the thirties the "condition of the workers" was no longer an issue of individual or institutional benevolence or a more efficient and enlightened functioning of government. Instead, militant workers believed that they constituted the class on which history had conferred a unique prestige. It was the worker who would lead the way toward the emancipation of humankind from millennia of economic and political bondage.

Therefore, two issues faced middle-class intellectuals. First, how were they to relate their ideas to the great economic and political issues of the decade? Were they to stay in or out of the Ivory Tower (or perhaps work out some more ambiguous relationship between themselves and the great issues of the decade)? The second, according to Bernard Knox, was "the problem which gnawed at the conscience of English left-wing intellectuals all through the period: personal and social relationships with the working class."[4] But this last problem was also faced by the workers. From their point of view, what kinds of relationships between themselves and middle-class intellectuals were necessary in a revolutionary world whose topography had been mapped by Karl Marx? On this new terrain, the worker, not his middle-class counterpart, occupied the high ground.

The vision of equality between the classes, which was hardly new but had never appeared so ideologically persuasive, was to receive an extraordinary test in unique circumstances. Would the two classes meet on what the worker-poet, Laurie Lee, called a "common shore"? The answer came, however, not in a revolutionary Great Britain but rather in an embattled Spain. On July 17, 1936, General Francisco Franco and his supporters rose against the democratically elected Second Spanish Republic. The failure of the military rising led to three bloody years of civil war that galvanized the attention of men and women throughout the Western world. Both Hitler and Mussolini provided abundant support to General Franco in the form of arms, men, and matériel. The Soviet Union responded by selling military supplies to the Republic and instructing the Comintern to recruit and organize an international volunteer army as a counterweight to German and Italian intervention.

The International Brigades, as they came to be called, eventually numbered some 30,000 to 40,000 volunteers, drawn from more than fifty countries around the world.[5] The Brigades quickly achieved mythic status as our century's most conspicuous example of disinterested idealism. The British Battalion, which included more than 2,000 volunteers, formed part of the English-speaking XVth Brigade. After its formation, the battalion fought in every major campaign of the war. Some 85 percent of its members were killed or wounded.

On October 29, 1938, in Barcelona, Dolores Ibarruri, known throughout the world as La Pasionaria, cried out to the departing volunteers, "We shall not forget you."[6] But many of the early remembrances were distorted by the fact that Spain was endowed with a virtually talismanic significance on both ends of the political spectrum. Consequently, "large parts" of the contemporary versions of these events were so heavily colored, the volunteer Jason Gurney believes, that they are nothing more than "a farrago of nonsense which has, nevertheless, passed into the mythology of the war as established fact."[7] Fred Copeman, the irrepressibly truculent commander of the British Battalion, said, "I always believe that history is a lot of old hogwash. It's what everybody makes it at the time it's written or at the time they're discussing it." The ex-sailor believed, and no postmodernist would disagree, that history "changes according to who has the power to change it at the time."[8]

When sufficient time had passed for more objective assessments of these remarkable years, studies appeared about middle-class intellectuals and Spain,[9] and then, with the emergence of history "from below," attention turned toward working-class volunteers. In recent decades, particularly in the years around the fiftieth anniversary of the war, working-class veterans of the Spanish struggle have cooperated by compiling oral histories of their experiences or writing their memoirs.[10] Now, a unique opportunity exists to rejoin the middle- and working-class volunteers, united by a shared vision and engaged in a common struggle, in a history they made together but which, until now, has been written about as if their experiences had been independent of each other.

The definitive account of British military operations in Spain remains *British Volunteers for Liberty*. Its author, Bill Alexander, a gifted and brave man, became the assistant secretary of the British Communist party after an outstanding military career both in Spain and in World War II. In addition, Alexander has been for many years the head of the International Brigade Association in Great Britain. He wrote in his book, "I have tried to tell the real story."[11] But, epistemic considerations aside, how close did he come to accomplishing his goal?

I do not intend to slight the important contribution that *British Volunteers for Liberty* makes. No one but Alexander could have written it. Nevertheless, among other issues, it is important to recognize and put into perspective what he left out or evaded about the role of the Communist party in the battalion. I would, therefore, submit that his is not the "real story" of the British Battalion, and this is much truer of Bill Rust's earlier *Britons in Spain* (1939). Although separated by almost fifty years, in each book the party in the Popular Front years "is presented simply as the most forthright and most consistent opponent of appeasement," and "uncomfortable facts" are quite often omitted. Consequently, the historian Kevin Morgan believes, "It would be unwise to leave the history [of the British Communist Party] entirely in its own hands just yet."[12] This still must be said of the British Battalion. Volunteers who were members of the Labour party or the Independent Labour party, those who were political agnostics or had anarchist sympathies, those who disagreed with party decisions or simply were maladjusted to military service deserve their place in the history of the Britons in Spain, a place they have not yet found in "official" accounts. For more than sixty years, Rust and Alexander have been the keepers of the story by which they wanted the battalion to be remembered.[13]

This study will incorporate some familiar and many new voices of this exuberantly noisy decade with its endless contentions about what, it must be admitted, were the most important issues the modern world had yet faced. In addition to published compilations of oral history, the archives of British volunteers in Swansea, London, Manchester, Edinburgh, and Moscow allow scores of workers to speak at length about their experiences. Certainly, it is no longer true, as the critic Samuel Hynes once remarked, that the "text" of the thirties can be read only in the works of middle-class writers because the lives of workers "did not find expression in language."[14] The inarticulate and the silent have, at last, found their voices.

Care must be taken in listening to them, however. Unusual enmities and loyalties, both ideological and personal, can still be heard after half a century. In addition (need it be said), even among the most scrupulous and retentive, memories are inevitably only representations of a partially understood and experienced reality, and this is particularly true in the case of war, one of the most isolating and disorienting events to befall a human being. Nevertheless, I am reminded of Maurice Barings' introduction to his autobiography. The old Etonian, sometime diplomat, and writer said, "Memory . . . is the greatest of artists. It eliminates the unessential, and chooses with careless skill the sights and sounds and the episodes that are best worth remembering and recording."[15]

Despite La Pasionaria's claim and the emergence of long-silent voices, the once overwhelmingly dramatic appeal of the Spanish Civil War has dimmed for many. The historian Eric Hobsbawm writes, "What Spain meant to liberals and those on the Left who lived through the 1930s, is . . . difficult to remember. . . . It now seems to belong to a prehistoric past."[16] Kenneth Morgan sounded the lament that the "memories of the Spanish Civil War and the International Brigade [have been] largely forgotten, save by labour historians at the universities."[17] Some argue that even they have said all that is necessary about the struggle. Tom Buchanan discovered in the course of his research on *The Spanish Civil War and the British Labour Movement*, "I became inured to the comment that nothing new could be found to be said on this subject."[18]

Yet if dust has settled over these old events and long-ago dramas (as well as most of their protagonists), it continues, nevertheless, to be disturbed. And for good reason. The Spanish Civil War was an event with protean and still-evident implications for our century. First of all, it conclusively revealed the refusal of democratic governments to act against fascism in behalf of their very survival; the Spanish Republic became part of the ransom paid by Great Britain and France to avoid confrontation with German and Italian totalitarianism, a policy that led finally to the most devastating war in human history. Second, Spain offered a bloody miniature of the titanic struggle between the left and the right that has absorbed the productive energies of most of the twentieth century. Third, the civil war in Spain challenged thousands of individuals to act independently from the policies of their governments. This suggested a critical distancing from and skepticism about institutional authority that have become enduring features of modern society. If governments were perceived to lie or to overlook economic injustice or political oppression, or in their timidity even to ignore their best interests, individuals still believed there was a public space in which they might join words and action.

III

In addition to studying the tentative junctions between words and action in the thirties, and hearing new voices challenge long-settled perspectives on a familiar landscape, the Spanish Civil War offers an unusual opportunity to examine the effect of politics and war on both elite and popular culture. The military historian, Michael Howard, has complained that cultural historians such as Paul Fussell, Samuel Hynes, Roland Stromberg, Robert Wohl, and Modris Eckstein have studied principally the impact of war in our century on high culture. He writes, "We still need to know how this high culture related to, and affected, popular culture and popular consciousness, if such studies are to be more than contributions to the history of ideas, rather than explanations of events."[19]

Therefore, popular as well as elite aesthetic representations will occupy a prominent place in this narrative. Gerald Brenan refused the youthful Raymond Carr's invitation to write the volume on Spain in the *Oxford History of Europe* because, he told Carr (who would ultimately write that book), "You can't get at the truth by history: you can only get at it through novels."[20] And one might add poetry, film, art, radio, personal recollections, and any other means men and women might choose to reflect their experiences during the thirties.

However, a "greater mystery" in getting at the truth, said Michael Jackson in his recent history of the International Brigades, "revolves around the relationship between middle-class intellectuals in the International Brigades and members of the working class."[21] The assumption has been that the interests between the two, if both shared a common political vision of society, would ultimately converge. As Tom Buchanan comments, "The usual context for studying this subject has been one that portrays the Civil War as the 'last great cause,' a radicalizing force uniting intellectuals and workers which generated mass enthusiasm in Britain."[22] This study will analyze this and other "mysteries" and, in doing so, discover members of the middle class and workers in critical and often overlapping relationships with each other, and with Spain. Paradoxically, the focus will sharpen further by expanding the traditional meaning of an "intellectual" and examining men and women of ideas regardless of class, whether Oxbridge aesthetes or accomplished autodidacts from the factories, mines, or the ranks of the unemployed.

This effort will be aided by new sources, which should put to rest some of the most egregious myth-making surrounding the foreign participation in the war. Michael Jackson observed that the "literature shows too little demonstrable interest in questioning and establishing facts to curtail myth." Moreover, he speculates that "if a cache of hitherto hidden documents about the International Brigades were unearthed, it would receive a mixed reception." Jackson believes that the legends surrounding the volunteers who fought in Spain are still too adhesive to be stripped away, even with the aid of new evidence. This belief can now also be tested. Just such a cache has appeared, and it will be up to the reader to determine if the myths about the International Brigades, in general, or the particular subject of this book, the British volunteers, will continue to survive. Ironically, this study will challenge Jackson's reinvigorated myth that the volunteers from the democracies, including Great Britain, were "marginal" men and social misfits.[23]

The newly opened archive of the International Brigades in the Russian Center for the Preservation and Study of Recent Historical Documents in Moscow contains materials long thought to have been destroyed. They do much to fill in the story that is already known in broad outline, and must have been known in detail by the leaders of the British Communist party. For example, few of the dissident volunteers could have defied Bill Rust's description of them as being "politically unreliable." But the purpose of Rust and his comrades, the files tell us, was more insidious; they sought to vilify any who challenged the communist line as "traitors" or "Trotskyists" or "cowards," or consign them contemptuously to what quickly became an omnibus category, that of "deserters."

Without impugning the idealism or heroism of those volunteers who explicitly or implicitly accepted communist domination of the British Battalion, I will offer evidence that supports Valentine Cunningham's contention that "truth . . . was deliberately and cynically distorted" in order to glorify the role of the Communist party.[24] I not only join Cunningham in resisting those who accuse him of unfairly criticizing the party, but will argue why his position is much closer to the truth than that of his critics.[25]

This book, then, will attempt to locate *both* working- and middle-class militants in the complex political and intellectual culture of the thirties, first in Great Britain and later in Spain. The book's outline can be quickly sketched. It is divided into three parts; the first two will attempt to establish British middle-class and proletarian intellectuals of the left in a meaningful political, cultural, and social context during the thirties. How did these men and women conceptualize and fulfill their relationship with political life? The third part focuses explicitly on the war itself. The rhetoric of solidarity would receive its great test *across* the Spanish frontier and finally resolve the question of whether a genuine "connection" between the classes could be reestablished for the first time in almost 150 years.

The cause of Spain in the 1930s evoked many of the same hopes and disappointments of a political unity between the classes, and the resulting creation of a new polity, as did that of the French Revolution in the 1790s. The English Jacobins—men such as the corsetmaker's son Thomas Paine, the shoemaker Thomas Hardy, the autodidact Thomas Holcroft, the attorney John Frost, Major Cartwright, and the poet, elocutionist, and friend of Wordsworth and Coleridge, John Thelwall — composed "an intellectual generation which had identified its beliefs in too ardent and utopian a way with the cause of France." E. P. Thompson believed that "the unity between intellectual and plebeian reformers of 1792 was never to be regained."[26] The 1930s, however, would offer a reprise of the 1790s. The poets and writers John Cornford, Julian Bell, George Orwell, Tom Wintringham, and Christopher Caudwell found in Spain a common cause with the East End garment workers Sam Masters and Nat Cohen, the boilermaker and communist leader Harry Pollitt, the ex-sailor and building worker Fred Copeman, the Liverpool docker Jack Jones—as well as similar disappointments.[27]

But if these "volunteers for liberty," so long immured in hagiography or demonology, depending on the point of view of the observer, are to speak to us today, we must understand the way in which they saw the great issues of their time. In so doing, we can see what measures of wisdom and folly there are for us to find in their bitter courage, self-sacrifices, and self-deceptions. This requires a voyage of our own. Upon landfall, we will see what it meant, in an uncertain and fractious world hurtling toward mass slaughter, to encounter the poet Laurie Lee sitting in a dark church on the eve of battle, his upturned face intermittently illuminated under a string of light bulbs, welcoming unfamiliar comrades. Lee remembers, "Some new Americans and British had joined our company. Wine was brought in, and we began to use the altar as a kind of bar. We were young and, as I remember, direct and trusting, even in our fights and excesses. Among us the young Spanish peasant, American student, Welsh miner, Liverpool dock-worker had met on a common shore."[28]

Despite all the political pedantry, the presence of the occasional adventurer, the often homicidal madness of the communists, and the inevitable savageries and brutalities that accompany the actions of human beings in a civil war, many of these men and women were the best of their time, and they have much to tell us still. This book will study particularly compelling examples of their stories, stories that were meant to evoke a sense of personal awakening to the realization of a larger and more generous concept of human existence, one that could bring a unique purpose and meaning to life and death—but also stories that manipulated and exploited those same sacrifices for purposes unintended by their victims. Perhaps, most importantly, the experiences of the British volunteers offer a unique opportunity for a case study of the relationship between theory and praxis, between the idea of radical democracy or socialism and its lived reality in a distinctively British political culture on the battlefields of Spain.

Acknowledgments

I am grateful for grants from the American Council of Learned Societies, Southern Methodist University's Fund for Faculty Excellence, its Office of Research and Administration, and SMU's Dedman College, which supported my research and writing. I wish to thank particularly the librarians and staff of the University's Fondren and Bridwell Libraries for their many and varied contributions to this book. Billie Stovall of the Interlibrary Loan office gave unfailingly helpful and sympathetic support over the years. I am also in debt to the staffs of the special collections at Brandeis University, the University of California at San Diego, Columbia University, the New York Public Library, and the University of Texas at Austin.

In London, I was equally well served by those of the British Library, the Communist Party Library, the Imperial War Museum (Sound Records Collection), the Labour Party Library, the Public Record Office, and, most significantly, the Marx Memorial Library in Clerkenwell Green, where the archives of the British Battalion are preserved. Maurice Pearton's friendship, learning, and assistance over many years meant more than he could ever know. Courtney Pinkerton interrupted her year abroad studies at the London School of Economics to resolve several important research issues.

The Manchester Studies Department of Manchester Metropolitan University, the Manchester City Library, and the Working Class Movement Library in Salford provided invaluable resources. I remember with particular warmth the assistance and hospitality I received from Hywel Francis and the staff of the South Wales Miners' Library in Swansea.

In Moscow, the librarians and staff of the Russian Center for the Preservation and Study of Recent Historical Documents cheerfully provided me with invaluable guidance under exceedingly trying circumstances. I am especially indebted to Leonid Waintraub for offering me his friendship, his compendious knowledge of the Russian archives, and, more practically, lodging during a lengthy stay in Moscow.

The Biblioteca Nacional and the Hemeroteca Municipal in Madrid possessed important contextual materials for this study. Tom Entwistle proved an irrepressibly stimulating and skillful guide to many of the battlefields where the British fought. Because of him, the Casa de Campo, University City, the valley of the Jarama, Brunete, Belchite, Pulburrel Hill east of Quinto, the Ebro, and Hills 666 and 481 in the Aragón became integral parts of my life. Ramón Buckley, Lourdes González-Bueno, and Casto Fernández lived the consequences of the Republic's defeat but, like so many Spaniards, refused themselves to be defeated. This book is meant, in part, to commemorate their victory.

I cannot express sufficiently my gratitude to my splendid colleagues in the Department of History at Southern Methodist University whose teaching and scholarship have been a continuing source of inspiration to me. I am particularly grateful to Ed Countryman, Tom Knock, John Mears, Dan Orlovsky, Bill Taylor, David Weber, and Kathleen Wellman for their friendship and counsel at crucial junctures in the writing of this book. Standish Meacham of the University of Texas at Austin took time from a busy schedule to offer early and cogent criticism. Norris Pope, the Director of Stanford University Press, gave me the confidence that this book had a future. His colleague, Peter Kahn, has exhibited quite extraordinary patience and skill in overseeing the long journey to print. Peter Smith has been the most tactful, efficient, and able of editors. Finally, over the many years of research and writing, my students incomparably sustained, stimulated, and enriched my life. Moreover, their gentle but persistent inquiries—"When will the book be finished?"—undoubtedly helped ensure that it would be.

My greatest debt, however, is to my family, especially Eric, Fiona, Cathy, Tod, and, most of all, to my wife, Patti LaSalle, to whom this book is dedicated. Her patience, love, and, not least, her wise editorial counsel, are present on every page. Most of all, she understood why the book was written.

J. K. H.

Contents

12 pages of illustrations follow page 178

Chronology

1924
First Labour government

1926
General Strike

1929–31
Second Labour government

1931
Formation of the National Government
Invergordon Mutiny

1932
Oswald Mosley's New Party becomes the British Union of Fascists
Publication of Strachey's *The Coming Struggle for Power*

1934
Revolt in Asturias
Fifth National Hunger March to London

1935
Clement Attlee elected leader by parliamentary Labour party

1936
February 16
Popular Front wins general election

July 17
    Generals' rebellion against the Second Republic
September 9
    Non-Intervention Committee convenes in London
October 4
    "Battle of Cable Street"
October 12
    International Brigades formed
November 8
    Arrival of XIth International Brigade in Madrid
December 17–19
    Counterattack at Boadilla del Monte by XI and XII International Brigades
December 24
    No. 1 Company, commanded by George Nathan, departs for Lopera on Córdoba front

1937
    Publication of Spender's *Forward from Liberalism*
January 9
    British government raises threat of prosecution of volunteers under Foreign Enlistment Act
January 31
    Formation of XVth International Brigade (which included the British Battalion)
February 12
    British Battalion goes into its first battle at Jarama
May 4–7
    POUM crushed in Barcelona
May 17–18
    Negrín succeeds Largo Caballero as prime minister
July 6–26
    British Battalion in action in the Brunete Offensive
August 24
    British Battalion at Quinto in Aragón Offensive

1938
    January 19
    British Battalion joins the defense of Teruel

February 16

British Battalion in attack on Segura de los Baños

March 9

Beginning of the Retreats

April 15

General Franco's forces reach the Mediterranean, cutting the Republic in two

July 25

British Battalion joins the Ebro offensive

July 27

British Battalion launches first assault on Hill 481 outside Gandesa

September 21

Prime Minister Negrín announces the withdrawal of all international volunteers

September 22

Last battle of the British Battalion in Sierra del Lavall

September 29–30

Chamberlain at Munich

October 29

Farewell parade for International Brigades in Barcelona

December 7

Arrival of British Battalion at Victoria Station

The ideas of economists and political philosophers, both when they are right and when they are wrong, are more powerful than is commonly understood. Indeed the world is ruled by little else. . . . I am sure that the power of vested interests is vastly exaggerated compared with the gradual encroachment of ideas.

— John Maynard Keynes

If you belong to the bourgeoisie, don't be too eager to bound forward and embrace your proletarian brothers; they may not like it, and if they show that they don't like it you will probably find that your class-prejudices are not so dead as you imagined. And if you belong to the proletariat, by birth or in the sight of God, don't sneer too automatically at the Old School Tie; it covers loyalties which can be useful to you if you know how to handle them.

— George Orwell

'What's your proposal? To build the just city? I will.
I agree. Or is it the suicide pact, the romantic
    Death? Very well, I accept, for
I am your choice, your decision. Yes, I am Spain.'

— W. H. Auden

Introduction
Myths and Memorials

We heard the blood-lust of a drunkard pile
   His heaven high with curses;
And next day took the boat
   For home, forgetting Spain, not realising
That Spain would soon denote
   Our grief, our aspirations;
Not knowing that our blunt
   Ideals would find their whetstone, that our spirit
Would find its frontier on the Spanish front,
   Its body in a rag-tag army.   — Louis MacNeice

I have . . . got the job of writing a history of the [British Battalion] and it is not an easy one I can assure you. . . . I would be very grateful if you and some of the lads out there could write out some of your experiences and accounts of incidents that took place. Do it in odd moments. With all this collective work on the book I am sure that it could become a real memorial to one of the greatest things that has ever happened in the history of British workers.
— Bill Rust

I

In recent years, historians have vigorously attacked the "myth" of the "hungry thirties" or the "low dishonest decade" or the "devil's decade." Instead of these dismal judgments, they remind us that the majority of the population was working and, moreover, was enjoying an unprecedentedly high standard of living.[1] One of the many literary itinerants of the period, J. B. Priestley, described this England as one "of arterial and by-pass roads, filling stations and factories that look like exhibition buildings, of giant cinemas and dance-halls and cafes, bungalows with tiny garages, cocktail bars, Woolworths, motor coaches, wireless, hiking, factory girls looking like actresses, grey-hound racing and dirt tracks, swimming pools, and everything given away for cigarette coupons."[2] Vulgar and uninspiring as this description may be, it illustrates the significant degree of prosperity and satisfaction that prevailed among the majority of the population. Political and economic discontents were recognized, of course, but, it is argued, they should not be allowed to distort the shape of a decade that was presided over by a competent if unimaginative National Government.

There was, of course, another England to be found; that is, if one chose to take the road to Wigan or any of the other routes of access into the distressed areas of South Wales, Lancashire, or the Clydeside, among others. In 1932, unemployment reached its high of 2,745,000 in the interwar years. By then, it has been estimated that 35 percent of the miners, 48 percent of steelworkers, and 62 percent of shipbuilders were without work.[3] Philip Bagwell, a historian who lived through the thirties, has suggested that if a student of the period were to say to "an older generation miner of the Rhondda, or cotton operative of Oldham, or boilermaker of Jarrow that the 1930s were prosperous [it] would be to invite unprintable language."[4]

David Goodman, a commercial traveler from Middlesbrough who fought in Spain, knew this England well, and judged: "Mass unemployment, economic depression and harsh treatment for the victims of Government policies were the hallmark of the period."[5] His views were shared by Harold Horne of Luton, who had been involved in protests against unemployment before joining the Communist party in 1930. "After six months drawing unemployment, you had to go on the relief, either to the workhouse or getting food tickets for things like bread, margarine and dripping, enough to keep you alive perhaps." Without work for three years, he was subsequently imprisoned for hitting a policeman, and afterwards left for Spain, saying, "I have a real hatred of oppression."[6] Bill Feeley, who worked in a bottle works in St. Helens and subsequently fought and was wounded in Spain, confirmed the experiences of his comrades: "It was a period of poverty, slums, works and pit closures, vicious means-tests and hunger marches."[7]

Most of the workers who went to Spain were on intimate terms with the conditions described by Goodman, Horne, and Feeley. Nor was the more fortunate Great Britain wholly unaware of their suffering. Julian Bell, the son of Clive and Vanessa Bell and nephew of Virginia Woolf, signaled his growing independence from the self-absorbed attitudes of Bloomsbury by recognizing this other England:

Down the black streets, dark with unwanted coal
The harassed miners wait the grudging dole;
The sinking furnaces, their fires damped down,
Depress to poverty the hopeless town. . . .

On every hand the stagnant ruin spreads,
And closed are shops and fact'ries, mines and sheds.[8]

A number of the inhabitants of the England of the dole queue, the means test, and the hunger marches, as well as those who were politically awakened by their suffering, formed a small but militant fraction of the British working and middle classes. They linked domestic with foreign oppression and achieved a genuinely radical, even revolutionary, vision of change. By 1936, the volunteers for Spain, regardless of the extent of their militancy, believed that their England suffered from the evident economic oppression of capitalism and the threat of political oppression by fascism. Mussolini had been in power for a decade. In his search for recognition and prestige, he had invaded Abyssinia in October 1935, almost three years after Hitler had come to power in Germany. Moreover, Sir Oswald Mosley's British Union of Fascists proved that not even Great Britain was immune to fascism's appeal.

There are those who believe, however, that too much attention has been lavished on this small, radicalized population of workers and their middle-class allies. "Measured in sheer numbers," John Stevenson has written, "the trade unions and the Labour Party remained the 'big battalions' of working-class political allegiance."[9] Nevertheless, this militant minority wielded a wholly disproportionate influence on the thirties. It became the catalyst for a host of initiatives that directly or indirectly challenged the domestic and foreign policies of both the Conservative and Labour parties. Further, Marxism gave their views a sophisticated ideological content—no matter how imperfectly understood or idiosyncratically interpreted—that was unlike that of earlier British radicalism, and, in a number of instances, brought a new conceptual coherence to their politics. Particularly susceptible to Marx's scientific appeal were young middle-class and proletarian intellectuals. Frustrated, however, by their inability to make significant headway against the Conservative governments of Baldwin and Chamberlain, and with the moderate Labour party, they and their comrades made the fate of the Spanish Republic, not a socialist Great Britain, their cause.

The more than 2,000 British who volunteered to serve in Spain saw themselves primarily as the manifestations of a certain core of political ideas, which could collectively be called antifascism. For many, including George Orwell, antifascism possessed a sublime simplicity, which was at once impressive and, as it turned out, dangerously naive.[10] For others, the decision to go to Spain possessed more complex ideological nuance, and with it, often inadvertent but ominous human implication.

Once in Spain, the battles fought by the international volunteers took place in cities and villages and across the great sierras, everywhere a modern nation struggled to be born. And their enemies were formidable. An extraordinary coalition of medieval and contemporary authoritarianism, led by General Francisco Franco, sought to still the birth cries of the Popular Front government elected in February 1936. The Popular Front attempted through democratic reforms to limit the power of the Church, to encourage Catalán and Basque nationalism, to address the fantastic inequities between the rich and the poor (particularly in the countryside), and to end the military's ability to take power by *pronunciamiento*. The center-left government was, however, crippled by its internecine antagonisms, and, morever, had succeeded in alienating the hegemonic trinity of the great landowners, the Church, and the army; in doing so, the government threatened the vision of a unified, Catholic Spain in which the ascendancy of the historic triumvirate was part of the natural order.

The Spanish struggle between the left and the right was to have profound international implications. Quickly into the conflict were Hitler and Mussolini, the first for reasons of ideology and the second in pursuit of strategic advantage against the liberal democracies. Watching, too, was Stalin, who carefully calculated how his own interests might best be served in this remote country.[11]

II

Any new study of the British who fought in Spain must be alert to old mythologies that still retain a remarkable resilience. One that asserts itself irrepressibly is that Spain was a poet's and a writer's war.[12] It is understandable that scholars have emphasized the role of middle-class intellectuals. George Seldes, a scrupulous reporter in Spain, wrote, "The overwhelming majority of the writers, poets, artists . . . of the world were committed to the Spanish cause, and not only did they vote for it, speak for it and raise money for it, but also thousands in a score of countries enlisted and fought for it."[13] But their sacrifices alone do not explain why they dominated the historiography of the struggle for such a preternaturally long time.

Jason Gurney, a sculptor who volunteered for Spain, offers the most obvious explanation. "The myth of an army of middle-class writers and poets has arisen from the . . . fact that these were the most vocal section of the organization and that their work forms the easiest form of source material for writers of a later generation."[14] Therefore, those who used their "voices," as did soldier-writers such as Esmond Romilly, Keith Scott Watson, Tom Wintringham, and George Orwell, effectively eclipsed the experiences and views of those who formed the majority of the volunteers. Arthur Koestler neatly and cynically demonstrates Gurney's point:

> Spain became the rendezvous of the international Leftist bohemia. Bloomsbury and Greenwich Village went on a revolutionary junket; poets, novelists, journalists and art students flocked across the Pyrenees to attend writers' congresses, to bolster morale on the front by reading their works from mobile loudspeaker vans to the militia-men, to accept highly paid, though short-lived, jobs in one of the numerous radio and propaganda departments, and "to be useful," as the phrase went, on all kinds of secret, undefinable errands.[15]

But in addition to unconscious self-aggrandizement, there was a second reason why middle-class intellectuals unintentionally consigned workers to anonymity. Poets and writers took a proprietary attitude toward Spain, in spite of or because of the unique status given workers by Marxism. They measured their own political self-importance against the fact that workers seemed such a strange and remote species, and could be conveniently and impersonally classified as the "proletariat." Allen Tate wrote in *New Verse*, "The well-brought up young men discovered that people work in factories and mines, and they want to know more about the people. But it seems to me that instead of finding out about them, they write poems calling them comrades from a distance."[16] After Julian Bell was elected secretary of the local Labour party organization in Glynde, not far from Charleston (where he spent much of his youth), in February 1932, he wrote to a friend, "The people are nice," and moreover, "seem ready to treat me as an ordinary human being—tho I am still horribly shy of them."[17]

In short, workers or "the people" were seen as a category, not individuals joined in a common struggle. There are several reasons for this. By the end of the nineteenth century the Education Act of 1870 and succeeding legislation had brought universal education to the British people, and with it, for the first time, mass literacy.[18] Culture was no longer defined by the educated elite. A vast new reading audience emerged with its own aesthetic tastes and intellectual needs. And not only were an unprecedented number of people reading, but new readers were reproducing themselves at a prodigious rate.

These two developments—mass literacy and the huge increase in population—inspired contempt and fear among the middle classes: contempt for the debased tastes of the newly literate and fear for their own hegemony in culture and politics. "Universal education," according to Aldous Huxley, "has created an immense class of what I may call the New Stupid."[19] While canvassing for the Labour party in Birmingham only a few weeks before his departure for Spain, and four years after his organizational work among the Glynde Labour supporters, Julian Bell referred to the workers as "just lumpish and dull."[20] Beatrice Webb genuinely found them contemptible. She was distressed by what she considered a lack of mental alertness and was horrified by their informal attitudes toward sexuality. She wrote, "To us, public affairs seem gloomy; the middle classes are materialistic, and the working classes stupid, and in large sections sottish, with no interest except in racing odds."[21] This is not far from the view of Virginia Woolf, who spoke of "self-taught" working men, "and we all know how distressing they are, how egotistic, insistent, raw, striking, and ultimately nauseating."[22]

In addition, many intellectuals feared that the emergence of a mass society with its own politics and culture might render them ineffectual and unnecessary. Beatrice and Sidney Webb's Benthamite[23] and positivist views happily led them to the conclusion that middle-class intellectuals would be required to understand and implement the political and economic solutions required by society,[24] thus supplying the necessary reassurance that they were equipped to play an important and relevant role in shaping the future. This also helps explain why George Orwell wrote that "during the Spanish Civil War the left-wing intellectuals felt that this was 'their' war."[25]

John Carey has argued that in addition to feeling contempt, fear, or insecurity about the intellectual's role in society's future, there was yet another strategy—to neutralize the threat the masses represented by sentimentalizing them. Figures such as the early Fabians, William Morris, George Gissing, H. G. Wells, Eric Gill, D. H. Lawrence, E. M. Forster, and George Orwell in *1984* (through his character, Winston) invented a form of the pastoral or "cult of the peasant" which had this effect. English intellectuals on the left adopted an urban variation of this by interpreting the masses "as stalwart workers or as the downtrodden and the oppressed." In January 1937, Charles Madge, a communist poet, and Tom Harrison, an anthropologist, established "Mass-Observation," an effort to apply scientific methodology to the study of "Mass-Man" by observing him in his many manifestations. As Neal Wood has written, "The very involvement in observing, compiling, and synthesizing facts [about the masses] was an emotional therapeutic."[26] These human beings inhabited a world, as Wells put it, "outside the range of ruling-class dreams, that multitudinous greater England, cheaply treated, rather out of health, angry, energetic, and now becoming intelligent and critical; that England which organized industrialism has created."[27]

In short, to understand why British middle-class intellectuals distanced themselves from workers, making "connecting" in the Forsterian sense[28] that much more difficult, it is necessary to recognize their reluctance to individuate those who made up the awesome new demographic reality that threatened traditional cultural and political forms. Workers would remain unthreatening and unknown, as long as they were consigned to cliché and stereotype. By separating themselves as a class from "the people of the abyss," as Jack London most famously called them, intellectuals were able to emphasize and legitimate their own superior qualities. James Hanley, the author of *Grey Children*, became particularly aware of the phenomenon on his visit to South Wales. What intellectuals on the left and right had in common, he believed, was that neither saw the workers for the individuals that they were, but rather as statistics or abstractions. "Men and women and children are problems, things. Feeling doesn't enter into the matter at all." A miner told him that "we're about fed up with people coming down here looking us over as though we were animals in a zoo."[29]

We now have a restored text that will allow a more closely mediated relationship with the lived experience of these often fiercely individual men and women in the thirties. And emendations are certainly necessary. Many have subscribed, to one degree or another, to the simple but compelling communist narrative that the Comintern forged a volunteer army of idealists and heroes from every group and class on the left, all of whom would willingly give their lives to defeat fascism while successfully suppressing their political and class differences in a united or popular front against Franco, Hitler, and Mussolini.[30] There is certainly a genuine measure of truth in this statement. But, to put it another way, there is more that is true than has been written. For example, in a photograph taken of a demonstration in February 1939 by the International Brigaders' Anti-Communist League, a worker holds a large sign that reads, "We Who Fought in the International Brigade Give You the Truth." Behind him is a demonstrator who carries a poster with the words, "Why Silence about Communist Spanish Atrocities[?]"[31] Theirs are the haunting obverse faces of those who swagger through the bravura accounts of the British in Spain, and little attention has been paid to them.[32]

Bill Rust, a correspondent for the *Daily Worker* in Spain and the author of *Britons in Spain*, explained the presence of the demonstrators in this manner. During the war he wrote that some British volunteers failed to live up to what was expected of them, which was certainly true. But, he continued shamelessly, "War has its seamy side, and some weak vessels who break under the strain return to cadge a few coppers from the gutter press by slandering the comrades they have so meanly deserted. Let them snivel, they will soon be forgotten."[33] His prophecy came true. But many of these "weak vessels" deserted in Spain, or returned to Great Britain embittered by their experiences, because of the ruthless behavior of party leaders like Rust, and they should be forgotten no longer. Prominent among them in the British Battalion, because their views defied the master narrative of the party, were those of independent mind. They have been written out of its history because they dared to criticize the leadership or the party line or the hypocrisies of a proletarian army that developed its own class system and even totalitarian tendencies.

The omission of workers from their own history was understandably difficult for them to accept. Syd Quinn, an ex-soldier and Hunger Marcher, fought at the early battle of Lopera in December 1936, where the novelist Ralph Fox and the poet John Cornford, died. He recognized their deaths as a "tragic loss." But Quinn told an interviewer, "Against the Cornfords and Foxes there are many other fine fellows who lost their lives in the first action." Then, Quinn pointedly remarked that he would not have his working-class comrades denied their "glory."[34] Something similar must have been felt by Tony Hyndman, a young worker and poet who fought at the Jarama and whose plight brought his friend, the middle-class writer Stephen Spender, rushing out to rescue him from the clutches of the Communist party. Years later Hyndman's patron wrote that "in the thirties antifascism was predominantly a reaction of middle-class young men brought up in a liberal atmosphere against the old men in power, of the same class, who while talking about freedom and democracy, were not prepared to denounce Hitler or defend the Spanish Republic."[35]

For Spender, the "real" thirties belonged to John Cornford, Christopher Caudwell, Tom Wintringham, Ralph Fox, and Julian Bell—middle-class writers all, four of whom died in Spain.[36] As I hope to demonstrate, any discussion of the "real" thirties will prove manifestly inadequate if it does not include those workers, like Hyndman, for whom "ideas and action were [equally] inseparable," and who as a class were overwhelmingly in the majority among British volunteers who fought in Spain.

III

Those who believe either that the Spanish War elicits the nostalgia of youthful idealism or is remembered today only because of the self-serving toil of professional historians may be surprised at the sense of urgency and fascination it can still evoke. The decade of the thirties, so different in its political enthusiasms from the Reaganism and Thatcherism whose legacies are with us still, makes new claims on our attention. This is, in part, because of the half-century commemorations held in 1986, and also, I would argue, because generations that were not alive in the thirties have discovered something of importance for themselves in the Spanish Civil War, as they face the forging of their own political relationships with their respective societies. Vincent Sheean wrote in 1939 that although the International Brigades counted for comparatively few in the Popular Army, "In the long epic of the war they not only did more than their material share, but suffused the total effort with a moral value more precious than their lives, the sense of a world not altogether lost, of peoples not completely stultified by their governments, of a common conscience in which whatever hope there is for any possible future must rise again."[37]

Even taking into consideration the contributions of the Italians and Germans to Franco's victory, and that of the Russians to the defense of the Republic, ultimately it seemed that the war's outcome would be decided by the conscious action of individual men and women. This was far different from the attitudes of those in World War II and the Cold War. To many of them, individuals seemed hostage to the overwhelming influence of technology and the ratiocinations of their leaders in Washington, London, Paris, or Moscow. Everyone remembers the culmination of this attitude of impotence and emptiness, Jimmy Porter's famous lament in John Osborne's *Look Back in Anger*: "There aren't any good, brave causes left. If the big bang does come, and we all get killed off, it won't be in aid of the old-fashioned, grand design . . . [but] about as pointless and inglorious as stepping in front of a bus."[38] It should also be remembered that this had not been the attitude of Jimmy's father, a veteran of Spain.

As he looked back, Stephen Spender wrote, "The 1930s saw the last of the idea that the individual, accepting his responsibilities, could alter the history of the time. From now on, the individual could only conform to or protest against events which were outside his control."[39] Spender continued, "This was one of those intervals of history in which the events make the individual feel that he counts. His actions or his failure to act could lead to the winning or the losing of the Spanish Civil War, could even decide whether or not there was going to be a Second World War."[40] "The Spanish Civil War," according to the volunteer Jason Gurney, "seemed to provide the chance for a single individual to take a positive and effective stand on an issue which appeared to be absolutely clear."[41]

The belief that an individual might still make a difference also profoundly affected working-class militants. Kenneth Bradbury, a typesetter from Oldham, left his job and went to Spain, where he was killed at the fierce winter battle of Teruel in January 1938. Bradbury wrote before his death that the "one thing Spain has done" was to give him "a lot more confidence," enabling him to have "a real say in the future shape of the world."[42] The itinerant poet, musician, and laborer, Laurie Lee, arrived in Spain in December 1937, after the battles around Madrid and before Teruel. He felt that an exclusive motive drew volunteers from his generation to Spain: "In our case," Lee said, "we shared something . . . unique to us at that time—the chance to make one grand, uncomplicated gesture of personal sacrifice and faith which might never occur again."[43]

Both middle- and working-class volunteers, therefore, believed that events had not yet exceeded their capacity to control them. What else, in the final analysis, can explain the decision made by the Clydesider, a miner from the Rhondda, an Oxbridge undergraduate, an East End tradesman or a boilermaker from Manchester to go to Spain? They left all that was familiar and took passage to a country that they could reach, in most cases, only by climbing the Pyrenees at night in circumstances of intense danger. It was a country whose history they did not know, and whose language they did not speak or write. If they lived long enough, and threw off the chrysalis of their illusions, they would find themselves caught in a political world more labyrinthine than they could ever have imagined or fully understood at the time.

These volunteers believed that Madrid would become the "tomb of fascism," as La Pasionaria promised, and that their presence might well decide the final outcome of the struggle. But they soon came to realize that the human cost would be dear. After the early days, volunteers knew that it was statistically probable that for all the fearful idealism that drove them to Spain, they might well find their last resting place in a mass grave, if the killing was sufficiently prodigious, or perhaps in forgotten solitude in a Spanish olive grove.[44]

The lasting appeal of Spain, then, is the belief that, despite the most improbable of odds and against every evidence, the individual can still affect the character of his times. Certainly, this was the principal attraction of Central America for *internacionalistas*. "For many European intellectuals," the historian James Wilkinson wrote in 1988, "Spain in the late 30s became a test of their own moral convictions . . . much like Nicaragua or South Africa today."[45] Another historian recently spoke along similar lines. "Spain became a prototype and a precedent for [future] involvement."[46] For example, one of the international work brigades formed in Nicaragua during the 1980s included volunteers from eighteen countries.[47] Their purpose was to protest U.S. efforts to overthrow the revolutionary Sandinista government. When asked his motives, a young international volunteer leaving Managua for the north of the country shouted to a reporter, "It's [just] like the Spanish Civil War."[48]

And to many it seemed so. La Pasionaria's famous slogan, *No Pasarán*, which had so inspired the defenders of Madrid in 1936, appeared almost everywhere in Nicaragua. A number of Spanish veterans, in fact, joined the *brigadistas*, seeing a direct link with their own experiences of half a century before. Lou Gordon, an American who had served in the Abraham Lincoln Brigade, reported that Nicaragua offered "the most dramatic deja-vu imaginable. I was suddenly transported back to . . . 1937 Spain."[49] The British volunteer, Dave Goodman, wrote, "Nicaragua is a key focal point today which in many ways evokes a response recalling that [of] the war in Spain."[50] In 1989 two British International Brigaders presented a check for £1,000 "to the people of Nicaragua." They explained, "We see it as our international duty—just as we did in Spain—to stand firm . . .

with the Nicaraguan people in their fight against external aggression."[51]

And there are more recent claims on individual conscience. The American writer, Susan Sontag, an inspiring artistic and personal presence during the siege of Sarajevo in 1993, wrote that the plight of the once beautiful city "is the Spanish Civil War of our time." Unconsciously repeating the legend, she asked, where are the intellectuals?[52]

IV

Both middle- and working-class volunteers, and the hundreds of thousands who actively supported them, saw the Spanish drama as a vivid morality play requiring that sides be chosen. There would be no acceptable intermediate positions between the antipodes of democracy (a coded word that also could signify socialism/communism) and fascism. Even one so discriminating as Stephen Spender could write in 1937 that Spain was a country in which "the issues are so clear and direct in a world which has accustomed us to confusion and obscurity."[53] The young Spender saw in the great German novelist, Thomas Mann, views similar to his own. Mann regarded "the Spanish Civil War as a microcosm of a Manichean conflict between the forces of good and evil in the contemporary world."[54]

The attitudes of Mann and Spender, and many others of their generation, represented an epistemological legacy that Paul Fussell in *The Great War and Modern Memory* has called the "*versus* habit." The distinctive character of trench warfare in World War I helped create in those who experienced its horrors, directly or indirectly, a dialectical mode of thought. It was "us" against "them" but without the Hegelian synthesis of reconciliation. In this world of binary opposition, one side was the repository of all things good and the other of all that was evil.[55] By the thirties "choosing sides"—right or left, fascism or antifascism, to stay in or out of the Ivory Tower—had become essentialized in its political discourse.[56] Two weeks after the war broke out in Spain, the *New Statesman* published an essay, "Trenches across Europe." Its author could see "the trench-lines drawn, that had divided us unperceived. They mean war, though no herald has declared it. The democracies face the dictatorships—it is a war of ideas. The workers face the owners—it is a war of classes."[57]

The most noted example of this tendency was Nancy Cunard's *Writers Take Sides on the Spanish War*. She proclaimed that "we have seen murder and destruction by Fascism in Italy, in Germany—

the organisation there of social injustice and cultural death—and how revived imperial Rome, abetted by international treachery, has conquered her place in the Abyssinian sun." Consequently, "we are determined or compelled, to take sides. The equivocal attitude, the Ivory Tower, the paradoxical, the ironical detachment, will no longer do."[58] In James Barke's thirties novel, *The Land of the Leal*, the clergyman brother of the hero (who dies in Spain) at last becomes convinced that "it is no longer possible to remain neutral."[59]

What remains undeniable is that few moments of human history have so stirred the outrage, in the Orwellian vernacular, of "decent" men and women as did Spain. Staring at the Republic's defeat, the French novelist, Albert Camus, could say without fear of contradiction that the war's eternal attraction would lie in the fact that those of his generation "have had Spain within their hearts . . . [and] carried it with them like an evil wound. It was in Spain that men learned that men can be right and yet be beaten, that force can vanquish spirit, that there are times when courage is not its own recompense. It is this, doubtless, which explains why so many men, the world over, feel the Spanish drama as a personal tragedy."[60]

And certainly this was true in Great Britain. The historian Neal Wood calls "Spain . . . the first and last crusade of the British left-wing intellectual. Never again was such enthusiasm mobilized, nor did there exist such a firm conviction in the rightness of a cause."[61] Noel Annan, who attended Stowe and Cambridge with John Cornford and went on to a distinguished career as a writer and educator, remembers: "No one can have a glimmering of the feelings of the intelligentsia of the left in the pre-war years who does not recognize that the Spanish Civil War obsessed them." He has written, "For that generation Guadalajara and Teruel sounded as mournful as the Somme and Ypres to their fathers."[62] The Spanish Civil War "provided for the generation of the thirties the emotional experience of their lifetime," according to the historian A. J. P. Taylor. He believed "it has been rightly said that no foreign question since the French revolution has so divided intelligent British opinion or, one may add, so excited it."[63] It might be noted that on at least one occasion Taylor himself spoke at a public forum in Manchester to denounce fascism.

All this and more can be said of thousands of working-class men and women whose feelings and perspectives are only now beginning to be heard and understood. Writing in the stylized political vernacular of the time, Glaswegian volunteers in Spain sent home a message, bristling with revolutionary enthusiasm, class pride, and confidence, to their fellow workers on the eve of a public event in behalf of the Battalion. "Glasgow boys, members of the 16th Battalion of the glorious 15th Brigade, send revolutionary greetings from the Battle-fields of Spain." They assured their fellow citizens, "We are proud to be sons of Glasgow, carrying on her fighting traditions, and we sincerely hope tonight's great gathering will mark a new stage in the advance of the revolutionary movement."[64]

So deeply felt was the Spanish Civil War that it could and did eclipse World War II in the minds of many. The American critic, Leslie Fiedler, said it was the Spanish War "which to those with memories like my own, made World War II seem when it came second-best, too-late, hopelessly impure."[65] Hugh Thomas agrees: "For intensity of emotion, the Second World War seemed less of an event than the Spanish War. The latter appeared a 'just war' as civil wars do to intellectuals, since they lack the apparent vulgarity of national conflicts."[66] In Olivia Manning's *The Levant Trilogy*, Harriet Pringle said of her husband, Guy, a young lecturer for the British Council with a working-class background, "He feels deprived. He feels he should have fought in Spain. He venerates the men who did go there, especially the ones who died. I don't know why it should have been more heroic to fight in Spain than, say, the western desert, but apparently it was. . . . They didn't want to be involved in anything so trivial as a Second World War."[67]

Although the British workers who went to Spain have been largely ignored by the country's elite culture for sixty years, they have never been forgotten by their own class. And their enduring place in proletarian culture has been aggressively reemphasized. In one recent year three plays were produced in England about the Spanish War. One of them played to "packed audiences" in the working-class environs of Glasgow. Similarly, Christie Moore's song, "Even the Olives Were Bleeding,"[68] was a huge success in Ireland. A Scots singer and song writer, Geordie McIntyre, wrote a ballad called "Another Valley" about the valley of the Jarama, the bloodiest killing ground of the war for the British. The last verse encapsulates its flavor:

Iron hearts and iron fists
Cannot smother the vibrant voice
That sings for peace and cries for
freedom
Calling us to make a choice.[69]

Over the years some fifty monuments to the British Battalion and the International Brigades have been placed throughout the British Isles. For example, in Glasgow along the Clyde, facing the Custom-house, is a bronze statue of La Pasionaria with arms raised and fists clenched. At its base is her famous cry of defiance to the people of Madrid, when it seemed that Franco and his troops would overwhelm the city: "Better to die on your feet than to live on your knees." A bronze tablet reads:

THE CITY OF GLASGOW AND THE
BRITISH LABOUR MOVEMENT
PAY TRIBUTE TO THE COURAGE OF
THOSE MEN AND WOMEN WHO
WENT TO SPAIN TO FIGHT FASCISM

1936–1939

2,100 VOLUNTEERS WENT FROM
BRITAIN, 534 WERE KILLED
64 OF WHOM CAME FROM GLASGOW[70]

The British veterans' traveling exhibit, "Anti-Fascist War, 1936–39," proved much in demand. In 1991 the Scottish Trades Union Congress took it all over the country during a series of Trade Union Weeks.[71]

Fewer than 100 British volunteers are still alive. Some are splendidly lucid about their Spanish experiences, others much more reserved, or burdened by the heavy weight of time. But they remind the communities in which they live of what they did when they and the world were younger. This is particularly true, as I discovered, of miners in South Wales. These men were the pride of the British working class, "the shock troops of the industrial workforce."[72] The fading presence of the miners' once-proud symbols of solidarity, such as their annual gala at which lodge banners were paraded and speakers once raised thousands to their feet, have become painful reminders of the power and prestige that was once theirs, and is no more. I attended a gala in Swansea after the end of the miners' bitter year-long strike in 1984–85, and along with many others was deeply affected by the sad eclipse of what had long been a principal public and civic ritual of the Rhondda. During previous weeks, I had spent a good deal of time in the company of several veterans of Spain, and was struck by the iconic status they possessed in their communities. This sense was reinforced when Neil Kinnock, the Labour leader, unveiled a memorial to the Welshmen who had fought in Spain, and in a few words offered them the benediction of a new generation.

But, as I understood, the thoughts of the men standing at attention before the memorial, wearing the uniforms of advanced age, were not in Wales but in Spain. They were remembering battles, not as old or fraught with legend as Thermopylae or Waterloo or the Somme, perhaps, but, for them, every bit as epic: the Casa de Campo, Boadilla, the Jarama, Mosquito Ridge, Belchite, Teruel, and Hills 481 and 666 in the Aragón. As Kinnock spoke, I thought of the prosaic reminders of these volunteer soldiers that are still scattered across their old scenes of struggle—the abandoned boots, the occasional buckle, a partially open can of rations, a rusted grenade casing, very occasionally a weapon, and everywhere, the abundance of expended ammunition, all that remain as testaments to such desperate hope.

But these Welsh veterans, and others with whom I spoke both in Great Britain and the United States, knew well that the journey to the Spanish War is an arduous one that cannot be eased by picking through its debris or dwelling on romantic symbols. Nor should the complexity of their experiences be reduced to legends or memorials. At the unveiling of the statue of La Pasionaria in February 1980, Jack Jones, former General Secretary of the Transport and General Workers Union, congratulated the city for remembering the volunteers who went to Spain so that "new generations can look upon it and understand what it was all about."[73] But a statue of La Pasionaria bearing one of her most resonant slogans obscures as much as it reveals about Spain and the British volunteers who fought there, and thus exemplifies the danger of such adamantine tributes. In the nineteenth century the artisan and essayist, Thomas Wright, warned of stereotypes imposed upon workers:

> The best of these portraits are idealised from observations necessarily superficial and generally made with a view to their suiting some preconceived theory, while others are "adapted" to the interests of parties, or boldly evolved from an inner consciousness or a rich imagination, by persons who wish to *father* their own interested designs upon the working man.[74]

As we shall see, there were those who for reasons of party or class inscribed powerful but badly flawed representations of the Volunteers for Liberty that persist to the present day.

PART I

Middle-Class Intellectuals
in the Thirties

CHAPTER I

The Leaning Tower

The 1920's were a generation to themselves. We were the 1930's.
  —Stephen Spender

That is your problem now, if I may hazard a guess—to find the right
relationship, now that you know yourself, between the self that you
know and the world outside. It is a difficult problem. No living poet
has, I think, altogether solved it.
  —Virginia Woolf to a Young Poet

I

Stephen Spender made the comment that during the thirties:
"the English anti-fascist writers became, as it were, honorary French
intellectuals."[1] British intellectuals had been historically uneasy
with those familiar staples of French intellectual life—abstract theory and an appetite for political confrontation. Rooted in the empirical traditions of Bacon, Locke, and Burke, British intellectuals owed
much to the distinctive character of the nation's political development, which fostered accommodation instead of confrontation between the classes, and, with it, the absence of the kind of alienation
between the intellectual and the establishment that developed in
France, the United States, and Germany.[2] Consequently, as Tony Judt
has remarked, the British intelligentsia never "coalesced into a common body defined negatively by its critical stance towards the status
quo."[3] The thirties, however, saw in Great Britain the emergence of
a radicalized cohort of intellectuals subscribing to a comprehensive
theory of change that rejected capitalism as an organizing principle
for the economic and political life of society.

Young writers in the thirties were well aware of the weight of their
historical legacy but explained its origins in intellectual and cultural
terms. "Politics were harmful," according to Cyril Connolly, because
"they were not artistic material of the first order." Therefore, "an
artist could not be a politician."[4] The future poet laureate, Cecil Day
Lewis, adopted a wider frame of reference. The "tradition of individualism and political indifference" was explained by two factors: the

150 years of freedom that British intellectuals enjoyed, and came to take for granted, and the Romantic Movement, which placed "the writer as someone 'above the battle,' as the high-priest of rites not to be shared by the vulgar."[5] This echoed the views of both the Romantic sage, Samuel Taylor Coleridge, and the contemporary French neo-Kantian, Julien Benda (who was widely read in Great Britain), each of whom argued in behalf of the intellectual's detachment from society, the former seeing him as one of the "clerisy," the latter as a "clerc," both terms meant to signify a virtual theological detachment from political and social problems.

By provoking a comprehensive rejection of received values, the Great War encouraged further contempt for politics. Therefore, the reasons for "the ivory tower attitude" arose, Connolly argued, not only from a traditional "disbelief in action" but "from the putting of moral slogans into action, engendered by the Great War." John Strachey, who was at Eton, declared that "the high explosives of war had done no material damage to English soil. Yet . . . their detonation has shattered most of the moral and social sanctions by which the British ruling class had guided its life."[6] Consequently, in the immediate postwar world, young middle-class intellectuals, afflicted by survivor's guilt, contemptuous of hypocrisy and bombast, and distrustful of parliamentary democracy judged to be complicit in the horrors of the war, turned resolutely away from the "reality" principle and toward the veneration and cultivation of male beauty, fantasy, and the unalterable supremacy of personal relations over all other loyalties. Noel Annan said of them:

> Every generation turns on its fathers; but the Great War, which most of Our Age considered was a war that could have been avoided and should have been stopped, made us preternaturally critical of what one of our number . . . called the Establishment—the network of people and institutions with power and influence who rule the country.[7]

Those of the twenties seemed "a generation to themselves," Stephen Spender remembered, one characterized by "despair, cynicism, [and] self-conscious aestheticism."[8]

The most brilliant and revealing expression of the moral, political, and aesthetic bankruptcy of the twenties was T. S. Eliot's *The Waste Land*. Eliot's sear vision made it necessary to face what Spender called "the destructive element," which, he said, is "a world without belief."[9] Christopher Caudwell thought that Eliot's poem was "brilliantly representative" of the twenties.[10] John Cornford wrote in *The*

Student Vanguard in May 1933 that it was a "perfect picture of the disintegration of a civilisation."[11]

For many of the interwar generation, the General Strike of 1926 became the first significant political event of their lives. But most regarded it, at least in the beginning, as little more than great theater. The Triple Alliance of the Railway, General Transport, and Miners' unions, which had long threatened such action, moved significantly, if ineffectually, on May 3, 1926, to express its support of the miners who faced a pay cut and longer working hours. Undergraduates treated the General Strike "as an exciting joke." A call went out for volunteers to replace the striking workers, to which students enthusiastically responded. Louis MacNiece remembers that "the most publicized blacklegs were the undergraduates of Oxford and Cambridge who regarded the strike as an occasion for a spree." To them, it was "a comic phenomenon due to the Lower Classes" which, moreover, was "a comet that came from nowhere and dissolved in rubble and presaged nothing to come."[12] A Cambridge undergraduate recalls: "The University fermented. Recruiting agencies opened all over the place, and undergraduates bicycled wildly from one to the next offering their services for such glamorous pursuits as engine driving, tram driving, or the steel-helmeted special constabulary."[13]

Student cooperation in breaking the strike, however, did not represent a politically self-conscious act of opposition to the workers, who lived in a world that was unknown to the vast majority of them. "I don't think there was any strong political feeling. Just Hurrah Patriotisimus or fun."[14] The future spy, Anthony Blunt, said later that the General Strike "was treated very largely as a sort of joke. . . . It did not impinge as a real event on us at all."[15] Rex Warner, Cyril Connolly, Alec and Evelyn Waugh, and Graham Greene were among those who explicitly or implicitly sided with the government against the workers.[16]

Nevertheless, as its significance quickly sank in, the General Strike became a defining political moment of the interwar period. "The impact of the strike," Hugh Gaitskell recalled, "was sharp and sudden, a little like a war, in that everybody's lives were suddenly affected by a new unprecedented situation, which forced us to abandon plans for pleasure, to change our values and adjust our priorities." He said, "Above all we had to make a choice. And how we chose was a clear test of our political outlook."[17]

II

The most difficult "choice" for many on the left was whether to join the Communists in seeking answers to the great questions of the day. The small British party was founded in 1920 from the British Socialist party and a coalition of left-wing groups. By the thirties, a Marxist society or cell had been established at several institutions: the London School of Economics, University College (London), Cambridge, and Oxford, as well as Manchester, Reading, Durham, and Leeds. To John Cornford the significance of communism lay in the fact that "it is the first systematic attempt by a working-class party to win over a whole section of the middle class."[18] Ironically, two middle-class writers, John Strachey and Stephen Spender, were to help immeasurably in the task. Their analysis of the political and economic crisis of the thirties would take both of them to Spain, as it would a number of their readers, to express their ardent support of the Republic.

John Strachey's *The Coming Struggle for Power* and Stephen Spender's *Forward from Liberalism* were strikingly successful in encouraging a new attitude of engagement. In the years between 1932 and 1935, Strachey published three books, *The Coming Struggle for Power*, *The Menace of Fascism*, and *The Nature of Capitalist Crisis*, all of which played key roles in the volatile political dialogue of the thirties. Hugh Thomas believes that Strachey's *oeuvre* quite likely "converted more people to communism, or to the communist way of thought, than anything else."[19]

The most significant of these, *The Coming Struggle for Power*, was published in November 1932, and its effect was everything that the British Communist party could have hoped. Kingsley Martin called it the "most influential single Marxist publication."[20] The astute Richard Crossman, politician, diarist, and the editor of *The God That Failed*, summed up its impact in this manner:

> To the Socialist generation of the 1930s, *The Coming Struggle for Power* came as a blinding illumination. Suddenly they saw the class war with Strachey's abstract extremism, jumped with him to the conclusion that capitalism was a doomed failure, and rushed to join the army of Socialist Revolution. So they dedicated themselves to the cause of the Spanish republic, of the hunger marches and of collective security against Fascist aggression. . . . This was a seminal book. Sown in the soil of the Hitler epoch, *The Coming Struggle for Power* produced a great tree of Socialist activity.[21]

"Strachey's book," observes the cultural historian Martin Green, "is generally considered to have had more effect than any other in causing the large-scale swing to the left of the English intelligentsia in the 30s."[22]

John Strachey's career on the left gave him the practical experience that most advocates of communism in the thirties lacked. Realizing this, he made it his purpose to combine economic and social analysis of the country's condition with political views rooted in his understanding of the manner in which capitalism actually worked. Strachey, however, was a man passionately, and often blindly, in love with ideas, and this love often obscured the realities that lay behind them. He moved from a brief dalliance with Sir Oswald Mosley's cryptofascist New party at the beginning of the decade to the embrace of communism. To Strachey, the formation of the National Government in 1931 appeared to provide incontrovertible proof that the political system had failed. Ramsay MacDonald's decision to lead the new government, following a cabinet crisis, left the Labour party leaderless and demoralized. In the summer of 1932, when Strachey wrote his book, millions were out of work, and both the Tory and Labour parties seemed thoroughly incapable of finding solutions.

Strachey's clearly written and often eloquent sketch of the history of civilization according to Marx becomes most compelling in the final section, which he called "The Political Struggle in Britain." According to Strachey, the thirty-five months in which the Labour party had been in office since 1924 had resulted in a betrayal of the workers, whose "strong and simple desire for an alleviation of their lot" had been thwarted by the leaders of the party they elected. This was accomplished by what Strachey called a kind of reverse alchemy in which the gold "of instinctive working-class revolt [was] somehow transmuted into the lead of working-class passivity and subservience."[23]

Unsurprisingly, the cabinet imbroglio in the summer of 1931 resulted in new elections, and the confirmation in power of the National Government. Capitalism, however, had proven that it could not solve its problems, Strachey charged. An economic philosophy based on individualism would always be diametrically opposed to the collective interests of the workers. For its part, the Labour party had established conclusively that it was not a socialist party but, in attempting to "rationalize" capitalism by promoting economic gradualism, had itself become a bulwark of the capitalist system.

Strachey's final judgment on Labour was ringingly contemptuous. He wrote that none

> of the leaders of the Labour Party, on whichever side of the House they may find it convenient to sit, ever falter before the expostulations of their supporters, however cogent, so long as they know that in the end the expostulator will remain a supporter. "The war and fortune's sons," they will "march indefatigably on," so long as life is in them, to ever new defeats, surrenders, deceptions, and betrayals.[24]

At this point, Strachey unfurled his sails and presented an alternative to his readers. He challenged them to abandon the Labour party and to join with the workers in overthrowing capitalism and beginning the task of building socialism. If the challenge to capitalism would not come from Labour, it must come from the followers of an economic and social philosophy that unhesitatingly opposed itself to economic individualism. These were, of course, the Communists. After unrestrained praise for the Soviet Union, the sweep of Strachey's exposition came home to Great Britain, which he believed to be a "particularly favourable ground for communism."[25] The reasons for this were the strength, education, and organization of the British working class, the country's heavy industrialization, and the absence of a large agricultural sector, whose workers were usually more politically traditional than were urban industrial workers.

In addition, the crisis that capitalism faced in Great Britain promised to weaken the efforts of the capitalists to defeat a proletarian revolution and would transform the psychology of British workers, which many believed, erroneously, to be incompatible with communism. Consequently, Strachey believed that "the intrinsic balance of class forces is certainly more favourable to workers in Great Britain than in any other major capitalist state." The revolutionary class in Great Britain had been given a mighty responsibility: "The immediate future of all humanity rests to no small degree in the hands of the workers of Great Britain."[26]

But if the workers were ready for the new world, intellectuals had proved reluctant to assume their roles and embrace the future. Strachey wrote: "The great majority of western intellectuals are engaged in the useless and indeed pernicious task of trying to carry on a little longer the culture of capitalism."[27] They should join the workers if they wished to be on the side of the future. Because a classless society eliminates the oppression of one class by another, "the barrier between mental and physical labour will be broken down."[28] Thus,

Strachey reflected the growing optimism among many intellectuals that the waste land could be left behind and a new society beckoned just an evolutionary step away.

III

Stephen Spender, although lacking Strachey's ability to synthesize and organize political ideas in a coherent and compelling manner, refused, unlike Strachey, to abandon fundamental tenets of liberal intellectual integrity: the importance of the individual and the right to criticize authority. The significance of each is manifestly present in his *Forward from Liberalism* which, like *The Coming Struggle for Power*, proved greatly influential in moving British intellectuals toward communism.

The Left Book Club promised that *Forward from Liberalism* "will mark a definite step in the breakdown of the traditional isolation of the creative writer from politics."[29] For the generation of the thirties, *Forward from Liberalism* possessed some of the same appeal as Lytton Strachey's *Eminent Victorians* in the twenties. Although a very different kind of book, Spender's *Forward from Liberalism* also became an emblem of generational rebellion. Brian Howard wrote that Spender's work possessed a special appeal to their class because it was "less a text which elderly beaks should be unable to blue-pencil, than an answer by one of themselves to the question as to *what they are to do* about a world that is rapidly becoming fit for tyrants to live in."[30]

Working-class readers were also powerfully affected by *Forward from Liberalism*. Dave Goodman, a commercial traveler from Middlesbrough and a volunteer for Spain, said that his political education came in a very brief, intense period, with much of his reading consisting of Left Book Club choices. Of these, Spender's was "one of the key books that influenced me."[31] According to him, "the message I got . . . was that the cherished Liberal freedoms depended for their full realisation on a basic economic freedom—freedom from exploitation."[32]

Spender, like Strachey, came from a distinguished Liberal family. When the poet left University College, Oxford, in 1930, he felt himself a "vague socialist." Soon he became active in politics. In 1936 he wrote to Christopher Isherwood, "It is true that I am rapidly enlisting myself as one of . . . the great 'stage army of the good' who turn up at every political meeting and travel about the country giving little talks, subscribe to things, do free articles etc. etc." He found the experience personally rewarding but believed "it's stupid to pretend that it will have the slightest effect on anything." On the other hand, he told Isherwood, "I still secretly believe . . . that a very good book about things one cares for is a potent instrument."[33]

He was correct. Though it may not be "a very good book," *Forward from Liberalism* became his "potent instrument" when it was named a selection of the Left Book Club in 1936 and, as such, gained immediate access to the homes of thousands of readers sympathetic to his views. His emerging political convictions found other literary expression—in his book of poems, *Vienna* (1934), *The Destructive Element* (1935), and his play, *Trial of a Judge* (1938). But none of these works was to influence the discussion of what an intellectual was to "do" in a time of crisis, as did *Forward from Liberalism*.

Spender began writing what he called his "Gollancz book" in March 1936 and completed it in July. The book was published in January 1937. Although Spender's work is not systematic in its argument, or beyond criticism on the grounds of historical accuracy, the author is reasonably hard-hitting in his criticism of capitalism. He attempts to make a case for communism as the next progressive step for liberals, yet shows that he will never concede his independence of thought to any ideology. He would always claim the right to criticize that which is arbitrary or unjust, regardless of whether it purported to serve any larger human purpose. Thus Spender announced his alliance with "communism" in a highly conditional manner, the wisdom of which was soon confirmed by his experiences in Spain.

Spender's general socialist views derived from Christianity, as did those of so many of his contemporaries on the left. Reading the Gospels in his youth, he was most affected by the teaching "that all men are equals in the eyes of God." The loneliness of childhood made him extremely sensitive to the need for and significance of human community, one that would enable individuals to break out of the world into which they were born and enter a larger and more inclusive existence. He wrote, "It seemed to me—as it still seems—that the unique condition of each person within life outweighs the considerations which justify class and privilege."[34]

His politics flowed naturally from the older radical traditions of Thomas Paine and William Godwin. He quoted the poet, William Blake, Paine's friend: "Religion is politics, and politics is brotherhood."[35] From this, all paths followed toward liberalism, socialism, and finally communism. The first two were way stations on the road to universal brotherhood, and communism signified the traveler's arrival at his destination. Liberalism had proved successful in achieving political democracy, but its reforms, instead of fundamentally transforming society economically and politically, had become nothing more than an apology for the interests of private property.

There could be no genuine democracy, then, without economic democracy, and this could occur only if men and women stormed the citadel of liberalism protecting the holy grail of private property. Liberalism, which held out the promise that reform would bring about a classless democracy, must at last be revealed as "the most dangerous of bluffs by which English capitalism diverted the working-class movement from revolutionary class-consciousness."[36] Fundamental change would occur only if a united front, consisting of all the progressive political forces in the country, including the communists and the ILP, fought to achieve the common goal of socialism. This had already happened in France and Spain, where Popular Front governments had come to power.

The reason, Spender believed, that intellectuals could not continue living in the ivory tower was that the very existence of civilization, which human beings had created over the centuries, was in peril. Consequently, "Communism or international socialism becomes an immediate necessity." In England, still a nation of the rich and the poor, the rich had found their natural political expression in the National Government, but "the other nation still exists, whose interests are freedom and internationalism." It was for this second nation that the "elect socialists," of whom the intellectuals were essential cadres, became "the guardians of an idea." Spender wrote, "After the revolution, during the transitional period, they assume a new and great responsibility: for they are the guardians of democracy, and the critics of the dictatorship." That their numbers were comparatively small was of little consequence, and could indeed be of enormous strategic benefit. A large party "dissipates all other energies and becomes an end in itself." But smaller numbers of individuals genuinely working to achieve socialism possess "moral qualities" that allow their energies to become concentrated "and by [their] irresistible strength accumulates all the support we shall need."[37]

John Strachey and Stephen Spender went beyond liberalism, and brought many with them. Scions of the intellectual aristocracy, they believed that it was the role of intellectuals to join the workers in making the future. But with new opportunities for the intellectual came new responsibilities. From his reading of Marx, John Strachey concluded that "the whole duty of the honest intellectual to-day" is to master a theoretical understanding of the progress of history. If this happens, the intellectual "can have no possible doubt as to the necessity of throwing in his lot with the workers."[38] And then the challenge would have to be faced. Marx had said famously, "the philosophers have only *interpreted* the world . . . ; the point, however, is to *change* it."[39]

IV

In the thirties the argument for communism or some sort of left socialism was founded on a still superficial but increasingly genuine understanding of the realities of unemployment and human suffering. The fact that young intellectuals felt themselves over-whelmed by a tremendous sense of personal and social guilt was due largely to the remarkable impact made by the unemployed who brought the sufferings of the country's distressed areas into the enclaves of Oxbridge class and privilege. If young middle-class intel-lectuals refused to come to them, then unemployed workers would confront them on their own terrain.[40] The illusions of "the middle class," Graham Greene wrote in his autobiography, could be sus-tained only as long as they "had not yet been educated by the hunger marchers."[41]

The arrival of the Hunger Marchers in Oxford and Cambridge proved to be a moment of epiphany for the undergraduate generation that succeeded the dandy aesthetes of the twenties. Organized by the National Unemployed Workers' Movement—and the most famous one, the Jarrow march, by the workers themselves—the marchers were the most conspicuous casualties of the economic battles that took place in the country's distressed areas, existing out of sight and sound of the relatively prosperous south of England.[42] Many who had seen their most productive years stolen by unemployment now had found a way to bring their plight to the attention of those who might do something about it. But they were not merely supplicants. There was an undeniable militancy at work. Asked why he had joined the marchers, an unemployed Scots communist said, "Well, conditions at that time were atrocious, really it was atrocious. In fact people were hungry. They talk aboot people bein' hungry now. But, God's truth, they were hungry at that time. And that's the only way. You tried to fight these people that were rulin' ye."[43]

For the first time, the workers laid moral siege to the ancient bastions of privilege and anticipated power along Kings Parade and Oxford High Street. For most students, the appearance of the marchers signaled the beginning of their understanding of what unemployment meant, as well as their first significant contact with workers. Frank McCusker from Dundee participated in the Third National Hunger March in 1930, which passed through Oxford. He remembers, "When we got to Oxford the students were standing on the side of the road wi' bundles o' walking sticks and handing them [to] us as we passed again after the police was away. They were sympathetic students, no' Communists or anything like that. But they seen what we were goin' through and they decided we needed sticks for walking."[44] Not long afterward the Oxford Union passed by sixty-seven votes the resolution that "in Socialism lies the only solution to the problems facing this country."[45] The young communist, Denis Healey, remembered that "the atmosphere [of Oxford] was like the early days of the French Revolution."[46]

In February 1934, a group of marchers from the northeast went through Cambridge on the Fifth National Hunger March to London. In the days before their arrival, the colleges were electric with discussion and anticipation. Young socialist leaders found themselves explaining "why students should be concerned with the militant working-class movement" to what must have seemed an endless round of undergraduate gatherings. All the colleges took up collections in order to provide the marchers with clothing and food, amounting to £120, a figure of sufficient magnitude that one called the response "an unheard-of thing in Cambridge at the time, before the sufferings of Spain made the raising of such sums almost an everyday matter."[47] A group of students from the Socialist Society met the marchers at Huntingdon and took them to Girton for refreshments prepared by female undergraduates.

Certainly for the students it was a distinctly unsettling and yet, at the same time, exhilarating experience. That cold afternoon in February, according to one in attendance, the students "had little knowledge of the working class, and of the militant working class almost none. It was a thrilling moment for them." One of those thrilled was the poet Charles Madge who, according to Kathleen Raine, "had never

seen the working-class" until that winter day.[48] Some remember
meeting

> the tired, shabby, cheerful column whose progress on the road they had
> followed day by day. Then the students and the unemployed formed up
> together and marched back down the long hill into Cambridge. At first,
> some of the students were a bit shy and self-conscious, wondering whether
> they had a right to be there, wondering whether it would be cheek to buy
> a pack of cigarettes for the men. Gradually, they began to enjoy it, singing
> *Pie in the Sky* and *Solidarity for Ever* and the rest of the marchers' songs.
> Going through the town, shouting "Down with the Means Test!" you
> would see some students you knew slightly, standing on the pavement,
> staring, a little frightened, at the broken boots and the old mackintoshes.[49]

Margot Heinemann, John Cornford's fiancée, was studying at Newn-
ham. The sight of these tired, desperate, unemployed workers evoked
a passion for the condition of the working classes that would change
her life forever.[50] Some of the marchers, however, could barely maintain a straight face at the sight of their new undergraduate comrades
singing, chanting, and marching with them.

The reaction in London was similar to that of undergraduates at
Cambridge and Oxford. When a group of Hunger Marchers on their
way to Hyde Park passed the wealthy American Michael Straight,
who was studying at the London School of Economics, he stared
wordlessly at them through the rain. Student leaders handed out
sheets with the appropriate slogans to shout, which included "Down
with the government of starvation and war!" Straight and his companion, the future Indian leader, Krishna Menon, found their voices
as they joined in behind the workers who, Straight thought, had
walked "all the way" from the Clydeside and Yorkshire to London.
"They were shabby and footsore. But they held their banners high,
and as they passed, we let out the yell." When the Hunger Marchers
began to sing the *International*, Straight felt embarrassed that he did
not know the words.[51]

A number of the undergraduates refused to be satisfied with the
momentary *frisson* of contact with the working classes, and experienced in the encounter a turning point in their political development,
moving with alacrity into the embrace of the Communist party.
Julian Bell, who deeply involved himself in the "No More War"
movement, wrote in the *New Statesman and Nation* that in Cambridge at the end of 1933, "We have arrived at a situation in which
almost the only subject of discussion is contemporary politics, and

in which a very large majority of the more intelligent undergraduates are Communists, or almost Communists."[52] Brian Simon, the distinguished historian of education and lifelong Communist, believed somewhat vaguely that 1,000 out of 8,000 Cambridge undergraduates were members of the party.[53] A few, such as Kim Philby, Guy Burgess, Donald Maclean, and Anthony Blunt, traveled even farther, into the employ of Moscow.

Among the militant students who played such an important role in this development, those at Oxford, Cambridge, and London were preeminent, and, among these institutions, Trinity College, Cambridge, became the vital center. James Klugmann, the roommate of John Cornford at Trinity and future official historian of the Communist party, wrote, "We, an extraordinarily erudite and arrogant generation of Cambridge students, who thought that we were the best intellectuals, and that the intellectuals were the wisest of the community, we were still lost at the beginning of the thirties, often with immense knowledge but no philosophy, immense mental effort and activity but no purpose."[54] It was at Trinity that Klugmann, John Lehmann, David Guest, Maurice Cornforth, John Cornford, Guy Burgess, Michael Straight, and the dons Maurice Dobb and Anthony Blunt made their academic homes and exercised a mutual influence. In addition, Bernard Knox lived in nearby St. John's and was friendly with both Cornford and Straight. Of these, Knox, Cornford, and Guest fought in Spain, and the latter two died there.

Straight has written a painful and candid memoir that helps us understand something of the climate at Cambridge during these years.[55] In the early thirties, James Klugmann and John Cornford dominated the emerging communist movement at Trinity, the college that had given birth to the Bloomsbury Group with its emphasis on personal relations and political detachment more than thirty years before. Klugmann and Cornford had little time for the scrupulous self-reflection and aestheticism of those of the previous generation. Neither of the two, Straight said, would "waste . . . five minutes in talking about themselves." Cornford wrote to his mother, "I have found it a great relief to stop pretending to be an artist."[56] Klugmann and Cornford founded the Socialist Society, which took its orders directly from the Communist party at King Street in London. According to Straight, there were 200 members of the society at Cambridge when he came up and 600 when he went down. Of these, one in four became members of Communist party cells.[57]

Straight joined the Trinity College cell, which numbered about twelve members in 1935, a decision that was to shadow his entire life. At the time, however, it seemed a perfectly natural step to take. Several of the largest trade unions were led by communists. "Most of the poets whom I admired," Straight wrote, "belonged to the Party or allied themselves with it." Both left socialists and communists shared the same goals and wanted a united front, which was the characteristic and dominant form of radical politics in most European democracies. The members met once a week in rooms at Trinity and discussed such issues as organizing a Cambridge protest against Mosley's British Union of Fascists, relief funds for Abyssinia, and how to combat pacifism in the Cambridge branch of the League of Nations Union.[58]

What is of particular interest about Trinity as a hotbed of Communist militancy is how little many of the students knew about Marxism. Party men such as Cornford, Klugmann, and Maurice Dobb were obvious exceptions, but Straight's ignorance was painfully exposed in a seminar chaired by John Maynard Keynes. In response to a question about Marx, Straight said, "I answered it in my unintelligible way but no one knew enough about Marx[ist] theory to dispute what I said." He felt he had eased himself through a sticky situation. "I was priding myself on carrying the day for the old German." He was firmly denied his triumph when Keynes bitingly observed that Marxism was so much "complicated hocus-pocus, the only value of which was its muddleheadedness." According to Straight, "It was the only instance that I can remember of a leading intellectual at the university challenging the new orthodoxy that had fastened itself upon the minds of the undergraduates."[59]

But if one were to look for the moment of permanent rupture between the postwar aesthetes and the politically engaged, it could well have come in a meeting of the Apostles, Cambridge's elite secret society, which had long been dominated by Bloomsbury's aesthetic philosophy, and included Keynes, G. E. Moore, G. M. Trevelyan, E. M. Forster, Julian Bell, and Straight, as well as Guy Burgess and Anthony Blunt. In the spring of 1937 Julian Bell arrived in Cambridge to deliver a paper to the Apostles. The son of Clive and Vanessa Bell, and the nephew of Virginia Woolf, Bell had been teaching in China but returned to England to join the International Brigades. While still in the Far East, he wrote to his great friend, John Lehmann, "I wonder where you are and where and when this will get to you. Spain most likely, I should think—it seems the right place to be if one can get there."[60] He told his mother, in what surely must be as clear a repudiation of Bloomsbury aestheticism as is conceivable: "It's too late for democracy and reason and persuasion and writing to the *New Statesman* saying it's all a pity. The only real choices are to submit or to fight."[61] This was a hugely symbolic moment in which the private world of Bloomsbury collapsed under the public pressures of the decade. The paper Julian read to the Apostles celebrated the soldier as his new ideal. On this point, Straight, listening intently, misunderstood Bell, thinking he was speaking metaphorically of the need to resign oneself to obey orders in an imperfect world. When he attacked him by saying that the Spanish War would not tolerate detachment, but required a sense of personal responsibility and the taking of sides, the child of Bloomsbury signaled his agreement with him. Talked out of serving as a soldier by his mother,[62] Bell left for Spain a few weeks later to serve as an ambulance driver for Spanish Medical Aid and was killed in July 1937 at the battle of Brunete.[63]

V

In addition to the rise of fascism on the Continent and in Great Britain and the economic distress of several million workers, hundreds of young men and women of the public schools and the university-educated middle classes turned to communism to find meaning in what they judged to be the meaningless world they had inherited. Orwell, in characteristic fashion, traced the origins of individual decisions to move to the left to a single cause, which was quite simply, "middle-class unemployment."[64] By this, he meant that in addition to literal unemployment or underemployment, the middle classes had lost the significance and meaning that had once attached themselves to their typical vocations. He wrote in "Inside the Whale":

> Unemployment is not merely a matter of not having a job. Most people can *get* a job of sorts, even at the worst of times. The trouble was that by 1930 there was no activity, except perhaps scientific research, the arts and left-wing politics, that a thinking person could believe in. The debunking of western civilisation had reached its climax and "disillusionment" was immensely widespread. Who now could take it for granted to go through life in the ordinary middle-class way, as a soldier, a clergyman, a stockbroker, an Indian Civil Servant or what not? And how many of the values by which our grandfathers lived could now be taken seriously? Patriotism,

religion, the Empire, the family, the sanctity of marriage, the Old School
Tie, birth, breeding, honour, discipline—anyone of ordinary education
could turn the whole lot of them inside out in three minutes.[65]

But once the old values had failed scrutiny, what would replace
them? "You have not necessarily got rid of the need for *something to
believe in*," Orwell said.[66] And this was the issue. As early as 1920
Bertrand Russell had perceived that "Bolshevism is not merely a
political doctrine; it is also a religion, with elaborate dogmas and
inspired scriptures."[67] Some, like Evelyn Waugh, found what they
were seeking in Roman Catholicism. Others turned to the Communist party. Gabriel Carritt, a member of an Oxford family of communists, suggested that the appeal of communism, if properly understood, possessed a similar potency for both workers and intellectuals.
He wrote, "I think a lot of the intellectuals and perhaps many of the
workers too wanted the Party to be the authority, to lay down how it
should be."[68] Charlotte Haldane agreed that the "authority" of communism appealed to much the same human needs that organized
religion once had, and in this sense the proselytization of both
workers and intellectuals was inherently ecumenical.[69] George Orwell wrote, "I do not think one need look farther than this for the
reason why the young writers of the 'thirties flocked into or towards
the Communist Party. It was simply something to believe in. Here
was a church, an army, an orthodoxy, a discipline."[70] Michael
Straight, who was converted to the Party at Cambridge, said, "We
were interested in ideas; we wanted to believe."[71] His contemporary,
Cecil Day Lewis, offered this summation of his generation's search
for new values and a new faith:

> We had all, I think, lapsed from the Christian faith, and tended to despair
> of Liberalism as an effective instrument for dealing with the problems of
> our day, if not to despise it as an outworn creed. Inoculated against Roman
> Catholicism by the religion of my youth, I dimly felt the need for a faith
> which had the authority, the logic, the cut-and-driedness of the Roman
> church—a faith which would fill the void left by the leaking away of
> traditional religion, would make sense of our troubled times and make real
> demands on me. Marxism appeared to fill the bill.[72]

In 1934 Karl Radek told the Congress of Soviet Writers that "in the
heart of bourgeois England, in Oxford, where the sons of the bourgeoisie receive their final polish, we observe the crystallization of a group
which sees salvation only together with the proletariat."[73] If the
bourgeois materialism of the older generation had failed and betrayed

them, then perhaps the answer to their disquietude lay with a political philosophy that put the worker, no matter how much an abstraction, at the center of history and life. Julian Bell reconciled the British and Continental intellectual traditions when he wrote:

> Like nearly all the intellectuals of this generation, we are fundamentally political in thought and action: this more than anything else marks the difference between us and our elders. Being socialist for us means being rationalist, common-sense, empirical; means a very firm extrovert, practical, commonplace sense of exterior reality. . . . We think of the world first and foremost as the place where other people live, as the scene of crisis and poverty, the probable scene of revolution and war.[74]

VI

Christopher Caudwell's movement toward the left is a particularly good example of the choice of Marxism as a system to replace a failed vision of the world. Caudwell saw humankind in the interwar years as victim of the last dying contortions of capitalism. He wrote in *Studies in a Dying Culture*:

> The War at last survived, there [came] new horrors. The eating disintegration of the slump. Nazism outpouring a flood of barbarism and horror. And what next? Armaments piling up like an accumulating catastrophe, mass neurosis, nations like mad dogs. All this seems gratuitous, horrible, cosmic to such people, unaware of the causes. How can the bourgeois still pretend to be free, to find salvation individually? Only by sinking himself in still cruder illusions, by denying art, science, emotion, even ultimately life itself. Humanism, the creation of bourgeois culture, finally separates from it. Against the sky stands Capitalism without a rag to cover it, naked in its terror. And humanism, leaving it, or rather, forcibly thrust aside, must either pass into the ranks of the proletariat or, going quietly into a corner, cut its throat.[75]

Caudwell, an ex-Catholic whose sister became a nun, expressed baldly what was implicit in the lives of so many intellectuals and workers of the period. In a remark that was published after his death, he said, "We both need a religion, but what religions are there to have nowadays? Communism remains, I suppose. . . . "[76] Thus he underscored the plight of his rootless generation and the enduring need to believe, if life was to have significance.

Although only one of Caudwell's poems was published in his lifetime, he left a great number in manuscript, some of which possess revealing passages on the theme of the loss of faith. In a poem on

Memorial Day, in which he commemorates the horrific slaughter of World War I, Caudwell renounced the God of the Victorians and the victorious.

> That was the climax of our faith:
> Let us admit it, who escaped—
> Still on the better bank of death,
> Shall we defend the God we shaped.[77]

In another poem, the narrator walks down a tiled corridor until he reaches "an office door and asked for God/The manager was bald and apologetic." He "told me God was out."[78]

In addition, Caudwell was fascinated by technology. As with John Cornford, part of communism's appeal for Caudwell lay in its prestige as a genuine science of society. Cornford's brother, Christopher, wrote that "it was partly through the search for a sociological or historical explanation for the nature of a poem that he came to consider contemporary society, and so to politics, and so to Communism."[79] Increasingly, young middle-class intellectuals possessed confidence in their ability to apprehend the truth, and a profound conviction that knowledge, once gained, must in some way be used for the benefit of humankind. This is yet another important reason why intellectuals of the thirties, convinced they had a leading part to play in shaping the political future, saw Marxism as a natural next step in the progress of society, offering them a confident understanding of their role in its accomplishment.

These young men and women had recovered the Enlightenment optimism that ideas were still, to use Max Weber's famous image, the switches on which history turned. If ideas, such as that of the class struggle, could be properly understood and embodied in the minds and spirits of men and women, the world might be changed sooner. In his opening speech at the Revolutionary Socialist Congress in Brussels in October 1936, Fenner Brockway, the Independent Labour party leader, said, "What the radio beam is to the pilot of an airplane, crossing mountains in the mist, the principle of the class struggle is to the Revolutionary Socialists, amidst all the complexities of social and international chaos."[80]

Karl Marx had supplanted G. E. Moore as the principal influence on the descendants of Bloomsbury, and the consequences were inescapable. Bell wrote:

We should cultivate all those valued states of mind that are produced by action. . . . For one thing, it is obviously prudent to dive in of your own accord rather than wait to be pushed. For another, action is the most potent of drugs, and battlefields and revolutions are usually fairly good at curing romantic despairs—and other diseases incident to life. For another, intellectuals often turn out to be good men of action, and would probably do so more often if they could keep their minds clear—could become intellectuals rather than emotionals—and if they acquired a hard enough outer shell of cynicism and practical common-sense.[81]

Bell would agree with John Strachey that there may have been a "very large element of rather neurotic personal salvation in our brand of Communism." But he added, possibly thinking of John Cornford, communism could also appeal to "minds a great deal harder." Regardless, it would be hard "to find anyone of any intellectual pretensions who would not accept the general Marxist analysis of the present crises." The most important issues now were ones "of tactics and method, and of our own place in a Socialist State and a Socialist revolution."[82]

The attitude of the poet Louis MacNeice was characteristic. When MacNeice departed Cambridge and embarked on his career, he found to his disgust that even some of the best-known figures of the left still maintained comfortable habitation in the ivory tower. While he was teaching in Birmingham, his landlady, an ardent socialist, often invited progressive luminaries such as Maurice Dobb, A. L. Rowse, John Strachey, and Naomi Mitchison to her home. The young poet could summon up little more than derision for their "armchair" reformism. "I felt that they all were living in the study. The armchair reformist sits between two dangers—wishful thinking and self-indulgent gloom."[83] He left the study and went to Spain with Anthony Blunt several months before the insurrection ("perhaps there will be a revolution when we are in Spain"[84]). After a second visit at war's end, he wrote his *Autumn Journal*, perhaps the greatest political poem of the era.[85]

The ivory tower not only leaned; it had been toppled. But gestures were hardly sufficient for the purposes of which socialists dreamed— the development of a genuinely egalitarian society and, as a crucial step toward securing it, the defeat of fascism in Germany, Italy, and, most of all, Spain. The events of the early thirties had shown that if the historical disengagement of British intellectuals continued, it could prove fatal. Intellectuals must organize if they were to avoid the fate of their German and Austrian counterparts. The Popular

Front, whose ambition was to join together all parties on the left, offered an opportunity for artists to break out of their isolation and establish "a sense of community" that would help them to discover the social function of art. Day Lewis said in one of his more hortatory moments, "Let us act now, before it is too late, throwing off our parochialism and political apathy in the interest of the civilization we have helped to build and can help to save."[86]

John Lehmann moved quickly beyond Day Lewis by answering somewhat differently the question, "Should Writers Keep to Their Art?" Unlike his fellow poet, he did not feel it necessary to argue in behalf of a public role for the intellectual. The question, rather, was what would be the most effective manner in which the intellectual could fulfill that role. He or she might turn to journalism or public speaking as had Shelley and William Morris at various junctures in their careers.[87] But Lehmann felt, as did MacNeice, that it was not necessary that a writer be an actual participant in the great events of his time.

Instead, writers could have more effect by developing qualities of imagination and thought and expressing them through their art, which would inevitably make "profound propaganda for [their] own view of life." This would be much more important than becoming a journalist, a mere transcriber of events, or a "committee man,"[88] or, for that matter, a member of the International Brigades. Above all, these young writers and poets believed they had the terrible responsibility of witness. Stephen Spender wrote, "One had the sense of belonging to a small group who could see terrible things which no one else saw."[89]

Cyril Connolly agreed. In 1938 he wrote that "we are living now in a transition period as suited to political writing as were the days of Ship Money or the reign of Queen Anne. Writers can still change history by their pleading, and one who is not political neglects the vital intellectual issues of his time and disdains his material." The writer need not become a "victim" of his age but rather "a person who can alter it." Moreover, Connolly continued, "By ignoring the present he condones the future. He has to be political to integrate himself and he must go on being political to protect himself." In periods of change, such as that in which Connolly and his contemporaries were living through, the writer must feel that he could affect the final shape of the times that would ultimately emerge.[90] "So," John Strachey wrote, "haltingly, unwillingly, blunderingly, we began to find ourselves propelled out of the ivory tower and toward—conceal the vulgar name as we might—politics!"[91]

Cyril Connolly had no doubt that if intellectuals stuck to their lasts, and yet at the same time looked beyond their ivory tower or work rooms, they might not only develop as artists but also exert a significant political influence on their age. In comparing the revolutionary poet, William Blake, and his great contemporary, Thomas Paine, he wrote, "The poet is a chemist and there is more pure revolutionary propaganda in a line of Blake than in all *The Rights of Man* [sic]."[92] But if a writer were going to realize himself at the same moment as an artist and a creator of his age, Connolly said by way of a conclusion, he must realize that "political writing is dangerous writing, it deals not in words, but in words that affect lives, and is a weapon that should be entrusted only to those qualified to use it." Speaking as one who had been to Spain a number of times, and, moreover, spoke Spanish, he meant that if "a burst of felicitous militancy with the pen may send three young men to be killed in Spain," the author is "responsible" for those deaths.[93]

Speaking in 1940 to a Workers Education Association group in Brighton, Virginia Woolf described the intellectuals of the thirties as clinging to what she called "the leaning-tower." Like those who had gone before them, they were "a small aristocratic class [crammed] with Latin and Greek and logic and metaphysics and mathematics." But now, she said, "they realized [the tower] was founded upon injustice and tyranny." Artists became psychologically divided, one part wanting to cling to the threadbare reassurances of class and privilege, the other part wanting to embrace the emerging new world of classlessness. To make them whole, they must "no longer . . . be isolated and exalted in solitary state upon their tower, but . . . be down on the ground with the mass of human kind."[94]

Those on the left who advocated disinterested reason, like Peter Quennell, were to find it progressively harder to express their opposition to fascism in the absence of concrete personal involvement. Increasingly, others like Louis MacNeice found it necessary to immerse themselves in the "destructive element." Ernst Toller, whose work was translated by Spender and Auden, and who was one of the Spanish Republic's most ardent supporters, put it unequivocally: "The young writer no longer wants to live in the ivory tower, which was the ideal of artists for decades. We became aware that necessity moved us more strongly than beauty. We understand that our task is to integrate this necessity in our own work . . . , in order to free reality from it."[95]

Edward Upward became something of a literary and political mentor to W. H. Auden, Stephen Spender, and Christopher Isherwood, and was perhaps "the most committed writer of his generation."[96] In his autobiographical novel, *In the Thirties*, Upward's principal character, the Marxist poet Alan Sebrill, expressed what it meant to leave the ivory tower and embrace communism:

> To be a Marxist [he] would have to take action in the external world, which meant that he would have to become a Communist. Then there might be hope for him. Communism was the only force in the world which was uncompromisingly on the side of the doomed and against those who wanted to keep them doomed. It was the enemy of his enemies: it aimed at the overthrow of a society which was dominated by poshocrats and public-school snobs and which had no use for the living poets. It demanded that its converts should believe not in the supernatural nor in anti-scientific myths but in man.[97]

But once the volleys of rhetoric had been expended, the next step, for a fewer number, was purposeful action "in the external world." One of these was Felicia Browne, a talented artist and sculptress, who joined a militia column in Barcelona and became the first Briton killed in the war. A eulogist called her "the very best type of the new woman." To a friend, she wrote:

> You say I am escaping and evading things by not painting or making sculpture. If there is no painting or sculpture to be made, I cannot make it. I can only make . . . what is valid and urgent to me. If painting or sculpture were more valid or urgent to me than the earthquake which is happening in the revolution, or if these two were reconciled so that the demands of the one didn't conflict (in time, even, or concentration) with the demands of the other, I should paint or make sculpture.

Browne expressed the dilemma felt by so many artists and writers of the period. One of her obituaries read: "Artist though she was, she knew she could not pretend to be Someone Apart from the common struggle."[98] Claude Cockburn, a combatant in the early fighting in Spain and later *Daily Worker* correspondent who had made his name with an insider's view of Westminster politics, understood why Browne resolved her difficulty as she did. He wrote that intellectuals who went to Spain or fought in the war "proclaimed, however briefly, that a moment comes when your actions have to bear some kind of relation to your words."[99]

Most middle-class intellectuals responsive to "the spirit of the age" rejected the historical tradition of "ivory tower escapism." Angela Guest found in her brother's papers a 1931 manuscript which, she was convinced, offered the only path for her generation.

> There is no passive attitude in politics. If one does not actively oppose a political system, then for practical purposes—if one is working in a system—one is supporting it. All men are linked together by a thousand bonds of social and economic intercourse. To talk as though these bonds were not existing, to abstract oneself from the human race and leave it to perish while one is engaged in the Higher Speculation of the Finer Arts, is simply *monstrous*![100]

For the majority of her contemporaries, the left, whether communist or noncommunist, beckoned irresistibly.

Looking back at the end of the thirties, Angela Guest, who also went to Spain, contrasted the twenties and thirties. "The outlook of the British intellectuals prior to 1930" was "a jumble of progressive and reactionary elements." But "the shock of 1930 struck this ill-assorted pile of grain and chaff with the force of a hurricane." The result, she said, was that "we became inspired missionaries for a new integration of thought and action, a new science of life" that would change the world.[101]

CHAPTER 2

Making Allies

I cannot regret that desire to be committed, that positive sense of
engagement, which our upbringing and the weather of the times
combined to produce. This was a period when it seemed possible to
hope, to choose, to act, as individuals but for a common end; possible
for us as writers, to bridge the old romantic chasm between the artist
and the man of action, the poet and the ordinary man.
— C. Day Lewis

Spain, the kulaks, the machinations of the Trotskyites, racial violence
in the East End—how antique it all seems now, almost quaint, and yet
how seriously we took ourselves and our place on the world stage.
— John Banville, *The Untouchable*

I

The thirties were to be the years of the British Communist
party's greatest influence.[1] The new prestige and success of the party,
which after 1933 had partially recovered from the sectarian divisive-
ness it had caused on the left, was due in no small part to the
leadership of the most able and creative working-class leaders of the
period. The British party played a leading role in organizing the
Hunger Marches and the unemployed, the struggle against Mosley
and his Blackshirts, the success of the Left Book Club, and the
creation of the British Battalion in the International Brigades, all of
which took place in the face of the indifference or the active hostility
of the parliamentary Labour party and most of the trade union
leadership.

Consequently, the CPGB became the most vividly radical force of
the decade, even though by no means did it take all the initiatives on
the left. This being said, it must be remembered that the party
remained numerically inconsequential, never rising above 18,000
members. David Caute has written sardonically that the British party
"lacked only one ingredient: workers."[2] What it did attract, as suggested earlier, were middle-class intellectuals (as well as militant
workers). Ironically, however, until the thirties the British party had

been the most hostile toward middle-class intellectuals of all Communist parties among the great industrial nations.

Young British intellectuals of the thirties earnestly looked to the founder of Soviet communism for support in their desire to ally with the workers. In 1902 Lenin argued famously in *What is to Be Done?* that workers could not transcend their trade union consciousness without the help of intellectuals who possessed a more cosmopolitan understanding of the state, social classes, and their relationships to each other, as well as a grasp of history and its ultimate direction. He wrote, "The teaching of Socialism . . . has grown out of the philosophical, historical, and economic theories that were worked out by the educated representatives of the propertied classes—the intelligentsia." He reminded his followers that the best examples were Marx and Engels themselves.[3]

In 1930 a University of London graduate, Freda Utley, reviewed Lenin's book, and wrote enthusiastically, "Might not Lenin have addressed this speech to the British Communist Party today?"[4] In return, she received a torrent of abuse from her worker-comrades. The reasons for this response lay in the belief of British proletarian leaders that middle-class intellectuals were irremediably individualist and competitive in their outlook and had a highly self-conscious sense of the superiority of mental over manual labor. Consequently, they were unsuitable as partners in achieving collective goals. Second, workers believed that the middle classes were too remote from reality and had little to offer a movement that would benefit primarily another class. Third, the comparative rigidity of the class system in Great Britain prevented middle-class intellectuals and workers from mixing and working together as freely as they did in Continental socialist movements. Consequently, stereotypes of each other were inevitable. For example, Hugh Dalton suggested to Julian Bell that he help Richard Crossman in a West Birmingham by-election "and meet real working men & women."[5]

Crossman himself came to believe that working-class communists possessed an instinctive resentment of the "intellectual convert." He wrote, "They not only resented and suspected him, but apparently subjected him to constant and deliberate mental torture." He concluded that the intellectual was consistently held to be inferior "before the true-born proletarian." His only hope was to undergo "mental training" in order to "achieve . . . the qualities which, as he fondly imagined, the worker has by nature."[6] There was a particular

suspicion on the proletarian left of "missionary intellectuals." In a
then unpublished story by Christopher Caudwell, a Jewish working-
class communist tells the middle-class Brian Mainwaring: "Oh, we
don't want you. Not down here. The workers distrust your sort,
deboshed intellectuals trying to save their souls! If you really want
to do propaganda, go back to your Mayfair drawing-room and carry
on with your old life."[7]

II

The British party presented its own particular ideological and
cultural obstacles to a genuine integration of middle-class intellectuals into the small but overwhelmingly working-class movement. In
the 1920s, only a handful of intellectuals were party members—figures such as R. Palme Dutt, Robin Page Arnot, and Emile Burns. Dutt,
a Balliol, Oxford, honors graduate and the leading British party
theoretician (and presumably himself a candidate for marginaliza-
tion), put the party's position in the most estranging possible manner.
He wrote that "bourgeois intellectuals" should be given every encouragement to join the party but each must agree to certain stipula-
tions. "First and foremost, he should *forget* that he is an intellectual
(except in moments of necessary self-criticism) *and remember only
that he is a Communist.*"[8]

As for Harry Pollitt, the general secretary of the British party, his
suspicion, if not hatred, of intellectuals was deep-rooted, despite his
close association with R. Palme and Salme Dutt. In 1923 he wrote to
Tom Wintringham, the Balliol graduate, a founder of the British
Communist party and, later, the *Left Review*, as well as the commander of the British Battalion in its first engagement in Spain:

> I know this little Party inside out, and up and down this country are
> working some of the best comrades in the world, only their praises are not
> sung from the house tops, but they are the people pegging away, unknown
> and unheard. These are the people who make the struggle worth the while,
> and the people to think of when things at King Street don't seem too
> pleasant, or when a lot of bloody fools are blathering about "the intelli-
> gentsia," because none of you are any better than us poor "workers," in
> fact the majority of you are a damn sight worse.[9]

What Pollitt's view meant in practice was that intellectuals were
to have no real influence in the party, but were intended only to
recruit nonparty professionals such as themselves. "Above all," Neal
Wood has written, "he must forget that he is an intellectual, sacrifice

his pride, and through self-denial, self-discipline, and humble but conscientious work become a militant fighter for communism."[10] There were those who prepared to meet Pollitt's demands, at least initially. Cecil Day Lewis expressed the inadequacy that many middle-class intellectuals felt when he wrote, "Why do I, seeing a Communist, feel ashamed?" thereby substituting "Communist" for "soldier" in the first line of Gerard Manley Hopkins' poem.[11] The distinguished biologist, J. B. S. Haldane, gladly prostrated himself before the proletariat. Intellectuals, he said, have mistaken words for reality. "They have not been manual workers, and have seldom realized that man's hands are as important as and more specifically human than his mouth." History has been made not by "those who thought about it, or talked about it, or impressed their contemporaries, but those who silently and efficiently got on with their work." The true revolutionaries, then, were not the intelligentsia. Rather, "the vast majority of them have been skilled manual workers."[12]

The intellectual, therefore, could escape his egotistical isolation and a pervading sense of ineffectuality only by allying with the workers.[13] In his novel, *In the Thirties*, Edward Upward's character, the poet Alan Sebrill, found the peace that passeth all understanding:

> He was no longer isolated, no longer worthless. He had found a place among people who wanted him and with whom, however inferior he might be to them in courage and in strength of will, he felt an affinity because they were members of the lower class to which he too, the would-be poet, in a sense belonged. He would do all he could to be worthy of them and of the great cause for which they were working. From now on he would be dedicated to the Revolution.[14]

Party attitudes began to shift in 1933, when Hitler came to power after having effectively captured the support of the petite bourgeoisie in Germany. Within a year the British Communist party offered a much warmer and less qualified welcome to middle-class intellectuals and professionals. Margot Heinemann remembered, "For the first time intellectuals, artists and professional people began to come towards the left and to ally themselves with the working class movement, not just as exceptional individuals but in quite large numbers and with wide practical effect."[15]

For many young intellectuals, most of whom knew little more about Marxist theory than did their working-class counterparts (and many a great deal less), it was above all the example that communists set in a time of economic and political crisis that proved persuasive.

George Bernard Shaw said as early as 1920, "A bolshevik is someone who does something about it."[16] Raymond Carr once commented, "Example, Dr. Johnson held, is always more efficacious than precept, and those of us who were tempted to join the party in the late 1930s were attracted less by the truths of Marxism than by the example of the selfless militants we knew who lived in that closed circle, that extended family of the party."[17] Communism promised an intellectual home, a new system of faith, and most important, a program of action for middle-class intellectuals and their new worker-comrades.

Moreover, party resistance began to thaw. In 1935, at the Thirteenth Congress, Harry Pollitt emphasized that a counterattack against the fascists must be mounted. This required that the party "see in these students, intellectuals, authors, doctors, scientists and professors, valuable allies who can be won for the working class."[18] In October 1936, communist Arthur Horner, the leader of the South Wales miners, emphasized the new line when he wrote an open letter in the *Left Review*, entitled, "The Arts, Science and Literature as Allies of the Working Class." He said: "I can assure you that the South Wales miners welcome every effort which aims to bring allies to the side of the working class in its struggle against Capitalism." Horner acknowledged that there had been differences with intellectuals in the past. "For too long have Arts, Science and Literature been used to impede and make more difficult the efforts of the workers to free themselves from the stranglehold of a contracting and sabotaging system of society." But there was a growing recognition of the mutual advantages to be gained by an alliance.[19]

Those in art and literature "can [also] be our allies in the great struggle to defeat reaction and to secure freedom," Horner said. Workers now understood that they could not be self-sufficient. They, as well as intellectuals (whose work depends on freedom), were equally susceptible to the threat of fascism. Therefore, he concluded, "the common suppression" provides a base for "a united struggle against the common enemy." Horner welcomed the *Left Review*, its middle-class contributors and readers, into the United Front "as an addition to the armoury of the exploited, an instrument which can do effective work in the urgent and imperative fight against fascism."[20]

The Scarlet Banner, one of the songs of the British Battalion in Spain, underscored this new alliance:

The People on the march
The road are treading,
That leads to freedom, that leads to freedom.
The hour of struggle's here,
Our courage needing,
Our banner leading
To victory.

Raise then the scarlet flag triumphantly
We fight for peace and progress and our liberty.
Oppression shall cease,
The people shall triumph.

From mines and factories,
From farm and college,
With strength of suffering and force of knowledge,
Come all who hope for life,
Their power conceding,
Our banner leading
To victory.[21]

But a union of those "from mines and factories, from farm and college," required more than ideological agreement or a common enemy. Somehow, the profound difference in life experience had to be recognized and bridged. When Spender's *Forward from Liberalism* appeared, Pollitt asked for a meeting with the author and traced the divergent paths that Spender, a product of the middle class, and he, a worker, had taken to communism. "What struck me about it was the difference between your approach to Communism and mine," said the head of the British Communist party. "Yours is purely intellectual. I became a Communist because I witnessed in my own home the crimes of capitalism. I had to see my mother go out and work in a mill, and be killed by the conditions in which she worked." The second difference, Pollitt said, was that Spender revealed no hatred of those who had exploited the worker. For his part, "he believed that hatred of capitalism was the emotional driving force of the working-class movement."[22]

Pollitt never felt that middle-class intellectuals were capable of this elemental feeling. The left-wing publisher, Victor Gollancz, wrote in his memoirs that Pollitt "distrusted, despised, disliked and occasionally even hated intellectuals as such."[23] For example, the leader of the British party never forgave George Orwell for writing in *The Road to Wigan Pier* that the middle classes believed (a distinction Pollitt missed) that workers "smelled."[24]

Pollitt was not being disingenuous, however, in the welcome he extended to intellectuals in the thirties. There was ample evidence that he could work successfully with them in a relationship of mutual advantage. For example, he ardently and successfully courted Spender to join the party, and then fully exploited the brief time that the poet spent as a communist. Certainly he admired and took maximum advantage of other left-wing intellectuals in the party, such as Ralph Fox and John Cornford, both killed early in the war, and the scientist J. B. S. Haldane. Too late, he attempted to recall Christopher Caudwell from Spain when he learned that Caudwell was a writer of growing distinction and would be of greater value to the party in Great Britain.

In the minds of the party leadership, however, there was a real question as to whether middle-class intellectuals could genuinely be counted upon to embrace and endure the workers' struggle. In 1931 Bob Darke saw his party cell in Hackney grow "from a loose-gathering of two dozen intellectual wastrels into a storm-troop of men and women drawn from all branches of working-class life."[25] If, as Day Lewis hoped, the thirties offered the hope of poets bridging the gap between themselves and "the ordinary man," then there would be considerable distance for both sides to travel.

To many proletarian Communists, Stephen Spender became the symbol of the intellectuals' general lack of endurance in making the journey. In his documentary novel, *Fellow Travellers*, T. C. Worsley offers a gloss on Spender's contentious and brief relationship with the Communist party, which to many militant workers appeared emblematic of the behavior of intellectual "types." Worsley's hero, "Martin"/Spender, is a principal speaker at a meeting in which the usual cast of left-wing pundits, such as Harry Pollitt, D. N. Pritt, and the "red" Dean of Canterbury, Hewlett Johnson, practiced their now well-polished exhortations for a receptive and enthusiastic audience. The chairman introduced Martin as "the most important of our younger novelists who had shown by his example that writing is no ivory tower business and that artists and cultural workers stand behind the working masses."[26]

But Martin determined that he would not allow himself to be used as a gramophone (to use Orwell's image) for left-wing slogans. While acknowledging that writers could not separate their art from the world, he told the audience that "a writer isn't a politician, he is looking for a very different kind of truth and his first duty is not to any Party slogan, but to the truth, the truth that he discovers in his writing and which makes his writing worthwhile." A party man then accosted Martin, haranguing him that the truth is "a very dangerous thing," and supplementing this with "the truth is what we believe." When Martin answered that "the truth always does good," he learned it was better "to keep off the subject." But Martin refused to retire and said that a writer cannot allow himself to be so throttled. Then the party factotum unwittingly delivered Martin's epitaph as a party member by saying, "Perhaps you'll realise, then, why we don't trust writers."[27]

III

It is understandable that working-class militants would be skeptical of those who claimed to be their new comrades. From the point of view of a worker, it was virtually impossible to conceive of a middle-class intellectual genuinely understanding the obstacles facing workers to obtain an education or maintain their self-respect in the face of chronic unemployment and the indignities of the Means Test. If such intellectuals all too quickly reneged on their promises and possessed little, if any, real understanding of the wellsprings of working-class anger, they also frequently let slip hints of class superiority that could both intimidate and permanently estrange them from militant workers, regardless of professed ideological affinities.

Certainly the intellectuals who fell into the last category knew Harry Pollitt's undying wrath. Speaking after Labour's great victory in 1945, he reflected on the pompousness and pretension among middle-class socialists. They seemed to be saying to working-class leaders: "You were never at Haileybury, Winchester, Oxford or Cambridge." Yet they, the intellectuals, had "never been in a strike or lock-out, hunger march or dole queue, . . . never preached the gospel of divine discontent or socialism at a street corner or market place, never known what it is to feel hunger or anger, and to passionately desire the overthrow of the capitalist system."[28]

If even the most well-meaning bourgeois intellectuals inevitably saw in abstract terms the daily issues of living and dying in the distressed areas, because such hardships had not affected them personally, the issue of political "disillusion" took on a very different meaning for a working-class militant in the thirties than it did for Stephen Spender or others of his class. The distance between middle-class intellectuals and workers remained dauntingly wide. This strikes particularly true when one learns from the biographer of the Hispanophile, historian, and quondam denizen of Bloomsbury, Gerald Brenan: "As extraordinary as it seems . . . Gerald never seems to have met, didn't even realise there existed, writers without private incomes."[29]

To some workers such as Martin Bobker, a Manchester Jew and waterproof-garment maker, who had by his own admission "a very, very hard life," the growing presence of intellectuals in the party appeared threatening. "I must admit that I was always a little bit scared of the Communist Party, not because I was worried about . . . what they were doing and what they stood for but I was always under the impression that [a Communist] must be very highly intellectual and that I couldn't possibly fit in with them."[30]

The party was forced to tread carefully so as not to alienate its natural constituency—men like Martin Bobker—but, at the same time, to continue to attract intellectuals. Christopher Caudwell recognized the problem. Upon his departure for Spain, Caudwell left behind the work that was to make his posthumous reputation, *Illusion and Reality*. It offered an intellectual, political, and artistic program that he hoped would genuinely fuse the interests of both middle-class intellectuals and workers in the Communist party. Emerging from the implosive forces tearing apart the old bourgeois order was communism, "a new system of social relations," which would make free the unfree, the once oppressed but now ascending proletariat. Freedom, however, would carry a heavy price. Caudwell wrote, "It costs the keenest of human pangs to produce a man; and events in Russia, Germany and Spain have only proved the correctness of the communist warning that a new society would be born only in suffering, torn by the violence of those who will do anything to arrest the birth of a world in which the freedom of the majority is based on their unfreedom."[31]

These historical developments had great significance for artists. Their attempt to delineate the authentic nature of history and the development of society led them confidently to the conclusion that "no one . . . can fail to see [the] relevance to contemporary art, and the importance of understanding the revolutionary transformation of the basis of society which is everywhere affecting art and the artist." Faced with economic crisis, the superstructure of capitalism was going through inevitable transformation. "The pole of the ruling class" had ossified because it had become estranged from the new economic base of society. "The bulk of artistic consciousness," Caudwell wrote, "cannot survive this fission." Capitalist art had lost its meaning and coherence and exploded into "fragments." This explained why modern bourgeois art was "decomposing and whirling about in a flux of perplexed agony."[32]

Some "part of the bourgeois artistic consciousness," however, "separates out, adhering to the pole of the exploited and revolutionary class. It fuses there with such consciousness as has already formed during the developing of their separation." The new aesthetic pattern emerging will be incomparably richer because it is the "creation, not of a limited part of society but of a class which had expanded to include the whole of concrete living." Thus, the new life of the artist would be inclusive of the whole of human experience and not exclusive of its majority.[33]

Artists must be conscious of the forces at work on society and themselves. Each had one of three choices to make: to oppose the new order of social relations, to ally with them, or to assimilate into them. Writers such as Day Lewis, Auden, and Spender had so far managed only to ally with the workers and, therefore, could correctly be called "fellow travellers." They were fatally limited by their inability to devise a "constructive theory" that would replace that of bourgeois art. It is only through the artist's conscious assimilation to the new proletarian order that theory and praxis, rhyme and history, will merge. This meant that artists would have to surrender their concern for individual liberties, a preoccupation of bourgeois artists. They must now be prepared "to some degree [to take the] marching orders of the proletarian general staff unless they are to condemn themselves to complete nullity in action."[34]

Thus, "crossing over" or "crossing the frontier" of class was not for the fainthearted or romantic. Intellectuals such as the writer and scientist must surrender their "lone wolf" tendencies, which were merely psychological artifacts of the crumbling bourgeois order, to the hegemony of the proletariat. Not to do so was to lead a divided and false existence. The artist's conception of freedom, Caudwell wrote, is an "illusion," determined by the consciousness of his bourgeois class. Intellectuals must understand the concrete world from which such concepts came, and in the instance of the bourgeois artist, see that they are limited to himself, at the expense of the majority of society.

The attraction of communism for Caudwell, as previously suggested, was that his own aptitude for applied science found its philosophical counterpart in Marx. The belief in reason and science and progress led him inexorably to the British Communist party, as he passionately believed it would many others. The price to be paid were the liberal values that Stephen Spender cherished. Caudwell, unlike Spender, had come to believe that the end justified the means.

IV

The burgeoning alliance between workers and intellectuals found its most brilliant literary exposition in the *Left Review*, which provided a continuous diet of left and communist perspectives on a variety of contemporary literary, social, and political issues to new and would-be allies. It appealed primarily, however, to a coterie audience. As John Lehmann said of it, "The politics came, fatally, first."[35] This was not the case with the Left Book Club. In February 1936, the publisher, Victor Gollancz, decided to take on the task of supporting a book club whose appeal would reach not just a few militant cognoscenti but, instead, a broad spectrum of the literate left, both middle- and working-class readers, in the country. It bore many resemblances to the *Universum Bucherei*, Willi Münzenberg's book club in Berlin.[36]

Gollancz was not immodest about the ambitions of the new club. It was meant "to help in the terrible urgent struggle for World Peace and a better social and economic order against Fascism, by giving (to all who are determined to play their part in this struggle) such knowledge as will greatly increase their efficiency."[37] Although avowedly nonsectarian (the majority of the membership was Labour), many, if not most, of the authors were communists. Richard Koch goes so far as to say "it was how Stalinist opinion was 'networked' in England."[38] In short, the club was yet another front organization.

But this charge seems exaggerated, in light of the fact that the Left Book Club published George Orwell's *The Road to Wigan Pier*, which made him "famous," as well as Spender's *Forward from Liberalism*, both of which encouraged an independent and critical stance on the left. Its list also included Leonard Woolf's *Barbarians at the Gate*, which energetically attacked Soviet policy, as well as Clement Attlee's *The Labour Party in Perspective*, which presented the case for Labour and the trade union movement.

Certainly the Left Book Club's positions generally paralleled those of the Communist party. James Jupp has written that the LBC was "the clearest example of a mass organization which voluntarily worked with the Communists, while independently organized and funded." It was easy to see how the distinction could blur, however. The Independent Labour party leader, Fenner Brockway, said in 1937 that "from the outset the Left Book Club has been recognisable as an instrument of Communist Party policy."[39]

Regardless, it succeeded beyond all expectations. Each month a new book appeared in its familiar bright orange paper cover, saving the member one-third to one-half of the regular price. Gollancz, the political scientist Harold Laski, and John Strachey made the selections. By the spring of 1939 membership had reached 57,000 and supported 1,200 discussion groups throughout the country. A probably typical example of the composition of a discussion group came from one participant who reported its membership as consisting of a draughtsman, a physicist, a printer, a dental technician, a teacher, a painter, and a road worker.[40]

Although the LBC's principal success was with progressive members of the middle class, the selections also found a place among serious working-class readers in the industrial areas and, later, in Spain. The club's selections played an important part in the intellectual life of the Welsh miner Jim Brewer,[41] who served with the British Battalion from the battle of the Jarama to the farewell parade in Barcelona. David Goodman, a volunteer from Middlesbrough, said that one of the reasons he became a communist was the influence of the Left Book Club, which constituted "a crash course in political education."[42] Nor was Goodman alone. Extensive questionnaires were given to volunteers in Spain. Among the questions asked were the level of education that had been attained, the languages spoken, and the cultural organizations to which the volunteer belonged. The Left Book Club was repeatedly cited as a strong political and cultural influence.[43]

On December 22, 1937, Gollancz wrote to the 50,000 members and hundreds of study groups of the Left Book Club that they each must do everything possible to promote the cause of the Spanish Republic. "There must . . . be many towns and villages in which there is one of our 750 Left Book Club Groups, but where meetings for Spain have not yet been arranged." He urged each convener to "take the initiative without a second's delay." In addition, "every one of our 50,000 members can do an immense amount to mobilize public opinion. They must themselves feel that every day that passes without some piece of activity is a betrayal." Finally, each of the club's constituents should appeal to friends and acquaintances with cogent, well-informed explanations of the truth about Spain. "If they would regard it as a paramount obligation to convert laziness and indifference, wherever they find it, into active enthusiasm for the Spanish cause," then "the issue would not be in doubt for a moment."[44] Gollancz said accurately that the Left Book Club members constituted "one of the strongest bodies of organised public opinion in the country." They had at their disposal "a vast network of activities—public and private meetings, cinema, theatre and the rest—all of which can be concentrated from time to time on such issues as Spain."[45]

Three weeks before his death Christopher Caudwell asked his CPGB branch "to raise money" so that, among other things, he and his comrades could receive "Left books and periodicals, *however few.*"[46] In the spring of 1937 Wally Tapsell, the able, tough cockney commissar, who was one of the four battalion commissars educated at the Lenin School, asked Harry Pollitt to send the Battalion 100 copies of the monthly selection.[47] A few weeks later George Aitken, the brigade commissar, wrote to Pollitt, requesting him to "be sure and get Left Book to send *all* publications."[48] Gollancz's brilliant creation made it possible for both middle-class and proletarian "thinkers" to find a common intellectual ground in Spain as well as Great Britain.

V

Despite their ceaseless activity, it would be wrong to exaggerate the prominence of the communists. At least half of those who went to Spain were not party members. David Blaazer argues that "too many studies of the non-Communist left in the 1930s seem to focus on the Communists themselves. The non-Communist Left itself is written about as though possessed of neither volition, reason, or history." He accuses George Orwell, the most read interpreter of the thirties, of a great historical sin of omission. In his political writing, Orwell unfairly neglected those on the left who were non-communist, leaving the impression in *The Road to Wigan Pier* and *Homage to Catalonia* that progressive British intellectuals had all fallen under the sway of Moscow, thus totally ignoring figures such as G. D. H. Cole and H. N. Brailsford,[49] who were much more cautious and prudent than were the Webbs, Shaw, and Charles Trevelyan when they looked toward the East. This charge possesses its own irony since Orwell himself was a quintessential product of the same radical tradition.[50]

Progressive intellectuals of the thirties, then, whether middle-class or workers, were not all Moscow's disciples. They emerged from a rich and historic culture, which, it has been said, "lived by ideas."[51] They supported the United Front and later the Popular Front for reasons more various than the simple reductionism encouraged by historians who have embraced the assumption of communist hegemony over the left in the thirties. Among the most influential of noncommunists on the left were, of course, Sidney and Beatrice Webb, who devoted their careers to exorcising the spirit of Marxism from British socialism. The Webbs were at the center of that singularly influential group of socialist intellectuals, the Fabians. They combined with the Independent Labour party and the trade unions in 1900 to found the Labour Representation Committee. "Starting from the present state of society," they wrote, our method "seeks to discover the tendencies underlying it; to trace those tendencies to their natural outworkings in institutions, and so to forecast, not the far-off future, but the next social stage."[52] They saw themselves as scientists of society.

It would be difficult to overemphasize their influence. During the interwar years, Noel Annan has said, "A schoolboy might begin to have subversive thoughts after reading Chesterton at thirteen, Wells at fourteen, Shaw at fifteen. But nearly all the time, if they were to form a loyalty to Labour, [they] came up against that ancient institution, the Webbs."[53] The Webbs continued to be influential in the thirties, as they refurbished their appeal to the young with their vigorous enthusiasm for the Soviet Union. This was based in part on their discovery in the course of a visit to Russia in 1932 that, at last, a "functional" society had been created. Their new attitude, however, represented a dramatic departure from their earlier condemnation of the Soviet Union. Six years before, they had written, "*We* regard Soviet Russia and Fascist Italy as belonging to one and the same species of government."[54] But as they began to make further investigations, their hostility thawed. Democracy had never been an end unto itself for them, but rather a means to achieve the goal of integrating the incomplete individual into the whole. Unfortunately, they, like so many before and after them, did not follow their own empirical precept—that one should look for objective evidence to support general conclusions. As with so many otherwise sensible souls, the Webbs found themselves swept off their feet by, at last, the great romance of their lives.

Reminding his readers of Julien Benda's warning against partisanship, the intellectual historian Ernest Gellner emphasizes in no uncertain terms that the Webbs' views of the Soviet Union did immeasurable harm to those seeking to find their political way in the thirties. "There can be few examples," he wrote, "of comparable *trahison des clercs.*"

> At the very moment when Stalin was turning the Soviet Union into one large gulag, Sidney and Beatrice chose to describe it as a "New Civilization". . . . Unbelievably, they had actually visited the Soviet Union twice. The slightest human or social curiosity should have alerted them to something that was perfectly obvious to observers such as Russell and Masaryk from the start . . .; all the apparatus, applied by persons accredited by the appropriate intellectual community, could lead to these morally, criminally and empirically absurd conclusions.[55]

An example of the remarkable influence of the Webbs' interpretation of the Soviet Union can be found in Stephen Spender's *Forward from Liberalism*. Spender's argument in behalf of communism as the logical next step for Liberals in their political development relied to a significant degree on the example of the Soviet Union. He smoothly digested the Webbs' *Soviet Communism: A New Civilisation?*[56] and used it to buttress his argument.[57] Their book, he wrote, was the "basis" for his discussion. "It presents a mass of knowledge as a coherent whole." Beyond anything else, their portrait of Soviet Russia "makes sense." Nevertheless, he emphasized that the choice of communism did not rest on the success or failure of the Soviet Union. It could stand alone and respond to its critics, although the Webbs "succeed in answering some of the main objections to communism."[58] In his essay on "Communism in the Universities," John Cornford wrote that noncommunist intellectuals such as G. B. S. Shaw and the Webbs had succeeded in refuting every conceivable prejudice of the middle classes against the Soviet Union, particularly the belief that fascism and communism were equally oppressive:

> Publicists like Shaw, social investigators like the Webbs, have a considerable influence on the middle classes. And when both proclaim that the Soviet system is in certain respects the highest form of democracy yet seen,

those students and intellectuals who are not too prejudiced to face reality at all begin slowly to revise their opinions.[59]

The Fabian conviction of their superiority to workers did not go unchallenged on the noncommunist left. The Independent Labour party, which was to accredit George Orwell for his journey to Spain and from whose ranks came some twenty-five other British volunteers, criticized the Fabians for their antiseptic and elitist views. Although the members of the ILP accepted Marxist analysis, they rejected communism. At the same time, however, they were prepared to forge a Popular Front with the party. Their distinctive contribution was to emphasize the importance of a socialist morality, which sprang from the ILP's nonconformist roots, giving their approach a passionate, evangelical character that would separate them from other socialist intellectuals who embraced Fabian or Marxist positivism in the interwar years.

Above all, the cry against fascism was heard over the din of ideological strife as the Popular Front campaign gathered momentum, even with the Labour party remaining officially neutral. A commitment to communism was not *de rigueur*. Shared values of a traditional kind—democracy, freedom, peace, and social, economic, and political reform—had become the common threads that drew together those whose elemental inspiration came from Great Britain's radical tradition.

But whether attracted to the Labour, Communist, or Independent Labour party, a growing number of young middle-class intellectuals rejected the distancing conceits of "the workers" or "the masses." For them, authentic human contact with their allies was the next step toward Spain. Socialist convictions required something more than simply cheering on the Hunger Marchers.

CHAPTER 3

Exploring the New Country

And, alone with his heart at last, does the traveller find
In the vaguer touch of the wind and the fickle flash of the sea
Proofs that somewhere there exists, really, the Good Place.
— W. H. Auden

I

The existence of a heroic, long-suffering proletariat, possessing a latent nobility, holding off despair with festive good humor, yet
bold enough to contemplate revolutionary change, obsessed young
middle-class intellectuals viewing the tumultuous history of the
thirties from its margins. Those who chose to test this assumption
made often tentative and, in fewer instances, genuine encounters
with the realities behind the stereotypes of the "proletariat." Adopt-
ing the dress, speech, and manners of the imagined "other," such
figures as W. H. Auden, Christopher Isherwood, and Michael Roberts,
as well as a number of their contemporaries,[1] invited the predictably
acerbic reaction of Wyndham Lewis:

> Great democrats they are, demotic tags
> Sprout from their mouths, they affect in public rags
> Almost, or homespun-sweatshirts and apache caps.[2]

Regardless of the affectation and posturing, there was indeed something unique about the minds and spirits of middle-class writers in
the thirties. "I do not think," Frank Kermode has said, "that any
English writers before them—or since—have felt as they did about
inequality and the absence of respect and affection between classes."[3]
But this feeling had to be oriented to a wholly unfamiliar terrain. J. F. C.
Harrison echoes many others when he writes, "The England of the
unemployed was largely unknown to the comfortable classes in the
suburbs of the south."[4] George Orwell confessed before his journey to
Wigan, "I knew nothing about working-class conditions."[5]

Middle-class intellectuals were stirred by the belief that if a true unity
were forged between the classes, it might, at last, result in an England
of which their forebears had only dreamed. The utopian prospect of

obtaining the unobtainable lay at the heart of Great Britain's radical aesthetic and political culture. The appeal of the "just city," the perfect society, took on a luster that proved irresistible to many.[6] Julian Bell offered a recycled Bloomsbury invitation to this "great good place."

> Through showering smiles and flowers you march
> Below the wreathed triumphal arch.
> The workers' city! Splendid there
> The houses mount the golden air;
> There sin and doubt are washed away,
> All pains that clog our heart to-day,
> The self-sick heart, the self-hurt mind,
> All the ills of human kind,
> Jealousy and hopeless love,
> While Cupid quits his throne above.
> Perfect in the worker's state
> Everyone is good and great,
> And perfect life at last you make
> With sport and poetry and cake:
> And free the naked bodies run
> In that city of the sun.[7]

The poet and publisher John Lehmann felt that he was being pulled "towards the heart of the fire." Lehmann wrote:

> The fire was the suffering, tension and bitterness the ordinary working men and women of the world were enduring, the creative despair and the revolutionary ferment that seemed to increase like a hammer beating louder and louder in the economic crisis of the 'thirties. A poet, if he was to accept all the implications of being a poet in our age, could not run away from that, but must set out towards it.[8]

The rhetorical strategies developed to "set out" toward the workers could sometimes be as embarrassing as fabricated dress and accent. The London School of Economics political scientist, Harold Laski, "the spearhead of the intelligentsia," was vastly experienced before working-class audiences, speaking widely and effectively in the days before the general election on November 14, 1935. Yet he was contemptuously denounced by the *Morning Post* as a Uriah Heep, debasing himself before an audience of miners by apologizing for his class origins and attempting to convince his audience that he, like them, was only "a member of the rank and file of the Labour Party."[9]

Stephen Spender thought less obsequiously of what an alliance with the working class might mean: "The attitude of the bourgeois communist or socialist to his proletarian ally is inevitably self-conscious and determines more than any other factor, his approach to the immediate and practical problems of communism." Spender believed that if a forthright manner were adopted, this self-consciousness could be overcome. "My own view is that I meet the worker, the worker meets me, as a fellow member of a future classless society, even though it is useless to pretend there is no gulf between us at present." Each must recognize he brings "different gifts to that society." The final test "for both of us is whether we are prepared to live for the same world which will unite both worlds."[10]

II

In the minds of a few middle-class intellectuals, the passage of this final test required proof that they were genuinely prepared to share the lot of workers. No other middle-class intellectual from the thirties is so closely identified with the working class as George Orwell. Orwell was one of a handful who did not satisfy themselves with general stereotypes of workers but insisted on a more realistic understanding of those with whom they were establishing a new relationship. *The Road to Wigan Pier* has been fairly called "the best possible introduction to the general topic of bourgeois intellectual attitudes to the condition of England in the Thirties."[11] In it, Orwell sought to penetrate the world of the impoverished, those whose lives, for the most part, went unseen and unheard in the south of England. In his own fashion, coolly and unblinkingly, Orwell persisted in advancing the evidence of his own observations and experiences. The selectors of the Left Book Club made *The Road to Wigan Pier* one of its monthly choices. Because of the club's large membership, the book was to have an immediate national impact. Without the journey to Wigan, it is hard to believe that Spain would have been the next destination for Orwell. And yet Orwell's idiosyncratic view of socialism, so resolutely grounded in the existential verities of his own life and thought, had little to do with the Marxist canon to which most of his left contemporaries subscribed. In a sense, much more revealing of their generation were the young middle-class volunteer, Christopher Caudwell, and the older novelist, Ralph Bates, whose origins were working-class.

III

For the genuinely committed, moving to the left meant that the personal and political implications of an alliance with workers had to be considered for the first time. Despite the success of his journeys, George Orwell became convinced of "the chiasmic, impassable quality of class-distinctions." One can pretend, he said, but it simply is not possible for the higher classes to be "really intimate" with workers.[12] Yet Orwell took his fellow intellectuals to task for their "emotional shallowness," a result of living in a world of ideas and having "little contact with physical reality." "So many" of England's intellectuals had severed themselves "from the common culture of the country," he said.[13]

Christopher Caudwell chose to connect himself intimately with "the common culture," becoming one of the few among his contemporaries to make a conscious decision to live among the workers. Christopher Caudwell, a *nom de plume* he chose for his serious work, or Christopher St. John Sprigg, his real name, proved neither a visitor nor an itinerant in the world of the poor.[14] Not that he wholly disapproved of those writers who sought to declass themselves but were devoid of a genuine commitment to their new comrades. Nevertheless, the "danger" they represented had to be acknowledged.

> Too often their desertion of their class and their attachment to another, is not so much a comprehension of the historical movement as a whole as a revolt against the cramping circumstances imposed on them by their own class's dissolution, and in a mood of egoistic anarchy they seized upon the aspiration of the other class as a weapon in their private battle. They are always individualistic, romantic figures with a strong element of the *poseur*.[15]

Caudwell worked hard to avoid the conventional typology. He left school before he was fifteen and became a journalist on a Yorkshire newspaper. Not going to university, apparently because of family financial constraints, he claimed that he learned all that he knew from the London Library.[16] In his twenties Caudwell already had a reputation as a prolific writer on technical subjects, often intended for younger readers, and usually explaining some aspect of aviation history. He turned to more serious themes at the end of his short life. His political *tour d'horizon* leads to some general views that will help us understand better what might appear as his otherwise impetuous decision to go to Spain.

Caudwell's poetry is particularly revealing about what he saw as the necessary relationship between the artist and society. Alan Young has written that Caudwell "advocated poetry's power to change society for the better. To understand language and emotion fully, he believed, is also to understand how they are bound up with social institutions and relationships."[17] His desire for teleological explanation expressed itself in a cohering myth, one that would make it possible to weave together the aesthetic imagination and the world in which the writers of the thirties lived into one intelligible and predictive whole.

Caudwell attempted to explain this to his great confidants, Paul and Betty Beard:

> Seriously, I think my weakness has been the lack of an integrated Weltanschauung. I mean the one that includes my emotional, scientific, and artistic needs. They have been more than usually disintegrated in me, I think, a characteristic of my generation exacerbated by the fact that, as you know, I have strong rationalising as well as artistic tendencies. . . . The remedy is nothing so simple as a working-over and polishing-up of prose, but to come to terms with myself and my environment.[18]

To achieve this integration, Caudwell used all the intellectual elements at his disposal, which were considerable—not only Marxist theory, but science, anthropology, psychology, and art. Like his contemporary, Day Lewis, he found that communism answered both his intellectual and emotional needs. After being beaten by the police in a demonstration, he wrote to his brother, "I could of course cease active Party work, and merely write, but how should I know how and what to write if I am not actively in touch with the movement?"[19] In Spain he said, "I am absolutely convinced of the correctness of the Communist Party line."[20]

Caudwell had first taken an interest in Marx at the end of 1934, and the following summer began to read him seriously. In December 1935 he went to live in East London. He learned: "One can never become accustomed to the anxiety of losing a job, the boredom of unemployment, the overwhelming pressure of the daily task, or the menace, like a secret cancer, of the end of one's days, without savings, with only the workhouse." With a knowledge that is at least as acute as Orwell's, Caudwell said, "These things are the nightmares and tortures of those who live in the dark depths of poverty."[21]

Caudwell kept away from party intellectuals and spent his time with working-class communists, joining them in the ordinary tasks and routines of party life.[22] Most of his comrades in the Poplar branch of the party were dockers, "quite aggressively proletarian," and they had a natural skepticism about the quiet new party member who supported himself by writing books. Caudwell overcame their prejudices by his lack of pretension, the obvious pleasure he took in their company, and his willingness to take on the same party chores as they did. Tony Gilbert, a young activist from the East End who knew Caudwell during this time, remembered that he and his friends "would hang on his every word," although acknowledging that he "wasn't quite one of us." The writer captivated his working-class audience by painting "a picture of what life would be like when we overcame some of the terrible problems that exist in our society."[23]

What Caudwell was attempting was something new. Frank Kermode believes that Caudwell (and Ralph Fox) "are valuable witnesses to a remarkable moment in literary history, an attempt to unify bourgeois intellect and proletarian culture."[24] This attempt took Caudwell into the ranks of the antifascist movement. For him, fascism was not an abstract evil. Its mephitic influence suffused the very textures of daily life, corrupting all that it touched. He decided to attend a large demonstration of 30,000 in Victoria Park, where some 4,000 uniformed members of Mosley's Blackshirts also had assembled. This was the first time he had seen the fascist Blackshirts in their serried ranks. Order quickly broke down. Caudwell was squarely in the middle of what became a vicious melee between supporters of the right and left. No longer would the crushing sound of a policeman's baton against a human head be the stuff of imagination. Attacked by Mosley's fascist militia, Caudwell wrote of the outcome to his brother, Theo:

> I am still sizzling with indignation from my experience on Sunday when I went to listen to Mosley in our local park (Victoria Park), was attacked by about twenty Blackshirts, picked up from the field of battle more or less woozy, arrested by the police who picked me up, beaten up again in the police van, and charged at Old Street with assaulting the police.

He added, "This last is particularly rich, I think."[25]

There was little question, as he thought of it, that Victoria Park was where he belonged that day. He wrote there was no possibility "of getting away quietly even if one wanted to. After a slosh in the face from a Blackshirt, I didn't want to, and I'm glad to say that before I took the count I got in some good ones." When he was brought before the court, "the magistrate ruled that there was no doubt I had assaulted the constable." He was found guilty and fined £2. He told his brother of the witnesses called to his defense, and the resoluteness of the workers who sang *The Red Flag* behind him.[26] For Caudwell, as for other intellectuals of the thirties, it was not enough to witness the developments in Victoria Park from some safe haven. Still, comparatively few were to do more than dally with the thrill of "real" life, and fewer still were to experience the consequences of the decision to embrace it.

The results of Victoria Park were to be of prime importance in Caudwell's political development and would locate permanently where his loyalties lay. He said, in a kind of ecstatic state, "It is wonderful how vivid a practical experience is." What he had seen and gone through had been the real thing, and he felt he had joined a rather exclusive fraternity. The young writer spoke of the "unusual" character of the violence he had witnessed and been victimized by, and said proudly, it was of a kind "not more than a hundred or so Party members have had." His conclusion proved unsurprisingly straightforward, and nicely ironic: "The experience has not made one exactly pro-National Government."[27] He warned his brother, "Unless the present [political] situation completely alters, . . . you may begin to feel revolutionary yourself—I mean revolutionary against the whole class of capitalists."[28] Caudwell told Theo that it was not enough to be a "sympathizer." Joining the Communist party meant more than just putting him "in touch" with the working class, but, rather, established him at the heart of a revolutionary movement.[29]

Caudwell thought he had sighted the new world. A member of the party was in Parliament, and the South Wales coal miners had just elected a communist by a large majority as president of the Miners' Federation. Aware that these few examples did not exactly make his case, he acknowledged the relatively small but growing numbers of the party, and aggressively asserted, "The Party's influence and following is out of all proportion to its numerical strength," which was true enough. But then he fell back on numbers by writing, "Even in France . . . the Party is now recruiting at the rate of a thousand a day."[30] This comparison was necessary to escape the usual charge of British political parochialism, Caudwell believed, and to demonstrate that he and his fellow communists were part of a great international movement.

In October 1936 Caudwell received a letter from Leningrad, admonishing the British workers for their insular complacency. "I must confess that I am very astonished by [the] indifference of [the] English working class in question of support of revolutionary Spain." But then he told his English friend, "Evidently conditions are very changed," acknowledging that "you write that [the] militancy of [the] English worker is rising rapidly. I believe that it is so. The time of new great class battles is coming."[31]

One of the most attractive aspects of Caudwell's personality as he prepared for "the time of new class battles" is that he never took himself with the heavy seriousness of so many of his comrades on the left. When his friend, Paul Beard, good-naturedly chided him as a left-wing poseur, writing, "So you are now a proletarian no longer in disguise— or is it an aristocrat in a new disguise? We send our best wishes for the adventure,"[32] he knew that Caudwell could laugh at himself. Later, when he was in Spain, happily occupied with the inner-workings of a machine gun and teaching what he learned to newcomers, Caudwell impressed Jason Gurney by his complete lack of pretension. "He was an exceedingly modest, pleasant man whom I knew simply as a private of infantry like anybody else." Gurney learned only after Caudwell's death of his accomplishments as a writer.[33]

Caudwell attempted to establish a life among the workers as an inexorable complement to his political views. Among the middle-class writers who volunteered for Spain, he was one of the few to live the unity sought on the left. Paul Beard understood that Caudwell's reason for going to live in the East End "was political, not literary." But it could well have been both, as with Orwell. After all, despite his tramping and living in filthy boardinghouses in the north of England, Orwell was continuously writing, first in his notebooks, and later for publication. Caudwell, with his typical refusal to have any special virtues attributed to him, told Beard that his decision to move to Poplar was based on his desire "to study conditions to get local colour." He offhandedly remarked to Beard that he was living there simply "as a change" and because he believed that it "may be more amusing" than his usual existence. Beard was not deceived by his friend's habitual self-deprecating casualness, attributing his comment to Caudwell's usual "way of hiding his feeling when taking an important step."[34]

But even Caudwell could not be wholly sanguine about the possibilities of a genuine connection with those of the lower classes. In his only serious novel, *This My Hand*, his protagonist, Ian, visits a prostitute's home, and meets her father, "Britain," who proves himself unctuously ingratiating to the middle-class stranger purchasing his daughter for the night. He then became painfully aware of "the quiet contempt" with which the girl's father saw him.[35]

Although Caudwell's decision to live in Poplar was unusual, he was not entirely alone. His fellow volunteer, David Guest, possessed gifts that were of the same order as his. After seeing the rise of Nazism as a student in Germany (and spending a terrifying two weeks in a Nazi jail), Guest returned to his studies of mathematics and philosophy at Cambridge, where he was deeply affected by the appearance of the Hunger Marchers, and helped establish a communist cell. Coming down from Cambridge, he moved with his sister, Angela, into the heart of working-class Battersea. Angela Guest assessed its impact on her brother:

> Here David learned things about working-class life that few who are not workers can appreciate to the full. He saw families sell their furniture stick by stick so that they could buy food. He saw families thrown into the street for the heinous crime of spending their rent money on food. He saw families refused relief without any cause.[36]

Determined not to be an "armchair socialist," Guest insisted on joining the Hunger Marchers on their way to Brighton to demand that the trade union leadership bestir itself on behalf of the unemployed.[37] He continued with a number of them to Spain.

Julian Symons speaks of the middle-class volunteers who sought in this strange and remote country the class unity they could not find in Great Britain:

> One unconscious motive behind their action was the wish to obtain that contact with the working class which was denied to them in their ordinary lives. The practical difficulties of association with what was, in the Thirties mythology, a great source of good, were great. What meeting point was there between poets like John Cornford and Julian Bell, scientists like Lorimer Birch, writers like Hugh Slater, and miners from Durham, cotton-workers from Lancashire? War melts away the barriers between classes, and also creates shared interests, bonds of knowledge and affection. Spain gave, then, a comradeship of class with class; but it gave it more than this. For a few months at the start of the Civil War, Spain seemed the image of a new world.[38]

If Spain was to be the new country, middle-class intellectuals who had not found their way to Poplar or Battersea, as had Caudwell and Guest, still could make common cause with the worker, who now had his own journey to make. None was more successful in making this journey than Ralph Bates, one of the most gifted novelists of the decade.

IV

Ralph Bates, the author of *Lean Men* and *The Olive Field*, was born in Swindon in the west of England to a working-class family, and left school at seventeen to join the Royal Flying Corps near the end of World War I. In 1923 he went to Spain for the first time, lived in the Pyrenees, and then moved to Barcelona where he worked on the docks and helped organize a fisherman's cooperative. His association with Spain was not accidental. Relatives on his father's side once included merchant captains with offices in Málaga who made regular voyages carrying cargo to Spain. But the firm had gone bankrupt about ten years before Bates was born.[39] The novelist told an interviewer that during World War I his great-grandfather died and was buried in Cádiz, and that it was his photograph that first drew him to Spain.[40]

Perhaps his roots in the West Country and recollections of past gentility made it possible for him to adopt a style with which he felt comfortable and confident, instead of one more characteristic of his origins. For Bates did not feel it necessary to emphasize or exaggerate his working-class background. He looked and spoke like an intelligent and cultured man, which, indeed, he was.

Moreover, he became a genuinely influential figure in Spain, unlike the much younger and unlucky Caudwell and Guest. An American interviewer described him as the most "prominent" of the thousands of English in Spain. He could say, on the one hand, Bates "knows the middle class of Spain. He has helped to organize its workers. He has been in close contact with its peasants. And when the war broke out, he fought side by side with his Spanish comrades in the common struggle against fascism." On the other, what was startling upon meeting Bates was that his manner of speech and gestures "are all the more suitable for the British countryside, than the Catalonian coast, or the central plain of Castile." The American could add no more than the puzzled observation that Bates "is an Anglo-Saxon from head to foot, inside and out."[41] Steve Nelson remembered that he "gave the impression that he knew everything that was going on in the world."[42]

Appearances hardly revealed the man, however. Bates himself speaks without bitterness about a class system that made it impossible for him to gain admittance to university. His father worked for the railway. After leaving school, Bates became an apprentice. He joined the Royal Flying Corps during World War I because he imagined that he would have an opportunity to learn to fly. Not only did he discover that he had little aptitude for flying, but he remembers, "I was not intelligent enough to know that no working man would ever get a commission."[43]

The officers with whom he came in contact were distinguished only by their inhumanity and injustice. Proof, if any were needed, came after the war's end. Not yet released from his regiment, Bates took advantage of living in what he took to be a relaxed state of discipline by attending in uniform a political lecture given by two Americans who had just returned from witnessing the Russian Revolution. Bates was immediately arrested. The authorities sentenced him to two weeks on the parade ground, marching in battle order for six hours a day. The impact lasted a lifetime. "I decided then and there that my judgment of the officer class was just. I had met only one or two decent men, or at least who decently employed their power."[44]

The novelist's identification with victims of the abuse of power was profoundly shaped by experiences such as these. "It was the humiliation, the constant humiliation, the way in which we were treated. And . . . the monstrous lying which was the basis of the power." The more experienced soldiers in his regiment were without his illusions and gave him the first chapters in his political catechism. One told him, "These people don't give a damn for you, they're concerned with their shooting lodges." Bates himself drew the obvious inference. "The class attitude was rigorously . . . [and] sharply defined as any Communist could have wished it to be. And it was sharpened from above rather than from below."[45]

The influences, then, that turned Bates into a self-professed revolutionary were the result of witnessing the soul-destroying effects of class oppression both in England and Spain. In the beginning, at least, his views had nothing to do with the young British Communist party. But Bates' attitudes began to take on a political character after he arrived in Spain: "I didn't think about theory," he said. What the writer wanted was to live in a society in which the kind of abuse of authority he had known in the British army did not exist. He worked on the docks in Barcelona and irregularly engaged in political organizing. His maturing philosophy, though powerfully felt, did not yet have a center. His belief was that human rights and the dignity of man were inherent and immutable. They could "not be conceded by these people." Moreover, he believed that any society that ignored or abused these rights was to be condemned and fought against, whether in England or Spain. In his own view, the vital power of these convictions "was much more revolutionary than the Communists." In that sense his political stance was "completely anti-ideological," wholly a product of his own experiences and the conclusions he drew from them,[46] although he would hew to the party line during the Spanish war, which included condemning the anti-Stalinist POUM (Partido Obrero de Unificación Marxista) in which Orwell fought.

At first, even with Bates' fluent command of the language, and the work he shared with his Spanish comrades, which included tin-smithing, harvesting olives, and participation in strikes that frequently had the character of a "free for all," he still found himself not fully taken into their confidence. The issue that crystallized these differences was his friends' refusal to ask him to make a contribution to the needy, perhaps a workman who had caught an arm in a loom or an indigent widow. Although he always volunteered to contribute, it was never requested, which made him feel acutely a sense of a fundamental separateness between himself and his friends and work-mates. When he became confident enough to challenge them, they at first offered distracting compliments, but then conceded, "We can't get it out of our heads that you are free and you can go when you want. We can't—we're here."[47] There was a difference between them, and Bates saw it.

He refused, however, to accept their judgment—in part because of his command of Catalán as well as Castilian, in part because of the dangers and hardships he shared with his friends over extensive periods of time, but, most of all, because a fundamental transformation had taken place. "My imagination had become Spanish, my whole existence was a rebellion against . . . suppressive traditions," and, moreover, "Spain was a volcano," and an explosive one. What fascinated Bates was the freedom that was being seized by the Catalán. One could say, "Down with the Church!" and "Up with this!" with impunity. In a word, it was possible to be "open." He said, "There was no need for all that mumbling hypocrisy," which he knew so well in England.[48]

Unlike any other foreign writer of the period, including Heming-way, Bates was able to enter into the world of the Spanish peasant and delineate its interior architecture with sympathy, understanding, and respect. At the same time, he understood the challenge he had taken up. In *Sirocco*, his revolutionary narrator, "Rafael," who was to be imprisoned after the failed rising in Asturias in 1934, disclosed that he had read few books, in part because he had little time for such activity. But there was a second reason. "I have never read a novel which seemed the remotest bit like life. Writers will not tell the truth."[49]

Bates set himself to tell the truth, as he understood it, about those who inhabited the world to which he had gained such intimate and unique access. His novels and short stories fully explore the abuses of authority in Spanish society. As much as an outsider could, he wrote about and understood the ordinary Spaniard, the rhythms and contours of his life. As a result, when one of his narrators refers to "our Spain,"[50] it does not seem to be a pretentious authorial claim.

Bates acknowledges the dignity and understands the challenges of his characters' daily lives and customs, and, moreover, comes to see how and why the arc of their political hopes was inscribed within that understanding. All of this is set in an atmosphere of revolutionary crisis that brings into necessarily exaggerated relief qualities that would have revealed themselves more slowly and discreetly in ordinary times. Bates put his ear to the ground of his adopted country and listened, but also was capable of looking upward:

> A good revolutionary must have a sense of locality; I mean that he should know and love the country he works in, the *little* country. The valley he tills, he must sing in it and listen to its peculiar echoes; the village whose gardens he tends, he must be concerned not only for its material welfare, but its decorum, its dignity; he should resent vulgarization of its tales, of its music, or even of the cry of its night watchmen. He must, in fishing a coast, know more than the reefs, the depths of the sea's bottom, and the mysterious currents, but the habits of mind and the hearts of the men who fish there.[51]

Although Bates professes never to have joined the Communist party or, indeed, even to have studied communism (with the exception of having read the *Manifesto*), his two great novels, *Lean Men* and *The Olive Trees*, are richly grounded in autobiography, and the leading figures of both are Communist party members. In *Lean Men*, an English communist, Francis Charing, goes to Spain at the orders of the Comintern to organize on the Barcelona docks. There is little question that the character may well strike the reader today as a tragic, perhaps even foolish anachronism. But alone among the English writers on Spain, Bates' vision of the good society genuinely transcends expostulation and touches that often subdued, but always living, restless dream that lies at the heart of human hope. One of the most interesting parts of the novel is Bates' analysis of Charing's world view. "The general doctrine of his philosophy," Bates writes, "was a system minutely and beautifully integrated by causality." History was not the manifestation of some crude mechanical system: "He believed that every event had its causal precedents, with which it was historically connected by some effective continuity."[52] In short, the Communist had adopted a teleological vision of life which, however, did not diminish the human intelligence and force required for its fulfillment.

To Francis Charing the Barcelona docks represented not a banal commercial tableau but rather a drama of human potential. For "the sensitive observer this drama, or tragedy, of the docks was magnificent in its grandeur of blind struggle and bitter suffering." Here Francis found "the restless and tormented spirit of man, straining to burst bonds, yearning for a nobler life, yet barely guessing what forms and likenesses that life could possess: the spirit of the man Prometheus." What he had found in Barcelona, however, could also be dispiriting. "Contrasted so terribly with the ideal, the romance of struggle was so belied by the meanness of the real." Sailing past the city's breakwater, however, he found his optimism returning.

> They were moving out towards peace, towards purity and innocence, and it filled him with the same quiet joy that he experienced in those rare moments of license when he permitted himself to think of what life would eventually be like in a society from which poverty, violence, the ceaseless battle of classes and war had been eliminated, where the spirit might drink as deeply as it wished of knowledge, art, of music and all things lovely that haunt the tormented spirit of man.[53]

PART II

Proletarian Intellectuals in the Thirties

CHAPTER 4

Living and Learning

The working-class intelligentsia is sharply divisible into two different types. There is the type who remains working-class—who goes on working as a mechanic or a dock-labourer or whatever it may be and does not bother to change his working-class accent and habits, but who "improves his mind" in his spare time and works for the I.L.P. or the Communist Party; and there is the type who does alter his way of life, at least externally, and who by means of State scholarships succeeds in climbing into the middle class.   — George Orwell

I

Amid the occasional adventurers, the congenital mavericks, and those looking for anything that would break the tedium of unemployment, the British Battalion included those distinctive but hardly isolated individuals whose decision to go to Spain was the product of serious intellectual and political development. "The British Battalion," one interviewer remarked, "was not made up of a crowd of radical romantics, as is often supposed. . . . Mainly they were working-class men who as *thinkers* [my emphasis] could see the Spanish conflict as a rehearsal for Fascist aggression throughout Europe."[1] Judith Cook, who knew a number of volunteers, writes:

> Most of them had been involved in the anti-Mosley groups of the "Thirties" and were well practiced in political activity of all kinds. Although they had left school early to go either into jobs or heavy manual labouring, or had found themselves in the dole queues through no fault of their own, they were well read and highly articulate. They went to night schools, WEAs, political meetings and they were politically educated in a way today's youngsters, with so many more opportunities, are not.[2]

The British working-class intellectual was typically an organizer and leader, one whom the Italian Marxist Antonio Gramsci (whose brother fought in Spain) recognized as being "specialised in conceptual and philosophical elaboration of ideas."[3] Among the British volunteers for Spain, they were most often school leavers at fourteen who then employed a variety of formal and informal means to continue their education. Orwell professed unreserved admiration for the self-educated workers who were busy improving their minds when not working, who might well join the Independent Labour party or the Communist party, and had no desire to alter either their accent or the milieu of their lives.[4] Jonathan Rée offers an evocative portrait of the proletarian autodidact: a person who

> with only the most rudimentary education, but possessed by a searing desire for knowledge, acquired massive, even ponderous, learning by boring through book after book, borrowed from clergyman or school-teacher, or from Trade Union or Chartist or Public Library, or even purchased with hard-earned money and gloated over with miserly pride: little boys reading by candle-light when they should have been asleep, or learning to write with improvised materials in snatched moments down the pit; tradesmen with a book always open beside them on the bench; devotees of evening institutes and working men's clubs and colleges or participants in educational self-help groups like . . . Tom Mann's "Shake-speare Mutual Improvement Group."[5]

It is easy to accuse some proletarian intellectuals of bibliomania or "university fetishism," but the ones who appear most prominently among the British volunteers possessed as confidently as any of their middle-class counterparts an understanding of "holistic social engi-neering," the ability intellectuals possess (according to Karl Popper) to apply theory to a reorganization of society.[6] For them, socialism or Marxism provided the philosophical underpinnings for their condem-nation of capitalist exploitation and Fascist aggression as well as an alternative to economic and political oppression.

Gramsci was impressed by the development of British "organic" intellectuals from their base in modern industrialism during the interwar years in England.[7] It was necessary now, he believed, for them to conquer ideologically those whose values and culture had lost their economic base, which had now passed to the workers. According to Gramsci, the "new intellectuals" needed by the work-ing class must unapologetically see themselves as part of an elite that would organize and lead their fellow workers, and therefore must become active participants in "practical life."

Gramsci's "new intellectuals" would include four of the British Battalion's commissars who attended the Lenin School in Moscow. One of them was Manchester's George Brown, who was killed in the Brunete campaign. A eulogist said:

> He was another example of how a worker, with just an elementary education and leaving school to start work at an early age, can grasp the essence of scientific socialism and apply it in the everyday struggles of the

class from which he sprang. He was able to impart the knowledge to other workers and to help them in their study of the science of Socialism.[8]

Tom Howell Jones, who lost his life in the Ebro offensive, was another exemplar. A fellow volunteer never forgot his first meeting with him at a class in economic theory in 1930, which was held every Sunday in the ILP rooms in Aberdare. He came to know Jones' well-stocked library from which the self-educated miner pulled down volumes of "the collected works of Lenin to the less well known works of Marx, Engels, Plekhanov, and other Socialist theoreticians." Jones' admirer added,

> Besides this attachment to pure Socialist theory, he was also very interested in history, economics and literature, especially poetry and the novel. He was exceptionally well read in the classics of English literature. He was a working-man with the culture of an intellectual and a poet.[9]

Others are not difficult to find, even if they have to be sought behind vague generalizations such as "intellectual types." The outstanding local historians and activists Eddie and Ruth Frow called the Mancunian waterproof maker, Bob Ward, "an intellectual type." Yet another "intellectual type" was Joe Lees of Oldham, who "loved good literature" and possessed a library of labour politics.[10] A barber from Aberdeen possessed a huge library and, according to Bob Cooney, was "what we would call a real natural working class intellectual."[11] George Leeson was one of two volunteers from the London Underground. (The other was Bill Briskie, a company commander at the battle of the Jarama.) Leeson was raised a Catholic and received a "classical education," rebelling against both. "I became interested in Socialism & read every book about it that I could get. Having been pumped full of Idealist Philosophy, I began to attempt the study of Materialism and Evolution."[12] Arthur Horner's mentor, Noah Ablett, differed from his student in that he was less impulsive, better read, in fact "a real philosopher" who was able to "sit there and listen to arguments and just stop the thing that didn't fit in and pick up the things that did fit in."[13] The key element was the working-class intellectual's relationship to working people. If the bonds of shared experience, of "a life in common" were present, then proletarian intellectuals might promote the best interests of the labor movement.

II

Whether communist or noncommunist, proletarian intellectuals took advantage of both informal and formal educational opportunities to understand the history, present, and future of their class. Such figures were the product of a working-class tradition that made them the most politically conscious British soldiers ever to shed their blood on a foreign battlefield. They had learned their politics from a culture they had created, and they were among its last graduates. After them came the ubiquitous influence of radio and television, and the death of the once-thriving and irrepressibly contentious world of the pamphlet and the radical newspaper.

The British volunteers received their informal education in three principal forms: print journalism, a general program of reading, and the open-air meeting. First, they read or had read to them pamphlets and newspapers, but particularly the latter, a longtime resource for workers. The growth of literacy in the nineteenth and early twentieth centuries generated a working-class readership that the *Daily Herald* and the *Daily Worker*, among others, took full advantage of during the years between the wars. These newspapers were "a formalised version of oral modes of transmitting and debating information prevalent amongst the uneducated."[14] Another publication that ignited or reinforced militancy was the communist *Imprecor* (International Press Correspondence), judged by Syd Booth to be "a marvellous piece of paper," moving him to join the Communist party.[15]

In addition to *Imprecor*, Booth was also deeply impressed by *Russia Today*, that Potemkin village of a publication, filled with pictures of smiling, happy, and prosperous Soviet workers.[16] And the Mancunian was hardly alone in succumbing to its mythologies. Julius Coleman, one of the earliest volunteers—who went out to Spain with John Cornford, the Cambridge poet and great-grandson of Darwin—admitted that he, too, was so moved by the magazine's rapturous pronouncements on the Soviet way of life that he mistook them for reality.[17] For those who had not yet adopted a sectarian frame of mind, there were more moderate, independent, and cerebral choices, with the *Manchester Guardian* at the head of the list.

The challenge to become "philosophers" and act on their new understanding was also realized through wide reading by a number of militant volunteers. One of them, Jim Brown, a construction worker, was among the best read of the volunteers for Spain. His self-education took place under the most wretched conditions. He walked the London streets at night to avoid the rats swarming across his bed in St. Pancras. Literature and ideas proved his salvation. He said, "I . . . had a great liking for poetry, for writers, for some thinkers.

I read some of the philosophers, most of the writers and I suppose I've read . . . almost a hundred thousand books."[18]

Brown's reading led him to a growing awareness of the distance between the classes, as did his experiences in life. He worked for a firm of fishmongers and "delivered at the houses of the really rich," including the Duke of Westminster, who had seventeen people working in his kitchen. When Brown returned home from a delivery, "Eight of us tried to maneuver three bloaters [a lightly salted and smoked fish] between us for dinner," and "you saw the terrific contrast" between the world of a St. Pancras slum and that of one of the great ducal households. Changing his occupation, Brown found the same fundamental inequalities between the possessors and the dispossessed. While working on a building site, he heard the foreman shout at a man who lit a cigarette, "Cut that out, those hands belong to me."[19]

Jim Brown did not see himself as unique or his understanding of the world unusually well informed. What he knew could be found in books that were available to anyone with curiosity and a vigorous mind. His reading included, in addition to poetry and philosophy, works by Adam Smith and David Ricardo, and Robert Blatchford's *Merrie England*. Most of all, he read Jack London, but then, he said, "Lots of people read Jack London."[20] Nor was he a passive reader. He was looking for reasons for the catastrophes that had befallen him and his class. His reading enabled him to transcend the particularity of his own misfortunes and to see them from a larger perspective. "The more I read the more I began to see things a bit clearer." The future took on a searing intensity as he contemplated what he believed to be the inevitability of a fascist England and Europe, if right-wing totalitarianism was not stopped in Spain. As he saw war coming, his understanding of Clausewitz and Liddell Hart convinced him that if the great human tragedy of war, waged with murderous new technologies, could be foreseen, it might also be stopped. In short, he came to understand intellectually what he instinctively believed. According to Brown, "the people knew, the ordinary person knew this was all wrong."[21] Brown's simple, earnest assertion is important as an example of unequivocal emancipation from the propaganda that England's leaders "knew best." The former fishmonger and insatiable reader became one of the earliest volunteers for Spain and fought with the No. 1 Company at Lopera, the Jarama, and Brunete.

Another proletarian intellectual was the Welshman Jim Brewer, who fought through all the major campaigns in Spain and was chosen to carry the flag of the British Battalion at the final parade in Barcelona in 1938. While growing up, he listened attentively to his grandfather's stories about the culture and political history of the miners of the Welsh valleys. Brewer remembered that he would talk "about the history of the working class movement and the beliefs of the average miner." When his health failed, Brewer left the mines and took full advantage of the educational opportunities that were beginning to open up for promising young working-class men in the early thirties. He was educated in Workers' Educational Association classes until he went to Coleg Harlech for a year at the age of nineteen and then won a Castle scholarship to Ruskin College at Oxford.[22]

Brewer supplemented his education with an active reading program that included membership in the Left Book Club as well as the works of Jack London, whose descriptions of unjust social conditions and egregious inhumanity influenced him deeply. Dickens, whom he read "from cover to cover," also opened new worlds for him. But his tastes were ecumenical. He read Lewis Mumford, Hardy, Wells, and Thackeray, all by the time he was fifteen.[23]

III

Outside of explicitly political texts, such as Marx and Engels' *Manifesto* or Robert Blatchford's *Merrie England*, only the *Ragged Trousered Philanthropists* had a greater impact on volunteers for Spain than Jack London's *People of the Abyss*,[24] which Jim Brown called "the book of all books."[25] In addition, he admired the American author's revolutionary novel, *The Iron Heel*.

In the summer of 1902 Jack London was on his way to South Africa as a correspondent under contract with an American news agency to cover the aftermath of the Boer War. When he received a cable suddenly canceling the agreement, he was forced to reconsider his plans. Instead of being dismayed by this dramatic change in his circumstances, he seized upon it as a challenge, deciding to move into the dreaded, pestilential East End to discover the living conditions of the poorest of the poor in the richest country in the world. As London himself said, "I went down into the under-world of London with an attitude of mind which I may best liken to that of an explorer."[26]

Unlike Charles Booth in London and Seebowm Rowntree in York, Jack London, anticipating Orwell, felt it necessary to live the life he sought to understand and describe. What he found was a world of suffering and degradation that had attained unimaginable proportions, constituting one of the greatest slums in the Western world. Combining both damning statistics and vignettes from his own experiences, he contrasted the conditions of the privileged in the great metropolis with those of the hundreds of thousands of human beings with whom he lived in the East End. "They are the stones by the builder rejected. There is no place for them in the social fabric, while all the forces of society drive them downward til they perish."[27]

Yet someday, London said, this submerged population would rise up "and the people of the West End will see them, as the dear soft aristocrats of Feudal France saw them and asked one another, 'Whence came they?' 'Are they men?'" And, at last, those who could have helped will hear "the cry of the people," London said. "From Ghetto and countryside, from prison and casual ward, from asylum and workhouse—the cry of the people who have not enough to eat." To answer this cry, according to him, required nothing more or less than the transformation of society.[28] All the numbers and experiences the author accumulated were intended to compose pieces of a mosaic with but one purpose, to show man's inhumanity to his fellow man. The world of the laboring poor whose inhabitants he had come to know on the streets and in the workhouses, whose hungers and hopes he had embraced, and whose stories he had memorized, must be made known to those who literally saw their fellow citizens in the East End as a strange and barbarous people.

Three years later, London completed *The Iron Heel*. Though little remembered today, the book moved away from sociological analysis to a full-blooded cry for revolution against the oligarchs who ground the "people of the abyss" into their miseries. London's book is a sub-Wellsian fantasy of small literary merit. Nevertheless, it enjoyed wide influence in Europe, particularly in France and Germany,[29] and exerted a very considerable impact on British militants, including the volunteers for Spain and, particularly, Harry Pollitt, who thought *The Iron Heel* the greatest of all revolutionary novels.[30] The Spanish Medical Aid Committee sent copies to its medical personnel in Spain. Anne Murray, a nurse who was one of three siblings to go to Spain, said that London's novel "brings out very clearly many of the dark facts and shows the methods by which many of our very successful business men reach the elevated positions in which they find themselves." According to Murray, "it is a very true book and I am all for the whole truth."[31] George Orwell called it "a . . . book of political prophecy" that foresaw the rise of fascism.[32]

London's novel purports to be a manuscript written by a daughter of the privileged, Avis, who falls in love with and marries a proletarian intellectual, Ernest Everhard. A self-educated "social philosopher," as well as an "ex-horseshoer," he easily proved himself the intellectual superior of his upper-class adversaries. But Everhard is above all the incarnation of London's fantasy of a Nietzschean superman who will show the workers the way to victory against their capitalist oppressors. After her husband's martyrdom at the hands of the "oligarchs," Avis wrote:

> His was a great soul, and, when my love grows unselfish, my chiefest regret is that he is not here to witness tomorrow's dawn. We cannot fail. He has built too stoutly and too surely for that. Woe to the Iron Heel! Soon shall it be thrust back from off prostrate humanity. When the word goes forth, the labour hosts of all the world shall rise. There has been nothing like it in the history of the world. The solidarity of labour is assured, and for the first time will there be an international revolution wide as the world is wide.[33]

London's two books established him as a political and moral force among British proletarian intellectuals who volunteered for Spain. His works helped them to identify the enemy, awakened them to conditions that must change, and provided them with examples of those who would be remembered for their attempts to build a just society. In addition, *The Iron Heel* held out the possibility that middle-class and proletarian intellectuals might forge a united front against political and social oppression.

IV

Like Jack London, Robert Tressell [Robert Noonan] was also an outsider, at least initially, in the world of working-class poverty. A son of a middle-class Irish family, he spoke several languages and received an education appropriate to his class. In 1902, upon his return from South Africa, he lived in the south coast town of Hastings. Turning his back on the professions, or the possibility of a teaching career, he became a house painter. His famous book, *The Ragged Trousered Philanthropists*, was the literary result of his life in the building trades.

The book's success was exceptional. In the first forty years of its publication, *The Ragged Trousered Philanthropists* sold over 100,000 copies, and was reprinted twice in the thirties. This was "an almost unbelievable figure" when one remembers that the typical working-class novel in the thirties was published in 1,500 copies and frequently only a third of that number actually sold. Moreover, as H. Gustav Klaus has pointed out, *The Ragged Trousered Philanthropists* "was *read by workers*."[34] Syd Booth, a carter from Manchester and a volunteer for Spain, was lent a "well worn copy" of Tressell's book by a Labour party workmate, and, he remembers, it quite literally changed the course of his life.[35] Harry Stratton, a taxi driver from Swansea and a veteran of the Jarama, whose conversion to socialism brought him into the world of fuel workers, dockers, coal-trimmers, and "others" in the thirties, summed up the book's importance. Tressell's book was their "bible."[36] Many believed that the novel played a role in the Labour victory in 1945.[37]

In his introduction, Tressell writes that his purpose was to offer his reader "a faithful picture of working-class life,"[38] more particularly of those working in the building trades in a small south-of-England town which he calls Mugsborough. The story centers on twenty-five workers who build a house called The Cave for a rich merchant, and their employers. Those working on the house were the foot soldiers of the great domestic armies—the plumbers, carpenters, bricklayers, plasterers, and painters—who were building the cities and suburbs of the bourgeoisie. They worked until they were fired or their job was finished. If they survived until old age, then the spiral downward into what Jack London called "the abyss" was inexorable.

Tressell's working-class hero, the socialist Owen, sought to understand the comprehensive human tragedy of which he, with his fellow workers, was a victim. Owen's attitude toward his workmates was, in the beginning, one of complete contempt. "Were they all hopelessly stupid? Had their intelligence never developed beyond the stage of childhood?" He attacked the idea, however, that most workers were lazy or drunkards. These stereotypes had been foisted on them by their oppressors, the middle class, who not only victimized them with their myths but chained them to their tasks, and had succeeded in dispossessing them of their common heritage, of their historical reality as a people.[39]

Owen believed that the real enemy was not the exploiter but his fellow workers who "quietly submitted" to their degradation and slavery, opposing anyone who spoke of change. As such, he called them "ragged trousered philanthropists," who freely gave their lives to uphold a corrupt system and who had no alternative vision of life. They could not or would not see a future in which a transformation of society might take place, one in which the productive classes, the workers, would supplant the unproductive classes, the capitalists and aristocrats. Moreover, he believed, the rich were right to despise the workers and to look upon them as "dirt." They deserved contempt.[40]

The different system required was socialism, which would prevent the domination of the productive by the unproductive. It would end private property and monopolies on the ownership of land, railways, gas and water works, factories, indeed all that should belong to society as a whole. Business competition perpetuated the inhuman conditions in which he and his workmates lived and labored. This was understandable because to gain a competitive edge over a commercial adversary, the capitalist was required to cheat and underpay his workers. Still, "nearly everyone seemed very pleased to think that the existing state of things could not possibly be altered."[41]

One of the workers grew sufficiently brave to say that he largely agreed with Owen, and that he had never before been able to find the words to express his dissatisfactions. Owen provided him and a few others with a conceptual strategy which enabled them to begin analyzing the social and economic trap in which they were ensnared and to encourage a growing confidence that their suffering was neither inevitable nor without solution. Owen explained that the socialist—very much against his will—finds himself in the midst of a terrible struggle and appeals to the other combatants to stop fighting and to establish a system of brotherly love and mutual helpfulness. But the socialist does not hypocritically pretend to practice brotherly love toward those who will not agree to his appeal and who compel him to fight with them for his very life. He knows that in this battle he must either fight or go under. Therefore, in self-defense, he fights, but all the time he continues his appeal for the cessation of the slaughter. The socialist pleads for change, advocating cooperation instead of competition.

Socialism, moreover, was synonymous with community. The only other group that preached the brotherhood of man, the Christians, "deride and oppose the Socialist's appeal." This, in a society that offers its benefits to those who possess the most amount of money, even though they may not be among its productive members. And Owen included in this category everyone from a thief to a bishop to a financier, all having in common the fact that they are "loafers." As a result, in a world in which worth is equated with money, "with the exception of criminals and the poorer sort of loafers," there was little wonder that "the working class are considered to be the lowest and least worthy in the community."[42]

There was quite literally nothing else like Tressell's novel in the proletarian canon. It alone had been written from "inside" the workers' experience of socialism. Alan Swingewood has called *The Ragged Trousered Philanthropists* "the first real novel of the working class."[43] Much of what was lacking in the novel must have been compensated for by the authenticity of the detail, the "recognition" of scenes that might have been drawn from the reader's own life, as well as the author's conviction that an alternative political culture—socialism—must lead to the downfall of the dominant system of bourgeois capitalism, which had degraded and exploited so many of England's men and women. Moreover, to have readily at hand the arguments for socialism and against capitalism must also have made the novel required reading for many.[44]

Like Jack London's *The People of the Abyss* and *The Iron Heel*, Tressell's novel spoke to the life experience and political culture of the working-class reader in a remarkably powerful manner. Its successful dramatization in 1927 by Tom Thomas and the Hackney People's Players resulted in the Workers' Theatre Movement.[45] In 1934 Frank Jackson, a veteran trade unionist, led a successful nine-day strike on a housing site in Putney. In the course of the strike Jackson began a series of discussions with his workmates on subjects of contemporary interest, as well as older issues of popular contention such as evolution. These bore a remarkable similarity to the "seminars" in *The Ragged Trousered Philanthropists*. After the strike ended, more than 200 copies of Tressell's novel were sold on the site.[46]

One of those bound for Spain, Bill Rowe, had a particular reason for cherishing Tressell's book. Rowe possessed "a soft spot for building workers" and denounced their employers as "the Scrooges of capitalism." When a building worker told him he wanted to murder his boss, Rowe chastised him, "Would that do much good? You boys first make your organisation so strong that you can take over the lot, foremen as well as machines. It's not just persons we want to shift, it's the sort of society that makes bullies and toadies."[47] For many workers, *The Ragged Trousered Philanthropists* offered an unforgettable picture of that society.

The books of London and Tressell were essential items in the intellectual inventory of working-class militants in the thirties, and, among them, many who volunteered for Spain. They enabled readers to see their lives within a clarifying intellectual, social, and economic context, thus giving a coherence and a legitimatization to the anger many felt so deeply at their years of unemployment, deprivation, and, most of all, political frustration.

V

And yet, "My best book," said Arthur Henderson, a leader of the Labour party, has "been my close contact with, and deep interest in the spiritual, moral, social and industrial affairs of life."[48] The life to which Henderson referred found its most vivid expression in the street-corner socialist orators who could hold audiences spellbound for hours in every city in the country, but particularly in the industrial North, Scotland, London, and South Wales. This rich and flexible oral tradition gave an insistent passion to the diverse elements of plebeian culture. The platform or street-corner orators shaped and evoked their audience's needs, grievances, humor, dreams, and simple delight in the sheer theater of the occasion. These speakers preached a doctrine of defiance to the regnant culture of the Victorians and Edwardians. We see their descendants on Hyde Park Corner today. But once they possessed an influence that only a Wesley or Whitefield or, later, a William Morris, could achieve, bringing moments of shattering illumination into their listeners' lives, and for many, changing them forever.

By 1914, the achievement of effective literacy by working men and women did not mean that oral culture was no longer important, but only that it had been powerfully complemented by the printed word. Robert Shields from Glasgow, who had been unemployed for six years before leaving for Spain, said that he became a militant first and foremost "by listening to street corner meetings," then reading, and finally by seeing a left-wing play with some friends.[49]

The militant, oral culture of the industrial cities of the North found its most receptive audiences in great public spaces such as Stevenson Square in Manchester. There, on Sundays, when as many as nine meetings might be taking place at any one time, huge crowds "of people who were discontented" circulated happily under a storm of political speech-making. Some of the speakers were "quacks" and "fakers." All, however, appeared to be aflame with some kind of grievance and found their "forum" in the square, hallowed, in part, because it was here that the Chartists had rallied their supporters in the nineteenth century.[50]

For Mick Jenkins, a leading Communist party organizer, the square became "a real hothouse" for breeding socialists.[51] This "hothouse," or any other civic space where workers gathered for conversation and enlightenment, helped join more tightly the intimate bonds of working-class community. Sam Wild, a former sailor and boilerman at the Paramount Theater who would command the British Battalion in Spain, remembered, "I'd listened to Harry Pollitt and other pro-Spanish Republican speakers in Stevenson Square and I came to the conclusion that I should do something about helping those people."[52]

Above all, it was necessary for the speaker to put his or her ideas into everyday words. Most workers found the language of continental socialism to be estranging. Imported concepts that were congenial to French and German radicals and revolutionaries often fell inertly into the political life of the British militant. David Caute has observed that the British constructed their world with a "vocabulary and concepts [that] were empiricist, positivistic, utilitarian, or pragmatic."[53] Even when socialism began making headway among Salford workers after World War I, Marxist language and ideology remained unfamiliar, too transcendental and abstract for their taste. Robert Roberts joined a group of fifty-four workers meeting over a bar to study the first nine chapters of *Das Kapital*. Within a month's time only three remained.[54]

There was, however, another factor that alienated workers from theoretical socialism: the powerful moral tradition of Christian brotherhood that historically helped to shape the ideology of the British radical tradition, inoculating it against foreign toxins. For many, a conservative interpretation of the Christian message, reinforced customary class attitudes of deference and accommodation. This was understood by Harry Quelch, a prolific speaker and journalist, who was wholly self-educated and "one of the outstanding working-class intellectuals in the history of the modern labour movement."[55] Quelch possessed a pessimistic view of the socialist potential of his fellow workers before World War I, ruefully concluding that among the working classes of Europe, the prewar English workers were "the most reverential to the master class."[56] The interwar years would see some changes in this proposition, at least among a militant elite.

Above the "lower" working class was "the cream of working-class society," those who were the most skillful, intelligent, well-read, and active in popular culture, whether it was the choir, cycling or rambling, or attending Methodist chapels or socialist Sunday Schools. Robert Roberts remembered, "Obscure men enough then, forgotten now, innocent perhaps in their hopes, they fought not only for self- or sectional interest but for the betterment, as they saw it, of a whole community." From them came the speakers who dedicated themselves to the "Great Debate" on socialism in the interwar years. They acted as "assessors, arbiters and makers of the common conscience, most, although having abandoned church and chapel, still espousing a Christian ethic." It was the power of their presence and language that permeated the psychological and intellectual defenses of working class life "and conditioned the minds of all."[57]

VI

The effect that these larger-than-life figures had on their audiences could be astonishing. Mick Jenkins remembered that in the presence of a good speaker, "You would stand with your mouth open . . . just glued to the spot and glued to him." But looking back on these great early occasions, Jenkins thought the messages were somehow insubstantial. This older generation of speakers, Jenkins observed, "carried an abstract sectarian message of Socialism divorced from immediate realities and [it seemed] very doubtful whether they convinced people in a permanent sense, although they must have set many people on the road."[58]

Another place of public education in Manchester was the Queen's Park Parliament, as it was called. Up to 400 people, including the youthful George Brown, met each week in the park to debate fiercely every conceivable issue, but typically contemporary political topics. The result was a carnival of language and contention. According to Mick Jenkins, "Well prepared arguments, delivered with oratorical ability, humor, repartee, devastating interjections, poetry, all entered into the afternoon's debate." Because Brown persisted in reading through the Marxist canon and mastering a "basic" understanding of Marxist theory, he became an effective and sympathetic spokesman for the party. He possessed a mastery of the well-turned phrase and sharp retort, but also had what every successful working-class leader required, the ability to put "in simple everyday terms" the principal issues of the day. This meant that he became equally at home in explaining party policy on a street corner or at a meeting of the Manchester and Salford Trades Council.[59]

Scottish militants breathed socialism in the open-air spaces of their towns and cities as well. The Mound in Edinburgh was a place where many Scots, including the volunteer Donald Renton, first began to formulate their political views. Renton later came into contact with the local Communist party organizer who encouraged him to read the great classics of Marxism and the publications of the Plebs League.[60] The blacksmith, Garry McCartney, received his political education in the exuberant political life of Glasgow in the thirties. On the weekend, Glasgow "was a forum of meetings, all over the city, at street corners, and in the centre of the city." Those in search of political enlightenment could find a rich variety of pundits from whom to choose—ranging from tramp preachers to recognized spokesmen for the Independent Labour, Labour, and Communist parties. "It was a whole seabed of discussion, all aiming in one direction," McCartney remembered. And that was, "How do we get socialism?" As a result of all the catechizing, he became "fully committed."[61] William Kelly, who was to be captured in his first action at Calceite, went at the age of fourteen with his father to hear the leader of the British Socialist party, the Glaswegian John Maclean. For Kelly, "that was the first inspiration I ever got in politics."[62] The same also applied to Alec Ferguson, whose father had been a member of H. M. Hyndman's Socialist Democratic Federation. At the age of twelve Ferguson heard a speech by John Maclean and promptly joined the ILP.[63]

Bob Cooney, perhaps the most popular commissar in the history of the British Battalion, came from Aberdeen. On Sundays he could be found at the Castlegate, a large open area in the city. Looking back more than half a century later, he remembered it as "a form of Open University." A wagon pulled into the square by a horse would serve throughout the day as a speaker's platform. Among those clambering up to address the expectant crowds were leading figures from the Communist party, the Reconstruction League, the Douglas Credit Association, and sometimes particularly memorable individuals such as the anarchist Guy Alred.[64] At one antifascist rally, Cooney himself spoke to an audience of 10,000. This public place, he said, "is our forum—the forum of the working class. It is to us the symbol of freedom of speech won by the struggles and sacrifices of our class."[65]

Although there was an undeniable breadth to the education a worker might gain from these open-air meetings, inevitably most of the talking was about politics, particularly socialist politics. Public spaces in Aberdeen, Glasgow, Manchester, Liverpool, the East End, the Rhondda, and countless others proved fertile recruiting grounds for socialists, most of them finding their homes in the trade union movement and the Labour party, others moving farther into the unknown by joining the Communist party, which became the most dynamic force on the left in the thirties. During this period, the Hunger Marchers offered cadres of speakers for socialist ideas as well as provided examples of working-class solidarity and militancy. Few who heard them were unmoved. One in the majority was Walter Gregory, who listened intently to the speeches of the marchers when they came through his home of Lincoln. Gregory believed they represented "the only organization with a real interest in helping the unemployed and [which] stood virtually alone in the battle to improve the position of the working class."[66]

For Tony Gilbert, a Londoner, the street corners of the East End were his Castlegate and Stevenson Square. "You could hardly go into any area of the East End and not see a street-corner meeting of one character or the other." The Labour party and various Christian organizations established a strong presence, but the dominant figures were Communist party speakers. Of particular importance to a young Jew like Gilbert was that the communists condemned the whole capitalist system, pointing out that the anti-Semitism of the fascist gangs that roamed the East End was only a "symptom" of the larger threat for which workers must be prepared. Consequently, young Jews flocked to the Communist party, explaining why "the East End of London supplied so many young people to enter into the struggle against fascism in Spain."[67]

VII

Harry Pollitt and Lewis Jones were the greatest extraparliamentary speakers of the interwar years. Fred Copeman, the commander of the British Battalion, said of Pollitt, "He'd bring tears to a glass eye."[68] Above all, Pollitt knew his audiences. A Mancunian boilermaker, Pollitt succeeded, first, because of his complete lack of affectation in front of an audience. He did not patronize his listeners or resort to rhetorical tricks; second, he carefully prepared and argued his speeches; third, he possessed a moral *gravitas* on the platform that inspired his listeners with a strong sense of the purity of his motives and the integrity of his views. His success was rooted in an ability to project a profound sense of class identity, and with it, a corresponding and quite genuine hatred of capitalism. Strongly influenced by his mother, who worked in a mill, he said, "I swore that when I grew up I would pay the bosses out for the hardships she suffered. I hope I shall live to do it, and there will be no nonsense about it . . . not that at that time I knew anything about systems, but I felt instinctively that something was wrong." The *New Statesman* said of Pollitt in 1940, "He is a man whom sincere Socialists want to follow whatever class they come from . . . because he is inspired with a moral fervor . . . utterly alien from the opportunism and Machiavellianism of current Marxism."[69] Pollitt developed a brilliant sense of timing that allowed him in the last part of his speeches to conclude his arguments and then bring his audience into an almost mystical communion with the "gleam" of the socialist promised land. No less a speaker than Michael Foot said, "The last ten or fifteen minutes of the speech, he would absolutely take the roof off and the whole thing would be extremely exciting."[70]

The genius of Harry Pollitt lay in the fact that he transcended two genres. On the one hand, he was the incarnation of the intuitive, evangelical street-corner socialist[71] who illustrated his remarks with examples from a working life. On the other, with the help of R. Palme Dutt, the Balliol-educated communist, he found a theoretical context in which he could place these same experiences, convincing both workers and intellectuals that the socialist "road" led to communism. Pollitt was an avatar of the last generation of proletarian intellectuals to have such a personal and often decisive effect on the political consciousness of working-class audiences. He was joined by hundreds of itinerant socialist speakers who made their way through the industrial cities of the North and their satellites, some of them men and women of considerable intellectual distinction, who had, above all, the ability to communicate in a familiar and effective manner with their audiences. These were figures such as John Maclean, Willie Gallacher, and Tom Mann, as well as those who heard them and in turn themselves became emissaries of their message.

John Henderson, a woodworker from Gateshead who was wounded at the battle of Brunete, demonstrated how a worker went from spectator to participant in this public discourse. "I went along to the open-air meetings at the Bigg Market in Newcastle, listened to the speakers there, [and] read a lot of books about politics and economics." Henderson began to attend CP meetings at a bookshop on Newcastle's Westgate Road. Then, he and a friend built a portable wooden platform that they could carry with them to address crowds at open-air meetings on Friday nights.[72]

If Harry Pollitt commanded legions of admirers, listeners, and some converts in London, the North of England, and Scotland, Lewis Jones similarly dominated the Rhondda. In a land that passionately loved the music of language, he was the consummate virtuoso, and was, consequently, perhaps a more naturally eloquent speaker than Harry Pollitt. On the day he died, he gave thirty speeches in behalf of the Republic.[73] As in the case of Pollitt, Jones was a communist, and like Pollitt, he learned politics not from theory but from what he saw and experienced. He went down into the pits at the age of twelve. In the next fifteen years he experienced the full range of a miner's life: the difficult and dangerous work, lockouts, strikes, efforts to organize, and confrontations with the authorities. Theory came only later, as it did for Pollitt. The role that Dutt played in influencing Pollitt was assumed in Lewis Jones' education by Noah Rees, who had received his Marxist training at Ruskin College, and subsequently became Jones' mentor. As the thirties began, Jones had a reputation as "an orator of unrivalled gifts, able to articulate the emotions of people with whom, in all other ways, he merged."[74]

His close friend, Mavis Llewellyn, said that Jones shared the joys and miseries of the working people of the Rhondda as no one else could. "You can say you're sorry for somebody, but there are ways in which you can identify yourself personally with suffering, and I think he did that."[75] He also believed, as did Pollitt, in an all-party alliance on issues as apparently disparate, but inherently linked, as the Means Test and Spain. Jones volunteered to fight in Spain, as did 160 Welshmen, but the party judged him too valuable to go, so he threw himself into the Aid Spain movement with all his formidable abilities and energies, dying in the week that Barcelona fell to Franco.[76]

Jones, like the men and women of lesser gifts and energies who traveled the country in the interwar years—as had Wesley's disciples 150 years before, preaching organization and salvation—reinforced the self-respect and potential of the working class at a time when the country's rulers counted them for very little. David Smith has written:

The forced creation of a South Walian working class from the late nine-teenth century meant that people wrenched from the closeness of personal and rooted traditions into an impersonal and a-historical world required—in order to have a sense of themselves as a proletariat—an identity that could only be their own if mediated through ballads, games, choirs, jokes and anecdotes which mirrored their own collective endeavours, courage and self-deprecation. That new tradition, for all its ambiguities, was neither crushed or passive. It spawned, in addition, an organically-related intelligentsia who were keenly aware of the self-making of this manufac-tured working class.[77]

Although the time and tempo of class formation differed in various parts of the country, as did the development of organic intellectuals, men such as Harry Pollitt and Lewis Jones announced a new dispen-sation, in significant ways a departure from the radicalism of the British past, but, as important, representing a continuation of the efforts of Thomas Paine, Robert Owen, and William Morris to under-stand and change the world. Pollitt and Jones were the last of their kind. After World War II, the leader of the British Communist party rebelled against the emphasis on abstract theory in the socialist message and warmed his hands over the fire that had once caused socialism to "gleam" in the dark night of capitalism. Pollitt said:

What was it that prompted Morris to go to the street corner? What was it that prompted Will Thorne to go every Sunday morning and never miss, wet or fine, to speak at Beckton Road in Canning Town extolling his conception of the gospel called Socialism? And do not be afraid of being sentimental in your approach even if you did go to a university. For alas in these days when pineapples and peaches pass for a British socialist epoch, we need to recapture something of the spirit that dominated this type of man.

All was not just sweet memory. Pollitt called forth "a return to the soap-box to blazon the principles and the cause of the workers at every street corner, market place and public hall."[78]

The degree of militancy that separated the more than 2,000 British volunteers and their hundreds of thousands of supporters from the majority, depended, then, on the informal oral and written culture of proletarian life. First was the workers' ability and willingness to read newspapers with a strong political bent, such as the *Daily Herald*, *Reynolds'*, and the *Daily Worker*, or have them read to them if they were not "good readers." Second, each in one way or another had likely been affected by the dynamic oral tradition of the working class. The combined effect was the creation of a political culture that helped to liberate men and women from the shadowing despair of the thirties by encouraging their understanding, passion, and sacrifice.

In February 1937, the British workers who hurried to protect the Madrid–Valencia road, the capital's lifeline, were men who had grappled with issues a good deal more complex than those that inspired their ancestors in the great struggles for workers' rights in the nineteenth century. They felt a self-confidence in themselves and their class that only the intellectual and political understanding they had made their own could bring.

CHAPTER 5

Learning and Living

The fact is, the majority of us had no more than the sketchiest grasp of theory. We did not bother to read the texts; we had others do that for us. The working class Comrades were the great readers—Communism could not have survived without autodidacts.

— John Banville, *The Untouchable*

As summer melted into autumn, Len and Mary devoted themselves with ever greater assiduity to the Circle. The subjects they discussed took on an increasingly Socialist bias, and under the guidance of John Library the Circle organised private and public lectures at which well-known Liberals and theoretical Socialists spoke. The experiment proved very popular, and political interest and discussion began to develop in the valley.   — Lewis Jones, *Cymwardy*

To have a knowledge of the great socialist writers, to be able to know their approach to the problems of life and politics, is to have a socialist culture. . . . Therefore, let us read.   — Ralph Fox

I

Depending on the susceptibilities of their audiences, as well as their own proclivities, open-air speakers might well part the ideological heavens and bring the audience to a moment of political revelation. This kind of apocalyptic exhortation was ever to be part of the repertoire of the left.[1] More lasting in its effect, however, was the kind of hardheaded, systematic analysis of socialism sought by Mick Jenkins and his party comrades. This became yet another reason that workers came to see Spain as a natural extension of their intellectual and political lives.

The listener's desire for analysis, facts, and figures that could be assembled into a meaningful philosophy, took on a more profound and lasting character when joined with a formal course of instruction in history, economics, philosophy, and political theory. The autodidact tradition saw workers pursuing their political and philosophical education through individual study, but also through the Plebs League, the Workers' Educational Association, the Extension and

Labour College movements (including the Central Labour College in London), and Ruskin College in Oxford.

Tom Mann described the typical working-class socialist as "a workman who through youth and early manhood has been battling against long hours in order that he might attend the institute, listen to lectures, and read the works of able men, and who by these means has succeeded in having a mind worth owning." In an introduction to a Left Book Club translation of a Russian work on dialectical materialism, John Lewis wrote, "If rulers must be philosophers that means that in a State where the workers rule the workers must themselves be philosophers."[2]

The WEA and other workers' educational institutions moved decisively away from preoccupation with discipline and rote memorization to subjects that encouraged the development of analytical skills and general learning. But the materials studied possessed a political content that students could apply to their lives and experience as members of the working class. Formal learning opportunities of this kind enabled the unemployed, particularly, to rediscover their sense of self-worth and to regain a measure of moral and intellectual control of their lives. The Workers' Education Association played a crucial role in heightening the self-esteem of workers. For example, instead of whiling away his days in unemployment, Walter Gregory enrolled in WEA classes. "I had long been aware of my educational limitations and had tried to overcome these through night school and now through courses run by the WEA, and it was these which set the political blood flowing through my veins." Courses on politics, government, and Marx, he wrote, "placed great emphasis upon opening its students' minds and sought to develop their analytical faculties." When Gregory moved with his family to Bulwell, a coal-mining village, he found "a derelict place of derelict men." This so alarmed him that he moved even more rapidly to the left, and, finally, into the Communist party.[3]

Other, less structured educational opportunities took the form of discussion groups organized by workers or perhaps by a middle-class militant. The Young Communist League attracted many because it recognized and met this need. The leaders of the local branches of the YCL might be a couple such as Ron and Mollie Body of Middlesbrough who "combined flair, imagination, patience, and down-to-earth practicality" in leading discussions and encouraging debate with a political content among young workers. One class was tutored by "a scientist comrade" who worked for Imperial Chemical.[4]

The branch secretary of the Young Communist League often arrived at meetings with an attaché case full of reading materials that could be purchased by members. One future volunteer for Spain who became a regular customer stayed up after the meetings until he had read through his new acquisitions "however late that might be."[5] The young Welsh communist, Edwin Greening, even devised a strategy to keep his books with him after volunteering for Spain. Once he joined the Battalion, Greening offered his comrades his cigarettes if they would help him transport his small library. As a result, "I had no trouble at all carting my books around Spain."[6] The historian Raphael Samuel has said of his mother, who worked ceaselessly for Spanish Aid in the thirties, that for her generation the party and its educational materials served as "a surrogate for a university."[7]

Margaret McCarthy recalls at YCL meetings that the names of revolutionaries imprisoned in various parts of the world were regularly remembered. When she heard their names called out, McCarthy felt as if she had overcome her insignificance. No longer was she simply one of millions who "were outcast, unwanted, untrained scrap, solely by reason of our working-class origin and our poverty."[8] Instead, she had become part of a movement that possessed an English past, but more important, an English present and future and, in turn, was linked to a transformation of the world outside her native country's shores.

II

One of the first volunteers to leave England for Spain was Charles Bloom, an ex-serviceman who studied dialectics with the itinerant Marxist educator, T. A. Jackson, at the Marx House School in Clerkenwell Green. Jackson was a key figure in the "university" whose purpose was to transform Great Britain and the larger world. His first book, *Dialectics: The Logic of Marxism*, appeared in 1936. Jackson became a protean force in worker education during the interwar years. He left school at age thirteen and worked in the printing trade until "a passion for book collecting and devouring" overwhelmed him. During a long lifetime there were inevitable changes in his ideas, but his original intention to incite and organize revolutionary socialism in Great Britain never wavered. A vivid teacher and writer, insatiably curious and relentlessly contentious in his polemics, the indefatigable Jackson was a unique figure on the proletarian left.[9] He remarked, "If it be not profane to say so, I will affirm that Communism—or Communist Propaganda—needs only one thing to make it triumph, viz., translating into English, the English of the workshop. . . . Let us speak the tongue our class uses."[10] And this he did, providing a satisfying philosophical picture of the world, in which unemployment, the Means Test, and the rise of fascism could be seen as parts of an intellectual whole.

To some workers, then, politics of a militant character did matter. On the left a substantial if minority stratum of articulate radicalism survived the defeat of Chartism in the 1850s, subsequently found its incorporation in a coherent vision of socialism espoused by William Morris and Tom Maguire, and then logically turned away in dwindling numbers from the "reformist" Labour party toward the socialist Independent Labour party or the small Communist party, which was founded in 1920.[11] The argument most commonly employed to "explain" the political ineffectuality of the rank-and-file support for Republican Spain is the intractable moderation and anticommunism of Labour's leaders, particularly Ernest Bevin and Sir Walter Citrine. These qualities proved sufficient to stop any challenge from the trade union membership, and particularly from the small but influential Communist party. K. W. Watkins has written that

> the tide, overwhelmingly as a result of the Civil War, was running strongly to the Left. . . . But it could only find a political expression which would truly reflect its magnitude through the actions of the two decisive bodies: the Labour Party and the T.U.C. It was at this point that the breakdown occurred. The mass feeling pulled in one direction whilst those who grasped the levers of the machine tugged in the other.[12]

Despite the undeniably dynamic and frequently creative leadership on the left, it is clear that, contrary to Watkins' view, the majority of organized workers and Labour party voters in the thirties remained moderate in their political loyalties. For most, their comparative economic wellbeing and the influence of their political culture, which made unconstitutional or revolutionary behavior unacceptable, protected them against initiatives advocated by the left.[13] Andrew Thorpe has concluded:

> This moderate line was not imposed by a treacherous leadership on a duped rank-and-file which would have preferred more unconstitutional action; far from it. The leaders understood pretty well the hopes and fears of their constituents, the majority of whom were never faring so badly under

capitalism as to want to rush headlong into a violent revolution the result of which no-one could have predicted.[14]

Yet, this is hardly all that needs to be said if militant working-class ideology is recognized as an emerging presence in the labor movement, and if it is acknowledged that the experience of Spain played a principal role in affirming and extending the influence of Marxism in popular as well as elite political culture. Franco was the symbol of oppression not just of the Spanish people, but also of English workers. It was said by a Welsh veteran, Dai Llewellyn, that "the face of the enemy" consisted of more than a palimpsest of images of Hitler or Mussolini or Franco, "the traitor general," but "it was also the mask of the fine English gentleman, the smooth manners and charm, and underneath, the savage ruthlessness and blood-thirsty readiness to use every means, however foul, to defend ruling-class profit and power."[15] Llewellyn himself sprang from what Hywel Francis and David Smith have called the "alternative culture" that had developed in the South Wales coal fields.[16] For that militant and able working-class minority in the Rhondda or Manchester or London or Glasgow who committed themselves to this vision, and wanted to continue their education in revolutionary politics, the Lenin School in Moscow was a next step.

III

The Lenin School, or the International Lenin University, in Moscow was established as the ideological finishing school for the most promising of the young Communist leaders from Great Britain and throughout the world. After the death of Lenin, the Fifth Congress of the Comintern felt a responsibility "to broaden and deepen the propaganda of the theory of Marxism-Leninism." This called for the major parties to send a small number of their most promising cadres to Moscow for an extensive theoretical education in a variety of subjects useful to communist agents and party officials. Margaret McCarthy remembered, "Almost every member of the Young Communist League in Britain who possessed any qualities of leadership at all went off to Moscow" to study at the Lenin School.[17]

After delays, the Lenin School is thought to have opened in October 1926 with students from Russia, France, England, and two German groups.[18] This uncertain beginning proved deceptive. The Lenin School became the "highest political school in the communist world" and grew to almost a thousand students. The most politically important representations came from the English-speaking countries, Great Britain and the United States, and then Spain, France, Germany, and China. The Spanish, German, and Chinese groups, however, were the largest, each sending around a hundred students.[19] They lived together in a residential setting and studied exhaustively in bright classrooms under a banner that read, "Without Revolutionary Theory, no Revolutionary Practice."[20]

The course itself lasted either nine months or two years. Generally, the classes consisted of "intensive propaganda," which nevertheless required a great deal of study. The core of the curriculum focused on Leninism, historical materialism, and the history of the Communist party in the Soviet Union. The practical application of theory was the characteristic that most distinguished the Lenin School from the Central Labour College in Great Britain. The former was intended to create revolutionaries who would make revolutions. The latter taught Marxist theory but "was not based on the necessity for the creation of a revolutionary party."[21] This difference in their attitudes toward the future was one of the factors that separated the British militants from their continental comrades.

Will Paynter, a major figure in the British Communist party, a leader of the South Wales Miners' Federation, and, later, a member of the International Brigades, was one of the chosen ones from Great Britain to attend the Lenin School in 1932. Its rigors had not been exaggerated. For the first three months he worked sixteen to eighteen hours a day, taking, among other subjects, political economy and social history. Hitler's accession to power in January 1933 and his offensive against the German Communist party, however, caused a weakening of the academic regimen as the Comintern found more pressing issues to address. Paynter's experience at the school, in any event, was a troubled one. He rebelled against the rigidity of its bureaucracy and leadership. For this he was called before the Central Committee. In addition, Paynter became convinced that the Moscow school was doing more harm than good to the British party. He believed that some two-thirds of the students from Great Britain who attended the school "were no bloody good when they came back here, and most of them left the Party,"[22] presumably for the same reasons that encouraged his contentious attitude: the party's rigidity and bureaucracy. One of those students was the volunteer Thomas Duncan, who came from a home where "proletarian politics prevailed."

At the end of his course he complained that both the Soviet Union and the school were too autocratic for his taste. When he returned to England, he planned to leave the working-class movement.[23]

What is less obvious, but equally if not more important than the endless hours of academic work, were the opportunities for travel and forming important ideological and personal relationships with young men and women from throughout the communist world. Most shared the same flaming idealism and, despite many of the disquieting things they saw and experienced in Russia,[24] knew the exhilaration of living in the country that had brought socialism to one-sixth of the globe. As one historian has written, Russia was "a reminder that in post-war Europe there was a new nation in which the workers ruled."[25]

Each of these threads of education, personal relationships, and travel were woven into new patterns of optimism and possibility. As inefficient and mindless as communism might seem in practice in Russia, all could be forgiven—the cruelties and inanities of the Soviets, the inequalities already being institutionalized between the people and the party leaders, the hypocrisies and lies—because the future promised the end of all such things. Nor, it must be remembered, did the living and working conditions in Russia, as appalling as they seemed to many foreign communists, appear so abysmal to many British students. In Margaret McCarthy's native Lancashire, such communities as Darwen, Oldham, and Bolton experienced unemployment of between 40 and 50 percent. In her wide reading as a young girl, she came to know well Engels' *The Condition of the Working Class in England in 1844*. Although she acknowledged that life had improved somewhat in the intervening ninety years, "the same atmosphere, the grimness, the unconcern for human life and values, even the very self-same factories, about which he wrote" still surrounded the inhabitants.[26]

One of the greatest British successes at the Lenin School was Bob Cooney from Aberdeen, who had joined the No More War movement in 1924 and two years later the Labour party. In early 1927 he became a member of the ILP Guild of Youth. He left the Labour party, however, when Captain Wedgwood-Benn, who had defected from the Liberal party and only recently joined Labour, was selected to stand at a by-election in Aberdeen. Cooney found it impossible to work for the candidate "because he wasn't a socialist as far as I was concerned." Cooney chose instead to devote himself to the communist candidate because, at least, he was the real thing.[27]

After hearing Harry Pollitt a year later, he decided to join the party and rose rapidly in its ranks. Cooney became a tutor organizer at the Aberdeen Labour College, where classes in economics, working-class history, political geography, and others were held two nights a week. When he was selected by the party to attend the Lenin School, it marked a turning point in his life. His roommate was the Welsh communist Harry Dobson, a future commissar in Spain.[28] One of his instructors was the novelist Ralph Fox, also a commissar in the Spanish War, who taught the history of the Western European labor movement and whom he discovered was "a very modest man,"[29] not an attribute that a revolutionary worker might have normally recognized in a Magdalen intellectual.

In addition, Cooney studied political economy, dialectics, and a practical course that was believed indispensable for a revolutionary: the means of communicating in jail. For Cooney and his generation of like-minded men and women, jail or prison was only to be expected, and with reason. Cooney had so many run-ins with the police that he thought the CPGB must have believed he was breaking into prison "because I was arrested so much."[30]

The theoretical training offered by the Lenin School was particularly important to members of the British party because of what was perceived as their relative lack of political sophistication. Cooney remembered, "In those days we were at local, district, and even often at national level amateurs, with more enthusiasm than deep theoretical knowledge." Cooney found that the school provided a sense of intellectual and personal self-confidence that built the foundation of his later success as political commissar of the British Battalion in Spain. For him, the school "really had an everlasting and revolutionary effect on my life because I felt a giant [by] the time I'd finished." Moreover, the Lenin School helped to correct what Cooney had objected to most in the British socialist tradition. This was the propensity to treat socialism as a "dream," which resulted in discussions within the labor movement that "were of a very philosophical nature and didn't have much to do with immediate problems." From this perspective, "socialism seemed to be a very far off thing," and militants could only "dream of a very, very distant future socialist idyllic Britain." Cooney's practical experience in the party and his theoretical training in socialist theory at the Lenin School had "dovetailed." As a result, he found himself able to analyze problems from both the point of view of their immediate effect and also their long-range consequences.[31]

Since the Lenin School allowed only boarders (although there were evening classes that enabled Margaret McCarthy to attend), it was inevitable, too, that close friendships would develop, particularly among students in the same language groups, such as the British and North Americans. For example, it was in Moscow that the American Steve Nelson and the Englishman George Brown came to know each other. They would not meet again until the eve of the battle of Brunete in July 1937.

At the end of the spring term, students normally made visits to collective farms and factories. But the visits were canceled in the summer of 1936, when the Spanish Civil War began. So were classes at the Lenin School. The "proposal" was made by the leadership that all students prepare to depart for Spain. Within a day, the Russians arranged an orientation, and the Lenin School "volunteers" were outfitted for the journey.[32] According to John Peet, the lack of imagination shown was monumental. The students were meant to travel clandestinely to Spain, but each was outfitted in "identical Comintern-issue blue serge suits" and given consecutively numbered forged Austrian passports.[33] No fewer than six of Bob Cooney's class of twenty (which included five women) went to Spain.[34]

IV

Many volunteers also were strengthened by their roots in the fraternal soil of Non-Conformity, as well as by that part of the British past which possessed particular meaning for working-class men and women. Jack Jones was profoundly shaped by his Methodist upbringing. Coming from a mixed family of Catholics and Protestants in Liverpool, he remembered, "I used to read the bible a bit and I was especially interested in ... the social teachings of Jesus Christ." Perhaps Jim Brewer's outlook most vividly illustrates the way in which religious values could reinforce or invigorate popular, radical culture. He came from a strict, Non-Conformist background, recalling, "One of the firmest things they ever taught was this necessity never to tell lies. Always to speak the truth regardless of what the consequences were, and you sort of take that attitude into politics and into everything you do." It was only natural that concepts such as the brotherhood of man came to be fundamental elements in his view of the world. As Brewer put it, the belief had been imparted into him "that you had to help other people and that you were part of a society and that you had to act according to your beliefs." This, he said, was "the basic thing," and it was necessary "to behave accordingly."[35]

But, in addition to his religious views, Brewer cherished the memory of his Chartist great-grandfather, who, he believed, set him on his journey to Spain. The historical tradition of plebeian militancy played a role of particular importance in the shaping of militant consciousness in the thirties. Lillian Buckoke, an indefatigable and courageous nurse, was a descendant of the fourteenth-century rebel, Jack Cade. She said, "The more I've read about him . . . , the more proud I am. In a small way . . . I tried to carry on his tradition" in Spain.[36] Harold King was one of the few experienced soldiers among the British volunteers, having served in World War I, where he was wounded at Ypres. He volunteered to act as a stretcher bearer at the Jarama and lost a hand when hit by an explosive bullet. Like others, he found in the English past a history other than that celebrated in his school textbooks. In World War I, he was in a constant state of contention with his sergeant major, who told him how proud he should be at the fame of his regiment. King's response was shaped by the popular narrative of the Norman Yoke, depicting the Normans who conquered England in 1066 as tyrants and usurpers, which played an essential part in Thomas Paine's political discourse. "I told him I'd got nothing to be proud [of] because the foundation of the regiment was a lot of bloody thieves and hooligans that joined up in the days of medieval times."[37] This inflamed the sergeant major because "he didn't like to mention this history."[38]

Margaret McCarthy, like Harold King, Brewer, and Buckoke, was deeply influenced in her political views by the powerful tradition of "this history" and its heroes and heroines. In her autobiography, she notes that when she was a child, a local socialist newsagent obtained a copy for her of a biography of Wat Tyler, the leader of the peasants' revolt of 1381. "With Wat Tyler . . . I first learned that Socialism too could be an adventure, a cause, a crusade, with ancient martyrs of its own, a cause in which we too might join and fight, living participators in something that was for the future, and yet deeply rooted in the English past." She said, "When I read Wat Tyler I felt English."[39] When McCarthy joined the Young Communist League, she discovered that not all martyrs for socialism were interred in the remote past. One of her comrades was jailed in 1926 for making a speech meant to stir "disaffection among the civil population." When released after a twenty-eight-day confinement, he was greeted as "a young class-war hero."[40] Another of her comrades was killed in Spain.

Finally, the career of George Brown confirms the connection many felt to exist between Spain and native radical traditions. When Brown was killed in his first action at Villanueva de la Cañada during the Brunete offensive in July 1937, the party lost one of its most valuable leaders. He was a member of the Manchester and Salford Trades Council, as well as the Communist party's executive committee. But his death could not be written of without emphasizing the continuities between the radical roots of the people of his city and the Spanish struggle. A eulogist noted with pride that Brown was "a true son of the working class. In the death of our comrade the great traditions of the Manchester people from Peterloo onwards are maintained."[41]

Nor did middle-class intellectuals hesitate to claim the heroes of popular history. James Klugmann, a contemporary of John Cornford at Cambridge and official party historian, believed that Great Britain's radical past belonged equally to middle- and working-class militants:

> We became the inheritors of the Peasants' Revolt, of the left of the English Revolution, of the pre-Chartist movement, of the women's suffrage movement from the 1790s to today. It set us in the right framework, it linked us with the past and gave us a more correct course for the future.[42]

Tom Wintringham, the poet, Balliol graduate, and commander of the British Battalion at the Jarama, had his own blood claims to the popular struggle against oppression.

> Eight or nine generations back before my birth one of my ancestors, a Nonconformist hedge preacher, had his tongue torn out by order of a royal court of justice. It was the only way to stop him "carrying on subversive propaganda," as we should call it today.

Wintringham said, "That hedge doctor had sent me [to Spain]."[43]

Workers reciprocated by seizing upon Lord Byron as an ally from the past. An early reviewer of Bill Rust's *Britons in Spain* wrote that Lord Byron's involvement in the Greek Revolution "is rightly hailed as the starting point of a glorious tradition." But "the men of the International Brigade have enlarged that tradition into something much bigger, filled with greater meaning."[44] The poet's theatrical, self-aggrandizing, and ultimately insignificant exploit did little to impress at least one working-class volunteer, Alec Cummings. The Welshman wrote, "*Es nada hombre.* We are all more than he." Moreover, to compare those whom Byron might have faced on the battlefield with Franco's forces was ludicrous. Cummings told a friend, "Here there [is an enemy] greater than the bastardized descendants of the Court of Byzantium."[45] Nevertheless, on the cover of a memorial souvenir of the battalion issued after the war, the flag of the British Battalion covered in its battle honors was crowned by a version of Byron's lines from *Childe Harold*:

> Yet, freedom yet, thy banner
>   torn but flying
> Streams like a thundercloud
>   against the wind.

Inside the program the audience read of the British Battalion:

> Out of the proud traditions of Britain's past they came. Part of the long struggle for freedom, carried forward from Wat Tyler through men like Byron and movements like the Chartists, through Keir Hardie to the present day. Our modern bearers of Britain's great traditions came forward in answer to the call, ready to give their lives that freedom might live.

Across from this inscription is an engraving of a trade union rally in Parliament Hill fields on April 21, 1834, protesting the harsh sentences meted out to the Dorchester laborers for their union activity. The relationship with a native radical tradition was reemphasized when the pamphlet's author wrote, "Those 2,000 men fought under a hot Spanish sun in a country strange to them for the same fundamental principles as John Ball and Wat Tyler fought [for] more than five centuries earlier."[46]

V

Most of all, it became increasingly clear that if the volunteers for Spain were to be worthy of their "great tradition," they must be prepared to address not the symptoms but the causes of all that oppressed them. This required fundamental change. The stark inequalities and injustices that proletarian militants encountered were undergirded by the widely shared assumption that a worker was held in almost literal bondage by his employer. They understood, however, that an act of individual rebellion was insufficient to achieve the liberation they desired. James Brown and others like him moved to embrace a radically different conception of society. When social theory combined with specific grievances, as in the case of Brown, the result could be life-changing.

Outside of personal considerations, which will be discussed at a later point, the influences that led a British worker to volunteer for Spain, whether inside or outside the Communist party, were many—the experience of oppression, newspapers, a vital oral culture, working-class educational institutions both at home and in Moscow, the influence of religion, and the authority of a plebeian past. In addition, there was a logical, sequential development of issues in the lives of many British militants: first, looking for explanations for the unemployment and repression they experienced; second, seeing the rise of fascism on the continent as an issue that concerned them; and third, seizing the opportunity to strike back at oppression, if not in Great Britain, then in Spain. The result was that the worker-volunteers discovered a new sense of their own worth. They need no longer be "subservient." They need no longer tolerate the contrasts between the rich and poor. Their hands were not anyone else's but their own. And, finally, they could throw off the legacy of generations of deferential behavior.

When the authorities prosecuted Walter Gregory for chalking antifascist slogans, he hated himself for the way he behaved in court. "Much to my consternation I found myself exhibiting a degree of humility and acquiescence which I did not feel, but which I seemed powerless to shake off."[47] But he and others like him were to find that power in Spain.

CHAPTER 6

Citizens of the World

Now I want to explain to you why I left England. You will have heard
about the war going on here. From every country in the world working
people like myself have come to Spain to stop Fascism here. So
although I am miles away from you, I am fighting to protect you and
all children in England as well as people all over the world.
— "A British volunteer to his daughter," Anon.

I

The British "volunteers for liberty" inherited both elite and
popular traditions of internationalism. The first derived from the
nineteenth-century radicalism of Cobden, Bright, and Gladstone,
which was imported into the Labour party by leading Liberals after
World War I. Its fundamental tenet was simple but endlessly ramify-
ing—the cause of liberty must be defended from oppression. The
chairman of the University of London Liberal Association, Hugh
Gosschalk, wrote after his return from ten days in Spain: "If Mr.
Gladstone had been alive to-day, he would have stumped the country
denouncing the barbarities committed by General Franco against the
civil population of Madrid." Comparing the efforts of the heroes of
the Italian unification movement with Spain's struggle to free itself
from fascism, he said, "Between the King of Naples and Mazzini Mr.
Gladstone did not hesitate. No more ought we to hesitate between
General Franco and President Azaña."[1]

Tom Wintringham, the commander of the British Battalion at the
battle of the Jarama, suggested the second tradition when he said that
the volunteers were "inheritors of an English tradition" of internationalism.[2] The historical roots of this "English tradition" reached
back to the English Jacobins during the French Revolution. "Mankind," Thomas Paine wrote in his *Rights of Man*, "are not now to be
told they shall not think, or they shall not read."[3] Paine's message
was clearly meant to lead to a universal diffusion of knowledge that
would empower the powerless, regardless of nationality. The author
of the *History of the International*, Julius Braunthal, believes that
Paine's *Rights of Man* "belongs to the history of the International,
because it implanted the idea of international solidarity for the

oppressed deep in the minds and hearts of English workers."[4] The exploited and oppressed of all nations, therefore, were bound together in a common fraternity with the British. The American and French Revolutions fused nationalism and internationalism, thereby establishing a new model of human brotherhood. In the May 1937 *Left Review*, Samuel Mill wrote that Paine's "indomitable courage, his thorough-going internationalism and his generous hatred of every kind of oppression, make his life a model for all who profess to be Communists."[5]

In the nineteenth century the Chartists demonstrated the power of a native radical movement uncompromisingly committed to internationalist goals. To the militants in Spain a century later, they were remembered as exemplars.[6] Drawing a parallel between Wales and Spain, a volunteer wrote home that "Wales in general & Newport in Particular [are] rich in the struggle for freedom & a better standard of life." It was at Newport, where troops killed twenty-four of the rebels, that the Chartists had led the only genuine revolutionary rising of the nineteenth century. Spain, the volunteer continued, "goes right back to the days of Chartism."[7] One British volunteer wrote down in pencil the lines of a poem saying that he and his comrades were the "offspring of Chartists" with "Red Blood in [our] veins."[8] Jim Brewer, who fought from the Jarama to the last battles of the Ebro, gloried in the fact that his great-grandfather had been a Chartist. According to Brewer, his commitment to Spain could not be fully understood except in terms of the internationalist ideals that the Chartist movement bred into its adherents and their progeny.[9]

The Communist party, with its internationalist appeal, "Workers of the world, unite!", was understandably seen as a contemporary incarnation of these ideals.[10] Ralph Fox asserted that the party was "the heir of the Chartists,"[11] thereby linking Communism with a native radical tradition. (Among other things, Fox was undoubtedly remembering the close friendships that existed between George Julian Harney and Friedrich Engels, and Ernest Jones and Karl Marx.) As he prepared to leave for Spain, John Cornford, the founder and leader of the Communist party student group at Cambridge, remembered the pledge of the Chartists when he said good-bye to his fiancée, "We are at one, and we will keep to each other."[12]

So powerful, in fact, was the identification of the British volunteers with the Chartists that they almost named the battalion after them, as other national groups identified their battalions with their own revolutionary heroes.

II

Further, by 1914 the anticolonial and anti-imperialist movements linked some members of the working and middle classes into a shared vision of internationalism. The greatest setback to this ideological partnership came with the outbreak of the war. Leading British and European socialists had refused to believe that workers would fight workers. The cruel disappointment to their hopes did not mean that lessons went unlearned, however.[13] The Cardiff volunteer and veteran of the Great War, Pat Murphy, found that it had turned him into a "passionate" internationalist.[14] After 1917, internationalists found a new enthusiasm in the success of the Bolshevik Revolution, which generated the "Hands Off Russia" movement opposing military intervention by Great Britain. This achieved its goal by successfully joining together labor's leaders with the rank and file in threatening the government with a general strike,[15] a strategy the labor movement never was able to realize against Chamberlain's nonintervention policy toward Spain.

In the twenties the Trades Union Council and the Soviet Union were to enjoy a cordial if sometimes difficult relationship until the adoption of the "class against class" policy at the Sixth World Congress in 1928, from which the relationship between the British Communist party and the Labour party was never to recover. Still, on the left, support for Russia became the litmus test of internationalism.[16] Communist parties were founded in each of the European countries under the auspices of the Comintern. John Strachey, as always, made the approving comment, "Communism is, in its very essence, internationalist."[17] C. Day Lewis joined in, prophesying a Soviet Union irresistibly crossing frontiers and, ultimately, enveloping the world in one proletarian whole. In his poem, "Letters in Red," he wrote:

Your republic, Soviet Union, is not contained
Between the Arctic floes and sunny Crimea:
Rather, its frontiers run from the plains of China
Through Spain's racked heart and Bermondsey barricades
To the factory gates of America. We say,
Whatever instinct or reason tells mankind
To pluck from its heart injustice, poverty, traitors,

Your frontiers stand; where the batteries are unmasked
Of those who would shatter Life sooner than yield it
To its natural heirs, your frontiers stand: wherever
Man cries against the oppressors "They shall not pass,"
Your frontiers stand. Be sure we shall defend them.

Finally, two developments—Hitler's rise to power in 1933 and the outbreak of the Spanish Civil War in 1936—brought together communist and noncommunist strands of internationalism. James Hinton has observed, "The advance of European fascism posed grim and urgent tasks for socialist and working-class politics in Britain. It was not without some sense of relief that working-class activists of many different shades of political opinion threw themselves as never before into the politics of the world struggle."[18]

The internationalism of the British militant, from Thomas Paine to Harry Pollitt, achieved its apogee in Spain. Pat Murphy wrote to the *Workington Star* after the battle of Villanueva de la Cañada, "Many well known and talented personalities and many good hard-working lads have fallen, realising that their sacrifice was for all lands and peoples."[19] A British volunteer said, "The cause of democracy in Spain and that of the British people were indivisible."[20] A letter from one of his comrades appeared in the *Daily Worker* on March 4, 1937: "I never knew until I left England what international solidarity meant, but if I give my life fighting in Spain I will be satisfied that I have done my duty. I will know that no worker can give his life for a better cause."[21] Moved by the deepest chords of history and memory, but also by the events surrounding World War I, as well as the very real, contemporary threat of fascism to Great Britain and the democratic states of the West, both the communist and noncommunist left saw working-class solidarity, antifascism, and the defense of Republican Spain as profoundly intertwined with Britain's best political interests.

On September 22, 1938, at a memorial meeting at the Central Hall on Renshaw Street, Oldham, in behalf of those who had died in Spain and their dependents, the speakers included Fred Copeman, the longtime commander of the British Battalion, Sir Peter Chalmers-Mitchell, who played a prominent role in Arthur Koestler's adventures in Málaga,[22] and Will Lawther, who had lost a brother in Spain. The speakers and audience were led in singing:

These things shall be, a loftier race
Than ere the world hath known shall rise;

With flame of freedom in their souls
And light of knowledge in their eyes.

Nation with Nation, Land with Land,
Unarmed shall live as comrades free;
In every heart and brain shall throb
The pulse of one fraternity.[23]

The older and newer traditions of internationalism that inspired
volunteers on the left to see Spain as their cause were epitomized in
one of the outstanding novels of the thirties, *The Land of the Leal*.
The title refers to the Scottish peasant's belief that a land existed
where oppression, injustice, and heartbreak have been vanquished.
Its author, James Barke, was a proletarian novelist from Glasgow, a
city that gave much to Spain. Among the 437 Scottish volunteers,
sixty-four of Barke's fellow Glaswegians died fighting for the Republic.

Andrew, one of the two brothers in the novel, was a self-educated
worker. Disillusioned by the collapse of the General Strike in 1926,
Andrew worked as an engineering fitter in the first years of the
Spanish War when he "found his old political faith re-awakening." A
speech given by a Spanish veteran awakened him to the dangers of
the rise of fascism on the continent. Spain, it seemed increasingly
clear, was "the battlefront . . . [where] the international forces of
fascism were gathered behind the puppet Franco." The horrors being
reported from Spain, "particularly the bombing of women and children," renewed him in his resolve. Suddenly all was clear. "The fight
against Fascism was the fight for human decency against human
beastliness."[24]

A speaker in *The Land of the Leal*, who had fought and been
wounded at the Jarama, told Andrew of the "magnificently heroic"
part played by the International Brigades in stopping the "Fascist
hordes" in Spain. Then, he lifted him to a renewed vision of human
solidarity, which was at once internationalist and at the same time
embraced or "connected" progressive elements of all classes. The
story of the International Brigades "was a deathless record of how the
best and bravest elements of the common people of the old world and
the new world had, together with writers and scientists and intellectuals, gone to the defence of the heroic Spanish people."[25] Thus, Spain
in the 1930s became for Andrew and others like him what France had
been to Thomas Paine and the English Jacobins in the 1790s. The
majority of British workers may have accepted the meleoristic tradi-

tions of the post-Chartist period, but a new post–World War I generation of militant activists was rediscovering a more generous and less
exclusive vision of radical change, which existed not only in England's "dark satanic mills" or her "green and pleasant land" but on
the sere landscapes of a remote country. The British volunteers
exuberantly rallied their comrades:

> Come workers sing a rebel song,
> A song of love and hate;
> Of love unto the lowly
> And of hatred to the great.

No longer was Spain a footnote to the histories of the great countries
north of the Pyrenees. It had taken center stage in the political and
moral imaginations of the militants of the decade. Sir Stafford Cripps
cried, "History has assigned to the Spanish people the glorious
mission of saving culture, civilisation and liberty, the highest values
of humanity."[26]

III

But history had not always been so clear about its intentions
for Spain or its people. In 1926 Herbert Read returned from a visit to
Spain, percipiently warning that Spain is a "place where the serpent
bites its own tail."[27] "Spain," wrote Wyndham Lewis in *The Wild
Body*, "is an overflow of sombreness. . . . A strong and threatening
tide of history meets you at the frontier."[28] Ezra Pound cautioned the
traveler for opposite reasons: he said there was *no* history waiting
those who crossed the frontier. Writing in the *New English Weekly*
in 1936, the poet resurrected the old canard, "Europe ENDS with the
Pyrenees." And then he added his own inimitable embellishment,
"Neither Spain nor Russia has ever contained more than a handful of
civilized individuals." To an American, he wrote in the same year,
"Spain is a damn'd nest of savages."[29]

For the overwhelming majority of British volunteers before 1936,
and the hundreds of thousands who were to support them, Spain
existed as a pastiche of historical, cultural, and political associations.[30] It was a country that most British had traditionally despised.
From the Reformation in the sixteenth century, Spain, the leader of
the Catholic Counter-Reformation, had been the *bête noire* of Protestant Europe, and particularly Great Britain. It represented "darkness and superstition," a country "where for so long the burning

stake, the torture rack, and the wheel held sway."[31] During Queen Elizabeth's reign, British volunteers rushed across the channel to assist the Protestant revolt in the Netherlands against Phillip II's rule.[32]

Over the centuries, hostility toward all things Spanish crystallized in the Black Legend, which, in essence, charged that by comparison with other European countries, the Spaniards were uniquely backward.[33] The Spaniard Julián Juderias, who first used the term in 1914, had no doubt that this "anti-Hispanic legend is not only a thing of the past" but "influences the present." A unique animus against Spain, he argued, could be found in virtually every European country. Although it might differ in individual details, the central theme was "that our country constitutes an unfortunate exception in the community of European nations in all that relates to toleration, culture, and political progress."[34] The historian Michael Alpert believes that in the imaginations of "many Christians" on the eve of the Civil War, "Spain remained principally the land of the Holy Inquisition."[35]

What is distinctive about the idiomatic rendering of the Black Legend by the English is that they were not concerned primarily with the intellectual or cultural backwardness of the Spanish but, rather, chose to create in the Spaniard a moral monster who comprised "most of the vices and shortcomings known to man," including, invariably, cowardly and treacherous behavior. The legend proved remarkably enduring. The writer V. S. Pritchett traveled to Spain for the first time in the early 1920s. Only after extensive contact with the remnants of the great literary generation of 1898 could even such a sensitive and discriminating traveler find himself "freed of the crude northern notion of the so called 'black legend.'"[36] Harry Pollitt tapped into the hoary tradition when he compared the fascists to "a new Spanish Inquisition . . . the horrors of [which] are known to every schoolboy."[37] One former schoolboy, Bernard Knox, was wounded near Boadilla in December 1936. A young *miliciano*, helping Knox to safety, said matter-of-factly that if it appeared the Moors were likely to capture them, he would first shoot Knox and then himself. In his somewhat delirious state, the young Englishman found himself repeating the words of a Tennyson poem he had learned at school: "Fall into the hands of God/not into the hands of Spain."[38]

Although travelers to Spain were few, it was not for lack of interest, but, more frequently, opportunity. George Orwell said that he had longed to visit Spain beyond any other country in Europe.[39] Whatever the reason for Orwell's fascination with the country, however, the historian Robert Stradling writes, he "was remarkably ignorant of all things Iberian in terms of 'background.'" Bernard Crick, Orwell's biographer, agrees that Orwell "seems to have had very little idea *where* he was."[40]

Orwell's ignorance was the rule rather than the exception among the British volunteers. Little enlightenment came from newspapers, the radio, or newsreels. The last, which accompanied the phenomenally popular new entertainment form of motion pictures, might have been expected to form at least some sensible impression of Spain in the minds of millions of British patrons flocking to the cinema in the thirties.[41] However, both newsreels and British feature films virtually ignored Spain until the outbreak of the war. In addition, until "talking pictures" appeared, coverage of major events in Spain was restricted to visual presentations with brief, explanatory captions. Even the crucial years of 1931–36 "seem to have escaped the notice of the British newsreels."[42]

Consequently, by 1936 the British filmgoer would have acquired only the most elementary knowledge of the country from the new medium, and that was riddled with cliché.[43] The first serious coverage of the war by Gaumont British News played on one of the most popular of stereotypes, the indolent Spaniard. On July 27, ten days after the military uprising, the Gaumont commentator told filmgoers of "a graphic story of bloodshed and violence in the one-time lazy south," and later, "the land of smiling tomorrow is grim today."[44]

If few middle-class intellectuals had direct experience with Spain, the country was even more unknown to workers.[45] The ex-sailor and buildings worker Fred Copeman said with his usual assurance, "Like all Englishmen, I had little knowledge of the Spanish background."[46] His comrade, Walter Gregory, wrote in his memoir, "It was astonishing how little I knew of Spain," adding, "In my ignorance, I was probably typical of the average British working-class man."[47]

The language barrier, as well as cultural and historical ignorance, presented another obstacle. The sculptor Jason Gurney wrote, "I was fortunate in being able to speak a certain amount of Spanish and was one of the very few British people who could communicate with them."[48] Unlike the Abraham Lincoln Battalion, which had a goodly number of Spanish speakers from Cuba and Puerto Rico, and some like John Gates and John Tisa who had taken Spanish in high school,[49] very few of the English volunteers spoke the language. The newspaper reporter and poet, J. R. Jump, was an exception.[50]

But there was another reason for the limited knowledge among British workers about Spain. Wracked by denominational rivalries, Spanish workers did not become widely visible to the British labor movement until 1934, the year in which the Asturian miners revolted only to be crushed by General Franco and his Moors from North Africa.

IV

In 1936, however, Spain became transformed in the British imagination. Upon his return from the embattled country, Ben Tillett, the venerable trade union leader, told the *Daily Herald*, "The greater the knowledge of Spain to-day by the man-in-the-street, the greater will be the respect with which the new Republic is held."[51] "Spain" was well on its way to becoming one of the great myths of the twentieth century.

Walter Gregory found it difficult to explain why he and his fellow workers felt so deeply about the country and its agony. "No other issue in my lifetime was to make such an impact upon public sympathies in Britain as did the Spanish Civil War." Abyssinia, Manchuria, fascism, the Depression, none of these "came anywhere near to rivalling Spain as a focus for working-class attention and indignation."[52] The reason, however, is not difficult to discover. The European working-class movement had experienced defeat after defeat in the two decades after World War I. In Great Britain the failure of the General Strike of 1926, the miscellaneous humiliations experienced by those both in and out of work, and the intransigent moderation of the political culture, as well as the ineptitude of both the left and the Labour party, had proved devastating to many workers. Moreover, in Germany the destruction of the trade unions and the Communist party, in Vienna the defeat of the socialist workers, and in Italy the persecution of communists and socialists added to the seemingly unending litany of working-class defeats.

From the standpoint of the left in Great Britain, the turning point in Britain's attitudes toward Spain began with the departure of Alfonso XIII in 1931, following the resignation of the dictator Miguel Primo de Rivera and the subsequent creation of the Second Spanish Republic. The country proceeded to adopt recognizable democratic institutions. Second, the failed rising of the Asturian miners in 1934, along with the brutal repression that followed, enlisted the sympathy of progressive Europe, particularly the working classes. In Great Britain, the Welsh miners, especially, felt an affinity for their comrades in Spain.[53] Thus, Emmanuel Shinwell, a member of the Labour party executive committee, could write that when the Popular Front was formed in 1936, "the news was received enthusiastically by Socialists in Britain. *Many of the new Government members were [now] well known in the international Socialist movement.*"[54] By coincidence, a few days before the insurrection, Francisco Largo Caballero was in London representing the Spanish trade union movement at the Seventh International Trades Union Congress.[55]

Within days of Franco's uprising in July, the Spanish workers were the principal figures in a new legend, that of a people who were fighting not just for themselves but for all Europe, indeed the whole of the Western world, against fascism. "Heroic Spain" became the new watchword of the left. The stories of bravery and self-sacrifice of the Spaniards began to capture the imagination of British militants. One said, "In 1936 Spain could no longer conjure up for many of us an image of a far-off land, locked into a romantic feudal past. Spain had unexpectedly given shape to many of our vague hopes and fears."[56]

The famous slogan, *No Pasarán*, exemplified not just the determination of Madrid to resist Franco, but of workers to resist the forces that opposed them and their interests. Therefore, when the CNT-FAI issued a call to the "Workers of England!" in November 1936, saying it was their "obligation" to come to the aid of the Republic, they were relying both on the international traditions of the British and the new visibility of the Spanish worker who "is to-day the admiration of the world."[57] John McGovern, the Independent Labour party leader and Member of Parliament, spoke in the spirit of the day: "Since the Russian Revolution in 1917 the one shining light in the long list of disastrous retreats by workers has been the spirit and organization of our Spanish comrades in their opposition to Franco and his bestial forces."[58] The result was the final metamorphosis of Spain from "backward" to "heroic," the incarnation of all antifascist and progressive virtues. One British volunteer wrote home, "The Spaniards are a great people, the more I see them, the more I admire their patience and courage. One reason is, it is the only country which has defied Hitler and Mussolini."[59]

If one is to accept the evidence of scores of interviews, memoirs, and Bill Alexander's history of the British in the Civil War, the transformation of Spain in the minds of British workers and left-wing intellectuals was complete by the time they arrived in Spain (although, as we shall see, some persisted in retaining the old myths). Perhaps Harry Pollitt best summed it up. After returning from a visit to the British Battalion, he wrote, "It has to be seen to be believed. Spain, the country of the siesta, kindly, hospitable, but a little lazy—this was the tourist picture in the old days." Now, he said, no one could think of the country in the same way. "The Spain of to-day has put up a resistance that has astonished the world. A resistance to fascism that one doubts whether the people of France or Belgium could surpass."[60]

Nor was this only a working-class enthusiasm. Stephen Spender wrote, "Within a few weeks Spain had become the symbol of hope for all anti-fascists." For those who responded, "it offered the twentieth century an 1848," when there was a "time and place where a cause representing a greater degree of freedom and justice than a reactionary opposing one, gained victories."[61] A British ambulance driver called Spain "a place that for many people was the centre of interest and importance of the whole world."[62] When the International Brigades ultimately departed Spain as a result of an agreement made by Prime Minister Juan Negrín with the League of Nations, one observer said that Spanish "is now the common language of all the men who have come from all countries of the world."[63] That is, Spanish had become the Esperanto of antifascists everywhere.

Therefore, once the struggle began, Spain emerged with startling clarity from the perceived darkness of its past. It was Spain where fascism would be stopped. Harry Pollitt, the most effective extraparliamentary speaker in the country, said, "The whole future development of the international situation is being worked out in the struggle between the popular forces of democracy, law and order and the bestial, terroristic forces of fascism in Spain." Therefore, any position except that of an active partisan was unacceptable. "There can be no neutrality in this life and death struggle."[64]

V

A volunteer, eager for a serious study of the country in which he was going to fight and quite possibly die, would find little before 1936 that was of real value to him. Raymond Carr once remarked,

"Imagine a major European country with no good book about it at
all!"⁶⁵ Nevertheless, for those intent on acquiring some genuine
understanding of what awaited them, one book became their *vade
mecum*. In 1936 *Spain in Revolt* was selected by the Left Book Club
for its members. Ronald Blythe calls it "a kind of thirties *Lillibulero*
which swept young men into the International Brigade."⁶⁶ A political
traveler to Spain, the poet Valentine Ackland, congratulated the Left
Book Club for selecting "such an important book." She said that it
"supplies us with what we need."⁶⁷ *Spain in Revolt* became the lens,
then, through which many British volunteers saw the events that
captured the attention of the world in 1936.

Dressed in the familiar yellow-orange colors, the book was dedicated "to those who died that Spanish democracy might live," thus
making its political stance clear. It succeeded in translating Spain's
confusing political world into a convenient but intelligently reduc-
tionist political idiom. The authors, Harry Gannes and Theodore
Repard, understood the significance of their accomplishment, asserting that "the importance of Spain at the present moment is perhaps
equalled only by the lack of accounts, reliable or otherwise, explaining the historical roots of revolt." The authors judged "there is no
coherent, systematic account of the history of Spain since 1933 in
any language."⁶⁸ They intended to fill this need for politically inquisitive readers on the left, as well as for others equally mystified by the
country's travail but who dwelled in other parts of the political
spectrum.

The authors of *Spain in Revolt* believed themselves responding to
the amazement that most British observers felt as they saw Spain
"exploding" into the world of European politics when the generals
rose on July 17, 1936. Clearly organized and informative about the
bewildering proliferation of Spanish political parties—so strange to
virtually all of the British—it offered enlightenment, if inevitably
superficial, to many of the volunteers and Republican sympathizers
in Great Britain.

The book first presented a general view of Spain and its history, so
long awash in mythologies and the brackish waters of general political and historical irrelevance in the modern era. Among other things,
the authors proved immensely helpful in supplying their readers with
the most rudimentary information concerning this virtually unknown country, shielded by the Pyrenees from the rest of Europe. It
then emphasized the antitheses that beset Spain, geographically,

economically, and intellectually, beginning with a description of Spain's physical "contrasts," alternating between mountains and vast, arid plains, and lush, fertile landscapes. The economic extremes that separated the wealthy and the poor were of staggering proportions. "Fabulously rich landowners, feudal lords over huge domains, live side by side with millions of land-hungry peasants." Similarly, economic and cultural divides that marked off the army and the church from the people also were mirrored by internal divisions in each, with the generals and the princes of the church monopolizing power and place over those beneath them who envied their ascendancy. Although the country had made immense intellectual contributions to Western culture, even if not internationally recognized—there was a plenitude of famous writers, scientists, and scholars to point to with pride—yet another contrast was that almost half the population was completely illiterate.[69]

The political crisis could not have existed without reference to the economic, cultural, and social gulf between the classes. Politics was the vessel into which generations of resentment and fear, as well as hope, found their most potent outlet. But their complexities either baffled the British volunteers, were ignored by them, or were reduced to slogans. Orwell referred to the various political groups as "a kaleidoscope of political parties and trade unions, with their tiresome names," which he found alien to the more straightforward political sensibilities of most Englishmen, not excluding himself. He wrote, "When I came to Spain, and for some time afterwards, I was not only uninterested in the political situation but unaware of it."[70]

The authors attempted to repair this ignorance by offering two threads through the labyrinth of Spanish politics. Most of those on the right were the great landowners, the army, and the church, which had traditionally supported the monarchy and were doing all in their power to bring about its restoration — or, perhaps in addition, to establish a fascist dictatorship on the Italian and German models, and, thereby, to destroy the Republic. They gathered themselves around the CEDA (Confederación Española de Derechas Autónomas) led by José María Gil Robles or around other right-wing groups such as the Agrarian party, the Conservative party, and various monarchist parties to which yet another group, the Carlists of Navarre, offered their own passionate if idiosyncratic devotional.

To the authors, the left consisted of workers and a small cohort of progressive politicians. It included both the comparatively small

Communist party, which had been banned under General Miguel Primo de Rivera's dictatorship, and a group of embittered defectors from the party led by Andrés Nin (at one time closely associated with Trotsky), who now constituted themselves into a new political group called the POUM (Partido Obrero de Unificación Marxista). The most dynamic force on the left, however, were the anarchists, who possessed an overwhelming presence in Catalonia. It was not Marx but Bakunin, his bitter enemy, who exerted the greatest influence over the new Spanish industrial proletariat in the nineteenth and early twentieth centuries. Why this should have been the case was not difficult to explain. The anarchists always flourished, according to the Marxists, in backward capitalist countries. And Spain was a particularly good example, "owing to the peculiar development of capitalism and the labour movement."[71]

Anarchist philosophy reflected the lack of political development among the workers. Because of the country's economic backwardness, class solidarity had not matured to the point that the anarchists grasped the historic role that the working class would play in achieving socialism. The anarchist principle, that politics were corrupt and, therefore, anarchists could not participate in the electoral process or serve in the government, was to be selectively applied as events unfolded, however.

If Bakunin proved victorious in his struggle for the soul of the Spanish worker before the Civil War, it was Marx (or the Soviet Union) who would reemerge in the role of Mephistopheles in the 1930s. The readers of *Revolt in Spain* were reminded that a "new society" had been created in the Soviet Union, a socialist society. The authors, however, were shrewder than many in assessing the motives for Russian interest in the Spanish conflict. It was a question of naked self-interest that drew the Soviets into what Franz Borkenau called "the Spanish Cockpit." The USSR realized that "a free-for-all" in Spain could well anticipate a larger struggle in which it might be the next victim of fascism. The huge country had much to fear if it were squeezed between a war in Europe in the West and the threat of Japan in the East. Then, "The foes of the Soviet regime could easily draw their forces together."[72]

If the status quo in Spain were to be challenged, the key issue would be agrarian reform. The authors repeatedly emphasized that root-and-branch change in the condition of life of the Spanish peasants was an absolute necessity. A "precondition" for industrial modernization, they said, was "a thoroughgoing agrarian revolution" that would "liberate the forces of production from the fetters of feudalism." (A version of this position would spell the death sentence of the POUM in the summer of 1937.) In 1931 a journalist wrote that Spain was "a people without land and a land without people." Gannes and Repard accepted the "aching and cutting indictment . . . that of all the countries of Europe its population is spread thinnest, while at the same time the land is concentrated in the fewest hands."[73]

In 1931 King Alfonso XIII fled the country, having been repudiated by the election results. The king warned that if he had attempted to save himself with force, it would have meant the end of the monarchy, the onset of revolution, and the destruction of the old regime. With the king's departure, the Second Republic was born. The atmosphere was one of enormous hope and celebration. The new constitution boldly announced that Spain would be "a democratic Republic of workers of all classes."[74] Church and state were separated, and a social program was promised that would comprehensively address the needs of workers.

Agrarian reform came before the new Cortes and was passed in September 1932. Unhappily, it was never implemented. Not long after its creation, the Second Republic found itself under siege by "the vested interests" of the old regime, who, though chastened by the new developments, were quick to regroup. The leaders of the right found solace in the consolations of Hitler in Germany and Mussolini in Italy. Gannes and Repard believed: "Fascism loomed as the only means by which the old order could be revived and kept intact." Not long after Hitler's accession to power in 1933, the Spanish workers, particularly the miners of the Asturias, rose up to prevent what they believed was an imminent right-wing takeover of the government. They heroically "tried to counter the danger of a fascist dictatorship by the establishment of a workers' and peasants' republic." The crushing in 1934 of the Asturias revolt by General Franco and his North African army resulted in the loss of several thousands of workers' lives, and thousands more were imprisoned.[75]

A martyrology for Spanish socialism had been created. The authors wrote, "October 1934, with all its mistakes, lives in the consciousness of the Spanish working class as a promise of ultimate and complete emancipation."[76] La Pasionaria told an interviewer fifty years after these events, "You cannot understand me if you don't first realize that I am the daughter and wife of Asturian miners."[77] The authors of *Spain in Revolt* enthusiastically agreed that the sacrifices of the workers had not been in vain. "Labour unity, weak at the beginning of the fight, came out of the fire like forged steel, which required only tempering and pointing."[78]

Slowly and painfully the realization dawned that if the left were to take power, it must act in cooperation with other parties. The Asturias rising taught the Spanish workers the necessity of cooperation. The Spanish Communist party adopted a popular-front strategy that helped bring a left-wing coalition to power on February 16, 1936. If any English readers doubted the significance of this event, they learned in no uncertain terms that this "was the most fateful election day in Spanish history. . . . Its aftermath was to shake the world." Although the authors ignore the comparative closeness of the vote, the Popular Front did indeed win a crushing electoral victory against the parties of the right. The reactionary tribune, Gil Robles, thundered in *El Debate* that the apocalypse was at hand. "The issue," he said, "was one of revolution against law and order, respect for religion, property, the family, and national unity, with socialism the real enemy."[79]

As the Popular Front struggled to govern in the spring and summer of 1936, dissident generals organized a "fascist putsch" that broke into the open on July 17. The reaction of the majority of the Spanish people thrilled the world. "As soon as the government began to arm the workers, it was able to draw upon inexhaustible military and human resources. Men and women, many of whom had never handled a gun, gladly sped to the front. A fascist victory under these conditions could only be a victory of total extermination." In an otherwise sober account of the events leading up to the Civil War, Gannes and Repard proved that they were not immune to the bravura mood of the period when they declaimed, "The people surrendered their arms only to death."[80]

The authors of *Spain in Revolt* told their tens of thousand of readers that any who thought that the events in Spain were an intramural dispute with little, if any, bearing on their lives were deceiving themselves. From the beginning, the authors saw the conflict as foreshadowing a new world war. Not that this was a novel perception. What was extraordinary, however, was that just as no one could believe that the death of an obscure Austrian archduke in Sarajevo in 1914 would touch off the first great war of the century, Spain "was the last place considered by political commentators" to precipitate a new world war. The authors warned, however, "that any pretext may serve for beginning the holocaust that is generally believed inevitable."[81]

The response of the great powers proved tragically inadequate. The Non-Intervention Agreement had quickly shown itself to be a fiction, little more than a convenient moral and political excuse for inaction by the British and the French. In effect, it allowed the fascist powers to supply the insurgent forces at will. At the same time, the pact denied desperately needed arms and matériel to the Republic. Spain received some aid from far-off Mexico, and from the sale of arms by Soviet Russia, which began when Stalin became convinced that Germany and Italy had no intention of abiding by the terms of the agreement. But more action was needed. Louis de Brouckère, the president of the Labour and Socialist (Second) International, said in August 1936, "Peace must be saved *now* by saving the Spanish Republic. If, for want of courage, we permit it to be crushed, war, pitiless war, undertaken in the most favourable conditions, will become practically inevitable."[82]

Gannes and Repard possessed little respect for British policy toward Spain. They called it "confused and contradictory," pointing out the strategic importance of Gibraltar to the Empire as well as the existence of a Spanish government friendly to English interests. Their fundamental point was that "a fascist victory could not be won without injury to British interests." So, whether one's political disposition was that of a high Tory or a socialist, there was ample reason for Great Britain to support the Spanish Republic in the hour of its peril.[83] Yet the folly of nonintervention unaccountably remained dogma in the British foreign office.

The British government's position was particularly difficult for militant socialists to accept because, at last, Spain was led by a government that proposed to incorporate into its social policies the welfare of the landless and those living on the economic margins of agrarian society. On August 22 *Mundo Obrero* spelled out the new government's programs:

> The democratic Republic means the rapid fulfillment of the division of land, the distribution of the lands of the nobility, the great landlords, and the high clergy to the peasants and the agricultural workers, special agrarian credits, tax reduction, annulment of debts, reformation of social legislation, [and] improvement of the conditions of life and work of the labourers.

The agrarian revolution, so long promised, so long postponed, would become reality. But only if the fascists were defeated. In the estimation of Gannes and Repard, the rising of the generals "was a desperate attempt by the landowners to regain what was decisively threatened after the February elections. A fascist victory would mean the end of land reform. A Popular Front victory would mean the acceleration of land reform." But the peasants were not the only ones to engage the new government's attentions. Its policies would also mean "measures for the protection of the small merchants and manufacturers and the legal dissolution of the reactionary and fascist parties."[84]

Finally, the authors of *Spain in Revolt* pointed out that in a country where there was one priest for every 900 people, as compared with one in 20,000 in Italy, the Church, one of the country's greatest landlords and oppressors, would play a leading role in the dramaturgy of the revolution. Dispossessed of its lands and discredited as an institution, the Church presented a ripe target for the accumulated resentments of the centuries among both the urban and rural poor. And yet an Englishman in Spain would be puzzled by the rigid piety of the Carlists of Navarre, who sided with Franco, and the equally devout church of the Basque region, which supported the Republic. The Basque provinces and their church did so because the region had been promised autonomy by the Republican government. Catalonia, too, possessed the same fiercely independent spirit of the Basque country. Autonomous for centuries, the Catalans, as had the Basques, developed a different language from Spanish and a vital regional culture. The working class was particularly strong in both regions because of the heavy concentration of industry.

As Russian aid and several hundred Soviet advisers poured into Spain in the fall of 1936, the Spanish Communist party began to evolve from comparative insignificance into the greatest political force in the Republic. Even in the early days of the war, Gannes and Repard understood the importance of the party, which they now were convinced "has become decisive."[85] Most important, as the volunteer Bill Feeley recalls, their book and other Left Book Club "progressive books on all sorts of political subjects" got readers "thinking about Spain."[86]

Spain

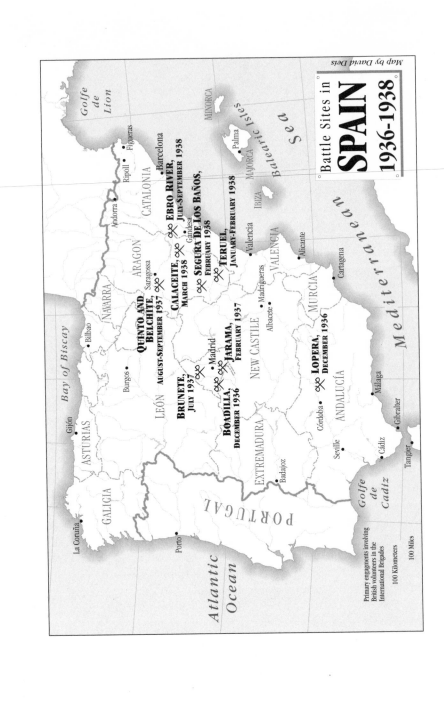

Battle Sites in
SPAIN
1936-1938

Golfe de Lion

MINORCA

Palma

Balearic Isles

MAJORCA

IBIZA

Sea

Mediterranean

Figueras

Barcelona

Ripoll

Andorra

CATALONIA

EBRO RIVER,
JULY-SEPTEMBER 1938

Gandesa

SEGURA DE LOS BAÑOS,
FEBRUARY 1938

TERUEL,
JANUARY-FEBRUARY 1938

CALACEITE,
MARCH 1938

ARAGON

Saragossa

QUINTO AND
BELCHITE,
AUGUST-SEPTEMBER 1937

NAVARRA

Bilbao

Valencia

VALENCIA

Alicante

Cartagena

MURCIA

Madrigueras

Albacete

NEW CASTILE

JARAMA,
FEBRUARY 1937

Madrid

BRUNETE,
JULY 1937

LEÓN

Burgos

Bay of Biscay

Gijón

ASTURIAS

GALICIA

La Coruña

BOADILLA,
DECEMBER 1936

LOPERA,
DECEMBER 1936

Córdoba

ANDALUCÍA

Málaga

Gibraltar

Tanger

Golfe de Cadiz

Cádiz

Seville

Badajoz

EXTREMADURA

PORTUGAL

Porto

Atlantic Ocean

Primary engagements involving
British volunteers in the
International Brigades

100 Kilometers

100 Miles

CHAPTER 7

Setting a Course

I see a boat slipping out of harbour & breasting the first waves beyond
the bar. The youth at the helm is so confident that he has made the
sheet fast; and while one hand is firm on the tiller, the other holds a
book, from which he glances up only now & then to set his course
closer to the wind that is driving him into the heart of the storm.
— Professor Francis M. Cornford

I believe that at certain moments in history a few people—usually
unknown ones—are able to live not for themselves but for a principle.
— Stephen Spender

Once the appeal for Volunteers for the International Brigade was made,
and, even more, once one's own friends had enrolled, every person who
had for the last ten years believed that this was the supreme issue of
our time, and that the war between Fascism and Socialism was the war
for the future of civilization, was confronted with the issue of whether
or not he should himself join.
— T. C. Worsley

I

In July and August of 1936, British volunteers began arriving
in Spain. The East End garment workers Nat Cohen and Sam Masters
crossed into Spain from France, as did John Cornford. Felicia Browne
was already in Barcelona for the Workers' Olympiad when the insurrection broke out. A scattering of other volunteers of varying nationalities soon followed, never numbering many more than a thousand.
Cohen and Masters joined the Tom Mann Centuria (which, despite
its name, was composed of a majority of Spaniards).

John Cornford, whom Esmond Romilly thought "a Real Communist,"[1] fought, ironically, with the anti-Stalinist POUM militia on the
Aragón front for a short time before returning to England to recruit
more British volunteers. Tom Wintringham, the *Daily Worker* correspondent in Barcelona, told Harry Pollitt, the general secretary of the
Communist party, "We ask you to encourage John to come back here
in a fortnight or three weeks. He has had a very bad time with the

worst organised gang on an unorganised front, but he can help us all the more by knowing the necessary comparisons."[2] On September 5 Wintringham wrote again to Harry Pollitt, emphasizing the importance of the symbolic presence of a British military unit in Spain, but encouraging "more volunteers to make it 'British' in fact as well as name." A week later he wrote to Pollitt in uncompromising terms. "We want a respectable number of English comrades, CP, LP or TU, to make a centuria."[3] Most of those trickling into the country, however, joined anarchist and POUM units, and a few were integrated into Communist militias. Some found a home in Enrique Lister's famous Fifth Regiment in Madrid.

II

The first British volunteer to die in Spain was the artist and sculptress Felicia Browne. She studied at the Slade School from 1924 to 1926, where her contemporaries included William Coldstream, Nan Youngman, Claude Rogers, Clive Branson (who was to serve in the British Battalion in Spain), and Henry Tonks.[4] Youngman said, "Felicia was much more aware of the political situation than any of us." In 1928 she went to Berlin to study sculpture, living with unemployed fellow artists. Witnessing the Nazis come to power led her to the Communist party, which she joined in 1933.[5]

Browne possessed a strong dislike of privilege as well as abstemious personal habits and genuine artistic talent. She donated her personal fortune to refugees, and, in a subsequent period of privation, took employment in a restaurant kitchen. Her ability to speak four languages eased her travels through some of the most remote parts of Europe. She made her living by sketching portraits of people in the villages in which she stayed, traveling as far as the Tatra mountains in Czechoslovakia. Almost always her artistic subjects were peasants and workers "whom she really felt with and for." In 1934, two years before her arrival in Spain, she received a prize from the Trades Union Congress for her design of a medal commemorating the 100th anniversary of the Tolpuddle martyrs, six Dorset laborers who were transported to Australia for giving illegal oaths to fellow members of their union.[6]

In August 1936, while still in Barcelona, Browne learned of a mission to blow up a fascist munitions train and boldly volunteered for it. However, the party attempted to dissuade her participation. According to a *Daily Express* reporter, she defied the orders and went to party offices, where she "demanded to be enlisted to fight on the Saragossa front." Browne reportedly said, "I am a member of the London Communists, and can fight as well as any man."[7]

A German comrade on the raid, George Brinkman, has left a fascinating typewritten report, describing their mission and the circumstances of the artist's death. According to Brinkman, the pudgy, bespectacled Browne was forced to clear a final gender hurdle before being allowed to accompany the raiding party. She went to its leader and asked if he would accept a woman comrade as a volunteer. After attempting to intimidate Browne by telling her of the dangers that awaited them, and failing, he accepted her as one of the ten who would attempt the hazardous mission. They left Tardienta by car and traveled to the farthest point of the front, where they disembarked and walked about twelve kilometers to the rail line. Browne and two others were told to keep watch and signal if there was trouble. The remaining seven moved close to the tracks. They set the charges with only thirty seconds remaining before the train passed.[8]

On their way back, the group stumbled upon a macabre scene, a crashed plane with the remains of the pilot in the cockpit. As they hurriedly buried the dead man, a dog suddenly appeared, and with him an oppressive sense of danger. Brinkman moved quickly up a steep incline where he saw thirty-five or forty enemy soldiers nearby. He signaled to the rest to take cover. To rejoin them, Brinkman had to run through heavy rifle fire. An Italian volunteer beside him fell with a bullet through his foot. Brinkman made him as comfortable as possible under the desperate circumstances and then ran to the others for help. Browne insisted on returning with first aid for the wounded man. When she reached him, the enemy concentrated its fire on the two of them, killing her with bullet wounds to her chest and back.[9]

III

Those who, like Felicia Browne, were among the first "spontaneous" volunteers included John Cornford, John Sommerfield, Bernard Knox, Jock Cunningham, and Esmond Romilly. They received their baptism of fire in Catalonia in the summer or the early battles around Madrid in the fall of 1936, when Franco drove to capture the great city. To John Cornford, the war initially seemed to be something of a lark. He wrote to Margot Heinemann, "I came out with the intention of staying a few days, firing a few shots, and then coming home. Sounded fine, but you just can't do things like that."[10] Waiting in Paris to travel south to Spain, the young Bernard Knox said, "We were glad that we were part of so great an adventure, sorry that we were so few."[11] Many of the first British volunteers were attached to the German Thaelmann or the French Commune de Paris battalions. Both of these units included a section of British machine gunners who were principally public schoolboys or university students who could speak French or German.[12]

The British journalist, Sefton Delmer, encountered a more varied group when he visited Romilly and about twenty of the early British arrivals in the trenches of the Casa de Campo, where the battle of Madrid reached its dramatic peak in November. He found students and public schoolboys but also miners, dockers, chemists, and clerks. The veteran journalist also noticed the company of German volunteers whom the British had joined. The contrast between the British volunteers and the exiled, tough, and embittered communist revolutionaries, some of whom Delmer had come to know while reporting from Germany, was startling. Each of the Germans wore a beret and gray overalls that passed close enough for "fighting clothes." In comparison "with those barrel-chested Germans, [the British] looked smaller and younger and less assured—like amateur beginners put down among a group of hardy old professionals." The difference in dress among the British also caught Delmer's attention. "Most of them wore the uniform of the British tourist, grey flannels, pullover, sportscoat, trilby hat and raincoat." Only one British volunteer, who wore the uniform from his days in the University of London Officer Training Corps, looked the part he had come to play.[13] But the days of informal soldiering would soon be over.

Having returned to England from Spain, where he had fought with the POUM militia in the Aragón, John Cornford obtained Harry Pollitt's agreement in September to recruit a small English contingent to take back with him, apparently unaware of the plans to form an international brigade. On November 21 "Frank Pitcairn" (Claud Cockburn) announced the formation of an international legion in the *Daily Worker*. Two weeks later Pollitt issued the call for volunteers, using the slogan, "Workers of the World Unite."[14] Then, with the formation of an international brigade, the few score Englishmen already in Spain became members of national groups attached to the Germans in the Thaelmann Battalion or the new French Marseillaise

Battalion until there were sufficient numbers to form their own unit. Among them was Esmond Romilly.

IV

A nephew of Winston Churchill, Esmond Romilly fled his public school at fifteen and published with his brother, Giles, a famous antiwar broadside called *Out of Bounds* before going to Spain in the fall of 1936. Romilly bicycled through the south of France, managed to take a boat from Marseilles to Barcelona, made his way to Madrid, and fought at Cerro de Los Angeles, University City, and, most famously, at the little village of Boadilla. His account of this short but fierce firefight became one of the first to reach England and has achieved the status of a minor but enduring classic of the war. He was nineteen when he wrote it.

After an amazing run of good fortune during the earliest fighting, in which all had come through unharmed, the twelve British still attached to the German Thaelmann Battalion found themselves on the outskirts of a small agricultural village fifteen miles from Madrid. It was here that their luck ran out.[15] Romilly offered the following inscription for the British who fought and died there, and one must remember that he did so in the epic spirit of the early days of the war:

> At Boadilla del Monte there are no graves nor tombstones. There were no burial speeches, no flags, processions nor trumpets. The bodies of the Englishmen who died there on that December morning lay unburied at the mercy of the Moors. But just as Madrid became a symbol throughout the world of the defence of democracy, so the men who died at Boadilla represent the desire of nearly every Englishman that liberty and justice should prevail.[16]

"The desire of nearly every Englishman that liberty and justice should prevail"—the ease with which these words spilled off Romilly's tongue can seem embarrassingly facile today. But to Romilly and his comrades who fought and died beside him, such words still possessed a pristine authority. Those with Romilly at Boadilla included Harry Addley, the owner of a Dover restaurant and a former sergeant in the Buffs in World War I, Joe Gough, a butcher and metal finisher, and Martin Messer, a student from the University of Edinburgh[17] and the son of a prominent shop steward from the Clydeside.[18] Also part of the British group on that morning was Lorrimer Birch, a rigid communist who "had never known hunger, nor oppression, nor fighting" but whose efficiency ensured that he would be elected group leader. An Oxford-educated scientist,[19] Birch had been one of the first to join the Tom Mann Centuria in Barcelona. Others included Sid Avner, a Jewish university student from London, and Raymond Cox, a clerk from Southampton. What struck Romilly most powerfully was the fact that in spite of their differing views and the separation of class, they discussed and argued all matters with perfect equality. He emphasized in his memoir that their endless grumbling was not to be taken for demoralization. "It only meant democracy in the Republican Army was something real."[20]

On that December morning in 1936, Addley, Gough, Messer, Birch, Avner, and Cox perished in the otherwise unremembered and insignificant battle. But Boadilla was, as Romilly said, "symbolic." Leaders were elected and friendships made and broken, not for reasons of class or educational background, but on the basis of ability and personal strengths and weaknesses. Ray Cox was one of those who died at Boadilla. Christopher Caudwell wrote from Spain to his brother, "I want to tell you of the tremendous pride and admiration the whole International Brigade feels for these few English comrades, including Ray, who were with the Thaelmann Battalion of the Brigade from the start." Because the early English volunteers were "so few, . . . they felt something outstanding was expected of them, and even among the foreign comrades I have met, you can tell that they were regarded as the very best the English Party could have sent." When the German writer, Ludwig Renn, under whom Cox served, was asked why the casualties of the English were so high, he replied, "because every one of them was a hero."[21]

Coming from Renn, who had played such a vital role in the defense of Madrid, this seemed heady stuff to Caudwell. The British writer appealed to Nick Cox to tell his mother "how Ray and his comrades have been the very best out of the best men who have come to Spain from all over the world to fight Fascism, and that we who came out so much later feel all the time the influence and inspiration of their examples."[22] As Romilly and several of the British who had served in the first weeks and months of the war prepared to return home, the commander of the Thaelmanns, Colonel "Richard," proved himself master of the martial homiletic, adding to Ludwig Renn's sentiments, "In the battles of the future, if we know that there are Englishmen on our left flank, or Englishmen on our right, then we shall know that we need give no thought nor worry to those positions."[23]

In the style of the overheated rhetoric of the ubiquitous propaganda genius, Willi Münzenberg, the party sought to take full advantage of Romilly and his comrades. Just as he and the survivors were mourning their friends in the Communist party offices in Barcelona, they heard the *International* being sung, accompanied by the sound of trumpets. Outside they saw hundreds of new international volunteers from Europe, America, and Australia marching through the streets. "From the ends of the earth they come. We have so often cried, 'Workers of all lands unite.' This fight that we wage here is the practical manifestation of that cry. Here we do unite. We shall not rest until Fascism is swept from the earth. The International Brigade grows daily. We promise you . . . you seven comrades . . . that we will fight on. They shall not pass."[24]

As Romilly and his fellow survivors moved through Albacete on their way out of Spain, they saw that the first members of the new British Battalion had indeed arrived and were beginning their training.[25] Christopher Caudwell wrote from Albacete on January 7, 1937, "An English-speaking Battalion is being formed within the International Brigade, although it is still partly scattered."[26] Three weeks later he said, "England seems centuries away."[27]

V

Despite the varying circumstances, temperaments, and proximate causes of the decision to fight in Spain, the great majority of British volunteers passing through Albacete shared some form of political idealism. Even in his youth, Romilly understood that the experience of shooting and being shot at on a winter's morning in a village in a foreign country required more explanation than that provided by a grab bag of heroic slogans. He believed that "it will be taken for granted that everybody who joined the International Brigade had 'political convictions.'" At the same time, he freely admitted that "these were not necessarily the only reasons why they joined."[28]

Romilly may have been young, but he would have been the first to say he was not a fool. Well aware that no one "ever does anything just for one clear-cut, logical (in this case political) motive,"[29] he acknowledged that a failed business venture in London helped him decide to go to Spain. But he faithfully recorded the words of one of his fellow volunteers, an old soldier from World War I. "As far as I'm concerned," Romilly's comrade said, "this is a war we know all about, we all know what we're fighting for and why we're fighting."[30] A good deal later Miles Tomalin, an artist and poet educated at Cambridge, wrote in his diary, "Undoubtedly the great majority are here for the sake of an ideal, no matter what motive prompted them to seek one."[31] Walter Gregory remembers the uncomplicated state of exultation that gripped him: "I was wild with excitement, I was going to Spain, I was going to fight for democracy, I was going to fight against Fascism."[32] Even the sculptor, Jason Gurney, who was bitterly disillusioned by his experiences in Spain, said of the volunteers, "The vast majority of them went to Spain of their own free will to fight for what they believed to be a moral principle. They were offered no reward other than the satisfaction of their own principles, and they suffered horribly."[33]

In his foreword to a collection of first-person accounts of the Spanish War, the trade union leader, Jack Jones, put the issue in the simplest and most straightforward of terms: "International solidarity required something more than reading about it at home."[34] In the same vein, Maurice Levine of Manchester said, "Being the sort of person I was, I think [of] the idea of [going to Spain] not so much as escapism or adventure but a feeling that there was something that had to be done and I should do it." He admitted, however, "It's very, very difficult to analyse one's actual feelings and what made one go . . . without any sort of experience whatsoever, to go and fight in another country, in somebody else's war."[35] Or, in words that would apply to Levine, there were those who went to Spain "to make explicit a conflict they felt was implicit in the circumstances of their lives."[36]

But of what did their "idealism" consist? For the most part, the British volunteers were not Marxist revolutionaries. Rather, they were men of the left who saw themselves as "the standard-bearers of British Democracy in Spain." One said, "Our claim to fame is this: that at a moment when Democracy stampeded, and when justice and liberty seemed to have perished from this earth—the men of the XVth Brigade — the men of the English-speaking nations —together with the liberty-loving manhood of other nations threw their bodies across the stampede and stopped it."[37] Above all was their insistence that they were fighting for the "rights" that every freeborn Englishman should enjoy. One of them was Charlie Goodfellow, a Lancashire miner, who was killed at Brunete. When he decided to go to Spain, his memoirist later said, "It was the natural step for him to take. He belonged to that section of the British workers who have fought continuously and bitterly for their rights."[38] For some, however, the struggle in Spain was a certain preparation for the revolution that was to come in England. One leading volunteer who fought at the battles of the Jarama and Brunete, attended Officer's School, and commanded a machine-gun company, found himself chafing at administrative duties. He admitted he had been fortunate to have such "varied" experiences, but "now I want to stabilise it all by another go at the front." "After all," he wrote, "we have many class battles to fight in the home country."[39] Joining him was George Drever, the eldest of eleven children whose father was a shipyard laborer in Leith. He received his bachelor's and doctoral degrees in chemistry at Edinburgh and became one of the few proletarian intellectuals to express explicitly revolutionary sentiments. He had two purposes in volunteering for Spain. In addition to fighting fascism, he wanted to become experienced with arms for the day of revolution in England. First and last, he wished to "act and behave in such a way that I can forward the struggle of . . . the working class people."[40] Finally, David Goodman, who came from a Jewish community in Middlesbrough, proved exceptional in that he saw his role in Spain in explictly ideological terms. He believed himself to be a member of a revolutionary "vanguard" whose task would be to sustain the workers "through this inevitable next stage of social evolution."[41]

The communists understood the political temperament of most of those to whom they appealed. The *Daily Worker* said reassuringly that the British Battalion is "fighting only for the right to Parliamentary methods of Government and democratic ideas and ideals. Their history will mean only a victory for these things and not as the millionaire Press in Britain would have its readers believe, to establish a 'Red regime.'"[42] This statement was not only tactically necessary if the battalion's critics were to be quieted, but for most of the British in Spain it represented the political sentiments fundamental to their vision of a just society. The British volunteers possessed a contractual understanding of the relationship between themselves and their governors. What the majority of them wanted was not to overthrow the traditional order but to have their rightful claims, and those of the international working class, recognized by those who ruled or oppressed them. Spain seemed the realization of the dream of a place where men could live, fight, and die on egalitarian terms and for consensual purposes, their sacrifices inspiring the script for a rewritten and renegotiated social contract. The communist nurse, Anne Murray, spoke for most when she said that the fascists would be defeated by "the seekers of contentment, fair play and happiness for the masses."[43] The mother of William Deegan wrote a poem in honor of her son's memory in which she claimed that he died for "freedom" and "right."

> He fought to set his kindred free,
> The working-class throughout the world.
> His task is done, tho' death his lot,
> Its end is triumph in freedom's fight.
> Dear Son, you'll never be forgot.
> Your life was given for peace and right.[44]

According to no less an authority than Sam Wild, the 500 British who died in Spain sacrificed themselves for "liberty, equality, and freedom from fear, superstition and want."[45] The majority of the volunteers, whether communist or noncommunist, possessed a view of the world that was shaped more by Paineite radicalism and internationalism than socialist dogma, which, in any event, "comprised little more than trade unionism, humanitarian sentiment and a belief in social justice and efficiency."[46]

Comintern publications such as *Spanish News* clearly understood how to couch the appeal of Spain to the British by emphasizing their distinctive political traditions. A special "Message to England" was characteristic of the approach. The struggle in Spain, the "message" read, was similar to England's Glorious Revolution of 1688 and the great French Revolution. "Faithful to their traditions, the English people understand us, encourage us and, as far as possible, support us. And this encouragement is proof of the fact that we are fighting for justice, that we are sacrificing ourselves for the triumph of democracy and that we are serving a desire for freedom."[47]

Even Charlotte Haldane, who wrote as a staunch ex-communist, would not deny the selflessness of those, like herself, who helped in the formative stages of the International Brigades or of the men and women who fought in its ranks. She organized the system for the vetting and transportation of the British volunteers from Paris to Spain. For many it was the first time they had been thrown into the company of those of a different class. Tommy Fanning met a young German student volunteer in Paris who was a "genteel type, not a rough-and-ready proly like myself, who had spent most of my time in workhouses, P.A.C. offices, and Labour Exchanges." Their meeting had been prearranged, and each saw the other as a future comrade "on our way to give assistance to our Socialist and Communist brothers."[48] Haldane said of men such as Fanning and his German comrade:

> The vast majority were men of splendid types, honest and brave, who in greater or lesser degree were conscious of being engaged in a crusade to rescue democracy from the grip of Fascism. They were not all Communists nor members of their respective parties, although the leadership was always entrusted to Party members, most of whom set a high example in discipline and devotion to the rest. To them, and to all the poorly paid workers in the organisation, the material reward was trivial. They were bound fast in the service of an ideal, which they believed with religious fervor to be embodied and exemplified with brilliant success in the Soviet Fatherland.[49]

The miner, Hugh Sloan, spoke for himself and his comrades:

> We became one people defending the
>   homes of Spain and our own
> With idealism in our minds we were no
>   romantics
> With fire in our bellies, we were no
>   warriors
> We were doing the job that life has thrust
>   upon us.[50]

VI

Even if it can be said that, for the most part, some form of political idealism was at the core of a volunteer's reasons for going to Spain, there were always specific circumstances in which that idealism was encapsulated. In Spain, a "convergence of personal and public crisis" might well take place.[51] The volunteer Charles Morgan was moved to say of his comrades: "There were 101 reasons for their being out there and many, many of them were buried with their reasons."[52] This is not apparent, however, when reading Communist party literature.

A masterpiece of this genre is *The Book of the XV Brigade*, which might be fairly called the party *Iliad* of the British volunteers.[53] Edited by Frank Ryan, the Irish leader, with assistance from Alonzo Elliott, a Cambridge teacher, and Alex Donaldson from Scotland, the book was a work of propaganda in which every volunteer appeared to be an antifascist hero. The reality was, of course, different. Tom Wintringham observed that most of the volunteers "were very much like the men you met in the crowd of a football match."[54] Jason Gurney said that "there were pure idealists, political opportunists, doctrinaire Marxists, adventurers and plain rogues, in varying proportions."[55] When Laurie Lee arrived in Spain in the winter of 1937, shortly before the battle of Teruel, he took this snapshot: "You could pick out the British by their nervous jerking heads, native air of suspicion, and constant stream of self-effacing jokes. These, again, could be divided up into the ex-convicts, the alcoholics, the wizened miners, dockers, noisy politicos and dreamy undergraduates busy scribbling manifestos and notes to their boyfriends."[56]

The usual estimate is that about one-half of the British Battalion was communist. The remainder varied predictably in their views. Charles Bloom, an ex-British soldier, was one of the first to reach Spain and fought for two weeks on the Jarama front before spending the rest of his war working in the post office. He offers a more specific political breakdown. Bloom felt he could say with confidence that in addition to the large communist presence in the battalion, there were also Liberals, Labour supporters, a few anarchists, some Trotskyists, as well as "a few adventurers [who would] go anywhere, fight anybody." As for the rest, Bloom said, "you name it." Interestingly, he believed that there was a "fraction" of twenty-five or thirty anarcho-syndicalists, which, along with the anarchists and Trotskyists, could well have made the battalion's response to the POUM uprising in Barcelona in May 1937 more complex than heretofore thought.[57]

Nevertheless, the overwhelming majority of the battalion consisted of workers, with about 25 percent of them unemployed. (David Goodman, a volunteer from Middlebrough, calculated the figure as closer to 20 percent.) The volunteers came from all parts of Great Britain, but most were from Scotland, the Manchester area, the valleys of South Wales, and London. In general, the volunteers can be grouped into fairly conventional categories. One was the unemployed, who were typically casualties of layoffs in the factories, building trades, or the mines. Another group consisted of instinctive rebels such as the ex-sailor Fred Copeman (who, however, went to Spain to impress his girlfriend),[58] the ex-soldier Jock Cunningham, the ex-sailor and boilerman Sam Wild, and the runaway public schoolboy Esmond Romilly. Tommy Bloomfield's views reflected those of working-class rebels of a less rhetorical temperament. While working on a building site in Kirkcaldy, he developed a strong distaste both for the working conditions and the foreman responsible for them. One day he told the foreman that "I'd had enough and that I'd be happier in Spain shooting bastards like him instead of working under him."[59]

Dedicated communists included such men as the mathematician Lorrimer Birch, the poet John Cornford, the Welsh miner Jack "Russia," the industrial chemist Bill Alexander, and Will Lawther's youngest brother, Clifford, a communist who in his last letter wrote, "I am going up into the line with men of every country and of none, men who like myself have given up good jobs at home."[60]

In addition, there were socialists or simply antifascists such as the Welshman Jim Brewer [61] and George Orwell. One volunteer, a friend of Syd Booth, was wounded and evacuated to England, staying for only two months before returning to Spain where he was killed. Booth explained in a letter home that "his hatred of fascism was bitter & he was determined to do his best to help bring about its defeat." He added that his friend did not belong "to any political party at all when he came to Spain. He knew nothing of politics but hated any form of oppression."[62] He was not alone. The miner Frank Cairns was judged at the time of the battalion's repatriation in 1938 to be "a good non-party anti-fascist."[63] A laborer from Dundee, Alexander McLanders, whom the commissars called "a sincere anti-fascist fighter," said that he came to Spain "for the Cause of Liberty."[64] Fred Borrino put his own antifascist views more expansively, saying that he was in Spain "to destroy fascism and establish [a] Worker State."[65]

Maurice Levine wrote home to Manchester:

> We were not dupes in coming to Spain; we quitted sound jobs and good homes; we were not lured by promises of big money, but came to fight with the knowledge that a defeat for international fascism meant a halt in its brutal aggression throughout Europe and would give time to the democratic countries of the world to unite and preserve world peace and democracy.[66]

For others, like Jim Brewer, fascism was simply one manifestation of injustice that had to be fought wherever it presented itself. Undoubtedly thinking of the American socialist Eugene Debs, he wrote to his friend, the Warden of Coleg Harlech, "To be silent in the face of injustice is to aquiese [sic]." Without a trace of self-consciousness, he continued, "Should one man be unjustly imprisoned, the place of all just men is in prison."[67]

Some volunteeers emerged from the powerful traditions of pacifism, which exerted a strong influence on the political culture of the thirties. Shortly after Hitler became chancellor of Germany, the

Oxford Union voted, "This House will in no circumstances fight for its king or country." Student groups throughout Great Britain adopted the resolution. The campaign for the Peace Ballot in 1934–35, "the largest and most sustained mobilization ever undertaken by a British peace movement," demonstrated, among other things, the support of millions for multilateral disarmament and the end of the private manufacture and sale of armaments.[68]

S. H. Charvet was one of the few volunteers who refused to renounce his pacifist views. In a letter to the command of the XVth Brigade, Charvet proved his fidelity to his principles by saying, "I do not want to kill. I should never make a soldier. I have a violent urge to save life." He demanded to be assigned to the medical unit at the front or be sent home.[69]

There were, of course, adventurers, such as Harold Davies from Neath, "a young man of no political opinions but he loved adventure."[70] Even they, however, "were bound together in most instances by their experiences of the Depression and the common cause of anti-Fascism."[71] Others with thoroughly pragmatic motives also made their way to Spain. The Scot Albert Smith went to Spain "because I was in debt to moneylenders."[72] A Glaswegian, John Smith, said that when he volunteered he had in mind a quite unholy trinity of "drink, women, and loot," confessing he had enjoyed little success in acquiring any of the three. Smith was later killed in the Ebro offensive not long after being commended for his bravery.[73] Another was Patrick Coffey, an Irish Liverpudlian laborer, who was called "a habitual drunkard," an "adventurer," and generally "a disruptive element." He admitted that he came to Spain only to obtain money for his wife and children. Moreover, he proved a bad influence on the younger men. A confidential report advised ominously, "You should treat him in the manner that he deserves."[74]

The frankly criminal element surfaced also. Two examples will suffice. One volunteer, John Coleman, had been jailed for nine months in Great Britain for breaking and entering. In addition, the English police wanted him for robbing a theater of £40.[75] When another volunteer, James Maley, was on his way to Spain, he recognized a fellow Glaswegian, a notorious "gangster" called Cheeky McCaig who directed the criminal activities of "the Cheeky Forty."[76] McCaig and his followers may have been the "Glasgow razor-slashers" of whom "Jimmy Younger" wrote to Stephen Spender.[77]

There were Jews, mostly from the East End of London and the industrial North, many of whom had already done battle with Mosley's Blackshirts in Cable Street or some other contested public space. They carried a special motivation. One volunteer said, "A feeling of kinship with the victims of Nazism was present throughout the Jewish communities in Britain."[78] Indeed, the Jews appeared to be so prominent among the international volunteers that an antibrigade diatribe, alluding to the "strong Jewish element" in the British Battalion, made the preposterous but revealing claim that 35,000 Jews had joined the International Brigades.[79]

A number of those with miscellaneous motives would include the nurse, Lillian Buckoke, neither unemployed nor political, and whose idealism was tempered by religious belief. In addition, it was no secret that there were British serving in Spain who were driven by some fantastic political confusion. For example, J. R. Jump remembers that "though the vast majority had strong political convictions," he met a Lancashire waiter called Joe Moran who told him he volunteered for Spain to fight "Franco and his bloody communists."[80]

Volunteers from any of these groups could anticipate, in addition to fighting against fascism or for an ideal, that they might find in Spain the answer to their personal problems, as Stephen Spender's friend, Tony Hyndman, hoped. A British ambulance driver confessed that he would have liked to have volunteered for "rational" reasons, but that instead his were largely personal.

> The truth was that I had run away from the difficulties of living in England. I hoped that by facing the superficially more difficult life in Spain I should more quickly achieve the integration which can only be achieved by self-discipline and faith, and which is easily, or hardly achieved in an office or a farm as on a melodramatic battlefield.[81]

Maurice Levine did the simple arithmetic: "Most of the people I met were very good types. There were a few scoundrels."[82]

VII

A comparison between the proletarian cultures of two industrial areas—Manchester and Salford, and Birmingham—reveals a good deal as to why some areas contributed a large number of volunteers to Spain and others did not. About 130 volunteers came from the Greater Manchester area, of whom some thirty-five were killed. Only eight joined from Birmingham. The "common element" linking working-class volunteers from the Manchester area was "a militant anti-fascism generated by a fusion of events in Europe and the experience of street politics in Britain."[83] These "events" in Europe included the increasingly confident antisemitic behavior of the Nazis, of which the considerable population of Jewish workers in Manchester and Salford and London was well aware, even if many of their fellow-citizens of the middle and upper classes appeared to be insulated from it through ignorance, complacency, or moral complicity.

To workers, Manchester's Sir Oswald Mosley made it very clear that there was a fascist threat at home as well as abroad. His British Union of Fascists transformed Hitler's threats into a disturbing immediacy. Mosley's meetings were a paraphrase of the garish and vulgar spectacles favored by the Nazis, complete with squadrons of Blackshirts carrying British flags and a fanfare of trumpets. Nor did Mosley ignore Hitler's antisemitism. At a mass meeting in October 1934 at Albert Hall, he cried out: "We declare that we will not tolerate an organised community within the state which owes allegiance not to Britain, but to another race in foreign countries."[84]

This is not to say that the economic conditions of the Manchester and Salford workers had no effect on their political views. Certainly the Trades Council records and the minutes of the Salford City Council reveal deep concern about unemployment and the application of the Means Test, which resulted in a demonstration by the National Unemployed Workers' Movement on October 1, 1931, and, subsequently, the so-called Battle of Bexley Square (which sent Eddie Frow,[85] among others, to prison). Trafford Park, which had once been the most active center for engineering in the world, "was slowly grinding to a halt." Each week the cotton mills laid off workers. Apprentices dreaded the approach of their twenty-first birthdays, knowing they would be sacked once they obtained the right to a tradesman's salary.

Even so, these social and economic grievances were not the cause but rather the context in which the Manchester and Salford workers decided to volunteer for Spain. More important than unemployment or the Means Test was their political understanding of the threat of fascism. This enabled them to overcome differences in politics, skills, and religion. A strong United Front in the Manchester area developed, linking political militants from the Labour and Communist parties. Reflecting the special conditions of the area, the Manchester Anti-Fascist Co-Ordinating Committee enjoyed the widest imaginable spectrum of supporters. There were Jews, trade unionists, militants from church organizations, and pacifists.[86]

Trades Council minutes reveal the dawning recognition of what was taking place on the Continent. On March 15, 1933, a very real concern was expressed over "the rise of this Fascist Dictatorship in Germany," which "inevitably implied a mighty social, revolutionary struggle, vast, crucial and decisive in importance for workers." Three weeks later Trades Council members resolved that the National Joint Council of Labour should be asked to "start at once a nationwide campaign to acquaint the workers of Britain with the full meaning of the German events."[87]

These views of working-class leaders and their constituents found vivid expression. Thousands of Manchester and Salford workers joined to disrupt a Mosley meeting held in Belle Vue on September 29, 1934. The Trades Council organized counter demonstrations, one of which attracted historian A. J. P. Taylor from Manchester University, who, according to the *Manchester Guardian*, "expressed [his] utmost horror and detestation of fascism, militarisation of the police and the open drilling and arming of hooligans."[88] Demonstrations and marches were common. One of the most famous acts of defiance against landowners and gamekeepers was the 1934 Mass Trespass on Kinder, in which workers, including Pat Kenny and Alex Armstrong, both volunteers for Spain, walked into parts of the countryside forbidden to them.[89] "Events like this demonstrated [that] class divisions were very much alive in our country." But there were compensations, too, for "they were lessons in unity and solidarity."[90]

In 1936 local antifascist concerns and Spain found a common focus. Ben Tillett and another former M.P. wrote in the *Salford City Reporter* on September 4, 1936, less than two months after Franco and the generals rose, "[We] want to stress that we in Salford have been discussing for a long time the necessity of holding protest meetings not only in relation to the Spanish Government but in relation to the increase in the popularity of fascism in Salford."[91] Films such as *The Spanish Earth* were shown at the Co-operative Hall, although the film with the greatest impact in the area was *The Defence of Madrid*. All this meant, according to Miriam Cunningham, that "never before had ordinary people" of such diversity of political and personal beliefs been so united.[92]

The Salford Labour party minute books record that over the course of the war its leadership purchased thousands of leaflets, such as *The*

Agony of Spain, Madrid, What Is Happening in Spain, and *Nazi Rule in Germany,* for distribution to its constituents. In fact, all the literature bought by the Salford party during this time focused on either the Spanish War or fascism. In the *Salford City Reporter* there was consistent opposition to fascism and support for the Spanish Republic. Moreover, the young proletarian intellectual of Irish descent, George Brown, had been elected to the Central Committee of the Communist party and proved influential at both the local and national levels. Harry Roland Heap, the first volunteer from Oldham, had fought in World War I. Like George Brown, he was an enormously persuasive force. "Well known for his love of political discussion," he had wide influence in Oldham, particularly on young militants, which may help explain why Oldham sent one of the greatest number of volunteers to Spain from the Manchester area.[93]

The Manchester and Salford experience was not, however, universal. Some industrial areas, such as Birmingham and the West Midlands, sent few volunteers, which, according to their historian, Peter Drake, reflected "the lack of working class militancy and unity which marked the political and industrial framework of the area." Birmingham's reputation among militants as a "city of reaction," the divided allegiance of Catholics, the comparative economic boom the city experienced in the mid-thirties, loyalty to the Labour party and, with it, distrust of the Communist party (which many saw as trying to thwart Labour's agenda), all played their part in dampening enthusiasm for service in Spain. In addition, the workers of the West Midlands, unlike the Welsh, the Scots, and the Mancunians, "shared very little in the way of a common culture."[94] Finally, many of the new industries responsible for the comparative economic prosperity of the area were not unionized, thus contributing to the lack of working-class militancy.[95]

Not surprisingly, one of the few who volunteered from Birmingham was chided for his lack of political leadership in the labor movement. In his "autobiography" Gerrard Doyle tells of being in and out of work in the twenties and thirties until "I got the idea into my head that it was only [a] waste of time working for what you got. That while Capitalism & Fascism reigned supreme the workers would be their slaves. There and then I abandoned all hopes of seeing anything good until fascism is crushed. So I came to help the boys in the crushing." One of the commissars observed, however, that although Doyle "has had a real worker's life in various trades," he "has not had an active political life."[96]

The 174 Welsh volunteers in Spain came from a world that had developed along very different lines from those in the coalfields of Durham or Yorkshire, or, for that matter, in the industrial area of Manchester. Resting on nonconformist foundations, Welsh militancy found its primary expression in the Communist party or, at least, a general set of Marxist views. The unique political development of the Welsh came from self-education, the Plebs' League, the National Council of Labour Colleges, which held classes in sixty-three centers in South Wales, the Central Labour College in London (partially owned by the South Wales Miners' Federation), and, of course, the Workers Educational Association. When James Hanley went to South Wales he found an unusually, perhaps uniquely literate population. When one miner discovered Hanley was a writer, he took him to his house to show him what he read, which included several volumes from the Left Book Club sitting at his bedside. The miner shared his membership with six others who, like him, could not afford to join alone. He told Hanley, "One of the most surprising things round here . . . is the enormous number of people who read,"; adding, "all miners read now. . . . They've got a real hunger to learn about things."[97] For a handful, the *summa* of their education was the Lenin School in Moscow.

But even though the Communist party had great influence on the South Wales Miners Federation, its strength tended to be localized in "Little Moscows" such as Maerdy and Bedlinog.[98] The Welsh volunteers, however, formed a working-class elite in Spain because they were comparatively better educated than many of their proletarian comrades in the British Battalion and, moreover, possessed the disciplining experience of active membership in the Communist party. Another factor that separated the Welsh from most of their fellow workers was the particularly bitter memory of the 1926 General Strike, when the miners stood alone, abandoned by the rest of organized labor. For many Welshmen, this experience was the beginning of their militancy, leading to a wide range of protest activities—riots, street demonstrations, stay-in strikes, and most memorably of all, the Hunger Marches, in which twenty-three Welsh volunteers for Spain participated. Education and protest were compelling alternatives to the humiliations brought about by an unusually high degree of unemployment and the Means Test.[99] Spain was to be the greatest protest of all.

Scotland, too, reacted strongly to Franco's efforts to overthrow the Spanish Republic. A Scottish journalist observed, "There is a litany of causes which have mobilised the generous indignation of the active Labour movement in Scotland, but none has compared with Spain for the multiplicity of activities called into existence." Flag days, collections for ambulances, and aid to Basque refugee children were some of the issues that were seized upon by Spanish Aid Committees (in Glasgow alone there were fifteen), which reached from the border mill towns to Aberdeen and Inverness and, most prominently, to the central industrial belt, which was the birthplace of Scotland's labor movement.[100]

The galvanizing influence among Scottish workers was the national conference of the Labour party, held in Edinburgh in October 1936. "Delegates had listened to some anaemic non-intervention resolutions while men fell like autumn leaves in the defence of Madrid." Isobel de Palencia, a delegate from the Spanish Republic, whose father was Spanish and mother Scottish, "took this conference by storm" when she spoke. As she gave the clenched fist salute at the end of her speech, the audience leapt to its feet and sang *The Red Flag*.[101] Fred Copeman, a commander of the British Battalion and a plainspoken ex-sailor, paid the Scottish volunteers his highest compliment. "These bloody Scotsmen are tough and I like them."[102]

VIII

Kenneth Bond, a proletarian intellectual from Bromley, was representative of many of the other militants from the London area and throughout the country. One of the founding members of the Bromley branch of the Communist party, he left for Spain in early 1938 and was killed in the Ebro offensive. Before his death, he was ceaselessly active in demonstrations, promoting the *Daily Worker*, the cooperative movement, and his union. For two years, he served as chairman of the Bromley Council Tenants' Association. He also managed to read widely. In addition to Marx, Engels, and Lenin, one of the authors he most admired was Jack London. Like George Orwell, he understood that comparatively few workers were committed political militants. When asked in Spain what question had been most on his mind, he replied, the "social revolution."[103] Unlike Orwell, however, he believed the Communist party could awaken the working class from its passivity. On July 11, 1938, he wrote to his comrades in Bromley that it was their duty, as it was his, to shake "the working class from their Slumbers." Later in the letter he asked,

"How's the branch going, have you all been able to settle down and turn Bromley red. I hope you are on the way for the working class must have their brains cleared or the rust cleaned off." His last words were, "*Salud* for red Bromley and red England. Salute to the workers that work for the benefit of the workers and the Community as a whole."[104] Bond's appeal to the "Community as a whole" symbolized the desire of the Party to attract noncommunist as well as communist volunteers.

The United Front, however, could in certain circumstances exacerbate class tensions. Jack Roberts[105] of South Wales, who was wounded at Quinto in the Aragón, felt little but outrage when he heard that a middle-class ambulance driver in Spain had pronounced himself "disillusioned." He saw his comrade's change of mind as an unwarranted indulgence by one who had never experienced the suffering that communism promised to end. Roberts thought, "I would imagine that anybody that would have finished his time in Oxford in those days were well blessed with world riches." By contrast,

> Us down here . . . we never had nothing. We had to struggle hard for what we were having and you could be as good a workman as you need and if you agitated too much one side you went. So your ability as a workman didn't count. It was what trouble somebody thought you created and that's the thing. You either created trouble and got kicked out or else you didn't say nothing and got kept down."[106]

"Disillusion" was never an issue for Roberts, who was a lifelong communist, known familiarly in the Rhondda as Jack Russia. Militancy flowed from his experience of life in a manner only a few middle-class Marxists would ever know.

Despite public pronouncements in Great Britain that the International Brigades were an all-party fighting force, the Communist party quickly tightened its control over the British volunteers. For those who had "military ambitions" in the war, the party was the sole route to positions of higher command and responsibility.[107] For example, George Nathan, who had brilliantly commanded the famed No. 1 Company, was the logical person to take charge of the British Battalion after Wilfrid Macartney's departure in February 1936. Instead, apparently because he was not a party member, Nathan was assigned to a position on the brigade staff. Ralph Cantor, who had campaigned for the Sheffield Youth Conference Against Fascism and War, and was described by Maurice Levine, a fellow Mancunian, as "a bright boy,"[108] confirmed the communist domination of leading roles among the international volunteers. He wrote in his diary, "Political leadership of our Brigade [is] entirely C.P."[109]

This remained true throughout the battalion's history. On the eve of his repatriation, Jack Carson wrote, "POLITICIANS ARE BAD OFFICERS." His view was shared by Edmund Updale, an electrician, who took part in six major engagements, was twice wounded, lost his leg at Batea, and was commended for his bravery. Although Updale fought with the Lincolns, his views are echoed to a greater or lesser degree in accounts from men in the British Battalion. Updale realized that a soldier's political ideals possessed a great practical value. He was convinced that "a sound knowledge of the cause for which one is fighting enables one to suffer hardships and deprivations which would otherwise cause discontent." But military and political leadership should not be confused, he said. "While a military leader must be sound politically, the knowledge of what a man is fighting for is not sufficient for entrusting to him the lives of men and the conduct of an important military operation. Officers must be soldiers & commissars politicians." In his own unit he found the political organization "often biased against men with no pol. background, giving preference to inferior men on account of their . . . pol. affiliations." Updale believed that "many expert soldiers served in the ranks on this account, and their value ignored, with unhappy results, for these men became disgruntled and prejudiced, and lost enthusiasm."[110] David Wickes agreed. A Labour party member since 1928, he believed that "political 'pull' was too much in evidence in the choosing of military command."[111]

Jason Gurney had known casually a few communists in London, and found them boring and unattractive. He now discovered in Spain that communists were not only socially discomfiting but could be intellectually and morally horrifying. Gurney believed the ostensible purpose of communism was to build a world of social justice in which each person would have the opportunity to realize his or her abilities to the fullest. But his communist comrades in the battalion dismissed this as bourgeois idealism. Gurney wrote, "It was only necessary to conform with a natural and inevitable process of history in order to assist rather than obstruct the inevitable." The laws of history were, of course, to be found in Marx, Engels, Lenin, and Stalin, whose works "were as much Holy Writ to them as the Bible is to Christians." In addition, Gurney said, "I now learned about the doctrine of 'revolutionary expediency,'" which was the foundation stone of ethics and morality. "In its simplest form it is that the end justifies the means, as long as the end is that of advancing and consolidating the Revolution."[112]

The anarchists, for all their catastrophic misjudgments in the war, warned early of what was to come. "The Spanish Revolution will serve the proletariat of the rest of the world as an example worth emulating, if it will avoid the errors of other revolutions, the errors of dictatorship."[113] But a Spanish revolution was the very thing the party did not want—Stalin had every intention of achieving effective dictatorship in Spain but behind an antifascist façade. The official line remained that the volunteers fighting in Spain were heroic antifascists, joined in a United Front in behalf of Spanish democracy against the forces of national and international fascism. Alonzo Elliott, a commissar who became a party member in 1934 while at Cambridge, wrote cryptically but revealingly in his notebook, "Unity most precious thing for us. Ban signs [of] separate Parties. No need to wear. In our Hearts."[114]

Looking at the country as a whole, J. R. Campbell contrasted the political caution of the labor movement's leadership with the urgency felt by its members. He argued that the "rank and file" have committed themselves to a "sustained effort on behalf of Spanish democracy," covering Great Britain "with a network of Spanish Aid Committees and Medical Unit Committees." Their efforts, however, were in sharp contrast to "the indifference of the leaders of the Trade Union and Labour Movement."[115] The enthusiasm of the "rank and file" for the cause of Spain did not, as Campbell believed, lead to an estrangement between them and their laborist leaders who accepted class collaboration as a means of attaining social change within the existing society.

Nevertheless, the Spanish War "was without any doubt the most widespread movement of international solidarity ever seen in Britain up to that time," said Nan Green in 1970. She concluded, "It united the most diverse sections of the British people and left a mark on the labour movement which is still perceptible."[116] Harry Pollitt concurred with Green: "The struggle of the Spanish people against fascism has evoked the greatest demonstration of international solidarity the world has ever seen."[117]

Still, there were those in Great Britain who failed to see why Spain was the chosen battlefield. A miner in South Wales asked, "Why should they be rushing over to another country to fight when there's all the fight they wanted here?"[118]

CHAPTER 8

When the World Seems on Fire

I believe that the experience of the struggle will give me just those qualities of practical life that I lack. My short experience of University life [as a lecturer] was useful. But in a world of wars and revolutions new tasks are on the agenda. Let us see that they are carried out. . . . It has required an incredible effort to concentrate on pure mathematics when the world seems on fire.
— David Guest

I have decided to go out in the new year, as soon as the book is finished, to join the International Brigade in Spain.
— W. H. Auden to E. R. Dodds

For long hours I debated with myself as to whether I should join the International Brigades. But I had not sufficient courage of my convictions to do this. Our Modern Democracy in its education conveys to youth singularly few convincing reasons as to why he should die to save it. There was also the element of physical fear. The chances of death were big. My body is not of a robustness calculated to survive long exposure, lack of food. I think now I was wrong. It would have been better to have joined up, feeling as I did.
— Henry Buckley

I

The origin of the International Brigades lay in the ambiguous and hypocritical world of European diplomacy. Even though Russia was a signatory to the Non-Intervention Pact worked out between England's foreign minister, Anthony Eden, and the French leader, Léon Blum, as were Hitler and Mussolini, ample evidence was rapidly accumulating that the German and Italian governments refused to adhere to the agreement.[1] Therefore, the Russians felt they were free to pursue their interests in a different direction. As a consequence of their fear of a rearmed and militant Germany in the west and the aggressions of Japan in the east, the Soviets reversed their foreign policy in 1935 and became ardent advocates of collective security and the Popular Front. This tactic succeeded in persuading much of progressive opinion in the West that an attack on the Soviet Union was a danger to all.

But Spain presented a particular difficulty for the Russians. "It exposed the contradiction in their new policy between the attempt to convince bourgeois democratic governments that the Soviet Union was no longer interested in exporting revolution on the one hand and their desire to continue to pose as the champion of the world proletariat on the other."[2] The dilemma was solved by finding an intermediate position. The Russians sent military supplies to the Spanish Republic but refused to be identified with any generally revolutionary movement for fear of alienating the Western democracies and thus compromising their own security against Germany. Therefore, the Popular Front policy adopted by 1935 demanded that the Soviets align themselves not with genuine revolutionary movements but with the established democratic order. This, of course, was to be most dramatically and memorably demonstrated in the destruction of the revolutionary POUM by the communists in May 1937.

Consequently, a number of communist fronts were established, most springing from the propaganda and organizational genius of Willi Münzenberg, who based his activities in Paris.[3] Examples were the Spanish Relief Committee and the Spanish News Agency. The most spectacular of their front organizations, however, were the International Brigades. The Soviets became convinced that without sizable military aid to the Republican government, the Popular Front would fall to the Spanish generals. If Franco could be defeated or if the demise of the Republic were delayed, a triple effect could be achieved: Russian influence in Western Europe would be greatly expanded; Spain could be used as a bargaining chip with Hitler; and Western antifascist opinion would be distracted from the Terror, which Stalin was about to unleash on his people.

The key to any or all three of these goals was the creation of the International Brigades. R. Dan Richardson, the author of *Comintern Army*, concludes that "the origins of the International Brigades are to be found in the working out of a Soviet-Comintern policy of worldwide scope and not, as some would have it, in the spontaneous response of world democracy to the threat of fascism in Spain."[4] Thus, he argues that the International Brigades, for all the idealism of many of their members, came into existence as part of the grand strategy of Soviet Popular Front policy. On October 16, 1936, *Pravda* printed the text of a telegram from Stalin to José Díaz, the secretary-general of the Spanish Communist party:

> The workers of the Soviet Union are only doing their duty in rendering all possible aid to the revolutionary masses in Spain. They are well aware that the liberation of Spain from the yoke of Fascist reactionaries is not the private concern of the Spanish but the general concern of all advanced and progressive humanity.[5]

The British Communist party was given the task of recruiting, organizing, and financing the journey of British volunteers to Spain. The party decided to name the battalion after Shapurji Saklatvala, the Indian national leader who became one of the first communist MPs. Ralph Fox doubted the wisdom of the choice. He wrote to Harry Pollitt, "Would Saklatvala have a wide enough appeal to non-Communists at home really to help the growth of the People's Front? If not, what propositions then?" The novelist had earlier supported the idea of naming the battalion after the Chartists.[6] Initially, however, the British did call themselves the Saklatvala Battalion, but Fox's concerns were valid: the name did not have sufficiently widespread appeal. So, alone among the various national groups, the British came to be known by their country of origin—the British Battalion.

Great Britain sent a smaller force of volunteers to Spain than did other countries. The largest group came from France, numbering approximately 10,000; Germany and Austria together sent around 5,000; the Poles, including Ukrainians, approximately 5,000; the Italians, 3,350; the United States, 2,800; and the British about 2,000. Probably the best figure, although there are several different estimates, is that the five International Brigades, XI–XV, consisted in all of approximately 35,000–40,000 volunteers with some 18,000 effectives at any one time.[7]

In addition to the British Battalion, the XVth International Brigade included, initially, the Franco-Belge Battalion, the Dimitrov Battalion (consisting of political refugees from Yugoslavia, the Balkans, and other countries), the Lincoln Battalion from the United States, and the Mackenzie-Papineau Battalion from Canada (although a number of Americans fought with them). In time, the XVth Brigade became all English-speaking, except for a company of Spanish Republican soldiers who comprised a part of each battalion. With the relentless casualties among the volunteers, and the slowing of replacements, the Spaniards ultimately achieved a numerical majority in the brigade.

Inevitably, the closest ties were formed between the British and the Americans. The result was a conflation of cultures that was perhaps best exemplified in the song that became most closely identified with the brigade, "The Valley of the Jarama." The music came from the American song, "Red River Valley," and the lyrics were written by a Glaswegian, Alex McDade, who was shortly afterwards killed at Brunete. The Americans and the British freely adapted the words to their respective moods and needs.

II

Auden's famous line that "poets [were] exploding like bombs" in Spain was not without foundation. The Spanish historian Angel Viñas believes the brigades possessed the highest proportion of intellectuals of any military force in history. Andreu Castells is more specific in his study of the international volunteers. He writes that 45 percent of the brigaders could be called intellectuals, another 44 percent were drawn from the professional classes and workers, and 11 percent could be referred to as "adventurers."[8] Jason Gurney, a Chelsea sculptor who served with the British and Americans in Spain, wrote that "the number of artists, musicians and writers amongst them was out of all proportion to their numbers in any of the societies from which they came."[9] Upton Sinclair, the American writer, contended that it was "probably the most literary brigade in the history of warfare."[10]

Agreement was not universal, however. André Marty, the leader of the brigades, took a different view. According to him, the volunteers consisted of an "overwhelming majority of workers" in which were "mingled intellectuals."[11] But then, as a Stalinist, he had the interests of the party to protect. Regardless, it would appear that the composition of the British Battalion was significantly different from that of other countries. The world of Nat Cohen and Sam Masters was more representative of the British volunteers than that of John Cornford and Christopher Caudwell. Workers made up 80 percent of the volunteers. And whether they were working class or middle class, coming from Great Britain or any of fifty other countries, the danger they faced was thoroughly democratic. The great majority of the volunteers were wounded or killed. At the early battle of Lopera in the south of Spain, for example, some 300 were killed and 600 wounded from nineteen nations.[12]

III

The volunteer Jason Gurney addressed the formation of the brigades from a different point of view than the historian R. Dan Richardson. The Comintern, he believed, simply took advantage of the fact that young men from all over the world were finding their way to Spain to fight for the Republic. He writes that "nobody invented [the International Brigades] at all. From the very day of the rising, all sorts of individuals set out for Spain to assist the embattled Republic. It immediately appeared as the symbol of a great number of things which men held valuable but which were being destroyed all over Europe." Once these feelings were tapped in Germany, Italy, France, Great Britain, and many other countries, "the Communists had the good sense to realize the terrific force of idealism that existed and climbed on the band-wagon to exploit it."[13] Fred Copeman, whom Gurney despised and who was the darling of the British party, said much the same thing. According to the ex-sailor, in the early days of the fighting, the British newspapers highlighted the role that students were playing. "And then the party suddenly got hold of it and said we will back this up."[14] Ultimately, Moscow would take possession of this idealism and shape it for its own purposes.

In any event, in the fall of 1936 the Comintern began a concerted drive to establish an international army in Spain and instructed the national parties to recruit and organize in each of their countries. In Great Britain "formal recruitment" by the party began as early as September 1936.[15] Usually, "Robbie" Robson,[16] a solemn World War I veteran and member of the party Central Committee, decided on each volunteer's suitability. When volunteers had reached a sufficient number, arrangements were made for a group to be taken to Paris on a weekend pass, a destination that did not require a passport. From there they would go to Spain.

Stalin did not instill the motives in volunteers, but through the Comintern he did establish a mechanism in each country by which volunteers could act on those motives. Thus, workers were enabled to inhabit a common space with middle-class intellectuals. Bill Alexander said, "We all know about the artists and intellectuals. Laurie Lee was already there. Ralph and Winifred Bates were already 'bumming' around Spain. . . . People like John Cornford and Esmond Romilly knew how to travel, how to get a passport, what to do." But, Alexander said, "It took longer for ordinary working men to organise themselves in this way but they went within a very short time."[17]

And, it should be added, with the assistance of the British Communist party.

Those who did not subject themselves to party discipline, whether communist or noncommunist, and made their way across the frontier independently, faced suspicion and danger upon arrival. For example, Laurie Lee's solitary climb over the mountains only made his motives suspect to the brigade functionaries who maintained party headquarters in Albacete.[18]

In addition to recruiting and processing volunteers, Moscow charged communist parties, including the British, with quotas to fill. It is clear, however, that with very few exceptions[19] the British in Spain were genuinely volunteers.[20] In any event, the British "quota" was small because of the party's size and comparative unimportance in the eyes of Moscow. As a member of a Young Communist League delegation to Russia in the late 1920s, Margaret McCarthy learned to her dismay of the little regard the Russians had for the British party. "It early became clear to me" that the British movement "was despised in the Comintern as a tiny, insignificant party which would neither grow [n]or die, as utterly supine and flaccid and intellectually incapable of revolutionary theory or practice." She said, "It used to be a joke that we should have a revolution in England only when one was imported," and she ruefully conceded, "There was, of course, a lot of truth in this."[21] Charlotte Haldane confirmed that Russian contempt for the British party remained even after the outbreak of the Spanish Civil War.[22]

IV

In the party's eagerness to get volunteers to Spain, Harry Pollitt allowed a number of unsuitable men to volunteer. In desperation, Ralph Bates wrote to Pollitt in late December 1936, complaining about the poor quality of the volunteers. "The proportion of duds, undesirables, and harmful types arriving here with Party cards or letters is far too high." The Germans, French, and Italians "repeatedly express their surprise at this, even disgust." Bates recommended that instead of sending out one or two volunteers at a time, "a body of military volunteers" should be "organized and controlled by the Party." He then told Pollitt, "I have, perhaps improperly, mentioned to leading Spanish comrades that there is just the possibility of an English battalion being formed, and they are all immensely pleased at the prospect."[23] The formation of a British battalion was, indeed, the party's goal, but the men would have to meet higher physical and political standards.

The party's man at Albacete, Dave Springhall, wrote on January 4 in the same vein as Bates, urging that the screening process at King Street be toughened. "We find that a number have never been in a W.C. [working class] movement, have never been in a trade union etc."[24] Two days later, Peter Kerrigan wrote from Albacete, "We are having to return a very high percentage from here." He urged that any romantic notions about the war be crushed. Volunteers should be told, *"This is war and many will be killed.* They must understand this clearly and it should be put quite brutally."[25] Shortly thereafter, Wintringham sent a final word. "About 10 per cent of the men are drunks and funks. Can't imagine why you let them send out such obviously useless material."[26] The inadequate screening process would remain an issue throughout the war.

The two principal communist representatives in Albacete when the British Battalion was formed were Peter Kerrigan and Bill Rust. Kerrigan had been the Scottish district secretary of the British Communist party and was now acting as political commissar. Bill Rust was publicly recognized as the correspondent of the *Daily Worker* but also served as base commissar. Neither Rust nor Kerrigan could be described easily. Kerrigan was a tough and imposing figure who served at the end of World War I, although he did not see combat. Tall and handsome, with crinkly gray hair, he spoke with a thick Glasgow accent. Alec Marcovitch, who knew him in Glasgow, thought him an arrogant bully.[27] Some, like Stephen Spender, managed to find a trace of humor in the formidable Scot,[28] although this was not a usual experience.[29] Walter Gregory, a brewery worker, admired him for his energy and effectiveness.[30] Apparently, the only time that "Big Peter" fired a weapon in Spain was when he wounded the first commander of the British Battalion, Wilfred Macartney.

Bill Rust also drew mixed reactions. He came from a working-class background, was a man of ability, and could, if he chose, be quite charming. Laurie Lee, for example, formed a good opinion of him.[31] But for the most part he was disliked and distrusted. In 1928, when Margaret McCarthy, an unemployed weaver, traveled to Russia with the British Young Communist League, whose leadership included Rust, she quickly grew to loathe him. The British mingled boorishly with other Comintern delegations, and McCarthy attributed this to Rust's influence. The former mill girl thought Rust "ill-bred, conceited and a bully," qualities that she believed were emulated by lesser figures in the YCL leadership.[32] Rust was above all an arch intriguer. The most recent biographer of Harry Pollitt writes that Rust was a man to "whose memory it is hard to be kind."[33] He became a YCL representative on the executive committee of the Comintern,[34] but devoted most of his time and energy to the *Daily Worker*. Charlotte Haldane, who organized the British arrivals in Paris, used her skills as a writer to teach Rust all that she could of the journalist's craft, perhaps unaware of his previous experience. He proved an apt and eager student.

Rust's climb from the East End of London to the highest ranks of the British Communist party left its mark. "What power came his way he used and enjoyed to the hilt," Haldane said. "He was utterly ruthless, and made use of me and my money with cynical matter-of-factness." Rust struck her nevertheless as intelligent, if undeniably "greedy for all the good things of life."[35] Alec Marcovitch, a Scottish volunteer, was outspoken in his dislike of Rust, one of many issues that would get him into serious trouble with the party. Rust's habit of wearing a leather coat made the Glasgow Jew think of the Gestapo. And, on closer acquaintance, he decided that Rust simply was not a likable man.[36]

Marcovitch was not the only volunteer whose opinion of Rust would come to the attention of the political *apparat*. William Benson was a twice-wounded veteran whose file in Moscow is missing two pages. A note from a SIM agent helpfully clarifies the omission by indicating that the pages "are at present in the hands of our service in the XVth brigade." The reason for the SIM's scrutiny, in addition to whatever other political infraction Benson may have committed, undoubtedly lies in an adjacent personal letter in his file, dated March 18, 1938. It is from Benson to a friend, in which he calls Rust "a bastard," continuing, "I never did think very much of him. Now I think less." The reason was that Benson held Rust partially responsible for sending a young volunteer back to the front line who did not belong there. He was "the one comrade who should have been sent back to England," but now "he will probably [sic] get killed and nothing will be said about him, while hero's [sic] like Kerrigan, Springhall, Aitken, and Copeman, will continue to be headliners in the D.W. [*Daily Worker*] shit."[37] The letter, of course, never reached its destination.

Members of the battalion admired Rust, however, if only because he brought the mail from London, and, alone among the international correspondents, always seemed to be at their side. He would even drive onto the battlefield in his automobile, as he did at Brunete. These actions put him a cut above his fellow correspondents who languished, as the brigaders thought, in the comparative security and among the various pleasures of Madrid, Barcelona, or Valencia.

V

The commissars at brigade, battalion, and company level were almost all communists. They represented the party's interests and were charged with looking after the morale and welfare of the men. David Anderson, who spent seven years in the Gordon High-landers and rose to second-in-command of the Canadian battalion, the Mac-Paps (Mackenzie-Papineau), spoke highly of the disciplined and brave example set by the communist leadership. "When things got very, very hard, there was always a member of the Communist Party [who] came to the fore and tried to explain things. They were always the ones that gave the lead and took the risks."[38]

The position of political commissar in the British Battalion was certainly not without precedent. Its ancestors could be found in Cromwell's army, among the French revolutionaries, and, of course, the Bolsheviks. In theory, the commissariat, which included the brigade and battalion commissars as well as ones assigned to each company, existed for several reasons. The first was to assist the commander in training while keeping up the morale of the troops by smoothing out differences. "He must settle their complaints and difficulties either amongst the men themselves or between the[m] and the military authorities. When hundreds of men are forced to live together under nerve-wracking conditions how much more smoothly goes the work if their troubles are settled quickly and they are not allowed to brood over them."[39] Sometimes small courtesies were sufficient. When commissar Tom Murray, a nonsmoker, received his cigarette ration, he waited until everyone had exhausted his supply, and then lined up the eighty smokers and gave each one-quarter of one of his twenty cigarettes.[40]

While serving in the Anglo-American battery, Sandor Voros jotted down in a small notebook his first impressions of the system. He began on a half-serious note. "The political commissar is a comrade whose job is to promise you everything you ask for and then blame it later on Albacete that he couldn't get it." He found the meetings conducted by his commissar to be much more productive than party meetings at home, however. "The agenda isn't prepared in advance . . . which gives plenty of room for surprises. You never know what's coming up next." The result was that the commissar held the attention of his men. "What's best of all, we don't waste our time in discussing high politics, economics, what not, we come right down to brass tacks—we take up . . . things that really matter." Last, "the meeting is conducted in a very democratic manner. Everybody can take the floor and our political commissar doesn't play any favorites."[41]

The commissar saw to it that the mail was delivered in timely fashion and ensured the punctual arrival of food. Most important, he helped to develop the political understanding of the volunteers, which meant explaining the party's position on every conceivable issue. In what seemed to be a self-defeating exercise from the standpoint of indoctrination, the commissars were "to awaken in the combatants a taste for study and reading, and an interest in intellectual questions." But, of course, the conclusions they reached would always be subject to the commissar's "vigilance."[42] For example, a British commissar would regularly visit a hospitalized volunteer to feed him a diet of communist newspapers and magazines[43] in order to ensure that his loyalties did not stray. Vigilance also would make him alert for espionage and other kinds of "provocation." Tom Murray spoke of the "fear" of spies infiltrating the battalion. "Identifying them and having them dealt with was a commissar's job, of course."[44] They also created and monitored "wall" newspapers on which the men of the battalion attached news clippings, stories, and poetry written by themselves, as well as various kinds of reminiscences.[45]

If a commissar proved himself in battle, then at least his proselytizing could be tolerated. Men such as George Aitken, Bert Williams, Wally Tapsell, and Bob Cooney were valued by most for their courage and steadiness of judgment, regardless of whatever flaws they may have had. Another who won admiration was George Brown, the leading Manchester communist whom the party made a commissar upon his arrival in Spain. Brown refused a position of safety in order to take part in the attack on Villanueva de la Cañada, part of the Brunete offensive, as an ordinary soldier, and it was there he died. Ralph Bates said what all acknowledged, "His was a very great loss."[46]

After Brunete, when the command structure did not function efficiently, a stern admonition was issued, instructing the commissars to fight apathy and "self-satisfaction." This, of course, would require more meetings, now on a weekly basis, discussing "political problems" with all officers of the battalion. The topics were to include commentary on "the vacillating, cowardly policy of France and Great Britain," which would then be contrasted with the disinterested peace policy of the Soviet Union as well as "its magnificent aid to the Spanish people." Other subjects to be covered were, significantly, "preparations for war against the U.S.S.R." by Fascist powers.[47]

The worst of the commissars saw the solution to any political or military problem in wholly ideological terms. In all, their record, particularly after Fred Copeman left, was uneven at best. Shortly after departing Spain in early 1937, Stephen Spender wrote to Virginia Woolf, "The political commissars . . . bully so much that even people who were quite enthusiastic Party Members have been driven into hating the whole thing."[48] On April 10, 1937, Ralph Cantor of Manchester wrote in his unpublished diary of the "grumbling" over the "favouritism" shown by the commissars in sending certain comrades back to England. Five days later he complained that the "news we get now [is] totally soaked in propaganda." The following day he wrote that "the political Commissars persist in treating us as children or political ignorants [sic]." On April 24 he said that the commissars were "badly chosen" and "succeed in provoking discontent." His ire reached its peak two days later when he wrote that the commissars had "all along fed us with lies. Political commissars are the most disliked men in the Brigade." He wrote there were even some "able" comrades who believed that the whole system of commissars should be abolished.[49] One of these was James Chalmers, a mechanic and self-described social democrat from Dundee who had been wounded twice, on the first day of the Jarama and at Brunete. Upon his departure from Spain, he said he had "never met a Political Commissar of any use." In his view the brigades could simply dispense with them.[50]

In part, Cantor and Chalmers were responding to the months of inactivity in the line that followed the furious fighting of the early days of the Jarama campaign. But they were also anticipating the ambiguous attitude toward political commissars that prevailed throughout the history of the British Battalion in Spain. At his repatriation in 1938, Alan Moulton, a member of the AEU, wrote that "political work" could have been more effective in the battalion. The commissars "were not able to win the confidence of the men."[51] Donald Melville, a worker who had been an organizer in the NUWM and who was described as "a good Party member and a good soldier," believed "at least in [the] later stages" that both the military and political leadership became "isolated [from the men] & unpopular with the great majority."[52] Certainly, the commissars were directly under party control, regardless of the wishes of the commander to whom they were assigned. Tom McWhirter learned, for example, that "a decision has been taken by our Party" that he was not to return to the front and would remain behind at the training base at Albacete.[53]

The propaganda role played by the commissars was to a considerable degree misguided. The party constantly reminded them of their ideological responsibilities to the men in the battalion who "must know always why they are fighting. The men of the People's Army are not mercenaries. . . . They are fighting for their freedom and that of their children [and] for the ideal of democracy throughout the world."[54] Military historians such as S. L. A. Marshall, however, agree that during the actual fighting, it is a soldier's devotion to his comrades and not to a cause that is decisive. In his affecting memoir, *Good-by Darkness*, concerning his combat experiences as a Marine in the South Pacific, William Manchester called his return to his unit after being wounded "an act of love." He wrote, "Those men on the line were my family, my home," adding, "Men, I now know, do not fight for flag or country, for the Marine Corps or glory or any other abstraction. They fight for one another."[55]

However, the ideological functions of the commissars had real, if limited, effect. The commissars affirmed and reaffirmed the invincibility of the volunteers in the face of their "fascist" enemies. Spain was not just a country undergoing a fearful political and military crisis. It was Armageddon. Here the crucial battle between antifascism and fascism was being waged. The former incarnated the democratic and social decencies, both actual and potential, and thus possessed all virtue. The latter presented a mortal threat to these values, and thus was demonized (as were its followers).

This kind of reductionism could backfire, however, if there were too severe a disjunction between the expectations the commissars encouraged and the realities the volunteers experienced. But the

International Brigades were, it must be emphasized, one of the most unusual armies in history. The overwhelming majority volunteered for ideological reasons, and most had already gone through considerable hardships to reach Spain.

John Gates, the commissar of the XVth Brigade and the highest-ranking American in Spain, agreed that the primary function of the commissars was political. But he would not have conceded that their effectiveness stopped at the threshold of the battlefield. Gates believed, "It would be difficult to explain how poorly armed men could fight a much more powerful army for so long and so well, if it were not for their political convictions."[56] A black Lincoln Battalion veteran said that the good commissars led by example as well as by word. They "gave the guys the strength to carry on."[57]

Erich Fromm makes a salient point about the practical benefits of persuading men who feel at odds with their society and consequently lead frustrated, boring, and unproductive lives, to become part of a new society or group that possesses heroic virtues. Such recruits are encouraged to replace with a kind of communal self-worship their frustrations, disappointments, anger, and consequent maladjustment to the distinctly unheroic world in which they live. The results are significant:

> The narcissistic image of one's own group is raised to its highest point, while the devaluation of the opposing group sinks to its lowest. One's own group becomes a defender of human dignity, decency, morality and right. Devilish qualities are ascribed to the other group; it is treacherous, ruthless and basically inhuman.[58]

Despite all their limitations, and virtues, the commissars strove ceaselessly to carry out their tasks. Other formal responsibilities included monitoring the well-being of the wounded, overseeing humane treatment for prisoners, and ensuring that the brigaders respected civilians and property. If "every kind of depredation" were avoided, it could be confidently said that "the productive population, workers and people" would be won over "from the enemy camp to the cause of the people." In theory, and not infrequently in practice, the commissar was to serve as an ideal of the communist working-class fighter "who set the example by being the first to carry out" orders. Finally, the commissar also had to be "capable of taking command of men in action" if the military commander should be killed or wounded.[59] Depending on who was battalion or company commander, the commissar might well offer military advice, and in the circumstances of the incapacitation of the combat leader, even take command himself, as did the American Steve Nelson at Brunete when Oliver Law was killed.

The principal problem among the commissars was that many of them wanted to be military leaders themselves. George Aitken, for example, referred to himself as "joint Commander of the Brigade."[60] On this sometimes delicate point, Tom Murray, the Scots commissar, said he would advise the commander on military matters only when "he felt that something required to be corrected." In the Ebro fighting he cautioned the able company commander, Jack Nalty, that they had lost their way, and "only on [this] one occasion did I exercise my authority as commissar against him." He halted the company and turned it around, overruling Nalty.[61]

VI

Whatever awaited them, first the volunteers had to reach Spain. Before the French closed the border in February 1937 as part of the Non-Intervention Agreement, volunteers crossed freely into Spain by bus or car. After February, a volunteer could reach Spain only by ship or by climbing the Pyrenees, which was the route taken by most of the British.

Typically, the British volunteers began their journey by traveling with a weekend ticket to Paris, which did not require a passport. After a physician examined a candidate, the British responsable in Paris, who for a significant period of time was Charlotte Haldane, established his political reliability. Of the 150 Haldane interviewed over a period of months, only five were returned to England. She would lecture them on subjects such as sexual hygiene and temperance, which many were shocked to hear about from a woman, even the wife of the famous scientist, J. B. S. Haldane. Their guides, often Basque smugglers, informed each contingent of the route to be followed, which would take them to southeast France and then across the Pyrenees. They wore their own clothes, with the exception of a French beret provided to them, which was meant to avert the suspicions of the inquisitive. Each volunteer took only a clean shirt and pair of socks, a toothbrush, a bar of soap, and materials for shaving. No suitcases or handbags were allowed.[62] Their journey continued on the famous "Red" train, which left each night from the Gare d'Austerlitz and made its way through the French countryside toward the Spanish frontier. The passengers often were recognized as volunteers by farmers in the field or by travelers at the various stations where the train stopped. They disembarked at towns such as Béziers, Perpignan, or other places close to the eastern slopes of the Pyrenees.

The solemn, timeless grandeur of the Pyrenees is both awe-inspiring and deeply forbidding. The mountains stretch 270 miles along the French–Spanish border, passable only at either extremity, and cut deeply by streams and waterfalls. The adventurous, such as Ralph Bates and his wife, Winifred, who came to know the mountains and passes intimately on their hiking expeditions before the war, were constantly stimulated by the endless tortured theatricality of the crouching mass that separated Spain from the rest of Europe. Winifred called them "the enchanted mountains."[63] The highest, Pico de Aneto, towers in the middle of the range, reaching 11,169 feet. There are three principal passes, each of them over 5,000 feet, with the easternmost being Puymorens. The most famous, however, is at lower altitude, the pass of Roncesvalles, favored by armies through the centuries and made famous by the *Chanson de Roland*.

Although there were variations to the journey, the volunteers typically climbed aboard buses and moved past sympathetic French border guards[64] to the base of the path they would follow. From there, they would begin their climb through the foothills of the Pyrenees toward the pass. The men were often shod in rope-soled *alpargatas*. The bark of dogs and the lights of houses broke through the silent, estranging darkness. Cognac helped ease the cold and difficulty of the nine-hour climb. Many of the men were not in good physical condition, so the hours of slipping, falling, and climbing could seem unendurable. As Jim Brewer moved through the pitch blackness, all he "could see was the faint gleam of somebody's feet" in front of him.[65] The American novelist Alvah Bessie remembers, "In the dark I passed a small man, moving doggedly ahead, sobbing quietly to himself."[66] David Goodman from Middlesbrough found himself behind an Austrian who gave him the courage to keep going. He "was an old man as he seemed to me then, short, squat, broad shoulders, kind of bullet headed, fairly bald, big pack on his back, shoulders very square and he appeared to march over those mountains as if he was on parade ground." Even with the Austrian's example, exhaustion forced the men out of a formal line. "It was a case of just keeping somebody in sight and going in the direction and it meant scrambling up rocks and being careful not to slip over a ravine here or there. And it went on hour after hour."[67] Occasionally, one or more of the volunteers simply did not have the strength to continue and had to be left behind to a wholly uncertain fate.[68]

As the light of dawn began to break, the men became aware of huge boulders streaked with snow and fierce winds streaming from the peaks. "We leaned against it, our overcoats flapping around us hampering our movements; our legs kept moving though our minds had already stopped far down the farthest slopes."[69] As they crossed the highest point, among the clouds, the men began to run past trees twisted into grotesque shapes by the unrelenting power of the wind until they threw themselves on the Spanish earth, crying and laughing. Then, they would look up to see the rich blue of the Mediterranean.

Before them lay the panorama of Spain stretched on a canvas fifty miles wide. The rivers in the distance seemed in the sunlight to be bright, delicate threads woven into its fabric. "You felt that you were in the presence of Time and Death, the top of the world and the end of it."[70] They laughed, they cried, they cheered, they sang, but most of all they felt overwhelmed by a sense of freedom they had never before known. It "seemed like stepping into a world where dreams had become reality."[71] Once an African-American who bore an uncanny resemblance to Paul Robeson began to sing a spiritual. The men joined silently behind him, "like following Moses," and made their way down the great mountain with their eyes fixed on "the promised land"—Spain.[72] Not far away was a white house. Inside, they found the walls next to the fireplace covered with the names of hundreds of men who had preceded them on their journey.[73]

VII

Tom Murray and Steve Fullarton's group bivouacked at a girls' school before reaching the fortress of Figueras. Once they had eaten and rested, some of them served guard duty for a detention center of disillusioned and malcontented brigaders, and, consequently, began to have second thoughts about their decision to volunteer for Spain. A sixteen-year-old from Glasgow now confessed that he lied about his age, thereby hoping to gain a reprieve from his decision. Murray had already judged him "far too immature to be mixed up in a business like" Spain. Two or three others "had taken cold feet." The next morning Murray and Mike Economides lined up the volunteers and gave each the option of returning to England, but insisted they must decide by the afternoon. When the men reassembled some hours later, several looked sheepish and pained. One said defensively that he thought he was going to drive an ambulance, and this obviously was not the case. Murray reminded all of the volunteers they had not come to a picnic. When the roll was called, five of the British raised their hands, including the young Glaswegian, signaling their intention to return home.[74] Quite simply, Spain was not their choice.

The others went on to Figueras. They, too, had made their choice. The destination of the exhausted men who climbed the Pyrenees in the night, and then kept to their decision, was an ancient fortress built by Ferdinand VI in the fifteenth century and occupied by Napoleon's troops in the Peninsular Wars. On one occasion the regular Republican troops stationed at the huge fortress took Walter Gregory and his group, who arrived on Christmas Day 1936, to see the grave of one of Wellington's officers who had been killed in the Peninsular campaign.[75] The new arrivals spoke and were spoken to in every language of Europe. One volunteer called Figueras the "stewpot of the world"[76] because men of so many nationalities were descending upon it. The huge interior courtyard was used as a parade ground to instill some modicum of order in the new soldiers.

Once the group that crossed the previous night was fed and rested, they assembled and another attempt was made to see if any volunteers had changed their minds. Very few had. The men soon left by rail for Barcelona and then moved on to the headquarters of the International Brigades at Albacete, an unattractive, squalid town, famous for its knife-making trade. Albacete, however, possessed two advantages. It lay astride the Madrid–Valencia road and was far away from the anarchist influences of Barcelona and Catalonia. The International Brigade leadership housed and trained the English-speaking volunteers, arriving by the hundreds, in villages outside Albacete. The British were assigned to Madrigueras and the Americans to Tarazona.

VIII

The first commander of the British Battalion was Wilfred Macartney. Although not a communist, he had been sent to prison in Great Britain for disclosing military secrets to the Russians. His account of his experience, *The Walls Have Mouths*, became a huge success.[77] He was, at first, highly regarded by both the men and the commissars. Springhall wrote, "McCartney [sic] has taken over as commandant of the Battalion. He is making a big hit with the lads & I think will do the job very well. . . . He has always acted with decisiveness & showed clear thinking and good military leadership."[78]

By January 6, however, there were hints of trouble. Peter Kerrigan believed that disciplinary problems and a bad cold had considerably affected Macartney's spirits. Kerrigan asked Pollitt if he would send Macartney a letter singing his praises. It would also help, he said, if the "DW [*Daily Worker*] . . . put [him] across big."[79] Kerrigan still was hopeful that Macartney would prove to be an effective leader. "He really is very capable indeed and in my opinion well respected by the men." Two weeks later Macartney's fellow writer and second-in-command, Tom Wintringham, reported that Macartney was "doing great work." But he echoed Kerrigan's concerns to Harry Pollitt that his commander labored "under a heavy load of discouragement, and you would be wise to try to get some cheering messages to him." Only now was the seriousness of the situation conceded by Wintringham. "He is not now talking about resigning, as he was a week ago, but he is still showing temperament." In addition, Wintringham believed his superior was too soft-hearted in administering discipline.[80]

On the same day that Wintringham wrote, Kerrigan told Pollitt more harshly, "Now McCartney [sic] is a problem and a worry." Kerrigan still believed he was the only one who could command the battalion, but the Scot's patience was wearing thin. "My impression about [him] is that he is far too irritable or querulous and I feel this has an effect on his ability to inspire the men with confidence in himself."[81] George Aitken, the steady political commissar who had been brought out from England, added with quiet understatement, "Mac is a rather difficult man to handle."[82] But the most damning indictment that Kerrigan lay before the head of the British Communist party was that Macartney had become "very critical of the Party." On February 1 Kerrigan told Pollitt that "the Zero hour is coming quickly,"[83] probably referring to the approach of battle but perhaps also to the crisis in the battalion leadership.

As a condition of his release from prison, Macartney was scheduled to make a quick visit to England to appear before the legal authorities, and then return to Spain to resume his leadership of the battalion. This meant that in his absence temporary command would pass to Tom Wintringham, a poet, founder of the *Left Review*, and former military correspondent of the *Daily Worker*. Wintringham wrote on February 7 to Pollitt, "Earlier this morning I learnt that tomorrow, moving up, the battalion will be temporarily commanded by myself. I'm very proud of this and hope I can carry the job well."[84] Thus, "the English Captain" was born.[85]

Given the increasing deterioration of confidence in Macartney's leadership, the accident that rendered him *hors de combat* could understandably be viewed with satisfaction by some. At a farewell dinner prior to his departure for England, Macartney and Kerrigan exchanged pistols. While the Scot was explaining how his weapon worked, the gun discharged, wounding Macartney in the arm. Kerrigan wrote to Pollitt on February 10, saying, "Mac will explain to you what happened in connection with his accident." Kerrigan then asked to be sent home with him, in effect offering his resignation, because "the accident was the result of a stupid mistake for which I was responsible and it was just chance that the consequences were not a great deal more serious." He recognized that, in any event, the wounding of one of the best-known writers in Great Britain would inevitably have "bad effects politically."[86]

Whether the shooting was accidental or intentional will probably never be known with certainty. Alexander, who knew Kerrigan well, defends him from charges of premeditation by arguing that "accidents with weapons were not uncommon among so many untrained men."[87] Yet both Macartney and Kerrigan were World War I veterans and, therefore, among the few "trained" men in the battalion. Fred Copeman, for one, refused to accept that the wounding had been accidental.[88] At any rate, given the party's displeasure with Macartney's political criticisms, and the waning confidence of the men whom he commanded, Macartney's departure from the scene was welcomed by most. Walter Gregory, whose father was a blacklisted carpenter and his mother a domestic, was certainly not displeased.

> I was never very impressed with Wilf. Somehow he lacked the aura which I associated with good leaders, he seemed unable to motivate those under him to give of their best, and I was left with the feeling that his abilities as an organizer and decision-maker were rather rudimentary. The problems of knocking us into a fighting unit proved too much for Wilf McCartney.[89]

Whatever "bad effects politically"[90] that might exist would be far outweighed by the benefits to be gained by Macartney's departure. Anticipating his quick recovery, however, Wintringham said, "I am

... very willing to keep the place warm for him."[91] But Macartney never returned to Spain.

In any event, the military leadership of a working-class battalion by a bourgeois intellectual had not begun auspiciously. Tom Wintringham was badly wounded on the second day of the Jarama. After him, the only battalion commander of his nine successors who might be described as an intellectual was the able and university-educated Bill Alexander (whose origins were, nevertheless, working class), who was wounded in the shoulder in the Teruel campaign shortly after he took command. Overwhelmingly, then, those who led the battalion were working-class militants who may not have had "an intellectual outlook," but nevertheless possessed the presence of mind, courage, and leadership qualities to succeed.

IX

A number of the first volunteers in the British Battalion believed that they were present at the creation of a new model army. A fellow party member told George Drever, the son of a shipyard laborer from Leith who had managed to win a doctorate in chemistry from the University of Edinburgh, that when his comrades in Spain found how clever he was, he would not have to worry about carrying his own pack. Drever turned and angrily called him "a bloody strange sort of Communist." In Spain, Drever felt certain there would be no artificial status based upon education or class.[92] Shortly before he left for Spain, Giles Romilly confidently told Tony Hyndman, "We shall have the right to question any orders with which we don't agree."[93]

Discipline, rank, differential pay, and separate dining for officers and men were all features of the capitalist armies, but not of a revolutionary one, many believed, especially the anarchosyndicalists. For a time this egalitarian spirit prevailed. Frank Owen luxuriated in the fact that "we are all paid the same, we eat together, we also sleep in the same quarters." Moreover, the officers did not have servants to take care of their personal needs, as in the British army, and they had no special privileges. "So you can see the harmony which prevails in the people[']s army."[94]

The "harmony," however, has been challenged by charges of antisemitism and racisim in the battalion. George Nathan was forced to contend with an antisemitic campaign launched against him and other British Jews, orchestrated by one of the malcontents in his No. 1 Company. David Springhall and Ralph Bates wrote at the end of

1936 to Harry Pollitt, "Today, steam from our Captain Nathan that anti-semitism is [beginning] to show itself." The response by the brigade leadership was, however, swift and exemplary. They immediately sent the ringleader home.[95] In another instance, a volunteer called one of his comrades "a dirty, stinking Yid." A "trial" was held, and the malefactor explained that he had used the expression in the heat of a disagreement. He was instructed to apologize, which he did, and left in the friendly company of the injured party.[96]

Fred Copeman was surprised when he met the new Lincoln-Washington commander at Brunete, Oliver Law. Law was the first African-American to command Euro-American troops in battle. Despite some dispute about his qualifications for command,[97] Jason Gurney found him to be "a very fine and intelligent black Communist."[98] Copeman agreed. The British leader, however, possessed certain understandable preconceptions about American racial attitudes, which Law's appointment helped soften. When Copeman first met Law, he thought, "We got a bloody darkie in charge of a Yankee battalion. I didn't think they had . . . any time for them." But Copeman found that "they did,"[99] adding, "They liked him. He certainly had their respect."[100]

The question has arisen, however, about the attitudes of the British themselves toward African-Americans in the brigade. John Peet, a former public schoolboy who had been recruited into the International Brigades by Esmond Romilly, was astonished to observe the American Walter Garland exercising authority. He remembered that "it was utterly unthinkable that a black man would be in charge of white men." Some even called the intelligent and able Garland "snowball" after a cartoon character.[101] When Paul and Eslanda Robeson visited the Lincolns, they were told by an officer that people of color had "quite a time at first with some of the southern white Americans and the British on this Negro question." He informed the Robesons that "the really difficult ones [are] the British. They refuse to eat in dining rooms with the Negroes, etc. and have to be dramatically educated, because neither the Spaniards nor the International Brigade will tolerate such heresy."[102] This charge of racism leveled against the British possesses little, if any, substance. Charlie Nusser, a Lincoln company commander who distinguished himself at Quinto del Ebro, has heatedly called it "a vicious slander of our British comrades." He knew the man who spoke to the Robesons, and argues that he was generally unreliable, given to bluster, and wanted to impress the famous couple by using the British as a foil so that his own enlightened attitudes on racial issues might be better appreciated.[103]

Other evidence supports Nusser. While Bob Cooney was at the Lenin School, he found a number of African-American communists among his classmates. When a student struck an African-American and called him "a nigger," Cooney was delighted to learn that he was deported from the Soviet Union.[104] In addition, there was the fact that the British Battalion was composed of a significant number of ex-servicemen who had been awakened by the racism they had seen in the colonies. J. R. Jump wrote in 1976 that cardinal sins in the battalion were unregulated drunkenness and venereal disease, each equal to a self-inflicted wound or some act of abysmal carelessness. Yet, "an even more serious offence in the International Brigades was racism, but there was little evidence of this." In the XVth Brigade there were Jews, African-Americans, Irish, French Canadians, Finns, and other nationalities. Jump said, "In the International Brigades all were equal, and I seldom came across any serious friction between men of different race and nationality."[105]

In reality, the most serious initial differences were among the various national groups from Great Britain. "Each came from ancient lines of people, fused now as Britain, but each with its own fierce traditions of courage, resistance to tyranny and unquenchable struggle for Freedom."[106] When the miner Harry Dobson was released from six months of hard labor for his part in disrupting a Mosley Blackshirt rally at Tonypandy, he became an instant legend in Wales by asking upon his release, "How do I get to Spain?"[107] The more than 120 Welsh miners, including Dobson, who volunteered for Spain, saw the decision in simple, universalist terms: "In Spain something was *happening*. In Spain you could do something definite to fight fascism. Over there was action, not words. And besides, to fight for the Spanish Republic was to fight for democracy in those glorious early days."[108] The poet Jack Lindsay told the British worker that Spain "is the pattern of the world to-day." He said, "The tale of the Spanish people . . . is also your own life."[109]

However, the internationalist tradition that bound British militants to the call of Spain received one of its greatest tests from the Irish. Bob Gladnick, an American volunteer, recalls that the spirit of nationalism could be even more powerful than the party. "The British Communists were still above all, an Englishman or a Scotsman. He was no goddamn bloody Irishman."[110] Frank Ryan, the revered Irish leader, wrote to his fellow volunteers, "We have come out here as soldiers of liberty to demonstrate Republican Ireland's solidarity with the gallant Spanish workers and peasants in their fight against Fascism." Although some Irish volunteers refused to join the British Battalion, preferring instead to fight with the Lincolns, the schism was largely healed, and Ryan could conclude, "We insist that the closest bonds of comradeship must unite us with all fighters against Fascism from other countries. Rival national war-cries will never be raised by us."[111]

Most, if not all, of the Irish volunteers were members of the Irish Republican Army. Their position was doubly difficult because the IRA was waging a war against the British at home while some of their most valued cadres were away on the battlefields of Spain, fighting as allies with the British. The question understandably arose as to why some of the IRA's best men were missing from the struggle to make Ireland free. Frank Ryan said in a prepared speech on November 1, 1937, that he and his fellow countrymen "are regarded in some circles merely as idealists, who come to fight another nation's battles." Ryan had no illusions concerning what was really meant by such accusations. "That is the equivalent of saying we Irish are deserting the fight at home." He vehemently rejected being called an "idealist" with all the sentimental, woolly connotations of the term, when quite a different case could be made for the Irish presence in Spain. "We are here because we are realists." The realism of the Irish volunteers lay in the fact that they understood "if Fascism triumphed in Spain, it would be the beginning of the end for human liberty and progress." Therefore, Ryan said of the Irish who were lying in their graves in Spain, and those who survived and honored them: "They came to break International Fascism here in Spain, and having broken it, the freedom of their own country would be more certain." Thus, for the Irish, the fight for human and political liberty in Spain was just another front of the war for Irish independence.[112]

When the test came, Ryan was proved right. It was known among the Irish volunteers, including Ryan, that George Nathan—a quickly growing legend in the International Brigades because of his leadership, military ability, and extraordinary personal courage—had been a member of the Black and Tans in Ireland.[113] So called because their uniform was khaki with the black-green belt and cap of the police force, the Black and Tans were mostly young veterans of the Great War with a taste for both adventure and brutality. They were recruited in 1920–21 to complement the police force, which was having an increasingly difficult time in its struggle with the IRA. The Black and Tans were popularly condemned as "the sweepings of English jails, sadists and perverts let loose upon the innocent countryside."[114]

Although these beliefs possessed more myth than fact, some of the Irish in Spain, including Frank Ryan, knew that Nathan had been implicated in the assassination of the Lord Mayor of Cork, who was also Commandant of the Cork No. 1 Brigade of the IRA.[115] Consequently, some of the Irish veterans wished to execute him, but cooler heads prevailed, a reconciliation was agreed upon, and Nathan continued to serve valiantly until his death at Brunete.

Peter Daly, a brave and aggressive leader, ironically relied on his native Ireland's struggles against the oppression of the British to motivate himself in Spain. In the heat of battle in Andalusia, Joe Monks heard him singing "Vinegar Hill," the story of the rising of the United Irishmen against the English in 1798.[116] Daly "came from a long line of Irish revolutionary stock." In Liverpool, his father was a member of the Tom Clarke Revolutionary Society.[117] Daly himself joined the Irish Republican Army and was wounded in the fighting against the British, as was Kit Conway who was killed on the first day of the battle of the Jarama. After Brunete, Daly joined the British Battalion and subsequently became its commander. His death at Belchite on the Aragón front served as an occasion to emphasize the international appeal of the Spanish cause. "Daly was swift to see that fascism and oppression was an international thing, only to be encountered by the international action of all the freedom-loving and progressive sections of humanity." The style of the ideological hack should not disguise the essential truth of the comment. Daly's best friend was William MacDougall, who served with the British Army in Ireland. The two even discovered that they had been on opposite sides of a number of military actions.[118]

When an ex-IRA officer such as Daly could win the leadership of the British Battalion, and enjoy the friendship of a once mortal enemy, the trite, ideologically inspired epitaphs become more persuasive than repugnant. Bob Cooney attempted to put the story of Ireland's travails at the hands of the British into a larger perspective. At Chabola Valley, where the brigades were preparing to join Modesto's army in the crossing of the Ebro, Cooney was constantly being called upon to speak on a variety of subjects in his winning manner. On St. Patrick's Day, instead of telling sentimental stories about Ireland, he put the country's history into context as "the latest chapter [in] the aged story of mankind and womankind for freedom." History told as the battle for "freedom" could bring sworn enemies into startling new alliances.[119]

X

If a veteran of the IRA could find it within himself to make common cause with the British in Spain against the forces of General Franco and his German and Italian allies, other suprising transformations were also possible. For Spain was preeminently an alchemist's laboratory, in which an individual could become someone quite different from whom he had been in his native country. George Kopp's masterful recreation of himself proved so thoroughly convincing to even an astute observer like George Orwell, that he memorialized it in *Homage to Catalonia*.[120]

There were other examples. In the British Battalion one of the middle-class volunteers who developed a remarkable aptitude for both combat and strategic planning was Malcolm Dunbar, who came down from Trinity College, Cambridge, in 1936. Jason Gurney knew him as an elegant, amusing, and cynical aesthete frequenting the purlieus of Chelsea in the thirties. When Dunbar learned that Gurney was going to Spain, he hunted him down in a club on the King's Road and asked how to join the International Brigades. Never dreaming that Dunbar had any serious intention of following him to Spain, Gurney was astonished to find him at the British training base at Madrigueras. "But," Gurney writes, "the Malcolm in Spain was totally different to the one I had known in the King's Road."[121] Dunbar discovered in himself a gift for military strategy and extraordinary personal courage; both were to make him chief of staff of the XVth Brigade in the final battles of the Ebro.[122] Fifty years later the commander of the Lincoln Battalion, Milton Wolff, remembered Dunbar as one of the two best soldiers in the brigade.[123]

Jock Cunningham was a Scot who had been cashiered from the British army for insubordination. His leadership and heedless courage helped save the day at the Jarama, and he became a regimental commander at Brunete. A Welsh volunteer said of Cunningham, "The lads would follow [him] to hell if necessary."[124] After an ineffectual performance at Brunete, however, he was called back to Great Britain by the party, where he gave a few ill-received speeches. He then disappeared, only to be spotted occasionally by old comrades in his random tramping around the country. Hugh Sloan has said, "It is amazing that out of the nowhere situation in the early '30s arose a person like that and then he subsided and disappeared back into anonymity again."[125]

Perhaps the most extraordinary transformation, however, was that of the dashing and fearless George Nathan. He began life in the East End, was one of the few working-class Jews commissioned in World War I, and became a casual worker in London, a hobo in Canada,[126] and a member of the hated Black and Tans in Ireland. In Spain, Nathan alluded to his service in Ireland, but he said, "We have all grown up politically. We are Socialists together now."[127]

Nathan was one of the earliest volunteers, informally dressed and personally unimpressive. Yet, in lieu of anyone else with significant command experience, he was given the British No. 1 Company. When he arrived to take command, the transformation had taken place. Impeccably turned out, he spoke in an obviously acquired upper-class accent, which, curiously, none of the rough-hewn types like Fred Copeman or Jock Cunningham seemed to mind.[128] In fact, Nathan was one of those ex-officers leading an anomalous existence of whom the critic Samuel Hynes has said: "He can speak like a gentleman, but he isn't one; he can do a working-man's job, but he isn't one of them, either."[129] When Nathan came up to congratulate the British Battalion on its performance at the Jarama, Tom Wintringham marveled that he was "cockney and gentleman, ex-hobo and now Chief of Staff of the Brigade."[130] The miner, Hugh Sloan, said that only in a people's army could workers such as Cunningham and Copeman function effectively alongside the elegant Nathan.[131]

In Spain, Nathan became an incomparable and universally admired leader, even by the IRA volunteers who knew of his past. Jason Gurney called him "the only personality serving with the International Brigades who emerges as an authentic hero figure, with a mythology of his own."[132] Nor was his devotion to the Republican cause dictated by whoever had cast him in his part. He was neither a communist[133] nor a mercenary. In some fundamental way the plight of the Republic had brought together all the fragments of Nathan's past and personality into one coherent whole, making possible his most heroic and convincing performance. For certain individuals, like Dunbar, the Trinity College graduate, and Nathan, the East End Jew, circumstances could produce a costume of the moment, and Spain was the greatest theater in the world. It was here that each found his finest and truest role.

But it was an ensemble cast, of different classes, temperaments, and, to a degree, motivations, each trying to find and play his part. The endless fluidity of the environment meant that if so disposed, volunteers such as Cunningham, Dunbar, and Nathan could literally reinvent themselves in Spain. The dramatic unities prevailed in Nathan's case. He was killed at Brunete, dying in the American Steve Nelson's arms, his legend not only intact but brilliantly embellished. Dunbar was not so fortunate. He survived, was denied a commission in World War II, and years later apparently committed suicide. On July 26, 1963, the following appeared in the British press: "MAN'S BODY IDENTIFIED —A man whose body was found on a deserted beach at Milford-on-Sea, near Bournemouth, about three weeks ago was identified yesterday as Ronald Malcolm Loraine Dunbar, aged 51, of Stanhope Gardens, S.W., son of the late Sir Loraine and Lady Dunbar, of Whitehall Lodge, Harrogate."[134] There was no mention of his service in Spain.

But Tom Wintringham's dream was realized. A British battalion had been forged in Spain, and it appeared that all of progressive Britain was eager to see this ostensibly classless society of volunteers in action against fascism.

Ralph Bates climbing in the Pyrenees. Courtesy of the
Marx Memorial Library.

Members of the Tom Mann Centuria in Barcelona. From the left are Sid
Avner (killed at Boadilla) and Nat Cohen. Tom Wintringham is kneeling
in the center (left). Courtesy of the Marx Memorial Library.

British volunteers in Albacete who would soon join the famous British No.
1 Company. Courtesy of the Marx Memorial Library.

British ambulance drivers in Barcelona. Courtesy of the Marx Memorial Library.

Standing beside a Spanish Medical Aid truck in Barcelona are Ewart Milne, Wogan Philips, Issy Kupchik (killed at Brunete), Stephen Spender, and George Green (husband of Nan Green, killed in the battalion's last battle). Courtesy of the Marx Memorial Library.

Courtesy of the Marx Memorial Library.

Courtesy of the Marx Memorial Library.

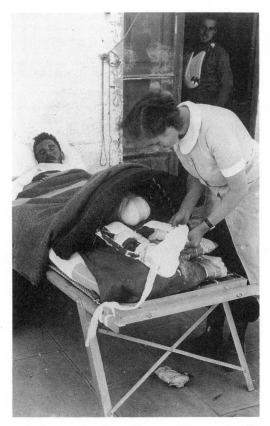

Ann Murray caring for a patient. Her two brothers, George and Tom, were also volunteers. Courtesy of the Marx Memorial Library.

Charlie Goodfellow, a miner from Scotland, who
became second-in-command of the battalion (killed
by the side of Fred Copeman at Brunete). Courtesy of
the Marx Memorial Library.

Bill Rust (left) preparing a story for the *Daily Worker*. Courtesy of the Marx Memorial Library.

Clement Attlee, the Labour party leader and future prime minister, visiting volunteers in December 1937. Courtesy of Archive Photos.

The leader of the British Communist party, Harry Pollitt, addressing the battalion on an early visit. Courtesy of the Marx Memorial Library.

The British Battalion moving out. Courtesy of the Marx Memorial Library.

Sam Wild (center) discussing strategy. To the right is Lt. Cipriano, an uneducated peasant from the Aragón who proved a "natural" leader and commanded the Spanish Company. Courtesy of the Marx Memorial Library.

A machine-gun position. Courtesy of the Russian Center for the Preservation and Study of Recent Historical Documents.

Holding the British Battalion flag. No. 1 Company was renamed the Major Attlee Company after the Labour leader's visit. Courtesy of the Russian Center for the Preservation and Study of Recent Historical Documents.

At ease. Courtesy of the Russian Center for the Preservation and Study of Recent Historical Documents.

The writer Hugh Slater (center), political commissar and, later, commander of the Anti-Tank Battery. He was chief of operations of the XVth Brigade at the Ebro. To the left is the poet and painter Miles Tomalin, who was put in charge of cultural activities for the brigade. To the right is Jim Sullivan from Glasgow (killed at the Ebro). Courtesy of the Marx Memorial Library.

Miles Tomalin playing his recorder for his comrades in the Anti-Tank Battery. Courtesy of the Marx Memorial Library.

Farewell parade in Barcelona for the International Brigades on Saturday, October 29, 1938. Courtesy of the Marx Memorial Library.

A demonstration by members of the International Brigaders' Anti-Communist League in London in February 1939. Courtesy of B. T. Batsford Ltd., Julian Symons' *Between the Wars*.

CHAPTER 9

The Battle of the Jarama

FEBRUARY 1937

I, the person called Tom, belonged to a quiet writing desk or the clatter
of a print-shop, little rooms where committees met, meetings in halls
with shadowed ceilings and the straining glare of bare lights, the
Garden House where my mother grew lavender and sweet briar, the
review I had edited and in which I had risked printing one or two of
my poems. . . . What on earth was I doing among these olive-trees,
dusty earth, cold February hills with hundreds of men to look after and
lead in unequal battle?

— Tom Wintringham

I

Once the Chamberlain government decided to enforce the
Foreign Enlistment Act of 1870 in January 1937, British volunteers
could no longer be recruited openly. The legal foundations for prosecution were extremely shaky, however, and the authorities found
themselves thwarted in their intentions to apply the act.[1] Nevertheless, the Chamberlain government sufficiently intimidated the party
that it temporarily suspended recruitment for the battalion.[2] New
precautions were now necessary, and they were spelled out at a
district meeting of the party at Shoreditch Town Hall on January 10,
1937. The details survive in a memorandum drafted by a Special
Branch detective who attended the meeting. A party leader, Norah
Brown, told the secretaries and branch organizers of the changes that
would have to occur. They would now be "obliged to resort to
subterfuge" in order to send volunteers to Spain. This would neces-
sitate much closer screening of candidates. According to the detective's notes, Brown criticized some of the earlier volunteers "because
they wanted to get away from their wives or families, or had a craving
for adventure, rather than because they were anti-fascists spurred by
a genuine political conviction."[3] Because of the new legal strictures,
the party could afford to work only with those whose political
motivations were certain. The manifest irony was that if every
volunteer had to be "100% Communist," as Brown insisted, the

dream of a United Front, consisting of all parties on the left, would be revealed as an invention of Moscow.

II

In January and February the British Battalion rose quickly to strength as volunteers arrived almost daily in Albacete. The new arrivals were quickly introduced to a military regimen. They would rise at 5:30, eat breakfast at 6:15, fall in at 6:45, and then carry out drills and rifle and machine-gun practice until noon. After the midday meal they resumed their training at 2:15 and finished at 5:00. They had free time from the conclusion of supper until lights were turned out at 10:10.[4] Adherence to this routine gave many of them the confidence that they could do what would be expected of them. Christopher St. John Sprigg pronounced himself satisfied with the training, albeit with reservations. "We have had plenty of field exercises & training in the theory of the machine gun." But "most of us have had no actual firing practice in rifles or machine guns yet. We hope to get some in the next three or four days."[5] Others, like Charlie Morgan, grew impatient with the incessant propaganda, and wanted more practical information. "We got lectures, lectures, lectures on Marxism—how many tractors the Soviet Union had produced, how many hectares of wheat were growing in the Ukraine." Finally, he could tolerate it no longer and shouted, "We don't want this bloody rubbish. We need training."[6]

As the British Battalion organized itself, a group of about twenty middle-class "intellectuals" formed around Giles Romilly, the brother of Esmond. Many were homosexual.[7] And most of them came from the London world of the left-wing intelligentsia, most typically from Chelsea, Bloomsbury, or Soho. The twenty-three year-old Alan Jenkins, living in Soho and unemployed, said: "Soho was full of young writers and out-of-work film extras who were asking each other: 'Have you seen Tony? He's been *under fire*.' And then: 'Are *you* going? Why not—are you a Trotskyist or something?'"[8]

Middle-class volunteers were often communists and would hold positions ranging from battalion commander to commissar to ordinary rifleman. The slim, bespectacled Tom Wintringham, with his high-domed head and scholarly stoop, proved an unpretentious and effective leader after Macartney's disappearance from the scene. Although he admired Macartney, Fred Copeman called Wintringham the "mainspring" of the battalion.[9] The new commander even drew praise from the hard-used working-class volunteer, Tony Hyndman, Stephen Spender's friend, who called him a "soldier and poet with infinite compassion." Despite all that had happened to him as the result of his resistance to party discipline, Hyndman could even add, "He was the man we needed. It took him only a few days to win the respect and loyalty of all under his command. He was cool, quick in deciding who did what, with a wry sense of humour."[10]

Even though Wintringham broke with the party toward the end of the war, his obituary in *Spain Today* was generous. "Those who took part in [the battle of the Jarama] will remember the calm and courageous bearing of Tommy Wintringham and the skillful way he deployed the units under his command in those first and most difficult hours."[11] Others felt the same way.[12] But the difference in class also emerged. When Sam Wild was asked for his opinion of Wintringham, he said simply, "good guy, middle class."[13]

III

As has been emphasized, many of the young middle-class intellectuals who came out to Spain were caught up in a romantic identification with workers. The barriers of class had prevented most of them from having any but the most superficial understanding of the men with whom they were to serve. And they were quite capable of putting absurd obstacles between themselves and workers. How could a proletarian volunteer see Julian Bell as a comrade when the son of Clive and Vanessa spent his spare time reading Racine, dressed eccentrically in khaki shorts, and wore a pith helmet? Or not find his humor "puzzling" when he talked of his hope that Spain would become a British colony, and said of his time in Spain, "It will sound well when I come to write my memoirs"?[14]

In place of direct experience, volunteers like Bell possessed the dramaturgy of Marxism, which awarded a unique prestige to these manual laborers, miners, industrial and building workers, and craftsmen. Working men, their middle-class admirers believed, were the cadres of the last great epoch in human history whose prologue had been thousands of years of victimization and exploitation by the owners of the means of production. This would be the age of the worker. And their middle-class comrades were at first awestruck by the glamour conferred by history upon these men with whom they would fight and die.

The diary of David Crook, an Englishman and Columbia University graduate, who most recently had been a private secretary to an MP, provides the best evidence of the growing realism that slowly began to erode the stereotypes. At first, Crook was simply giddy with the prospects that lay before him. He had felt some guilt at leaving his parents, who depended on him for financial support. On January 2, 1937, he wrote, "Yet beside the tremendous sweep of history and social development these personal problems become trivial." He thought, "Any creative undertaking from art to sex is a satisfying experience. What could be more creative than shaping history or building society[?] It is like possessing a thousand women in one night." A few days later, as he and other volunteers were leaving Barcelona, women factory workers gave them the antifascist salute. He thought gleefully, "What would the cocktail drinkers say to this?"[15] He found life imitating art. The Russian film, *Three Women*, had made an enormous impact on him. A scene from the film seemed to have been almost exactly replicated among his comrades. "There actually occurs here the process shown in the pub scene in Three Women—a crowd cleansed and raised from dullness and despair to confident determination—by the singing of the *International*."[16]

At brigade headquarters at Albacete, the heroic strains of the *International* began to die away. Crook found himself appalled at the obsessive attention to material needs exhibited by working-class volunteers. "All along a number have been astonishingly concerned about money matters and food—as if Beethoven had been worried about putting his tie straight in the middle of composing the 9th symphony." On January 9, just a week after his first rapturous pronouncements, Crook adopted a more realistic mood. "In a way, I suppose I am disappointed." He came to Spain "expecting to find the very pick of the working-class and anti-fascists of the entire world." This, he acknowledged, "meant setting a pretty high standard." But the distance between the comrades who existed in his imagination and those who occupied his reality was disconcertingly large. "When these same people contain habitual drunkards and petty thieves one feels terribly let-down." Yet Crook remained optimistic. "Action will elevate and purge them."[17]

IV

Crook was momentarily cheered when he attended a Burns night celebration, a few weeks before the battalion went into action.

The large number of Scottish volunteers in the battalion ensured that the anniversary of Robert Burns' birthday on January 25, 1937, would be celebrated with special exuberance, and with as much wine as could be obtained. Even in ordinary times it is an evening of great significance for Scots at home and abroad. Typically, there is a special meal, a Burns Supper, consisting of haggis, turnips, and potatoes. In the absence of these ingredients, the boisterous volunteers ate sardines with their bayonets.

On this night, which would be the last such celebration for many Scots in the battalion, Peter Kerrigan remembered that Burns' "lovely haunting love songs and folk ballads were sung. We even permitted the English, Welsh, and Irish to make their contributions, and right well they did."[18] Several Scottish brigaders actually wore kilts, much to the consternation of the Spaniards. The gravest difficulty arose, however, when no copies of Burns' poems could be found.[19] Nevertheless, some of the men remembered the words to his poems. And none of the more than 100 Scots celebrating the evening would have forgotten Burns' poem, "A Man's a Man for A' That." Certainly not on this night.

> The honest man, tho' e'er sae poor,
> Is king o' men for a' that.
>
> That man to man, the warld o'er,
> Shall brithers be for a' that.

To quote from and speak on Robert Burns was much more than an evening of cultural reminiscence. Burns was the poet laureate of Scotland's poor, as well as any other reader who believed in the artificiality of Britain's class distinctions and could agree with Burns that, ultimately, "rank is but the guinea's stamp." Consequently, no one had to be prompted to emphasize the political importance of Burns to the volunteers.

Victor Kiernan points out that in contrast to the English workers many volunteers from Scotland possessed an *instinctive* rather than an intellectual internationalism, attributing it to Scotland's historically greater openness to continental influences and interests.[20] But the Burns' Night celebrated in Spain suggests that their poet spoke to his fellow countrymen of a world that was one because all men were brothers, a concept that was equally powerful to militants on both sides of the Tweed.

David Crook wrote to friends in England of this January night in 1937. There were "excellent talks" on Burns "as a poet of the poverty-stricken Scottish peasantry." Crook said that his comrades spoke powerfully on Burns' "revolutionary equalitarianism, his support of the French Revolution and international outlook." With an astonished pleasure as he remembered those gathered for the occasion, Crook wrote, "All are honest to God British proletarian types." When Crook said, "Never has there been such a Burns night,"[21] surely he was correct. Facing battle, could British soldiers previously assembled from different classes, ethnic backgrounds, and ways of life, agree: "That man to man, the warld o'er / Shall brithers be for a that"? In less than three weeks many of those who attended this most extraordinary of Burns' Nights would be lying dead or wounded a few miles away on their first and final battlefield.

Crook was assigned to Fred Copeman's machine-gun section. As he took up his new responsibilities, he continued to scrutinize himself and his surroundings with the eye of a keen observer. Dave Springhall, the brigade commissar, impressed him by a talk he gave to the men. Yet, Crook had some reservations. "He seems a working-class type but uses a great many polysyllables." Although Crook found that "the profanity here is truly phenomenal," he rejoiced in the fact that "a complete democracy" existed in his section.[22]

Crook came to like as well as admire Fred Copeman, which put him in a distinct minority. As he settled down to his duties, much of the earlier strangeness of his surroundings began to fade. Even "the novelty of the clenched fist salute is beginning to wear off." On January 24, he repeated his displeasure at the lack of self-discipline among the working-class volunteers. "Nothing has disgusted me more than the drunkenness." When he was invited to the home of a peasant family in Madrigueras, he found that the village was well aware of the indiscipline of the British. One child looked at him apprehensively throughout the meal. "Apparently [she] expected me to rise in a state of wild drunkenness and commit some terrible act." He ruefully observed, "It must be admitted that up to now the International Brigade has not lived up to the somewhat ideal picture I had painted of it in my mind." Yet his optimism remained irrepressible. "This [is] of necessity a trying time, waiting—waiting for arms and ammunition. Once we get into action the standards are bound to change."[23]

In addition to Kerrigan and Copeman, Crook was impressed by another working-class comrade. His new friend had left school at thirteen, become "a professional bum," but was extremely articulate. "He has read Marx and learnt some by heart." Yet even he proved disappointing because he had "no capacity for original or ordered thinking or concentration." Despite his disappointments, Crook insisted that when the battalion left for the front, he wanted to take with him "a hopeful progressive attitude towards society despite having very idealistic illusions shattered by this first class contact with the masses." A few days before their sudden departure, he jotted down, "Sometime[s] I feel that reading, or gaining knowledge, or this diary, may be of little use—there may be little time left."[24] He was right.

On February 7, the volunteers finally heard the call they both longed for and feared: "Fall-in, full marching order, we leave tonight." They gathered up their haversacks, blankets, packs, and overcoats. All of Madrigueras turned out for their departure. The men made their way clumsily down to their trucks, sweat streaming down each face. The villagers lined up by the trucks "shouting, saluting, laughing and crying."[25] A volunteer remembered the remarks of the normally laconic Scottish commissar, George Aitken, who pronounced it "a great and historic occasion." "In the past," Aitken said, "many Battalions of British soldiers had left the shore of Britain to fight in foreign lands. But ours was the first Battalion of British workers which had left Britain to fight for freedom and democracy." Aitken exhorted them, "The eyes of the workers of Britain and of the whole world [are] on us."[26]

The afternoon of their departure from Madrigueras was remarkably beautiful, clear and windy. The countryside was a canvas of colors, from a sandy yellow to a rusty red. Adding richness to the scene were the different colors of the pines, the olives, and grapes.[27] Suddenly, life seemed almost overwhelmingly vivid and precious.

V

Franco still believed that he could capture Madrid by the spring. Consequently, he decided to strike east of the city and cut the Valencia road, the city's lifeline to the outside world. This would be accomplished by coordinating his offensive with the Italians, who would move on Guadalajara from the north under General Roatta at the same time that General Mola's forces crossed the Jarama River.

The January weather made it impossible to coordinate the two attacks, but Franco decided to begin the Jarama offensive without waiting for his allies. He was forced to abandon the strategy of maneuver which had been so successful in the fall and face the Republican forces in conditions reminiscent of World War I, thus neutralizing his forces' advantage in tactics and experience.

The village of Chinchón sits above the valley of the Tajuña, some fifteen miles from Madrid. It reminded David Crook of Kendal in the Lake District of England.[28] Across the valley are the hills of the Sierra Pingarrón. In the second week of February 1937, they rumbled with the sounds of artillery. When darkness fell, the flash of weapons could be clearly seen. On the night of February 11, the British Battalion suddenly received orders to climb aboard trucks that took them across the valley to the edge of the village of Morata de Tajuña.

The British established their headquarters in an old but picturesque farmhouse close to the Chinchón–San Martín de Vega road that belonged to a famous Spanish wit and cartoonist whose work appeared in *El Sol*. More ominously, the house long had provided a country retreat for a famous torero, whose death in the bull ring had inspired García Lorca's most famous poem, "Lament for José Mejías Sánchez." The verses include the incantatory refrain, "a las cinco de la tarde," the hour of Mejías Sánchez's death.[29]

Sometime before dawn, large amounts of coffee were served to each man. They assembled in conventional military formation, which included the battalion commander, his second-in-command, a political commissar, an adjutant, three companies of infantry, a machine-gun company, scouts, and a quartermaster and cookhouse staff. Each company had three platoons, which in turn were divided into sections of ten men. As the sun rose, each of the four companies of the battalion began to march in single file up the hillsides of the village. Their destination was the valley of the Jarama.

In the clear, cold morning air of February 12, 1937, the Jarama valley seemed to have been scrubbed to a radiant loveliness, contrasting sharply with the grim domestic miseries of the British base at Madrigueras that had so recently been left behind. Scattered over the graceful landscape of hills, valleys, and plateaus were olive trees, silver oak, pine, and cypress, while the step of each volunteer stirred up a rich perfume from the odors of gorse, marjoram, and sage.[30]

When the men of the British Battalion stared up at the luminous blue sky above the Jarama valley and saw Russian fighter planes effectively engaging the air force of the insurgents, when they held in their hands newly issued rifles that bore the imprint of the hammer and sickle, when they read of Russian food ships evading Italian submarines and making their way into Barcelona's harbor, there was no doubt which of the countries of the world had earned their gratitude, and which political party, perhaps, their loyalty.

As they climbed, the volunteer, and mostly amateur, soldiers began to abandon packs and encumbering effects of all kinds. Among their scattered belongings were a variety of reading materials. Marxist textbooks proved particularly heavy and were the first to be discarded, although the proletarian intellectual T. A. Jackson loved telling the story of an International Brigader whose life was saved because he refused to abandon Jackson's *Dialectics*, which weighed in at exactly two pounds, and proved impervious to a bullet.[31] Less cumbersome were copies of the Left Book Club's *Spain in Revolt* by Harry Gannes and Theodore Repard.

As they advanced up the steep incline to the plateau on which the battle would be fought, they continued to unburden themselves of other books, many of which could have been found in the library of any undergraduate: poetry of all kinds, Nietzsche, Spinoza, language primers, and even a copy of Rhys Davids' *Early Buddhism*.[32] In addition to the Oxbridge graduates and intellectuals who have pushed their way to the fore in elite mythology, these books belonged to working-class militants who were "thinkers,"[33] or, as Robert Roberts called them, members of "the working-class intelligentsia."[34]

When they reached the top of the plateau, a messenger gasping for breath told them that the military situation had changed dramatically, that a fascist offensive had broken through the Republican lines, and the British would immediately go into a blocking position. There was little initial tension because the British volunteers were informed they would be held in reserve. The 600 men of the battalion, few in really good physical condition and all made increasingly uncomfortable by the hot sun as the morning wore on, laboriously made their way through the olive groves to the plateau above.[35]

Recovering from the climb, the men formed up and began to disperse over the terrain to prepare to engage the enemy. Those who had five weeks of training, as many did, felt supremely confident, despite the deficiencies of their weapons and the sudden replacement of their battalion commander, Wilfred Macartney, by Tom Wintringham. They then passed between two hills, one on the left crowned

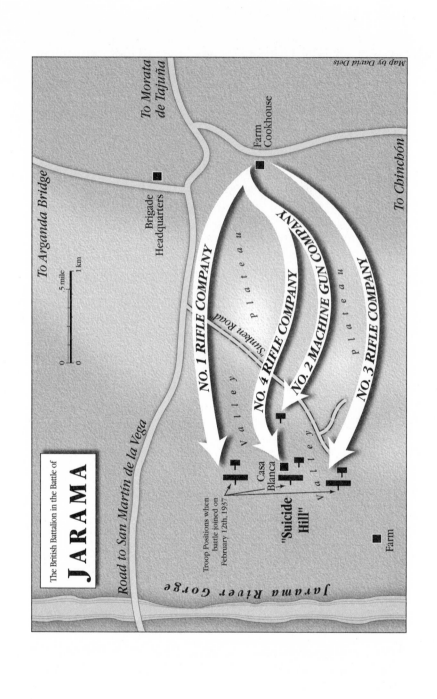

The British Battalion in the Battle of

JARAMA

Road to San Martín de la Vega

To Arganda Bridge

To Morata de Tajuña

To Chinchón

0   5 mile
0   1 km

Brigade Headquarters

Farm Cookhouse

NO. 1 RIFLE COMPANY

NO. 4 RIFLE COMPANY

NO. 2 MACHINE GUN COMPANY

NO. 3 RIFLE COMPANY

"Sunken Road"

p l a t e a u

p l a t e a u

v a l l e y

v a l l e y

v a l l e y

Casa Blanca

"Suicide Hill"

Troop Positions when battle joined on February 12th, 1937

Jarama River Gorge

Farm

Map by David Deis

by a white house and one on the right which was conically shaped. There were no indications of panic or disorder.[36]

Battalion headquarters was established in a sunken cart road running at right angles to the San Martín de la Vega road. No. 2 Company with the machine-gun section was under the command of Harry Fry, who placed his men some fifty yards in front. No. 1 Company moved to the right, taking up positions on what came to be called Conical Hill. On the left, Companies 3 and 4 moved around White House Hill, but soon faced withering fire from the Moors and were forced to fall back to its comparative protection. In a few hours White House Hill would be renamed Suicide Hill.

The Franco-Belge battalion was some 800 long yards to the right of the British, positioned across the San Martín de la Vega road. The British left flank, amazingly, remained open.[37] But nothing could detract from these first moments. One volunteer remembered, "We looked magnificent, we felt magnificent, and we thought that if only our colleagues back home, who had made it possible for us to be there, could see us now, how proud they would be that we had started to repay them for their efforts."[38] The repayment would be in blood unimaginable. The fighting was so intense that the Moors came within thirty yards of the British lines. One volunteer remembered that "men lifting their heads to fire were shot through the face."[39] On seeing his first casualties, another said, "Everywhere men are lying. Men with a curious ruffled look, like a dead bird."[40]

Sam Wild and David Crook found themselves isolated in the slaughter. The two were all that remained of No. 1 Company, which had been positioned on the Conical Hill. A breastwork of stones partially protected them, but Wild was hit by machine-gun fire. The former sailor said, "I felt I was dead because one [bullet] had just rolled around the back of my spine [and] semi-paralysed me." Then, Wild remembered, "This kid . . . caught hold of me." He began carrying Wild to the rear, despite his protest that he be left to die. Crook was hit in the leg as he got Wild to safety. Thirty-eight of their comrades in No. 1 Company remained behind.[41]

Once they had obtained the correct ammunition, Harry Fry and Fred Copeman were able to position their machine guns properly and use them to devastating effect. Battalion after battalion, brigade after brigade, was hurled into the inferno by both the Republic and the Insurgents. "The unceasing action of attack and counter-attack exacted a toll upon both sides that can only be described as horrible."

Arthur Landis has written, "There are few battles of World War II that can even begin to equal the ferocity of the clash of opposing forces on those few square kilometers of the valley of the Jarama."[42] Paul Preston calls it the most violent battle of the entire war.[43]

At the end of the first day, less than half the battalion remained, and only 125 of the 400 in the rifle companies. A Merseysider wrote home:

> I shall never forget my first night in action: a machine-gun bullet ripped off the top of my steel helmet. Such a narrow escape from being put clean out. I have not experienced anything like it in my short life. I am very fortunate to be here writing these few lines. . . . In fact it [sic] may be my last, but I want you to tell all the fellow comrades that no matter what may befall me, it is all in the cause of Humanity and Freedom against Fascism and all that it brings in its train. I am enclosing a photo of myself taken with some of the comrades. I hope you will keep this for the children, as a memento of me . . . in case I get killed.[44]

Books, abandoned either because of their weight or the death or wounding of their owners, lay scattered among the debris on and near the battlefield. One page of *Spain in Revolt* left fluttering in the winter wind promised that the laurels of the Republic's sacrifices would fall on the shoulders of "the poorest and humblest layers of society," and if the Republic won, "the greatest transformation of all would take place among the working-class and revolutionary parties."[45] Rhetoric that had once thrilled the 500 volunteer soldiers, so far from their homes, families, Oxbridge colleges, and workmates in the British Isles, now must have seemed cold comfort to the survivors on this rough and heavily indented landscape, made grotesque by the shattered olive trees and the oddly contorted and sundered bodies of their comrades.

VI

On the second day, the survivors were cheered by the efficiency of Aitken, "the only Political Commissar who was effective without becoming sanctimonious," who brought up to the front not only stragglers but food and hot coffee.[46] Disaster struck, however, when Harry Fry's machine-gun company, lying about 100 yards in front of the sunken road, was infiltrated and captured by the Moors. Upon the orders of General Gal, the arrogant and inept commander of the XVth Brigade, Wintringham was forced to make an assault. As "the English Captain" stood up to lead his men, he immediately was felled by a bullet.[47] George Aitken succeeded him in command. He was joined by Jock Cunningham, who left the hospital to be with the battalion.

On the third day of the battle, faced with tanks as well as rifle fire, the British were told to retreat. Two who disobeyed the order were a motor mechanic named Len Bibby and a young student from the University of Reading, Bill Ball, who stayed behind to prevent any more of their Maxim machine guns from falling into enemy hands. Bibby was killed as they returned to their own lines and Ball fell several days later.[48]

The inadequacy of their weapons, the shortage of ammunition, the impact of the horrifying slaughter on inexperienced leaders and their troops, should have proved completely demoralizing. But the British found some last reserve of courage and stamina and managed to hang on, although sustaining losses that should have rendered them completely ineffective as a fighting force. Inevitably, without officers, and in shock, many volunteers began to drift back to the sunken road where Wintringham had established his headquarters. Others straggled back to the farmhouse in hopes of finding water and food. In the minds of even the most dazed was the realization that being inspired by high ideals did not make them invincible on a battlefield, which came as a huge surprise to many of these volunteer soldiers.

The edge of disaster had been reached. Only 215 remained of the nearly 600 who had begun the battle. The men were demoralized and retreating, leaving the whole of the Tajuña Valley open to Franco. General Gal came up and told Jock Cunningham of the danger. Jock said, "The next ten minutes would decide" if the Moors would have the Valencia road—Madrid's lifeline.[49] Though mercenaries, the Moors were superb, battle-tested soldiers who lived and died by their own code of professionalism.

Oliver Green remembers, "The events which followed were among the most glorious in the long history of the struggles of the British workers." Exhorted by Cunningham and Frank Ryan to return to their positions, a few, and then more and more volunteers began to march up the crest of the hill. At Ryan's insistence, the volunteers began to sing the *International*. Retreating men turned around. "The whole of the hillsides echoed with the song, the song of struggle." Crawling on their stomachs and then moving in short rushes, they forced the fascists back. "Inch by inch they advanced."[50] But the toll continued to be heavy. On February 29, the Australian nurse, Una Wilson, wrote in her diary: " . . . and so it goes on, day after day, this awful slaughter. We heal their wounds and back they go to the front to be shot to bits. . . . How I hate war, hate it like hell. I feel tonight I could never smile again."[51]

After the Jarama, the inevitable victory of "good" against "evil" would never again be so easily believed, at least not by those who survived these days of February. The British played a key role in holding the Valencia road and, in so doing, established the lines between the Republican and Nationalist forces in the valley of the Jarama for the remainder of the war.

VII

It must have seemed to some that Goya's visions of the horrors of war could have been painted from the carnage that took place at the Jarama. Along the Sunken Road, near the Suicide and Conical hills and the valley that stretched between them, a terrible human tragedy had been played out. For the young artist Jason Gurney, the images would prove overwhelming and unforgettable.

At Wintringham's instructions, Gurney made his way down the Sunken Road to the battalion's left flank in order to reconnoiter the position, exposed as it was to the enfilading fire of the Moors. He had traveled about 700 yards "when I came on one of the most ghastly scenes I have ever seen." Lying in a hollow were approximately 50 wounded volunteers from the battle on Suicide Hill. "They were all men whom I had known well, and some of them intimately." One, a cheerful young Jew who had kept up the men's spirits at crucial times, lay conscious and apparently without pain, in spite of a gaping stomach wound, exposing loops of his intestines that twitched slightly as flies began to settle on them. Another, with whom he was particularly close, had taken nine rounds in his chest. He asked Gurney if he would hold his hand. They talked briefly, and then the hand went limp.[52]

It was a scene of such unmitigated horror and suffering that it etched itself forever on Gurney's mind. "To this day I do not know what I could have done to help those poor wretches as they lay awaiting death in the twilight of that Spanish olive grove." He, as a sculptor and ardent lover of women, had worshiped the perfection of the human body. Now, he saw what war could do to its logic and articulation. Gurney felt that he "had suffered some permanent injury to my spirit from which I would never recover."[53]

Gurney went into battle with his mind conditioned by martial narratives from films, which powerfully shaped his anticipation of what was to come. He and his fellow volunteers had assumed their places in a mythic discourse, which Samuel Hynes has called the reromanticizing of war that took place in the thirties.[54] Philip Toynbee wrote of his generation, "It seems to me now that our picture of war was as falsely romantic, in its different way as anything which had stirred the minds of Edwardian boys, brought up on Henty and the heroics of minor imperial campaigns."[55] For Gurney, the images were now in a state of disarray, and he had lost the narrative thread of his life as a soldier. As he, and later Paul Fussell, reminds us, no one who has not been in combat can truly understand its diabolical horror. And those who have tried to anticipate the experience of war in film or prose have inevitably submitted its chaos and discontinuities to the seamless discourse of story, thereby sentimentalizing and falsifying its reality.

But psychological defenses woven out of fantasy were not necessarily a bad thing. Films and books and plays were a ubiquitous frame of reference in which the chaos could be contained and the participant enabled to distance himself emotionally by becoming an observer of his own story. Sam Wild said, "I was a bit like James Cagney portrayed in his films."[56] While on convalescent leave in Madrid, David Crook saw "The Sailors of Kronstadt," which though "not one of the best Russian films," the audience found riveting. "It was their life of the last half-year."[57] As Charlie Morgan from Manchester prepared to go into an attack on the first day of Brunete, he remembered "It was like a panorama." Then, a close friend turned and said, "Charlie, it's like being in the pictures isn't it," and was immediately shot dead.[58] When Tom Clarke was being treated for a head wound he received at the Jarama, a large crowd gathered around him watching the extraction of the bullet. Suddenly it reminded him, too, of a scene from a film.[59] T. C. Worsley beheld with stunned amazement the thousands of refugees fleeing Málaga. "We had viewed the procession as one views a film unrolling itself in front of one, so that the stream of people was outside us, performing with the unrealism of actors."[60] As the youthful Esmond Romilly first saw enemy troops advancing on his position, he could not believe the threat was real. "We were only playing at soldiers, we were only amateurs."[61] But the time for amateur theatricals had passed, and within minutes Romilly would see the appalling reality of his British comrades dying one after the other in a matter of minutes.

Emotional adjustment to the reality of war, as opposed to its fictions, had proved impossible for Tony Hyndman, as it would for Jason Gurney. On the first day of bloody combat on the Sunken Road and around Suicide Hill, Gurney wrote, "I had finally grown up into the reality of war only when I stood amongst that ghastly collection of dead and irretrievably mutilated men left behind in the retreat. This was the reality—not fear or excitement or drama—just pure horror and the knowledge that I was utterly powerless to do anything about it."[62] An unidentified ambulance driver at Brunete felt similar shock at war's "reality"—"buttocks, penis, ears torn off by shell fragments; eyes destroyed; ear drums broken; leg or arm smashed; face mashed to pulp."[63]

Surveying the battlefield somewhat later, "Martin," in Cuthbert Worsley's memoir of his visit to Spain, found cinematic memories comforting. "It was all just like what one had seen in films out of the last war, the olive trees torn and shattered by bullet or shell, the corpses between the armies, the stray shots, the enemy somewhere over there crouched in similar positions." He said, "I recognised it as if I had always known it."[64] What is interesting about this statement is its almost total falsity. No film had ever shown what "Martin" saw on that day—the stinking and dismembered corpses, the latticework of intestines covering a dead soldier, heads without bodies, bodies without heads. But for "Martin," who knew only, "I must keep out of it," the manner in which he confronted such a scene and shaped it in an emotionally acceptable manner was to impose the ordered, and therefore sense-making, images of World War I films over a landscape at once cacophonous, funereal, and, above all, replete with horror. It was either that or suffer as Gurney had and would.

Several months later, in the summer of 1937, Hugh Sloan, a miner from Fife, looked over the Brunete battlefield, and saw, too, what no film could have prepared him for: "There was nothing but dead men and dead mules rotting in the sun. The smell of death was unbearable. The decapitated body of a man lay with a board on his chest. On the board . . . was the name of a miner from west Scotland."[65] This was war's reality and perhaps a miner could face it more squarely than a middle-class aesthete. Jim Brown, unquestionably one of the best-read working-class volunteers, could find nothing in his compendious literary inventory to which he could relate what he experienced at

Brunete. He told an interviewer, "This went on and it went on and it became a surrealist world. It became a kind of insane world, an unreal world."[66] Brown's response was not unlike that of the historian Marc Bloch, who served in a French infantry battalion in World War I, and remembered his initial battles as "a discontinuous series of images, vivid in themselves but badly arranged like a reel of movie film that showed here and there large gaps and the unintended reversal of several scenes."[67]

As a veteran of World War I, George Aitken did not need to grow into the "reality" of war, nor did he have to unburden himself of the illusion that war possessed the coherence of dramatic narrative. But even he admitted to being stunned by the sheer ferocity of the fighting in Spain. Aitken, the able commissar of the British Battalion and later of the Brigade, who was recalled to England after Brunete, spoke of his experiences at a memorial meeting for a veteran from Swinden in 1939: "Never before had such savagery and brutality been witnessed. Nothing comparable to it had been seen in the wars of Carthage and the war in Spain was in many respects worse because science had been allied to savagery."[68]

That early emotion upon first hearing the *International* would never be recaptured. The British volunteers for Spain had started their long journey, which had taken them to the valley of the Jarama, and for those who survived and for those who would join them, on to the battles of Brunete, Teruel, the Aragón, and the Ebro. At the same time, they marched also into a political world that teemed with its own dangers and could be every bit as deadly as the battlefield. George Leeson acknowledges the many battles that were to be fought by the British Battalion in Spain. "But it is generally agreed," he writes, "that this first action has a glory all of its own."[69]

VIII

Others were also eager to taste the "glory." Spain became a magnet for those whom Hans Magnus Enzensberger would later call the "tourists of the revolution."[70] Indeed, so many political and cultural luminaries came to visit that a Canadian volunteer sighed that "everybody was there but Shakespeare."[71] The phenomenon of the visiting delegation or individual who comes to find "the truth" has been a regular feature of contemporary conflicts ranging from Indochina to Central America.

Visitors brought to Spain a lexicon of stereotypes that they had no real desire to test against reality. Among these was the "red" Dean of Canterbury, Dr. Hewlett Johnson, who added his own trope to the saga of "heroic Spain." The Dean reported that during an air raid in Santander, he would "never forget" the falling sound of the bombs or "the working people pushing us to safety." The Dean added, "These poor people had not seen meat, bread, butter or milk for three weeks." Since then, they had been visited by a food ship "and all foodships [sic] must go there." A university professor wrote gushingly, "It is quite difficult to tell the plain unvarnished truth without seeming to produce passionate propaganda for the Spanish government." Monica Whately added her self-confident voice to the chorus of the delegation, when she said they had found in Spain "a war between the forces of reaction and the forces to keep the freedom and democracy we enjoy."[72]

But from the point of view of propaganda, the visit of Clement Attlee, the Labour party leader, on December 6, 1937, proved of unique significance. After the Edinburgh conference in October 1936, the Labour party declared its support of the Spanish Republic and endorsed its right to buy arms wherever they could be procured, although the party continued to waffle on the issue. Attlee was accompanied by Philip Noel-Baker and Ellen Wilkinson, both members of the Labour party executive committee. Invited by Prime Minister Negrín, the delegation visited Barcelona, Valencia, and Madrid, interviewing Spanish officials at each stop. But their most significant decision was to visit the British Battalion itself. When they arrived after dark, the faces of the British and American volunteers, as well as the crowd of Spaniards, were illuminated by flickering yellow torches. One speaker cried out that the extraordinary scene was nothing if not a reminder of the meetings at which the Chartists "had demonstrated by torchlight for their demands" in the nineteenth century. The battalion leadership then surprised Attlee by naming the famous No. 1 Company for him. "We are proud," he told the British volunteers, "of the deeds of those who have died and those who still live." Attlee further ensured the warmth of his welcome when he called the Non-Intervention Agreement, which prevented the Republic from buying arms, a "farce."[73] In an unguarded moment, the future prime minister had evaded the caution of the trade union movement at home and had identified the parliamentary Labour party with the sacrifices of the British volunteers in Spain.

The reactions of other political travelers could prove a good deal more complex and purposeful, culminating with Orwell's decision to leave the comfort of a journalist's seat and join a Marxist militia group in Barcelona. Others included W. H. Auden, who left England on January 12, 1937, to spend six weeks in Valencia and Barcelona. He wrote to his great confidant, Professor E. R. Dodds, "I shall probably be a bloody bad soldier but how can I speak to/for them without becoming one."[74] According to the *Daily Worker*, he hoped to serve as an ambulance driver. He apparently did some propaganda broadcasting in Valencia. While there he jubilantly reunited with Cyril Connolly, who was carrying a letter of introduction from Harry Pollitt, which proved helpful when he was questioned by a Comintern agent.[75]

Although disillusion ultimately took place, during the early days of his visit Auden could summon up an apparently genuine enthusiasm for the cause of the Republic. He wrote an article in Valencia that appeared in the *New Statesman* on January 30, 1937: "For a revolution is really taking place. . . . In the last six months these people have been learning what it is to inherit their own country, and once a man has tasted freedom he will not lightly give it up."[76] But on March 4 the poet was back in London. In May, his great poem *Spain* appeared as a sixteen-page pamphlet, selling for a shilling, with all proceeds going to Medical Aid for Spain. Nevertheless, the experience of Spain caused Auden to revise his early left-wing enthusiasms.[77] In March 1939, Auden told Louis MacNeice

> that it was not his job to be a crusader, that this was a thing everyone must decide for himself, but that, in his opinion, most writers falsified their work and themselves when they took a direct part in politics, and that the political end itself, however good, could not be assisted by art or artists so falsified.[78]

The revision of the text of the "engaged" intellectual of the thirties had begun.

More accessible to us, however, is Stephen Spender, whose greatest literary strength lay in autobiography. With the publication of *Forward from Liberalism*, Spender met with Harry Pollitt, the British party leader. Pollitt conceded their differences, said the party could live with them, and persuaded Spender to accept a membership card. After traveling to North Africa on a ludicrous party mission, Spender returned to Spain to take up a job in Barcelona. He hoped to broadcast for a socialist radio station, but found upon his arrival that the

position had been abolished. With this setback, his thoughts immediately turned to the plight of his friend "Jimmy Younger"/Tony
Hyndman in Albacete. Although Spender's purposes were more personal than political, his subsequent visit to Albacete and the Jarama
killing ground would profoundly affect his attitude toward the Communist party.

After a domestic contretemps with Spender, Hyndman had departed England and joined the British Battalion, participating in the
battle of the Jarama. Deeply affected by the appalling bloodshed in
those February days, he attempted to leave the battalion, but found
himself detained by the party in Albacete. The ex-Guardsman wrote
to Spender, "I can still see the blood and the dead faces; worse still,
the expression in the eyes of the dying. I felt no anti-fascist anger, but
only overwhelming pity." Spender attempted to gain Hyndman's
release by asking that the party allow him to appoint his friend as his
secretary. But this proved unsuccessful. Spender was able, however,
to extract a promise from commissar Peter Kerrigan that Hyndman
would not be sent back into combat. When the brigade command
determined that all able men were needed for the Guadalajara front
in March, Kerrigan forgot his agreement. Rather than face the prospect of returning to combat, Hyndman deserted.[79]

After interviews with the British embassy and the Republican
foreign minister, Julio Alvarez Del Vayo, Spender stirred Kerrigan to
take further interest in his friend's case. More threats and false
accusations came from the party. Nevertheless, the medical officer
verified that Hyndman had a duodenal ulcer, and he was finally
allowed to return to England.[80] Spender found himself both appalled
and frightened by the dangers that had engulfed his friend.

A second crucial event in Spender's visit to Spain occurred when
he was invited by George Nathan, whom he much admired, to visit
the Jarama front. After being persuaded to fire a few machine-gun
bursts at the Moors from the British trenches, Spender walked back
to lunch with a young former public school boy who came from a
staunch Liberal family, as did Spender himself. He told the poet that
the XVth Brigade was under the control of the Communist party.
Even if this were true, Spender replied, the cause of the Republic
remained liberal. Upon the boy's further protests, Spender offered to
assist him in returning to England because of his youth. He refused
his help, however, and prophesied, "My life is to walk up to the ridge

every day until I am killed." He did die some weeks later, but on a different battlefield.[81]

The third stage of Spender's disillusion with the party came when he returned to Spain later in 1937 for the meeting of the Second International Writers' Congress for the Defence of Culture, which opened in Valencia. At the conference he found the great French writer, André Gide, being pilloried for his *Return from the U.S.S.R.*, published in November 1936. In the book, Gide asserted his right to criticize the Soviet Union and party dogma.[82] Only a brief time before, he had been lionized by the party for his admiration of the ideal of communism. The intolerance shown toward the French author seemed particularly profane to Spender when the official purpose of the congress "was to discuss the attitude of the Intellectuals of the World to the Spanish War."[83] Apparently, the party would be satisfied with nothing less than a membership of submissive minds parroting whatever each was told to say— of course, and always, for the good of the Republic.

In addition, Spender grew increasingly offended by the opulent treatment the Republic gave him and his fellow writers when ordinary people were suffering acutely from every conceivable shortage. He wrote, "This circus of intellectuals, treated like princes or ministers, carried for hundreds of miles through beautiful scenery and war-torn towns, to the sound of cheering voices, amid broken hearts, riding in Rolls-Royces, banqueted, fêted, sung and danced to, photographed and drawn, had something grotesque about it."[84]

Finally, in Valencia he found himself being chastised at dinner by an intelligent young correspondent from a communist paper who took issue with a piece that Spender had written recently for the *New Statesman*. In his article, Spender charged that communists controlled the International Brigades, and that this should be clearly stated to all volunteers. According to Spender, the response from his dinner companion was that in essence "the facts in my article were true, but he said that nonetheless I should not have written them." The argument was an increasingly familiar one to the poet. Spender's self-appointed adviser told him that he "should consider not the facts but the result which might follow from writing them," concluding, "the truth . . . lay in the cause itself and whatever went to promote it." Although Spender had departed from the party months before, he had come to see increasingly and irrevocably that communism could never be the next step from liberalism, if what was precious about the liberal tradition—the right to independent thought and criticism—was to have any meaning. He chose as his final judgment on the party: "Apparently, truth, like freedom, lay in the recognition of necessity."[85]

The writers Sylvia Townsend Warner and Valentine Ackland, whom Spender mercilessly caricatured while he was travelling with them in Spain,[86] are sometimes seen as just another example of left-wing "day trippers." Sylvia Townsend Warner had already demonstrated, however, a genuine degree of political seriousness by taking part in the East End demonstrations against Mosley and the Fascists. In addition, her novels showed increasing commitment to society's marginalized. In *Lolly Willowes: or the Loving Huntsman*, which was published in 1926, her heroine, a forty-year-old unmarried woman, abandons her upper-middle-class existence to live with the poor in a Chiltern village. *Summer Will Show*, a historical novel published on the eve of the Spanish War, offered hope that communism would prove to be the new form of economic and social organization that would eliminate classes and ensure a sufficiency for all.[87] Her Spanish Civil War novel, *After the Death of Don Juan*, has been rediscovered and much praised.[88] Moreover, both she and her partner wrote widely on antifascist issues, most significantly in the *Left Review*.[89]

What further separated Townsend Warner and Ackland from the run of dilettantes is that they were both dedicated communists who had been asked to come to Spain by Tom Wintringham, an old friend, to do administrative work for the medical units. When they arrived in Barcelona, they were both dismayed and uplifted by the dizzying whirl of events. They wrote a letter to Pollitt complaining that Wintringham was too preoccupied with his journalistic duties, and the party, consequently, was badly disorganized. The city itself, however, captivated Sylvia. "Barcelona, by the time we saw it, was I suppose the nearest thing I shall ever see to the early days of [the] USSR." Having made their report to Pollitt, they believed their duty done, and promptly returned to England.[90] Valentine was offered an opportunity to drive an ambulance back to Spain, which she quickly accepted, but illness prevented her from doing it.[91] The two, however, returned to Spain in July 1937 to attend the International Writers' Conference.

One scientist, J. B .S. Haldane, provided an encouraging example for other travelers. A distinguished geneticist, Haldane became the most famous foreign scientific figure to identify himself directly with the cause of the Spanish Republic. Haldane's passionate interest in political and economic questions, which was to last the remainder of his life, however, was a recent development. He had been an officer in the Black Watch in World War I, carrying from it a strong legacy of contempt for the high command, an enthusiasm both for the comradeship of war and the heightening of the senses it produced, and a deep feeling for the suffering of others. Moreover, he had close associations with working-class people and neither romanticized nor patronized them. Yet, according to John Strachey, Haldane had once believed politics was "nonsense."[92] It was his strong and growing conviction that science should benefit humanity that ultimately moved him into politics and the Communist party. His biographer, Ronald Clark, believes that the principal attraction of communism for Haldane was that the communists "had . . . been among the first to see science as a utilitarian subject directed towards the needs of the many rather than as a philosophical discipline understood by the few."[93]

Haldane made three trips to Spain, advising the Spanish government and the British Battalion on anti-gas measures, hitchhiking to his destinations, and taking manifest pleasure in sharing the comradeship and dangers of the front. In the course of his visits to the British Battalion, and, indeed, for the remainder of his long life, he demonstrated "commonsense and [a] genuine feeling for ordinary people." From this, his biographer concludes, "a mutual and lasting respect" grew up between the famous scientist and working men and women.[94] This, even though the Manchester volunteer, Ralph Cantor, could wonder after meeting Haldane, "Why do professors stutter? Eccentricity!"[95]

Clark observes, however, that "it is remarkable how rarely [Haldane] is mentioned even in the accounts of the fighting later produced by the British members of the International Brigade." He forgets that those who produced the accounts were middle-class intellectuals who were comparatively few in number. In fact, interviews with the brigaders are replete with references to Haldane, his bizarre appearance,[96] his impromptu and riveting lectures, the small pistol he produced to help repel an anticipated attack, and his ability to talk about science to ordinary working men. Fred Copeman was particularly grateful for the lectures he gave on theories of crossfire, which he put into practice.[97] In 1937 Haldane became the science

correspondent for the *Daily Worker*, contributing some 350 essays by
1950. What made him a success, as a Fife housewife put it, was that
"he had no airs about him."[98]

One of the least likely figures to visit Spain was the future Conservative prime minister, Ted Heath, who as an undergraduate at Balliol
became president of the Federation of University Conservative Associations. While at Oxford the young Heath, the son of a carpenter,
came under the influence of A. D. Lindsay, the remarkable Master of
Balliol, who "taught democracy to a generation of undergraduates
alarmed by the march of fascism and subject to the contrary tempta-
tion to respond by embracing communism."[99] Heath received his
political education by traveling on the continent and seeing firsthand
the crude brutalities of Nazism. He broke with Chamberlain's appeasement policies, became a leading Oxford antifascist, and subsequently defeated a pro-Franco rival for the presidency of Oxford's
Conservative Association.

While in Spain with a student delegation, Heath narrowly escaped
death or serious injury on at least three occasions.[100] He said, won-
deringly, after meeting the British Battalion, "Their morale was high
and they still genuinely believed that they were going to throw back
General Franco's troops. . . . One could not but admire these men,
civilians at heart, who had to learn everything of a military nature as
they went along. They would go on fighting as long as they could,
that was clear."[101]

Upon his return to Oxford, Heath became the university's leading
undergraduate Conservative and antifascist. At Cambridge, hundreds
of undergraduates were embracing both antifascism and communism. In Spain, however, George Orwell and his Independent Labour
party comrades in the POUM militia would soon discover the naïveté
of the assumption that an antifascist and a communist were necessarily fighting the same battle.

CHAPTER IO

Barcelona and the Battalion

EARLY SUMMER 1937

George Orwell judged matters by the standards of his own life, which
in politics were as exacting as those of a saint.
— Stephen Spender

People don't know, can't ever know what it is like here.
— Anonymous

The legend of intellectuals and workers marching together had been
created.   — Noel Annan

I

After the bloodletting of February, the opposing armies maintained static positions through the spring and early summer until
General Franco developed a new strategy to take Madrid. Before he
could implement his plan, however, "a civil war within a civil war,"
as George Orwell described it, broke out in Barcelona in the first days
of May 1937.[1]

The origins of these endlessly controversial developments in separa-
tist Catalonia lay in the growing tension on the left between revolutionaries—the POUM and their much larger allies, the anarchosyndicalist
CNT-FAI (Confederación Nacional del Trabajo-Federación Anarquista
Ibérica)—and antirevolutionaries—the PSUC (Partit Socialista Unificat
de Catalunya), a coalition of Catalan organizations controlled by the
communists. The first ardently believed that a genuine social revolution, necessitating the collectivization of the means of production, and
the defeat of the Nationalists went hand in hand. The second was
concerned that a revolutionary socialist agenda would alienate the
bourgeois democracies, whose aid was needed to win the war. Therefore,
they insisted that victory could be achieved only if moderate social
policies prevailed and all energies were devoted to the war's prosecution.

When Soviet supplies began arriving in October 1936, the prestige and influence of the Spanish Communist party soared. In December the PSUC felt strong enough to move for the dismissal of the POUM leader, Andrés Nin, from the Generalitat, the regional government of Catalonia. The deteriorating situation came to an end in May when the PSUC and the government succeeded in crushing the POUM and their anarchist allies in heavy street fighting, precipitated by the government's effort to reclaim the control of the telephone exchange, which had been in the hands of the anarchists. This fratricidal struggle abolished the hopes of the Catalonian revolutionaries, and turned one of the witnesses of the fighting and the repression that followed, George Orwell, into a lifelong anticommunist and the author of one of the enduring classics of the war, *Homage to Catalonia*.

Orwell (or Eric Blair, his given name, by which he was known in Spain) arrived in Barcelona in December 1936 as a journalist accredited by the Independent Labour party. Established in 1893, the ILP became one of the founders of the Labour Representation Committee in 1900 and of the Labour party in 1906. It disaffiliated from its offspring in July 1932 after a cabinet crisis in the second Labour government which led to the resignation of Ramsay MacDonald and the formation of a National Government of Liberals and Conservatives. MacDonald's decision to follow opportunity instead of principle (as perceived by his critics) and lead the new government resulted in his expulsion from the Labour party. To the ILP, however, MacDonald's behavior appeared the final evidence needed to persuade revolutionary socialists to reaffirm their independence of thought and action from the increasingly right-wing Labour party. This led to the ILP's decision to leave the Labour party and join the International Bureau of Revolutionary Socialist Parties, also known as the London Bureau, and to recognize the POUM as its Spanish counterpart.

After the outbreak of the war, the POUM appealed to its sister parties in the Bureau for aid. In September the ILP representatives, W. B. Martin and Bob Edwards, drove an ambulance bearing the name of the POUM to the Aragón front. Moved by the gravity of the situation, Martin, a veteran of World War I, immediately took command of an artillery section of sixty men. Edwards, a member of the party's National Administrative Council, returned to England to raise a group of ILP volunteers. In doing so, Edwards forswore his own pacifist beliefs and overcame the antimilitarist position of the ILP.[2]

Shortly after his arrival in Spain, Orwell joined the POUM militia on the comparatively quiet Aragón front. He quickly established himself as a brave and effective leader among his largely untrained British, Spanish, and European comrades. The author of the recently published book, *The Road to Wigan Pier*, won the admiration of Bob Edwards, who remembered him "as a very brave man." Orwell suffered "dreadfully" from asthma and bronchitis but "he was quite fearless."[3] The youthful Stafford Cottman saw Orwell as "different from the rest of us," in part because he wrote each day after breakfast, in part because of his Eton accent. But Cottman admitted that he "was a person capable of influencing" his comrades, that he possessed the "common touch."[4]

We now know that Orwell was especially singled out for attention by the communists. Orwell's is one of two files on British volunteers who served in the POUM militia in Moscow's former Central Party Archive. Dated July 7, 1937, it identifies him both as a member of the ILP and a "Trotskyite."[5] A communist, in all probability the commissar, Wally Tapsell, wrote in an official report that "the leading personality and most respected man in the [ILP] contingent at present is Eric Blair [Orwell]. This man is a Novelist who has written some books [on] proletarian life in England." But, "he has little political understanding." According to the report, Orwell said that he "is not interested in party politics, and came to Spain as an Anti-Fascist to fight Fascism."[6]

The irony of it all, as readers of *Homage to Catalonia* well know, is that a few days before the outbreak of the Barcelona fighting, Orwell and other disaffected British volunteers had decided to transfer from the POUM to the International Brigades because of their impatience with the disorganization and inactivity of the POUM.[7] Orwell wrote that he approached "a Communist friend" with Spanish Medical Aid about the possibility of transferring to the British Battalion. "He seemed very anxious to recruit me and asked me, if possible, to persuade some of the other ILP Englishmen to come with me."[8]

It was at this point that Orwell was put in contact with Tapsell. Certainly, a party representative talked to a number of the ILP volunteers when they took leave in Barcelona on April 27, 1937. He reported to his masters, "The general impression gained from some of the men is that in the first place they were tricked by the P.O.U.M. into going on to the Aragon front. They believed when coming out to Spain that they would be enlisted in the ranks of the International

Brigades." After eight days in the Lenin barracks, the volunteers began to complain. The ILP representative, John McNair, quickly found them uniforms and sent them to the POUM, telling the newly arrived British that the International Brigades had a unit fighting with the POUM, and they would be attached to it. Because "the general political level of the members of the contingent [was] very low," the volunteers were easily fooled. But "many of them quickly realized that [they were] being used as a pawn in a game played by the P.O.U.M. [leaders], with the agreement of John McNair of the I.L.P. who must justify his existence in Spain."[9]

"In a conversation with the writer on the 30th," the report adds, "Blair enquired whether his association with the POUM would be likely to prejudice his chances of enlisting in the International Brigade. He wishes to fight on the Madrid front and stated that in a few days he will formally apply to us for enlistment when his discharge from the POUM has been regularised." We read in Orwell's file that he had come to see the hopelessness of continuing as a combatant with the POUM. Orwell "has grown to dislike the POUM and is now awaiting his discharge." Blair's name is then listed along with eight other members of the ILP who did not wish to remain with the POUM.[10]

The Moscow files are revealing about Orwell in both small and large ways. In *Homage to Catalonia*, Orwell writes that once the purge against the POUM began, his hotel room in Barcelona was burglarized; all items of personal correspondence on *The Road to Wigan Pier*, other memorabilia, his notes on the war, and even his dirty laundry had been taken. In his file is a report dated July 10, 1937, which details these very items as being confiscated.[11] The intruders, probably SIM agents, had been particularly interested in a letter of support he had courageously written on behalf of the imprisoned POUM leader George Kopp, as well as other correspondence with his former commanding officer. In addition, the party agents purported to have found a letter revealing that Eileen Blair, Orwell's wife, was under the discipline of the POUM.

Finally, the political report on Orwell charges that he had played an active role in the Barcelona fighting in May. This contradicts his account in *Homage to Catalonia*, in which he describes himself as a passive and troubled bystander who was not drawn into the actual fighting. From the party's point of view, however, the conclusion was inescapable: Orwell and his wife were enemies of the Republic. In the uncertain political climate of the summer of 1937, Orwell could have hardly exaggerated his peril at the hands of his "fellow anti-fascists," the Catalonian communists. By labeling him a Trotskyist, the communists had in effect signed his death warrant if he remained in Spain.

The issues were further complicated by the views of a member of the ILP contingent, Frank Frankford, who was one of those who wished to transfer with Orwell to the British Battalion. Frankford's file in Moscow indicates how confused he was by the fighting in Barcelona, and, consequently, why even the better-informed and more independently minded members of the British Battalion could be so quick to judge the conduct of the POUM as traitorous.[12] In a long statement, Frankford verified all the Communist party's accusations against his former comrades. He claimed to have been so deceived by the POUM during the May fighting that only later did he realize he had actually been on the fascist side. When Frankford returned to the front he found "open fraternization" between the POUM and the fascists. Frankford wrote that he even received orders not to return fascist fire. But the most spectacular of his accusations was directed against George Kopp, Orwell's revered friend and commander. In his interrogation by party officials, Frankford said that he had learned from a patrol that Kopp had been seen climbing over the wire one night, returning from Franco's lines.[13]

Despite Kopp's *bona fides* as yet another mystery man in Spain, Frankford's last accusation appears particularly implausible. The man who won George Orwell's undying admiration and who survived torture in communist cells in Spain to fight in the French Foreign Legion in World War II is not a likely candidate as a traitor. Stafford Cottman remembered him as "quite a brave sort of bloke" who "gave confidence and encouragement." Like Orwell, Kopp was the sort of man that one followed "happily."[14] It is certainly clear, however, that the communist-controlled PSUC believed that Kopp possessed information they wanted.

A last irony is that because the nine volunteers had shown "leanings toward Trotskyites [sic]" since coming to Spain, the party contact recommended that their application for transfer to the British Battalion be turned down.[15] Soon, there were hundreds of bodies in the streets of Barcelona, casualties of the successful PSUC effort to destroy the POUM. The communist oppression only confirmed Orwell's loyalty to the POUM. He returned to the front, and was soon badly wounded, and evacuated back to Barcelona for recuperation.

Within a short time every follower of the POUM was either dead, in prison, or, like the wounded Orwell, on the run.

The communists relentlessly pursued their witch hunt. In the *Daily Worker* of May 11, 1937, "Frank Pitcairn" linked the uprising in Barcelona with Russia's internal enemies:

> In the past, the leaders of the POUM have frequently sought to deny their complicity as agents of a Fascist cause against the People's Front. This time they are convicted out of their own mouths as clearly as their allies, operating in the Soviet Union, who confessed to the crimes of espionage, sabotage, and attempted murder against the government of the Soviet Union.[16]

The Independent Labour party leader, Fenner Brockway, met Eric and Eileen Blair in a small village in France on June 26 after their successful escape from Barcelona. Two days later he saw them off to London. Brockway wrote in his diary on July 2, "C.P. papers contain wildest attacks on POUM as [a] Fascist organisation and demanding death penalties." The following day he recorded that Francisco Largo Caballero, the prime minister, told him the "C.P. is using every means to destroy its political opponents, not refraining from manipulating 'justice' and power over [the] police."[17] The ILP Member of Parliament, John McGovern, said that "to oppose the anti-revolutionary line of the Popular Front and to criticize Moscow puts your life in serious danger at the hands of the Communists in Spain."[18]

The events of May 1937, of course, bitterly disillusioned Orwell. The arrest of several of his comrades by the communists, including the death in prison of Bob Smillie,[19] the son of a famous Scottish labor leader, did not turn Orwell into a dedicated reactionary, as somewhat similar experiences ultimately did to the American novelist, John Dos Passos. (The communists murdered a close friend of Dos Passos in Madrid.) Instead, Orwell remained a socialist, but one who recognized the totalitarian nature of Stalinist communism. Much of his mood is captured in a letter he wrote to his friend Rayner Heppenstall. After the jaunty irony of the opening, Orwell quickly reveals his bitterness:

> It was a queer business. We started off by being heroic defenders of democracy and ended by slipping over the border with the police panting on our heels. . . . But though we ourselves got out all right nearly all our friends and acquaintances are in jail and likely to be there indefinitely, not actively charged with anything but suspected of "Trotskyism." The most terrible things were happening even when I left, wholesale arrests,

wounded men dragged out of hospitals and thrown into jail, people crammed together in filthy dens where they have hardly room to lie down, prisoners beaten and half starved etc. etc.[20]

That Orwell faithfully recorded what he saw and believed to be true does not mean that he necessarily understood all the complexities of the political situation in Barcelona. But he was one of the few intellectuals in the thirties to escape the "versus" complex. Not for him the easy antitheses of traveling intellectual poseurs in Spain who thrilled to the sound of "fascist" shells at the Second International Writer's Conference in Madrid. Reality could not be so easily or quickly grasped. Consequently, upon his return from Spain, Orwell refused to contribute to Nancy Cunard's questionnaire, "Authors Take Sides on the Spanish War." He considered this kind of either/or simplification of complex issues to be nothing but "bloody rubbish." Cyril Connolly said of him, thinking back to their childhood, "The remarkable thing about Orwell was that alone among the boys he was an intellectual and not a parrot[,] for he thought for himself."[21] In a recently discovered letter to Cunard, written shortly after his return from Spain, Orwell explained his position. In doing so, he separated himself from his left contemporaries in often violent language.

> I am not one of your fashionable pansies like Auden and Spender, I was six months in Spain, most of the time fighting, I have a bullet hole in me at present and I am not going to write blah about defending democracy or gallant little anybody. Moreover, I know what is happening and has been happening on the Government side for months past, ie that Fascism is being riveted on to the Spanish workers under the pretext of resisting Fascism.[22]

In a decade awash in middle-class rhetoric about workers, Orwell was one of the few intellectuals who purposefully set out to make contact with their world, and to test his general views against the reality of his experiences, whether in Wigan or in Barcelona or the battlefields of the Aragón.

II

To complete the remarkable cast of British characters appearing in the struggle between the POUM and the communists, the young Englishman, David Crook, who had saved Sam Wild's life at the Jarama in February, surfaced in Barcelona in August 1937. Orwell and his wife had fled Spain; George Kopp remained in prison; and

Crook quickly realized that the luminous egalitarianism of the Catalonian capital had greatly darkened. In the aftermath of the crushing
of the POUM, and the pervasive atmosphere of suspicion which
descended upon the Catalonian city, Crook was himself detained and
his belongings searched.

Agents discovered in his possession two letters from the ILP leader,
Fenner Brockway. Most incriminating was one from Eileen Blair in
which there was a reference to George Kopp. With this in hand, his
interrogators apparently hoped to play a cat-and-mouse game with
Crook by putting him in the same cell as Kopp, allowing him to go
free, then rearresting him with the hope that the young volunteer
would be sufficiently unsettled that he would reveal any information
Kopp may have given him in prison. Kopp's incarceration by the
Catalan communists and the danger facing anyone who had associated or corresponded with him proves his importance to them—but
hardly that he was a spy, although other questions about Kopp
remain.[23]

In such perilous circumstances, Crook must have been possessed
of a mad impudence. He told his interrogators that although he was
not a Trotskyist, he agreed with certain of their views, and, moreover,
was writing a book critical of the Republic.[24] One can only speculate
about his motives. What conceivably saved Crook was that (it appears) he was secretly working to buy arms for the Republic, which
his jailers may have learned before taking further action against
him.[25] As for Kopp, he was released eighteen months later. The
POUM provided a unique target for the communists. But, fortunately,
they possessed in George Orwell a writer who would effectively put
their case before the world. In the end, what had delighted Orwell
about the POUM, despite its military inefficiency, was its classlessness, a quality he also found in the extraordinary atmosphere of
Barcelona in late 1936 and early 1937.

III

None of the political or ethical complexities of the struggle
in Barcelona appear to have registered with the battalion. On June 20,
even the usually circumspect Jim Brewer referred to those in the
POUM militia as "the cafe-lizard type who made trouble in Barcelona
the other day, ably seconded by the half-dozen I.L.P.ers present in
Spain."[26] The brigade newspaper, *Volunteer for Liberty*, told its
readers that the POUM was infested with spies who had been in direct

contact with Hitler.[27] Most if not all of the battalion had nothing but contempt for Orwell and the British volunteers in the Aragón. One veteran asked rhetorically, "How many of the ILP were killed on the Aragon front?" Although a number were wounded (Orwell most famously), the answer, as he knew, was none.[28]

Most important, members of the British Battalion heard only the Communist party's version of the suppression of the POUM in Barcelona. This is a point that requires some development. Regardless of contingent motives, the majority of the British volunteers made a conscious political decision to go to Spain. For them, it was a choice freely made, based on their experience of life, their reading of books and newspapers, and the kind of open exchange of ideas that they had known on street corners, in great public spaces, and in their educational classes. They believed that this same intellectual freedom would exist in the British Battalion.

The core of political discussion among the volunteers consisted of monthly selections of the Left Book Club, the *Daily Worker*, and battalion and brigade news bulletins.[29] In ideal circumstances, the XVth Brigade newsletter, *Our Combat*, published in English, French, and Spanish, appeared regularly. In addition, they also received the English-language version of *Volunteer for Liberty*, which remained the official International Brigade organ. Each of these, with some exceptions from the Left Book Club, reflected the Communist party "line."

The reaction of a few nonparty and party "thinkers" was often very hostile. They felt themselves held hostage to communist propaganda, and thus unable to gain the facts on which they could make informed and rational decisions. The goal of seeking objective truth was subordinated, unconsciously or consciously, to politics. It was for good reason that George Orwell told Arthur Koestler that history stopped in 1936. He wrote: "Early in life I had noticed that no event is ever correctly reported in a newspaper, but in Spain, for the first time, I saw newspaper reports which did not bear any relation to the facts, not even the relationship which is implied by an ordinary lie."[30] The American correspondent, Herbert Matthews, agreed: "Journalistic faking reached great heights in that war, as readers gradually began to realize."[31]

Claud Cockburn, the former *Times* reporter, editor of *The Week*, and *Daily Worker* correspondent (under the name of Frank Pitcairn) who had been one of the first to fight in Spain, contributed his own remarkable abilities to this campaign of propaganda and distortion. Willi Münzenberg's henchman, Otto Katz, suggested to Cockburn that the Republic needed news that would have "a clear psychological impact." The English journalist then proceeded to concoct a story of a revolt against Franco in Morocco. He wrote unapologetically, "In the end it emerged as one of the most factual, inspiring and yet sober pieces of war reporting I ever saw, and the night editors loved it."[32]

Examples of this kind of travesty are numerous. Peter Kerrigan, himself reporting for the *Daily Worker*, took Harry Pollitt to task for a false story the British party leader had planted. According to the CPGB organ, Kerrigan heroically swam the Ebro bearing crucial reports. Kerrigan said Pollitt knew this was "a phony story," and, moreover, "there was already too much butter in [the *Daily Worker*]."[33] On October 18, 1938, Pollitt again angered Kerrigan as arrangements were being made for welcoming the British Battalion home. He told Pollitt that the *Daily Worker*'s report that the battalion was at the strength of 1,000 was "incredible." "This phony figure of 1,000 in the battalion . . . you must know [to be] wrong." And, more pragmatically, "The boys' reaction here was very bad when they saw it."[34] Thinking of the *Daily Worker*, Orwell said, "I saw great battles reported where there had been no fighting, and complete silence where hundreds of men had been killed." Remembering his experience with the POUM, "I saw troops who had fought bravely denounced as cowards and traitors, and others who had never seen a shot fired hailed as the heroes of imaginary victories." He concluded by writing, "I saw . . . history being written not in terms of what happened but of what ought to have happened according to various 'party lines.'"[35]

The reviewer of Bill Rust's *The Story of the Daily Worker*, the newspaper with which Rust had so long been associated and which Orwell held in such contempt, emphasized its role in creating the "story" of Spain. His dishonesty or denial achieves remarkable proportions when he explains why the *Daily Worker* had a "very special place in working-class journalism." The British volunteers in Spain had suffered the intellectual inconvenience of reading other newspapers but "there were no complaints about the *Worker*. It did the job a newspaper should do—told the people of Britain the truth."[36] According to Harry Pollitt, in his foreword to the memoir of the Spanish hero, Jack Coward, "The *Daily Worker* is the only paper that Jack Coward, and the hundreds of thousands of the best of the working class from which he sprang, trust. They trust its news. They trust its views, which are fearlessly expressed and accurate in their forecast."[37] If so, it was a wholly misplaced trust. The newspaper of working-class militants consistently misled or lied to them. Even George Murray, a SIM agent and soldier in the Anti-Tanks, wrote to his brother in Edinburgh, "I am sure you are far better served with news, not only of home and world events but of the Spanish War itself, than we are."[38]

Not all succumbed to the *Daily Worker*'s version of history by any means, suggesting that there were those in the battalion who established some kind of independent space for themselves. The middle-class Mancunian, Leslie Preger, who had visited Russia before the war and drove an ambulance in Spain, remembered that the only paper he trusted was the *News Chronicle*. "I realised very early on that the first casualty of war is truth."[39]

If the *Daily Worker* told the "truth," then, as Orwell understood better than most, anything could be said to be "true." Jack Jones has written, "So many good men died, believing to the end in the cause of democracy." This belief was cultivated and sustained by the Communist party through a deliberate campaign of propaganda and censorship, and was helped immeasurably by the inability of the British to escape their native insularity despite their internationalist traditions. "Anyhow," Fred Thomas of the Anti-Tank Battery remembered, "anything not immediately and obviously affecting our daily lives—bitter cold or searing heat, hunger or thirst, mail and cigarettes—seemed remote and unreal."[40] As a result, the battalion lived in an ideological cocoon of unreality.

The party achieved this isolation in several ways. First, the leadership cut off the British volunteers from the larger world by censorship of newspapers and mail, making it impossible for the majority of the volunteers to separate party myths from reality. Although George Brown and others found it possible to subscribe to the *Manchester Guardian*[41] and other papers, the reading material available to most of the members of the battalion was carefully controlled by the party. As for personal correspondence, scores of letters sit in the Moscow files, never sent to their destination, providing mute testimony to the ardor and efficiency of the brigade censors and the corresponding inability of the volunteers to write honestly to their comrades and loved ones, or they to them. According to one disaffected volunteer, "When writing home . . . the only news we were allowed to send was a lot of lies praising the Communist Party, and for this reason there were a number who never wrote at all."[42]

Another volunteer, who was wounded at the Jarama and subsequently worked at brigade headquarters in Albacete, wrote in block letters on his repatriation papers that he "OPENLY OPPOSED MILITARY CENSORSHIP OF BOOKS, PERIODICALS ETC."[43] Charles Wagner also became concerned about what he called "the newspaper problem." He accused the political leadership of failing to disclose "that stopping the papers has been going on for some. I feel you should not stifle our opinions . . . , as you have done, but as comrades and Communists we should be able to discuss" issues freely.[44] Even when on leave the men had little opportunity to learn anything of the political situation. Then, their minds focused on sleep, clean clothes, eating regular meals, and other comforts.

It would not be unreasonable to have expected the men of the battalion to learn more about the political complexities of Spain from the Spaniards themselves. Despite the compulsive attraction "Spain" had for the left, however, volunteers came to know remarkably little about the country or its people during their time in Spain. Thus, there is great irony in Bill Alexander's accusation that George Orwell was ignorant "of the realities of Spanish life."[45] Rather, it was the men of the British Battalion, not Orwell, who were sheltered from reality. After all, Orwell and his handful of fellow Englishmen were not fighting in an English-speaking unit. Orwell, who first became a squad leader and then the equivalent of a platoon leader of Spanish militiamen, possessed an excellent facility for languages, learning sufficient Catalán to communicate with his comrades so quickly that he was promoted to corporal shortly after arriving at the front.[46]

On the other hand, in the British Battalion, at least in the beginning, most volunteers spoke little, if any, Spanish. An administrative staff member in Albacete said that in the American and British battalions "nobody knew a word of Spanish. . . . I mean, people like Bill Lawrence[47] or Will Paynter[48] never learned a word of Spanish all the time they were there." He felt justified, too, in adding that "they never met a Spaniard."[49] On August 28, 1937, a recommendation was made to begin a course in Spanish for the British volunteers, but not acted on until more than four months later. On December 16, 1937, six months after Orwell and his wife had fled Spain, Arthur Nicoll wrote a memorandum indicating that a start would be made on teaching the British to speak the language of the country in which they were fighting and dying.[50] Success toward meeting this goal always remained modest. Alec Ferguson, exceptionally, learned the language and spoke it "like a native." But, after twenty months in Spain, he could report that the "majority" of the British never learned Spanish.[51] As late as May 1, 1938, the *Volunteer for Liberty* announced "it is the duty of every volunteer to make what efforts he can to acquire at least a working knowledge of Spanish."[52]

Nor was the language barrier broken by an active program of personal contact with Spaniards. The American Leonard Lamb, who served with the Lincolns in the XVth Brigade, remembered "how isolated the internationals were in [the war]. The only place I imagine [they] met some of the Spanish people were in some of the smaller towns where they may have been quartered."[53] George Brown refers to one such instance in a letter home. It pleased him to report that "the Battalion is getting very close to the people in the District, winning their friendship as they did in the early days in the village where they trained." He added, "Already our comrades have volunteered to help in bringing in the harvest and the Popular Front committee is considering how best to harness the men."[54] The base commissar, Will Paynter, however, hinted in his farewell letter to the battalion in October 1937 at problems: "We have . . . to remove bad habits of the past and attain a more intimate knowledge and relationship with our Spanish comrades."[55]

These "bad habits" were still in evidence at the time of repatriation. In his final report on the battalion, Alonzo Elliott concluded that by the end of their time in the war most of the British had learned "a certain minimum of Spanish."[56] But there were a number, including "comrades who have displayed outstanding qualities in Spain in the military or political fields,"[57] who refused to accept the importance of speaking the language, and, consequently, were unable to form close ties to the Republic's political and social life. In part, Elliott conceded, this was because the British had never completely overcome their prejudices against the Spaniards. He attributed this to a deeply ingrained feeling of British superiority to foreigners, as well as an inability to shed the stereotypes about Spaniards that some volunteers brought with them and insisted upon retaining.[58]

In addition, the British could prove so tribal in their habits that they often demonstrated little desire to know even the Spaniards serving in the battalion, as Jason Gurney observed to his amazement.[59] Matters were hardly helped when the redoubtable battalion com-

mander, Sam Wild, got along so badly with the Spaniards under his
command that it was made a matter for his permanent record.[60] Some,
of course, did make sincere attempts to understand the Spanish
people better. The Spaniards, however, did not always welcome their
overtures. One anarchist, who had impressed an IB officer with his
intelligence, snapped, "Why are you foreigners here?", causing the
volunteer to conclude from this and other incidents that the Spaniards were a "xenophobic" people.[61]

The fundamental tragedy was that most in the battalion, regardless
of class, did not have enough independent information about the role
of the Communist party, Spain, or its people to establish the factual
basis on which an intelligent political life could be led. Those who
did either deserted, felt themselves trapped, entered a state of denial,
or believed that the cause of antifascism was more important than
the treachery of the party. W. K. MacGregor could write contemptuously to Peter Kerrigan on November 19, 1937, that in "my opinion
. . . the only action [the ILP contingent] ever did was to engineer along
with the POUM the rising in our rear at Barcelona."[62] Whether based
on inadequate information or political faith, it became axiomatic that
the ILP and the POUM were seen as disrupters of the war effort and,
by most, as traitors to the Republic.[63]

The *Spanish News Bulletin* put the lie in its classic form, congratu-
lating the PSUC, the Comintern-controlled party of Catalonia, for
tearing away "the trotskyist mask" of the POUM and revealing "the
hideous grimace of fascist counter-revolution." This was accomplished when the communists allegedly discovered hoarded weapons
and documents incriminating the POUM in a fascist intrigue. Judgment followed swiftly. "The documents prove that the trotskyist
spies were in direct contact with the spy agencies of fascist states and
before all with Germany." Therefore, "All this material shows the
role which German and Italian fascism played in the trotskyist
uprising in May."[64]

The communist line did not go unchallenged by the POUM and
the ILP. Worried that the POUM version "is widely quoted in certain
organs of the British working class press," the Communist party fired
another salvo against "the uncontrollables . . . , often criminal types,"
justifying their "liquidation."[65] The *Labour Monthly* declared that
the POUM was "one of the most valuable propaganda agencies the
Nazis possess behind the Republican lines."[66]

IV

The battalion had other issues on its mind than the fighting in Barcelona, however. It began readying for the July engagement at Brunete, whose intensity would rival the Jarama and the battles of World War I in the memories of veterans of both conflicts. After the fall of Francisco Largo Caballero in May and the accession of the respected scientist, Juan Negrín, the communists exercised significantly greater control over Republican strategy. The long-planned Republican offensive was directed at the village of Brunete, thirty kilometers to the west of Madrid, reflecting the communist obsession with the defense of the great city where so many of their cadres had died. All five of the International Brigades were thrown into the battle.

The British commander was Fred Copeman, a former sailor who enjoyed great prestige among the workers because of the prominent role he played in the Invergordon mutiny.[67] In this single respect, he was like André Marty, the oddly ridiculous but thoroughly murderous head of the International Brigades, who became one of the leaders of the mutiny against the French Black Sea fleet, which had been ordered to support the White Russians in 1919 in the Russian civil war.[68] Some exaggeration of their respective roles in the two insurrections undoubtedly helped to influence their acceptance among working-class volunteers in Spain. Copeman's part is worth briefly exploring, however, because of the criticisms that have been leveled at his leadership of the battalion. Jason Gurney believed that "he made himself out to have been the leader of the Invergordon mutiny in 1931, but in fact he must have played a very minor role as he was never charged with any offence after the mutiny was subdued." In Gurney's view Copeman was a master of self-aggrandizement.[69]

The Invergordon mutiny, the greatest in the modern history of the British fleet, took place shortly after the National Government announced substantial pay cuts in the navy. Copeman writes in his autobiography that the mutiny "sprang from the spontaneous reactions of the men of the Fleet against injustice."[70] When the mutiny broke out in the autumn of 1931, the Atlantic Fleet was due to begin exercises in the deep-water channel of Cromarty Firth, near Invergordon. Although Copeman was certainly not the leader of the mutiny—indeed, it was too diffuse to have a single leader—his role was not as insignificant as Jason Gurney supposes, nor did he emerge from it unscathed, as the sculptor suggests. Serving on the *Norfolk*, along with Len Wincott and George Hill, Copeman could fairly claim to be one of the mutiny's leaders.

At a pivotal moment in the crisis, his fellow seamen asked Copeman to speak. Climbing upon the roof of a pavilion, Copeman encouraged support throughout the fleet for those who wished to lay down their tools. The argument that successfully swept the lower decks was one of class solidarity. Even men whose grievances were not as great as others were persuaded to cooperate.

Once the mutiny was settled, and despite Chamberlain's pledge that there would be no punishment, Copeman, Len Wilcott, and others were discharged to barracks as "subversives." After the election called by Chamberlain, they were expelled from the navy itself.[71] For Copeman, the mutiny stood as "a turning point. . . . I began to understand the meaning of leadership and—even more important— the meaning of politics." He wrote, "At Invergordon I had tasted leadership and felt the thrill of power, which came from the willing support of thousands of followers."[72]

Copeman found work in the dockyards. He was kept under surveillance by naval intelligence and lost at least one job in London because of suspected communist sympathies.[73] The poet Laurie Lee caught a glimpse of him in London where he had become a steel erector and union activist, and, of course, was to see him again in Spain. Lee wrote:

> Veteran of Brunete, and once my strike leader when I was a builder's labourer in Putney. Here in Spain I saw again that hard, hungry face, even more shrunken now by battle and fatigue than by his struggles back home in the early Thirties. When he recognized me his hard eyes glittered with frosty warmth for a moment. "The poet from the buildings," he said. "Never thought you'd make it."[74]

Lee described Copeman as a "rough-cut, hollow-cheeked, working-class revolutionary, and archetype of all the Commanders of the British Battalion."[75] Copeman said of himself with unintentional irony, "All my life, I [had] an instinctive dislike of anybody who has authority, anybody who looks as if they are going to give an order."[76] Charlotte Haldane wrote of him, "He was a natural rebel . . . a rough diamond, with a heart of gold." His lack of deference to authority was legendary. Haldane said in her sometimes painfully chipper manner, "He gave the rough side of his tongue and a merry stream of nautical oaths to his political superiors as blithely as to his foreign colleagues in the Brigade command."[77]

This kind of behavior would help, in part, to explain Jason Gurney's view of the ex-sailor. When Gurney, the Chelsea sculptor, arrived at the training base at Madrigueras, he found himself thoroughly repulsed by Copeman and quickly came to loathe him. None of the working-class volunteers appeared to share his sentiments. According to Gurney, however, everyone was frightened of Copeman because of his fighting prowess. "He charged around the place threatening to beat everybody's brains out, and looking as if he was quite capable of doing it."[78]

Gurney's judgment of Copeman speaks as much to the difficulties of integrating men from very different worlds into one fighting unit as it does to Copeman's boorish bellicosity. A Chelsea artist accustomed to sophisticated company and a London steel erector with a truculent attitude were not likely to get on. But it was a question of temperament, not class prejudice. For, by contrast, Gurney came to admire Harry Fry, a Glasgow shoemaker with little formal education, but who possessed a "natural genius for organization." Similarly, Gurney held in high regard William Briskey, a London bus driver, who also commanded one of the battalion's companies.[79]

Now, Copeman the "natural rebel " was in the strange position of seeing that discipline was respected and orders obeyed. His advice to his troops on the eve of battle did not spare the more delicate sensibilities, and could have hardly come from the mouth of a regular British officer. He cautioned his men that if they were preparing to go "over the top and you are messing around with your bloody self or going to Madrid and having it off, then you will find it is harder to get over the bloody parapet."[80] But there was a quality of compassion that cemented his relationship with the rank and file of the battalion. If a patrol returned without completing its mission because of the danger, Copeman would tell his comrades he would have been as frightened as they were; nevertheless, the job had to be done, and he explained that he would have to send them out again. This empathy helped establish an essential democracy in the battalion, despite the hierarchy that developed.

The relationship with the battalion commissar was understandably crucial for the commander. Copeman decided to challenge his power immediately. He told Wally Tapsell, the quick-tongued Cockney commissar,[81] that he would no longer accept his authority. "This was revolutionary[,] as the party commissars had the power," Copeman said. But Tapsell, who had been an important YCL leader and a member of the party's Central Committee, accepted Copeman's point, obtained a weapon, and took up the duties of an ordinary rifleman. He told Copeman, "I'm not going to be hanging around like these other blokes."[82] Nor did he. At Calaceite, Walter Gregory's last sight of Tapsell was firing at enemy tanks. In his view, Tapsell was "surely the greatest of all those who served as political commissars in Spain."[83] To many he epitomized the slogan of the commissars, "I was first to advance and last to retreat."[84]

Although some may have obeyed Copeman out of fear, most followed him willingly. Charlotte Haldane visited Copeman when he was hospitalized on the eve of the battle of Teruel in December 1937. She had worked clandestinely in Paris, taking on the critical party responsibility of reporting on the personal and political reliability of British volunteers as well as arranging their transit to Spain. She had heard much about the former naval rating, great stories "of his physical and moral courage, and his devotion to the men under his leadership, which they reciprocated." Haldane, who had personally interviewed more than 150 of the British volunteers in Paris on their way to Spain, and stayed in close contact with those veterans who returned to Britain, said, "I did not want to leave Spain without having brought him the affectionate greetings of his comrades at home."[85]

Tom Wintringham had no hesitation in saying, "Fred Copeman is one of the strongest men, physically and morally, that I know."[86] But although Copeman may have had a warm place in the hearts of many under his command, he was indeed a "rough diamond." A confidential assessment of Copeman in his file in Moscow reported that "he had both good and weak points," noting particularly, "he had little military knowledge." But "when he wants, he is able to command."[87]

Copeman's philosophy of leadership was both effective and simple. Meeting with each company commander, "My job was to tell him what I wanted done and then he had to do it. And he was the same with his section leaders. And it was the same with the machine gun crews." Ultimately, Copeman said, "The discipline came from individuals who themselves were leaders in their own way." He also knew that a commander's words had to be backed by action. "They take advantage of somebody that's not what [he] should be. They don't take advantage of a fellow that's all fire and bloody go and not just bluff." He said, "There's a vast difference with a fellow who gets among them when the bullets are flying and gets on with it. And they want to be with him."[88]

Copeman's first action was to clear the trenches of Spanish women who had accompanied their men into combat, or who themselves had come to fight.[89] From his point of view, the women threatened military efficiency. Syd Quinn had been astonished to see women in action at Lopera.[90] Walter Gregory said that in the early battles for Madrid he saw women in the front line.[91] Alf Salisbury confirms that he fought alongside women in the first days.[92] Later, at the Jarama, Tom Clarke from Fife remembered that when elements of the British Battalion fell back in retreat, he and his comrades saw a machine gun being fired resolutely by three Spanish women, which both shamed them and considerably stiffened their resolve.[93] Copeman's decision to send the women away "caused a riot among the Spaniards."[94] Once the women were ousted, Copeman set about establishing disciplinary rules for the volunteers, who regarded themselves as an army of equals. Jason Gurney had already found that during the training at Madrigueras, discipline was "extraordinarily slack."[95] Copeman's rules were meant to be "simple." He called a general meeting and explained that if the Republic was going to win, discipline must be accepted by each man, especially since the International Brigades had now become part of the Popular Army. Walter Gregory admitted that "his firm, almost authoritarian, style was probably one which the Battalion needed most at the time."[96] This style required saluting, which was anathema to many volunteers. The party explained, however, that "a salute is a sign that a comrade who has been an egocentric individualist in private life has adjusted to the collective way of getting things done."[97] When he became Jock Cunningham's second-in-command, Copeman told the battalion in his typical blunt fashion, "If you don't like saluting me, I will salute you first but you must salute because that's now the order. You have been ignoring officers but we are now in the Spanish army, so salute."[98] In the middle of May he knocked out a drunken Scot who would not return his military greeting.

Copeman made two other inflexible rules. First, no one in his command was to be shot for desertion.[99] Copeman understood that there were those who simply could not function effectively on a battlefield: "I never judge a fellow who can't stand it." He said, "You can or you can't, and in a volunteer army [it's] bloody ridiculous to shoot everybody who doesn't go marching on and on," as the Russians were accustomed to doing.[100] Yet, when the military situation dictated it, Copeman acted decisively. After the murderous first day of the Jarama, Copeman told a number of men who had taken refuge in huge wine vats, and who refused to listen to his remonstrations, that he intended to drop grenades underneath them, which achieved the desired result of immediately restoring a number of effectives to the battlefield.[101]

The worst that could happen to a volunteer under Copeman's leadership was to be sent home in disgrace, which some feared more than Franco's bullets. For example, Albert Cole, a sailor turned soldier, had been mistakenly jailed for overstaying his leave. He wrote to Bill Rust, asking him to clear up the misunderstanding, or "I don't think I would ever go home to face the Liverpool workers if I thought for one moment, that they would be able to say I done [sic] anything detrimental to the Republic or committed any act at all that classed me as an enemy of the Spanish people or government."[102] Typically, Copeman would order a deserter to dig a trench as punishment. Because men would often overstay their leaves, or simply decamp for a week or two to Madrid or Barcelona, each month Copeman would send three lorries to the two cities and round up those who were missing, usually easily located in the brothels and cafes. Again, the punishment was to "dig the old trench."

The second "hard and fast rule" was that no prisoners taken by the battalion were to be harmed. Copeman was aware that other battalions in the International Brigades took a very different view. The German and Italian volunteers knew what it was like to live in a fascist dictatorship. "So they had a ruthlessness when they arrived, which wasn't in the British, American, [and Canadians]."[103] Nevertheless, Copeman believed that all the national battalions, including the Americans and Canadians, resorted to executions for disciplinary reasons.

It was true that Copeman's military abilities were limited.[104] Other commanders of the battalion such as Peter Daly had more military experience. But Copeman, and later Sam Wild, both with glaring personal shortcomings, exemplified Correlli Barnett's definition of a leader who possesses

> a psychological force that has nothing to do with morals or good character or even intelligence: nothing to do with ideals or idealism. It is a matter of relative will powers, a basic connection between one animal and the rest of the herd. Leadership is a process by which a single aim and unified

action are imported to the herd. Not surprisingly it is most in evidence in times or circumstances of danger or challenge. Leadership is not imposed like authority. It is actually welcomed and wanted by the led.[105]

Tom Wintringham, the battalion's first commander and later a well-known commentator on military affairs, wrote: "The commander of the English battalion was partly, as any commander is, a creation of his battalion, a person trying continually (if seldom consciously) to be what his men needed and unconsciously desired."[106]

The Oxford-educated Wintringham was to be in command only a few days before being wounded. The ten men who followed him in command had working-class backgrounds, proving "the English Captain's" point that a commander was the "creation" of those who followed him. After Wintringham was wounded on the second day of the Jarama, Jock Cunningham succeeded him. When Cunningham fell, Copeman took command, although he had been hit twice himself. He acknowledged that the party "appointed" him to command the battalion, but "it would have been a bit funny if anybody else was." Whoever was in command, he said, the men had to approve it. "Once we'd got over the early stages of old Tom Wintringham and Macartney the battalion commanders were almost [always] elected by the men."[107]

This did not mean, however, that an officer class in the customary sense developed. The respect was accorded to each officer as an individual. According to Jim Brewer, "You'd be prepared to regard them as an officer because you knew they were prepared. They weren't prepared to put you where they wouldn't go themselves." The former Welsh miner could say quite dispassionately, "I have had vast experience of warfare . . . and these chaps were definitely born leaders."[108] One veteran of Spain who served in the British army in World War II remarked at the contrast with Spain, "There were no classes and no 'sirs' [in Spain]. . . . We built our army from nothing. Its laws and regulations we developed to suit our needs, the needs of the people."[109]

Nevertheless, in daily life, the battalion appeared very similar to a capitalist army. The leadership established separate eating facilities for officers and other ranks. Although Sam Wild, who was to command the battalion after Bill Alexander was wounded, significantly relaxed Copeman's rules, the segregation of meals continued, much to the anger of some who insisted they had volunteered to serve in a revolutionary army.

V

Before the battle of Brunete in July 1937, Copeman feared that his command was disintegrating. No fresh recruits were coming in. The long months in the Jarama trenches after the great battles in February had taken their toll on morale. It was then that Alex McDade from Glasgow wrote his famous lyrics to "The Jarama," which was sung to the tune of the American song, "Red River Valley":

> There's a valley in Spain called Jarama
> That's a place that we all know so well,
> For 'tis there that we wasted our manhood,
> And most of our old age as well.
>
> You will never be happy with strangers,
> They would not understand you as we,
> So remember the Jarama Valley
> And the old men who wait patiently.

New cadres did arrive to join the "old men," however, and the British Battalion was back up to strength by July, enabling Copeman to be at his most optimistic before the battle. "Brunete was an action where we had everything. We had the arms. . . . Every man was trained and the commanders knew their job. And they were all in the right place." Each leader, from the sections to the platoons to the companies, and the adjutant occupied their positions of responsibility "because they were that much better than the next one below. And they were there because they were better than the fellow below them."[110] Copeman believed that these appointments demonstrated that leadership was not a matter of courage alone. It required intelligence as well, a quality not exclusive to middle-class comrades.

Copeman would demonstrate this conviction by the men he chose to fight beside, to socialize with, and most of all, by the manner in which he isolated middle-class and some working-class intellectuals in the battalion from their comrades. As a result of the uneasy mixing of temperaments before Brunete, Copeman decided to impose a kind of apartheid. He created a new unit, the Anti-Tank Battery, separate from the battalion and reporting to the brigade command. The Anti-Tanks were composed of "good-looking students," all chosen by Copeman. They lived separately from the battalion for the simple reason that Copeman thought they would be more comfortable with comrades of their own interests—and, correspondingly, volunteers in the battalion with more usual interests would not be made to feel inferior. One of the latter, Tommy Fanning, an ex-soldier, had once said, "I never talk about what I don't know. . . . I'm not claiming to be an intellectual Marxist."[111] Copeman wanted men such as Fanning to know that the battalion belonged to them.

Copeman called those middle- and working-class volunteers assigned to the Anti-Tanks "intellectuals." As such, "They tended to discuss with each other and not with the mass of blokes." To him, the issue seemed to decide itself. "If they're going to do a job, why not give them a job they'll like. They'll be together. They'll talk much higher intellectually than us." Also, this separation would make life easier for Copeman. "If they've got any problems, then they'll sort them out among their bloody selves." The acutely observant Fred Thomas, who served with the Anti-Tank Battery from the time of its creation to its dissolution, neatly parsed Copeman's difficulty: "For years we had sung, and some even believed, that 'The emancipation of the Working Class is the task of the Workers alone' and everyone [realized] that intellectuals were not workers."[112]

To command the Anti-Tanks, Copeman selected from the young middle-class volunteers "the best-looking one of the lot," Malcolm Dunbar. It was an unbelievably fortunate choice. Dunbar became one of the most exceptional strategists and fearless soldiers in the International Brigades. From Fred Copeman's point of view, however, he was just the sort of man who would make an ordinary worker feel insecure about his abilities. According to the proletarian commissars, Dunbar took "an intellectual approach and argued for the sake of argument."[113] Officially, the appointment "was a tribute to Dunbar's capacity . . . to command the unit," although it was admitted "he had not previously served with the artillery."[114] Of more importance to Copeman than his potential as a soldier were his university accent, the neatness of his appearance, and his romantic good looks—all of which reminded the American reporter Vincent Sheean of a young officer in the long-running London play, *Journey's End*.[115]

In a few handwritten pages in Dunbar's Moscow file, we learn more about this enigmatic figure. Dunbar revealed that behind his irresponsible Chelsea façade was a serious man. He first became interested in the labor movement while working as a photographer and journalist from 1933 to 1936, when he "made many friends in the left wing movements, chiefly the C.P. though [he himself] was not actually a member of the Party." The police arrested him while demonstrating against Mosley in the "Battle of Cable Street," although his press card got him released almost immediately.[116]

Understandably, Dunbar did not communicate easily with those who did not share his intellectual and cultural interests, and there apparently was an element of genuine shyness in him. The American John Gates believed he had a "fear of people."[117] Jack Jones thought him "aristocratic."[118] He became a close friend of the American volunteer Leonard Lamb, however, who remembered, "It was good to talk to him; he was an intellectual; he knew something about books and we could sustain a conversation." For Lamb, who had graduated with a degree in English literature from Brooklyn College, the British volunteer "was quite a change."[119] Frank Graham, whose background was working class although he studied at Kings College, London, believed that the very qualities that attracted Lamb to Dunbar prevented him from becoming an effective leader. The equation was simple. He said, "Dunbar was an intellectual; [therefore] he couldn't lead anybody."[120]

Malcolm Dunbar's commissar and successor in command of the Anti-Tanks was the writer Hugh Slater. Asked to describe him, Sam Wild replied, "Middle class, college education, accent."[121] Slater attended Tonbridge and London University before working for *Imprecor* and contributing to the *Left Review*. He later became a novelist.[122] Slater, like Dunbar, was "extremely good-looking."[123] The miner-poet Hugh Sloan, also in the Anti-Tanks, found Slater remote and difficult to know. But, in a view not universally shared, Sloan believed that he was one of the best men in Spain.[124]

Another factor that may have motivated Copeman to form a separate unit was the homosexuality of some middle-class volunteers. Copeman sturdily asserted that he had no prejudice against volunteers of this sexual orientation, citing his years in the navy as proof of his wide knowledge and acceptance of the varieties of human behavior. But there is no doubt that general ignorance of and aversion to homosexuality was an aspect of working-class culture. Most workers, even including a middle-class writer such as Orwell, invariably denounced a "nancy." Within some working-class communities, a worker who developed a pronounced interest in books, music, or the arts was judged to have revealed his true sexual nature. Robert Roberts writes that such interests were sufficient to make anyone suspect in his native Salford and went so far as to say, "This linking of homosexuality with culture played some part, I believe, in keeping the lower working class as near-illiterate as they were."[125] At any rate, this assumption could have been yet another reason for segregating middle-class intellectuals and the better educated among the workers from the rest of the battalion.

Fred Copeman may have thought he had solved his command problems by establishing the young students, graduates, and educated workers in a separate military unit, but this was not the case. Although the morale of the Anti-Tanks was consistently high because they saw themselves as an elite and highly effective unit, they were not the harmonious group that Copeman imagined them to be. For instance, Dunbar's attitudes could be all too representative of his class. According to the plainspoken American John Murra, who later became an anthropologist, Dunbar held John Gates, the brave, tough, and effective American commissar, in contempt, not for his shortcomings, but rather because the Cambridge intellectual "couldn't stand . . . this tailor Jewish boy from New York."[126]

That the writer Hugh Slater knew his job, there was little doubt. But his ability to understand and gain the cooperation of his working-class subordinates was severely limited. A Durham miner who had been with the battalion from the start, and was described as a "good proletarian type," was forced to leave the Anti-Tanks "because of differences with Slater."[127] Another comrade in the Anti-Tanks, Jim Brewer, despised the young officer. Brewer had gone into the pits at fourteen but then took advantage of virtually every working-class educational opportunity available to him, including Ruskin College at Oxford, before volunteering for Spain. The former miner was one of the most independent thinkers in the battalion. One of his friends, whom Brewer knew to be a brave man and one of the few among the British volunteers who could speak Spanish, got into a political argument with Slater. As a result, the imperious commissar threatened to have him shot. In Brewer's view, Slater had exhibited the temperament of a Danton or Robespierre. Brewer's friend managed to escape from Spain, and in his farewell, said he had not volunteered to defend the Republic in order to be threatened "by a bloody fool like that" just "because he dislikes my attitude."[128] In its final evaluation of Slater, the commissariat lauded him as "a leader almost of genius" but "with insufficient judgement of men." In addition, he was not reluctant to seek his own comforts, "which had a bad effect on his unit."[129]

Brewer reserved his praise for those who, in addition to being good soldiers, were without pretension. He warmed to the Merseysiders because "they were all people that I instinctively liked as dependable people, devoid of a lot of flummery."[130] One of Brewer's fellow soldiers, Hugh Sloan, despite his admiration of Slater and, one presumes, of Dunbar, also recognized that neither made any effort to disguise his contempt for working men. According to Sloan, the two constantly made fun of and condescended to their worker-comrades. It is easy to imagine the reaction this kind of attitude would elicit. Harry Stratton, a taxidriver from Swansea who fought in Spain, said, "Public school accents and the assumption of superiority by some types always got up my nose. I didn't see why anyone, myself included, should be treated as an inferior being."[131]

Regardless of the tensions in the Anti-Tank unit, it was enormously effective in battle. Jim Brewer, who fought throughout both the Spanish War and World War II, wrote to Bill Alexander, a commander of the Anti-Tanks, subsequently of the British Battalion, and later a captain in World War II, that the Anti-Tanks were "the best unit we ever served in."[132]

Copeman, understandably, was pleased. He was particularly impressed, and perhaps surprised, by the Anti-Tanks' behavior under fire. "They had plenty of courage. You know, they weren't dodgers." From his perspective, "They just happened to be intellectuals who in my opinion had a job to do and could do it better among themselves." Otherwise, they "would just be lost among a bunch of roughnecks. And that's why they were there." However, among the repertoire of International Brigade songs was one expressing the belief that, ultimately, the battle was that of the workers to fight and win.

As man is only human,
He must eat before he can think.
Fine words are only empty air
And not his meat and drink.

As man is only human,
He'd rather not have boots in his face.
He wants no slaves at his beck and call,
Nor life by a master's grace.

And since a worker's a worker,
No class can free him but his own;

The emancipation of the working-class,
Is the task of the workers alone![133]

The traditional ascendancy of the middle and upper classes in British society had been successfully challenged in the British Battalion. And Copeman intended to secure his victory when he recruited in England. When reminded of the popular view that the battalion was composed mostly of young intellectuals, Copeman conceded that "in the early days" many of the men were indeed students. But when returning to Great Britain, he said, those "I recruited weren't students at all. There might have been a few. But most of them were . . . ordinary working-class lads, lads who I had known on hunger marches and things like that."[134]

The latter were the men he felt he could depend upon. One of the Hunger March veterans who fought in Spain spoke of the class solidarity that the marches encouraged. "The coarseness of a single blanket seem[ed] a small price to pay for membership in such a marvellous band of men."[135] This was the kind of experience for which Copeman was looking.[136] He knew that unemployment was not their choice, and certainly did not define them as men. George Orwell understood that "the English are a conscience-ridden race, with a strong sense of the sinfulness of poverty. One cannot imagine the average Englishman deliberately turning parasite, and this national character does not necessarily change because a man is thrown out of work."[137] The unemployed were, nevertheless, victimized twofold—by their economic plight and by middle-class stereotypes imposed upon them. Now, in Spain they could fight back. Benny Goodman of Manchester said, "You've got to fight to live and if you don't fight you're a dead duck."[138] A Middlesbrough comrade said that the call for reinforcements of the battalion toward the end of 1937 was simply a matter of a transfer "from the struggle at home to the struggle there."[139] Both volunteers discovered working-class comrades who were fellow fighters against an unjust and exploitative system.

Copeman knew his men and they knew him. Social identification and class pride possessed enormous power for those who had experienced the despair of powerlessness. His praise for one of his class who had demonstrated qualities of leadership and courage knew no bounds. "Jock Cunningham," he said, "was kind of worshipped. He was the bees knees mate. This lad was some thing and [had] the courage of a bloody lion; and the fellows liked him, followed him, would do anything for him." The Dubliner, Joe Monks, who fought with Cunningham in the battles for Madrid, added that Jock was one "of the makers of that military magic" who saved the great city.[140]

Copeman felt much the same way about Sam Wild. It was with Cunningham, Wild, and other working-class comrades who had proved themselves in the "struggle" that he found his proper milieu and helped to forge in Spain an alternative culture, based on leadership, ability, and courage, and not on education and privilege. Copeman said, "We are not going to save any bloody system. We want a different system . . . where people work for each other, not work for bloody profit that [is] immoral."[141] As the historian Victor Kiernan once wrote, "The workers' revolution feared by so many conservatives after the Great War was now breaking out under Spanish skies instead of British skies—the single armed uprising in the history of the modern British working class."[142]

Copeman understood, therefore, that the British needed "down-to-earth" leaders. This contrasted with the Lincolns, whose officers, he said, "were top intellects." According to him, "Ours were the opposite." The results proved impressive. The British became "the finest battalion in the brigade. . . . In every action they were the last to be withdrawn. Commanders don't use a battalion like that unless it's a good one."[143]

Manchester's Ralph Cantor also felt a new confidence in his class. Cantor was a twenty-one-year-old working-class musician and poet who became a militant antifascist through his work with the Sheffield Youth Congress against War and Fascism. He was one of the first from Manchester to volunteer, and fought under George Nathan's command at Lopera.[144] Cantor confided in his diary that all who had been "sent out direct to big positions fail," something that the "boys [were] all conscious of." Men who had been "boosted" such as Macartney, Wintringham, Kerrigan, and others had proved themselves to some degree or another lacking. But "men from the ranks produce the best and most courageous leaders [such as] Nathan, Cunningham, Copeman, Goodfellow, [and] Meredith." On April 12, 1937, Cantor quoted Lenin, "Only the working class can bring about its own emancipation." He added, "It appears that only workers who are free from bourgeois influence and upbringing can really lead such sharp struggles."[145] And, Cantor would have agreed, only a proletarian intellectual could write about them. The next day Cantor was pleased to note that an American publication had accepted one of his poems, although he would not live to see its publication.

Copeman and Cantor believed that in Spain, at last, the working class had become the creators of its own culture (as well as its literary representations).[146] Under Copeman's leadership, then, the battalion became self-consciously working class. This did not mean, however, that military egalitarianism prevailed. On May 2, 1937, Ralph Cantor, who (as we have seen) admired the proletarian leadership of the battalion, wrote in his diary that a "disturbing feature of the war is the distinctions [sic] which are too acute for justification. A Sergeant receives more than double a volunteer. An officer more than 4 times as much and higher officers more." Cantor also complained about "acute distinctions in food and accommodation" between officers and the ranks, and acknowledged that there was "grumbling over separate doors for officers and men in one case." As for the brigade newspaper, *Volunteer for Liberty*, it was "almost a fashion plate weekly for the officers."[147]

When Billy Griffiths joined the battalion in the spring of 1938, he found the regular meal served to the ranks to consist of beans, lentils, bread, and coffee. Upon sitting down to lunch with the battalion staff, the ex-miner found a very different cuisine. Bread fried in olive oil, a fried egg (the second one he had had since arriving in Spain), and lamb chops, all topped with cherries and cream. Supper was "of the same standard." The table was set with knives and forks, cloth and china. Wine was served. After three days of this treatment, to which he was entitled as secretary of education of the party, although bearing only the rank of a private, he encountered a friend who had become ill because of the harsh diet served to the rank and file. Reflecting that he was "living like a lord," Griffiths returned to the fare provided for ordinary soldiers but, as a good party man, refused to criticize the battalion leadership (although he would do so freely later).[148] One can only conclude that men of the British Battalion, for the most part, accepted the unequal situation.

Regardless, there was a profound sense of class pride in the battalion. When a section of the British line was withdrawn for a rest at Brunete, they were asked to return immediately to prevent a fascist breakthrough, which, after an exhortation from Jock Cunningham, they agreed to do. The battalion commissar, Wally Tapsell, said afterwards, "If it was a tough job, well we reckoned we were a tough mob."[149] And so they were.

Copeman recognized the obvious, of course. There *were* class differences among those he led, but he believed that class segregation would make men on both sides of the barrier more comfortable, while helping them both to achieve the common goal of defeating fascism. This did not mean, however, that such barriers were always in place. When men were off duty, Copeman encouraged the classes to mix. "We meet every night and talk about every bloody thing in heaven and hell." These conversations included "the finest brains in the world and the dumbest brain[s] there." Figures such as "Haldane, scientists, poets, authors" and Copeman's fellow workers were "all equal to one another."[150]

Workers, not their middle-class comrades, felt at home in this new society. Both, however, were to achieve a liberation from the constraints of class that they had never before known. Jason Gurney expressed the awkwardness felt by his middle-class comrades among the workers, but also the resulting new freedom:

> The position of a middle-class person in a working-class movement is always anomalous, particularly in such a class-obsessed country as England. It involves an elaborate pattern of pretence on both sides which is embarrassing and absurd. It is ridiculous to pretend that class differences do not exist; above all, in a movement which is primarily concerned with the class struggle. One is constantly embarrassed by the fear of appearing to patronize and of being patronized.

Yet, he said, "here in Spain one was free of the whole thing." He tasted the same sweet exultation as Spender, when he wrote, "In Spain I was simply one of an undifferentiated mass, joined together in a common cause to fight and struggle for an ideal that was infinitely larger than any of us."[151]

CHAPTER 11

We Are Not After All Alone

BRUNETE—JULY 1937

QUINTO—AUGUST 1937

BELCHITE—SEPTEMBER 1937

TERUEL—DECEMBER 1937

SEGURA DE LOS BAÑOS—
    FEBRUARY 1938

[There were] all kinds of people in the battalion. We had playwrights, writers, quite a number of university dons [who] dabbled in all sorts of things, and we also had quite a few working class philosophers [who] during the days of unemployment and bumming around the world had secured quite a philosophical outlook.
— Sam Wild, Commander of the British Battalion

I

In the end, however, Copeman allowed himself to be blinded by his class prejudices. There *were* examples of middle-class volunteers who could successfully assimilate into the life of the battalion. John Cornford, the brilliant young Cambridge historian and great-grandson of Darwin, was one. Cornford already possessed a formidable reputation for having been one of the first to fight in Spain in the summer of 1936, and then to have left the country and returned with recruits for the bloody battles around University City in November. When he arrived at Madrigueras, he joined his fellow volunteers in sleeping "very rough." Tom Wintringham, serving on the battalion staff, discovered Cornford's presence among the rank and file, and sent one of his runners to invite him to dinner at battalion headquarters, an invitation not extended to any of Cornford's working-class comrades. Maurice Levine of Manchester, who slept on the same floor with Cornford, remembered "very clearly" the young poet's response. He "politely turned him down."[1]

There were others, too, who made the connection. Like Orwell, Lewis Clive had been educated at Eton. A descendant of Clive of India, he went up to Christ Church, rowed for Oxford, and won a gold medal for England in the 1932 Olympics in Los Angeles. He then worked for the New Fabian Research Bureau, wrote a book, *The People's Army*, and became a Labour councillor in North Kensington.[2] Unlike Malcolm Dunbar and Hugh Slater, Clive was utterly without condescension and, because of his manner and efficiency, maintained a particularly good relationship with the trade union leader, Jack Jones, with whom he often talked. They did disagree, however, on how to address Jim Middleton, the secretary of the Labour party, Clive holding out for "dear Middleton," which Jones thought "snobbish and upper-class." Jones wanted to call him "comrade Middleton." Clive won. By the time Middleton received the letter, however, Clive was dead and Jones was wounded, both on Hill 481 in the Ebro battle.[3]

Another who "connected" was David Guest, who took a first-class honors degree in mathematics at Cambridge. Son of the Islington Labour M.P., he had seen fascism at work in the streets of Germany and subsequently joined the Communist party. He made a place for himself in the working-class movement as a delegate to the Trades Council and an indefatigable worker for the party in Battersea. In reviewing his reasons for going to Spain, Guest said, "There is . . . the need to show that there is no division between party 'workers' and 'intellectuals' over this matter, particularly in view of the large number of young workers who have gone from Battersea."[4] He, like Cornford and Clive, bridged the two cultures. The young mathematician was thinking of Auden's poem, *Spain*, when he wrote home: "I have . . . a lively desire to explore whole fields of theoretical work, mathematical, physical, logical. . . . But, of course, this is not possible now—'to-day the struggle.'"[5]

There is further evidence that life in the battalion did not remain as compartmentalized as Copeman planned. Jim Brewer, who served from the Jarama to the final parade in Barcelona, believed that there was a real contrast between the British and other International Brigade battalions. In the latter, the officer corps formed a class apart, while among the British "there was that intimate contact all the time."[6] The men in the British Battalion felt that their officers, for the most part, had earned their right to lead. They had to do so because there was a fundamental "anti-officer complex" among the British volunteers. Upon meeting leaders who commanded respect, regardless of class—such as George Nathan, Fred Copeman, Malcolm Dunbar, Sam Wild, and George Fletcher—the men naturally accorded it, and accepted the distinctions that emerged.

J. R. Jump, a twenty-one-year-old journalist and poet, arrived late in Spain and no longer wondered if a connection between the classes was possible. He found himself serving with "miners, shipyard workers, sailors, students, shop assistants, clerks, waiters and former members of the British army and the R.A.F. I remember two Labour councillors, three poets and one author."[7] Walter Gregory judged that in Spain "our intimacy was genuine, not contrived," by contrast with his lower-deck experience in the navy during World War II, which he found to be a recapitulation of all the petty class divisions in English life, "a microcosm of British society."[8] Certainly, then, volunteers from both working- and middle-class backgrounds found a new polity emerging whether the working-class leadership wanted it or not. One who had worked and waited and sacrificed for most of his adult life to see this was the novelist, Ralph Bates.

II

Ralph Bates joined Fred Copeman and Ralph Cantor on the battlefield of Brunete. Bates was one of the most gifted, interesting, and politically influential Englishmen in Spain during the early part of the Civil War. His introduction to "Frank Pitcairn's" *Reporter in Spain*, therefore, strikes the reader as more than a little disingenuous. Bates writes, "I shall be expected to speak as a novelist, not as a politician, which indeed I am not."[9] In one sense this was true, but in other respects quite the opposite. Bates said publicly that by virtue of his vocation and his support of democracy and its institutions, he bore a responsibility to play a part in the Spanish War. Having alerted society to the dangers that threatened it, writers were "responsible for the fact that hundreds of thousands are now dead because they refused to live under fascism."[10] In "bearing witness," Bates, too, had made a political choice, which was to involve him in much controversy regarding his role in Spain.

Bates is perhaps known chiefly today, and unfairly, because of George Orwell's bitter denunciation of him in *Homage to Catalonia*. Orwell excoriated Bates for accusing the POUM militia of irresponsibly abandoning its military positions and playing football with the fascists in no man's land. This, at a time, "when, as a matter of fact, the POUM troops were suffering heavy casualties and a number of my personal friends were killed and wounded," Orwell writes.[11] Bates acknowledged much later that he had been misinformed by his wife, Winifred, a devout Stalinist, concerning the activities of the POUM.[12]

As the assistant political commissar of the XVth Brigade, Bates carried important responsibilities. He was, however, in certain respects a shadowy and mysterious figure, and therefore easy to misunderstand. Stephen Spender once felt moved to say that Bates was an example of a good writer and a good man whom the Communist party turned into a killer.[13] In his autobiography, Spender is apparently referring to Bates when describing a fellow delegate at the Writers' Congress in the summer of 1937. Although reeking a bit of conceit, Bates seemed to Spender an attractive and cultivated man. Therefore, the poet felt particular dismay when Bates confided in him that he had recently sent a reluctant young volunteer into a sector of the fighting in which he was certain to be killed. Spender did not believe that Bates could have the authority to make such a decision, but, in fact, he did. (On this point, an early British volunteer bitterly remarked that the commissars "hold in their hands the power of life and death."[14]) Spender concluded that Bates' "telling was the showing off of a literary man who had tasted a little power."[15] Far from simply being a literary man in Spain, however, Bates was well aware of his political importance. At an early stage of the formation of the British Battalion, Bates wrote to Harry Pollitt, reminding him that he was "the leading English party member here now that T. W. [Tom Wintringham] has gone." Bates informed Pollitt that as a matter of policy, "At the front deserters are shot, if caught, whether foreign or Spanish."[16]

Bates professes, however, not to have actually been a member of the party. Yet in his public role in Spain he appeared indistinguishable from a high-ranking communist. He had lived for years in Catalonia, where he came to have a special affection for and political working relationship with the anarchists. With this experience, one would have expected a more acute understanding of the events leading to the liquidation of the POUM by the communists in May 1937 than he appears to have had. When he spoke to the battalion, as he did on several occasions, he merely reiterated the standard party clichés about the perfidies of the POUM. Ralph Cantor records in his diary on May 14, 1937, that in Bates' lecture on "Disorders in Catalonia," the novelist presented the case that the "P.O.U.M., Trotskyists and spies engineered it." A week later Bates reassured the battalion that the government was well in control of the situation, which Cantor refused to accept. He wrote, "It is clear that despite Bates['] denials that the Government problem [in Catalonia] is still unsettled." Nevertheless, Cantor conceded that Bates had delivered a "very able speech."[17]

Certainly, there was no one else like Ralph Bates among the British in Spain. Alone among the British intellectuals who played an active role in the war, he had made his home in Spain for many years, spoke several of the Iberian languages with idiomatic fluency, and knew virtually the entire Spanish political and intellectual establishment. He was already the author of two enduring novels about Spain, *Lean Men* and *The Olive Field*.[18] The American, Edwin Rolfe, wrote home that Bates "knows more about Spain than any Englishman or Canadian or American in the country."[19] Bates wrote:

> My memory goes back to the dictatorship of Primo, Berenguer, of Alonso. Just before the monarchy fell [April 14, 1931] I walked month after month, throughout a year, twelve hundred miles, through the immense, almost unknown, the "lost" Cordilleras of Spain, to find how Spaniards live. I dare to say that I know more about the life and work of Spanish shepherds, olive workers, ploughmen, peasants, than these Englishmen whom I find talking of a "glorious Spanish tradition" and its fascist champions. I believe I know the real tradition, the way olives are grown, wine made, cork gathered, what songs are sung for the picking of figs, or the herding of cattle. I know, because I have followed them, by what immemorial tracks the sheep flocks go up in summer from the red choking plains to the hills.[20]

Although his novels had been translated into a number of foreign languages, Spanish, oddly, had not been one of them. His unique access to the highest levels of the Republican government was due more to his general reputation as a well-traveled intellectual with an astonishingly intimate knowledge of Spain than to any specific acquaintance with his work among the Spaniards.

Early in the war Bates held the effective rank of a subcabinet officer in the Spanish government. He also was named the first editor of *Volunteer for Liberty*, the official newspaper of the XVth Brigade. A whirlwind of energy, florid in complexion, and with a neat shock of blond hair and a carefully maintained mustache, he possessed an evangelical temperament and a natural fluency of expression that made him a powerful advocate for the Republic in virtually any milieu.[21] For example, Leo Gordon, a tough Brooklynite who had worked odd jobs wherever he could find them throughout the United States, met Bates in Spain and described him as a "regular guy."[22] This was no small tribute. Gordon undoubtedly knew little, if anything, about Bates' background, and therefore must have assumed his accent to be upper class, thus identifying him with the stereotypical English "gent."[23]

Bates also impressed the sardonic Keith Scott Watson. A young Englishman educated at the University of London and widely traveled in Germany and Soviet Russia, Watson took part in the early fighting, and subsequently fled from it. He then became a secretary to journalist Sefton Delmer, departed Spain, and promptly wrote a book about it all.[24] Watson found Bates to be a man of exceptional parts, a conclusion he arrived at when he observed the English writer sort out a leadership crisis which had flared up in the small English group assembled in Barcelona. He struck Scott Watson as "tall, stout, about forty, looking more like a master plumber than a revolutionary leader." The crisis was resolved, and the usually acerbic young writer confessed that he and his fellow soldiers were impressed by the Englishman, who had "won everyone completely in the few minutes he had been in the room." Comparing the demoralization created by the rusticated ex-leader with the effect of Bates' intervention, he said, "Just as our absent leader created distrust, so, with the same spontaneity, this ex-soldier, skilled artisan and revolutionary, whose novels are the finest on modern Spain, inspired it." Bates then offered some general remarks about the significance of the international presence in Spain, and Scott Watson offered the final encomium: "His analysis of the historic base of the war was brilliant in its simplicity." Bates endeared himself to them further when he saw them off on the train, and said in confident farewell, "I hope we shall meet in Madrid—and later in Seville or Burgos, best of luck to you all."[25]

Bates came to possess a remarkable prestige among both the Americans and English of the XVth Brigade. An American broadcast on November 17, 1937, called "A Letter from the Front" offered a retrospective on the English writer, spelling out the effect that Bates could have on those an American might say "knew the score." The broadcast extolling Bates' qualities was an extraordinary tribute, considering the tensions that existed between the British and American battalions.[26] Those listening on that early winter evening heard of a meeting between Bates and the George Washington Battalion that took place in June 1937. Gathered behind the Jarama trenches, the men of the Washington Battalion, who were to be virtually wiped out the next month at Brunete, waited for Bates to address them. They knew him from previous visits. And by now, these were not the untested boys and men of the previous February. The furious blood-letting that month in the valley of the Jarama, caused in no small part by the ineptitude of the higher command, and the long, slow attrition that took place in the trenches in the spring and early summer, had encouraged the cynicism felt by every soldier. But Bates had earned a special place in their affection and esteem. His books "were known to us." The Americans were fascinated by the fact that, unlike most of the traveling literary men, he was a soldier who had experienced danger and spent years acquiring an understanding of Spanish life and customs. "He had fought at the front during the early days of the war." He had penetrated "deeply into the life of the masses." But, more than anything else, "his personality was of a type that appealed to us very much."[27]

His remarks were not those of a political gramophone, as Orwell said of other commissars, but a remarkable mixture of analysis, facts, and memory, the last consisting mostly of vignettes revealing the character and customs of the lives of Spanish peasants. Bates held the Americans spellbound. Even when he drifted away from his theme with other stories, not a noise was heard "because their taste was thick and sweet in the mouth of the man who recited them."[28]

The novelist's voice was at odds with his mature and thickening appearance, and hardly what one would expect from a speaker of such reputation. It "resembled the high, quick, eager, and uneven tones of a growing English school boy." But Bates commanded respect not only because of the unique authority of his experience, but also the fact that he himself had suffered class discrimination, and because his political views were rooted in a profound sense of individual worth.[29] Like his friend Malraux, Bates possessed the inestimable advantage of being able to present himself as a man of action as well as an artist. When he spoke and wrote of the war, he was not reluctant to reveal his private feelings and personal loyalties, yet was not preoccupied with them. Or rather, he saw them as something to be controlled and, if necessary, repressed if they were impediments to action. This was not the case with the poet Stephen Spender, who in unsparing Bloomsbury fashion condemned himself as a coward when staring across the frontier toward Spain from Port Bou. Later, Spender said he thought a dead soldier on the Jarama battlefield more suited for a kiss than a bullet.

In E. M. Forster's novel, *Howards End*, Helen Schlegel commented to her sister, Margaret, "The truth is that there is a great outer life that you and I have never touched—a life in which telegrams and anger count. Personal relations, that we think supreme, are not supreme there."[30] No British intellectual in Spain understood this better than Bates. The all-importance of personal relations—which Bloomsbury had embraced in order to win independence from the soul-destroying, busy hypocrisies of the Victorians, and which had brought Spender to the battalion in the first place—seemed disposable in this violent, politically dangerous world.

As a literary intellectual, Bates mediated through language the horrors that all but overwhelmed him. As the product of a working-class background, from which he fled to Spain, he brought to his lightly fictionalized account of the hellish battle of Brunete an exceptional empathy with ordinary people as well as an artist's ability to speak of that which Copeman and most of his comrades could only suffer silently. In addition, he was remarkably brave in action. After Brunete, Edwin Rolfe said, "He hates to do important work that involves no danger."[31] And yet he remained the artist. During the July battle, Bates spent an evening discussing one of Malraux's novels with a German friend. The following day his position was hit by a shell, and his friend fell upon him mortally wounded. As he stared in horror at the broken body, Bates mindlessly repeated a fragment of an old verse, "your bowels are like jeweled lizards . . . , your bowels are like jeweled lizards." And then he thought with a kind of dazed wonder, "It was the fragility of this body of watery cells and delicate filaments, and the hard sharpness of metal, which made me think of that verse."[32]

The explosion had burned off his eyelashes and part of his mustache, leaving him in a state of shock. "My brain was a kaleidoscope of red glass, shifting around, presenting a different pattern at every moment, but always of sharp triangles and pentagons of red glass." Bates nevertheless was able to help rally Spanish troops who were beginning to abandon their positions. He then stumbled upon a mortally wounded comrade whose pain had proved so unbearable that he had bitten through his lips. "I drew my pistol and held it to his ear and blessed him with sweet death." Bates' drugged mind wandered until he became barely coherent: "Sweet death," he thought, "that is comfortable as polished china upon white linen; beautiful as golden evenings and the hoot of outgoing ships upon a gleaming estuary."[33]

As Bates moved away from the dead soldier to straighten out the line, he found himself with four Belgians, two of whom were sisters who had disguised themselves in order to accompany their lovers to Spain. One of the girls was wounded. Bates bent over the young woman, whose breast was exposed:

> God, the contact of smooth skin upon hot, trembling fingers, tears were coming to the surface of my husk of flesh. In that moment I saw all their story, the four of them setting out from a slum in Antwerp, the tender, strong, shaven-headed girls in their lovers' clothing, crossing a fog-hidden canal by night into France. Dodging through France, hiding by day from the French police, at the command of despicable men. Crossing the phantom hills of midnight into Spain, and the months of fighting, of hurried loving, of fear, of weeping during the "nightwatches" and now this approaching thunderstorm of death. . . . Tears were watering my inner self, washing away the lacerating crystals of fatigue.

Bates, knowing they would stay until they were overrun by the enemy, ordered the four of them to evacuate the white house in which they had established themselves, even though it meant revealing an important position. What he had done was militarily irresponsible. But "[I] turned upon [my] conscience and my will and cast them out of me like alien things." The rewards proved sufficient: he had recovered his humanity. "I staggered across that brazen hill, but in my heart was the love, and the awareness of man's need of man, by compulsion of which we were fighting."[34]

This, beyond any other appeal of Spain, was the most important—the existence of an emerging society of men and women, bound together not by the artificial ties of class or race or nationality, but by their shared humanity. This is what the revolution and socialism meant to Bates. In the noble and timeless simplicity of this vision, ideology was of little importance. In *The Lean Men*, his character, Francis Charing, said that "the final value, deeper than love, is [the] realization that we are not after all alone. . . . If only we could understand—no, come in contact with one another—all duties, all privileges, all rights would disappear, all wrongs."[35]

III

Fred Copeman's active service came to an end at Brunete, as did that of his sternest critic, Jason Gurney. Both had breakdowns. In Gurney's case it was because of several incidents in which friends were "reduced to meat fragments."[36] Copeman commanded with his customary bravery and energy until he too began to collapse psycho-logically.[37] An incident that would have shaken the strongest was the death of Charlie Goodfellow. Copeman and Goodfellow were side by side when an artillery round took off his friend's head. After forty years the shock can still be heard in Copeman's voice. "His bloody brains are in my lap. His head is off. He has only got his neck."[38] Syd Quinn, who had fought at Lopera and the Jarama, spoke plainly about Copeman's deterioration in the latter stages of the Brunete offensive, which decimated the British Battalion. As the casualties mounted, Copeman "went off his nut." It became so bad that a soldier "couldn't take a crap without his permission," Quinn said. He wrote to Maurice Levine in 1975, "Copeman was breaking up—we could all see it coming. The poor bugger was on his own [and] didn't know which way to turn."[39] Quinn made this judgment without malice because, as an ex-serviceman, he undoubtedly realized that under the relent-less pressure of command responsibility even the bravest could falter. He said of Copeman, "We all had great admiration for him."[40]

After Brunete, Fred Copeman, Jock Cunningham, George Aitken, and Wally Tapsell were called back to England. After Copeman crossed from Boulogne to Folkeston on August 15, 1937, a Special Branch constable at Passport Control interrogated him about his service in Spain. Copeman told him that he commanded the British in the International Brigades. Asked if he was returning to Spain, Copeman replied, "I don't think so. It is a very responsible job and a great strain. I don't feel equal to it."[41] For Fred Copeman, this was an extraordinary admission.

By all accounts, the men found the greeting by the party leaders at King Street unrelievedly hostile. There was a ruthless examination of the leadership with particular venom directed at Jock Cunning-ham, who clearly had been overwhelmed in trying to control three battalions at Brunete. The humiliation heaped on this extraordinary warrior was a singular warning, unforgettable to those like Copeman who later broke from the party. In addition, the British had virtually mutinied over the incompetence of General Gal, the commander of the XVth Brigade. During the battle, the fiery Wally Tapsell charged Gal with not being "fit to command a troop of Brownies, let alone a People's Army."[42] The threat of the British Battalion's machine-gun company prevented Gal from executing the furious commissar on the spot.[43] After the King Street interview, only Copeman and Tapsell were allowed to return to Spain.

Copeman's stay in Great Britain after Brunete helped him recover his habitual élan. He was in demand as a speaker, possessing the oratorical skills essential to working-class leadership in Great Britain as well as Spain. His language was unadorned with rhetorical embellishments and frequently vulgar, but flowed from the experiences of working-class life. Skills that had proved so persuasive at Invergordon enabled Copeman to become one of the most effective advocates for the antifascist cause and the British Battalion. The Special Branch detectives who followed him from meeting to meeting recorded the scope of his speaking engagements and the manner in which he approached audiences, whether in Hyde Park or in the various meeting halls of London.

First and foremost, Copeman talked simply but rivetingly about his experiences in the war. Often, he would include anecdotes about volunteers from the particular locality in which he spoke. If there had been deaths, the parents often would be present and he would offer an undoubtedly bowdlerized version of how their sons had died, linking them and his audience in the most intimate way to the battlefields of a far-off place. In death as well as in life, class consciousness could be promoted.

Finally, Copeman's instinctively humane nature made his accounts of fascist atrocities or bombings in Spain almost unbearably moving. To one audience of a thousand, Copeman began with an account of what he had recently seen in Tortosa in the Aragón: "Not a wall in that town has been left standing as a result of the dastardly work of the Franco bombers. Every woman and child in the town has been killed. I walked along one street and I counted seven hundred and thirty dead bodies, all were those of women and kids. You could smell the town from miles away as the ruins were full of dead bodies which had lain there for days."[44] The remainder of his talk focused on his experiences as a combatant and commander in Spain. Thus, Copeman offered a powerful narrative to accompany the still photographs of the staring eyes of dead children or the faces of despair in a throng of refugees in films shown at Aid Spain rallies. Moreover, he was not fictional, but the real thing, a working-class hero.

On October 15, 1937, Copeman addressed a meeting of the Joint National Committee for Aid for Dependents at Kingsway Hall in London. Sitting in the audience was Sergeant Minikin from Special Branch, who listened attentively to Copeman's account of his fighting in Spain. According to Miniken, Copeman "went on to say that every volunteer who went to Spain had to break the National Government's laws to do so." He did not mean this as a warning, but as a challenge. The British commander said, "Bugger their laws—we want a spirit of rebellion in this country."[45]

IV

The appalling heat and casualties of Brunete, which ended in a stalemate, were followed in August by the Aragón offensive, in which the XVth Brigade played a small but significant part. The offensive was intended to take pressure off the northern front, where Franco was closing in on Santander and the great Basque industrial city of Bilbao. After the Lincoln Battalion took Quinto in the Aragón, the British found themselves in a savage fight for Pulburrel Hill, a strategically important position just east of the village, which resulted in success with the help of supporting fire from the Lincolns, Republican artillery, and, not least, the thirst of the defenders.

The battle of Belchite followed, engaging the Anti-Tanks heavily and leaving the town a monument to the viciousness and deadliness of modern warfare. It remains so today, appearing largely as it did in 1937, with stacks of rubble in the street, only the façades of many houses remaining, staircases reaching blindly for what once had been the floors above, and rooms whose ceilings disappear into spiraling clouds and the crystalline, blue Spanish sky.

Despite an ill-starred Republican operation against Fuentes de Ebro in October in which Spanish troops were clumsily and disastrously carried into battle by Soviet tanks, thereby outpacing the Canadians and British who both suffered heavy casualties, the battalion had recovered a good deal of its élan. One of its leaders told Peter Kerrigan that the battalion had finally managed to eliminate "our slovenly methods of training and general attitude toward discipline" which had crept in after Brunete.[46] Another wrote to him that "the situation here has improved considerably and the new leadership pulls better than the old."[47] When Copeman returned to Spain before the December battle of Teruel, he was in splendid form. Tom McWhirter, at the time base adjutant in Albacete, wrote of meeting him upon his return. "Fred has developed a lot since his journey home and a new man has returned to the struggle," concluding, "more power to his strength and he will be twice as usefull [sic]."[48] Shortly afterward, one of the base leaders wrote that the brigade leadership was so impressed by the improvement in the battalion that it called the British "the best" in the brigade. "The spirit," he said, "is grand."[49]

At the same time, certain things did not change. Copeman was endlessly profane, treating with perfect familiarity all of his comrades, regardless of rank, as if they were mates on one of his old ships. He believed that the quickest way to settle an argument was with his fists, a view shared by one of his successors, Sam Wild. But he, Jock Cunningham, Frank Ryan, and Sam Wild had each earned legendary reputations for their courage and leadership, and much was tolerated in them that might have been unacceptable in others.

Copeman would never again command the British in action, however. He came down with an acute case of appendicitis on the eve of Teruel in December 1937. There were few illusions left about where the journey of the British volunteers had led them. Spain was a killing ground. By this time, most of Syd Booth's friends who were politically active, including one with a wife and three children, were on their way to the war or already there. His epitaph for them read simply, "Most of them got killed."[50]

V

On December 17, 1937, the Republic launched an offensive in the snow and cold of Teruel during the worst winter Spain had experienced in twenty years, and took the small city with heavy losses. The attack was intended to thwart another Nationalist offensive aimed at Madrid. The town itself sits on a hill, oddly grand in the bleak terrain surrounding it, and yet irrepressibly prosaic, reminding the English correspondent, Henry Buckley, of "a sort of Spanish Buxton."[51]

During the assault on Teruel by Spanish troops, the XVth Brigade was held in reserve east of the provincial capital. The apparent victory caused the battalion to be sent by rail to the Aragón, only to hurry back in time to help contain what proved to be a successful counterattack by the Nationalists. In all of this blooding the British consolidated a well-deserved reputation for courage and efficiency. They were commended especially for their valor by Colonel José Modesto. Teruel, however, remained in the hands of the enemy.

Bill Alexander, an industrial chemist from a working-class background, received a battlefield promotion to captain and took command of the battalion. In the XVth Brigade's effort to prevent the recapture of Teruel, the British carried out a diversionary attack and

Alexander was wounded. Sam Wild replaced him, and became the last commander of the British Battalion. Wild had been a member of Copeman's machine-gun section at the Jarama and later a company commander under his leadership. He too was "a born leader," and, as such, saw no reason to emulate his predecessor. The ex-sailor and boilerman from the Paramount Theater in Manchester possessed his own special genius as a commander of men, as well as his own optimism that a new relationship was being forged between the classes on the battlefields of Spain. Wild once remarked that what bound together "workers and intellectuals . . . trained and untrained soldiers . . . all fighters for a new social order" was "unshakable unity."[52]

Unlike Copeman, Wild was comparatively indifferent to the trappings of leadership. According to Jim Brewer, who was to serve in the Western Desert and Italy as an officer, "Sam didn't give a damn whether he shaved or not, or whether his boots were polished or anything like that [because] he was too busy getting on with the job. He behaved like a real first class British officer in battle."[53] Yet it is difficult to imagine that an English officer would share Wild's philosophy of leadership: "I've always been a man that thought all human beings are beautiful until I find them out, then when I find them out I'll . . . kick them to death."[54] Nor was his toughness dissimulated. At the time of this comment, Wild had been wounded five times.

Certainly his anger at oppression was beyond question. During his travels in the British navy Wild saw native people "degraded." He said, "These experiences accentuated the sympathy I had for minorities and a feeling that something was terribly wrong with the world." Consequently, he took a greater interest in books and political change, particularly the Russian Revolution. Ultimately, his sense of estrangement from the symbols and institutions of British hegemony was complete. He "became anti-Queen, anti-King, anti-ruling class, [and] anti-officer." He deserted from the navy and was discharged "with ignominy," which Wild said, "was quite O.K. by me."[55] Brewer contrasted Wild with the middle-class commissar and later commander of the Anti-Tanks, Hugh Slater, who "was a travesty of an officer." An intimidating ideologue, Slater paid more attention to appearance than the importance of the task he was to perform.[56] This was not the case with Wild. Under his command, the British continued to fight bravely and well.

VI

The absence of Fred Copeman's vaunted discipline apparently made little difference to the effectiveness of the battalion, as the volunteers faced the battles and endured the hardships that awaited them with the aid of their own individual resources, new leaders, and, finally, the informal but highly effective leadership of Sam Wild. When J. R. Jump reached the Internationals in 1938, however, efforts were being made to restore saluting, which Copeman had once insisted upon. But, as far as Jump could tell, "nobody took much notice." The rank and file called their officers *Camarada* if they didn't know their Christian names. Moreover, "Off duty there was no gulf between officers and men. This camaraderie was even more apparent in the front line where everything was shared—food, tobacco and danger." In May 1938 Jump could say that despite the difficult conditions in which the battalion was living, including having to face the ubiquitous and undefeatable enemy of every combat soldier, lice,[57] "our discipline was good, though it was seldom imposed from above or, if it was, it was so skillfully done as to be hardly noticed." There were no fights, little drunkenness, even though spirits and wine were inexpensive, and "in fact, an almost puritan attitude to drink and sex."[58]

Despite Copeman's intentions, battalion life inevitably drew men from very different worlds together. In the battalion, which after Brunete included one Spanish company and in each company one Spanish section, 50 percent of the Spaniards were illiterate and 40 percent semiliterate.[59] The volunteers who were able gave literacy lessons to remedy this as well as held general discussion groups among themselves. If a man possessed some specialized knowledge of a subject, he might well be asked to speak to his comrades. The Spanish-speaking Jump talked about a newspaperman's life. A Welsh brigader explained dialectical materialism. An ex-IRA soldier offered his version of the history of Ireland to his mostly British audience. And, on another occasion, a trade unionist discoursed on the General Strike of 1926, undoubtedly with a complete and vivid dramaturgy of its heroes and villains, from the miners to J. H. Thomas and Winston Churchill.

One of the battalion's most popular figures was Miles Tomalin, a Cambridge graduate, artist, and poet, who delighted his comrades with his lyrical and somewhat whimsical nature, and ease of friendship. Cooney called him "the genius behind the wall-newspapers . . .

who, in addition to the soul of a poet, possessed a flair for organisation not usually associated with devotees of the muse."[60] A comrade called Tomalin "a grand chap . . . an intellectual, but with his two feet firmly on the ground."[61] In this battalion of mostly working-class men, the personal qualities of one such as Tomalin were sufficient to destroy many of the traditional stereotypes and barriers between classes, but working class-consciousness would always define the battalion's character. It was up to the middle-class intellectual to find his place within it.

VII

Wild, who fought and distinguished himself in all the engagements involving the British Battalion, was fortunate to have the experienced Bob Cooney as his political commissar. An ex-sailor like Copeman, Wild also resembled his predecessor in being an energetic leader. But he had a lengthy list of shortcomings as well. Wild could be so verbally violent to his subordinates that the uninitiated departed with their confidence shaken. Also, like Copeman, Wild had virtually no knowledge of military tactics. In addition, his judgment of men was often flawed, suggesting a difficulty in seeing those under his command as separate individuals with distinctive strengths and weaknesses. Moreover, he had a virtually complete inability to work effectively with the Spaniards in the battalion. Finally, and most seriously, like many of the British volunteers, Wild also had a drinking problem. Nevertheless, Sam Wild became the best of the British commanders and was regarded by his followers as the most outstanding in the brigade. What overcame his weaknesses, including his lack of military knowledge, was his "great heroism," his coolness in dangerous situations which inspired trust in his men. In combat Wild led by example, and his men found his example irresistible.

Although Wild's leadership abilities were unquestioned, it was unclear if he was going to have a sufficient number of men to lead. It became critical that the party recruit from outside its badly decimated ranks if the United Front strategy was to prove effective and the battalion remain viable as a fighting unit. The party leaders intended the battalion to become the very incarnation of the United Front against fascism, regardless of what ideological differences might divide volunteers. Therefore, when King Street was notified that the Labour councilor from Liverpool, Jack Jones, had volunteered for Spain, they were jubilant for two reasons. First, Liverpool was strongly Catholic, "and in the past numerous attempts have been made to prevent the Liverpool Labour movement from supporting the Spanish Government on the grounds of the alleged persecution of the Catholic Church." As Tom Buchanan has emphasized, the Church retained considerable authority in the lives of Catholic workers and was one of several reasons why the leadership of the labor movement was reluctant to support Republican Spain.[62] Second, the arrival of Jones in Spain was not a solitary commitment. Jones was a prominent enough catch himself. He was a leading member of the Transport and General Workers Union, the largest in the country, and a member of the national executive committee of the Docks Committee (as well as a working docker). His real importance lay, however, in the fact that he explicitly came as a "representative" of the militant noncommunist labor movement. A party memorandum observed, "The fact that the influential Liverpool Trades and Labour Council now takes this step of approving J. L. Jones' decision to join the International Brigade and looks upon him as their representative in Spain is an act of very great significance."[63]

In this case the party was not exaggerating. The Liverpool Trades Council wrote on May 18, 1938, that "we have followed from the start with great admiration the struggle which the Spanish workers are making for liberty and against fascist dictatorship. We regret, owing to the cowardly attitude of the capitalist Government here in England that we can only give you our deepest sympathy, some small financial assistance and our sincere hope for your ultimate victory." And, of course, they "gave" Jack Jones to Spain, whose appeal was also enhanced by the fact that he had married the widow of the leading Manchester communist, George Brown, who had been killed at the battle of Brunete. Their letter concluded on a bravura note, "The workers of the world will yet march together, will destroy capitalism, and will establish in full security, the socialist state."[64] The ward Jones represented felt that the principle of the all-party United Front could not be sufficiently stressed. The leaders passed a resolution "recognising that [Jones'] action is not a personal matter, but a gesture from the whole of the Labour movement of support and confidence in the ability of the Constitutional Government of Spain to conquer Fascism."[65]

In Great Britain, Jones had been in charge of arranging travel documents and raising money for Merseysiders, aided by his connections with the Spanish UGT (Unión General de Trabajadores).[66] He volunteered for Spain because he wanted to make it clear that there were Labour leaders who disagreed with the Non-Intervention policy. Jones said, "It was so vital to demonstrate that we supported the Republic and were against non-intervention."[67]

Ernest Bevin, the general secretary of the TUC, insisted upon seeing him before he left. Bevin asked Jones, "Have the communists been after you?" Jones said, "No," that "the issue affects a lot more people than the communists." He was seen off by Tom Mann and Ben Tillett, both of whom professed their wish to volunteer.[68] Jones arrived in Spain in time for the Ebro offensive. He joined three other Labour party councillors in the battalion. When asked if, by the time he arrived, the party had effectively taken over the battalion, Jones replied, "I don't think you can ignore that." He was not an innocent about the party; he had felt the ridicule hurled at him by YCL and CP members who called him a social fascist before 1935, "which I thought was a terrible mistake." But Jones was convinced "that we were fighting the same battle."[69]

The activity of the party in the battalion, moreover, was not particularly apparent to him. "Within the Battalion . . . it wasn't all that evident. People didn't [flaunt] their membership of the Communist Party so much." From the point of view of the "rank and file," they "weren't anxious to be involved too strongly in . . . political activity. They supported the idea of a democratic government."[70] In short, Jones found in the battalion a simulacrum of the United Front mentality that possessed sufficient power to bring him and a dwindling number of others to Spain. Ordinary soldiers, it seemed, simply wanted to get on with it and tried to ignore the more egregious of the party's machinations. They could do so, it seems, with a fair degree of success unless, as we shall see, they possessed an incorrigibly independent and irrepressible tongue. Jones did not disappoint his comrades. He was wounded at the Ebro, and Sam Wild rated him as "an outstanding comrade" at the time of the battalion's repatriation.[71]

A third reason for recruiting Labour party volunteers was that the Communist party simply could not sustain the continuing losses of its most effective cadres. At a Central Committee meeting held in October 1937, Harry Pollitt said, "Our party is not in a position to be allowing so many of our finest members to go. We have to try to get non-party people, the trade union and Labour Party types, to help restore the Battalion to its former strength." Pollitt's success was to be mixed at best, particularly because, as he realized, "the romanticism is gone and so many know the suffering and the difficulties."[72]

The lengths to which the leader of the British party was prepared to go in making the United Front a reality are well documented in the case of Tom Murray, an Edinburgh political leader. Murray's file in the International Brigade archive in Moscow reveals that while sitting as a Labour councillor, he was, in fact, "always [an] underground member of the C.P.," having joined in 1931. It was the decision by the district and central committees that "a special effort" was needed "to break through [the] lethargy of official labour leadership and as a gesture to stimulate recruiting for the Brigade from L.P. and T.U. circles."[73] The "special effort" was to send Tom Murray to Spain.

In a memorandum, the party leadership enumerated its reasons. Murray was general secretary of the Temperance Society. As a result, he "has great influence in the national and international organisations of this movement." He already inhabited a strategically important and highly visible position of political and trade union responsibility. As a Labour member of the Edinburgh Town Council, he "possessed growing influence in the Council Labour Group, and increasing influence on group policy and tactics." Finally, "his influence in wider Labour Party circles [was] growing considerably and [he was] likely to play an increasing part in [the] Scottish Labour Party Conference."[74] Murray had been elected to the Edinburgh Trades and Labour Council with the highest number of votes of any candidate. But he did not have to be reminded of his increasing prominence and influence. Each reason raised by the party for him to go to Spain, he believed, could also be seen as a reason for him to remain where he was, and thereby, clandestinely, better serve the party's interest.

On March 3, 1938, Murray wrote a letter to R. W. "Robbie" Robson, who was the head of vetting volunteers but also an important party official, which was to be hand-delivered: "It is very important at this juncture that the Labour Party members be stimulated into greater activity and I am perfectly willing to play whatever part the Party think[s] is most suitable for me." The report concluded that although Murray believed he would be more useful by remaining in Edinburgh, "he feels he is not necessarily the best judge in the matter and that the Party ought to take final responsibility for a decision."[75]

And so they did. "Party district and Central (British) Committees decided [Murray] should volunteer for I. Brigade as a special effort to break through lethargy of official labour leadership." Moreover, it would be seen "as a special effort to stimulate recruiting for the Brigade from L. P. and T. U. circles."[76] Tom Murray, therefore, would go to Spain. On March 23 the Aberdeen Labour and Trades Union Movement wrote to Murray, expressing "our keen appreciation of the sacrifice you are making in going to Spain to play your part on behalf of democracy." On April 8, 1938, the *Daily Worker* cast Murray in a heroic pose. Murray announced (shamelessly), "I have become alarmed to an increasing extent at the lack of vigour on the part of the leadership of my Party, and have resolved that I must take the initiative in breaking through this lethargy and indecision by offering my personal services as a fighter in the ranks of the People's Army of Democratic Spain." Murray then quickly issued a rousing letter to his Labour supporters:

> For some time I have experienced a growing consciousness of the menace of Fascism and the need for the most vigorous action which we can take to defeat this vile manifestation of reaction. Consequently, I have decided to offer my services, without reservation, to the Spanish people at this time of crisis and dire need and hope to proceed to Spain almost immediately.[77]

A little more than two weeks later he circulated another letter, in which the apparently eager warrior said, "I simply cannot describe in words how keen I feel about my participation in the war . . . in the battalion with which I will soon be right in the front line." To those with raised eyebrows, he insisted, "This is no mere propaganda splash. I never felt just quite so enthusiastic about anything as I am about this great struggle."[78]

In fact, as he and Pollitt both knew, there was a mutually accepted "reservation": he would remain in Spain no longer than the end of September, when he would return to Edinburgh for elections.[79] The party could not afford for him to lose his seat on the council or the immediate benefit of his propaganda work. His service in Spain lasted from early April to late August 1938, when he and Jack Jones, who had been wounded, were sent home.

The veterans who returned to England and spoke publicly of their experiences in Spain certainly gave the impression that all political differences in the battalion had been overcome by the common devotion to antifascism. Freedom of discussion, the abolition of class and caste distinctions, and a common purpose that subsumed political differences were the themes emphasized to explain why the International Brigades were different from any other army in history. The historian, Ben Pimlott, has noted, "Reports from members of the

International Brigade, in particular, appeared to present a shining example of the possibilities open to socialists if they were able to forget their differences and act together in their struggle against fascism."[80] Fred Copeman agreed. "The strength of the British came [from the fact that] we respected one another and every lad had a point of view and it would be listened to."[81] Frank Owen from Maerdy, one of the "Little Moscows" in South Wales, wrote to his wife on May 18, 1937, that in contrast to the repression existing among fascist troops, he found that in "the Workers['] Army . . . you can take up any matter of grievance with the Political Commissar, with the lives and well-being of each and every individual being one of the first considerations."[82] George Brown was convinced that the men of the battalion were exposed to a "vast field for expression" unlike that of any other army, except that of the Soviets.[83] Upon repatriation in the fall of 1938, David King, a mechanic from Yorkshire, said of the British volunteers, "there has been the broadest democracy within its ranks," even adding, perhaps "a little too much."[84]

But, as we will see, this was at best a very partial truth. The British Battalion suffered from its own kind of caste system. It, too, hid behind illusions, and unity could be strained to the point of breaking, and beyond.[85] In the British Battalion, it was much more likely that a volunteer would be disciplined for independence of thought or outspoken opposition to battalion policy or leadership than for recognized political differences. But the latter could happen as well. Even the bitterly critical Jason Gurney, whose memoir underscores the insidious influence of the party on the battalion, was not above denouncing another volunteer (a fact he does not mention in his book) on the grounds of his past political associations. He accused his comrade, Edwin Hall, of having been a member of Oswald Mosley's British Union of Fascists, and, moreover, of having taken part in the beating of a left-wing speaker. Events proceeded swiftly. After receiving the charge in the morning of June 1, 1937, Hall was promptly arrested and brought before the party authorities. Statements were taken. The accused finally admitted that for six weeks in 1933 he had indeed been a member of the British Union of Fascists, but denied the accusation of political thuggery. The unfortunate Hall said, not unreasonably, "Hardly anyone then knew anything about the Fascists, and they were not even [thought to be] anti-Jewish." Nevertheless, Hall was placed under guard as a suspected spy until the battalion leadership received instructions from Albacete on the disposition of the case.[86] Much more pressing than the threat of "spies" in the battalion, however, was the large number of desertions.

Bob Cooney, the last commissar of the battalion before its withdrawal, was described in his final personnel evaluation as "the best commissar we have," and "the best battalion commissar in the brigade."[87] It was Cooney's belief that "there was never a more disciplined unit than the British Battalion of the International Brigade." He felt he could add, "There was never an army in history that had so few bad lads, so few deserters."[88] Jim Brewer sharply disagreed with Cooney's views. He believed the number of desertions was much greater than the rank and file knew.[89] If a comrade was absent from the line, the leadership encouraged the belief that he had been wounded. According to Brewer, "there were desertions on [a] scale that we didn't dream about," and the party covered them up. He was correct. Moreover, Brewer said, officers would periodically come around and announce they had been given the authority to shoot anyone who did desert. And, Brewer added, what genuinely appalled him was that they seemed to say it "with such relish."[90]

The heretofore insuperable obstacle to writing about the dissidents within the British Battalion has been that existing records have been under party control, either in London or Moscow. "Official" historians such as Bill Rust and Bill Alexander each produced valuable books, particularly in Alexander's case. But both were intent on protecting the battalion's and the party's reputations.

Until the opening of the Moscow archives, it has been impossible to offer a less simplistic and more human understanding of the experiences of the more than two thousand men and women who served in Spain. Now, the careers of the hundreds of deserters can be restored to the history of the battalion. The personnel records of the British brigaders reveal that at least 271 volunteers deserted (Alexander puts the figure even higher at 298, hardly the "handful" to which he later refers[91]), and many deserted more than once. The lower number has been derived from ten surviving lists prepared during repatriation of the volunteers in the fall of 1938. The lists included not just those who deserted, but volunteers who were considered "bad elements." In all, they contain 400 names, making up what the battalion leadership called the "black list." In addition to those labeled deserters were men identified by the leadership as undesirables, drunks, cowards, the disaffected, criminals, one *Poumista*, one Trotskyist (as well as another who was suspected of such tendencies), a fascist, and no fewer than thirteen "spies."[92] Thus, if one subtracts the 526 killed from the total of 2,063 volunteers, an extraordinary 26 percent of the remainder consisted of men whose behavior and performance were considered worthy of condemnation.

The judgments followed accordingly. One volunteer was summed up as being a "Deserter. Rotten, lumpen element. Absolutely worthless."[93] This is a characteristic description of the "volunteers for liberty" who were considered unsatisfactory; it would be repeated, in one way or another, time and again. This is important to note because although some deserters were unquestionably scoundrels, it would be absurd to believe that all were. There were a number who for one reason or another were maladjusted to military life, regardless of their political convictions. One, a landscape gardener, wrote to Will Paynter a few weeks after the battle of Brunete, "I implore [you] to send me home before I have a complete nervous or mental breakdown. There are times, I'm ashamed to admit, when I feel that I could end my life. . . . Please! Send me home quickly."[94] For most others, the principal issues were home leave and the desire to be discharged from the battalion after a stated period of service. As will also become clear, in many instances those who deserted did so because of political views that would not allow them to submit to party control of the battalion. The tradition of a "free born" Englishman did not coexist easily or at all with authoritarianism of any kind.

Will Paynter, the brigade commissar, wrote to Harry Pollitt with his own explanation for the high number of desertions. He had recently gone to a prison where a number of British deserters were being held, and had interviewed twenty-five of them. He talked to two prisoners who were British army reservists and had pay coming to them but, despite reassurances when they volunteered, they were not allowed to return to England to collect it. Three of those Paynter interviewed had families who had received no Dependent Aid support, despite having reported their concerns to Springhall and Kerrigan. But, Paynter believed, most of the men deserted because of the battalion's refusal to allow leave to England.[95]

This last complaint was the most prevalent. Paynter summarized what he heard. First, the soldiers had begun the war as volunteers but now, since the brigade had merged with the Popular Army, had been turned into conscripts. Second, they were convinced that, having been stigmatized as "bad elements," they would be held in Spain until they were killed. Third, they told Paynter that deserters were not necessarily those who had lost their nerve. Even some of the most courageous volunteers were saying openly that if they were not given leave, they would take it. Fourth, by being denied leave, it was clear to those with whom Paynter spoke that they believed "the political people" had no confidence that they would return. Finally, Paynter told Pollitt what was most disturbing was that these complaints were "not confined to a few, but are widespread, and are therefore serious."[96] Consequently, Paynter immediately recommended home leave for all those who had been in Spain for over six months. "All the leading comrades share this opinion and support the request." To refuse to make this change in policy, Paynter said, would be "to perpetuate the ideology [sic] that the only way to leave is via a coffin or bandages."[97]

While the battle for Brunete was raging, Paynter wrote again to Pollitt that never had the battalion been so hard-pressed. He explained the unpleasant realities and revealed, as he had throughout his tenure as brigade commissar, his genuine decency. He told Pollitt, "The toll of desertions has been heavy." More than twenty had been detained in Albacete, "and there were more in Madrid and Valencia," he said. "The whole problem," however, "is being treated with [the] greatest possible degree of humanity." He told Pollitt, "I have argued that while we must condemn this . . . form of conduct we must also understand it." Those who were breaking down had all been in Spain more than six months. "Almost without exception" they had been with the battalion since the first day of the Jarama, and "many" had been wounded. "All are exhausted and in bad nervous condition. Many of them have previous excellent records . . . [which] prove they are not just cowards."[98] Paynter told Pollitt, "Our dead and wounded are more than double those of the two other English speaking Battalions together." The battalion went into action at Brunete with 331 in their ranks. Only forty-two effectives remained at the end. Both Fred Copeman, the battalion commander, and Wally Tapsell, his commissar, suffered breakdowns, the former being in effect removed from command of the battalion by brigade headquarters.[99]

Unfortunately for the future of the battalion, Paynter's attempt to understand and rehabilitate those who fled the fighting reflected an unusual sensitivity and humanity among the commissariat. Not that his motives were unalloyed by practical considerations. An embittered deserter who reached England might well damage the reputation of the volunteers by going to the press, as some did. In addition, it was important for both military and political reasons that the battalion remain viable as a fighting unit, particularly with the number of volunteers diminishing after Brunete, when there was even talk among the leadership of "liquidating" the battalion and forming a new unit with the Americans. Paynter recognized that if the British Battalion ceased to exist, there would be "a resultant political scandal and concern in England." To the political leadership, "It is this which is the real issue." On July 21 Paynter reported to Pollitt that "our aim is still to keep as many men as possible serving in Spain. . . . The record and continued existence of our Battalion is a tremendous lever for agitation against the Gov't" and is of great "importance upon the movement at home."[100]

As a result, any lack of ideological harmony in the battalion that might create a "political scandal" had to be stamped out or discredited. This attitude led to the persecution and defamation of "political unreliables" such as Alec Marcovitch and George Wattis.

CHAPTER 12

"Political Unreliables"

To romanticize the Spanish war would be worthless and wrong. To hide men's fears and failings would be, I think, the worst kind of insult.
— Esmond Romilly

I remember learning from both German and British Internationals that after the battle of Morata [the Jarama] none of them quite knew which of their comrades had been killed by Franco and which by Stalin. And it was the same story in battle upon battle after that. The stone cairns put up as memorials for the "Heroic fighters for Freedom," however, carried the names of all the fallen without differentiation as to who had killed them.
— Sefton Delmer

Alec Marcovitch

I

The cloak of anonymity that descended over the British volunteers who appeared on some form of the "black list" has remained in place for sixty years. The political ideals and internationalist motives that drove most of them to Spain, and alone should have preserved them from vilification, were obscured by their failure to accept party control of the battalion or to adjust successfully to the extraordinary challenges facing a volunteer army at war. The careers of Alec Marcovitch and George Wattis and others will help illuminate the experiences of this army of the forgotten.

The official newspaper of the XVth Brigade, the *Volunteer for Liberty*, claimed that the soldiers of the International Brigades served in an army that insisted on freedom of discussion. This contrasted sharply with the British army, in which "everything is done to preserve the illusion of sanctity around the officer caste and to maintain wooden discipline, which kills initiative." Further, this rigidity has the effect of stifling "individual self-respect."[1] As we have seen, the freedom of discussion allowed among the British volunteers was severely circumscribed by the political culture of the battalion.

And, also, despite its special character, the British Battalion developed its own "officer caste."

A fundamental point that Will Paynter and his successors failed to recognize was the alienation of those who increasingly rejected the Stalinization of the battalion and its leadership. Alec Marcovitch from Scotland is one of the few working-class veterans to speak publicly of the reasons for his disillusionment over his experiences in Spain. He declared his enmity not only against the party for its influence on the battalion but against some of the most revered figures in its leadership.[2] It was an enmity heartily reciprocated. Marcovitch was one of seventy-five party members in the battalion singled out for special censure when the brigades were being repatriated, because they either deserted or had "exceptionally bad records."[3]

Born in the Gorbals, Marcovitch was a Jew of Russian and Polish extraction who later became a member of the national executive of the National Union of Tailor and Garment Workers. During the years between the wars, Marcovitch found Glasgow a hotbed of political activity, and the Communist party, particularly, achieving great prominence. It was an environment made for a young man of ability and a distaste for authority, as well as one with a passionate interest in finding a radical solution to the poverty, unemployment, and general hardships that surrounded him.

Early in life Marcovitch's skills as a political orator made him locally famous as the "boy speaker." He claimed to be able to put a soapbox down and within a few seconds draw an audience of between 400 and 500 people. In Spain, Alan Gilchrist conceded that Marcovitch "is something of an orator and his glib tongue makes him dangerous."[4] "Trained" in Marxism by Eddie McNally, he joined the Communist party and subsequently received various inducements from the Independent Labour party and the Labour party to disaffiliate from the CPGB. Marcovitch rejected their overtures, however, because he did not believe that either party offered a genuine alternative to capitalism. He felt particular contempt for the ILP leader James Maxton, whose emotional oratory and gradualist program left Marcovitch frustrated and uninspired. "I mean old Jimmy Maxton and his long hair and his finger forbidding you crying."[5]

What did stimulate Marcovitch, however, were the Communist party publications, particularly *Imprecor*, which he admired for "not only . . . condemning the old system but in trying to establish a scientific basis for the new system." To Marcovitch, it was the kind of "good stuff" on which a thoughtful young militant could build a political life. Unlike some other volunteers, he did not confine his reading to the usual canon of Marxist classics. He also read the Webbs, the Fabians, and, of course, selections of the Left Book Club.[6] This suggests something of the openness and inquisitiveness of mind that would cause his downfall in Spain.

The first signs of Marcovitch's independence from the party line appeared in the early thirties. Glasgow communists became aware of a specific instance of Stalin's persecution of the Jews through the legal system. The incident appeared sufficiently serious for the Glasgow party to ask Peter Kerrigan, a member of the party's Central Committee, to explain the Kremlin's actions. Kerrigan's report focused on Russian law, the nature of the accusations, and the fact that the accused had received a fair trial and thus deserved guilty verdicts. Marcovitch found this explanation unsatisfying. He told Kerrigan that the party's version of Stalin's actions was "all very well," but it fell to him to carry this rationale to nonparty Jews. "I can't go to Jewish comrades or Jewish people and tell them because I've got faith in the Soviet Union and in the fairness of the legal system, that there should be no question at all as to the validity of the trials that took place."[7] He warned Kerrigan that his fellow Jews would want to know the exact charges, the reasons for the accusations, and what degree of guilt was admitted by the accused.

Despite Marcovitch's dissent, Kerrigan hoped for unanimous approval of his report by the Scottish Communist leadership. Anything else, Marcovitch remembered, was "not good, you know." But instead, a large minority refused to accept the official explanation. Then, and later, Marcovitch demonstrated a remarkable ability to translate latent dissidence among his comrades into public opposition. The party considered the matter to be of sufficient seriousness that leaders called another meeting, this time with Pollitt in attendance. Marcovitch's spirited intervention was a portent of the difficulties in which he would find himself in Spain, difficulties that were precipitated, he believed, by the long memory and undying enmity of Kerrigan. In his file in Moscow, one of the shortcomings enumerated is that the young Glasgow Jew "alleged anti-semitism in [the] Soviet Union."[8]

Marcovitch arrived in Spain in October 1937. He trained as a rifleman and ammunition feeder for a machine gun, fighting at Teruel

when the battalion was called in to stop the Nationalist counteroffensive. From the beginning, Marcovitch appears to have been fiercely
critical of headquarters conduct. He saw the battalion command as a
"closed shop" receiving special privileges denied to others. At one
point, he rose at a political meeting being run by Cooney and complained of the difference in treatment between the rank-and-file and
the command staff. Marcovitch spoke out because he believed it was
his "prerogative" at an open meeting to say what he pleased, including leveling accusations at his superiors. "I mean there were no
fascists there. I had a point of view which was not entirely in
sympathy with the way things were as I saw them. I felt it was my
right."[9] He was specific about his complaints, which included the
rations, compassionate leave, differences in living standards between
the officers and men, and the incidence of venereal disease, which he
believed was crippling the fighting efficiency of the battalion and,
therefore, should be considered a military crime.

The consequences of his outspokenness proved fateful. Cooney
said "this matter" was too serious for the battalion and had to be sent
to brigade. In Marcovitch's file in Moscow, there is a handwritten
note by Cooney in which he says Marcovitch "has shown an anti-
party attitude" both in Scotland (undoubtedly referring to the run-in
with Kerrigan) and in Spain. Elsewhere in the note Marcovitch is said
to have confessed to being a Trotskyist.[10] This demonic typology was
characteristic of the battalion, as it was of virtually any communist
organization. And, unfortunately, Marcovitch played into Cooney's
hands.

Despite his estimable qualities, Cooney, like all devout communists, was quick to see a follower of Trotsky behind any criticism of
or independence from the party line. In his unpublished autobiography, "Proud Journey," he makes his bondage to the communist line
abundantly clear. He writes that while a tutor at the Aberdeen Labour
College, "I also took every opportunity of exposing the Trotskyists
who served as lieutenants of fascism within the Labour movement."
At one speaking event, "I spoke to a crowded hall and went tooth and
nail for the Trotskyists."[11] Therefore, Cooney required no belabored
reflection to identify the threat that Marcovitch represented.[12]

Among the commissars, only Alan Gilchrist refrained from the
usual political mugging given to a dissident. Gilchrist had known
Marcovitch at the training camp in Tarazona "where he was a leading
political figure." Despite shortcomings, according to Gilchrist, "he

was generally regarded as a potential leader." Gilchrist did not have personal knowledge of him again until June 1938, when Marcovitch was a member of No. 1 Company. According to Gilchrist, he had succeeded in organizing "a large, influential, and effective group of agitators on the questions of discipline and repatriation." Again, he could give the devil his due. Marcovitch, he said, "posed very successfully as a champion of the oppressed." His views were confirmed in another report stating that Marcovitch "had a great deal of influence among those comrades who thought as he did." The commissars called one of them, Robert Middleton, also of Glasgow, a "Trotskyist and dangerous," and "a real bad egg." But undoubtedly Middleton's real shortcoming was that he had "defended Marcovitch, known Trotskyist."[13] It would have been interesting to ask virtually any member of the battalion, even Cooney and particularly Sam Wild, exactly what a "Trotskyist" was, or how a volunteer from the Gorbals had managed to become one.

According to Marcovitch, after he challenged Cooney in front of the battalion he was ordered to brigade headquarters and put under close arrest. He was then sent to a correction camp where he found himself to be the only member of the British Battalion in a group of about thirty detainees, including Germans, Italians, French, Belgians, and two Americans. He was quick to recognize that none of them was a criminal. "They were all men of integrity, all men of profound political conscience, all men with background[s] in the revolutionary movement." He found his fellow prisoners to be not only worthy militants but good and decent, even heroic men. This realization left Marcovitch stunned. "The seeds of discontent can't just be as narrow and exclusive."[14]

To most volunteers, these camps and labor battalions were an ominous mystery, but there is ample evidence from the literature and documents in Moscow that they existed. Witness comes from the disaffected, such as Tony Hyndman, who made "a steady progress through jails, camps, then more jails."[15] One British volunteer found himself detained for weeks in circumstances of indescribable filth, in the company of brigaders of other nationalities, several of whom were killed for trying to escape. "I began to wonder," he said, "whether we were suspected of Fascism, or what we were supposed to have done, and I often thought of what the English democrats would say if they knew how we were treated by the so-called democracy which we had come to Spain to defend."[16] A London tailor, Reuben Lewis, complained that "a prisoner should have a trial before being sent to jail."[17]

The existence of one detention center for the disaffected, Camp Lucas, lying ten miles from Albacete, was widely known of—although it was not mentioned in Bill Rust's account of the British volunteers in Spain. John Angus, later a student of the historian Eric Hobsbawm and a university lecturer, became political commissar of the camp after the battle of Brunete in July 1937. His specific duties were to supervise the 60–70 British prisoners, many of whom were bitterly critical of the battalion leaders who were allowed to return home after the horrific battle. "They were just ordinary chaps who thought they had been conned and whose morale had been reduced by seeing a number of commissars, one after the other, stay with them for a few weeks and then return to England."[18]

Marcovitch was never formally charged with misconduct. According to him, he and the men in the camp in which he was detained, which was close to the Ebro, were sent on special, hazardous missions across the river. The ostensible purpose of these forays was to collect information before the last great Republican offensive, but Marcovitch believed there was just one real reason—to get them killed. He concedes that this was only his assumption, and there was no declared policy to this effect. He felt, however, that under the circumstances it was sensible to believe that the overall goal was to silence the "politically contentious." He and other prisoners were therefore often behind fascist lines, waging guerrilla warfare. The death rate was appropriately high, from 40 to 50 percent. Over a two-month period, he made eight to ten raids.[19]

Marcovitch survived the odds. With understandable satisfaction, he said, "The wee man came back every time." When he was finally allowed to return to the battalion, his fellow soldiers believed "they'd seen a bloody ghost." No one, however, called him "a bloody traitor" or "a fascist swine" or a "Trotskyist or a deviationist," or any other of the standard litany of party denunciations. Instead, the men of the battalion were civil and sympathetic to him. Yet none of them wished to be seen talking with him. "They were afraid that big brother was looking and my association with anybody . . . would [make them] . . . potentially suspect."[20]

All affability, Peter Kerrigan approached Marcovitch upon his return, but the young Glaswegian refused to be appeased and cursed his enemy. It was Kerrigan, he was convinced, who had made the decision to send him to the camp. Later, Marcovitch was segregated from the battalion again. According to his account, at the end of the war he made a fighting retreat into France with a motley assortment of other International Brigaders. On August 17, 1938, the final judgment was rendered on his behavior—when he was named by the commissariat a provocateur, a Trotskyist, and a generally pessimistic element.[21]

In retrospect, Marcovitch said he was probably "impetuous. . . . I should have kept my mouth shut" and "let sleeping dogs lie." But he maintains that the grievances he felt against the battalion leadership were more than minor irritants. "It was the principle that was involved." Marcovitch attempted to sum up his philosophy, which became more explicit as the years passed. "I believe that each person in his own right . . . is entitled to as full a life, as full of opportunity of expression as it's possible to obtain without it in any way affecting the rights of other people."[22]

II

Marcovitch's story is important because, as the Moscow archives of the International Brigades reveal, there were many like him who became disaffected, often deserted, and were conveniently summed up as being "demoralized" or "undisciplined" or "inactive" in the discharge of their duties.[23] For example, the police arrested Archibald Jack Campbell in Valencia for "making derogatory statements against the Spanish army" and deserting. Arthur Teasdale, although secretary of his Communist party branch in Great Britain, was in and out of trouble in Spain. The party judged that he "had become an enemy of the working-class." Thomas Carlisle, noted for his personal courage, was judged to be "talkative anti-party." He too later deserted.[24] All had been effectively silenced.

Therefore, Marcovitch would have agreed with John McGovern, the ILP leader, who predicted in 1937 that communism "would still the tongues, shackle the limbs, and mould the robot minds in every militant fighter throughout the world."[25] Upon his return to Spain, the young journalist and former volunteer, Keith Scott Watson, wrote to his editor that in the Republic "political reliability has become a virtue far above military utility."[26] The purge of the "political unreliables" by the party proved relentless. Jack Carson, an auto mechanic from Manchester who was wounded at Gandesa, found himself thrown "into jail without trial." He "suffered 19 days in a terrible lice infested, cold, damp, hell hole." Defending himself against some charges and admitting others, he wrote to Harry Pollitt, "I stand condemned, and despised as a deserter and saboteur. Little wonder my one desire [h]as been to get out of it, not because of Spain, not because my mind has changed about Fascism, but because I am not prepared to take so much shit from so called 'comrades.'" On his final evaluation before repatriation, his "faults" were listed as "constant criticism of command and [being] a ringleader against order and discipline." He refused to be silenced, telling Pollitt further that there could be only one explanation for not receiving mail from his wife. "I am despised, black-listed or something." In his own final statement, he confessed himself to be "very bitter" about his "unjust" treatment.[27]

Judgments poured forth on those who had soldiered successfully but still had provoked the party. Even a "good" and "brave" comrade such as Alfred Christie from Aberdeen, who spent nine months at the front, could be damned by inference. The battalion leadership concluded that he could be depended on to support the party line only "generally." Patrick Toal arrived in Spain on December 11, 1936, and joined the No. 1 Company under Nathan, fighting in all the major campaigns from Córdoba to Brunete, where he was wounded, suffering a fractured arm. Toal had "a good record in the line," but he too was judged "politically unreliable." According to Arthur Nicoll, Fred Thomas was "a first class soldier," thus admitting him to a handful of the military elite who received such praise in their final evaluations. In addition, he edited the wall newspaper, suggesting that he was more independently minded than many. His shortcomings were that "he tends to be cynical." Moreover, he "is openly critical of the C.P. membership in Spain"—half of whom, Thomas was reported as saying, "make him sick."[28]

Frank Farr came to Spain with the first British ambulance unit. He made no secret of his views that the military and political organization of the International Brigades was "very amateurish." For their part, the commissars accused him of "over-valuing himself" as well as becoming hypocritical and cynical. The commissar, Alonzo Elliott, a Cambridge teacher, concluded that Farr had become an "enemy." In a sensitive letter to his wife that she never received, Farr wrote, "The wheels of the War Machine grind exceeding small & they have ground my spirit & my power to hope right away." He said he would have thought that "the theory that wounded men can live, thrive, &

mend on bad political speeches was exploded . . . but they still try to work it."[29]

One of the great ironies lay in the fate of John Lepper. Any reader even passingly familiar with the poetry of the Spanish Civil War knows the famous, haunting verse drawn from his experiences on February 12, 1937, the first day of Jarama:

Death stalked the olive trees
Picking his men
His leaden finger beckoned
Again and again.

The poem was included in Spender's and Lehmann's collection, *Poems for Spain.* But after the battle Lepper attempted to desert with Spender's friend, Hyndman. According to the report of the American SIM agent, Tony De Maio, they were arrested by Spanish police in Valencia when the two went to the British consul for help in returning to England.[30]

This was one of several junctures at which Spender attempted to intervene in Hyndman's behalf, even suggesting to the brigade that Hyndman be given an appointment as a private secretary. So infuriated was De Maio that he wrote, "a report has been made against Spender for recommending a deserter for such a confidential job." As for Lepper, he complained of painful cataracts but was not believed. According to his file, he finally admitted to his real crime, that he was a coward.[31] Despite the intense pain his eyes were causing him, Lepper was sentenced to a labor and reeducation camp for two months. Worse fates befell others.

III

For the genuinely unfortunate, death could be the penalty. Billy Griffiths, the party secretary of the battalion, discovered on the eve of the Ebro offensive that a number of men, sentenced at the brigade level for desertion, were awaiting execution.[32] It is clear that such sentences were being delivered, and if not carried out, were in practice suspended only for a short time. Tom Murray, who sat as a Labour party councillor in Edinburgh but was an "underground" member of the Communist party, came to Spain as a company commissar after Copeman had relinquished command. He tells of the leader of a machine-gun crew, "quite a capable bloke, too," who refused orders to relocate his gun and threatened Murray with a grenade. He was immediately removed from the front and demoted in rank. According to Murray, the party discovered subsequently that he had a brother serving in the Nationalist ranks, and he "had a very strong anti-Soviet and anti-Socialist background." These two damning revelations, coupled with his disobedience on the battlefield, were sufficient to ensure his execution. "He was got rid of, just shot in the back of the neck."[33]

The Australian nurse, Agnes Hodgson, recorded in her diary on October 19, 1937, a meeting in Barcelona between one of her friends and a British volunteer who "is sick of it all," and was attempting to desert. He appeared to be in an anxious state, however, because "he fears he will be shot."[34] According to Copeman, after his departure the unvarying rule of the British against executions was broken when two members of the battalion, who had deserted from the front and imperiled their comrades, were executed.[35] The XVth Brigade commander, Vladimir Copic, who had a penchant for singing opera and staying away from the front lines, ordered the executions, Copeman said, and they were reluctantly carried out by Sam Wild, the battalion commander.

The perspectives on Copic were predictably varied. Jason Gurney believed he was "an utterly unprincipled brute who would swear that black was white if it suited his convenience, and his only genius lay in his capacity for intrigue."[36] Robert Merriman, the commander of the Lincolns, loathed Copic's arrogance and held him responsible for the decimation of the American battalion on February 27, 1937, by forcing it into an impossible attack.[37] On the other hand, from a British commissar's perspective, Copic "symbolises proletarian strength," an example of the kind of man "our class produces."[38] Copeman, who was back in England when the executions occurred, would have none of it. When he heard of the executions, his reaction was unambiguous: "I thought that was just bloody awful." But he had no illusions about party behavior in the brigades. He later said that if André Marty had been allowed to execute all those who deserted, "there'd have been a few thousand shot."[39]

There were less direct ways of disposing of those who were judged for one reason or another to be "undesirable." Charlotte Haldane's close friend, an American communist called "Jack," crossed swords with the intolerably difficult French party until "matters finally came to a show-down." He was ordered to the front, not with the Lincolns, but rather to an obscure Spanish infantry unit. And there, she believes, he was murdered. Haldane wrote, "I am convinced that Jack was not a war casualty, but a victim of political bigotry, envy, malice, and intrigue." Bill Rust told her frankly that "he was sold down the river by his own Party."[40]

Bert Overton may have suffered a somewhat similar fate. The brigade court-martialed Overton, an ex-Guardsman who failed abysmally as a company commander at the Jarama, costing the lives of many because of his fear and incompetence. He was then sent to a labor battalion. At Brunete, he was killed while carrying ammunition "to a forward position."[41] Some wondered if putting Overton in harm's way wasn't simply an expedient means of getting rid of a soldier who had become a dangerous embarrassment. Another suspicious case was that of Patrick Glacken, a member of the Labour party from Greenock who was arrested for desertion on January 8, 1938, and "sentenced to execution for this crime." The leadership commuted his sentence, but twelve days later Glacken was killed in action. The commissar Wally Tapsell managed to lodge a protest about the handling of the case, but with Glacken's death it apparently became a moot point.[42] A third incident paralleled the first two. William Meeke had been in Spain since October 1937. He was twenty-eight, Irish, and judged an "incorrigible, useless type." In his file the commissariat noted tersely that Meeke was shot while attempting to escape.[43]

In the overwhelming majority of instances, however, deserters, who could legally be condemned to death, were sentenced by court-martial to imprisonment in labor camps. One example is a guilty verdict rendered on a British volunteer who was reminded that he could have received the death penalty. Instead, he found himself in a special penal section of a labor battalion for the duration of the conflict. After the war such men were told they were *"to be judged by their comrades."*[44] And yet, in some instances, redemption could be achieved. Another deserter, George Coyle, left the front at Jarama and subsequently took leave in Madrid without authorization. He was sentenced to a term in a labor battalion but subsequently restored his reputation at Brunete and became a battalion commissar.[45]

The experience of George Green in Spain (not the musician of the same name) was representative of many. He served in the British army until 1935 and then became an ambulance driver at a hospital in Surrey. Upon volunteering, his "one desire" was to serve in hospitals, but "my applications have been either torn up or burnt by

... officers [who are] supposed to be out and out Communists." At one time attracted to the party, he said, "now that I have seen all that I want to see, I don't wish to become one"—at least not as he saw Communism practiced in Spain. He took part in the Retreats. "After this I got a little fed up," and he attempted unsuccessfully to desert. The commissariat typically called him "a thorough rotter, drunkard and one of the worst elements to have been here."[46]

Party leaders were not the only ones who served as recording angels of the fate of the British volunteers. The steadfast J. R. Jump, for example, made inquiries about the disposition of certain "bad elements" and discovered they had been sent to a prison or a labor battalion, sometimes for homosexual activities, but probably more often for repeated misconduct or political heterodoxy.[47]

When Tom Murray first arrived in Spain, he was told to find guards for prisons inhabited by "people we couldn't identify—there were fascists, there were all kinds of people" being detained "until they could be investigated."[48] These were probably incarcerated somewhere in the dreaded SIM empire, "with its secret prisons and torture chambers for political opponents of the left and the right."[49]

Given the variety of individuals who volunteered for Spain, it was inevitable that some would believe they had made the wrong decision and attempt to leave, as was the case with Tony Hyndman. Others were motivated by the unfolding truth of their own experiences, arriving at the conclusion that the war simply did not offer them anything for which it was worth fighting and dying. As D. F. Springhall, a member of the party's Central Committee and a commissar in Spain, admitted, "There were those who argued that they had come to Spain to learn to be soldiers and not politicians."[50] In a long letter to the Warden of Coleg Harlech, Jim Brewer demonstrated that even he had little understanding of the reasons his fellow volunteers had for fleeing Spain. Brewer accused some of the "deserters" of spreading "all sorts of lying reports" once they returned to England. He wrote to his old friend, "The *truth* about them is that they deserted in the most trying hours. . . . One in the course of an advance is known to have stopped, taken a few pounds from the pocket of a comrade who had fallen and quit. Later he wrote a letter to the *Times* about rotten treatment by the Spanish authorities."[51] Since Brewer's own motives and conduct approached the ideal of a brigader, his testimony offers unimpeachable evidence that even the most perceptive in the battalion had little idea of what actually was occurring.

Contrary to party propaganda, then, many volunteers who deserted the battalion were not cowards or wastrels. Their reasons for departing Spain or speaking out against the influence of the Communist party proved well grounded, lending support to Alec Marcovitch's lonely testimony. This becomes clear from a number of other specific instances of disaffection, further revealing that the party did not practice the political tolerance promised by the Popular Front. A former naval rating deserted, to the chagrin of the commissars who in a confidential "observation" reported that "no investigation took place," even though "he was suspected of having Trotskyite tendencies." An English miner from Musselburgh, the commissars noted, was "suspected for his politics," and thought to have "Trotskyite tendencies."[52] On another occasion, a British officer overheard the American socialist, Hilliard Bernstein, criticizing Stalin. Enraged, he called Bernstein a "Trotskyite" and forced his transfer to another battalion.[53]

In his final report on the British Battalion, Alonzo Elliott said it was the intention of the leadership to evaluate politically and militarily as many volunteers as possible. The evaluators included a military leader, a commissar, the secretary of the party, and occasionally others. The following are examples of the political surveillance to which the British volunteers were subjected, even those against whom no direct action was taken. James Arthur, a miner from West Lothian and member of the CPGB, was judged "a first class soldier" who, however, "took no interest in political work whatsoever." Moreover, on several occasions he showed "anti-officer feeling." Alan Gilchrist, a London schoolteacher and commissar, recommended that Arthur be "carefully watched" because he had exhibited "anti-party tendencies in the past." The commissars criticized Reuben Gainsborough, wounded in the Sierra Pandols, for his "constitutional opposition to the command, and anti-party attitude." It was conceded that Gainsborough was "brave at the front," but "he is unreliable" and an "anti-party element to be watched."[54]

If a volunteer was suspected of "anti-party tendencies," it was imperative that his mail be carefully monitored. The party accused a contentious brigader from Newcastle, who claimed to have been a party member since 1934, "of continuous slander of the command" and making "cheap jokes about the party, the army and government." Even worse, he refused to keep his grievances to himself. He was "writing very bad letters home"[55] which were read and confiscated by the censor. Another volunteer was also writing "bad" letters in which he asked his wife to help get him out of Spain. He suggested that she approach the *Daily Express* with his story. The letter, however, was intercepted. Peter Kerrigan wrote that his "line" was not to consider the volunteer's "possible innocence." The party, he said, must be prepared for bad publicity because others of his letters may have reached England. Unfortunately, there was little that could be done about the situation now. "He cannot disappear without an explanation."[56]

A few "unreliables" allowed their true feelings to be expressed implicitly or explicitly only upon repatriation. Some of the strongest open criticism of the party came from James Nixon, a printer from Lancashire, who was a member of the Labour party and had been wounded at the Ebro. Upon the withdrawal of the brigades from Spain, he wrote in his final assessment of the IB that "political organization [was] not sufficiently elastic to allow airing of grievances without fear." A note was attached to his statement which said, "Should be watched." Since his behavior had been judged to be "good," this could only have been a reaction to his comments. The remarks on Nixon concluded with the comment that he was "politically developed," in itself an almost singular recognition, "but does not agree with the C.P. In fact during the 6 months I have known him he has always opposed the Party line." John Beaumont was judged to be "politically nowhere" and a "would be wise guy." When asked to give his opinion of the IB and its political and military organization, he wrote a succinct, "no comment." Clarence Wildsmith, an electrician from Doncaster, was more explicit in his response to the same question. "I cannot answer this question here in Spain or on paper." Philip Goodman, a chemist from Manchester, who was a sergeant in the Anti-Tanks and fought from the Jarama to the Ebro, said in almost identical words, "This is not a question that can be answered in Spain or on paper." Thomas Mitchell from Edinburgh did not submerge his views in silence, however. The commissariat wrote of him: "His general political attitude is that Communism is a good thing, that communist parties support the correct policy, but that individual communists, almost without exception are no good." He "regrets having come to Spain."[57]

The men of the battalion, then, were kept under political observation from their arrival until they were killed or repatriated. In a war in which it would seem that no political comment went undocumented, a final one will suffice. Ronald Bates, a relative of Ralph Bates and a clerk from Gloucester, reported a discussion he had with two disaffected volunteers which, he believed, required action from the commissar to whom he wrote:

> They say . . . that they have lost most of their illusions since receiving first-hand experience of the I.B. Newspapers at home had boosted it as a democratic army infinitely superior to any imperialist army. Actually, they say, it is much more incompetently organized, and more hypocritical than an imperialist army. It is hypocritical, they say, in that they are given a political commissar who is presumably to be their representative, whereas in practice he is nothing more than an apologist for the incompetence of the military command.

Bates concluded that what was needed was "a first class talk from yourself on the I.B."[58] If the British example is representative, then it is hard to believe that any army that has ever taken the field relied more on political "talk," first class or not, than the International Brigades.

The consequences of a volunteer's questioning or criticizing the party line would usually be a stern reproof from a commissar and, of course, a record of the incident. One possible response, whether sincere or not, was to abase oneself before the party hierarchy. Charles O'Neal, a transport worker from Scotland who questioned a party policy, answered his critics in a pathetic handwritten note. He abjectly apologized to Commissar Dave Springhall for being "guilty of neglecting my C.P. line and have allowed my Personal feeling to get the [best] of me." He thanked Springhall for his "straight talk," pledging himself in the future to "always place the Commius [sic] Party first in my life."[59] Others, however, refused to seek absolution from the party. A volunteer who made his way through the detention centers stopped writing home because "the only news we were allowed to send was a lot of lies praising the Communist Party, and for this reason there were a number who never wrote at all."[60]

For those who did not cause political trouble, a tolerant attitude was possible. For example, most of the battalion believed that Taffy Foulkes, a popular ex-sailor, had been absent from the battalion for so long that he had deserted. Jack Jones caught sight of him in the Barcelona docks and persuaded him to return to the battalion. The commander, Sam Wild, "simply told him not to be a bloody fool again."[61]

These records enable us for the first time to get behind what a recent history of the war still refers to as the "legendary International Brigades."[62] Those of the right and the left have draped the bunting of their respective ideologies over the brigades for the past sixty years. The "legend" can now be seen as the infinitely more compelling and complex human experience that it was. The characteristics of moral and intellectual independence that caused a middle-class or working-class "thinker" to volunteer for Spain were sufficient to bring about character assassination, surveillance, imprisonment, and, in isolated cases, worse.

George Wattis

I

Despite the testimony of Alec Marcovitch, perhaps the most damaging evidence of the extent of communist domination of the British Battalion came from George Wattis. Unlike Marcovitch, Wattis was lionized by the party. He was one of the few British volunteers to have had extensive military experience before Spain[63] and, subsequently, a distinguished record as a fighter and leader throughout the Spanish War. His career is one of the most fascinating and revealing of all those in the British Battalion, and purposefully buried by the keepers of its "story."

On the morning of February 27, 1937, in the valley of the Jarama, as the Lincolns prepared for their first battle, Robert Merriman, commander of the American battalion, challenged Lt. Col. Copic's suicidal orders to attack the heavily defended Pingarrón Hill. Copic, the brigade commander, gave instructions to two British members of his staff, Captain D. F. Springhall and Lieutenant George Wattis, to carry his instructions personally to Merriman and to remove him from command if he refused to carry them out. Wattis had previously communicated an order from Copic that Merriman found so unreasonable that he wrote in his diary, "No such order ever came out of the general's staff before."[64]

The two men made their way to Merriman's command post by motorcycle. Once they arrived, Springhall and Wattis came to understand the Lincoln commander's reasons for questioning the command. Yet they did not have the authority to cancel the order they were carrying. Moved by Merriman's resolution to lead the attack himself, the two decided to go over the top with the Lincolns. Wattis joined No. 2 Company, and Springhall stayed with Merriman. As the madness of the order became apparent, the Lincoln officers could not persuade all of the young, untried Americans to leave their places of safety. Wattis, who was already famous for his coolness under fire, walked up and down the trenches, touching the shoulders of the reluctant with his swagger stick and motivating the more recalcitrant with his pistol.

As Merriman waved his troops on, the Lincoln commander fell almost immediately, badly wounded in the shoulder. Springhall received an appalling blow to his face, carrying away his upper teeth from one ear to the other. Wattis, however, was touched with George Nathan's special grace and luck that day. He paced the battlefield "upright and cool," encouraging the slackers into action. "Though a perfect target, he was not hit and never lost his *sangfroid* or his swagger stick."[65] His reputation as a brave, experienced, and resourceful officer was confirmed.

With Merriman down, David Jones succeeded to command, but he blurted out, "I don't know about military things a fuck."[66] Wattis then effectively took over the leadership and attempted to get the survivors back into their trenches. Unfortunately, as the Lincolns withdrew, they provided the Nationalists with perfect targets as the February sky darkened over the Jarama valley. It was two weeks later that Wattis, who was an excellent shot, left the trenches to snipe at the Fascists. D. R. Davies marveled at his bravery, particularly when Wattis took a bullet through his beret, which succeeded only in cutting off a lock of his hair. In the course of Wattis' heroics, one man was killed beside him and two wounded.[67]

Wattis emerged unharmed from this first blooding of the Americans, but not unscathed. Because of charges that he had forced men into the attack at gunpoint and had badly positioned a machine gun, he was forced to face "a Communist party trial." Sandor Voros wrote in his diary, "Charge against Wattis worked up [by] Madden whom he ordered over the top." The Lincoln commander, Martin Hourihan, "fought ag. it," seeing it as the "venom of one man, . . . the type who'd rather stay in the trenches than go over the top."[68] Wattis was exonerated.

At the beginning of March, the Lincolns, or what remained of them, assembled to select a new commander. Copic nominated Wattis (or another British volunteer of like ability) to succeed to the battalion command, but his British nationality proved an understandable obstacle.[69] Wattis also received prominent mention in the *Book of the XV Brigade*, which celebrated the exploits of the heroes of the brigade. The British, Irish, and Americans gave the editors names to "play up." Then, they divided the nominations into three categories, indicating the prominence the respective figures were to receive. Sandor Voros said that the difficulty "was how to glorify all those selected elite" and yet find space for the rank and file "without whom the Brigade would have had no history at all."[70] Wattis was selected as one of the battalion's "elite." His sniping exploit was remembered, and his refusal to withdraw brought the encomium: "Comrade Wattis displayed extreme bravery by staying in this position."[71]

II

When Harry Pollitt toured an American hospital after the battle of Teruel he met Wattis, who was recovering from wounds. Obviously impressed with him, Pollitt reported that Wattis was "brimming over with enthusiasm," having "splendid things to tell about the British comrades with whom he had been fighting at Belchite." The British party leader saw him as the very epitome of the wounded hero. "He made light of his wounds and his one wish was to get back quickly to the boys."[72]

Wattis even managed to impress mightily one of the old sweats from No. 1 Company. Syd Quinn had arrived in time to fight at Lopera with Nathan, John Cornford, and Ralph Fox. By Brunete, Quinn had seen the best and worst of his fellow countrymen in action. To him Wattis was "the most outstanding" of them all. Though he remembers the ex-British officer as being "superb" at the Jarama, particularly when he helped lead the Lincolns into battle, it was Wattis' performance at Brunete that overshadowed all else. In the inferno of the July heat of the furious battle, at a point where the shelling was extremely intense, and British resolution was beginning to erode, Wattis decided that his peaches-and-cream complexion required a shave. He put a mirror on a tree, lathered, and applied a razor to his face, explaining that he hoped to make an impression on the fascists. In fact, as Quinn well understood, he "made men realize all was not lost."[73] Steve Nelson, who succeeded Oliver Law in command of the Americans at Brunete, had equally high praise for Wattis, particularly because the Englishman's leadership and heroics did not seem to be sustained by deep political conviction. Nelson admitted, "Sometimes I wondered what kept him going because politically he didn't seem to fit and yet in every crisis . . . he stood his ground with a pistol in his hand," adding "that solid, determined stand was the stamp of this man." As for "cracks about his lack of political comments and knowledge, . . . the guys respected him. There were times when he was the last man to come out of the line."[74]

Wattis was badly wounded at Brunete, however. He recovered in time to play an important role in sorting out the confusion of the Retreats. On the morning of March 9, 1938, a huge Nationalist offensive was unleashed. Its purpose was to slice across the Aragón and into Catalonia in order to cut the Republic in two. Efforts to hold Belchite were unsuccessful, and the XVth Brigade made a fighting withdrawal. Those who survived the onslaught, along with retreating Americans, made a valiant stand at Caspe, but they were unable to hold the town. A significant number were lost in the running fight, including Robert Merriman, the commander of the Lincolns, who was probably captured and executed on a dirt road outside Corbera.

The retreats were, for the most part, orderly, but in light of the overwhelming strength of Franco's forces, many found themselves separated from their units and forced to make their way back into Republican lines alone or in small groups. A number were forced to swim the Ebro to reach the Republican lines on the north bank of the great river.

Another tragedy occurred when, after regrouping, the British Battalion marched to relieve the troops of Enrique Lister and unexpectedly encountered a deep penetration force of Italian troops while rounding a bend toward Calaceite in the early morning of March 31, 1938. The equally surprised but larger and better-armed force of Italians turned out to be advance elements of the massive Nationalist offensive. The unexpected attack, although heatedly contested by the British, including the destruction of several Italian tanks, resulted in the capture of 150 British volunteers.

The battalion had been decimated. Sam Wild was in hospital, and George Fletcher wounded. Consequently, Wattis was appointed to take command, but for only a short time. Wild hurried back from the hospital, acknowledging he was under the veteran officer's authority until the battalion was officially restored to him.[75]

III

The reason for this recitation of Wattis' martial virtues is to establish that he cannot be dismissed as a malcontent, shirker, drinker, or reluctant warrior, which were the usual charges made against disaffected volunteers such as Alec Marcovitch. Wattis and Dave Springhall, with whom he had once charged into battle at the Jarama, were now beginning to part company. Springhall, brave in action and badly wounded when he went over the top with Merriman, eagerly promoted the party line about the battalion. In a speech at the Communist party's London District Congress, Springhall acknowledged the misperception that the battalion was "a red army." To this, Springhall felt it necessary to point out "that it was a Spanish People's Army composed of all honest elements prepared to fight against Fascism." The party definition of "honest elements" was, of course, the sticking point.[76]

Not knowing that Wattis was already back in England, Harry Pollitt wrote on April 16, 1938, that he wanted to "facilitate" the veteran's return in light of his serious wounds. Further, as an ex-British army officer, his pension was in danger of being cut off. But, undoubtedly of most importance, Wattis possessed significant propaganda value. As a former officer he "can exercise influence in certain circles." Bill Rust, however, found Wattis' attitude to be "bad." Conceding that "he is a brave man and an excellently trained officer," he believed "he has had enough and cannot be strongly trusted." Rust reassured Pollitt he had "given him a straight talking to." In a moment of sublime self-deception, Rust said, "I think I have him where I want him just now."[77]

Among his other concerns, Wattis desired reassurances that once he had straightened out his financial affairs in England, he would be allowed to return to Spain. Rust wrote Pollitt on April 20, 1938, that "it seems to me undesirable that he should come back. Make good use of him there is the best thing."[78] In this expectation, both he and Pollitt were to be sorely disappointed. Despite Pollitt's intervention to have him repatriated, Wattis left Spain in April and was officially reported as a deserter on May 15, 1938.[79] Captain Wattis, Alonzo Elliott wrote, had now become one of the "agents of the class enemy."[80]

When Wattis returned to England after eighteen months in Spain, angry and disillusioned from his experiences, he learned that a question had been raised in the House of Commons about the activities of the Communist party in the battalion. He telephoned the M.P., Sir John Smedley Crooke, on April 9, 1938, giving him evidence of how deeply the Russians had compromised the independence and integrity of the battalion. A day later he put his remarks in writing. This brought a waspish reaction from Home Secretary R. A. B. Butler, a Franco supporter,[81] who scribbled across the bottom of a note: "Capt Wattis seems to be a student of Hudibras,"[82] referring to the satire by Samuel Butler inspired by *Don Quixote*.

Wattis refused to retreat into silence after writing to Smedley Crooke. At the end of April, he went to the foreign office, asking for assistance in evacuating the British volunteers from Spain and, at the same time, expanding his charges.[83] Fred Copeman, who was to criticize the party ten years later for "its ruthless opposition to a contrary point of view,"[84] wrote to his companion-in-arms and fellow communist Sam Wild about Wattis, "who no doubt you have heard has joined the Fascists. He speaks these days on behalf of the Friends of General Franco."[85] André Marty judged the situation serious enough to write Harry Pollitt concerning the former British army officer.[86]

The defense of the battalion's "story" was well under way. Three months after Wattis contacted Smedley Crooke, Bill Rust, the first and only historian of the battalion for forty years, sent a sounding shot across the bows of any veteran who chose to question the image of antifascist solidarity and democratic commitment of the men of the battalion. If they wanted their place in working-class history secured, the best decision was to keep silent. In return, he would write, "The people of England owe a debt of gratitude to the men who marched away in the ranks of the British Battalion to fight in the cause of peace and democracy. It is one of the most glorious episodes in the history of the working class."[87] Although in many ways accurate, this statement shielded darker truths, ones with which Rust unquestionably had the widest familiarity.[88]

The lines of John Cornford's famous poem, "Full Moon at Tierz: Before the Storming of Huesca," which seemed so faultlessly pure in the early days of the war, now rang hollowly:

> Freedom is an easily spoken word
> But facts are stubborn things. Here, too, in Spain
> Our fight's not won till the workers of all the world
> Stand by our guard on Huesca's plain,
> Swear that our dead fought not in vain,
> Raise the red flag triumphantly
> For Communism and for liberty.

Freedom was indeed "an easily spoken word," and "facts" proved to be intractably "stubborn things," which defied any linkage between "Communism and liberty."

IV

There were those who justly drew a distinction between the behavior of the Soviets and the British party. For example, Copeman said he knew that the Russians "were up to all the tricks in hell,"[89] implying a distance between the British and Russian communists in Spain. But he and Harry Pollitt were extremely close, and Copeman was named a member of the British party's Central Committee. One must conclude that the British party leadership must have known, officially or unofficially, something of the increasing Russian terror in Spain.

Also, it is hard to believe that at some level the volunteers them-selves did not know what was taking place. The British in Spain had a short period of innocence. At the battle of Lopera near the end of December 1936, Lt. Col. LaSalle, commander of the Marseillaise Battalion, to which Nathan and the No. 1 Company were attached, was tried and executed on charges of spying for the fascists. That he was an incompetent leader and lost his nerve seems clear, but in the confusion of the early fighting this was hardly unusual. LaSalle's commissar, who himself was executed for treachery by the Resis-tance during World War II, formally denounced his commanding officer. There are suggestions that André Marty was behind the charges against LaSalle because of his growing paranoia about spies, as well as to settle an old score. Despite other evidence that he may have been guilty, the Marseillaise commander died insisting upon his innocence.[90]

LaSalle's execution, however, was not just an internecine political intrigue among the French. What is troubling is the role that the British political and military leadership may have played. On January 3, 1937, Ralph Cantor wrote in his diary, "Trial of our Commandant De LaSalle [who was] proved to be receiving money from the Italians." General Walter instructed Maurice Levine and Syd Quinn to take charge of the prisoner until the court martial proceedings began. There were two British observers[91] at the "trial" itself, one of them apparently the commissar, Bob Elliott. Not only this, Cantor wrote cryptically, "Nathan chief witness." He added, "Verdict and sentence and execution within 20 minutes."[92]

Maurice Levine also places the commander of the English Company at the trial.[93] Nathan may well have testified to the military incompetence of the accused, but, since he was not a communist, it is not easy to understand the principal role he allegedly played in the judgment passed on his commanding officer. And the British themselves were divided on the matter of what should be done with the French commander. The old soldier, Jock Cunningham, believed it was wrong to carry out the execution. Typically, Copeman speculated that LaSalle could have just been frightened and "perhaps he was fed up and drifted a bit." Neither agreed with the summary justice administered to the French commander, and Copeman believed that the commander of the International Brigades, André Marty, was behind it.[94] The point, nevertheless, is that from their earliest service, the British did not stand back from the politicization of justice, nor did they question the Communist party's authority in its administration.

It must be recognized, however, that much of the political intriguing could go unrecognized if a volunteer was not in the party, did his job, and kept his mouth shut. Unquestionably for some volunteers, much could be accepted in order to achieve the purpose they had come for — to defeat fascism. As Raymond Carr has written, "Without passports and with no help from their embassies, the discontented and disillusioned ('they told me this was a revolution, but it's nothing but a f— war') soldiered on."[95]

V

With this background in mind, we can move to the accusations made by Wattis. In his letter to Smedley Crooke, Captain Wattis charged that the Russian NKVD[96] had thoroughly infiltrated both the Spanish Popular Army and the International Brigades since the outbreak of the war. Although this may have been known or guessed by the volunteers, very few, if any, could have imagined the scale of Soviet penetration, which went down to the cadre level. To evaluate properly the plausibility of Wattis' revelations, it is necessary to put them within the context of Soviet espionage strategy in Spain. Fortunately, we know much more about NKVD activities in Spain since the Russian archives have been opened, and particularly the role played by General Alexander Orlov in promoting Soviet interests in Spain.

Several months after the war broke out in July, the influence of the Soviet secret police began to expand throughout Spain, eventually operating outside the control of the Republican government. Its chief was the Soviet spymaster, Alexander Orlov, who arrived at Gaylord's Hotel, where the Soviet mission was housed, on September 16, 1936. Although in reality he was head of the Madrid station of the Soviet NKVD, General Orlov presented himself to the Republican government as a political attaché. In fact, he possessed immense authority, justified by Moscow's charge to conduct counterintelligence and oversee internal security as well as Soviet supplies making their way to Spain. His chief functions, however, were to conduct intelligence operations. One of the ways he chose to do this was to encourage the burgeoning power of the SIM, the Spanish Republican secret police, which Orlov helped shape into the mirror image of the NKVD, and to which George Murray of the Anti-Tank Battery, for one, reported. The head of the SIM in the International Brigades answered directly to André Marty, but he and his organization were a power unto themselves.[97]

The American, Anthony De Maio, represented SIM's interests in the XVth Brigade. His reports on the political conduct of British volunteers appear frequently in their personnel files in Moscow. For example, Brendon Moroney, a laborer from Great Britain, was judged guilty of "insubordination and mutiny." Because of this, De Maio accused him of being "an out and out fascist" who "should have been shot for the disruption he has caused here."[98] It might have been pointed out to De Maio that if the British navy or army had implemented such a policy, at least two of the British Battalion commanders, Fred Copeman and Sam Wild, as well as the battalion's finest combat leader, Jock Cunningham—each of them guilty of "insubordination and mutiny"—would not have had an opportunity to volunteer for Spain. After the war, in hearings before the House Committee on Un-American Activities, De Maio was accused twice of murdering prisoners for whom he was responsible. He responded to the charges in a circumlocutory manner, and then decided to take the Fifth Amendment.[99]

It is possible to obtain a glimpse into the paranoid and murderous world of the SIM in the case of the English sailor Geoffrey Byng (Geoffrey Marshall), who served in the Republican navy. A rumor had been started that Byng was a British secret agent, which, in a letter to his family that was intercepted, he vociferously denied. "Anyone

who has served with me knows quite well that I have never been
anything but fanatically loyal to the Republican government." He
was nevertheless arrested and detained on a prison ship for a week.
Before taking him to SIM headquarters in Barcelona, a guard bran-
dishing a machine gun told Byng that he was going to be executed
immediately, "and I believed him." Instead he was imprisoned with
150 officers "of all sorts," some of whom had been incarcerated for
six months without charges. As far as he knew, his fate, too, remained
undetermined.[100]

Orlov recruited promising communists in the International Brigades to join the international NKVD network. To facilitate this,
Orlov set up a secret center in Spain, of which the Republican
government knew nothing, to train agents. Several of its graduates
would pay rich intelligence dividends to Moscow during World War
II and the Cold War. The Soviet spymaster was not only interested in
placing reliable agents in strategically important places in Europe and
the United States. He and his associates recruited other International
Brigaders for undercover activities in Spain. Their purpose was to
move against those political factions that Moscow believed possessed
Trotskyist associations. As a result of Orlov's manifold activities, his
operational correspondence spills over with reports of the apprehen-
sion of "spies" throughout Republican Spain.[101] Walter Krivitsky, a
key figure in the NKVD (OGPU), who defected to the West only to
die under mysterious circumstances in Washington, D.C., in 1941,
said that the NKVD

> had its own special prisons. Its units carried out assassinations and kid-
> nappings. It filled hidden dungeons and made flying raids. It functioned,
> of course, independently of the Loyalist government. The Ministry of
> Justice had no authority over the OGPU, which was an empire within an
> empire. It was a power before which even some of the highest officials in
> the Largo Caballero government trembled. The Soviet Union seemed to
> have a grip on Loyalist Spain, as if it were already a Soviet possession.[102]

But it did not require a high-ranking Soviet agent to reveal the truth.
When the Labour MP and Republican supporter, James Griffiths,
visited Spain in 1938, he confided to his diary that "the secret police
is still an unpleasant feature on the Government side."[103] This horror
was Stalin's price for Russian support during the defense of Madrid
and subsequent Soviet arms shipments, which, despite widespread
belief to the contrary, were not benefactions but bought and paid for
by Spanish gold.

The refusal or inability of communist volunteers in the battalion to see the web of deceit, paranoia, and brutality in which they were enmeshed was to last beyond the end of their military service in Spain. At the end of World War II, in what can only be called a state of continuing denial, Sam Wild angrily denounced those who perpetuated the legend of a Red Spain, when, in fact, he said, there were never more than two communist ministers in the government. For Wild it was indeed a war in which the simplicity of antifascism explained all. Tom Murray, who served as a commissar, said of the stories of the Stalinization of the battalion, "None of that was true. I certainly wasn't aware of Soviet state security men dominating our battalion or any other with which I had contact."[104] In view of the fact that Murray was an "underground" communist in Spain, sent there under party discipline while posing as a member of the Labour party, that his sister was a communist nurse in Spain, and his brother, George, worked for the SIM, this denial appears to be somewhat disingenuous. Other members of the battalion were unquestionably engaged in intelligence activities. For example, Thomas Brazell, a tin-plate worker from Llanelly who was killed at the Ebro, described his military duties as "inteligence [sic] C.P. work," in addition to soldiering.[105]

VI

Those who spoke for the British volunteers have persisted until the last in denying the independent power of the Communist party in Spain. The combined service of Nan Green and Alonzo Elliott in Spain lasted from September 1937 until February 1939. In a 1977 joint publication, *Spain against Fascism, 1936–39: Some Questions Answered*, the two acknowledged that "stories about 'NKVD' agents in Spain" have been widely believed, even by "progressive historians." Yet, they themselves tended to think "that most of them are apocryphal." Considering the length of time they spent in Spain, they could have been expected to hear of individuals who had fallen into the clutches of the Communist intelligence apparat. But, "We never did."[106]

The unspeakable irony of this statement is that Nan Green herself was one of those who fell into its hands. A hospital administrator in Spain and the wife of George Green, who was killed in the last action of the British Battalion, she became for more than forty years the much-loved and esteemed secretary of the British International Brigade Association. Green's Moscow file, however, offers some remarkable reading. In it is a denunciation of her by Bill Rust, the *Daily Worker* correspondent in Spain, but, more important, a member of the Central Committee of the CPGB. He charges her with being an "adventurer" and then urges that she be expelled from Spain.[107]

Rust's accusation reflects much about the man and the time. He submits, first, that Green had a sexual liaison with a hospitalized International Brigader whom Rust judged to be "either a Trotskyist or Fascist," and who later deserted. Second, her superior, Dr. Krushmar, made a report "very critical of her work." Third, Krushmar found a letter in her room that was "full of criticisms of the Soviet Union," even though it was unclear who had written it. Rust admitted that "the only criticism" that he could bring with certainty against Green was her friendship with "the very bad element." In a dizzying display of communist logic, he found this sufficient to conclude that "in any case, it is clear that Nan Green should not be permitted to undertake any party work."[108] Not to put too fine a point on it, she could no longer be trusted by the Communist party.

Green herself was under no illusions as to how her behavior might be seen. But Rust knew only the outlines of the story of the troubled hospital where she worked. In her unpublished memoir, which is painfully honest, Green reveals a complex tale of intrigue and deception. Her medical chief, Kushmar, was an addict who was consuming the hospital's supply of morphine. Green's signature was required to order more narcotics. He made sexual advances to her, "not I am sure for my *beaux yeux* but to neutralise my hostility." The hospital commissar, Frank Ayres, a Yorkshire railwayman who had been a member of the party since its earliest days, had himself become a victim of a whispering campaign because he refused to remove anarchist reading materials from the patients' library. When Ayres returned to England, he left behind a confidential assessment of the hospital personnel with a trusted employee. One of the staff reported Ayres' confidant to be a spy and accused her of having stolen the report, which resulted in her imprisonment. Only after "days of interviews, depositions, counter-depositions, enquiries and table-thumpings" was Green able to obtain her release.[109]

Upon their return to the hospital at Valdeganga, Kushmar counter-attacked by firing Ayres' assistant and accusing Green of financial mismanagement. He took Green to Albacete "where he made God knows what allegations about me to the authorities (some of [whom] followed me round to my later jobs though I did not know it until much later)." As a consequence of the charges she was dismissed from the hospital. Green refused to do the "wise" thing and "fight my way through the sinister series of events that had led to my dismissal from Valdeganga, and demand vindication." In part it was because she knew she could find work in Barcelona where she was "believed in," and also because the war was at a critical stage, and "I would be wasting every one's time just to put myself in the right again."[110]

There was, however, another reason for her reluctance to fight the injustice that had been done to her. She felt "a stain on my conscience," and with her characteristic honesty described it. In her memoir she wrote, "In the last turbulent days of Valdeganga I had fallen victim to an ephemeral affair with a patient, a man much younger than myself, which in that over-charged atmosphere . . . had exploded—and gone out like a rocket." She realized that it must have become widely known. "I was feeling deeply guilty and wanted to put it behind me." She realized that her retreat from the arena of vilification "was not wise." Kushmar, she knew, "had filed a scurrilous report on me which had reached, not perhaps the medical services but a much higher and more powerful authority, charged with the scrutiny of Communists from all countries."[111] Bill Rust was a member in good standing of this "much higher and more powerful authority," and was close to the center of this "sinister series of events."

Nan Green, a woman of exceptional quality by any standard, was one of the fortunate ones. At the time of the repatriation of the International Brigades in 1938, her party reputation had been restored. The final critique of her read, "I believe she is a genuine and sincere Communist and wants to give the best of her abilities. She is brave and never seeks her own personal comfort. She is the type of Communist who is always working to keep up the morale of those around her." Her previous difficulties with the party were caused by "irresponsible gossips." The grievances against her were "false and actuated by jealousy."[112] Probably by the time her file arrived in Moscow Green was on board a ship, chartered by Wogan Philips[113] and paid for by British contributions, taking 5,000 Spanish refugees to Mexico.[114] At the same time her would-be nemesis, Bill Rust, may have been seeing his book, *Britons in Spain*, through the press. Both the idealism and the mythmaking were moving swiftly ahead. Rust wrote his book before the war ended. After Spain, he assumed full-time labors with the Communist party. The world of deceptions, lies, and ruthless ambition in which he moved with such agility in Spain became lost for sixty years.

VII

Wild, Green, and perhaps Murray appeared not to want to know what was really taking place around them, even when they themselves were in harm's way. But information perhaps unavailable to them must have been accessible to Nan Green's co-author Alonzo Elliott. For him to say that he knew nothing of NKVD activities in Spain seems implausible.

Elliott became a member of the party in 1934 while a student at Cambridge. In Spain he worked under Luigi Longo in Madrid at the headquarters of the political commissars and subsequently served in the Foreign Cadres Commission of the Spanish Communist party in Barcelona. His notes appear prominently in the files of the British volunteers. Interestingly enough, in Elliott's file is a formal portrait of "Gallo" (Luigi Longo), Inspector General of the International Brigades, dated January 1, 1939, and obviously meant as a farewell gift. On his picture Gallo wrote an appreciative note concerning Elliott's service. Elliott had worked closely with André Marty as well as Longo during the repatriation of the brigades. Subsequently, he stayed behind to help organize the departure of scattered brigaders still in Spain. Some of them had to fight their way to the French border, and then evade their chief, André Marty, if he believed them to have sensitive information about his or the party's activities in Spain.[115] Because of his unique status, Elliott wrote a lengthy history of the British Battalion in Spain for the party, which is thorough, detailed, and convincingly suggests that he is one of those who "knew." But Alonzo Elliott was the man to keep the secrets.

The account by Nan Green and Alonzo Elliott of the British in Spain presents a stunning contrast to the accusations Wattis made in his letter to Smedley Crooke. Writing from the Endsleigh Hotel close to Euston Station, Wattis named the chief NKVD officer "for all the Brigades," as one "Major Stefanovitch."[116] According to Wattis, next in the chain of command was an NKVD Moscow-trained operative assigned general responsibility for each of the brigades. To facilitate his work, three agents reported to him from within the individual brigades. Additionally, he planted "spies" in every "group" of twelve men. Each of these "secret agents" was a communist, known to his counterparts in the battalion.

Their masters instructed them to overhear the conversations of soldiers and prepare secret reports for the NKVD. Wattis wrote, "As a result of their activities officers and men are liable to arrest, to be held incommunicado, tried secretly, and disappear." On a larger scale, he said, NKVD personnel operated in such cities as Valencia and Barcelona. There, agents would actively cultivate conversations with men and officers on leave and report back in detail "to the chief of the Service," presumably Orlov. If the agent discovered something sufficiently incriminating about one of the volunteers, action of a direct or indirect nature soon followed. "In those cases where it would cause a scandal for the man to be executed secretly[,] arrangements are made for him to be disposed of during an action."[117]

All this resulted in a growing disillusion within the battalion. Wattis believed that communist members had "contracts" that specified a length of service, allowing them to take leave and, ultimately, return to England, while noncommunists were expected to serve for the duration of the war. In a subsequent interview at the foreign office, in which he sought the means to evacuate his former comrades from Spain, Wattis enlarged upon his comments to include the reasons for the incompetence of the Spanish Republican Army. He felt it was due in part "to the undermining of discipline by the political commissars and agents, and to the growing belief that communism was no better than fascism."[118]

The close relationship that Wattis felt existed between the battalion and the SIM finds support from the British consular service. In a memorandum dated June 9, 1937, a consular official alleged that "the delegation of the International Brigade in Madrid . . . appears to be closely connected with the secret service organisation." He reported that a staff member of the consulate went to make an inquiry at IB headquarters and "was given a rather ugly hint that his presence in their offices was not desired and might lead to unpleasant consequences for him."[119] This reception would not have surprised Fred Copeman. Copeman was so convinced that the Soviets acted independently of any authority but their own that he believed (erroneously, it would seem) that Bob Merriman and Wally Tapsell did not die in battle. Instead, he thought they were liquidated by the Russians because, as senior officers, they "found out something. They had their teeth in something which was rotten and they weren't bloody well letting go."[120]

G. D. H Cole, one of the comparative handful of intellectuals on the left who distanced themselves from the methods of the Soviet Union, described the work of the NKVD in Spain with classic British understatement: "A body which is even partly engaged in espionage and terrorism is not one which lovers of freedom can contemplate with pleasure."[121]

VIII

Another of those who must have known of the parallel authority that developed in the International Brigades was Harry Pollitt, head of the British Communist party and frequent guest in the Soviet Union. More than any other individual, he had stirred the British working classes to concern and sacrifice for the Spanish Republic. Kevin Morgan has written, "In the first heady months of the war there was no greater stimulus to solidarity with the republic than Pollitt's passionate oratory and his regular appeals for recruits and donations in the *Daily Worker*."[122] Pollitt made five trips to Spain to visit the battalion and his devotion to the welfare of the volunteers was both moving and incontestable. Copeman said of him, "He thought only of the battalion, . . . and he wouldn't give a damn about Russian commissars or anything like that." Later, when Pollitt made it clear that he would follow the Moscow line wherever it led, Sam Wild wrote to him. He stated his "confidence that the Pal and Comrade I loved and trusted for his devotion to the Battalion will emerge from this fully conscious that the line he takes is for the benefit of the class he had sacrificed so much for."[123] Yet the British commissars, such as Will Paynter, regularly sent Pollitt reports that demonstrated the difference "between the official version of events . . . and the reality."[124]

There is only one way this paradox can be resolved. Kevin Morgan argues what can be inferred from Wild's letter, that it is necessary to understand Pollitt's absolute conviction that the interests of the Soviet Union were indistinguishable from those of the working classes of the world. Stalin's activities inside or outside Russia could not be seen within traditional categories of abstract political morality. Thus, Pollitt remained a Stalinist all his life, his blind devotion to the Russian leader rooted in the class hatred that drove him throughout his long political career. Since the word "intellectual" has been employed in this study in both the Gramscian sense as well as more traditionally, Raymond Aron speaks to Harry Pollitt as well as to D. N. Pritt and John Strachey when he asks, "How many intellectuals have come to the revolutionary party via the path of moral indignation, only ultimately to connive at terror and autocracy?"[125]

When La Pasionaria's letters and speeches were published in England shortly after the war, a reviewer parroted the now familiar themes, "The Government's cause is that of democrats all over the world, and conversely . . . the rebels are assisted by Fascists and reactionaries in every country."[126] It had not yet occurred to him or to many others that Spain was indeed a battleground of totalitarianism—of the left as well as the right—and that cynics and idealists found lodging on both sides of the conflict. The unfortunate Alec Marcovitch never doubted that freedom of expression was the right of every volunteer in Spain, as did all those supporters of the Republic outside Spain who believed that the "cause" of the Republic was that of all who believed in democratic expression. To compound the problem, there were those who departed from Spain before their illusions were shattered, and who helped reinforce the conventional stereotypes.[127] But the reality remained that the battalion was firmly in the grip of the party, whatever the political affiliations of individual volunteers.

When Harry Pollitt wrote to the secretariat of the Spanish Communist party arranging for the return of the volunteers, including Marcovitch, to England, he addressed specifically what was to be done with volunteers "who are in prison for offenses against military discipline." They "will receive very little sympathy in this country."[128] Pollitt wrote that nevertheless the practical problem remained that the "relatives and friends" are "sympathetic to us, and they tend to become embittered by their inability to get news and by the fact that all the men are returning home." Therefore, "from the point of view of its political and propaganda effect," the miscreants should be returned either with the battalion or "shortly" afterwards. If they were left in Spain, it would only stimulate "anti-Republican" feeling. He assured the Spanish communists in words that should be fully measured. "It is by no means due to any concern with the men themselves," he said, "but out of consideration for political values."[129] Pollitt, who in most respects was a genuinely compassionate man, simply could not see the volunteers in prison, including the wounded, as anything but traitors to the cause to which he and his party had devoted so much.

Therefore, the makers of the "legend" of the British Battalion as an example of the United Front in action stand sadly revealed. The Communist party, in practice, stood in opposition to virtually every political instinct—democratic pluralism, the rights of the individual, freedom from oppression—that was incarnate in the British progressive tradition. "Winning the war against Fascism" would mean little, many now understood, if the victors were indistinguishable from the vanquished.[130] And yet, as we shall see, for a proletarian intellectual such as Billy Griffiths, the party possessed a theological claim on his soul. His experience would offer the clearest evidence of the manner in which inherent intelligence, decency, and courage could become sacrificial offerings to the British party.

CHAPTER 13

The True Believer

THE RETREATS—MARCH 1938
THE EBRO OFFENSIVE—JULY 1938

Our fight's not won till the workers of all the world
Stand by our guard on Huesca's plain,
Swear that our dead fought not in vain,
Raise the red flag triumphantly
For Communism and for liberty.
— John Cornford

I

In the spring and summer of 1938 the party attempted to make the battalion more efficient by initiating an "activist" movement whose purpose was to "challenge" the other national groups of volunteers to achieve a series of goals which the ex-public school boy John Peet regretfully said "had no relation to reality." They ranged widely from abolishing illiteracy to establishing choirs, theatre companies, and dance groups, as well as developing special military training. In addition to determining "who could be the most active activists," it was necessary that "every activist was going to recruit a new activist." Less explicitly, each activist was meant to encourage morale and to look for indications of "defeatism."[1]

This well-intentioned but misguided and often ludicrous waste of effort was symptomatic of the party's determination to reemerge as a coherent presence among the British volunteers. Despite controlling the battalion, the party had refused to establish a visible and separate organizational presence since the early days in Albacete for two reasons. First, it might well jeopardize the United Front policy, which promised the unity of all antifascists. Second, the minister of defense, Indalecio Prieto, attacked the system of commissars in October 1937 and made it illegal for an officer in the Popular Army, which now had absorbed the International Brigades, to engage in political work. The British were reluctant to defy the law of the Republic. Even when Prime Minister Negrín made it easier for the party to function openly, "It was done in a very obvious & clumsy fashion," understandably harming the "unity" among "the non-party, anarchist and others." The leadership of the brigade decided it was the responsibility of the commissars to provide contact on an individual basis with those volunteers who were communists. But, inevitably, the work of the party "was carried out in a haphazard way."[2]

This meant that the battalion possessed little organized defense against internal criticism of British party policy. The most serious issue was repatriation. This arose because "for a long time" the volunteers believed that they had agreed to serve six months and then be sent home. This impression was fostered both in England and confirmed at Albacete by prominent members of the brigade leadership. Quite understandably, many of the men believed it to be true; in fact, the policy had changed when the battalion had become part of the Popular Army. This offered an easy target to the dissatisfied. As a result, "The weak, disruptive, alien and cowardly elements in the Brigade took advantage of this failure to understand the fascist demagogy to increase demoralization and weaken the Brigade."[3]

In the spring of 1938 the CPGB decided to disregard "legalisms." Billy Griffiths, a miner from Tonypandy,[4] played a key role in the party's late attempt to regenerate itself in the battalion. Ironically, Griffiths, like Tom Murray of Edinburgh, had no intention of volunteering for Spain, although he was a leading party activist and organizer in the Rhondda, who devoted himself to the cause of Spain. Nevertheless, he said, "I hesitated to take the final step." He did not see himself as good military material and believed that his effectiveness as an organizer and party leader was more important to the Republic's survival than anything he might accomplish with a rifle. Moreover, he was candid enough to admit that he liked what he was doing. As with so many able workers, political leadership offered an avenue to upward mobility and a kind of success he had never known before, particularly in South Wales, where the party exercised widespread influence. "It gave me power[,] status and responsibility." In "an ever widening circle," Griffiths found himself "a person of some substance with a brighter future." Therefore, he at first "resented" the party's decision that he should go to Spain. But the more he thought about it, the more he came to believe that it was wise. "Politics was no longer a game. Slogans became clothed in flesh and blood."[5]

Griffiths was not the only Welsh stalwart to resist the invitation to fight in Spain. The Welsh had suffered grievously on the Spanish battlefields. According to Griffiths, "recruiting was not easy. There was a certain reluctance among leading comrades to volunteer." Arthur Horner, a communist and president of the South Wales Miners, attempted to clarify what was expected of a loyal comrade by putting the experience of militants in historical perspective. In the twenties, he said, when management victimized a communist worker, the party considered their man's dismissal a necessary sacrifice for the coming victory over capitalism, and expected the victim to feel the same. Subsequently, a stint in prison became the mark of loyalty staunchly offered as tribute to the party and to the future of the working class. But a new time had come. "Now it was expected that one should die for the party." Thus, the cup was passed to Griffiths and to Jack Jones, another miner from the Rhondda, more experienced and older than Griffiths, who had been a student at the Labour College. Neither was an impressive physical specimen. "It would require a great deal of political courage to make up [for] what we both lacked in the normal faculties of other men," Griffiths said.[6]

In the early spring of 1938 Jones and Griffiths found a sufficient number of other recruits to organize a group and begin their journey to Spain. The new band of volunteers departed by boat train from Euston. They submitted themselves to the usual physical inspections in Paris. When it was discovered that some of those being rejected "were good men, sound political types, fully dedicated," the party leadership quietly consulted the examining physician and all were passed as fit. The group of about forty men, including Griffiths and Jones, arrived in Béziers near the frontier. Two guides led them in single file onto the mountain trails. Griffiths remembered "the climbing became more difficult and seemed never ending. Hour after hour we pushed and scrambled, slipped and pulled, up and up . . . in the dark of the night. When dawn broke the worst was over. We rested and looked down. It seemed impossible." Going down the pass proved comparatively easy, and, twelve hours after starting, they had arrived, at last, in Spain.[7]

The worst of the journey was not over for Griffiths. The little miner was to become the innocent victim of the revolutionary discipline he later advocated so energetically to his comrades in the battalion. When he sat down to eat at Figueras, shortly after arrival, he found the food put before him "atrocious." Unable to consume a portion of rice, he attempted to return it to the kitchen staff, and "much to [his] surprise and consternation" found himself immediately arrested and taken to the guard house. "I spent a number of anxious hours wondering what was going to happen." Jack Jones interceded on his behalf, suggesting that a misunderstanding had occurred.[8]

The commander, Mike Economides, a Cypriot whom Jones had known in London, judged that in view of the shortage of food, what Griffiths had done was "most serious." Then he came to the real point. Economides told the newcomers that the war in Spain was being waged in two directions—"the enemy in front and the Fifth Column in the rear." Moreover, "a clever agitator could exploit the food situation, fan discontent, and undermine morale." It was as if Griffiths and Jones had entered Camus' city of plague and found themselves immediately contaminated, in their case by party paranoia. Jack Jones agreed to take personal responsibility for Griffiths, which was the miner's only way out of the perilous situation. Griffiths understandably wondered "what would have happened if the circumstances had been less favourable," adding, "it was a sobering thought."[9] In spite of this greeting, party discipline prevailed for Griffiths. Not only did he refuse to condemn the suspicions of his hosts, but he agreed that such precautions, which might have cost him his life, were justified. The worlds of conspiracy and *agents provocateurs* were the very foundations of a party loyalist's life, and, therefore, Griffiths found nothing objectionable about his treatment.

He was to take these views into an important new party initiative when he joined the battalion on the eve of the Retreats.[10] After Franco's recapture of Teruel, the following month the Nationalists launched the greatest offensive of the war in the Aragón. Their intention was to separate Catalonia, its industries, and reserves of manpower, from the rest of the Republic. Skillfully combining air and artillery power, and deploying an overwhelming concentration of force, the attack sent the Popular Army reeling into retreat, gathering up Griffiths and the newly arrived volunteers in its fury. Although Major Johnson, the American commander of the brigade training center, told Griffiths, Jones, and the other new arrivals that they would be in his charge for three to sixth months before they were ready for action, they were packed into food vans before dawn, traveling until noon of the following day. Other vehicles then took them on a sixteen-hour journey until they caught up with the battalion, or what was left of it after its fighting retreat from Belchite to

Caspé. Sam Wild had returned as battalion commander after treatment for a wound in the hospital, and he was in a foul temper, chiefly because of his displeasure with the performance of his men. Wild spoke bluntly. A number of comrades had abandoned all discipline in order to save themselves: bugging out, deserting, and, worst of all, throwing their rifles away, thus helping to create a panic. Wild told his men that more retreats were coming, but that the battalion's withdrawal must be both controlled and orderly. If the men had to break and run again, there would be a place and time for a rendezvous. No time was available for a democratic discussion of alternative plans. Those who would not accept this course of action, turned up late, or without their weapons, would be "instantly shot."[11]

Sam Wild halted the battalion's disintegration by imposing a convincing measure of order and control under bewildering circumstances, thus restoring a feeling of group solidarity, and reducing the individual soldier's sense of facing the terrors of the battlefield alone. But only training could establish a sense of oneness with the battalion, and Griffiths and the other newcomers had been denied this.[12] One of the arrivals, John Peet, joined the battalion "or what remained of it" in an open field close to the Ebro. His new comrades hardly seemed the stuff of which heroes were made. "They sat or lay there, exhausted beyond all limits, after weeks of defeat, confusion, hunger. Most of them appeared apathetic. They stared at us with empty eyes—the odds and sods, the men back from hospital, the rookies fresh from Britain, and most of them turned away if you questioned them."[13]

Committed communists like Griffiths and Peet could accept Wild's orders with equanimity because the battalion was part of a larger movement to which they had long devoted themselves. Another volunteer might not. For example, John Lambert, a noncommunist who refused to be swept up in the Retreats, submitted a sworn statement to the Special Branch shortly after his return to England: "I think it is all wrong that young boys should be recruited for service in Spain without any military training at all and be sent to the front line a day or two after they arrive in Spain."[14]

After joining the battalion, one of the first volunteers Griffiths saw was Harry Dobson, another miner from the Rhondda whom he had known for years, and who was also a party loyalist of the first order. With Dobson's help, Griffiths began to learn the rudiments of a soldier's life under less than ideal circumstances. But Griffiths "had plenty of energy and drive," was very intelligent, and reacted quickly to challenges.[15]

The battalion was on the move through the village of Calaceite in the early morning hours of March 31. Dawn was breaking, and Griffiths saw light flickering in the distance. He and his comrades advanced into the village, when firing suddenly broke out and Italian tanks and soldiers appeared. Fortunately for Griffiths, he was in the rear of the column and was able to slip down a high embankment which offered temporary cover. It was extraordinary how calm this instant soldier felt in the madhouse that erupted all around him. The experienced comrade he was assisting on a machine gun took off, leaving Griffiths fumbling to set up the weapon properly. Nevertheless, he was able to establish a firing position and began blasting away at the Italians. Then, with the hopelessness of the situation apparent, one of the leaders ordered Griffiths to exfiltrate with others.

In his desperation and disorientation, he suddenly saw Malcolm Dunbar, now the brigade chief of staff, sitting calmly on a low wall of a stone bridge, taking notes and apparently "oblivious of the shells which shrieked over head, or of the planes which swooped down from time to time to strafe." For Griffiths, "the effect was startling."[16] The tall, shy Cambridge graduate, who within moments would be wounded, communicated to Griffiths a confidence and reassurance that conditions hardly justified. Griffiths and others managed to escape the fate that befell 150 of their comrades, including Jack Jones, who had been captured in the debacle. Griffiths and Syd James tried to get one of the others in their group to help them with the heavy machine gun and ammunition they were carrying, but to no avail. It was each man for himself.

With important exceptions, demoralization was now destroying what remained of the battalion. Griffiths' group dropped to three. When they finally made contact with brigade transportation, and waited to be picked up, the miner saw an acquaintance from the Rhondda walking past them. When Griffiths told him they intended to return to the line, he laughed, shrugged, and then waved good-bye, moving in the opposite direction. Griffiths' Spanish education had now entered a new phase. Despite all the propaganda at home, the British volunteers were not all working-class heroes. "It was our first experience of deliberate desertion."[17] Under the gifted leadership of Lt. Cipriano, the commander of the Spanish company in the battalion, they made their way back to the lines of the Americans and the

Canadians. The Nationalist offensive, however, forced Griffiths and James to take to their heels again.

Syd James believed the war was almost over, and the moment had come to make their way out of Spain. Griffiths refused, and James accused him of being "too class conscious." Finally, James left him to find medical treatment, and Griffiths was completely alone. Untrained, certain only of his lack of aptitude for the military life but with the consolation of his political beliefs, Billy Griffiths had received his blooding in the Retreats, and acquitted himself well. But when he wrote home, he recognized the difficulty of explaining his experience to those left behind. "The separation was not of distance alone. There was an unbridgeable gap of experience which I would have had some difficulty understanding had I not lived through it."[18]

The wreck of the battalion finally settled, and it was now up to replacements, many of them Spaniards, to salvage the remains. In a few days Sam Wild felt confident enough to parade his command and address them. He told the battalion that their orders were to resist the Nationalist advance at all costs. They must prepare for what was to come. Wild then asked for volunteers to dig trenches.

Wild's instructions were typical of his command style. These were men of his class, and he knew how to talk to them. There were no histrionics or rhetorical flourishes of any kind, such as a Macartney or perhaps a Wintringham might have employed. He said, "Those who volunteer will receive no thanks. But those who don't can look out."[19] Not a member of the battalion asked for further explanation. The simplicity of Wild's style, which essentially was one of leading by example, was dictated, too, by the paucity of leadership opportunities available to men of his class. As one volunteer said, "The pattern of working-class life in Britain between the wars had done little to inculcate leadership skills."[20] But fortunately, as Jim Brewer said, Sam Wild was a "born leader."

As the British were resting and training in the early summer of 1938 before the Ebro battle in July, David Guest joined Griffiths in the battalion. He had been a principal party organizer in Battersea, and unlike many middle-class intellectuals who went to Spain, knew many of the working-class volunteers personally. He felt he had talents to offer the battalion, such as his organizing abilities. More important, he wrote in notes found after his death, "There is also the need to show that there is no division between party 'workers' and 'intellectuals' over this matter." Like Griffiths, Guest did not look like a soldier. He was thin and emaciated. The two volunteers—the brilliant Cambridge and Göttingen philosopher and mathematician, and the miner from the Rhondda—were similar in other ways. Both were dedicated Communists and anti-Trotskyists. One of Guest's closest associates in the YCL, Dorothy Woodard, wrote that he "showed us the dangers of Trotskyism and how it disrupts the ranks of the workers."[21]

In Spain, Griffiths was amazed at the inner resources Guest commanded, and was perhaps unconsciously reminded of himself. The newcomer, who had taken such a circumlocutory journey to the Spanish battlefields, made an increasingly profound impression on the tough little Tonypandy native as he performed "herculean tasks" in the final fighting. Guest's friend, Bill Davison of Battersea, was not surprised to hear of his exploits. "He had some guts, did Dave."[22]

With the reconstitution of the battalion, Billy Griffiths became battalion secretary of the Communist party, charged with rebuilding the party from within the battalion. This posed difficulties. The Spanish government still forbade the existence of party organizations in the Popular Army, of which the International Brigades were a part, so the work the party assigned Griffiths to do was illegal and necessarily clandestine.

II

The situation Griffiths faced was complex. The brigades, in the tradition of the Popular Front, recruited "anti-fascists," which included liberals, social democrats, political agnostics like George Nathan, as well as communists. Anarchism had a strong appeal for some of the volunteers. For example, Walter Gregory said that "like so many of those who had volunteered to go to Spain to fight for the Republic, I had developed strong leanings toward Anarchism and a fraternal bond with its advocates."[23] Nevertheless, a serious attempt would be made to organize a party structure within the battalion. Previously, the party had depended on the individual commissars to carry out its instructions independent of any formal organization. "The aim was to build a Party which could function in action. [One] which would strengthen the command and maintain discipline and the morale of the rank and file." Essentially, this meant tightening the communist network in the battalion to the extent that in the next action, the overall discipline and effectiveness of the troops would prove more cohesive. "How to do this no one knew." The only thing that was clear to veteran organizers like Griffiths and Bob Cooney, the commissar, "was that the organization had to be built from the top down, had to be flexible, with the final power centered in the Battalion committee of three."[24]

Griffiths unconsciously enumerated the difficulties that lay before him. He was not appointed by the rank and file, but by the party. Second, the goals and the means to achieve them were vague. And third, as will be apparent, a parallel command structure would be set up that was certain to subvert the effort to make the battalion more militarily efficient. Griffiths was also handicapped, as George Murray said, by being too "doctrinaire," a quality that repelled some of the men who felt he did not consider "the human element."[25]

The effort to establish a party organization in the battalion was kicked off by "an extraordinary meeting" at brigade headquarters. Lt. Col. Copic, the XVth Brigade commander, chaired the meeting. One of his interpreters summed up the opera-loving Copic as "a first class politician but not the best of commanders."[26] This was just one of numerous examples of leadership positions in the International Brigades going to those who could be politically trusted rather than to those who were militarily competent. Battalion and company commanders who were party members attended. In addition, party representatives from division, two members from the Central Committee of the Spanish Communist party, and the party secretaries (of whom Griffiths was one) from each of the five battalions of the brigade also took their places. They spent a good deal of time analyzing the disastrous events of the Retreats.

What became increasingly apparent in the course of the meeting was that the authority of the party was being reaffirmed, even if it meant rejecting the judgment of the military leaders. For example, Joe Gibbons, Griffiths' counterpart with the Canadians, known as the Mac-Paps, felt free to criticize his commander, Major Edward Cecil-Smith, for giving him military duties with the machine-gun company as well as the responsibility to correct problems in the cookhouse. This forced him to neglect party responsibilities. As far as Gibbons was concerned, his commander's behavior indicated "an anti-party mentality."[27] But this was the issue in a nutshell, Griffiths believed. The problem would be resolved only when Cecil-Smith understood that the strength of the party organization was as critical to the success of a military operation as were the duties Gibbons had been assigned with the machine-gun company and the cookhouse.

Despite the astonishing altitude to which his party prominence had taken him, Griffiths remained an ordinary rifleman, and an initially reluctant one at that, with little military experience. His behavior at Calaceite and during the Retreats had been exemplary, but it must have seemed more than a little presumptuous to some senior fighting leaders for him to expound on what he believed the battalion needed to function effectively. Yet, they listened and apparently made no demurrals. There was the unalterable fact of his party prominence.

Cecil-Smith was not the only leader in the brigade to have an "anti-party mentality." Griffiths was assigned to the company of the able and courageous Captain Jack Nalty[28] from Dublin, who had fought with the No. 1 Company under Nathan at Córdoba. Unfortunately for Griffiths' plans, Nalty "felt that the Party was a waste of time." He gave him routine duties which left little time for applying himself to party organization. "This was the last straw."[29] Griffiths arranged a meeting with Sam Wild, who was much more a warrior than a political man,[30] and Bob Cooney, the battalion commissar, to plead his case. Cooney and Harry Dobson, a brigade commissar, were enthusiastic about Griffiths' plans to form a party organization within the battalion, but Sam Wild's cooperation was necessary. Wild insisted on thinking it over, but he inevitably came around. Griffiths was duly transferred to battalion headquarters, reporting only to Wild and Cooney.[31]

With time now on his side, Griffiths established party committees in every company and maintained contacts down to the platoon and section levels. "On paper our organisation was perfect. We could exercise influence at all levels." So perfect did the structure appear that it was copied throughout the brigade. But Griffiths was a realist as well as a committed communist, and he had to admit, "We were soon to find out that the organisation was as fragile as the paper on which it was written."[32]

Nalty's disdain for the party was not unique. Griffiths spent his hours "spreading the idea of the Party" and organizing discussions on the proper relationship between the party and the military command. He admitted, "On this point we were somewhat vague. The correct relationship . . . still eluded us." Despite his ceaseless activism, Griffiths had to concede that "there was a general feeling that the Party was superfluous." Fred Thomas, who served with the elite Anti-Tank Battery, remembered that "he drove us barmy" with his lectures on Marxism. Nevertheless, Griffiths proved himself useful. He and

Dobson made a comprehensive tour of the battalion positions, identifying personnel needs as well as some tactical misalignments. This tour gave Wild and Cooney the best overall view of the battalion they had received since the men had taken up their new positions. Some practical benefit also came to needy individuals, one of whom had fruitlessly sought new eyeglasses from supply but without result, until Griffiths' intercession. Griffiths reported that a "careful selection and training of cadres" was necessary if the battalion was to attain maximum efficiency. Each of those selected would develop "the habit of thinking as a Party member and accepting responsibility not only for leadership, but the closest possible contact up and down the line."[33]

III

Griffiths' influence as battalion party secretary demonstrated how thoroughly political were the considerations affecting personnel and tactical decisions on the eve of the Ebro offensive. Further, the old Rhondda comrades, Griffiths and Dobson, each of them brave, intelligent, and resourceful, could be ruthless in achieving party goals. One of the British officers from Albacete reported to Griffiths, as battalion party secretary, that he had sustained a chest wound at Brunete, his nerve had failed him, and he had consequently been made a staff officer. While telling Griffiths his story, he became excited, probably at the Welshman's obvious lack of sympathy, and threatened to desert if he was sent into action again (circumstances not unlike those of Stephen Spender's friend, Tony Hyndman, after the Jarama). According to Griffiths, he asked only for "justice." Griffiths, the private soldier, said he would take the matter under advisement and discuss it with Cooney and George Fletcher, who was commanding the battalion in Wild's absence. Dobson came down from brigade to join in the conference to determine the best course of action. Because of the officer's rank and past record of misconduct, Dobson and Griffiths argued in behalf of a court-martial, with the recommendation that he be shot. Cooney and Fletcher, however, would not agree to it. Consequently, no action was taken, and the officer disappeared, to reemerge on the eve of repatriation.[34] One can only surmise that Fred Copeman would have put Griffiths and Dobson firmly in their place, and found some noncombatant duty for a volunteer whose nerve had cracked.

One would like to know what part George Murray played in this and other party matters. Murray was a printer from Scotland who served as the battalion agent for the SIM (Servicio de Investigación Militar), which had been established after the May fighting in Barcelona.[33] General Orlov had forced the creation of the intelligence service on Prieto, which Soviet agents now controlled.[35] The SIM's responsibilities included looking for spies and acting as a political police. Murray acknowledged that he guarded against the "insertion of enemy agents."[36] The Scot also participated in the entire campaign in the north, including the Ebro battles, and thus it remains unclear why he did not work closely with Griffiths and Dobson. Because he was actually assigned to the Anti-Tank battery (although its members had rejoined the battalion after the Retreats when they were unable to acquire more guns), it may be that his physical separation from the battalion prevented any significant contact with the two party men.

The activities of Griffiths and Dobson suggest an attitude of suspicion and denunciation, which were classic hallmarks of Communist-party behavior. A particularly offensive example of this was the case of Lillian Buckoke. A young nurse from a working-class background, she wrote on her application papers for Spain that she was "politically disinterested." If this did not guarantee distrust toward her, then her outspoken refusal to condemn all capitalists out of hand undoubtedly did. Her reasons, she said, lay in her own experience, not in ideology. Instead of laying people off during the Depression, the firm that employed her father devised a rota by which each employee worked a reduced schedule, rather than face unemployment. This, she believed, was a sensible and humane response to a horrendously complex situation.[37]

Although only nineteen when she arrived in Spain, Buckoke had great confidence in her own judgment. In the Aragón she and another nurse decided to attend wounded Spaniards. This apparently harmless initiative resulted in commissars accusing them of acting without proper authorization. Other nurses and other medical personnel were instructed not to speak to either of them. A contributing factor, or perhaps the prime factor, in their persecution was, as far as Buckoke knew, that she and her colleague (who later changed her mind) were the only nurses in Spain not to have joined the party. Regardless, both of them fell into "great disgrace" with the other volunteers. Buckoke's fiercely independent spirit was hardly appeased when rumors began to be circulated by other nurses that she was a spy. For the most part, she viewed her chief tormentors, the commissars, with contempt. They earned her respect only "when they downed their books and pamphlets and picked up the rifles and bayonets and [fought]." After the war, this courageous and idealistic young woman voluntarily went into a French concentration camp to help care for Spanish and IB refugees. "I gave them everything I had except the rags I wore."[38]

IV

As the brigade trained in Chabola Valley (with Wattis back in London), the great Ebro offensive loomed. Prime Minister Negrín believed that a spectacular action was needed to gain world attention, thus improving his negotiating position with Franco, and, in addition, to bridge the corridor to the sea that the Nationalists had wedged between Catalonia and the rest of Republican Spain in their March offensive.

Griffiths "worked ceaselessly to build the Party." And success appeared to be growing. He found that with the disciplined example being shown by party men, "the orders from above were being met by an enthusiastic response from below." He felt a measure of self-congratulation was in order. Others had begun following the example of the British Battalion, demonstrating "an expression of the power of political ideas which was a constant product of our work."[39] The question remained, however, as to how effective punishment could be meted out to those who did not conform to the new regime. In the weeks before the crossing of the Ebro, a number of minor misdeeds and disturbances required attention. Griffiths became concerned about Wild's informal style of administering justice, and the fact that his punishments usually consisted of simply digging a latrine. The Welshman did not believe this was "fair," arguing that a real court with a prosecutor and defense should be set up. This was done, but in the face of an ineffectual prosecution and an effective counsel for the defense, the next miscreant was found not guilty. "That was our first and last Court Marshal. Sam had no faith in it anymore so they were discontinued."[40]

The British commander's methods remained more straightforward. On one occasion, Wild happened to pass by as two of his men engaged in a lively fight. He immediately challenged whoever won, although both were considerably bigger than he. The second fight was as vigorous as the first, and Wild proved, as he had many times, why his

304 The True Believer

manner was so well suited to a proletarian army.[41] No one doubted Sam Wild's personal courage or leadership abilities, but he was also capable of impetuously stiffening the loose discipline that prevailed in the battalion with potentially devastating consequences. When some of the men became drunk in a neighboring village and threw several hand grenades, fortunately with no injuries, Wild adopted draconian measures. There would be no more wine in the battalion for anyone, and the village was off limits to all. This was particularly hard on the Spaniards in the battalion, for whom wine was a customary part of their diet.

Griffiths was outraged. "Mass punishment was indefensible. The innocent were being punished with the guilty." Disaffection grew in the battalion with such startling rapidity that Griffiths believed there was no time to lose in getting Wild to change his mind. He called a meeting of the battalion and company party committees, in all about twenty volunteers, who met in a wooded area away from the other men. There were angry words. Not a few of them were directed at the hypocrisy of Wild's behavior. For despite his indisputable merits, the British commander himself had a serious drinking problem. From the standpoint of his men, there had been too many nights when their commander returned to the battalion in an inebriated condition. Benny Goodman, who had worked in the clothing trade in Manchester, was a great admirer of Wild's leadership. "If somebody says you have to reach it . . . he'd just have to reach it." By this time, Wild's personal courage was legend. "He was fearless." But this did not mean his conduct was beyond reproach. Goodman remarked, "If you've known Sam, you've never seen him sober." Yet he added, this remarkable man was never drunk in combat.[42] For the older veterans, however, Wild's habits stood in stark contrast to Fred Copeman's abstemiousness.

A second meeting was convened, consisting of Dobson, Cooney, Griffiths, and Wild. From the military and party perspective Wild had to be persuaded to withdraw the order or be replaced. Griffiths said, "This would be my job." He decided to be "brutally frank. No details were left out and no feelings were spared."[43] Wild was deeply embarrassed and had little to offer in his defense. Cooney stepped forward in behalf of Wild as being the best man for the job, and the party, therefore, had to play a constructive role in helping him overcome his weaknesses. Thus, the men and their commander reached a reconciliation through the mediation of a private soldier, which would have been unimaginable in a bourgeois army.

Griffiths and Dobson were ever alert for heterodoxy. One day they saw an editorial on discipline attached to the wall newspaper of No. 4 company. The wall newspapers had been an important cultural and political outlet for the battalion from the beginning. Art work, poetry, announcements of various kinds, news, and editorials could all be found there. In this instance, the editorial attacked bourgeois discipline imposed from the top in favor of proletarian discipline "from below." Dobson and Griffiths judged the article to be "dangerous." Despite the eloquent opposition of Lewis Clive and David Guest, Dobson and Griffiths responded that in the abstract their arguments were sound but military necessity required that discipline come from the top, which apparently ended the dispute. Thus, the two Welsh miners told the Oxbridge graduates what the limits of free speech would be in the battalion.

Perhaps the most astonishing example of Griffiths' influence came when he received a message from division headquarters "to recommend the best young officer in the Battalion for special duties at Division level." Griffiths writes, "I selected my man, spoke to him and told him not to breathe a word." Several days later orders arrived transferring him. This, apparently, without Sam Wild knowing anything about it.[44]

When the Ebro offensive began, Griffiths found himself assigned to military duties as a runner, reporting to a Spanish sergeant. He protested to Sam Wild, but this time in vain. Griffiths said, "This was fantastic and contrary to all Party instructions." He then appealed to the authority of brigade headquarters, which duly countermanded Wild's orders, telling Griffiths he was to have complete freedom of action. Once again, he would devote full time to party work, and report only to Wild and Cooney.[45]

V

The battalion had been rebuilt to 650 men, two-thirds of them Spanish. Largely forgotten were the losses and demoralization that had resulted from the Nationalist breakthrough in the spring. The attire of the battalion was so ragtag, however, that years later the only comparably dressed army that came to the mind of the journalist and volunteer John Peet was the Viet Cong.[46] Sam Wild, the battalion commander, took a perverse pride in the contrast between the efficiency and morale of his men, and their dress. He said, "I don't know whether it's working class snobbery[,] but it made you feel proud."[47]

The men of the British Battalion were intensely pleased about going over to the offensive, and confident that no one could stop them. The Army of Catalonia, supplemented by small cadres of survivors of the XVth Brigade, assembled on the Ebro. Plans were laid for the last Republican offensive of the war. The brigade went through a period of training, reorganization, and refitting, with a few new recruits arriving and virtually every able-bodied volunteer in Spain reporting for duty. Most of all, these precious weeks were a time of healing, for restoration of body and spirit from the terrible events of March and April 1938. At the end of July, the Army of Catalonia and the Internationals began crossing the Ebro, catching Franco by surprise. As one of the British remembered, "I did not meet a single individual who entertained the thought of defeat."[48] The Mac-Paps were the first across, neutralizing the initial resistance, which made the passage easier for the British.

As the brigade moved out toward Corbera and Gandesa, there was a collective sense of exhilaration. Then, the realities set in. Walter Gregory, a seasoned campaigner, saw his old comrade, George Stockdale of Leeds, die, the first in his company. Although Gregory, who had arrived in Spain in December 1936, had seen and experienced more suffering and sacrifice than most, he found himself almost unbearably shaken by the death of his friend. Stockdale had been hit just above the left eye by bullets from a hidden machine gun, leaving one side of his brain exposed. The fatally wounded man attempted to speak to his friend, but Gregory, try as he might, could hear only the death rattle in his throat. "I thought of his wife back home in Leeds of whom he had spoken so often and so tenderly, and for a moment I wished she could be beside him. . . . If I could have wept for anyone in Spain, it would have been for George." Earlier, before Teruel and the savage battles of the Ebro, Gregory had written:

> Within the space of little more than ten months the Battalion had seen action at Jarama, Brunete and Belchite and had gained a reputation for dependability and courage. Yet of the men who had marched with such optimism and cheer to the heights of Pingarron [in the Jarama] in January 1937 only a handful remained, all of whom had now graduated with alarming speed to the category of war veteran.[49]

But in certain moments of vulnerability, even the "war veterans" felt the need to shed tears for a friend or perhaps for a long-lost sense of their own immortality.

In the first part of the battle of the Ebro, Griffiths found himself in constant motion, carrying orders to company commanders from Wild. When he made his way back to battalion headquarters, he and Harry Dobson took refuge from shelling and opened a can of tuna fish for their meal. As they ate their rations, Dobson told him that Sam Wild still did not understand how his fellow Welshman was to be used. Griffiths was not just a runner, Dobson said, and hinted ominously that Wild might have had sinister motives in exposing him to such danger. "To sum it up Sam was told to lay off." The next day both Dobson and a comrade were caught by the same machine-gun burst. Dobson's wound was judged less serious, and he was not evacuated until hours later. He died in the base hospital. Dobson may have been, as Griffiths eulogized him, "one of the bravest, coolest and most dedicated of men,"[50] but he also demonstrated the politicization of the battalion and managed to compromise severely Wild's authority.

Although Griffiths could be ruthless in his recommendations, he was not like some of his comrades in the party hierarchy, who stayed clear of harm's way. "One should appreciate what being a Party secretary meant. I was asking men to carry out almost impossible tasks. I could only do it honestly if I was prepared to take as big or even bigger risks. I owed this to myself—to my own conscience." Later, he thought, "I was proud to be a Communist—to be a member of the Party—to call these men comrades."[51] Griffiths had quickly become an excellent soldier.

The British Battalion was ordered to take Hill 481, about a mile from Gandesa, and the key to capturing the town. Seventeen-year-old John Richardson wrote to a friend, "At dawn we went over the top. And the world went mad."[52] Half a century later, the American Bill Bailey remembered watching helplessly from a hill about half a mile away. "We could watch the action. We could see the whole [panorama], like watching on a TV set. . . . The British came out of their trenches. . . . They're now trying to work their way up the hill. They got half way up the hill—the Fascists just waited. Then [they] just rolled out hand grenade after hand grenade, just rolled it down the hill at them. It was a massacre."[53] The Nationalists repulsed attack after attack by the British, who faced four feet of barbed wire, booby traps, "showers of hand grenades," the errant rounds of captured French 75s, and a determined enemy. Despite sacrifices and exertions on an epic scale, the capture of the hill would never take place. The

Nationalists, behind their well-fortified positions, successfully re-buffed the British attacks for the next six days. Griffiths and one of his fellow runners came as close as any of their comrades to reaching the crest.

The failure of the battalion to take the position on July 27, 1938, was a turning point. Here David Guest died. Here, too, after so much blood and sacrifice, in the arid Aragón landscape on a small but strategically located hill between Gandesa and Corbera, the war for the British achieved its symbolic conclusion. There would be more bloodletting, particularly on Hill 666, rising high above them in the Sierra Pandols, and later battles, before their withdrawal in October with the rest of the International Brigades. But on this hill, victory seemed to lie tantalizingly within their grasp, only in the end to elude them.[54] After a last desperate attack, which brought a handful of British to within a few yards of the summit, the effort ended and what remained of the British Battalion went into reserve. If courage should have its just reward, it would have been presented on the top of Hill 481 to the British Battalion on that scorching July day in 1938.

These meticulously remembered months in Spain found their expression in a memoir that Griffiths handed into his adult education tutor almost thirty years later:

> When all is said and done, and a great deal will be left unsaid forever, [Hill] 481, that scrub of a hill, was the altar on which all the ideals, the passions, which symbolised the political climate of the 30's, reached the zenith of their powers to drive men from a choice based upon open conviction to superb examples of self-sacrifice and courage, in the belief that this was decisive. And decisive it was. Courage, conviction, bravery, self-sacrifice was [sic] not enough. The rock remained as a permanent monument not only to self-sacrifice and courage, but to the treachery of those who denied us the means to wage modern war.[55]

The Nationalist troops now moved to the offensive. Franco was at the head of an army of 100,000 men, with huge material advantages over the Republican Army of the Ebro, including the incomparable German 88mm gun. He began his counteroffensive in the Sierra Pandols, overlooking Gandesa and Corbera, and, importantly, the river crossings of the Ebro. A key position was Hill 666, which the Americans held for an all-but-unendurable twelve days.[56] The British joined the Lincolns and on August 24 replaced them on the hill. They repulsed a furious enemy attack, for which they were to be decorated, and a day later, a Spanish unit relieved them.

VI

Though driven by his ideals and courage, Griffiths' unwavering loyalty to the party, which had given him a place in his world, also led him into disloyalties to those comrades who were not party men, as well as to Sam Wild who knew better than Billy Griffiths what was needed to win a battle. Griffiths wrote an after-action report on the battles, in which he gathered the experiences and observations of party members in the battalion. It included a good deal of criticism of the command. When he gave a copy to each of his superiors, Cooney challenged his right to send the report to the brigade, and Wild ordered him not to. But Griffiths refused to obey Wild's order. "As far as I was concerned it was a Party document,"[57] Griffiths said. He met with the brigade party secretary, an American who had spent eighteen months at the Lenin School, and turned the report over to him.

Griffiths' behavior was a matter of contention and controversy not only for Wild and Cooney, but also to his fellow soldiers. Jim Brewer was one of those "who got fed up with all the preaching" by Griffiths, who, he believed, was always busy promoting the communist cause when he should be learning how to soldier. "He'd be telling you what Marx and Lenin thought of this, that and the other thing." Griffiths believed that he "knew all the answers." Brewer, who was outside the loop of power and influence, despite his formidable qualities as a soldier and man, could only suppose that Griffiths and his fellow communists "had their little cells" in the battalion.[58]

With the last great offensive across the Ebro blunted by Franco's troops, Prime Minister Negrín was reduced to playing the few cards left to him. He decided unilaterally to withdraw the volunteers, hoping that Hitler and Mussolini would follow suit. Unhappily, this final effort to win international support for a withdrawal of all foreign troops from Spain came to nothing. As repatriation loomed, and yet the fighting continued to rage, it became more and more difficult to keep up the morale of the troops. To Griffiths, this simply meant "the responsibility and influence of the Party grew." If morale was to be sustained, it had to be on the bedrock of political conviction. "One had to believe that this fight was inevitable, it was dictated by the logic of history, and that the final victory must be ours." No one could doubt him when he said, "I was ready to die for it."[59] All this Griffiths believed and preached with the zeal of a speaker in Castlegate Square in Aberdeen.

For the British, the last battle began on the night of September 22, 1938, the day before their evacuation from the Ebro. They were called upon to face yet another Nationalist offensive against the crumbling Republican resistance. The struggle proved both vicious and deadly—forty-eight of the remaining 106 British were killed, taken prisoner, or missing in action. Much of the final fighting took place hand to hand. On September 24 the British Battalion stood down for the last time. The forces of the Republic continued to struggle until November 16, when they were finally pushed back across the Ebro. By that time, however, defeat had become inevitable.

After a bout with fever, Griffiths rejoined the battalion at the town of Ripol in the foothills of the Pyrenees close to the French frontier. The gathering of the battalion prior to repatriation was the penultimate moment of its history in Spain. And Griffiths was pleased to see that, although an army had ceased to exist, the battalion hierarchy was in place. Officers and the ranks continued to live and eat separately from each other. Men identified themselves in terms of their place in the military hierarchy. It was not what had been imagined twenty-eight months before. Griffiths said, revealingly, "Tomorrow or the next day, or the next day, we would become Tom, Dick or Jack with no distinction."[60]

Griffiths' last task was to set up a commission to evaluate the conduct of each party member in the battalion. The purpose was to make recommendations concerning who would receive membership in the Spanish Communist party. No one would be recommended for this high honor, which would bring instant acceptance by communists throughout the world, unless his "conduct was beyond reproach." Griffiths said, "In other words we were to purge the Party of disreputable elements." There were to be no exceptions. "Even Cooney had to toe the line." Each man was "being investigated and judged. By amateurs it is true, but what we lacked in skill and experience, was more than balanced by honesty and sincerity."[61]

A private soldier was once again telling well-known figures in the battalion that they must submit to his authority. Billy Griffiths was afraid of losing his status and prestige when he was ordered by the party to Spain. But the party ensured that he remained "someone" after he arrived. Upon repatriation, five of the battalion received signed notes from Dolores Ibarruri, La Pasionaria, a devout communist who beyond any other single figure symbolized the Republic's resistance to Franco. Billy Griffiths, who entered Spain a private and left a private, joined Sam Wild, Malcolm Dunbar, Alex Gilchrist, and Alex Donaldson in this signal company.[62] In addition, he was among a handful picked by Alonzo Elliott for special praise in his final report on the battalion's performance in Spain.[63] While Griffiths accepted his rewards from the party, Alec Marcovitch languished in jail.

The British volunteers had come a long way since Esmond Romilly's romantic belief that men fighting for ideals would inevitably, swiftly, and cleanly rout their enemy. At the end of the war Walter Gregory could write: "Despite talk of nobility and valor, in reality the battlefield is a place where survival is the paramount objective. To survive it is necessary to kill; but often to kill effectively it is necessary to numb the senses and see the enemy as simply a figure that must be eliminated rather than as a fellow member of the human race." The experience of combat, he said, "paralyses the emotions and suspends rationality."[64] Neither S. L. A. Marshall nor Paul Fussell could have put it more cogently. But if the reasons for going to Spain dissolved in the crucible of combat, they were never far away.

The *Times* and *New York Times* correspondent in Republican Spain, Lawrence Fernsworth, wrote, "Even upper-class England is learning—if it ever learns anything—what ordinary Englishmen always knew, that the men who went to Spain went out of loyalty to England."[65] As the role of the British Battalion in the war wound down, its leaders knew that they would return home with a unique prestige, and they would have to begin planning how they could convert all they had endured and sacrificed into political influence. In the wake of the Ebro offensive, Fred Copeman wrote to Sam Wild of the phenomenal crowds that were turning out to raise money and express solidarity with the battalion in Glasgow and Liverpool. There were even some 200 MPs at a special meeting in the House of Commons, "the largest that has ever been held there." Copeman wrote, "The Government advance on the Ebro sector has done much to again put the question of Spain and as far as I am concerned, of course, the British Battalion on the front page again." He urged Wild to "remember what I said in the last letter. You must take the opportunity now whilst holding the position that you do to study politics and to use the meetings of the Battalion Command as a training ground for future leading political discussions."[66]

The importance of the battalion to militants in Great Britain could not be overestimated. Copeman urged, "Go on with the fight, Sam, and remember that your work and that of the men you lead is being followed by the whole progressive movement." He concluded by telling his successor, "I hope that when the job is done to see you and them return to our country to continue the struggle for freedom, peace and social progress."[67]

On Saturday, October 29, a farewell parade for the International Brigades was held in Barcelona, the city that had seemed to encapsulate the kind of society these thousands of volunteers had dreamed of in the early part of the war. Led by Jim Brewer, the British volunteers marched past President Manuel Azaña while hundreds of thousands applauded, Republican aircraft circled overhead, and military bands played. Most memorably, however, La Pasionaria gave the Republic's farewell to those who had sacrificed so much for its struggle to survive.

> You can go proudly. You are history. You are legend. You are the heroic example of democracy's solidarity and universality. We shall not forget you, and when the olive tree of peace puts forth its leaves again, mingled with the laurels of the Spanish Republic's victory— come back.

The British foreign office agreed to coordinate with Paris-based George Leeson in returning the volunteers to England. They traveled through France in a covered train. Each received a bill from the British government for the cost of the journey.[68]

On December 7, 1938, the remnants of the British Battalion returned to England, proudly displaying both the flag of the Spanish Republic and the Major Attlee banner carried by members of No. 1 Company. They were greeted by thousands at Victoria Station. The 300 veterans who stepped off the train, led by three of their wounded comrades, one on crutches, responded to a crisp command and marched into working-class mythology. They represented what Bill Rust called "the real Britain." The next day the Liberal *London Star* reported:

> Led proudly by their wounded comrades, the men marched into London. With them marched the spirit of Byron, the Tolpuddle martyrs, the Chartists, Keir Hardie . . . , Britain's bravest fighters for liberty through the centuries. Behind and around them marched twenty thousand British democrats.
>
> Men as well as women wept and cheered alternately. It was no political affair, for all parties were represented, both on the platform and in the crowd. It was British democracy spontaneously expressing its abhorrence of Fascism and its appreciation of bravery.

These men have made history, by forming part of the greatest international democratic army the world has ever known. They have inspired the world by their example. Something of this seemed to enter everyone who was at Victoria Station last night, and the memory of it will never be eradicated.[69]

Attlee, accompanied by Sir Stafford Cripps, Norman Angell, Will Lawther, and the Labour peer, Lord Strabolgi, addressed the returning veterans and the huge throng, speaking first of the shared pride that all the assembled felt. The future prime minister then declared, "You have stood for the cause of the workers."[70] He welcomed them home as "heroes of the democratic faith, back once more to continue the struggle in this country." Others who spoke to the crowd were Cripps, the Communist MP William Gallacher, Tom Mann, and Will Lawther, president of the Miners' Federation who had lost a brother in Spain.[71]

It was no accident that workers gathering in all major cities of the country to pay ceremonial tribute to the British Battalion concluded by singing "Jerusalem." At Manchester Free Trade Hall on September 28, 1938, Paul Robeson led in singing the famous verses:

And did the Countenance Divine
Shine forth upon our clouded hills?
And was Jerusalem builded here
Among those dark Satanic Mills?

I will not cease from Mental Fight,
Nor shall my Sword sleep in my hand,
Till we have built Jerusalem
In England's green and pleasant land.

This suggests a very different spirit from that which the historian Gareth Stedman Jones found a generation earlier. He has written of workers who buried their millennial dreams and adopted a defensive strategy to fend off the aggressions of employers of the 1890s. For those who gathered to sing "Jerusalem," Stedman Jones says, "it was not as a battle-cry but as a hymn."[72] But for those caught up in the passion play of Spain, and still eager to recapture lost ideological positions, it had become a battle cry.

PART IV

Legacies

CHAPTER 14

The Musketry of Thought

I came back a different person, and I've stayed that way ever since. I've never consciously let down my class from that day to this, and I learned it the hard way—not from textbooks and lectures—but from Spain.
— Sam Wild

Spain was different—it was not only the head but the heart that was affected. . . . Those years in Spain were the finest hours of the British left, of the British labour movement, I saw in my lifetime.
— Bill Feeley

My susceptibility to the heroic, played upon by Russian films in which the worker, mounted upon his magnificent tractor, chugged steadily towards the new dawn and the new world, joined up with my natural partnership [with] the underdog to create a picture, romantic and apocalyptic, of the British worker at last coming into his own. There was generosity as well as absurdity in this, for my friends and I did at least make some attempt to imagine the conditions we did not share, the unemployment and malnutrition which had been rotting the heart out of a million working-class families, and we were prepared to help destroy a system that perpetuated itself by such hideous human wastage, even though our own pleasant way of life would be destroyed in the process.
— C. Day Lewis

Only connect.
— E. M. Forster

I

As we have seen, if the men of the battalion sought to live their political ideals on the battlefields of Spain, they were betrayed by the party that made it possible for them to be there. When the remainder of the battalion was in transit back to England, the chairman and general secretary of the central committee of the Workers Circle Friendly Society sent a telegram: "Defenders of Democracy (stop) Your noble and heroic deeds kindled many hearts now striving for liberty and well being of mankind."[1] In a memorial meeting on January 15, 1939, at City Hall, Newcastle, twenty-five volunteers from Durham and Northumberland who had fallen in Spain were remembered: "They Died for Democracy and Us."[2] Well intentioned, in certain respects true, but misleading and oversimplified, as myth is. One of its makers was John Peet, a veteran of the British Battalion, who later went to Eastern Europe and became a propagandist for the party. He said at a reunion of the International Brigades in Florence in 1976, "Spain was the last occasion on which everything was simple and clear. There was a right and a wrong, a black and a white. There were no grays. And you know, it really was so. We *were* right." But after Spain, Peet said, "everything became complicated."[3] What he failed to acknowledge, then or later, was that Spain, too, was "complicated."

Other middle-class intellectuals often fared little better, and with the passage of time and the sharpening of perspective, had less excuse. Michael Foot, an activist in the thirties at Oxford, biographer of Aneurin Bevan, and former leader of the Labour party, insisted in 1986 that "Madrid was held in democratic hands from the beginning of the Civil War right to a few months before the Spanish War became engulfed in World War."[4] Eric Hobsbawm looks back over the decades in a similarly misty light: "For many of us the survivors, now all past the Biblical life-span, it remains the only political cause which, even in retrospect, appears as pure and compelling as it did in 1936."[5] Those young intellectuals who made the same choice in the thirties would have echoed their agreement with Foot and Hobsbawm. But sixty years later, few would agree with Foot, one of Great Britain's most distinguished public intellectuals, or with Hobsbawm, one of his generation's greatest historians, that the fate of the Republic "was held in democratic hands," nor that the Spanish Civil War was as "pure and compelling" as it seemed to most in 1936. That two of Great Britain's most gifted and creative figures on the left continue to think so is reason enough for students of the period to continue their labors.

But, despite the opportunistic advancement of "truth" and the persecution of those who opposed it, worker and middle-class volunteers "connected" in a wholly new manner. The abstract figure of the worker and that of his middle-class comrade had collapsed under the influences of shared ideals, danger, hardship, and a common life. For example, John Angus, an insurance underwriter from London who described himself as "petite bourgeois," won Alex Donaldson's highest political approval. Donaldson wrote that "this comrade is perhaps the finest political cadre developed in Spain." Sam Wild called him "an outstanding comrade."[6] But politics, not military effectiveness, too often remained the party's litmus test for success or failure in Spain. Having broken with the party in 1938, Tom Wintringham wrote on May 22, 1941:

> Spain woke me up. Politically I rediscovered democracy, realising the enormous potentialities in a real alliance of workers and other classes. . . . I was disgusted by the sectarian intrigues of Marty & Co. . . . Two bullets and typhoid gave me time to think. I came out of Spain believing . . . in a more radical democracy, and in revolution of some sort as necessary to give the ordinary people a chance to beat Fascism. Marxism makes sense to me, but the "Party Line" doesn't.[7]

Others drew similar conclusions about the "party line." Orwell wrote, "The thing that frightens me about the modern intelligentsia is their inability to see that human society must be based on common decency, whatever the political and economic forms may be."[8] It was the absence of a moral center in communism and, therefore, what the party asked its adherents to believe and do, that drove Orwell to his own vision of socialism.

In 1956 John Saville and E. P. Thompson founded *The Reasoner* as a forum for the discussion of ideas the party would not tolerate. On the title page they chose a quotation from Marx, "To leave error unrefuted is to encourage intellectual immorality."[9] In the same year both Thompson and Saville left the Communist party, as did many others, emphasizing the fundamental incompatibility between the party and those intellectuals who refused to accept their roles as ideological mendicants.

II

The experience of Spain, both lived and imagined, had a profound impact on working-class consciousness in Great Britain. At the funeral of the redoubtable Pat Murphy, a Cardiff seaman and veteran of the Somme as well as Spain, his mourners heard the following words spoken as a summation of his seventy-six years:

> Man's dearest possession is life, and since it is given to him to live but once, he must so live as to face no torturing regrets for years spent without purpose; so live as not to be scared by the shame of a cowardly and trivial

past; so live that dying he can say: "All my life and my strength were given to the finest cause in the world—the emancipation of mankind."

Murphy's lifelong credo had been simple. "'Was it for or agin' the interests of the working class." The answer could be yes or no but "never any 'maybes.'" The example of Murphy and those of his class was not lost on the generations that followed them. Murphy's biographer wrote:

> I learnt the most profound lesson of my life from Pat, that history was something that actually lived. Our history [of the working class] can all too easily be seen as long past, unconnected to the present and irrelevant to the future. When I talked to Pat of the things he had done in the past, and that we are both trying to achieve for the future, I began to become aware that the International Brigade, the General Strike or whatever, was not just his history, but mine too: it belonged to me, and I belonged to it.[10]

What emerged most powerfully from Spain was that in the minds of the British volunteers and their supporters, socialism no longer seemed a ravishing dream. Instead, it had taken on an exhilarating reality, even if subsequently tempered or modified. Above all, the Catalonian city of Barcelona in the fall and early winter of 1937 located itself unforgettably on the imaginative map of the British volunteers, and, for many, would always be the "good place," so long dreamed of, so long desired. At the beginning of the war there was little indication of the mythic stature the city would assume. The fighting between the insurgents and the political militias for control made it seem terrifying and forbidding. A young American living in the city, Megan Laird, kept a diary during these days. She wrote, "We are in the midst of Revolution. Or Hell. Or perhaps only a bad dream. I do not know. It is impossible to understand what is happening—what key had turned to release pandemonium on a tranquil world."[11] Soon the disorienting turmoil would subside, and Barcelona began to reshape itself along its new political and psychological contours.

The "time" and "atmosphere" of the city became the stuff of utopian fantasy.[12] Franz Borkenau, the Austrian socialist who scrupulously cultivated the objectivity of a social scientist, was stunned as he arrived in Barcelona from Port Bou. "As we turned round the corner of the Ramblas (the chief artery of Barcelona) came a tremendous surprise: before our eyes, in a flash, unfolded . . . the revolution. It was overwhelming. It was as if we had been landed on a continent different from anything I had seen before."[13] Orwell wrote, "When one came straight from England the aspect of Barcelona was something startling and overwhelming." He said, "It was the first time that I had ever been in a town where the working class was in the saddle. . . . Every shop and cafe had an inscription saying that it had been collectivized." All manifestations of servility and economic status had vanished. "In outward appearance it was a town in which the wealthy classes had practically ceased to exist."[14] Orwell excitedly wrote to his old St. Cyprian and Etonian classmate, Cyril Connolly, "I have seen wonderful things & at last really believe in Socialism, which I never did before."[15] Orwell was convinced that for the first time he was seeing socialism function in human terms. Jason Gurney agreed. "What was exciting was the glorious feeling of optimism; the conviction that anything that was not right with society would assuredly be put right in the new world of universal equality and freedom which lay ahead."[16]

The British volunteer and Columbia University graduate David Crook[17] went through Barcelona in January 1937 and also felt "a peculiar electrically equalitarian atmosphere."[18] So, too, did T. C. Worsley. He said of the city, "It is everything we've worked for, everything we've dreamed about in all our Cell meetings and our Demos—so drab and dull as they were. But they've flowered here and blossomed into a perfect world."[19]

Workers felt the same. The early Scots volunteer Donald Renton remembered upon his arrival in the Catalonian capital "the sense of freedom in the air, of workers' power."[20] The dreams of Thomas Paine and Robert Owen and Ernest Jones and William Morris appeared to have been realized in the Catalonian city.

III

In whatever political configuration they might manifest themselves, the coalition of antifascist forces from Great Britain, jarred into unity by Spain and shaped by both the Communist party and the progressive tradition of the British "left,"[21] helped reestablish an antihegemonic mentality. In the spring of 1938 an Emergency National Conference met in London to discuss ways to aid the Spanish Republic. The high point of the huge conference was a speech by Harry Pollitt, who had been in Spain the previous week and now was determined to allay fears that Franco neared victory. Toward the end of his remarks he told his audience:

> A week ago to-night I stood in the trenches of the *Major Attlee Battalion* [sic] of the *International Brigade*. They were tired, strained, and had gone through terrible experiences. Many of their comrades killed and wounded; many taken prisoner by Franco. Here were Liberals, Labour men and Communists, trade unionists and co-operators, united, without regard to political differences, in their resolve to defend Democracy and Peace.[22]

One of the largest crowds of any May Day since 1926 assembled a few days later. The theme was "Spain above all." The tricolored Spanish flag waved everywhere among the tens of thousands entering Hyde Park. A red banner, stirred by the breeze, declared that "Spain's fight is our fight." The huge throng enthusiastically greeted each of the special deputations winding their way into the park. The greatest applause went to a group of wounded British volunteers who were followed closely by a squadron of nurses from the Spanish Medical Aid Committee. Eight platforms were set up so that the vast crowd could hear from every sector of the labor movement. Herbert Morrison said from one platform, "Let us remember the heroic Spanish people and their fight against foreign invasion for the freedom of the whole world."[23]

In Spain, for the first time in the history of the British working class, workers had successfully taken up arms for the purpose of creating an alternative society, which emerged in the culture of the British Battalion. The Liverpudlian, Jack Edwards, put the collective accomplishment of the British volunteers in Spain in striking form. While at Madrigueras, he found that he and those being trained with him took it all so seriously because they "were looking for another type of life . . . than what we've had." There would be no unemployment. "We could live in fairness with everybody else. You know there wouldn't be this scraping for halfpenneys and penneys. There wouldn't be this bloody battle on the bloody streets all the time—arguing against unemployment, arguing against cuts and all this. This is what we were after. There'd be no means test. Everybody would have a decent standard of living." This, Edwards said, "was a Socialist principle." And, "when you saw the unity in Spain that . . . was the answer to it."[24] Workers in the battalion felt, at last, that they "were treated as intelligent men."[25] Copeman wrote of Bob Elliott, a member of the Blyth Borough Council, one of the leaders of both the National Unemployed Workers' Movement and the Hunger Marchers,[26] that "his undying faith in the working class was an inspiration to the whole Battalion. He died [as] he lived—in the struggle."[27] Frank

Owen from Maerdy said a few weeks before his death at Brunete, "I must say that, what I have found here, is Comradeship in its truest sense. Anything no matter what it is, he has only to ask and it is at hand," and later, "it is Comradeship from the Top down to the lowest rank."[28] Frank Brooks from Battersea wrote in a more lyrical and allusive vein, "Amongst the Brigade there is such marvellous comradeship that I sometimes believe that here is the 'brotherhood of man' which Tennyson wrote about."[29]

Denied every outlet for their convictions except through laborist institutions, the ILP, and the Communist party, workers had proved beyond question that within their ranks was a cadre of leaders who were both brave and efficient,[30] earning them and the men they led in Spain the sobriquet of the "shock" battalion. The American Bill Bailey said of the British, "Every place they've been, they got the worst of the worst." They could almost always be found "in the thick of the battle."[31] For his part, Frank Owen was continually amazed by the fact that "our Officers are Workers like all the other comrades."[32] Morris Miller, Sam Wild's adjutant, said of Wild's leadership at the Ebro, where he won the Republic's highest decoration, the Medal of Valor: "Day and night he was at the telephone directing operations, ordering advances here, withdrawal there, regrouping the companies, reacting quickly to changing circumstances, never ruffled by the fact that he was receiving half a dozen reports at once." Miller concluded, "He was a model of resource and coolness." Bob Cooney, Wild's commissar, said of him, "No words could possibly convey what Sam's leadership meant to us. He was an inspiration to every man."[33] Despite the fact that some volunteers saw Wild only as a warrior, his military exploits were nevertheless informed by strongly held political views sharpened by his contact with fellow workers in Spain. He remembered:

> It impressed me to talk to somebody who could explain about education outside of the capitalist set-up and the way we'd been compelled to follow attitudes towards religion, personal behaviour, sex etc. Whereas before you'd never thought of nationalism, chauvinism, sexism—things that were outside the scope of ordinary people; you started thinking about it and getting ideas.[34]

The ties that bound middle- and working-class volunteers were formidable and yet, as we have seen, a genuinely egalitarian society did not develop among the British in Spain. Jock McKelvey, a character in James Barke's *Land of the Leal* and a veteran of the British

Battalion, spoke not of equality between the classes, but the *superiority* of workers to their middle-class comrades in a speech that could have been given by Harry Pollitt:

> I came across a lot of intellectual and bourgeois types. Pretty fine types some of them. But taking them by and large they're vain, petted and ridiculously childish. They've got to be treated like spoiled children. It takes donkeys years to knock the old school tie stuff out of them. They mean well[,] of course. But they've got to be spoon-fed politically. Often it's only a thin layer of their grey matter—such as it is—that's affected: they don't respond with their blood and guts. They just don't know what it is to hunger and want and know persecution. They've never seen their fathers and mothers work themselves into the grave. Or suffer and endure hardship—that's all objective social phenomena to them. It's so very different with a worker. A worker knows what it is to suffer—and he's prepared to suffer for his political beliefs.[35]

For the working-class volunteers, Spain provided an education beyond compare. Tom McWhirter, who was carrying out base administrative duties after he had been wounded, wrote not long before his death, "At last they have agreed to let me back to the front. . . . I feel I need more experiences up there to back up the further theoretical training I have picked up in the rear."[36] Theory and praxis combined to create a new self-confidence in themselves and their class.

After his service in Spain, Bill Alexander won the Sword of Honour at Sandhurst for his military efficiency, and subsequently commanded a reconnaisance unit in World War II. Alexander believed that "our experience in Spain gives us the answer. In the working class are men for every job—the working class, given the urge and the enthusiasm, shown the direction, can storm the world." Never had ordinary British working men been given such an opportunity to demonstrate their capabilities. "Everyone in our battalion could study and develop himself because he knew that his ability would be recognised and used—no matter birth or education." He urged: "Let these people turn to us, members of the working class. We could produce the leaders to carry out any job put to us in Spain, and to-day we can produce the men to defend the people of Britain."[37] Walter Greenhalgh, who came from the north of England, said his service in Spain "has given me a pride in my working class origins that nothing and nobody had since been able to shake."[38]

As one reads through the citations given for actions on September 23, 1938, at the Ebro, Alexander's confidence in working-class courage and leadership becomes remarkably powerful. Alan Gilchrist "returned to front line from hospital after being wounded and displayed great energy and courage in carrying out his duty whilst obviously sick." John Loban was cited for "repeated heroism, during whole of action until wounded." John Power's superiors commended him for his "efficient leadership and bravery under heavy fire. Magnificent record of duty during 21 months service in the anti-fascist fight." Liam McGregor must have helped restore faith in the political commissars, although his citation sounds suspiciously like a textbook example of how the party believed each commissar should behave in battle. He "carried out his duty as Commissar. Was first to advance and last to retreat. Died as he lived, a model anti-fascist fighter."[39] It is not difficult to understand why Sam Wild once said:

> Spain made me a working class snob. I've had experiences of all kinds, but the happiest days of my life were spent in Spain. For the first time I recognised the dignity, the goodness and the bravery of ordinary people, in this case the Spanish people. I also experienced the comradeship of my own people—the British—which I had not believed possible. I've been through life, joined the navy, been all over the world, and seen the poverty, degradation and exploitation of peoples everywhere, but I've never met people I could appreciate like the Spanish people and the British who went to Spain.[40]

The British left found its iconography in the returning veterans, who made it their password to say that they had returned to England to fight fascism on a different front. Bill Alexander has written that he and his comrades felt a special charge. "We who had gone to Spain from the organizations of the working people should upon our return take our places, as individuals in those organizations."[41] The British Battalion's reputation for valor and efficiency served a crucial psychological need for what in many respects remained a dependent class. When the survivors returned, they took on a larger-than-life role in plebeian culture. As shop stewards, trade union officials, town councilors, and other "figures" in their communities—from the coal mining valleys of Wales, to London, to the industrial North and Scotland—they became symbols of a working-class radicalism whose last full measure of devotion was manifestly to "another kind of life."

Jack Jones became general secretary of the Transport and General Workers' Union. Jim Brewer was a prominent figure in his local Labour party and served as a town councillor. Peter Kerrigan continued to play an important role in the British Communist party, as did Michael O'Riordan in the Communist party of Ireland, and Roderick

McFarquhar in the Scottish Nationalist party. Frank Deegan was in the forefront of the dockers' struggle after the war; Jim Prendergast played a similar role for the railwaymen. Charlie Goodman led the fight in the East End for low rents and more abundant housing. Lord Milford, the only Communist member in the House of Lords, who was wounded as an ambulance driver in Spain, and Dr. Reg Saxton, worked in a variety of peace organizations. Dr. Harry Bury was one of a group of International Physicians for the Prevention of Nuclear War who received the Nobel Peace Prize in Stockholm.[42] Tony Gilbert was for many years secretary of the Movement for Colonial Freedom.

Bill Alexander answers those who would diminish the importance of the Spanish veterans in their working-class communities and in the larger world. He wrote, "Service in the International Brigade is a badge of high honor and distinction in the British labour and progressive movement."[43] Many, if not most, of the veterans insisted that even after a lifetime crowded with event and disputation, their coffins be covered by the International Brigade flag.[44]

IV

It must be remembered, too, that the British volunteers were only the spearhead of a huge army of support for the Republic in Great Britain. This can be said even if one takes Tom Buchanan's point that "in practice, apathy towards, support for, and opposition to the Spanish Republic were all visible" among British workers, and, moreover, that the term "mass movement" disguises the many differences among supporters of the Republic. Nevertheless, there remains a good deal of substance in Jim Fyrth's claim that the cause of Republican Spain became "the most widespread and representative mass movement in Britain since the mid-nineteenth-century days of Chartism and the Anti-Corn Law Leagues, and the most outstanding example of international solidarity in British history."[45] Certainly, supporters of the Republic would make their views felt during the General Election of 1945.

It is, of course, true that the triumph of Clement Attlee and the Labour party was due to a number of factors, including the party's careful plans for postwar renewal, Churchill's embarrassing and disastrous campaign, and the fact that Labour's win was part of a general movement throughout Europe in support of governments that promoted social reform. On this last point, Lord Beveridge, the author of two reports that became the foundation stones for the policies of Attlee's government, acknowledged that "the most general effect of war is to make the common people more important."[46]

Nevertheless, the "mentality" represented by those who supported the British Battalion and the Dependents' Aid Committee established to assist them, as well as the many others who contributed to and worked for such organizations as the Spanish Medical Aid Committee, the National Joint Committee for Spanish Relief, and the TUC and Labour party's International Solidarity Fund, must be considered in any inquiry into Labour's defeat of Churchill and the Conservatives in July 1945.

The grievances of antifascists against the great war leader had deep roots. In a speech given in Rome in 1927, Churchill expressed his sympathies with Mussolini's regime. In a passage that was to provide a constant supply of ammunition for his enemies in the coming years, he told his fascist audience, "If I had been an Italian, I am sure I should have been entirely with you from the beginning to the end of your victorious struggle against the bestial appetites and passions of Leninism."[47] Harry Pollitt railed against the Non-Intervention Agreement, asserting his belief that "our British 'gentlemen'" might well have intervened on behalf of the Republic, as they had in Russia "when after repeated denials it was at last admitted that enormous quantities of munitions had been sent by Winston Churchill to help the counter-revolutionaries."[48] Spanish veterans and supporters of the cause of Republican Spain had no difficulty remembering Churchill's attitude toward the Republic. Churchill, called "THE Imperialist of Imperialists," had argued against intervention on the side of the Republic, which was self-contradictory, they believed, because a Franco victory would imperil British economic interests in Spain and threaten the Empire. This was additionally difficult to understand because ordinarily Churchill "with fountain pen in hand, would rush into the fray" should anyone "attempt to even manicure the toenails of the British lion." The only plausible explanation lay in the fact that he opposed the holding of power by the "common people." And "the fate of the common people of Spain" rested, as it had since German and Italian intervention, "in the hands of the common people of all countries."[49] Moreover, less than a month after the uprising of the generals against the Spanish Republic, Churchill had said, "It is idle to claim that a constitutional and parliamentary regime is legally or morally entitled to the obedience of all classes, when it is actually being subverted and devoured from day to day by Communism."[50] A. J. P. Taylor remembered, "Churchill failed to become the champion of democracy against fascism as many British people wanted."[51]

Although his hostility toward the Republic softened, in *The Gathering Storm* he made no apologies for his position, "Naturally I was not in favour of the Communists. How could I be, when if I had been a Spaniard they would have murdered me and my family and my friends."[52] On May 25, 1944, he told the House of Commons that the people of Great Britain had reason to be grateful to Franco for his neutral attitude toward Gibraltar. Consequently, "I am here to-day speaking kindly words about Spain. . . . Internal political problems in Spain are a matter for the Spaniards themselves. It is not for us—that is, the government—to meddle in such affairs."[53] Harry Pollitt had warned during the Spanish struggle:

> Winston Churchill, who so loudly parades his claims of being the only person really alive to the danger of Nazi Germany, has been an implacable enemy of the Spanish Government from the day civil war was forced upon the Spanish people, and his language and arguments are precisely the same as will be used against any future Labour Governments that attempt to serve the interests of the majority of the people.[54]

Sam Wild said in late 1940, "We who served in the Brigades know that Hitler, Mussolini, Petain, and others do not speak for the workers of those countries any more than Churchill does for us."[55]

If the left's memory of Churchill's attitude toward Spain was enduring, so too was theirs of Attlee, who had visited the British Battalion and allowed the famed No. 1 Company to be named after him. Bill Rust wrote at the time that the future prime minister's gesture was "historic because everybody felt a new unity between the Britishers fighting in Spain and the Labour Movement at home." This unity seemed to be confirmed when Attlee wrote back: "I would assure [the volunteers of the British Battalion] of our admiration for their courage and devotion to the cause of freedom and social justice. I shall try to tell the comrades at home of what I have seen." Then this most restrained of men brought himself to cry out awkwardly, perhaps predictably, and, in the end, even movingly, the old challenge,"Workers of the World unite."[56]

The Labour party flooded the electorate both in Great Britain and the services with a number of powerful Victor Gollancz tracts such as *Guilty Men*, *Your M.P.*, and *When the Men Come Home*, each of which spelled out its differences with the Conservatives on a variety of foreign and domestic issues, and particularly the National Government's policy toward Spain. In *Can the Tories Win the Peace*, Konni Zilliacus claimed that "class hatred determined the Government's resolve that the Spanish Government should in no circumstances be allowed to win the war." As the election on July 5, 1945 approached, Labour supporters were told to ask each Tory candidate, "Do you endorse the friendly attitude of Mr. Churchill toward the Franco government in Spain?"[57] Those who had suffered and sacrificed so much for Spain, and, in addition, for what their dreams for Spain might mean for postwar Britain, were not heartened by Churchill's election-eve call to "leave these socialist dreamers to their Utopia of nightmares."[58]

Labour's victory in 1945 was a euphoric moment for the left, even those who had quarreled bitterly with the party's early support of Non-Intervention in Spain when Walter Citrine had argued that any other course of action would lead to war with Germany and Italy.[59] The communist Nan Green compared the "air of enthusiasm, energy and confidence" of wartime Madrid with London on "the day we knew Labour had got in!"[60] At last, out of the ashes of so many individual and collective defeats, from the General Strike to Invergordon to the Rhondda, from the Clydeside to the Ebro, Labour had found the parliamentary strength to do more than dream of a socialist millennium, no matter how evanescent the reality was to prove.

As late as 1977, two years after Franco's death but with Spain's experiment in democracy at a very fragile stage, the National Conference of the AUEW (Constructional Division) passed the following resolution:

> This National Conference congratulates our EC and the TUC and the Labour Party on its splendid stand in support of the Spanish Workers fighting to free themselves from fascist dictatorship. Conference recalls with pride the outstanding role played by some of our members who served in the International Brigade and we call upon our EC to support in every possible way solidarity and action to end fascism and for peace, democracy and a free Spain.[61]

The left, however, would never genuinely capture the Labour party. Harold Laski's hope that "at long last we are going to be in a position to do full justice to our Spanish comrades" would continue to go unfulfilled—with Labour out of power during the thirties or in power in 1945–51. But the sacrifices that the labor movement had made for Spain were assimilated into its conception of itself. The dreary acceptance, pessimism, and insularity found in Walter Greenwood's *Love on the Dole* (1933)[62] or Walter Brierley's *Means Test Man* (1935) received a challenge. The volunteers for liberty, and the multitudes who supported them in Great Britain, expanded the sense of what might be achieved by the laborist consensus in the postwar years.

Perhaps, after all, it is Sam Wild, great in his virtues and his faults, who can still remind us of the hope and challenge and anger that lay at the heart of those in the thirties who proposed to find or build the just society. In the battle of the Ebro, Wild received the Republic's highest decoration for bravery. The citation read, "His untiring energy and efficiency gave an example of bravery to the whole battalion."[63] His memorial ceremony in Manchester began with the socialist hymn "England Arise." Those assembled sang of the England that had allowed itself to become a subject nation:

> Over your face a web of lies is woven,
> Laws that are falsehoods pin you to the ground.
> Labour is mocked, its just reward is stolen,
> On its bent back sits Idleness encrowned.
>
> How long while you sleep,
> Your harvest shall it reap?
> Arise, O England, for the day is here!

The mourners assembled to hear what they had known for fifty years, that Sam Wild "was a hero in his time, a leader of men who, when the call came, was ready to answer it." Addressing Wild's three sons and daughter in the audience, his eulogist said, "Looking around the world, there is still much that angered Sam that is left for them to fight and change." Sam's daughter, Dolores, then read La Pasionaria's famous farewell speech to the International Brigades. Finally, it was time for "all of us here to pay our last respects to Major Sam Wild, Commander of the British Battalion, International Brigades." Moreover, "We promise that in our turn we will hand on the banner of democracy, of comradeship and international solidarity and friendship so that peace will be achieved throughout the world." The ceremony ended, as it only could, with the singing of the *International*, which included the verses that moved so many in the thirties from fear to hope:

> No saviours from on high deliver,
> No trust have we in prince or peer;
> Our own right hand the chains must sever,

Chains of hatred, of greed and fear,
Ere the thieves will out with their booty
And to all give a happier lot,
Each at his forge must do his duty
And strike the iron while it's hot!

We peasants, artisans and others
Enrolled among the sons of toil,
Let's claim the earth henceforth for brothers,
Drive the indolent from the soil.
On our flesh too long has fed the raven,
We've too long been the vultures' prey:
But now, farewell the spirit craven,
The dawn brings in a brighter day.[64]

A mourner at Sam Wild's memorial service said that Wild's death "marks the end of an era in working-class politics."[65] Lost was the political culture in which the street-corner orator possessed an honored place and with his words could change the whole course of a listener's life. Gone, too, were the verbal, personal politics made passionate by the vision of socialism and its capital in Moscow. But much had been learned, and much had been taught by the "Volunteers for Liberty" to their working-class comrades about the qualities they possessed. Wild received a tribute from an admirer:

Sam,
You'll be in all the history books
And each subsequent generation
Will equate, with proper adulation
You, Sam Wild, with, say Wat Tyler
And other freedom fighters
Through all the centuries
Sam,
You may not like the thought
But you will enter history.
You'll be a hero to future people.
And so you ought.
For many you inspired,
And you're admired
For all the things you taught.[66]

A plaque was inscribed and placed on his council house in Manchester to commemorate his service in Spain. As all know who walk the streets of London and other urban centers, including Manchester, such recognition is normally reserved for the writers, politicians, philanthropists, artists, and other middle- and upper-class worthies who have shaped the dominant culture of their times. Sam Wild, too, will be remembered for his contribution to the culture of his age, but that culture would be part of the collective creation of the class to which he, Sam Masters, Nat Cohen, Jock Cunnigham, Fred Copeman, and thousands of other working-class militants belonged. Their sacrifices burn in memory, not the least in that of Bill Scott. A bricklayer from Dublin, Scott fought with the Thaelmanns in the battle for Madrid, and remembered a friend who lies amidst the olive groves of the Jarama: "Even now, as an old age pensioner, my thoughts often go back to the spot where they buried him in the Valley of the Jarama. That war never ended."[67]

Among the lasting words written about the decade of the thirties are those of Stephen Spender: "The peculiarity of the 1930's was not that the subject of a civilization in decline was new, but that the hope of saving or transforming it had arisen, combined with the positive necessity of withstanding tyrannies."[68] For all of its betrayals the cause of the Spanish Republic will always be a reminder of that hope. From the point of view of Republican Spain, the tragedy is clear. Great Britain's National Government never deviated from the Non-Intervention Agreement. The Labour party and the majority of its members were moderate and not militant in their views. Only belatedly did Labour end its support of Non-Intervention. And those who moved toward communism found themselves in the grip of an ideology that made a mockery of their idealism, and proved capable of eliciting from Harry Pollitt a statement that must rank as one of the greatest self-delusions ever uttered by a British working-class leader. He said, "The British workers, too, would have done their duty to Spain if they only had a Stalin at their head and not a Citrine or a Dalton."[69] One worker, among many, who would have disagreed said after his return to England, "Looking back on things, it seems to me that as soon as we passed the Spanish frontier we ceased to be volunteers and became conscripts in the interests of Communism."[70]

V

If militant workers had discovered the role that they might play in shaping a new society, so too did their middle-class allies. One of the greatest novels of the period, and the century, Malcolm Lowry's *Under the Volcano*, is saturated with the Spanish War and brilliantly evokes the choices that middle-class intellectuals saw before them in the thirties, as well as the enduring legacy of the responses they made. Lowry's political sensibility was profoundly shaped by the months he spent at sea before going up to Cambridge, and by the radical generation of which he was a part. Afterwards, his close friendship with the novelist and volunteer John Sommerfield possessed an effect that Sommerfield himself did not even fully appreciate.

Lowry's friend was one of the first of the British to fight in Spain, and he wrote an evocative account of his experiences, *Volunteer in Spain*, which he dedicated to John Cornford. Lowry inscribed a version of a poem entitled, "Song About Madrid, Useful Any Time," to the "Persistence of the memory of Madrid: To John Sommerfield and Julian Bell." A discarded line alluded to "The Live phantoms of University City," where Sommerfield and Cornford had fought in the early great battles for Madrid. The last two stanzas of his final version of the poem speak of Madrid as a city in which "life must be the winner."

> Nor shall death pass to that town,
> Where life finally stands guard;
> Though swollen death with death be grown,
> And the dead ride hard.

> Since life must be the winner,
> Though even a recruit,
> Though but a rank beginner,
> In the musketry of thought.[71]

In a letter to Jonathan Cape, written in 1946 from Cuernavaca, Lowry confirmed Sommerfield's importance and influence on his life, referring to him as "my old pal John (*Volunteer in Spain*) Sommerfield."[72]

Although one of his biographers, Douglas Day, did not believe that Lowry developed any political views of importance in his early years, he speculates, presumably on the strength of *Under the Volcano*, that later, "Lowry felt some degree of guilt at not having joined those friends who fought for the Republic in Spain."[73] But Day, unlike Gordon Bowker, offers no real explanation for how this dramatic change in outlook might have occurred. Stephen Spender, with admittedly less biographical material at his disposal than either Day or Bowker but with a sure psychological understanding, compares the alcoholic and self-destructive Lowry with the irreproachable Orwell. They were alike, Spender believed, because each was relentlessly independent in his political judgments during a time when the politically active could largely be described as conformist.

In *Under the Volcano*, the British consul, Geoffrey Firmin, has a brother, Hugh, who had gone to Spain as a journalist sympathetic to the Republic, and is on the verge of returning. Instead of becoming wiser about the political complexities and betrayals of the war, however, Hugh continues in full possession of his innocence about Spain. The consul's refusal to subscribe to Hugh's idealistic clichés results in his adoption of a political quietism which, Spender believes, possessed its own integrity, and thus, genuine political significance.

If one accepts Spender's point, then the consul is not unlike the example held up for emulation by Julien Benda's "clerks." If Hugh was the "man of action," then his brother was the man who had chosen scrupulously self-reflective inaction (this despite or because of the dashing and heroic "man of action" role he had played in World War I). But in reality, both the "man of action" and the man of inaction coexisted uneasily in Lowry himself. He wrote, "Hugh and the Consul are the same person." Lowry said in a letter, "Hugh may be a bit of a fool but he none the less typifies the sort of person who may make or break our future: in fact he *is* the future in a certain sense."[74] The consul could see, as well as Hugh, the fundamental differences between the Spanish Republicans, for all their faults, and the values that Franco represented. It was their response that differed.

In Bowker's view, the great struggle of Lowry's aesthetic, moral, and political life was dominated by the influence of two writers. Each represented the extremes of the spectrum that lay before the artist of the thirties. The first was the poet and novelist, Conrad Aiken, who believed the intellectual's only obligation was to his art, and who served for a lengthy period of time as Lowry's guardian. The second was the antifascist Norwegian writer, Nordahl Grieg, whose work Lowry greatly admired and whom he once sought out in his home in Norway.

Lowry believed Grieg to be "a man of action and a man with a social conscience," the total antithesis of Aiken. When the Spanish Civil War broke out, the struggle in Spain became central to Lowry's imaginative world. While his friends were fighting and dying in Spain, and while he traveled in Mexico with a wounded Abraham Lincoln volunteer, Lowry announced that he would join the International Brigade, which, of course, he did not do. On one occasion in Mexico he boasted of having been a pilot for the Spanish Republic and, consequently, was arrested by the police as a communist.[75] In *Under the Volcano*, Bowker interprets Hugh who had done what Lowry boasted he would do but did not, to be the author's "good angel" while the "dark angel" of Aiken was constantly beckoning him to the destruction of his political ideals and, through alcohol, his very existence.[76]

Bowker judges that "Orwell, Spender and Auden set out to find the alternative society through organized political action." Unlike them, however, "Lowry embarked on a lonely and seemingly undirected search for an alternative identity in and through literature."[77] This, however, is a false antithesis. Auden and Spender were first and last artists whose politics flowed from their imaginative encounter with their times, and therefore each was profoundly individualistic. It is, of course, true that Orwell called himself a socialist, but he was one of the least ideological imaginable. Each functioned most persuasively as individual critics of the group thinking of their times.

Although Bowker has cleared up any doubts about Lowry's politics, he has, by his "good angel"/"bad angel" dichotomy, oversimplified Lowry's position. By his refusal to act, Geoffrey Firmin turned away from the facile political pieties of his brother, Hugh, who "still dreamed, even then, of changing the world . . . through his actions."[78] If the "engaged" intellectual seems a dominant figure of the thirties, Geoffrey Firmin in *Under the Volcano* established a criterion for truth that occupied a "disengaged" position of reasoned integrity, which the writer Peter Quennell, among others, would have recognized.

Thus, the man of inaction was not indifferent to, but very much implicated in, the life of his time. The consul made a different choice from Bell, Cornford, and Sommerfield, those who, like Hugh, shared "that absurd necessity . . . for action." He lamented the follies of "you people with ideas!" But he too lived in a fabulous world of "ideas," and the choice he made, as a consequence of them, was not an ignoble or cowardly one. At the moment of his death at the hands of the police who, among other things, had mistaken him as a veteran of the International Brigades, an old musician leaned over his body and called him "compañero," the Loyalist greeting. Lowry writes, "It made him happy."[79]

Unlike the communists or the fascists, Lowry tells us that the death of one man is significant; it does diminish each of us. When the Mexican police throw the consul's body into a ravine, and then follow it with that of a dead dog, the reader sees in one man's ignominious and anonymous death the meaningless destiny that each of us faces. The consul chooses alcohol as an anesthetic against this knowledge. Most of us prefer something else—self-deceptions of infinite variety, or, as in the example of Hugh, an identification with causes that confer meaning on our individual lives. A few find the courage to turn away from opiates and bromides and face the prosaic truth of their insignificance, but, in so doing, perhaps find or create a certain modest but authentic nobility out of their blinking honesty. The consul's architecture may be of a much larger scale than our own. Yet in its collapse, Lowry makes us feel a reverberation that must be acknowledged by each of us. A human being has died. And in this affirmation of the worth of one man, Lowry's vision attains a genuine universality. Thus, Spender was right. Lowry does indeed have an "affinity" with Orwell, who himself can be seen as a more honest conflation of Hugh and Geoffrey Firmin. Goethe's words appear as one of the epigraphs for *Under the Volcano*, "Whosoever unceasingly strives upward . . . him can we save."

"Only Connect": Clem Beckett and Christopher Caudwell

The story of the friendship and deaths of Clem Beckett and Christopher Caudwell on the first day of the Jarama captures in miniature the experience of the British volunteers in Spain.[80] The two men symbolized the genuine possibilities in Spain of moving beyond the barrier of class and into a new fraternity of shared ideals and mutual respect. As important, there was a foreshadowing of the role of the Communist party in destroying this first enthusiasm on finding, at last, the "great good place."

Oldham's Clem Beckett, the famous dirt-bike rider, became one of the best known figures in the popular culture of Great Britain in the interwar years. Upon first meeting Beckett, the most striking personal characteristics were his determination, lack of pretension, and air of good-humored civility. In appearance he was muscular and short. Those who followed his career knew him to be absolutely fearless, with an astonishingly high threshold for pain. His signature was the stub of a cigar that always seemed to be hanging from his mouth and a penchant for looking as if he had just emerged from a garage.

By 1928, in dirt-bike riding's early days, he was "the idol of the crowd." At the height of his career he raced on three different tracks in a single twenty-four-hour period. A year later he toured France, Denmark, Russia, the Balkans, Germany, and Turkey. He became so popular in Scandinavia that he remained there for months at a time. Not that he was unappreciated at home. The manager of an English speedway said, "He rode as no-one else has ridden." Joe Norman, a former naval engineer from Manchester who fought in Spain, never forgot seeing Beckett break the Flying Mile record at White City.[81]

Beckett also was highly conscious politically and possessed a deep resentment of injustice. Dirt-track racing was, of course, the central interest of his life. But his career had already proved considerably varied. He became an apprentice card fitter for a company that made textile machinery. His interest in another form of transportation, horses, led him to an apprenticeship with a smith who had contracted to shoe the Oldham Railway van horses. Beckett joined the Blacksmith's Union and met a smith who introduced him to socialist thought. After hearing Tom Mann speak in Oldham in 1924, he joined the Young Communist League, and he took its principles seriously.

When he became aware that some dirt-track promoters were taking advantage of the lesser-known riders by underpaying them and ignoring their contracts, he organized the Dirt Track Riders' Association. He wrote articles in the *Daily Worker* on January 14 and February 17, 1931. One of them was titled "Bleeding the Men Who Risk Their Lives on the Dirt Track." His outspokenness provoked a suspension from the race track managers which, though withdrawn in 1933, earned Beckett the sobriquet, "the outlawed rider." After an altercation with the manager of the Sheffield track over poor racing conditions he received his second suspension, this one permanent.

During his first suspension, he found work assembling engines for the Ford plant at Dagenham, where unions were not allowed. Beckett and some of his comrades attempted to organize their fellow workers from inside the plant. These efforts lasted until he fell afoul of company spies and was fired after eight months. Beckett also became increasingly involved in representing his sport. In 1932 he became vice president of the Workers' Sports Federation and received an invitation to the Soviet Union in the company of other British sportsmen. They arrived in Leningrad on June 3, 1932, and gave exhibitions continuously in the country. Beckett proved so popular that he was asked to stay an additional four months. When he returned to Manchester he bought a cycle shop and married a young communist he had met on his Scandinavian tour.

Clem Beckett's life as a popular legend and political militant might have continued seamlessly if the Spanish War had not intervened. At the end of 1936 he and Arnold Jeans were among the first to volunteer from Lancashire. His wife, Leda, said at a memorial meeting held at the Coliseum, Ardwick Green, Manchester, that her husband "understood that people could live freely and happily only if they took power into their own hands, that was why he was a Communist. He saw the fight in Spain as part of the fight of the British workers."[82] When Beckett arrived at the British base at Madrigueras in November, he was quickly enlisted as a mechanic and a driver. But Beckett also had acquired military skills, serving for a time in the Territorial Army. When asked to take over a truck repair depot, he refused, saying, "I came here to fight Fascism."[83]

One of Beckett's closest friends at Madrigueras was "Christopher Caudwell," or Christopher St. John Sprigg (like Orwell, he chose not to be known by his *nom de plume* in Spain), who had driven an ambulance out from England a few weeks before. To Maurice Levine, the friendship that developed between them was unlikely. The "tough working-class" Beckett "for some reason or other teamed up with this writer."[84] But there was nothing feigned about the relationship that developed between them. Frank Graham from Sunderland knew them well and testified to the fact that the two were "very close friends."[85] Others saw that "a deep comradeship developed between them." The writer and the dirt-track driver were spectacular contrasts to each other in every obvious way. Sprigg was as tidy in his appearance as Beckett was informal. He did not smoke, and his natural manner was a studious reserve. The two men shared the same deep political convictions, however, and an interest in anything with moving parts. Further, "Each was a man of character and ability and they were attracted by their complementary qualities."[86] In addition to their close work in the machine-gun section, Beckett and Sprigg often took guard duty for their comrades, and their friendship must have flourished on those long cold nights on the Castilian plain.

Beckett quickly came to the notice of the British leadership. "He became one of our best tutors on the use of the machine-gun, for he seemed to have a natural gift in picking up mechanical parts." John Lochore, who knew them both, remembers, "Clem I first met at Madrigueras when he was billeted in the same building and he was eventually selected as the leader of our group, with Christopher St. John Sprigg as his next-in-command and myself as the political delegate."[87]

Nevertheless, in an ominous portent of what was to come, someone made "an inaccurate report" to the battalion command that resulted in Beckett's arrest. When protests were made, the authorities released him. Beckett remained "bitter" about the incident, although he returned to the leadership of his section. His arrest may possibly have had something to do with a letter he wrote on November 26, asking for leave to return to Manchester for two weeks. Beckett was convinced that the British government would confiscate his business, leaving his wife and mother destitute, unless he sold it. In the same letter he insisted that he wanted to be assigned to the infantry and not a garage.[88]

Beckett's independence of spirit lay at the bottom of the growing contention between himself and the party leadership. Dave Springhall and Peter Kerrigan, the Albacete commissars, wrote to Pollitt of their concerns about Beckett. They said of the man whom the party hagiographers would promote to the status of a working-class martyr: "We have . . . & am sure will have more trouble with your friend Clem Beckett. He is a dolt as honest as he is big but as confused & muddled as it is possible to be." The two party stalwarts then made it clear to Pollitt their real criticism of Beckett. "He is setting himself up against the Party leadership & become the voice of all the rotton [sic] dissident elements."[89]

As for Sprigg, what gives his views an especially authentic grounding is that he chose, without moral posturing, the kind of life he would lead and who would share it with him. And he freely accepted the consequences of his choice. His politics may have been the product of a creative reading of his left-wing contemporaries, Marx, and the cohort of socialist writers. But his decision to go to Spain was a spontaneous one. He wrote to his brother, Theo, on December 9, 1936: "I expect it will be a surprise to you, but I am leaving for Spain on Friday. I did not know there was any chance of this till yesterday afternoon. They are badly in need of drivers who are in the Party or close to it[.] I have passports, & I therefore volunteered." He drove in a caravan of vehicles across France to the Spanish border. There, on December 17, 1936, he wrote to his brother, "Just arrived at [the] frontier. Convoy had engine trouble all through France. Spain tomorrow." He stamped the card in Perpignan.[90]

To hold this postcard in one's hand decades later, in a chastely elegant, virtually silent library, knowing the outcome of his journey, carries a special poignance. Sprigg would not return to England, where *Illusion and Reality* was awaiting publication. He knew his book had exceptional qualities, but he adopted his habitual self-deprecating mannerisms in describing his *chef d'oeuvre*. "It is a super-technical copper bottomed piece of literary criticism, too frightfully fundamental, very revolutionary and disgustingly erudite."[91] Subsequently, it would bestow upon him the posthumous reputation of being the most acute of English Marxist literary critics.

Once in Spain, he abandoned ambulance driving and joined what was at first called the International Column. The party had told him to use his own judgment as to whether he should remain or return to England. The decision would turn on whether he thought he could be of more use to the party in Spain or in Poplar. The reasons for his decision to stay were several, which he explained in a letter to the party. First, he learned that a British battalion was being formed "where Party experience apart from military experience would be valuable." Second, even though he had no military experience, he possessed technical knowledge that "could be of use on the unfamiliar type of machine gun supplied to the Battalion." Third, he believed that, all in all, he could pull his weight militarily and still do important party work. Finally, of fundamental importance, it seemed clear to him that the Poplar branch was functioning satisfactorily without him, and thus his conscience was clear on this count.[92]

In Spain he came to be known as "Spriggy" by his comrades, or in some instances "John." The persona of the writer and the political activist had at last fused. He was charmed by the strangeness of the country and felt keenly the remoteness of England. "It is all tremendously interesting and one thing is certain; it is impossible in England to form any idea of what it is like to be in Spain." He wrote to his friend, Nick Cox, on December 30, "England seems miles and miles and years and years away already." He included greetings to his party branch in Poplar, urging his comrades "to get the Government's arms embargo lifted as soon as possible." More practically, he asked them "to raise money to send us English cigarettes, chocolates, Left books and periodicals, however few."[93]

He found that his party duties had, indeed, not ceased with his arrival in Spain for, as he said, "the party never sleeps." He wrote, "I thought when I came out here that I should throw off the responsibility of Party member and writer too, as far as spare time was concerned." This, however, was not to be. "I'm a group political delegate—strictly speaking, a non-party job instructor to the Labour Party fraction (we have a Labour Party organisation) and joint-editor of the Wall newspaper."[94]

The young writer had a special regard for the British volunteers who preceded him. He wrote to his friend, Nick Cox, on the death of Cox's brother, Ray.[95] On the same day, in another consolatory letter, he spoke bitterly of the effect of the arms embargo on the Republic's effort to defeat the military uprising. It was his belief that "the freedom to get all the machine-guns and ammunition we wanted would transform the war into a rout along large sections of the front." Writing about the same time to a wounded friend whom he jokingly addressed as "you careless bastard," Sprigg expressed his regret that he had not been able to see action with him. But it was coming soon. He learned that the new British unit would be leaving for the front in five days (which, in the event, turned out to be overly optimistic). Madrid seemed a possible destination "as that seems the centre of action."[96]

One of the reasons things were going well in general, he told his brother and sister-in-law, was the prestige (and, therefore, the brigade's expectations) of the British volunteers, as well as the large number of ex-servicemen who had volunteered. These factors, along with the egalitarian nature of this army of revolutionaries—as they would have described themselves before Moscow's strictures were laid down—made Sprigg feel excited and optimistic.

The uniforms they were issued and the novel methods used for training served as symbols of the new kind of army he had joined.

> Our uniform is a pair of baggy trousers (khaki), khaki tunic, khaki great coat & khaki beret. Of course there is no distinction between the uniforms of officers & men & the discipline, although strict, is entirely different to the discipline of the ordinary army. The morale & discipline within the ranks is based on different methods from the accepted army practice, which make it possible, given the type of men you have here, to shorten very considerably the period of training. In addition there is a high proportion of ex-soldiers in our ranks.[97]

As one reads the cheerful accounts of his stimulating new encounters with military life, it is impossible to forget that he and 300 of his comrades had less than a month to live.

Unlike others preoccupied with their various discomforts and prospects for survival, Sprigg took a keen interest in the extraordinary new environment in which he was living and in the war raging about them. Most importantly, he had found himself among an aristocracy of the brave and committed, some of whom had proven their qualities in memorable fashion. "I am beginning to understand how it has been able . . . to build up a big reputation & a special tradition."[98]

Yet another friend in England heard of his delight that sufficient volunteers had arrived for an English-speaking battalion to be formed. He could welcome them as a more considerable figure than the complete neophyte he had been only a few weeks earlier. "We have been here nearly four weeks training and waiting for new drafts to arrive and bring us to battalion strength." He had now qualified as a machine gunner and been assigned to a crew and subsequently become an instructor. "Len [Cockran] and I are Nos. 1 and 2 on the same machine-gun. We have been here so long that we give instruction." He was beginning to feel like quite an old soldier. But, he admitted, "no rifles yet—the arms shortage is urgent here—but we should get them very soon now and will then go to the Front."[99]

Sprigg felt it was important that the members of his Communist party branch in Poplar be kept apprised of his activities, because of the personal and ideological links that had been forged between them, but also to encourage them to struggle in their own way for Spain. "We know you are behind us in England, fighting for us," he wrote to his Poplar comrades. "We feel the benefit here of every penny you raise. And if you can force the lifting of the Arms Ban so that we can chuck away our obsolete weapons and buy all we want, then Fascism will be conquered in Spain in a few days." Sprigg, whose qualities as a writer and critic were to be fully appreciated only posthumously, concluded by saying to his working-class comrades three weeks before his death, "I'm confident that Poplar is pulling its weight in the campaign for the Brigade and for Spain. I am always proud to be able to say that I belong to the Poplar Branch."[100]

Nor was this windy rhetoric. Sprigg, as much as anyone of his class could, had managed to find the "other country" both in Spain and in England. Unlike the communism embraced by writers such as Spender and Day Lewis, he bore the burden as well as the glory of his own hopes for the future. To a friend and party organizer who needed reassurance he wrote, "We all feel our lack of experience at times, sometimes very acutely—as I am doing here in Spain, with totally new Party responsibilities of a kind that we in England have not had experience of." He responded with sensitivity and tact when his friend lamented that he was unable to join him. "Don't worry about not being able to come out here. All of us would like to get out, only a few lucky ones can manage it, but they will be enough if those at home, with the lousy end of the stick, can do the necessary." He closed with his own particular benediction on his friend, "Family responsibility is a very real thing—I had a lot of it once, so I know—and it is absolutely right for you to keep the home fires burning."[101]

His brother and sister-in-law heard from him two weeks before the battalion left for the valley of the Jarama, where the International Brigades would throw themselves against Franco's attempt to control the Valencia road, and thus to cut Madrid off from the outside world. He felt encouraged by the fascists' inability to take Madrid. "So far it has failed to come off, in spite of the scale of operations; & it seems to me that Madrid cannot be taken now." He felt that the tide of battle was changing. "It will soon be our turn to take the offensive on a wide scale." He wrote, "We still feel keenly[,] however[,] the disadvantage of being short of weapons, & those not the best, while Franco has all the latest in rifles, machine-guns & artillery."[102]

The sense of impending action runs through his last letters with adrenal intensity. Another friend, Peggy Sound, heard that "things are starting to get active here." The battalion had been formed. "In fact," he wrote to her on January 30, "we expect to move off very soon." He felt encouraged by the presence of George Nathan, the larger-than-life leader of No. 1 Company, and believed him erroneously to have become the "commandant" of the brigade. What he could not understand were the dim echoes of English politics that he was picking up in Spain—the reluctance of the Labour party to accept a broad front against Franco seemed to him incomprehensible. "Out here, where our Labour Party Group meets in the Communist Political Commissar's room in the offices of the local Anarchist trade union, it is difficult to imagine the frame of mind of the Labour Party leadership at home."[103]

Once the volunteers of the British Battalion had been loaded into lorries at the farmhouse where they had been served coffee in the early morning of February 12, they drove over rutted roads to their drop-off point at the bottom of a hill leading to a plateau. Within hours one-half of the battalion had been killed or wounded. Among them were Beckett and Sprigg. Eyewitness accounts vary about how they

died. Frank Graham said the two friends "advanced towards the
Moors to cover our retreat. . . . I saw them open fire, several Moors
fell, their guns jammed and they were overwhelmed by more advancing Moors."[104] About half of their comrades made it through as a
result of their covering fire. Len Cockran, who called Sprigg "John"
and thought of him as "my best pal out there," wrote three weeks
after the battle:

> On the first day John's section was holding a position on a hill-crest. They
> got it rather badly from all ways, first artillery, then gunned by aeroplanes,
> and then by three enemy machine-guns. The Moors then attacked the hill
> in large numbers and as there were only a few of our fellows left, including
> John who had been doing great work with his M.G., the Company Com-
> mander—Briskey, the Dalston busman —gave the order to retire.

Cockran later interviewed one of the wounded survivors, who told
him that Sprigg (and Beckett) were still covering their retreat when
the Moors were fewer than thirty yards from their position.[105] In a
subsequent letter Cockran admitted there were "conflicting reports"
of how the young writer died but reconfirmed his own account.[106] A
month after their deaths, Harry Pollitt returned from Spain and added
that Sprigg had refused to carry out the order to retreat. He did not
challenge any other aspect of the story of the deaths of the two men.

Fred Copeman, however, sent a somewhat less heroic account to
the writer's brother, Theo. In his customary self-confident manner,
Copeman wrote that he knew "the exact circumstances" in which
Sprigg and Beckett died. He said there had been heavy fighting early
in the afternoon. Three of the four British companies were engaged
when a Moorish breakthrough threatened the left of the machine-gun
company, forcing it to withdraw. "One gun manned by Clem Beckett,
your brother and George Bright, had been strongly fixed and the crew
found it almost impossible to move it when the time came to
withdraw." With the Moors apparently on the verge of penetrating
the British front, a "slight panic" occurred. Some of the volunteers
began to run, others to fall back in more orderly fashion. Sprigg and
Beckett were forced to abandon their machine gun. Apparently the
two friends realized that they had not removed its lock, thereby
rendering it useless to the Moors. They ran back to the gun. When
they reached it one of the Moors threw a grenade, killing both Beckett
and Sprigg. Bright managed to retrieve the lock. On entering the
British lines, however, he too was killed.[107]

After Sprigg's death, his agent wrote to Theo, "What a tragedy life is! When we are all of us involved in wholesale murder—before very long—we shall have more and more of this sort of tragedy on every side, but the noblest of them all will be those who, like Chris, went first, of their own free will, in the hope they would be able to divert the catastrophe and save humanity."[108] So it seemed to many in the thirties that the moment had come not only to find the blessed land but to save it from its ravening enemies, and the cost proved necessarily a heavy one.

In the relentlessly fluid and terrifying moments of battle, particularly with casualties as staggering as those suffered by the battalion on February 12, 1937, it is inevitable that no single story of two men's deaths will be agreed upon. But someplace along what came to be known as Suicide Hill, the young author of a book that would soon make him famous, and a working-class hero from Oldham, each of whom had forged an unusual friendship in the weeks that led to this February day, died together.

In London, Theo had tried to have his brother recalled to England. When it became clear that Sprigg would remain in Spain with the battalion after delivering his ambulance, Theo did everything he could to persuade Harry Pollitt to have him return, arguing that his brother would be much more valuable to the party as a writer in Great Britain rather than a soldier in Spain. Theo sent an advance set of proofs of *Illusion and Reality* to King Street, where a member of the party's political committee read them and then sent a cable recommending Sprigg's "immediate recall" to England. "But it was too late."[109] Copeman wrote to Theo that his brother had been buried with some eighty others on Hill 231, just above the Tajuña Valley near the village of Morata.[110]

Sprigg left an unpublished letter, however, to Aldous Huxley that testified to another kind of legacy. In *Ends and Means*, Huxley argued that "good ends can be achieved only by the employment of appropriate means. The end cannot justify the means, for the simple and obvious reason that the means determine the nature of the ends produced." Sprigg called this a "policy of constructive passivity." He criticized Huxley for refusing to acknowledge that means and ends are rooted in specific situations. If the situation in which the means are embedded changes, then a new means can be selected, even if not compatible with the end. Huxley believed that because the Soviet Union was born in coercion and violence, the end was necessarily a nation in which coercion and violence ruled. Sprigg answered that in the USSR, "violence *has* begotten peace." He told Huxley that he quite simply did not know what he was talking about. Huxley had never been to Russia or "read any detailed study of its administration such as the Webbs' *Soviet Communism*."[111] Of course, it was Sprigg who was uninformed about Russia, not Huxley, and Sprigg whose moral reasoning was to ally him with the oppressors as well as the oppressed.

On September 16, 1938, the Fifteenth Congress of the Communist Party of Great Britain met in the Birmingham Town Hall. Part of the proceedings included a memorial service for all those who had fallen in Spain. The delegates sang "Far from their Homeland":

> Far from their Homeland our comrades are lying.
> Yet as they died 'twas with brothers they stood,
> Fighting the cause of our common humanity,
> Healing its wounds with the gift of their blood.
>
> They who have fallen are building the future,
> We who remain are their head, hands and heart;
> They saw a new world and strove for their vision,
> We swear to keep their trust and each play his part.[112]

In Spain, the inequalities between classes ended. Charles Morgan, who had originally volunteered in order to escape the dole said, "We had the finest, bravest men in the world out there. We had the ordinary workers, the scientists, the poets and the writers, and in Spain they were truly equal to one another." Sam Wild remembered that "there was a kind of mutuality which became blessed."[113] The Scot, Donald Renton, said of the author of *The Road to Wigan Pier* and *Homage to Catalonia*, "I don't agree with everything Orwell said but to me, though we never met, he was a comrade in the same struggle. The important thing was what he did and where he was in 1936–37." Even Malcolm Dunbar could step outside of himself. Tommy Bloomfield, the building worker and miner, remembers Dunbar cutting a cigarette in two in order to give him half. "That to me summed it up, when you think from what different homes and backgrounds we had come from."[114]

Bill Feeley had no doubt of the significance of his experience in Spain. "Those years in Spain were the finest hours of the British left, of the British labour movement, I saw in my lifetime."[115] Perhaps Jim Brewer should be allowed a final word. He wrote to his friend, Ben

Bowen Thomas, "Ours is the first army since the Crusades which knows what it's fighting for and is utterly confident of success."[116]

The widow of Harold Fry wrote to Tom Murray, thanking him for his letter of condolence after her husband's death. Fry was a shoe repairer from Edinburgh and an ex-sergeant in the British army. He had commanded the machine-gun company at the Jarama until his unit was infiltrated by a contingent of Moors who killed a number of his men and took the rest prisoner. Tom Wintringham called him "the coolest man among bullets I have seen."[117] Subsequently, Fry was sentenced to death by a military court at Salamanca and then freed in an exchange of prisoners in May 1937. Fry decided to return to Spain. He was given command of the battalion and was killed in the first moments of the battle at Fuentes de Ebro. In a letter written on December 15, 1937, his wife captured the motives of many of those who worked for Spain in Great Britain and those who fought and died on Spanish battlefields:

> My husband went to Spain because he realized the danger of Fascisim [sic], and believed that his military experience could best be used in fighting it. He joined the International Brigade because he thought it was the job he could do best. His experience of Fascist method[s] of warfare and the brutal treatment of prisoners behind the lines only helped to strengthen his determination to carry on the fight untill [sic] Franco, Hitler and Mussolini were beaten. This is why he went back to Spain again after a short period of leave, his wound hardly healed, and without even seeing his baby boy which was born the day after he left. I would not has [sic] stopped him even if I could, because I believed he was right, and I am sure that his last thoughts must have been of regret that he could not live to see the final triumph of the forces he fought for. Please excuse me comrade, if I don't write any more.[118]

To E. P. Thompson, whose older brother, Frank, was drawn into the Communist party in the thirties because of Spain, "Christopher Caudwell" represented "the most heroic effort of any British Marxist to think his own intellectual time." Thompson thought of R. F. Willets' "Homage":

> I see a man
> Last heard of alive on a hill-crest
> In Spain, expecting to die at his gun.
> Alone, his youth and work over,
> His stars and planets
> Reduced to yards of ground.
> Hoping others will harvest his crop.[119]

CHAPTER 15

Ideas and Politics

A year ago, in the drowsy Vicarage garden,
We talked of politics; you, with your tawny hair
Flamboyant, flaunting your red tie, unburdened
Your burning heart of the dirge we always hear—
The rich triumphant and the poor oppress'd.
And I laugh'd, seeing, I thought, an example
Of vague ideals not tried but taken on trust,
This would not stand the test. It sounded all too simple.

A year has pass'd; and now, where harsh winds rend
The street's last shred of comfort—past the dread
Of bomb or gunfire, rigid on the ground
Of some cold stinking alley near Madrid,
Your mangled body festers—an example
Of something tougher.—Yet it still sounds all too simple.
— Frank Thompson

It was the most decisive point in my life. If I were on my deathbed and
anybody said, "What is the most valuable thing that you've done in
your life?" I should say, "The day I decided to go to Spain."
— George Leeson

I

Samuel Hynes has argued that the "myth" of the Great War
had assumed its enduring place in English culture by 1930. War—men
and women believed—was meaningless, and betrayal inevitable. As
Great Britain prepared for another world war, Hynes wrote of those
who would fight it: "They would go without dreams of glory, expecting nothing except suffering, boredom and perhaps death—not cynically, but without illusions, because they remembered a war: not the
Great War itself, but the Myth that had been made of it."[1]

Curiously, Hynes makes no comment about Spain. Those who
went to Spain were enveloped in a countermyth—that war could be
noble and meaningful if it was waged against the very forces that
brought about World War I. Therefore, a battle would be fought not
in the interests of the few, as the Great War had been, but in the

interests of the many. Bob Cooney said, "It was OUR war, and we gave it all we had."[2]

Many of the men of the British Battalion who survived Spain, regardless of class, were worthy successors of "thinkers" such as Ralph Cantor, George Brown, and John Cornford, who believed that ideas and choice were inseparable. So, too, were many of the 400 who served in the battalion and, knowingly or unknowingly, found themselves named on the "black list." They had also made a decision. There is little question that many such men possessed an independence of mind that made them targets of party retaliation.

II

But even in a world divided between "good" and "evil," was it necessary to reside either in or out of the Ivory Tower? The writer Gerald Brenan found another way— other than soldiering in Spain or becoming a political gramophone—to connect ideas and politics. Brenan was a middle-class intellectual and supporter of the Republic who, with the exception of Ralph and Winifred Bates, knew contemporary Spain better than any of his generation. Brenan's first exposure to the country came in 1919. Subsequently, he lived for many years in the remote village of Yegen outside Granada. For the first three months of the Civil War, he found himself in the thick of events. His letters during these weeks reveal his belief that the struggle was between tyranny and liberty, with no suggestion of the emerging role of communism. His pro-Republican political views, however, did not prevent him from hiding a village friend who was a devout Falangist, thereby saving his life.[3]

Brenan agreed to serve as a correspondent for the *Manchester Guardian*. The reporter Jay Allen, who broke the story about the massacre of Badajoz in the *Chicago Tribune*, wrote to him, "I admire your guts staying on," but urged him to get out if he heard the Moors were advancing. Brenan and his wife did leave and returned to England. On November 9, 1936, Brenan addressed a packed Albert Hall of Republican sympathizers and subsequently provided assistance to Sylvia Townsend-Warner and the Association of Writers for the Defence of Culture. He also helped raise money for Spanish Medical Aid.[4]

Yet, as deeply as he felt about the Spanish tragedy, Brenan would not allow himself to be used, no matter how good the cause. When Sir Peter Chalmers-Mitchell and others signed a letter to the *Times*, maintaining that Republican forces committed no atrocities in Málaga, Brenan refused to join them because he was not certain that the statement was true. In February 1937 efforts were made to enlist him to go to Madrid and help with the evacuation of refugees. He declined the request because he, the veteran of World War I, had determined to fight the war in a different way, on his terms. Endowed with a rare understanding of the Spanish people and their history, as well as a deep hatred of violence, he set out to discover why the tragedy of the Spanish War had occurred. Brenan early came to understand that the roots of the war were in the history of the peninsula itself, not in Berlin, Rome, Moscow, or London.

Brenan's "method of fighting for the Republicans," as Jonathan Gathorne-Hardy put it, would be to write a book delineating the causes of the war. With the knowledge gained from a lifetime of reading about and living in Spain, further research in the British Museum, and information from sources such as Luis Araquistáin, he withdrew himself from the daily and exhilarating passion of the struggle to write his brilliant and lasting study, *The Spanish Labyrinth*. Brenan sought to make his book fair. To a great extent he succeeded. And it was with some surprise, he said, "On finishing it I saw that what I had written was really an indictment of the follies and illusions of the left, with whose general aims I sympathized." Brenan combined being a self-described "socialist at long range" with being "a conservative at short range."[5] Consequently, he attained a degree of political understanding that the old mandarin, Julien Benda, and the overwhelming majority of his generation found impossible to achieve. Brenan provides evidence that in this most passionately partisan of decades, the reading and writing of history could have a steadying influence, enabling him to provide lasting service both to the House of Intellect and the country he loved.

III

After Spain, many intellectuals came to a reconsideration of their political commitments. Auden, Isherwood, and Spender regretted their embrace of the political left. Auden concluded at the end of the decade that poetry can make nothing happen. After Spain, Spender wrote, "What can I do that matters?" The answer was nothing. Cyril Connolly, who had made three trips to Spain during the war, and whom Jacques Barzun once called "a representative modern mind," also changed his views about what a writer can "do."

In October 1939, he wrote an article for the *New Statesman* entitled "The Ivory Shelter." In it he asserted that writers should devote themselves to their writing and turn their backs on the outside world. It was his view that events had outstripped the ability of writers and artists to influence them, and his brilliant editorship of *Horizon* paid tribute to this belief. The decision of Auden and Isherwood in January 1939 to leave England and settle in America seemed to many of their contemporaries to represent a repudiation of all conviction that art could change anything. Connolly wrote that "the departure of [the two poets] to America a year ago is the most important literary event since the outbreak of the Spanish War."[6] But one could equally well argue that the two were continuing their pursuit of "connections" which, they knew, would never be realized in Great Britain. The historian A. L. Rowse, who knew Auden from his undergraduate days at Christ Church, remembers a comment the poet made: "The attractiveness of America to a writer," Auden said, "is its openness and lack of tradition. It's the only country where you feel there's no ruling class. There's just a lot of people."[7]

Certainly, the legacy of intellectuals who lived through the thirties was a cautionary one. In his poem, "Remembering the Thirties," Donald Davie wrote, "A neutral tone is nowadays preferred," intimating that the proper role of writers was to stay out of politics. Ian Hamilton recalls that in 1960 when he, as president of the Oxford University Poetry Society, invited Stephen Spender for a visit, both Spender and the thirties seemed distinctly *démodé*. "Indeed, the nineteen-thirties were ... seen as a tragicomic literary epoch in which poets had absurdly tried, or pretended, to engage with current politics — one in which pimply young toffs had linked arms with muscular proletarians in order to 'repel the Fascist threat' when they weren't at [Sissinghurst or Garsington] for the weekend, sucking up to the Bloomsbury grandees." But Spender was a good deal more than a poseur or sycophant. His tentativeness and ambivalence saved him from a fate that befell many others of his generation. T. C. Worsley, who accompanied Spender on one of his journeys to Spain, reportedly said, "He's in the clouds, but he has radar."[8] That radar guided Spender away from any political position that offered the individual as a sacrifice to revolutionary ends. It also helped him join Brailsford and, of course, Orwell, in proving that the intellectual could make decisions and commitments that possessed intellectual and moral integrity.

Not all proletarian or middle-class intellectuals, who when faced with what they believed to be the inescapable political consequences of their ideas, disavowed their youthful enthusiasms or turned their backs stagily at the empty shrine to the God that failed. Some, like George Orwell, Margaret McCarthy, and, indeed, Stephen Spender were, in their own fashion, to stay the course and leave a legacy of progressive independence of thought for the future. The career of the historian, E. P. Thompson, who served as president of the Ralph Fox Memorial Committee in Halifax, would be impossible to conceive of without the examples of the intellectuals of the thirties. Of course, there had been radical British intellectuals throughout history, figures such as Milton, Swift, Shelley, Wordsworth, and William Morris (all named by Thompson himself in order to place the roots of his radicalism within a specifically English historical tradition[9]). But never before the thirties had there been a generation of middle-class British intellectuals who so passionately identified themselves with the forgotten.

Orwell chose the marginalized in society as his subjects—the coal miners, the tramps, the unemployed, the traveling salesmen, the Italian volunteer in Spain—and used them as evidence to indict those in authority who were indifferent to their plight. He did this so that members of his class might not escape an encounter, even if only a vicarious one, with those whom they had traditionally ignored or from whom they had resolutely turned away. In *Keep the Aspidistra Flying*, Orwell's character Gordon Comstock, a successful advertising executive and unsuccessful poet, announced that "he was going down, down into the sub-world of the unemployed,"[10] and so he did, as did Orwell with more fruitful results.

The identification of ideas with life made Orwell and Thompson the supreme examples of the "engaged" intellectual in their respective generations. Like Orwell, Thompson saw the timeservers and the uncritical ideologues for what they were and, like Orwell, turned his back on communism without abandoning socialism.[11] Each, in his distinctive manner, leaves a legacy of enormous importance that springs from the essential Englishness of his intellectual and moral life, which in a fundamental sense are one and the same. Fred Inglis captured the genius of this achievement: "Insisting always on the power of radical thought and the necessity of socialism, [Thompson] also speaks in an idiom which can conserve the moral ideas capable of stirring men and women to acts of courage, ardour, faithfulness—of love, joy, peace, long suffering, gentleness, truth. The history he has written backwards is the ground for political moves forward."[12]

This study has attempted to examine the collective efforts of those men and women who responded to the "choice" of Spain and did so from the learned and lived experiences of their culture. The result was the creation of an antihegemonic ideology that significantly challenged the dominating political culture of the thirties and afterward. Those who went to Spain, or who supported the Republic but remained in Great Britain, were participants in a struggle not only for a free Spain, but also to challenge the moderation of both the National Government and the labor movement.

Yet the disillusion felt by many young intellectuals of the thirties, whether middle or working class, should not allow us to forget that in their grasp of social injustice and the menacing politics of their time, they were lonely voices in their respective cultures. Most generally averted their gaze from the historical situation, not by philosophical choice but through indifference, ignorance, or simple human inanition. For them there were no struggles of conscience or disillusion because they never asked or attempted to answer the difficult moral and political questions of their time.

Spender, who delighted almost as much in the *luxe* life as Connolly, effectively struck back at a *Times* editorial titled "Eclipse of the Highbrow," which the poet believed to be an attack on his generation of intellectuals. He reminded its author that many of the "high-brows" among his contemporaries were "the prophets of the present conflict between Democracy and Fascism at a time when . . . your leading articles were advocating a policy of appeasement and surrender." In attempting to find a balance between the claims of art and politics, the poet wrote in *Horizon*: "The artist cannot remain aloof from the short-term issues of his time, but his position is not to lose himself in them."[13]

Frank Kermode has argued that Auden's *Spain* offers a point of view that deserves not only to endure but to triumph. He writes of the poem, "Life is now boldly identified with Spain, which at this critical moment offers itself to human choice." In life, as illuminated by Auden, the important thing is "to choose, not what to choose. The whole of history, evolutionary as well as cultural, culminates in this moment, and in Spain—a figure for crisis and necessary choice, a reef or mole between past and future." Nor is Kermode prepared to accept that individual neurosis or the particular character of our lives renders political choice invalid. "We have always projected our individual crises on to history, so Spain is caught up in a typology, and it is the nature of typologies to transcend history; because we all at times have to make more or less desperate choices, the urgency of that Spanish moment does not disappear with that moment itself."[14] In this book, we have lived with individuals who felt compelled to make "desperate choices," and we cannot leave their company without raising again the issue with which they struggled, the relationship between the intellectual's moral and political values and the "good society."

IV

Stephen Spender believed that a reconciliation between engagement and critical distancing was impossible. What is required, he once wrote, was either a Dostoevsky who submerged himself "in the spiritual blood and mire of his time," or a Voltaire who, though revolutionary in his views, "ruthlessly satirized both sides."[15] The poet could not bring the two together. What he had established, however, was the emptiness of theory without facts. The historian David Caute sees the tragedy of the left in the thirties lying in the fact that intellectuals allowed theory to dominate facts. Asked if they could ever be "effective politicians," he answers "no." Caute believes that "the intellectual's proper function is a critical one: his theories require factual support, but if he fixes facts then the theories lose all credibility."[16]

Archie Cochrane, a Spanish veteran and pioneering epidemiologist, became impatient with the grand political pseudosciences that mesmerized his generation of intellectuals in the thirties. He said, "I have given up any attempt to change the world as I once wanted to do and this is where I disagree with my Marxist friends. I feel that I should just concentrate on changing a small bit of it. It's a bit more effective if one does that."[17] Born of a privileged background, Cochrane attended Cambridge, where he took a first in both parts of the natural science tripos. He worked at the "English" hospital in Grañen. After a year in Spain, he returned to University College Hospital in London to complete his medical studies, no longer the callow young student but one who had played a part in five major battles, and, moreover, with his Spanish tan and red beard looked the man of experience he had become. The most politically conservative of the physicians on the staff said to him, "Ah, Cochrane, back again. Had an interesting weekend?"[18]

After finishing his medical course, Cochrane went to the Rhondda, which had sent large numbers of its young men to Spain. It was here in the valleys of South Wales, where the suffering was so acute in the interwar years, and the Communist party and Spain seemed so woven into the very fabric of politics and culture, that Cochrane chose to practice medicine. Ultimately he revolutionized the science of epidemiology, for which he was much honored. He became a Fellow of the Royal College of Surgeons and received the MBE and CBE. He returned to his hospital in Spain forty years later, and found it turned into a bar and apartments. "I moved towards a window and suddenly found myself in our old so-called 'operating suite.' It was now a sitting room and two bedrooms, but it was unmistakable, and from this stable point I was able to recognize much else."[19]

Above all was the feeling of having done something against fascism, even as comparatively insignificant as he believed his efforts were, instead of simply talking about it. And unlike some other veterans, he had not transformed Spain into a land of constant nostalgia. Rather he knew it to be an essential stage of a larger journey on which he had embarked, and, nearing the end, acknowledged that it had gone well. Archie Cochrane asked that his obituary read, "He lived and died, a man who smoked too much, without the consolation of a wife, a religious belief or a merit award. But he didn't do so badly."[20] What he said of himself could have been said of many others who had volunteered for Spain. In spite of it all, they hadn't done too badly, and, for many, their lives and political education did not stop when the British Battalion was welcomed home at Victoria Station, or when Franco marched triumphantly into Madrid on May 19, 1939.

V

In a sense both Orwell and Thompson are the "amateur" intellectuals whom Edward Said believes our society so urgently needs. These are men and women who are not beholden to the state or institutions, but who "organically" identify themselves with the powerless, and thus live on the margins of society and play the role of its critic. Most of all, no gods will fail them because they have come to understand that there are no gods to serve. He writes, "The true intellectual is a secular being. . . . The intellectual has to walk around, has to have the space in which to stand and talk back to authority, since unquestioning subservience to authority in today's world is one of the greatest threats to an active, and moral, intellectual life."[21]

But the British are still uneasy with intellectuals *in* politics, as Paul Johnson's shrill *Intellectuals* suggests; or, for that matter, *out* of politics. When Edward Said announced the topic of the prestigious Reith Lectures, "Representations of the Intellectual," he discovered "that it was a most 'un-English' thing to talk about. Associated with the word 'intellectual' was 'ivory tower' and a 'sneer.'" Raymond Williams wrote in *Keywords*, "Until the middle twentieth century unfavourable uses of *intellectuals*, *intellectualism* and *intelligentsia* were dominant in English," and, he adds, "It is clear that such uses persist."[22]

The British scholar Timothy Garton Ash has written acutely on the intellectual in contemporary politics. In part, this is because he became one of the earliest students of the Polish Solidarity movement and has followed with sensitive and discriminating attention the intellectual and political careers of the Polish electrician, founder of Solidarity, and former president of Poland, Lech Walesa, and the Czech playwright and politician, Václav Havel. Thus, he observed at close range organic intellectuals playing a prominent role in the dramatic changes that transformed Central and Eastern Europe in the 1980s.

Garton Ash agrees with David Caute and Edward Said that the intellectual's chief contribution to society is that of its critic. The exercise of power should be left to others. He argues that as we look back at our century it is clear that intellectuals have been the least suited of all of society's groups to hold power. "Indeed, as the twentieth century closes, the catalog of the *trahison of the clercs* is a thick volume; the list of those who preserved real independence is a thin one." This is because intellectuals "are among the least likely to resist the insidious poison [of political corruption], precisely because they are the most able to rationalize, intellectualize, or philosophically justify their own submission or corruption by referring to higher goals or values." Instead of the intellectual *engagé*, he asks for the *spectateur engagé*, who though intimately connected to the issues of his or her time does not seek a role as a public figure.[23] There is, of course, a danger in this. In his new introduction to his autobiography, Stephen Spender writes, "Today we have become spectators of reality, which has become a photograph."[24] As Spender understood, intellectuals who observe history by turning pages in an album will lose their "organic" relationship with their times. And, of course, Garton Ash knows this too. He wrote in his diary on Christmas Eve,

1980, "Poland is my Spain." In his most recent book, he adds, "I tried always to be strictly accurate, fair to all sides and critical of all sides. Impartial I was not. I wanted Solidarity to win. I wanted Poland to be free."[25]

A further consideration is that as the Enlightenment project comes to a close, and with it the demise of utopian intellectuals who believe in universal truths, perhaps never again will we hear a figure of the stature of André Malraux say, "By fighting on the side of the Spanish Republicans and Communists, we were defending values that we held (that I hold) to be universal."[26] Nevertheless, Havel argues that we should listen to those intellectuals whose views are formed with a profound sense of ethical responsibility "with the greatest attention, regardless of whether they work as independent critics, holding up a much-needed mirror to politics and power, or are directly involved in politics." He submits, "After all, who is better equipped to decide about the fate of this globally interconnected civilization than people who are most keenly aware of these connections, who pay the greatest regard to them, who take the most responsible attitude toward the world as a whole?"[27]

VI

Fred Copeman's decision to recruit exclusively from the working class was significant. He believed that middle-class intellectuals were transgressors of space that rightfully belonged to working men. At the beginning of the war such intellectuals had been disproportionately represented among the British volunteers. And then, increasingly, as we have seen, the British Battalion in Spain became almost exclusively a working-class fraternity, one with which figures such as Christopher Caudwell, Jason Gurney, Malcolm Dunbar, Hugh Slater, Miles Tomalin, and Lewis Clive had to negotiate a relationship.

Miles Tomalin, a Cambridge graduate in English literature who later studied working-class history at Marx House, served with the Anti-Tanks in Spain, and by common agreement edited the best wall board in the country. On the form given to Tomalin at the time of repatriation he wrote at length about the strengths and weaknesses of the International Brigades.

> I am confirmed in my opinions on such obvious matters as the value of unity on a broad basis to fight fascism at its present strength. The necessity of discipline, the same—though I observe that many men accustomed to

a life of working-class protest seem unable to drop the habit when authority is on their side. I see the importance of morale in struggle. I have been
much impressed by the spirit of comradeship among our men, which
seems to last through all ups and downs, and is a powerful argument for
the community life of socialism. It has succeeded to this extent because
it has been based on a practical purpose. From this . . . one can foresee a
subtle but complete change in general psychology once socialism has been
established.

Yet, upon repatriation, he named Malcolm Dunbar and Hugh Slater
as his references—both, like him, middle-class intellectuals and
university graduates. In his file there is the statement, "As an intellectual he found it difficult to submerge himself in the working class
movement."[28]

British workers had become social actors on a world stage in a
manner unprecedented in their history. And despite everything, they
found "a career open to talents" for the first time in their lives. In the
detailed evaluations that were made out on volunteers, one can
suffice for many. Harry Bourne, a self-taught accountant and factory
worker, was described as a "very keen comrade who rapidly acquired
military knowledge." He possessed "good spirit" and was "very
popular," with "possibilities of leadership." Intellectually active, he
was "well informed politically and [was] keen to study." Most important, Bourne, a machine gunner, proved himself "brave while in
action & a definite inspiration to his comrades."[29]

Another volunteer wrote to his mother, "To live at such a time as
this and take part in so magnificent a struggle is the greatest honour
that can [fall] to anyone. This is one of most decisive battles ever
fought for the future of the human race and all personal considerations fade into insignificance by the side of it."[30] Such an experience
possessed an intensity that was sufficient to enable a worker to
reimagine himself. Charles Goodfellow, who fell at Brunete, wrote,
"We are making history that will inspire the workers of the whole
world."[31] When Tom Murray took part in his first action at the Ebro,
he remembered: "There was a real battle there and we were winning.
. . . It was a bit of an experience for those of us who had never been
in action before. But at the same time," he proudly said, "we scared
them."[32]

With bullets flying and wounded all around, Murray stumbled upon
three dead comrades in the Sierra Pandols who had been killed by the
same shell. Charlie McLeod of Aberdeen lay with his head on George
Jackson's chest. Malcolm Smith of Dundee lay an arm's length away.

One of those who died had come with Murray from Scotland and refused to turn back after arriving in Spain when he had the chance. With pride, Murray, once a farm worker, said of their sacrifice, "The crossing of the Ebro is now regarded in military circles as one of the most brilliantly composed military operations in the history of the war."[33] But, it should be recalled, it was an operation planned in part by Malcolm Dunbar, the onetime Chelsea boulevardier and "good looking young man" whom Fred Copeman had pulled out of the ranks and made commander of the Anti-Tanks, who was now Chief of Operations for the XVth Brigade. But to Murray, the crossing of the Ebro would always mean the sacrifices of his fellow workers, McLeod, Smith, and Jackson. Jim Brewer, a miner from Rhymney in South Wales, found in the Anti-Tank battery a miner, factory workers, an industrial chemist, students, a schoolmaster, and building trades workers. He conceded they were a "motley crowd" but were "true comrades all." Most of all, he wrote, "I don't think any of us knew such pride before."[34]

Miles Tomalin believed that the intervention of the brigades showed the Spaniards that they were not alone in their struggle against fascism. "Democracy can command a loyalty that does not stop at national frontiers." And one might add, class. But Spain gave to the volunteers an equally precious gift which, Tomalin said, would remain with them throughout their lives. "War compels a man to feel deeply, and if his cause is humane, it gives him a foundation on which to build his feelings."[35] Sam Lesser, a student who saw himself as an intellectual "worker" and fought alongside Esmond Romilly in the battles around Madrid and at Boadilla, was then wounded at Lopera and succeeded Peter Kerrigan as *Daily Worker* correspondent (as Sam Russell), wrote of what Spain meant to worker solidarity in the defense of Madrid: "The common people of all countries . . . were showing what common people can do. Madrid inspired the whole of Spain. And Spain taught its lesson to the world."[36]

When the memorial service was held for Lewis Clive—the scion of a great family, an Oxonian, an Olympic hero, and one of the most fashionable and available young men in London in the thirties—at St. Martins in the Fields, almost the only members of his class present were his family. It was impossible for a worker-comrade to withhold bitter comment: "What led him to let the fashionable hostesses down so badly that scarcely a single one of his countless socialite acquaintances, old and young, even cared to join with the throng of his working-class comrades, who were proud of him, in attending the memorial services"?[37] The larger solidarity between workers and the middle classes, of which British socialists had long dreamed, had been forged, if imperfectly. Of middle-class intellectuals like Esmond Romilly and Lewis Clive, Huw Williams remarked that he "was equal to them" and they were "equal to me."[38]

Though class barriers were breached, they did not fall in Spain. An unprecedented egalitarianism prevailed, but on the terms of the workers and not the middle-class volunteers. In his hospital bed recovering from wounds, Tom Donnelly wrote on March 15, 1938, that he saluted the dead "whom I know will live long in the memory of future fighters for Peace, Democracy, and *the abolition of classes* [my emphasis]."[39] While recovering from wounds, David Crook felt optimistic about the possibility of a genuine socialist unity taking place in Spain:

> The feeling of being neither flesh nor fish, which so many of us in the middle class know only too well, is resolved over here. There are occasional discouragements, disappointments, shattering of false ideas—but those which one retains are all the stronger, in fact, tougher. And as soon as one sees this war in its historical framework one is filled with a feeling of tremendous pride, as well as a joy and gratification at the privilege of taking part in it.[40]

Despite their hatred of capitalism, the overwhelming majority of the volunteers accepted democratic institutions as a way of achieving socialist goals. Stafford Cripps, who would greet the battalion when it returned to England, said:

> The violent revolutionary alternative I am convinced is hopeless. With modern mechanised armed forces, armed revolution has not the ghost of a chance, even if it were desirable. I should in any event oppose it with all my power, but in present circumstances I look upon the suggestion as sheer lunacy. Our only alternative then is to attempt to rid ourselves of capitalism by the machinery of democracy.[41]

This was a judgment largely shared by working-class members of the Battalion.

VII

The experiences of those workers who had gone to Spain resonated with the power of myth. Joseph Campbell once wrote, "It has always been the prime function of mythology and rite to supply the symbols that carry the human spirit forward, in counteraction to those other constant human fantasies that tend to tie it back."[42] The working-class volunteers lived a drama whose narrative construction conformed to the myth of the hero. This "archetypal monomyth" gave a genuine familiarity to the great adventure of those who left their homes and crossed the Pyrenees to a strange country, fought for the noblest of ideals—democracy and freedom—and then returned, bearing the testimony of their struggles and adventures. The difference was that unlike the traditional actors in the heroic myths of the past such as the Grail quest, these were working men. And, not unnaturally, the "myth" obscured many of the "facts."

The working-class communities from which the overwhelming number of the British volunteers came integrated the memories of their dead into their culture in distinctive and public ways. An important feature of the grieving for those who died in Spain came in highly ritualized ceremonies. Jack Lindsay was a fertile source of poetry meant for mass recitation:

Call out the roll call of the dead, that we,
the living may answer, under the arch of peace
assembled where the lark's cry is the only shrapnel,
a dew of song, a sky wreath laid on earth
out of the blue silence of teeming light
in this spring-hour of truce prefiguring
the final triumph, call upon them proudly,
the men whose bones now lie in the earth of freedom.

Then, fallen volunteers would be singled out and the narrator would ask:

Where now is he, that tramping on means-test marches,
knew that the road he had taken against oppression
led to the front in Spain? For he was marching
in country lined with harlot-hoardings of menace,
England seared into slums by the poison-bombs of greed.
That road of anger and love must lead to Spain,
the shouts in Trafalgar Square to No Pasaran.
Where is Tommy Dolan of Sunderland?[43]

In a gathering of hundreds and sometimes thousands, the memorial programs took on a mournful, liturgical character as the names of working-class heroes were slowly chanted. Fred Jones "will be remembered by many as the assistant cook at the first Unemployed Holiday Camp held in Oxford." Thomas Gibbons was a building laborer "who played a very active part in the struggles of the unemployed." Johnnie Stevens was killed at the Jarama. He was "one of the leading and best liked young Communists of St. Pancras, always in the fore of anti-fascist activity." William Seal was a baker's roundsman and a van driver who "was always ready to do any hard work in the struggle against the employers." Steve Yates, an electrician, became "a veritable landmark in the fight against fascism in this borough during 1935–36 and was arrested and fined many times." Two who died at the Arganda Bridge, Madrid's lifeline to Valencia, were George Bright, "an uncompromising fighter for Trade Unionism," and Anthony Yates "who was always in the thick of any fight or agitation against the Fascists and served time for his activities."[44]

Yet if these working men who died in Spain were to be remembered, it was not only as a series of ideological bas-reliefs. The homely associations, the heartbreakingly prosaic ways in which their lives and deaths were recounted, made them live again in their communities. Those who gathered for the memorial ceremonies remembered their fathers and sons, brothers, husbands, comrades, men whom they knew well, loved, quarreled and worked and organized with, whose lives had now taken on a larger meaning. They gave back to their communities not just the glamour of their faraway deaths, but the truth that they had fought and died for their own class, and an alternative vision of the world in which political and economic exploitation would end. In a poem meant for mass recitation, Jack Lindsay wrote in the voice of a Spanish worker to his British comrades:

> Can you dare to know your deepest joy
> All that is possible in you?
> Then what you see in Spain's heroic ardour
> Is your own noblest self come true.[45]

We find in another poem an expression of the need to commemorate not only a proletarian leader and intellectual who died at Brunete, but the international cause that drew militants from the working and middle classes together into a sense of passionate fraternity against a "system" that denied men and women work, forbade them opportunities to realize themselves intellectually and politically, and which appeased fascism.

Where shall we find you, George Brown?
We shall find you laughing in the mountains of the Guadarrama
When we come back.
We shall find you at Teruel
When there's dancing in the streets.
We shall find you again in the streets of Madrid,
When Manchester and Brunete
And Villa Nueva de la Canda [sic] have become
One and the same.
We shall come again, lorry after lorry, man after man,
In extended order, marching forward,
To find you where we left you,
Always George Brown.
Glory! What a day that'll be,
Wonderful, glorious,
What a day of wonder!
Every man will be a poet then
And every poet be free of his poetry;
Finding no song is made
For such a morning![46]

In the International Brigade archives in Moscow an anonymous
poem, "To England from the English Dead," has lain for sixty years:

Dishonourable England! We in Spain
Who died, died proudly. But not in your name.
Our friends will keep the love we felt for you
Among your moist green landscapes and smooth hills,
Talk of it over honest window sills
And teach our children we were not untrue.
Not for those others, more like alien men,
Who, quick to please our slayers, let them pass,
Not for them
We English lie beneath Spanish grass.[47]

Notes and Bibliography

Notes

Preface

1. Quoted in Fussell, *The Great War*, 335.

2. Graves and Hodge, *The Long Week-End*, 334.

3. George Orwell used the term "intelligentsia" to describe the British intellectuals of the thirties. See his essay, "Looking Back on the Spanish Civil War" in *A Collection of Essays*. A. J. P. Taylor is quite wrong, however, to claim that the issue of Spain "remained very much a question for the few, an episode in intellectual history," *English History: 1914–1945*, 398.

4. Knox, *Essays*, 218.

5. Michael Jackson has provided the most recent estimate that the total number of volunteers was approximately 36,000, of whom 32,000 served in the ranks. See his *Fallen Sparrows*, 68. However, the British volunteer John Peet maintained index cards at Brigade Postal Service at Albacete. "One slack night [in February 1938] I got the idea of counting the cards to determine how many foreign volunteers had actually come to Spain." Even after eliminating double entries and addressing other problems, he concluded "that any count would be a pretty vague estimate." Nevertheless, he believed that the number of volunteers could not have been lower than 40,000 and was possibly as high as 50,000, thus contradicting "the number of 32,000 often mentioned." His calculation did not include the 1,200 Russians in Spain. See "Spain: Some of the Nuts and Bolts," MML, 10–12.

6. Quoted in Low, *La Pasionaria*, 110.

7. Gurney, *Crusade in Spain*, 13.

8. Interview with Fred Copeman, SRC, 1976, 794/13, 3.

9. Examples include Benson, *Writers in Arms*; Ford, *A Poet's War*; Guttman, *The Wound in the Heart*; Hoskins, *Today the Struggle*; Stansky and Abrahams, *Journey to the Frontier*; and Weintraub, *The Last Great Cause*. Auden's poem, "Spain," set the relationship between poets and Spain in stone.

10. Early into the field with selective examples were Cook's *Apprentices of Freedom* and Corkill and Rawnsley's *The Road to Spain*. Francis wrote an excellent study, *Miners against Fascism*, in which he made pioneering use of interviews with Welsh veterans. MacDougall edited a volume, *Voices from the Spanish Civil War*, which records the personal recollections of a number of Scottish volunteers. Fyrth and Alexander have done the same with *Women's Voices from the Spanish Civil War*. Gurney's *Crusade in Spain*, although factually flawed (indeed libelous in certain instances), is nevertheless an intelligent and sensitive account of the author's experiences in Spain. Gregory was a Hunger Marcher and a volunteer who fought in most of the war's major battles. His memoir, *The Shallow Grave*, offers important perspectives on the war. Such locally printed books as Stratton's *To Anti-Fascism by Taxi* and Monks' *With the Reds in Andalusia* have appeared with frequency.

11. Alexander, *British Volunteers for Liberty*, 16.

12. Morgan, *Against Fascism and War*, 9.

13. See Williams, Alexander, and Gorman, *Memorials of the Spanish Civil War*, for a remarkable example of exclusive history.

14. Hynes, *The Auden Generation*, 11.

15. Baring, *The Puppet Show of Memory*, 1.

16. Hobsbawm, *The Age of Extremes*, 160.

17. Morgan, *The People's Peace*, 191.

18. Buchanan, *The Spanish Civil War and the British Labour Movement*, xi. As this book was going to press, his important new study, *Britain and the Spanish Civil War*, appeared, expanding the range of his concerns and replacing K. W. Watkins' *Britain Divided* as the definitive work on British attitudes toward Spain.

19. Howard, "Patriotism at a Dead End: The Point of Wars for the People Who Fight Them," *Times Literary Supplement*, January 6, 1995, 5.

20. Quoted in Gathorne-Hardy, *Gerald Brenan*, 356.

21. Jackson, *Fallen Sparrows*, 81.

22. Buchanan, *The Spanish Civil War and the British Labour Movement*, 3.

23. Jackson, *Fallen Sparrows*, 20, 52. A famous version of this view was expressed by Hugh Thomas in the first edition of his history of the Spanish Civil War. Thomas believed that "many" of the volunteers from Great Britain "desired some outlet through which to purge some private grief or maladjustment." (See *The Spanish Civil War* [New York and Evanston: Harper and Row, 1961], 299). The statement was repeated in the revised edition (1965) but not in his canonical third edition (1977) which devotes less space to the International Brigades.

24. Cunningham, Introduction, *The Penguin Book of Spanish Civil War Verse*, 74.

25. I do not mean to suggest that Cunningham's introduction is unflawed. As John Saville observes, there are factual misstatements, as well as a superficiality in his understanding of the war in Spain and a significant amount of implausible hypothesizing (*Socialist Register*, 1981). A veteran

entered the debate and summarized the disagreements. See "'Spanish Civil War Verse' Provokes Violent Debate," typescript, David Goodman, Salford. All who work on this subject owe an enormous debt to Cunningham for making elusive primary materials available, as well as for his indispensable *British Writers of the Thirties*.

26. Thompson, *The Making of the English Working Class*, 115.

27. A handful of Englishmen fought with Franco. The best known is Peter Kemp, a self-described "radical Tory," who after leaving Cambridge served first with the Carlists and then the Spanish Foreign Legion. He was a prominent critic of the Sandinistas in Nicaragua during the 1980s. Some fifty years after Spain, Kemp's views remained unchanged. He said, "I've no doubt whatsoever that I fought on the right side." See *Spanish Civil War Collection*, 166–67, and his very interesting memoir, *Mine Were Of Trouble*. However, the Francoist volunteers who received the most attention were those who joined General Eoin O'Duffy in an Irish unit that served briefly and ineffectually in Spain.

28. Lee, *A Moment of War*, 114.

Introduction

1. Thorpe, *Britain in the 1930s*, 1–5, 121–26. See John Stevenson, "Myth and Reality: Britain in the 1930s," in Sked and Cook, eds., *Crisis and Controversy*. For another brief summary see Constantine, *Social Conditions in Britain, 1918–1939*.

2. Priestley, *English Journey*, 401.

3. Powell, *British Politics and the Labour Question*, 99.

4. Philip Bagwell, "The Left in the Thirties," in Rubinstein, ed., *People for the People*, 224–25.

5. Goodman, "From the Tees to the Ebro: My Road to Spain," typescript, Salford, 2–3.

6. Winter, "My Fight for Freedom," *Luton News*, December 4, 1975.

7. Baldwin, *Bill Feeley*, 12.

8. Quoted in Stansky and Abrahams, *Journey to the Frontier*, 82.

9. Stevenson, "The United Kingdom," in Salter and Stevenson, eds., *The Working Class and Politics in Europe and America*, 142.

10. Stansky and Abrahams, *Orwell: The Transformation*, 211.

11. Koch believes that as early as 1933 Stalin and Hitler had come to an agreement to provide each other mutual assistance. Consequently, Stalin had no serious interest in allowing the Republic to win. This is a highly arguable thesis, suggesting the care that must be taken in properly digesting the vast new materials pouring from the Russian archives. See Chapter Two in *Double Lives*.

12. For example, Knight begins her recent book, *The Spanish Civil War: Documents and Debates*, which is intended to underline the major themes of contention about the war, by proceeding through the litany of well-known British poets and writers who flocked to Spain, implicitly reminding her

readers of the moral glamour it possessed for the young middle-class intellectuals of the decade but without referring to workers. Similarly, in Kenwood's *The Spanish Civil War: A Cultural and Historical Reader,* a section on "British responses" is limited to an essay on "Poets of the Thirties."

13. Seldes, *Witness to a Century,* 319.

14. Gurney, *Crusade in Spain,* 69.

15. Koestler, *The Invisible Writing,* 398.

16. Quoted in Cunningham, *British Writers of the Thirties,* 224. Margaret Cole writes that the absence of a fundamental change in class attitudes meant "the British upper classes [could] think and write of the classes below them as though they were a different species — a species of 'natives,' to use the language of imperialism, who should be well treated and have their more serious disadvantages remedied where possible, but with whom one could not possibly associate on terms of equality." See "The Labour Movement between the Wars," in Martin and Rubinstein, eds., *Ideology and the Labour Movement.*

17. Stansky and Abrahams, *Journey to the Frontier,* 104.

18. Although see Roberts' *The Classic Slum* for the very uneven response to the new educational opportunities offered in Salford.

19. Carey, *The Intellectuals and the Masses,* 3, 5–6, 16.

20. In a letter to his mother, Vanessa, quoted in Stansky and Abrahams, *Journey to the Frontier,* 392.

21. Quoted in Foote, *The Labour Party's Political Thought,* 31.

22. Bell, ed., *A Moment's Liberty,* August 16, 1922.

23. Beatrice Webb pointed to Bentham as "Sidney's intellectual god-father." She suggested that Marxist dialectics should be scrapped for "the utilitarian calculus, by which I mean the greatest good of the greatest number, a calculus which I believe controls the Soviet Gosplan, in its planned production for community consumption." Quoted in Caute, *The Fellow-Travellers,* 243.

24. Quoted in Beilharz, *Labour's Utopias,* 63.

25. Orwell, *The Collected Essays, Journalism and Letters,* 2:52–53.

26. Wood, *Communism and British Intellectuals,* 64.

27. Quoted in Carey, *Intellectuals and the Masses,* 150.

28. The famous epigraph of E. M. Forster's *Howards End* was "only connect."

29. Hanley, *Grey Children,* 79–80, 106, 1.

30. See Richardson's *Comintern Army* for a decisive rebuff to this mythology.

31. Symons, *Between the Wars: Britain in Photographs,* No. 173.

32. These men were in all likelihood members of the International Brigade League. According to Bill Alexander, they consisted of only ten members. He writes, "The organization and its members soon vanished from the scene." See *British Volunteers for Liberty,* 249.

33. Rust, *Spain Fights for Victory,* 16.

34. Interview with Syd Quinn, SRC, 801/3, 73.

35. Spender, "Writers and Politics," in Kurzweil and Phillips, eds., *Writers and Politics*, 221.

36. Ibid., 15.

37. Sheean, *Not Peace but a Sword*, 234.

38. Osborne, *Look Back in Anger*, 84–85, 58. As a child, watching his father die for twelve months, Jimmy said, "I was a veteran" of Spain too.

39. Spender, *World within World*, 290.

40. Spender, *The Thirties and After*, 10–13.

41. Gurney, *Crusade in Spain*, 36.

42. Frow, "Kenneth Bradbury," in *Clem Beckett*, 19.

43. Lee, *A Moment of War*, 46.

44. John Cornford wrote to Margot Heinemann on November 21, 1936, that "the losses are heavy, but there's still a big chance of getting back alive, a big majority chance." If this was his real assessment of the situation, it presumably would have changed if he had lived to see the killing grounds of the Jarama and Brunete that were soon to come. See Galassi, ed., *Understand the Weapon*, 186.

45. Wilkinson, "Truth & Delusion," 5. His essay appears in a special section titled, "Remembering the Spanish Civil War."

46. Quoted in Carroll, *Odyssey of the Abraham Lincoln Brigade*, 369.

47. Jones, ed., *Brigadista*, 130. This was the Maurice Bishop Brigade named after the slain Grenadan leader.

48. Carson, "With the International Brigades in Nicaragua," *Village Voice*, 17.

49. Carroll, *Odyssey of the Abraham Lincoln Brigade*, 373.

50. Goodman, "From the Tees to the Ebro," 23. Also see Maury Colow, "Ambulances for Nicaragua," in Bessie and Prago, eds., *Our Fight*, 349–56.

51. *Morning Star*, January 6, 1989, MML, Box A-32 Tg/7.

52. *New York Times*, August 19, 1993, A3.

53. Quoted in Wilkinson, "Truth & Delusion," *Salmagundi*, 3.

54. Spender, Introduction, in *Voices against Tyranny*, 7.

55. Fussell, *The Great War and Modern Memory*, 79–82.

56. Kevin Foster, "'Between the Bullet and the Lie': Intellectuals and the War," in Kenwood, ed., *The Spanish Civil War: A Cultural and Historical Reader*, 20.

57. August 1, 1936, quoted in Mowat, *Britain Between the Wars: 1918–1940*, 578.

58. Quoted in Cunningham, ed., *Spanish Front*, 51.

59. Barke, *Land of the Leal*, 577.

60. Quoted in Guttman, *The Wound in the Heart*, x.

61. Wood, *Communism and British Intellectuals*, 57.

62. Annan, *Our Age*, 183.

63. Taylor, *English History: 1914–1945*, 395.

64. "To All the Workers of Glasgow" [loose sheet], MML.

65. Fiedler, "The Two Memories," in *Proletarian Writers of the Thirties*, 16. See Alexander's comments on this point in *British Volunteers for Liberty*, 11.

66. Thomas, *The Spanish Civil War* (1961 ed.), 616.

67. Manning, *The Levant Trilogy*, 498.

68. This is an apparent reference to the words of the Irish poet, Charles Donnelly, spoken a few moments before his death at the Jarama. Donnelly took refuge behind an olive tree and began squeezing olives that were lying on the ground. In the lull between bursts of machine-gun fire, a Canadian volunteer heard him say, "Even the olives are bleeding." He died minutes later. (In the Canadian account of 1937 he is erroneously called "Charles Connelly, Commander of the Irish Company.") See "The Mackenzie-Papineau Battalion in Spain," *Marxist Quarterly* 18, 1966, 33.

69. Bill Alexander, "From Our British Comrades," *The Volunteer*, 13, 2 (1991), 5–6.

70. Joseph B. Russell to *The Volunteer*, 12, 1 (1990), 27.

71. Bill Alexander, *The Volunteer*, 6.

72. Powell, *British Politics and the Labour Question*, 71.

73. "Glasgow's Tribute to the Brigade," February 25, 1980, unnamed newspaper, MML.

74. Quoted in Alastair Reid, "The Essays of Thomas Wright," in Winter, *The Working Class in Modern British History*, 174.

Chapter One

1. Spender, "Writers and Politics," in Kurzweil and Phillips, eds., *Writers and Politics*, 225.

2. Crick, *George Orwell*, xix. Also see Wood, *Communism and British Intellectuals*, 97, on this point. Any argument that convincingly seeks to analyze this phenomenon further must do so within the context of Great Britain's distinctive political culture. In Great Britain, unlike the Continent, the relationship between power, institutions, and the law had been largely decided by the beginning of the twentieth century. From this perspective, one must take into account the unique ability of the landed aristocracy of the nineteenth century not only to survive but to preserve its hegemonic values by forging an alliance with the emerging industrial bourgeoisie. The aristocracy made strategic political concessions to the middle classes, most notably in the instance of the Reform Bill of 1832. In exchange, the great landowners imposed their values on this dynamic new sector of society. The medium for the survival of the attitudes of this outmoded elite was the British educational system, which socialized each succeeding generation in its values. Consequently, a British intelligentsia disaffected from the ruling order did not develop, as in those European countries whose landed classes had confronted rather than conciliated the bourgeoisie, or, as in the case of France, where intellectuals saw themselves as both critics and mediators between the state and the rest of the nation. See Nairn, *The Break-Up of Britain*, 24–52; Anderson, "Origins of the Present Crisis," *New Left Review*; Annan, "The Intellectual Aristocracy," *Studies in Social History*; Jennings and Kemp-Welch, "Century of the Intellectual" in *Intellectuals in Politics*, 2–5, and Wiener, *English Culture*. Heyck offers an etymology of "the intel-

lectual" in Victorian society, arguing that the intellectual saw himself as a member of an aesthetic elite, or, as George Gissing wrote, "a separate and learned class." See "From Men of Letters to Intellectuals," 183.

3. Judt, *Past Imperfect*, 249.

4. Connolly, *Enemies of Promise*, 96.

5. Day Lewis, "English Writers & A People's Front," *Left Review* 13, 1936, 672–74.

6. Strachey, "The Education of a Communist," *Left Review* 3, 1934, 64.

7. Annan, *Our Age*, 10.

8. Spender, *World within World*, 139.

9. Spender, *The Destructive Element*, 14.

10. Quoted in Pawling, *Christopher Caudwell*, 10.

11. Galassi, ed., *Understand the Weapon*, 45. Also see Stansky and Abrahams, *Journey to the Frontier*, 174–75, 182. Evelyn Waugh chose a famous line from the poem for the title of his novel, *A Handful of Dust*.

12. MacNeice, *The Strings Are False*, 134.

13. Symons, *The General Strike*, 67–68.

14. Ibid. Hugh Gaitskell and his fellow undergraduates at the London School of Economics proved an exception. See Annan, *Our Age*, 174.

15. Stallworthy, *Louis MacNeice*, 183.

16. Hynes, *A War Imagined*, 421–22. See Fisher, *Cyril Connolly*, 75.

17. Hugh Gaitskell, "At Oxford in the Twenties," in Briggs and Saville, eds., *Essays in Labour History*, 9.

18. Galassi, ed., *Understand the Weapon*, 102.

19. Thomas, *John Strachey*, 129.

20. Ibid., 130.

21. Quoted in Newman, *John Strachey*, 62.

22. Green, *Children of the Sun*, 270.

23. Strachey, *The Coming Struggle for Power*, 302. Nan Green said that she and her husband, the musician George Green, joined the Communist party because of Strachey's arguments. See Interview with Nan Green, Manchester, August 7, 1976, 3.

24. Ibid., 307, 322.   25. Ibid., 361.

26. Ibid., 363, 396.   27. Ibid., 157.

28. Ibid., 348.

29. *Left Review* 15, 1936, cover advertisement.

30. Green, *Children of the Sun*, 290.

31. Corkill and Rawnsley, *Road to Spain*, 96.

32. Goodman, "From the Tees to the Ebro," Salford, 12, typescript. Also, see Interview with Goodman, n.d., 7, Manchester, in which he calls *Forward from Liberalism* "one of the key books."

33. Stephen Spender to Christopher Isherwood, October 30 [1936] in Bartlett, ed., *Letters to Christopher*, 122–23.

34. Spender in Crossman, ed., *The God That Failed*, 231–32.

35. Spender, *Forward from Liberalism*, 3.

36. Ibid., 43.

37. Ibid., 191, 208, 229–31.

38. Strachey, *Coming Struggle for Power*, 377.

39. Marx, "Theses on Feuerbach," Tucker, ed., *The Marx-Engels Reader*, 109.

40. See Kingsford, *Hunger Marchers in Britain*.

41. Greene, *A Sort of Life*, 175.

42. For an account of the NUWM, see Croucher, *We Refuse to Starve in Silence*.

43. MacDougall, ed., *Voices from the Hunger Marches*, 1: 38.

44. Ibid., 33.

45. Wood, *Communism and British Intellectuals*, 52.

46. Quoted in Cloud and Olson, *The Murrow Boys*, 139.

47. Stansky and Abrahams, *Journey to the Frontier*, 214–15. See Branson, *History of the Communist Party*, 207–10.

48. Cunningham, "Marooned in the 30s," *Times Literary Supplement*, 4768, August 19, 1994, 4. See also his *British Writers of the Thirties*, 242.

49. Quoted in Stansky and Abrahams, *Journey to the Frontier*, 214–15.

50. MML, Box D-4 He/1.

51. Straight, *After Long Silence*, 52–53.

52. Stansky and Abrahams, *Journey to the Frontier*, 109.

53. Annan, *Our Age*, 187.

54. James Klugmann, "Introduction: Crisis in the Thirties: A View from the Left," in Clark, Heinemann, et al., eds., *Culture and Crisis*, 29.

55. Straight's brother-in-law was Gustavo Durán, one of the most successful of the Republican commanders, and the model for Manuel in André Malraux's *Man's Hope*, arguably the greatest novel of the Spanish War. Straight went on to become a speech writer and adviser to President Roosevelt and a longtime editor of the *New Republic*, which his parents founded. When he learned the Kennedy administration was preparing to name him chairman of the new National Endowment for the Arts, which would require an FBI background check, he went to the Bureau and told them of his early communist associations at Cambridge. This led to the unmasking of Anthony . See *After Long Silence*, 266, 316–28.

56. Quoted in Spender, "Writers and Politics," in Kurzweil and Phillips, eds., *Writers and Politics*, 233. Louis MacNeice wrote to Anthony , "I really must congratulate you on your university for producing this Cornford boy because obviously he is the one chap of the whole damn lot of you who is going to be a great man." See Stallworthy, *Louis MacNeice*, 182.

57. Straight, *After Long Silence*, 60.

58. Ibid., 60–61.

59. Ibid., 67.

60. September 25, 1936, Folder 15, Berg.

61. Quoted in Straight, *After Long Silence*, 108.

62. Stansky and Abrahams, *Journey to the Frontier*, 397.

63. Straight, *After Long Silence*, 108.

64. On the issue of middle-class unemployment also see Wood, *Communism and British Intellectuals*, 88–89.

65. Orwell, "Inside the Whale," in *A Collection of Essays*, 236.
66. Ibid., 237.
67. Quoted in Blaazer, *The Popular Front*, 143.
68. Quoted in Morgan, *Harry Pollitt*, 122.
69. Haldane, *Truth Will Out*, 306.
70. Orwell, *The Collected Essays*, 1: 515.
71. Straight, *After Long Silence*, 61.
72. Day Lewis, *The Buried Day*, 209.
73. Quoted in Wood, *Communism and British Intellectuals*, 51.
74. Stansky and Abrahams, *Journey to the Frontier*, 280.
75. Caudwell, *Studies in a Dying Culture*, 72.
76. Hynes, "Introduction," in Caudwell, *Romance and Realism*, 6.
77. Caudwell, "November the Eleventh," in *Collected Poems*, 40.
78. Ibid., "The Kingdom of Heaven."
79. Galassi, ed., *Understand the Weapon*, 13.
80. Brockway, *A Lead to World Socialism*, 4.
81. Quoted in Stansky and Abrahams, *Journey to the Frontier*, 95.
82. Ibid., 109. A minority on the left were outspoken in their opposition to intellectuals becoming "men of action." The young writer, Peter Quennell, expressed his agreement with the French neo-Kantian, Julien Benda, the author of *Betrayal of the Intellectuals*. "I still believed," he wrote, "a belief I have never lost—that the writer, if he deliberately espouses a cause, is bound to curtail, and perhaps distort his vision." Quennell felt that it was the duty of the intellectual to stand aloof from politics and to contribute to society's general well-being by addressing liberal and humane themes that transcended specific political issues. Quennell realized, however, as did Benda, that some degree of political involvement on his part was inevitable "since every work that [the writer] produces must reflect the spirit of his age, and reveal his attitudes towards its values." He concluded that the intellectual's "most effective criticisms are not expressly stated so much as subtly and quietly implied, and form part of a picture of the human condition that transcends the problems of the present day." But among those on the Left, Quennell's scrupulous detachment proved an exception. See *The Marble Foot*, 242.
83. MacNeice, *The Strings Are False*, 3.
84. Quoted in Stallworthy's *Louis MacNeice*, 177.
85. See his thoughtful essay, "Comments on Spain," in *London Forward* 8, March 4, 1939, 3. He acknowledged that "there is plenty of black on the Government side and plenty of white on the Franco side." But "Franco represents dead tradition and the Government represents living tradition." Great Britain bore a particular responsibility for the defeat of the Republic. The refusal of Chamberlain's government to send arms and food contributed to Franco's victory. MacNeice, like many of his contemporaries, such as David Guest, Julian Bell, Ted Heath, Felicia Browne, Stephen Spender, John Lehmann, W. H. Auden, and Christopher Isherwood, was doing an extraordinary amount of traveling. Vienna, Berlin, Hamburg, Barcelona, Madrid, and

Valencia—each was a step toward identification with the community and traditions of the European intelligentsia. See Hynes, *Auden Generation*, and Fussell, *Abroad*.

86. Day Lewis, "English Writers & A People's Front," *Left Review*, 671–72, 674.

87. Lehmann, "Should Writers Keep to Their Art?" *Left Review*, 882.

88. Ibid., 884.

89. Spender, *The Thirties and After*, 12.

90. Connolly, *Enemies of Promise*, 97–98.

91. Strachey, "The Education of a Communist," *Left Review*, 67.

92. Connolly, *Enemies of Promise*, 101.

93. Ibid., 104.

94. Virginia Woolf, "The Leaning Tower," *Collected Essays*, 2:180, 172, 176.

95. Quoted in Caute, *Fellow-Travellers*, 51.

96. Parker and Kermode, *Reader's Guide*, 523.

97. Upward, *In the Thirties*, 41.

98. "Felicia Browne: Killed in Defence of Democracy," *To-Morrow*, December 1936, 4.

99. Cockburn, *In Time of Trouble*, 250.

100. Haden Guest, *David Guest*, 87–89.

101. Ibid.

Chapter Two

1. If there had been any ambiguity over how British socialists envisioned the emergence of a socialist society, the Communist party's ideology and behavior in the interwar years decided the issue. The Labour party refused to cooperate with the CPGB in achieving socialism and conducting a "socialist" foreign policy for four principal reasons: first, the communists condemned parliamentary democracy, except as a means to achieve a workers' state; second, the Zinoviev letter, purportedly an instruction from the Third International to British workers to revolt, effectively smeared the Labour party with "Bolshevism" and consequently played an important role in bringing down MacDonald's government in the General Election of 1924; third, the Communist National Minority Movement, initally accepted as an ally by the trade union movement, attempted to disrupt it and thereby earned the undying enmity of Ernest Bevin, who with Sir Walter Citrine was to be one of the two most powerful figures in the labor movement in the thirties; fourth, there was never any doubt that the party's first allegiance was to Moscow and not to the national interests of Great Britain. The authority of Moscow was confirmed in 1928–29 when the Comintern imposed the disastrous "class against class" line on its national parties. This required the CPGB to sever links with the Independent Labour party and any other groups on the left that allowed membership to both communists and noncommunists. From 1929 to 1933 the British communists ended whatever slight chance they may have had of reconciling with Labour by stigmatizing the

party and its leaders as "social fascists," as well as traitors to the working-class movement. At the 1935 Seventh World Congress, however, the Comintern abruptly changed the party line. Concerned by the German threat and the destruction of working-class parties and trade unions in Italy, Germany, and Austria, the Comintern abandoned the "class against class" strategy and called for a Popular Front "against war and Fascism." But memories could not be so easily put aside. When the British communists called for a United Front of all parties, the invitation was summarily rejected by the laborist leadership.

2. Caute, *Fellow Travellers*, 166.

3. Lenin, *What Is To Be Done?* 62–63.

4. Quoted in Rée, *Proletarian Philosophers*, 88.

5. Hugh Dalton to Leonard Woolf, July 30, 1937, Berg. When Roderick MacFarquhar was in the midst of organizing amubulance support for the wounded at Brunete, he was astonished to see Bell, "the man of letters," wearing a topee or light helmet which originated in India. Although excellent for protection in the scorching July sun, Bell's headgear, MacFarquhar said, was the only one of its kind "I saw throughout the Spanish revolt." Becoming one with the workers had its limits. See his "In Spain," *Railway Service Journal*, 105.

6. Crossman, ed., *The God That Failed*, 8.

7. Quoted in Sullivan, *Christopher Caudwell*, 20. Those who believed they had "gone over" to the workers could be as excoriatingly critical of middle-class intellectuals as workers themselves. Ralph Fox, a product of Magdalen, Oxford, and the author of *The People and the Novel*, among many other books, echoed party suspicions of intellectuals. After leaving Oxford, Fox went to Russia with a famine relief expedition, not as a touring literary lion like the Webbs or George Bernard Shaw, and he remained to teach at the Lenin School. When he joined the Communist party, it was seen as a genuine statement of solidarity with the workers. According to him, "intellectuals are in fact dreamers." In the last months of his life he thought of the "great refusal" of contemporary writers "to face reality as a whole." See Ralph Fox, "Lawrence the 20th Century Hero," *Left Review*, July 1935, 391–96. After his death in battle, the Magdalen intellectual found an honored place in the iconography of the British volunteers. Harry Pollitt said Fox "was able to foreshadow the alliance between mental and manual worker in the fight against Fascism and war." The American Michael Gold called him a writer who had "come out of the rancid atmosphere of the Ivory Tower into the strong winds of nature and society." See *Writer in Arms*, 3, 10. The *Left Review* (February 1937) proclaimed, "He helped to win the support of many intellectuals who had previously clung to the tradition of the incompatibility of art and politics." His epitaph read, "He lived with and taught and organised working men."

8. Branson, *History of the Communist Party*, 204–6.

9. Harry Pollitt to Tom Wintringham, quoted in Kevin Morgan, *Harry Pollitt*, 43.

10. Wood, *Communism and British Intellectuals*, 173.

11. Abel, *The Intellectual Follies*, 39–40.

12. Haldane, *On Being the Right Size and Other Essays*, 84.

13. For this desire to abolish the "I" in favor of the "we," see Cunningham, *British Writers of the Thirties*, 219–20.

14. Upward, *In the Thirties*, 68.

15. Margot Heinemann, "The People's Front and the Intellectuals," in Fyrth, ed., *Britain, Fascism, and the Popular Front*, 157.

16. Quoted in Caute, *Fellow-Travellers*, 7.

17. Carr, "Heroes and Guerrilleros," *Times Literary Supplement*, December 17, 1993, 5.

18. Quoted in Branson, *History of the Communist Party*, 207.

19. *Left Review* 13, October 1936, 670.

20. Ibid.

21. "The Scarlet Banner," *Songs of the Spanish Civil War, The Oldham Men Who Fought in Spain, 1936–1938*, Salford. This was a program presented on Saturday, February 15, 1986.

22. Crossman, ed., *The God that Failed*, 230–31.

23. Quoted in Kevin Morgan, *Harry Pollitt*, 123.

24. See Orwell, *The Road to Wigan Pier*, 127–28.

25. Wood, *Communism and British Intellectuals*, 30.

26. Worsley, *Fellow Travellers*, 54–56.

27. Ibid., 59.

28. Quoted in Morgan, *Harry Pollitt*, 159.

29. Gathorne-Hardy, *Gerald Brenan*, 321.

30. Interview with Martin Bobker, October 7, 1977, Manchester, 5.

31. Caudwell, *Illusion and Reality*, 19, 275.

32. Ibid., 279, 281.

33. Ibid., 282.

34. Ibid., 281, 283, 285.

35. Lehmann, *The Whispering Gallery*, 232.

36. Koch, *Double Lives*, 192. Among the many sources on the Left Book Club, see Betty Reid, "The Left Book Club in the Thirties," in Clark, Heinemann, et al., eds., *Culture and Crisis*, 193–207.

37. Quoted in Jupp, *Radical Left in Britain*, 96–97.

38. Koch, *Double Lives*, 192.

39. Jupp, *Radical Left in Britain*, 97.

40. Branson, *History of the Communist Party*, 215.

41. Interview with Jim Brewer, November 29, 1969, Swansea, 5.

42. Goodman, "From the Tees to the Ebro," Salford, 12.

43. See, for example, the questionnaire completed by Karl Boden, Fond. 545, op. 6, d. 108, ll. 5v, Moscow.

44. *Left News* 21, January 1938, 636.

45. Ibid. 20, 1937, 592, 594.

46. Christopher Caudwell To "Bottle," January 24, 1937, Texas.

47. W. Tapsell to Harry Pollitt, April 25, 1937, MML, Box C 12/4.

48. George Aitken to Harry Pollitt, May 8 [1937], MML, Box C 13/2.

49. See Brailsford, *Socialism for Today*.

50. Blaazer, *The Popular Front and the Progressive*, 4–6.

51. Ibid., 57. Blaazer applies Peter Clarke's analysis of the New Liberalism to the Progressive tradition.

52. Ibid., 45.

53. Annan, *Our Age*, 178.

54. Caute, *Fellow-Travellers*, 88–89.

55. Ernest Gellner, "No School for Scandal: Dahrendorf's LSE and the Quest for a Science of Society," *Times Literary Supplement* 4808, May 26, 1995, 3.

56. The question mark was subsequently removed.

57. Robert Oppenheimer, the director of the atomic bomb project at Los Alamos, was also influenced by the Webbs' adulation of Russia. See Caute, *Fellow-Travellers*, 292.

58. Spender, *Forward from Liberalism*, 251–52. If Spender had talked to Sir Walter Citrine, he would not have been so sanguine. Citrine's *I Search for Truth in Soviet Russia* demonstrated that a man of very considerable limitations was quite capable of seeing that "Russia . . . has suppressed all political opposition. Liberty of speech, freedom of the press and public meeting are denied to all but the Communist Party," 286.

59. Galassi, ed., *Understand the Weapon*, 107.

Chapter Three

1. For examples, see Green, *Children of the Sun*, 253, 284, 293; Cunningham, *British Writers of the Thirties*, 252–253; Spender, *World within World*, 204.

2. "One Way-Song" (Section XXVII).

3. Kermode, *History and Value*, 42.

4. Harrison, *The Common People*, 371.

5. Orwell, *The Road to Wigan Pier*, 149.

6. Cunningham, "Introduction," in Bates, *The Olive Field*.

7. Bell, *Julian Bell*, 222. In the poem, "Bypass to Utopia," Bell emphasizes the damage that modern war and "restored old tyrannies" have done to this dream of "the golden town."

8. Lehmann, *Whispering Gallery*, 199.

9. Quoted in Kramnick and Sheerman, *Harold Laski*, 349–50.

10. Spender, *Forward from Liberalism*, 180–81.

11. Kermode, *History and Value*, 91, n. 6.

12. Carey, *The Intellectuals and the Masses*, 40.

13. Orwell, *Collected Essays*, 2: 74.

14. Hynes, *Romance and Realism*, 3–28. Hynes' introduction remains an extremely useful biographical essay on Caudwell.

15. Caudwell, *Illusion and Reality*, 90–91.

16. Pawling, *Christopher Caudwell*, 7.

17. Ibid., 9.

18. Hynes, *Romance and Realism*, 13.

19. Christopher Caudwell to Theo [T. Stanhope Sprigg], June 11, 1936, Texas.

20. Quoted in Lewis, "Christopher Caudwell," *Spain Today*, 8–9.

21. Caudwell, *This My Hand*, 173–74.

22. He was one of a handful of middle-class intellectuals who took this route. Others included Ralph Fox, David Guest, Hugh Slater, Edward Upward, and, of course, to a certain extent George Orwell.

23. Interview with David "Tony" Gilbert, SRC, 9157/10, Reel 5.

24. Kermode, *History and Value*, 96.

25. To Theo, June 9, 1936, Texas.

26. Ibid.

27. Ibid.

28. To Theo, June 11, 1936, Texas.

29. Ibid.

30. Ibid.

31. Alex A. Compasor to Comrade [Caudwell], October 17, 1936, Texas.

32. Paul Beard to Christopher Caudwell, November 17 [1935], Texas.

33. Gurney, *Crusade in Spain*, 71. Caudwell's last novel, *This My Hand*, was a complete departure from anything he had done before, and is his one significant work of fiction. The novel is a psychological study of a war veteran, Ian Venning, who kills his emotionally unstable first wife, drives his second wife, Barbara, to suicide, and, finally, murders his mistress, a crime for which he is executed. Despite this lurid and melodramatic plot, it is, from the point of view of this study, an interesting novel. Published after Caudwell became a communist and the year he went to Spain, it provides insight on several issues of importance for both himself and his generation. For example, there is an interesting interplay between the imagined and the lived experience in the lives of several of his characters. Also, the book reveals Caudwell's attitude toward pacifism and morality, which is relevant to any convincing interpretation of his character, as well as of his anticipation of the intensity of the experience he would soon undergo in Spain.

34. Paul Beard to T. Stanhope Sprigg, February 22, 1939, Texas. Beard refers to a letter he received from "Chris" on November 21, 1935.

35. Caudwell, *This My Hand*, 248.

36. Angela Haden Guest, "David Guest: A Memoir" in *David Guest*, 108.

37. Ibid., 109.

38. Symons, *The Thirties*, 120–21.

39. Author's interview with Ralph Bates, April 11, 1991.

40. D. M. Miller, American Broadcast, March 4, 1938, DMWC.

41. Ibid.

42. Author's interview with Steve Nelson, May 13, 1989, Truro, Mass.

43. Author's interview with Ralph Bates.

44. Ibid.

45. Ibid.

46. Ibid.

47. Ibid.

48. Ibid.

49. Bates, *Sirocco*, 158.

50. Ibid., 243.   51. Ibid., 204.
52. Bates, *Lean Men*, 59, 226.   53. Ibid., 114.

Chapter Four

1. Norman Jackson, "The Men Who Fought for Peace," *Manchester Evening News*, February 14, 1975, 8.
2. Judith Cook, "For Freedom's Sake . . ." *Western Mail*, March 3, 1979, Swansea, S. C. 671. Cook is the author of *Apprentices of Freedom*.
3. Gramsci, *Prison Notebooks*, 334.
4. Orwell, *The Road to Wigan Pier*, 163.
5. Rée, *Proletarian Philosophers*, 6.
6. Quoted in Havel, "The Responsibility of Intellectuals," 36.
7. Gramsci, *Prison Notebooks*, 18.
8. Quoted in Mick Jenkins, *George Brown*, 16.
9. "T. Howell Jones the Man," Swansea, S.C. 183, 1–2.
10. Edmund and Ruth Frow, *Manchester's Memorial to Members of the International Brigade*, 2–3.
11. Interview with Bob Cooney, August 5, 1976, Manchester, 26.
12. Fond 545, op. 6, d. 162, l. 38, Moscow.
13. Interview with D. D. Evans, August 7, 1973, Swansea, 25.
14. But see Roberts, *The Classic Slum*, 128–29, and Vincent, *Literacy and Popular Culture*, 242.
15. Interview with Syd Booth, December 10, 1976, Manchester, 5.
16. Ibid.
17. Interview with Julius Coleman, November 20, 1977, Manchester, 14.
18. Interview with James Brown, August 8, 1976, Manchester, 2.
19. Ibid., 2, 4.
20. Ibid, 2.
21. Ibid., 4.
22. Interview with Jim Brewer, November 29, 1969, Swansea, 3, 2.
23. Ibid., 31.
24. H. G. Wells had first used this term to describe the "great useless masses of people." See Carey, *The Intellectuals and the Masses*, 123.
25. Interview with James Brown, August 8, 1976, Manchester, 2–3.
26. London, *The People of the Abyss*, 11.
27. Ibid., 36.
28. Ibid., 167, 175.
29. West, *Orwell: The Lost Writings*, 122–24. Orwell believed the book was virtually ignored in Great Britain but evidence suggests otherwise.
30. Crossman, ed., *The God That Failed*, 237.
31. Anne Murray to Frankie, April 26, 1937, Edinburgh, Box 1 (3).
32. West, *Orwell: The Lost Writings*, 122.
33. London, *The Iron Heel*, 6.
34. Klaus, "Socialist Fiction in the 1930s" in *The 1930s: A Challenge to Orthodoxy*, 22.

35. Interview with Syd Booth, December 10, 1976, Manchester, 2.

36. Stratton, To Anti-Fascism by Taxi, 9. It is of interest that Alan O' Toole and John Nettleton of the Robert Tressell Museum wrote the introduction to the autobiography of the Spanish Civil War veteran, Jack Coward, *Back from the Dead.*

37. Mayne, "Ragged Trousered Philanthropists," *Twentieth Century Literature*, 1967, 83.

38. Tressell, *The Ragged Trousered Philanthropists*, 1971, 11. The edition read by militants in the twenties and thirties is a much abbreviated version of the one we know today. First published in 1914, the book comprised approximately two-thirds of the original manuscript. Four years later, a still shorter version was published which became known as the "abridged edition." It was this version that was read and circulated during the interwar years.

39. Ibid., 1918 edition, 7, 10.

40. Ibid., 25–26, 48.

41. Ibid., 94.

42. Ibid., 157, 165.

43. Swingewood, *The Myth of Mass Culture*, 52. I am indebted to him for his stimulating discussion of the novel, 50–58.

44. In addition to Swingewood, see McKibbin, "Why Was There No Marxism in Great Britain?" *English Historical Review*, April 1984, 325. The Leninist stance of the British Communist party in the interwar years was undoubtedly a factor in the novel's success. From this perspective, a socialist minority was necessary to move the inert majority to revolutionary action.

45. Andre Van Gyseghem, "British Theatre in the Thirties," in Clark, Heinemann, et al., eds., *Culture and Crisis in Britain in the Thirties*, 212; and Jon Clark, "Socialist Theatre in the Thirties," ibid., 220.

46. Bert Hogenkamp, "Making Films with a Purpose," ibid., 263. Also see his *Deadly Parallels.*

47. Sam Wild, "In Memoriam: Bill Rowe," in *Volunteer for Liberty* 2, February 1949.

48. Vincent, *Literacy and Popular Culture*, 260.

49. Fond 545, d. 199, ll. 43, 43v, Moscow.

50. Interview with Mick Jenkins, July–August, 1977, Manchester, 1.

51. Ibid.

52. Typescript, remarks made at Sam Wild's memorial service, Salford. See MML, Box D-4 Wi/i, for Wild's visits to Stevenson Square to hear the Fenians. Also see Corkill and Rawnsley, *Road to Spain*, 19.

53. Caute, *Fellow-Travellers*, 222.

54. Roberts, *The Classic Slum*, 220.

55. Bellamy and Saville, eds., *Dictionary of Labour Biography*, 8:199.

56. Roberts, *The Classic Slum*, 30, note.

57. Ibid., 178, 183.

58. Interview with Mick Jenkins, July–August, 1977, Manchester, 14.

59. Jenkins, *George Brown*, 8–9.

60. Bellamy and Saville, entry on Donald Renton, *Dictionary of Labour Biography*, 9: 244.

61. MacDougall, ed., *Voices from the Spanish Civil War*, 241.

62. Interview with William Kelly, August 2, 1976, Manchester, 1.

63. Interview with Alec Ferguson, August 1, 1976, Manchester, 2.

64. Interview with Bob Cooney, August 5, 1976, Manchester, 2, 6.

65. Bob Cooney, "Proud Journey," MML, Box A-15/3, 23.

66. Gregory, *The Shallow Grave*, 167.

67. Interview with David "Tony" Gilbert, SRC, 9157/10, 6. Jews were also quick to remind their fellows that Spanish fascists had promised a reenactment of 1492 when the Jews had been expelled from Spain. On October 10, 1936, General Gonzalo Queipo de Llano announced, "Our war is not a Spanish Civil War, it is a war of western civilization against the Jews of the entire world. The Jews want to destroy the Christians." Henry Srebrnik, "Jewish Communist Activity in London," *Michigan Academician*, 1984.

68. Cook, *Apprentices of Freedom*, 74.

69. Morgan, *Harry Pollitt*, 89–90.

70. Ibid., 119.

71. The patrician, R. Palme Dutt, who was exercising great influence on Pollitt at this time, apparently had nothing but contempt for this kind of public speaking. In a report adopted at the Communist party's Fifth Congress in October 1922, which Dutt and his wife, Salme, seem to have been largely responsible for, he ridicules the "barren ritual" of the street-corner meetings and the "local speaker" who served as a spigot for any idea that came to his head and would appeal to an audience. Pollitt seems to have given his approval to the report in which these remarks appeared, indicating a belief in the centrality of the party in the new political culture he hoped to institutionalize. But he never escaped his origins in the tradition, and continued to be an extraordinary public speaker throughout the rest of his life. Whatever the influence of the Dutts, Pollitt could never abandon the sense of fellowship and connection that these occasions gave him. See ibid., 29–30.

72. Interview with John Henderson, MML, A-12 He.

73. Jones' novel, *Cwmardy*, was sent out to the battalion and made a great impression on the Welsh volunteers. J. S. Williams said, "I am reading it and its [sic] great." He had a difficult time obtaining his copy because "all the Welsh boys wanted to read it." He subsequently put the novel in the battalion library so it would be available to all. See his letter to Idris Cox, July 7, 1937, quoted in Francis, *Miners against Fascism*, 280. Arthur Horner, the leader of the South Wales miners, gave the Hackney native and volunteer, Fred Thomas, a copy of Jones' book when he visited Spain. See *To Tilt at Windmills*, 50.

74. Smith, "Introduction," in Jones, *Cwmardy*.

75. Interview with Mavis Llewellyn, May 20, 1974, Swansea, 20.

76. Smith, "Introduction," to Jones, *Cwmardy*.

77. Smith, "Introduction," to Jones, *We Live*.

78. Morgan, *Harry Pollitt*, 158.

Chapter Five

1. John Strachey was particularly critical of what he called "a socialism of the hereafter." He judged that "verbal socialism, like religion, can . . . become the opium of the people." Moreover, it was being preached around the country by "hundreds of competent orators," *Coming Struggle for Power*, 297, 299.

2. Quoted in Rée, *Proletarian Philosophers*, 8, 114.

3. Gregory, *The Shallow Grave*, 164, 170–71.

4. Goodman, "From the Tees to the Ebro," Salford, 13.

5. Ibid.

6. *Spanish Civil War Collection*, 169.

7. Samuel, "Lost World of British Communism," *New Left Review*, 1974, 53.

8. McCarthy, *Generation in Revolt*, 93.

9. MacIntyre, *A Proletarian Science*, 102–5.

10. Rée, *Proletarian Philosophers*, 44.

11. For working-class resistance to Marxism see McKibbin, "Why Was There No Marxism in Great Britain?", *English Historical Review*, 1984, 306. On the passivity of the unemployed in the thirties also see Brown, *English Labour Movement*, 276–77. For a convenient summary of the historical debate concerning politics and the British working class, see Savage and Miles, *Remaking of the British Working Class*, 2–20. Also see Stevenson and Cook, *Britain in the Depression*, 290–308, and Saville, *The Labour Movement in Britain*, 74, 14, 19.

12. Watkins, *Britain Divided*, 181.

13. Stevenson and Cook, *Britain in the Depression*, 293–94.

14. Thorpe, "Labour and the Extreme Left," in *The Failure of Political Extremism*, 27.

15. R. Bourne, typescript, "The Promised Land," December 1973, MML, 4.

16. Francis and Smith, *The Fed*, 350.

17. McCarthy, *Generation in Revolt*, 177.

18. Carr, *Socialism in One Country*, Vol. 3, Pt. 2, 1018–19.

19. Tuominen, *Bells of the Kremlin*, 7, 77. The following account of the Lenin School is taken primarily from the autobiography of the general secretary of the Finnish Communist party and member of the Presidium of the Comintern who was a student and later an instructor at the school. A second source is McCarthy's *Generation in Revolt*.

20. McCarthy, *Generation in Revolt*, 177.

21. Interview with Idris Cox, December 23, 1969, Swansea, 5.

22. Interview with Will Paynter, March 6, 1973, Swansea, 7–8.

23. Fond 545, op. 6, d. 126, ll. 62–63, Moscow. Nevertheless, Duncan volunteered for Spain, where his comments in Moscow caught up with him, upon applying for OTS. In a memorandum dated March 8, 1937, John Lochore asserted it was necessary "to start an investigation of him and to evaluate his integrity."

24. While in school in Montreal, Suzanne Rosenberg remembers meeting a fellow member of the YCL who had recently returned from the Lenin School. His reticence in talking about his experiences in the school and evasiveness in response to her questions about Russia, caused a "doubt" to creep through her armor of certainties. See *Soviet Odyssey*, 31. Also Corkill and Rawnsley, *Road to Spain*, 28.

25. Hynes, *A War Imagined*, 356.

26. McCarthy, *Generation in Revolt*, 100.

27. Interview with Bob Cooney, August 5, 1976, Manchester, 4.

28. Bob Cooney, typescript, "Proud Journey," MML, Box A-15/3, 109.

29. Interview with Bob Cooney, Manchester, 22.

30. Ibid., 30, 24, 4.

31. Ibid., 27.

32. Ibid., 79, 87.

33. John Peet to Bill Alexander, November 7, 1987, MML, Box C 4/11, 2.

34. Interview with Bob Cooney, August 5, 1976, Manchester, 24.

35. Ibid.; interviews with Jack Jones, August 25, 1978, Manchester, 2–3, and Jim Brewer, November 29, 1969, Swansea, 2–3.

36. Interview with Lillian Buckoke, February 28, 1978, Manchester, 15, 12, 2.

37. This was also Ralph Fox's position. He told the American Michael Gold, "The British upper class is, even racially, a foreign group of invaders; the true historic nation was always oppressed by them, and always had to fight them for its liberties. It is the masses who are England." See Gold's "Till We Have Built Jerusalem," in Fox, *A Writer in Arms*, 11.

38. Interview, n.d., Harold King, Manchester, 5–6.

39. McCarthy, *Generation in Revolt*, 49.

40. Ibid., 77.

41. *These Men Have Died*, Salford, 9, 15. The famous massacre of workers in St. Peter's Fields, Manchester, August 16, 1819, has always been known as Peterloo after the Battle of Waterloo in Belgium five years before.

42. James Klugmann, "The Crisis of the Thirties: A View from the Left," in Clark, Heinemann, et al., eds., *Culture and Crisis*, 25.

43. Wintringham, *English Captain*, 98.

44. A., "Britons in Spain," *Labour Monthly*, 1939, 180–81. The most brilliant contemporary example of the Byronic tradition was the great Liberal dissenter, H. N. Brailsford, who left England with other volunteers in the spring of 1897 to assist the Greeks in their revolt against the Turks. Although his internationalist idealism foundered upon the prosaic and tawdry characteristics of the struggle between the ancient enemies, Brailsford lived to volunteer for service with the International Brigades. See Leventhal, *The Last Dissenter*, 27–33, 249–52.

45. Alec Cummings to Frank Crabbe, December 12, 1937, MML, Box A 15/11.

46. Ibid., *Memorial Souvenir*, 7, 10.

47. Gregory, *The Shallow Grave*, 176.

Chapter Six

1. "The Republic," in *Spain Assailed*, 22.

2. Wintringham, *English Captain*, 16.

3. Quoted in Henry Collins, "Thomas Paine and the Beginnings of Modern Radicalism," Rubinstein, ed., *People for the People*, 43.

4. Quoted in Weisser, *British Working-Class Movements and Europe*, 6, n. 4. For four stimulating essays on working-class internationalism see Gregory Claeys, "Reciprocal Dependence, Virtue and Progress: Some Sources of Early Socialist Cosmopolitanism and Internationalism in Britain, 1750–1850," in Van Holthoon and Van der Linden, eds., *Internationalism in the Labour Movement, 1830–1940*; Vol. 1, 235–58; Christine Latek's "The Beginnings of Socialist Internationalism in the 1840's: The Democrat Friends of All Nations," ibid., Vol. 1, 259–82; Peter Gurney's "'A Higher State of Civilisation and Happiness,'" ibid., Vol. 2, 543–64; and John Saville, "Britain: Internationalism and the Labour Movement between the Wars," ibid., Vol. 2, 565–82.

5. Mill, "The Rebellious Needleman: Tom Paine," *Left Review*, 1937, 207. Waiting impatiently for repatriation, the volunteer Fred Thomas was reminded of the warning of "old Tom Paine" that "these are the times to try men's souls." See *To Tilt at Windmills*, 155–56. Also see Ian Dyck, "Local Attachments, National Identities and World Citizenship in the Thought of Thomas Paine," in *History Workshop Journal* 35, 1993. Dyck makes an interesting contrast between the "steadfast Englishness" of William Cobbett and the "world citizenship" of Tom Paine, 130.

6. Henry Weisser, however, believes that only an "advanced segment" of the Chartists can genuinely be called internationalists. See his *British Working-Class Movements and Europe*, 168. The Paris Commune also drew great support from British workers. See Royden Harrison, "The Journeyman Engineer: The English Working Classes and the Paris Commune," in his *English Defence of the Commune*, 133–44.

7. Bill Morrissey to Edward Thomas, n.d., Swansea, S.C. 613, 2.

8. Fond 545, op. 3, d. 413, l. 103, Moscow.

9. Interview with Jim Brewer, November 29, 1969, Swansea, 1.

10. There is no intention to overestimate the role of working-class internationalism. As Hobsbawm has observed, "Working class consciousness, however inevitable and essential, is probably politically secondary to other kinds of consciousness. As we know, whether it has come into conflict in our century with national, or religious, or racial consciousness, it has usually yielded and retreated." See "What is the Workers' Country" in *Workers*, 59. In addition, Buchanan has emphasized that many British Catholic workers were alienated by the persecution of the Church and played a significant role in moderating trade union support for the Spanish Republic. See Chapter 5 in *The Spanish Civil War and the British Labour Movement*. In the case of those workers who volunteered for Spain or supported the Spanish Aid

Movement in one form or another, however, it is clear that working-class consciousness was a preeminent consideration.

11. Fox, "Marx, Engels and Lenin on the British Workers' Movement," in *A Writer in Arms*, 167.

12. Straight, *After Long Silence*, 97.

13. See Jolyon Howarth, "French Workers and German Workers: The Impossibility of Internationalism, 1908–1914," *European History Quarterly* 1, January 1985.

14. MacMillan, "Pat Murphy," Swansea, 25.

15. L. J. MacFarlane, "Hands Off Russia: British Labour and the Russo-Polish War, 1920," *Past and Present* 38, 1967, 127, 132, 145, 149–50.

16. Saville, "Britain: Internationalism and the Labour Movement between the Wars," in Van Holthoon and Van der Linden, *Internationalism in the Labour Movement, 1830–1940*, 2:567–68.

17. Strachey, *Coming Struggle for Power*, 350.

18. Hinton, *Labour and Socialism*, 155.

19. MacMillan, "Pat Murphy," Swansea; see loose page of the *Workington Star* between pages 23 and 24.

20. Goodman, "From the Tees to the Ebro," Salford, 3.

21. *Save Peace! Aid Spain*, 4–5.

22. See Koestler's *Spanish Testament* and Chalmers-Mitchell's *My House in Málaga*.

23. *Programme, Commemoration Meeting to Men in the International Brigade Fallen in Spain*, Salford. This was distributed for a meeting at the Central Hall, Manchester, Renshaw Street, September 22, 1938.

24. Barke, *The Land of the Leal*, 507–8, 566–67.

25. Ibid., 567–68.

26. Thomas, *To Tilt at Windmills*, 59; *National Emergency Conference on Spain*, April 23, 1938, 24, 27.

27. King, *The Last Modern*, 84.

28. Quoted in Powell, *Messengers of the Day*, 194.

29. Carpenter, *A Serious Character: The Life of Ezra Pound*, 554.

30. For a full discussion of perceptions of Spain by the left and right, see Tom Buchanan's "'A Far Away Country of Which We Know Nothing'?" *Twentieth Century British History* 1, 1993, 1–24.

31. Pollitt, *Save Spain from Fascism*, 10.

32. Kiernan believes that the Dutch Revolt was the only foreign war that attracted significant numbers of British volunteers before Spain. See his "Labour and the War in Spain," 7.

33. Maltby, *The Black Legend in England*, 3.

34. Julián Juderias, "The Black Legend, 1914," in Gibson, ed., *The Black Legend*, 194.

35. Michael Alpert, "Humanitarianism and Politics," *European History Quarterly* 4, 1984, 435.

36. Pritchett, *The Spanish Temper*, Introduction.

37. "The Truth Behind the 'Red Atrocities,'" *International Press Correspondence* 37, August 24, 1936, 1001.

38. Knox, *Essays*, 259.

39. Orwell, *Homage to Catalonia*, 203.

40. Robert Stradling, "Orwell and the Spanish Civil War: A Historical Critique," in Norris, ed., *Inside the Myth*, 106. Stradling quotes Crick's remarks in the *Times Higher Educational Supplement*, February 24, 1984, 12.

41. Harrison, *Common People of Great Britain*, 376. For example, at the end of the thirties twenty million cinema tickets were being sold each week. In Liverpool it has been estimated that 45 percent of the population went once a week, and 25 percent two or more times.

42. Aldgate, *Cinema and History*, 95.

43. However, the Liverpool volunteer, Joseph Leo Byrne, attributed his decision to go to Spain directly to cinema newsreels. Interview with Byrne, 1992, SRC, 12930/3, Reel 1.

44. Aldgate, *Cinema and History*, 105. The Anglo-American film, *The Spanish Earth*, brought to completion by the Dutch director Joris Ivens and the American novelist Ernest Hemingway, was the only film on the Spanish Civil War to be distributed commercially in England. It was, however, shown only at selected cinemas, even though British documentaries, such as Ivor Montagu's *The Defence of Madrid*, had proved highly effective for the purpose of fund raising. See Hogenkamp, "Film and the Workers' Movement," *Sight and Sound* 45, 1976, 74.

45. The Workers' Olympiad in Barcelona generated a good deal of attention among the British. Organized as a response to the Berlin Olympics, it attracted twenty-eight competitors from Great Britain. In addition, the Workers' Travel Association had recently been organized. The WTA was sufficiently confident of interest in Spain to organize a cruise that was to begin on July 18. See Buchanan, "'A Far Away Country'," *Twentieth Century British History* 1, 1993, 4.

46. Copeman, *Reason in Revolt*, 74.

47. Gregory, *The Shallow Grave*, 19–20.

48. Gurney, *Crusade in Spain*, 59.

49. Tisa, *Recalling the Good Fight*, 13.

50. J. R. Jump, "International Brigader I," in Toynbee, ed., *Distant Drum*, 112.

51. Salford, "Ben Tillett Finds New Spain," newspaper clipping, n.d.

52. Gregory, *The Shallow Grave*, 13, 20.

53. This was particularly true in Wales. See Francis, *Miners Against Fascism*, 67–68, 141, 265–66. Before World War I Spanish miners were brought to Wales as scab labor. Spanish communities subsequently established themselves in Dowlais and Abercave and were to prove an excellent conduit for information concerning repression in Spain. After an initial period of political and racial hostility, the Spanish miners integrated into Welsh life and became enthusiastic members of the trade union movement as well as strong socialists and communists. Three Welsh-Spaniards fought in the British Battalion in Spain; all of them were killed. See 35–36, 203–4.

For initial animosity to the Spaniards see interview with D. D. Evans, November 1, 1970, Swansea, 2. The antagonism was based on the inability of the Spaniards to speak Welsh and their comparatively free and easy ways, contrasting sharply with the wishes of the chapel hierarchy. This resulted in the Spanish miners being cheated of part of their wages, among other forms of discrimination. By the Spanish Civil War, this spirited antagonism had vanished. Four thousand Basque children were evacuated and brought to Great Britain, creating perhaps the single most romantic legend of the war in Great Britain. Mrs. Fernandez, "one of the Spanish Dowlais colony," was named warden of the colony of refugees. See Cyril P. Cule, "Spanish Civil War: A Personal Viewpoint," S.C. 158, Swansea, 8.

54. Quoted in Watkins, *Britain Divided*, 145. Kiernan points out how effectively Watkins refutes Hugh Dalton's statement in his memoirs that "Labour had no knowledge of or interest in Spain before the civil war." See "Labour and the War in Spain," 14. Dalton, however, does not go this far. He simply says how little he and the Labour executive knew of the leaders of the Spanish left.

55. Watkins, *Britain Divided*, 146.

56. Coward, *Back from the Dead*. Preface by Patterson. When Coward, a Merseyside seaman, decided to return to Spain, he used Patterson's passport.

57. *The Fighting Call*, 2, November 1936, 12.

58. McGovern, *Terror in Spain*, 3.

59. Quoted in Rust, *Spain Fights for Victory*, 6.

60. "If We Fail the Spanish People Now, Who Will Help Us?" *International Press Correspondence* 24, May 17, 1938, 590. The stereotypes died with difficulty, however. In his final report on the battalion's history in Spain, Alonzo Elliott wrote that some of the volunteers persisted in believing that the Spanish were principally "matadors and guitar players." See Fond., 545, op. 6, d. 22, l. 33, Moscow.

61. Spender, *World within World*, 187.

62. "C. 1823," "Close-Up of a Battle," *Supplement to the Adelphi*, February 1940, 14.

63. Lefebre, "Departure of Disabled Members of the International Brigade," *International Press Correspondence* 27, May 28, 1938, 659.

64. "To the Aid of the Spanish People!" *International Press Correspondence* 36, August 28, 1936, 959.

65. Quoted in Gathorne-Hardy, *Gerald Brenan*, 348. Certainly for those who had seen something of the world, or dreamed of doing so, Spain held an inherent fascination. There were many readers familiar with nineteenth-century Bible vendor George Borrow's handsome tribute to the "spirit of proud independence" of the ordinary Spaniard. Several decades later Scotswoman Fanny Inglis Calderón de la Barca left a memorable account of the intrigues of court society as well as of her encounters with famous sites such as the sombre palace of the Escorial, known for centuries as the eighth wonder of the world, and which became a hospital during the war. A visit by Lady Gertrude Bone to Santiago in 1925 resurrected the spirit of the great

medieval pilgrimages that had once made Spain the destination of Europe's devout, and which she described with lively enthusiasm in *Days in Old Spain*. The remarkable Irish scholar Walter Starkie shared Borrow's fascination with the gypsies, and communicated it with unmatched vividness to his readers on the eve of the Spanish Civil War. For samples of each of their work, see McGann's *Portrait of Spain*. E. Allison Peers' *The Spanish Tragedy*, published in October 1936, may not have been a good book but it was widely influential. The author believed that the Republic had been a catastrophe for Spain and that Great Britain should not become involved in its death throes. Peers was a professor at Liverpool University and considered the preeminent Hispanicist of his time.

66. Blythe, *The Age of Illusion*, 116.
67. Valentine Ackland, *Left Review*, 16, 1937, 914.
68. Gannes and Repard, *Spain in Revolt*, 5.
69. Ibid., 16–17.
70. Orwell, *Homage to Catalonia*, 46–47.
71. Gannes and Repard, *Spain in Revolt*, 30.
72. Ibid., 183.   73. Ibid., 213–14.
74. Ibid., 50.   75. Ibid., 57, 77.
76. Ibid., 93.
77. Author's interview with Dolores Ibarruri, January 24, 1986, Madrid.
78. Gannes and Repard, *Spain in Revolt*, 81.
79. Ibid., 90, 114–15, 117.   80. Ibid., 153.
81. Ibid., 167.   82. Ibid., 184.
83. Ibid.   84. Ibid., 224, 197.
85. Ibid., 263.
86. Interview with Bill Feeley, 1976, SRC, 848/4, Reel 1.

Chapter Seven

1. Ingram, *Rebel: The Short Life of Esmond Romilly*, 142.
2. Tom Wintringham to Harry Pollitt, September 13, 1936, MML, f. 3.
3. Alexander, *British Volunteers for Liberty*, 52, 64.
4. See Morris and Radford, *AIA*, 30–52.
5. See "The First Volunteer," in *Spain Today* 16, September 1949, 6; "Felicia Browne," in *Left Review* 13, October 1936, 688. Also see "Felicia Browne: Killed in Defence of Democracy," *To-Morrow*, December 1936, 4.
6. Ibid.
7. MML, Box A-12 Bro.
8. Ibid.
9. MML, Box A-15, f. 8. Further biographical details on Browne rely on material in *Drawings by Felicia Browne*, a typescript by Lynne Humberston entitled "Woman and War—The Experience of Some of Britain's War Artists," as well as Brinkman's account of the raid and her death.
10. Galassi, ed., August 16–30, 1936, in *Understand the Weapon, Understand the Wound*, 174.

11. Sloan, *John Cornford*, 186.
12. Haldane, "International Column," *Spain Illustrated* (1937).
13. Delmer, *Trail Sinister*, 310–12.
14. Branson, *History of the Communist Party of Great Britain*, 230.
15. When I visited Boadilla in July 1985, it was no longer as isolated or somnolent as it seemed when Romilly fought there in 1936 or when Hugh Thomas revisited it years later. Thomas gives his impressions of the village in his introduction to the 1971 reissue of Romilly's book, 7.
16. Romilly, *Boadilla*, 14.
17. Scott Watson, *Single to Spain*, 140.
18. Peter Kerrigan, ms., "Spain, 1936–1938," MML, f. 3.
19. There is some confusion in Romilly's account concerning Birch's academic backround. He identifies him both with Cambridge and Oxford.
20. Romilly, *Boadilla*, 39–45, 132. An indispensable companion to Romilly's book is Mitford's *Daughters and Rebels*. This hugely entertaining autobiography tells of her meeting with Romilly, their elopement to Spain, marriage, and their return to England on a warship especially sent to reclaim the runaway couple.
21. To Nick [Cox], January 7, 1937, Texas.
22. Ibid.
23. Ibid.
24. "The International Brigade," *Spanish News Bulletin*, January 1, 1937, 14.
25. Romilly, *Boadilla*, 195–96.
26. To Peggy [Sound], January 7, 1937, Texas.
27. Ibid., To Peg [Sound], January 30, 1937.
28. Romilly, *Boadilla*, 22.
29. Ibid.
30. Ibid., 146.
31. Miles Tomalin, ms (unpublished diary), 7, quoted in Thomas, *Spanish Civil War*, 455.
32. Gregory, *The Shallow Grave*, 19.
33. Gurney, *Crusade in Spain*, 13.
34. Jack Jones, Foreword, in Cook, *Apprentices of Freedom*, viii.
35. Interview with Maurice Levine, February 10, 1977, Manchester, 23.
36. Muggeridge, *The Thirties*, 248.
37. Fond 548, op. 3, d. 478, l. 96, Moscow.
38. R. Bourne, "The Promised Land," December 1973, MML.
39. [N.N.] to Peter Kerrigan, December 5, [1937], MML.
40. MacDougall, ed., *Voices from the Spanish Civil War*, 277, 287.
41. Corkill and Rawnsley, *The Road to Spain*, 97.
42. "What I Saw in Barcelona," *Daily Worker*, April 9, 1938, 7.
43. Anne Murray to Tom Murray, April 16, 1937, Edinburgh.
44. *Daily Worker*, July 18, 1938, 5.
45. Sam Wild, *Spain Today* 3, March 1949, 14. This comment appears in Wild's review of Copeman's *Reason in Revolt*.

46. Thorpe, "Labour and the Extreme Left," in *The Failure of Political Extremism*, 16.

47. "Message to England," *Spanish News*, 12, April 5, 1938.

48. Tommy Fanning, "Little Albert," *Volunteer for Liberty* 5, May 1941, 18.

49. Haldane, *Truth Will Out*, 122.

50. Quoted in Bill Alexander, "News from Britain," *The Volunteer*, 1, Summer 1992, 4.

51. Cunningham, *British Writers of the Thirties*, 421.

52. Cook, *Apprentices of Freedom*, 74.

53. The weekly newspaper of the International Brigades was *Volunteer for Liberty*. First edited by Ralph Bates, the inaugural issue appeared on May 24, 1937. Subsequent editors and staff managed to publish it sixty times in its sixteen months of life. The editors claimed "that its pages have accurately mirrored both the life of the Brigade and the outstanding events in Spain" during its history. See "The 'Volunteer for Liberty'" in *The War in Spain: A Weekly Summary*, 55, February 4, 1939, 221. The importance of the *Book of the XV Brigade* and *Volunteer for Liberty* is undeniable. Nevertheless, it must be remembered that no deviation from the Communist party political line was permitted.

54. Symons, "The Betrayed Idealists," *Sunday Times Magazine*, July 23, 1961, 21. Also see Symons, *The Thirties*, and Goodman, "From the Tees to the Ebro," Salford, 4.

55. Gurney, *Crusade in Spain*, 66.

56. Lee, *A Moment of War*, 45.

57. Interview with Charles Bloom, 1976, SRC, 992/6, Reels 1, 2.

58. Christopher Darman, "The Red or Dead Brigade," *The Guardian*, February 13, 1965, 6.

59. Interview with Tommy Bloomfield, *Scottish Labour History Society Journal*, 11, May 1977, 28.

60. Lawther, *Spain and Ourselves*, 14.

61. According to records in the former Comintern archive, however, Brewer did join the party in Spain. There were divergent views on the manner in which he carried out his responsibilities. George Fletcher, while commanding the Battalion, wrote that as No. 1 machine gunner, Brewer had performed his duties "very well." Sam Wild called Brewer a "good, active comrade," and a "good example." These evaluations by his military commanders stand in contrast to criticism leveled at him by the battalion commissar, Bob Cooney, and by Benny Goldman, the party secretary. They judged Brewer to lack leadership qualifications and to have a "slightly nervous disposition." The resolution of these contrasting views may lie in his final evaluation before repatriation, when Wild, among others, said he only gave "fair support for leadership and Party." Arthur Nicoll added that Brewer liked to discuss political questions "but did very little political work in his unit." Earlier, George Fletcher, although admiring his ability as a soldier, believed that he "needs coaching politically." Nevertheless, whatever his shortcomings, real or imagined, the leadership chose Brewer to carry

the battalion flag during the farewell parade for the International Brigades in Barcelona in October 1938.

The former miner was at war continuously from 1936 to 1945. He was one of the few members of the British Battalion to be commissioned in World War II, where he served in the Western Desert and Italy. Moreover, after the war, he played an important role as town councilor of his native Rhymney for many years. Consequently, the party evaluations can most charitably be called wrongheaded. Perhaps Brewer's life as a "student" weighed against him or, even more likely, his native good sense in the face of party propaganda. See Fond 545, op. 6, d. 110, ll. 62–76v, Moscow.

62. Syd Booth to Edward Thomas, S. C. 608, Swansea.

63. Moscow, Fond 545, op. 6, d. 113, l. 7.

64. Moscow, d. 171, l. 5v.

65. Moscow, d. 108, l. 57v.

66. *Manchester Guardian*, April 14, 1937, quoted in Miriam Cunningham, "What the People of Manchester Did to Help the People of Spain in their Struggle Against Fascism," 1981, Salford.

67. To Ben Bowen Thomas (n.d.), quoted in Francis, *Miners Against Fascism*, 282.

68. Hinton, *Protests & Visions*, 94.

69. Moscow, Fond 545, op. 6, d. 114, l. 43.

70. Eaton, *Neath and the Spanish Civil War*, 53.

71. Gregory, *The Shallow Grave*, 36.

72. Moscow, Fond 545, op. 6, d. 202, l. 12.

73. J. R. Jump, "International Brigader I," in Toynbee, *Distant Drum*, 113.

74. Fond 545, op. 6, d. 116, l. 10, Moscow.

75. Ibid., l. 78.

76. Quoted in Willy Maley, *Scottish Labour History Review*, 5, Winter 1991/Spring 1992, 15.

77. Spender, *World within World*, 213.

78. Goodman, "From the Tees to the Ebro," Salford, 12.

79. "Wayfarer," "The International Brigade," reprinted from *Weekly Review*, MML, 19, 31.

80. J. R. Jump, "International Brigader I," in Toynbee, *Distant Drum*, 113.

81. "C. 1823," "Close-Up of a Battle," *Supplement to the Adelphi*, February 1940, 15.

82. Interview with Maurice Levine, 1987, SRC, 9722/6, Reel 6.

83. M. E. Kirk, "An Examination of the Motives Prompting the Volunteers from Manchester and Salford to Join the International Brigade in Spain, 1936–1939," (thesis submitted to the University of Manchester, May 1980), Salford, 44–45. For his conclusions, Kirk relies on the Trades Council records; the Labour Party Minute Book, 1936–1939; as well as the local newspapers of Manchester and Salford and the interviews with volunteers in the archives of the Manchester Metropolitan University.

84. Ibid., 2–4.

85. Eddie and Ruth Frow were the founders of the Working Class Movement Library.

86. M. E. Kirk, "An Examination of the Motives," Salford, 6, 8. See Miriam Cunningham, "What the People of Manchester Did to Help the People of Spain in Their Struggle against Fascism," 1981, Salford, 1.

87. Kirk, 9.

88. Ibid., 9–10.

89. Edmund and Ruth Frow, *Manchester's Memorial to Members of the International Brigade*, Salford, 2.

90. Miriam Cunningham, "What the People of Manchester Did," Salford, 2.

91. M. E. Kirk, "An Examination of the Motives," Salford, 14.

92. Miriam Cunningham, "What the People of Manchester Did," 10.

93. Edmund and Ruth Frow, *Manchester's Memorial to Members of the International Brigade*, 4–5.

94. Drake, "Labour and Spain," 265, 146, 191, 231, 235, 266. South Wales sent some 160 volunteers to Spain. By contrast, only twenty-two went from Birmingham and its surrounding districts. Drake spent three years looking for survivors of the Spanish conflict in the Birmingham area, apparently missing the last one, Ted Smallbone. See Fred Norris, "The Survivor" (newspaper clipping), MML. According to Drake, those who volunteered were all working men with the exception of John Cornford (whom Drake counts as a recruit from Birmingham because of his political work in the city and his relationship with Margot Heinemann who was teaching school there, and whom Cornford often visited) and a well-known doctor, Charles (or Colin, as Bill Alexander calls him) Bradshaw. Also see MML, Fred Norris, "The Spanish Secret War" (newspaper clipping).

95. Jones, *Union Man*, 58.

96. Fond 545, op. 6, d. 125, ll. 124–25, Moscow.

97. Hanley, *Grey Children*, 64–65.

98. See MacIntyre, *Little Moscows*.

99. Francis, "The Background and Motives of Welsh Volunteers," *Journal of Oral History* 2, 1981, 87–95, 103.

100. Wood, "Scotland and the Spanish Civil War," *Cencrastus*, 14, and "Homage to the Fifteenth Brigade," *Weekend Scotsman*, June 30, 1979.

101. "Homage to the Fifteenth Brigade."

102. Interview with Fred Copeman, August 2, 1976, Manchester, 28.

103. See Moscow, Fond 545, op. 6, d. 108, l. 21.

104. K. P. Bond, "Letter from a Revolutionary," and H. J. Belsey, "Note on Kenneth Bond," in Toynbee, ed., *Distant Drum*, 109–11.

105. See Felstead, *No Other Way*.

106. Interview with Jack Roberts, n.d., Swansea, 9.

107. Gurney, *Crusade in Spain*, 72.

108. Levine, *Cheetham to Cordova*, 31. Edmund and Ruth Frow add that he was "sensitive." See *Manchester's Memorial to Members of the International Brigade*, 3.

109. Diary of Ralph Cantor, entry for May 9, 1937, Salford. Maurice Levine has annotated several pages of Cantor's diary, correcting mistaken dates, pointing out how little frontline service he actually saw, and attributing his disgruntlement with the Communist party and particularly the commissars to his extended stay in the Jarama trenches, which resulted in "living in dug-outs, monotous [sic] food, lack of comforts and being infected with body lice." See his typescript, "Ralph Cantor."

110. Fond 545, op. 6, d. 209, ll. 3v., 4–4v., 5, Moscow.

111. Ibid., d. 215, l. 2.

112. Gurney, *Crusade in Spain*, 73.

113. *Boletín de Información*, 13, October 28, 1936, 1. This is the bulletin of the CNT and FAI, translated into English for the consumption of readers in Great Britain and the United States.

114. Fond 545, op. 6, d. 129, l. 95, Moscow.

115. Campbell, *Spain's Left Critics*, 1.

116. Green, "The Communist Party and the War in Spain," *Marxism Today*, October 1970, 316. A volunteer hospital administrator in Spain, Nan Green was the longtime secretary of the International Brigade Association in Great Britain and a much-loved figure on the left. It was she who perhaps did the most to ensure that the Marx Memorial Library would become the repository of the British Battalion's records.

117. Pollitt, *Spain: What Next?*, 5.

118. Hanley, *Grey Children*, 106.

Chapter Eight

1. For an interesting recent discussion of the relative culpability of Great Britain and France in initiating the Nonintervention Agreement, see Stone, "Britain, France and the Spanish Problem," in Richardson and Stone, eds., *Decisions and Diplomacy*, 129–52.

2. Richardson, *Comintern Army*, 10.

3. See Koch's *Double Lives* for a bravura interpretation of Münzenberg's influence.

4. Richardson, *Comintern Army*, 14–15.

5. Quoted in Alpert, *A New International History of the Spanish Civil War*, 73.

6. MML, Box C 8/2.

7. Thomas, *Spanish Civil War*, 982–83.

8. Angel Viñas, "Los Condicionantes Internacionales," in Tuñon de Lara, ed., *La Guerra Civil Española*, 154. See Andreu Castells, *Las Brigadas Internacionales de la Guerra de España*, 97.

9. Gurney, *Crusade in Spain*, 17.

10. Quoted in Weintraub, *The Last Great Cause*, 9.

11. "The International Brigades," in *International Press Correspondence* 24, May 17, 1938, 586.

12. Monks, *With the Reds in Andalusia*, 18.

13. Gurney, *Crusade in Spain*, 62.

14. Interview with Fred Copeman, August 2, 1976, Manchester, 8.

15. O'Toole and Nettleton, "Jack Coward, Merseyside, and the International Brigades: A Hero Named Coward," intro. to Coward, *Back from the Dead*.

16. Branson, *History of the Communist Party in Great Britain*, 341.

17. Judith Cook, "Under the Red Banner the Old Brigaders Meet to Make History," *Labour Weekly*, August 13, 1976.

18. There is a note in Laurie Lee's file in Moscow that "he did not come through the usual channels." The young poet told the party that he was subject to epileptic fits, which he feared would have caused him to be rejected by the brigades if he had come in the normal way. As a consequence, although he later claims to have fought at Teruel, he told his interrogators that he didn't think he would be of any use at the front. "He agrees that the added excitement would be too much for him." Lee is described as an artist and a violinist. Despite the seriousness of the circumstances in which he found himself, the party believed that "his sympathies [are] all with the Republic." The fact that he knew Fred Copeman also must have helped. See Fond 545, op. 6, d. 162, l. 33, Moscow.

19. Interview with John Murra, June 26, 1981, Brandeis, 31. Murra, an American, worked at IB Headquarters in Albacete with figures such as Wally Tapsell and Will Paynter. According to him, "Some of the British were . . . shipped," meaning that they hadn't volunteered.

20. Haldane, *Truth Will Out*, 87.

21. McCarthy, *Generation in Revolt*, 125.

22. Haldane, *Truth Will Out*, 89.

23. An addendum to a letter to Pollitt, dated December 21, MML, Box C 8/3.

24. MML, Box C 9/2, f. 4.

25. MML, Box C 9/3.

26. MML, Box C 9/7.

27. Interview with Alec Marcovitch, September 20, 1977, Manchester, 39.

28. Spender, *World within World*, 222. See Worsley, *Fellow Travelers*, 214–15, 220–21, for a portrait of "Seton"/Kerrigan as a threatening communist functionary in Spain.

29. Gurney, *Crusade in Spain*, 63. Gurney remembered him "as dour and ill-tempered as only a Scot can be, utterly devoid of any trace of humour. Calvin would have loved him."

30. Gregory, *The Shallow Grave*, 29.

31. Lee was grateful to Rust for getting him out of a Barcelona jail and putting him up for several days. His brief acquaintance persuaded the young poet that "he was a quiet, gentle man, tough with bureaucrat bullies, but a kindly uncle to such strays as myself." See *A Moment of War*, 174–75.

32. McCarthy, *Generation in Revolt*, 134.

33. Morgan, *Pollitt*, 148.

34. Branson, *History of the Communist Party in Great Britain*, 36.

35. Haldane, *Truth Will Out*, 132–33. For the details on Rust's career in the Communist party see Branson, *History of the Communist Party in Great Britain*, 53, 234.

36. Interview with Alec Marcovitch, September 20, 1977, Manchester, 37.

37. Fond 545, op. 6, d. 105, l. 103, Moscow.

38. MacDougall, ed., *Voices from the Spanish Civil War*, 96.

39. "The Heroism of the Commissars," *Spanish News Bulletin*, No. 10 (n.d.): 12.

40. MacDougall, ed., *Voices from the Spanish Civil War*, 316.

41. Fond 543, op. 2, d. 200, Moscow. These remarks are taken from a draft letter that Voros wrote in an unpaged spiral notebook in June 1937.

42. *Tasks and Duties of Commissars*, 5.

43. N.A., *In Spain with the International Brigade*, 11.

44. Interview with Tom Murray, *Scottish Labour History Society Journal*, 11, 1977, 35.

45. MacDougall, ed., *Voices from the Spanish Civil War*, 314.

46. Jenkins, *George Brown*, 16, 30.

47. *Bulletin of the Political Commissars of the International Brigades*, 4, 1937, 11–12.

48. Stephen Spender to Virginia Woolf, April 2 [1937], Berg.

49. Diary of Ralph Cantor, entries for April 10, 15, 16, 24, 26, Salford.

50. Fond 545, op. 6, d. 114, l. 13, Moscow.

51. Fond 545, op. 6, d. 175, l. 102, Moscow.

52. Fond 545, op. 6, d. 172, l. 13, Moscow.

53. Tom McWhirter to Peter Kerrigan, November 26, 1936, MML.

54. Ibid.

55. 391. In his recent study, James McPherson carefully analyzes the motivations of soldiers of the North and South in the American Civil War. He emphasizes the importance of ideals in motivating combatants and, at the same time (as we have seen in the Spanish Civil War) concludes that primary group cohesion was inspired by mutual dependence and support. See *For Cause and Comrades*, 77–89.

56. Quoted in Carroll, *Odyssey of the Abraham Lincoln Brigade*, 96.

57. Ibid. Also see Fond 545, op. 6, d. 165, l. 7, Moscow, for a comment on the Canadians.

58. Quoted in Holmes, *Acts of War*, 50.

59. MML, Instructions on "The Tasks and Duties of Commissars," December 21, 1937 (Commissariat of War of the International Brigades); "Strengthen the Work with the Military Command," *Bulletin of the Political Commissars of the International Brigades* 4 (October–November 1937); "A Year's Fight Against Fascism," *Bulletin of the Political Commissars of the International Brigades*, August 15, 1937, 10–14.

60. MML, Box C 17/7, f. 4. This is Aitken's statement defending himself from Wally Tapsell's charges after Brunete.

61. MacDougall, ed., *Voices from the Spanish Civil War*, 312.

62. Haldane, *Truth Will Out*, 113.

63. Interview with Winifred Sandford, August 1, 1976, Manchester, 1.

64. The official position of the French was to be as stringent as possible in regulating the frontiers. The British Foreign Office received a communication from French authorities, dated January 20, 1938, that despite the claim made by the British consul general in Barcelona, "a great number" of British nationals had recently crossed the frontier into Spain. The policy of the French government was that the "points of passage" across the frontier were being guarded with "particular rigor" [my translation]. See PRO, FO371/22636 W886/83/41. The British were not impressed. In an unsigned note to a memorandum from Sir George Mounsey, the author writes, "Evidence of French bias on the side of the Spanish Gvt., amounting almost to intervention, is getting stronger and stronger." See FO371/21322 W2507/7/41.

65. Interview with Jim Brewer, November 29, 1969, Swansea, 18. See Jones, *Union Man*, 63–64.

66. Bessie, *Men in Battle*, 22.

67. Interview with David Goodman, n.d., Manchester, 29.

68. PRO, FO 371/22651 152833. A young volunteer, subsequently disillusioned by his experiences in Spain, returned to tell his parents of the ordeal of the climb and that two men had been lost from his group, 158. The Non-Intervention Inspection Committee claimed to have found the remains of 200 volunteers who had fallen from the rocks or succumbed from exhaustion while on the journey. See Carroll, *Odyssey of the Abraham Lincoln Brigade*, 125.

69. Bessie, *Men in Battle*, 23.

70. Ibid.

71. Symons, "The Betrayed Idealists," *Sunday Times Magazine*, July 23, 1961, 21.

72. Interview with Vince Lossowski, June 1, 1980, Brandeis, 13.

73. John Winter, "My Fight for Freedom," *Luton News*, December 4, 1975. On the wall of the white house Harold Horne found the inscription, "J. Gough, Luton." Years later Horne learned that Gough was known in the Vauxhall plant where he worked, and that he had been killed at Boadilla. For more on Gough, see Romilly's *Boadilla*, 39–40, 143–44, 185–86, 191. Also see Goodman, "From the Tees to the Ebro," Salford, 18–19.

74. MacDougall, ed., *Voices from the Spanish Civil War*, 310.

75. Gregory, *The Shallow Grave*, 25.

76. Fond 545, op. 3, d. 478, l. 30, Moscow.

77. Thomas, *Spanish Civil War*, 591, n. 1. See *Walls Have Mouths*.

78. MML, Box C 9/2, January 4, 1937, ff. 10–11.

79. MML, Box C 9/3.

80. To Harry Pollitt, January 19, 1937, MML, Box C 9/7.

81. Kerrigan to Pollitt, MML, 9/8.   82. MML, Box C 9/12.

83. MML, Box C 10/1, f. 2.   84. MML, Box C 10/4, f. 1.

85. See Wintringham, *English Captain*.

86. MML, Box C 10/6.

87. Alexander, *British Volunteers for Liberty*, 91.

88. Interview with Fred Copeman, August 2, 1976, Manchester, 9–10.

89. Gregory, *The Shallow Grave*, 159–60, 29.

90. Peter Kerrigan to Harry Pollitt, February 10, 1937, MML, Box C 10/6.

91. Tom Wintringham to Harry Pollitt, February 7, 1937, MML, Box C 10/4, f. 1.

92. MacDougall, ed., *Voices of the Spanish Civil War*, 279.

93. T. A. R. Hyndman, "International Brigader 2," in Toynbee, ed., *Distant Drum*, 122.

94. Frank Owen to his wife and children, May 24, 1937, in R. Sydenham, "Did They Die in Vain: The International Brigade, A Compilation of Facts," typescript: 9, Swansea.

95. Dave Springhall and Ralph Bates to Harry Pollitt, December 21 [1936], f. 2, MML, Box C 8/2. Also see Box C 9/6 for more on the "campaign" against Jews in the emerging battalion.

96. J. R. Jump, "International Brigader I" in Toynbee, ed., *Distant Drum*, 117.

97. For biographical information on Law, see Collum, *African Americans in the Spanish Civil War*, 5, 13–14. The question about Law's competence in Spain was raised most controversially in Herrick's novel, *Hermanos!*, 322–29. He calls Law "Cromwell Webster"; interview with Bob Gladnick, January 21, 1980, Brandeis, 154, 173, 192–93, 206. (Cecil Eby apparently relied heavily on Gladnick as a source in his critical *Between the Bullet and the Lie*, 133–35; Rosenstone, *Crusade of the Left*, 110, 184–85, and Carroll's *Odyssey of the American Abraham Lincoln Brigade*, 135–39. Lincoln veterans with whom I have spoken, including Steve Nelson, who succeeded Law in command after his death at Brunete, vehemently defend the African-American volunteer. Even if Law was a generally respected leader, however, there is evidence that other African-Americans were given responsibilities for political reasons that they were unable to carry out. See interview with John Murra, June 26, 1981, Brandeis, 53, 55.

98. Gurney, *Crusade in Spain*, 136.

99. Interview with Fred Copeman, August 2, 1976, Manchester, 75.

100. Interview with Fred Copeman, 1976, SRC, 794/13, 90.

101. Interview with John Peet, 1976, SRC, 800/9, Reel 1.

102. Collum, *African-Americans in the Spanish Civil War*, 33–34.

103. Charlie Nusser to the editor, *The Volunteer*, 1 (Winter 1993), 21.

104. Interview with Bob Cooney, August 1, 1976, Manchester, 23.

105. J. R. Jump, "International Brigader I" in Toynbee, ed., *Distant Drum*, 116–17.

106. R. Bourne, "The Promised Land," December 1973, MML, 1–6.

107. Quoted in Francis, *Miners against Fascism*, 94.

108. Dan O'Neill, "Crusade to Spain: Welsh Memories of the Civil War," unnamed, undated newspaper, MML.

109. Jack Lindsay, "On Guard for Spain: A Poem for Mass Recitation," in Cunningham, *The Penguin Book of Spanish Civil War Verse*, 253.

110. Interview with Bob Gladnick, January 21, 1980, Brandeis, 111.

111. Quoted in O'Riordan's *Connolly Column*, 68.

112. "Extracts from a Speech by Frank Ryan," DMWC.

113. Joe Monks, *New Statesman*, March 31, 1961. Also see Manus O'Riordan, "Portrait of an Irish Anti-Fascist," published in the *New York Morning Freiheit*, September 18, 1983. The typescript of the article is in the Working Class Movement Library in Salford.

114. Lyons, *Ireland since the Famine*, 415, 413.

115. Richard Bennett charges that Nathan was a member of the so-called Dublin Murder House gang and linked him with the assassination of the Lord Mayor of Limerick and the ex-Lord Mayor of Cork. See "Portrait of a Killer," *New Statesman*, March 24, 1961, 471–72. Bennett received this information from two former Black and Tans who had served with Nathan in Ireland. In addition to being a "killer," they both described him as "notorious" for his homosexuality. In a note attached to a clipping of the story in the Marx Memorial Library, the editor of the *Irish Democrat*, Desmond Graves, told Peter Kerrigan that he had reviewed Bennett's book on the Black and Tans and found it full of "errors of fact and suppressions." He believed Bennett's article was "a blatant effort at imperialist whitewash." See C. Desmond Graves to Peter Kerrigan, March 20, 1961, MML. Regardless of Graves' defense, there is extensive evidence that Nathan served as a member of the Black and Tans.

116. Monks, *With the Reds in Andalusia*, 47.

117. The English executed Clarke as a result of the 1916 Easter rising.

118. *These Men Have Died*, 15–19.

119. Interview with Bob Cooney, August 5, 1976, Manchester, MML, 8.

120. Kopp was Orwell's commanding officer. Orwell wrote in *Homage to Catalonia*, "I knew his history. He was a man who had sacrificed every-thing—family, nationality, livelihood—simply to come to Spain and fight against Fascism." In fact, the "history" that Orwell "knew" was largely fiction. Instead of being a Belgian engineer with prior military experience, Kopp's true nationality was Russian and he had never served in the military. In addition, he was neither a graduate engineer nor a devoted husband and father as Orwell believed. It would also appear that Kopp's claim that he was forced to flee Belgium because he was fabricating illegal munitions for the Spanish Republic was false. Orwell risked his life in an effort to free Kopp, a man whom he literally did not know. See Shelden, *Orwell*, 271–72.

121. Gurney, *Crusade in Spain*, 66–69.

122. One of the characters in Norman's autobiographical novel, *The Fell of Dark*, is modeled after Dunbar.

123. Wolff, *Another Hill*, 358. The other was the legendary American Joe Bianca, who died on Hill 666 in the Sierra Pandols during the Ebro offensive.

124. J. S. Williams to Doris and Idris Cox, July 7, 1937, quoted in Francis, *Miners Against Fascism*, 280.

125. MacDougall, ed., *Voices of the Spanish Civil War*, 210.

126. Wintringham, *English Captain*, 30–31.

127. Monks, *With the Reds in Andalusia*, 8.

128. Ibid, 12.

129. Hynes, *A War Imagined*, 361.

130. Fond 545, op. 3, d. 480, l. 169, Moscow.

131. MacDougall, ed., *Voices of the Spanish Civil War*, 209. Significant information can be found here on Jock Cunningham during and after Brunete.

132. Gurney, *Crusade in Spain*, 94.

133. Hugh Slater claimed that Nathan told him of his intention to join the party. This, of course, is possible. But Slater disclosed this after Nathan's death in *The Book of the XV Brigade*, 176. The book is indispensable for some types of information but one must not forget that its purpose was party propaganda.

134. MML, Box D-4 Db.

Chapter Nine

1. The government was embarrassed by the persistent disregard of the law by volunteers. In a conversation with the German chargé d'affaires on January 7, 1937, Eden told him "to impress" on the German government "British determination to find means to prevent [the] flow of volunteers to Spain in order that [the] conflict not spread." See PRO, FO 371 W495/7/41, 233. Lord Halifax commented on the "unfortunate impression" the departure of groups of men for Spain was having on signatories to the Non-Intervention Agreement. If it appeared that the government was "ineffective in preventing persons leaving in considerable numbers to fight in Spain," then the chances "of an international prohibition of volunteering might be seriously impeded," particularly "if such an impression were to gain ground." Halifax then insisted that "a careful watch . . . be kept on the activities of recruiting agents in this country," so that proceedings might be brought against the lawbreakers. See PRO, FO 371/21321 W1954/7/41, February 8, 1937, 132.

2. PRO, FO 371/22651 152833, 157. The MP from Bury St. Edmonds conceded that the act "is completely out of date." Moreover, "there is some doubt whether it can be applied in the case of a civil war, and it appears to be impossible to use it to stop the enlistment of a volunteer, or to stop the action of any body of individuals assisting that volunteer." A successful prosecution, he pointed out, would depend on a contract of service being drawn up in England. This formality, however, did not occur until the volunteer reached Spain. He accused the irrepressible Ellen Wilkinson of Jarrow with complicity in the illegal recruiting, a charge which she robustly denied, but added for the edification of her fellow members, "I have nothing but the greatest admiration for the men who have played so great a part in fighting the battle for democracy in face of the Fascist invaders." Ibid., 162.

3. PRO, FO 371/21320/152833. This is a memorandum from Chief Constable A. Canning. On July 27, 1938, an MP rose in Parliament and complained, "It is over two years since the Home Secretary announced that the Act would be put into operation, but there has not been a single prosecution."

4. Frank Owen to his wife and children, May 24, 1937, in R. Sydenham, "Did They Die in Vain: The International Brigade—A Compilation of Facts," typescript, Salford, 10.

5. To John Larmour, January 6 [or 7], 1937, Texas.

6. Cook, *Apprentices of Freedom*, 65.

7. Gurney, *Crusade in Spain*, 66–67.

8. Sherry, *The Life of Graham Greene*, 1: 611.

9. Copeman, *Reason in Revolt*, 80.

10. T. A. R. Hyndman, "International Brigader 2," in Toynbee, ed., *Distant Drum*, 130, 124.

11. *Spain Today*, 8 (1949), 10. It was written by George Naylor.

12. Gregory, *The Shallow Grave*, 50.

13. Interview with Sam Wild, Manchester, BBC Tapes, 1974, 47. Copeman believed that he was "higher" up in the party than Wintringham. In fact, Wintringham was present at the creation of the British Communist party and was a key member of an early intrigue to overthrow the "old guard" in 1923 and install Harry Pollitt as party secretary. See Morgan, *Pollitt*, 33.

14. "C. 1823," "Close-Up of a Battle," *Supplement to the Adelphi*, February 1940, 11–12.

15. Diary of David Crook, entry for January 6, 1937, MML, Box D4 Cr, ms.

16. Ibid., January 9, 1937.

17. Ibid.

18. Peter Kerrigan, "Spain, 1936–1938," typescript, MML, 3.

19. *Spain at War*, September 1938, 198.

20. Kiernan, "Labour and the War in Spain," *Scottish Labour History Society Journal* 11, 1977, 10.

21. David Cook [or Crook] to Jimmy, January 24, 1937, in Acier, ed., *From Spanish Trenches*, 100–101.

22. Ms. diary of David Crook, entries for January 10, 11, and 12, 1937, MML.

23. Ibid., January 12, 24, and February 3, 1937.

24. Ibid., January 27 and February 3, 1937.

25. Ibid., February 8, 1937.

26. Contemporary accounts, MML, Box D-7 E.

27. Ms. diary of David Crook, February 8, 1937, MML.

28. Ibid., February 10, 1937.

29. Gurney, *Crusade in Spain*, 90.

30. The description of the flora of the Jarama valley comes from Herrick's *¡Hermanos!*, 137. Herrick fought with the Lincolns and was wounded on the San Martín de la Vega Road.

31. Rée, *Proletarian Philosophers*, 128.

32. Gurney, *Crusade in Spain*, 112–13.

33. Norman Jackson, "The Men Who Fought for Peace," *Manchester Evening News*, February 14, 1975, 8.

34. Roberts, *The Classic Slum*, 179.

35. "I Was Fighting Hitler Six Years Ago," *Volunteer for Liberty*, 1943, 9–11.

36. There are numerous accounts of this first great battle, but Bill Alexander's is the most carefully considered. See *British Volunteers for Liberty*, Chapter Eight.

37. The summary of the disposition of forces can be found in O'Toole and Nettleton's introduction to Coward's *Back from the Dead*.

38. *The Observer*, June 22, 1986, 17.

39. O'Toole and Nettleton, introd., in Coward, *Back from the Dead*.

40. Cook, *Apprentices of Freedom*, 4.

41. Interview with Sam Wild, BBC Tapes, 1974, Manchester, 49.

42. Landis, *Death in the Olive Groves*, 17.

43. Preston, *Franco*, 222.

44. O'Toole and Nettleton, introd., in Coward, *Back from the Dead*.

45. Gannes and Repard, *Spain in Revolt*, 277.

46. Gurney, *Crusade in Spain*, 117. "Evening Advertiser," typescript, June 8, 12, 1939, MML, 5. Also see MacDougall, ed., *Voices from the Spanish Civil War*, 117.

47. Wintringham, *English Captain*, 113.

48. "Evening Advertiser," typescript, June 8, 12, 1939, MML, 5.

49. Contemporary accounts, MML, Box D-7 E.

50. Ibid.

51. Quoted in Fyrth, *The Signal Was Spain*, 78.

52. Gurney, *Crusade in Spain*, 113–14.

53. Ibid.

54. Hynes, *The Auden Generation*, 21.

55. Toynbee, *Friends Apart*, 91.

56. Interview with Sam Wild, BBC Tapes, 1974, Manchester, 1.

57. Ms. diary of David Crook, entry for March 3, 1937, MML, Box D-4 Cr.

58. Judith Cook, "For Freedom's Sake," *Western Mail*, March 3, 1979.

59. MacDougall, ed., *Voices from the Spanish Civil War*, 64.

60. Worsley, *Behind the Battle*, 183.

61. Romilly, *Boadilla*, 113.

62. Gurney, *Crusade in Spain*, 116.

63. "C. 1823," "Close-Up of a Battle," *Supplement to the Adelphi*, February 1940, 16.

64. Worsley, *Fellow Travellers*, 213.

65. MacDougall, ed., *Voices from the Spanish Civil War*, 204.

66. Interview with James Brown, August 8, 1976, Manchester, 24.

67. Holmes, *Acts of War*, 156.

68. "Evening Advertiser," typescript, June 8, 12, 1939, MML, 5.

69. George Leeson, "There's a Valley in Spain," in *Spain Today*, February 1947, 5.

70. Caute, *The Fellow-Travellers*, 416. When T. C. Worsley went to Spain with Stephen Spender, he wrote, "I only thought of myself as a kind of tourist. Here was one of the great events of our time in progress. I should do, what all the while I had really been wanting to do — see what it was like." See *Behind the Battle*, 14.

71. Quoted in Wyden, *The Passionate War*, 321.
72. Typescript on visiting delegations to Spain, MML.
73. "British Labour Delegation Visits Spain," *Volunteer for Liberty*, 26, December 13, 1937, 1. Attlee's account can be found in *As It Happened*, 133–34. Harris offers a misleading version of this incident in his biography of the Labour leader. See his *Attlee*, 138.
74. Quoted in Mendelson, *Early Auden*, 196. Auden's experiences in Spain are most conveniently summarized by Jenkins in "Auden and Spain," Bucknell and Jenkins, eds., *W. H. Auden*, 88–93.
75. Fisher, *Cyril Connolly*, 152–53.
76. Monteath, *Writing the Good Fight*, 83.
77. It should be remembered, however, that Auden was one of the few of his Oxbridge contemporaries to support the General Strike of 1926. He drove a truck for the TUC. See Spender, *The Thirties and After*, 6. In addition, after he left England, he contributed to an Aid Spain banquet in New York, sending in the cost of the dinner for a friend but not expecting to pay for his own. This suggests that he was continuing to play his role as a supporter of the Republic. See Wystan Hugh Auden to Herman Shumlin, n.d., Columbia.
78. Quoted in Hewison, *Under Siege*, 8.
79. Spender, *World within World*, 214, 226–38.
80. Ibid., 212–38.
81. Ibid., 223–24.
82. See Caute, *The Fellow-Travellers*, 30, 181.
83. Stephen Spender, *World within World*, 240.
84. Ibid., 241.
85. Ibid., 244.
86. Ibid., 244–45.
87. Barbara Brothers, "Through the 'Pantry Window': Sylvia Townsend Warner and the Spanish Civil War," Brown, et al., *Rewriting the Good Fight*, 161–71.
88. Gillian Beer, "Disperse As We Are," *Times Literary Supplement*, 4813, June 30, 1995, 7.
89. See Mufford, *This Narrow Place*, 70–134.
90. MML, Box C 7/1, n.d.; Harman, *Warner*, 153.
91. See Harmon, *Warner*, 152–56.
92. Strachey, *Coming Struggle for Power*, 185.
93. Clark, *J.B.S.*, 116.
94. Ibid., 125. Of all the well-known visitors who came to Spain, including Paul Robeson, Nehru, and Hemingway, Haldane made the most memorable impression on the medic Huw Williams from South Wales. Interview, SRC, 10181/5, 1988, Reel 5.
95. Ms. diary of Ralph Cantor, entry for March 30, 1937, Salford.
96. The outfit he believed appropriate for wartime Spain consisted of a black leather jacket, breeches, and caps of varying description. This ensemble of clothing was not always able to contain his great girth, and even by wartime standards his low level of hygiene drew attention. Moreover, his

wife, Charlotte, from whom he was estranged (a conclusion drawn from their independent sexual lives), lumped her husband in with other thrill-seeking intellectuals "who were having a lot of fun and frivolity and pseudo-military excitement in that heroic city." See Haldane, *Truth Will Out*, 96.

97. Interview with Fred Copeman, 1976, SRC, 794/13, 25.

98. Clark, *J. B. S.*, 119–21, 125, 136.

99. Campbell, *Edward Heath*, 22.

100. Ibid., 32–33.

101. Quoted in Jones, *Union Man*, 69–70. Also see "British Students Went to Spain," Salford, which includes a resolution from the deputation asking all British students to contribute to food for Spain, with Heath being one of the signatories.

Chapter Ten

1. See Chapters 42 and 43 of Bolloten's discussion in *The Spanish Civil War: Revolution and Counterrevolution*. He writes of May week in Barcelona, "No historical episode has been so diversely reported or defined," 429. Chomsky's "American Power and the New Mandarins," reprinted as "Objectivity and Liberal Scholarship," in *The Chomsky Reader*, 83–120, remains the classic, contemporary response to historians who argue that the destruction of the POUM, though revealing the ruthlessness of the communists, was necessary if the war was to be won. The film "Land and Freedom" (1995), which won the Felix award for the best European film of the year, follows a young Liverpool volunteer to Catalonia whose disillusions with the communists roughly parallel those of Orwell.

2. See Thwaites, "The Independent Labour Party," *Imperial War Museum Review* 2, 1987, 50–61.

3. Christopher Farman, "The Red or Dead Brigade," *The Guardian*, February 13, 1965, 6.

4. Interview with Stafford Cottman, 1986, SRC, 9278/7, Reel 4.

5. Fond 545, op. 6, d. 107, ll. 22–23, Moscow. Much of the Moscow file appears to be duplicated in a police report in Valencia which calls the Blairs "known Trotskyites" and "linking agents of the ILP and the POUM." See Robert Low, "Archives Show How Orwell's 1937 Held More Terrors Than His 1984," *Observer*, November 5, 1989, cited in Michael Shelden, *Orwell*, 269–70.

6. "Report on the English Section of the P.O.U.M.," MML, Box C 13/7.

7. Stansky and Abrahams, *Orwell: The Transformation*, 213.

8. See Orwell, *Homage to Catalonia*, 116–17.

9. "Report on the English Section of the P.O.U.M.," MML, Box C 13/7.

10. Fond 545, op. 6, d. 135, ll. 35–37, Moscow.

11. With the exception of his laundry.

12. A version of Frankford's story, which undoubtedly settled the matter for most in the British Battalion, appeared under the headline, "Trotskyist Traitors," in *Volunteer for Liberty* 14, September 13, 1937, 9–10.

13. Fond 545, op. 6, d. 136, ll. 35–37, Moscow. Frankford's charges were made to Sam Lesser in an article which appeared in the *Daily Worker*. Orwell surmised that "all these wild words . . . were put into Frankford's mouth by Barcelona journalists, and that he chose to save his skin by assenting to them." Frankford repeated his accusations to Bernard Crick forty years later, however. See Crick, *Orwell*, 232–33.

14. Interview with Stafford Cottman, 1986, SRC, 9278/7, Reel 4.

15. Immediately after the fighting concluded, Orwell reported that he was again approached to join the IB. It was only several weeks later, when the purge began, that his presence in Spain became untenable. See Orwell, *Homage to Catalonia*, 145.

16. Cockburn, *Cockburn in Spain*, 184.

17. Fenner Brockway, "Personal Report of Visit to Spain," loose papers, MML. Brockway told Blair that he had spoken to a German who had seen Bob Smillie in prison, and that he was indeed ill.

18. McGovern, *Terror in Spain*, 5. After the war, the writer, former commissar, and gifted strategist, Hugh Slater, expressed his agreement in *The Heretics*. His novel tells a grim cautionary tale, comparing the fate of three children in the Children's Crusade in the thirteenth century with that of three English students who went to Spain. The heroine's brother, Paul, fights with the POUM while their friend, Simon, becomes a member of the British Battalion and the SIM. In all probability Simon denounces Paul as a Trotskyist, resulting in his death.

19. See Buchanan, "The Death of Bob Smillie, *The Historical Journal* 2 (June 1997), 435–61."

20. To Rayner Heppenstall, Texas.

21. Connolly, *Enemies of Promise*, 164.

22. See Andy Croft, "The Awkward Squaddie," *New Statesman and Society* 294, March 18, 1994, 57.

23. See Shelden, *Orwell*, 271–73. Also see letter from Bert Govaerts to Bill Alexander, February 12, 1984, MML, Box A-12, Orw. Govaerts concluded after studying Kopp's career, "All in all, Orwell's famous gift for observation was grotesquely beaten by this very very curious man."

24. Fond 545, op. 6, d. 120, ll. 85–86, Moscow. Crook had been detained before, in Kentucky where he had been investigating coalfield conditions. After Columbia, and his return to England, he worked as a part-time private secretary for a Labour MP.

25. A note by Bill Alexander states that after serving in the battalion, Crook was recruited to buy armaments for the Republic. "This had to be carried out in a clandestine manner." MML, Box D-4, Cr/1.

26. To Ben Bowen Thomas, Warden of Coleg Harlech, June 20, 1937. Quoted in Francis, *Miners against Fascism*, 275.

27. *Volunteer for Liberty* 10, August 16, 1937, 3.

28. Author's interview in London, December 1, 1981, with an International Brigade veteran who wished to remain anonymous. Bill Chambers was killed after he transferred to another militia unit. See Thwaites, "The

Independent Labour Party Contingent in the Spanish Civil War," *Imperial War Museum Review* 2, 1987, 60. Bob Smillie died in prison.

29. J. S. Williams to Doris and Idris Cox, July 7, 1937, quoted in Francis, *Miners Against Fascism*, 280.

30. Orwell, "Looking Back on the Spanish Civil War," in *My Country Right or Left: 1940–1943*, 2: 256.

31. Matthews, *The Education of a Correspondent*, 130.

32. Quoted in Watkins, *Britain Divided*, 56.

33. To Harry Pollitt, September 12, 1938, MML, Box C 25/1.

34. To Harry Pollitt, October 18, 1938, MML, Box C 26/3.

35. Quoted in Woodcock, *Orwell's Message*, 79. Koestler could well have told Orwell a corroborating story. While writing *Spanish Testament*, he was interrupted by Willi Münzenberg who "would pick up a few sheets of the typescript, scan through them, and shout at me: 'Too weak. Too objective. Hit them! Hit them hard! Tell the whole world how they run over their prisoners with tanks, how they pour petrol over them and burn them alive. Make the world gasp with horror. Hammer it into their heads.'" See *The Invisible Writing*, 407.

36. A. D., "The Story of the Daily Worker by William Rust," in *Spain Today*, March–April, 1950, 14.

37. Harry Pollitt, Foreword, in Jack Coward, *Back from the Dead* (London, n.p., n.d.), MML, 4.

38. George to Tom Murray, May 15, 1937, Edinburgh. Also see John Angus on this point. Any reporting unfavorable to the Soviet Union or its "line" was regarded as "enemy propaganda." See N.A., *In Spain with the International Brigade*, 5.

39. Corkill and Rawnsley, *The Road to Spain*, 33.

40. Jones, *Union Man*, 75; Thomas, *To Tilt at Windmills*, 110.

41. George Brown to Mick Jenkins, June 27, 1937, in Jenkins, *George Brown*, 24.

42. N.A., *In Spain with the International Brigade*, 26.

43. Fond 545, op. 6, d. 200, l. 8v, Moscow.

44. Ibid., Fond 545, op. 6, d. 211, ll. 1–2.

45. Bill Alexander, "George Orwell and Spain," in Christopher Norris, ed., *Inside the Myth*, 96–97.

46. Shelden, *Orwell*, 254.

47. A prominent American Communist party official and base commissar at Albacete.

48. A leader of the South Wales miners and British base commissar.

49. Interview with John Murra, June 26, 1981, Brandeis, 33.

50. Fond 545, op. 3, d. 444, ll. 15–15v., 77, Moscow.

51. Interview with Alec Ferguson, August 1, 1976, Manchester, 8.

52. *Volunteer for Liberty* 19, May 1, 1938, 12.

53. Interview with Leonard Lamb, March 19, 1980, Brandeis, 34.

54. George Brown to Mick Jenkins, June 27, 1937, in Jenkins, *Brown*, 25.

55. Will Paynter to the British Battalion, October 5, 1937, quoted in Francis, *Miners Against Fascism*, 282.

56. Fond 545, op. 6, d. 22, l. 33, Moscow. This is a fifty-three page study of the British Battalion made by Elliott for the party. He wrote in French, calling it "Rapport du Camarade: Les Volontaires Anglais en Espagne—Studies au Point de Vue de Cadres."

57. Fond 545, op. 6, d. 87, l. 29, Moscow.

58. Ibid., Fond 545, op. 6, d. 22, l. 33.

59. Much the same was said about the Americans. Ralph Bates accused them of knowing nothing about the realities in Spain and, as a result, they "existed in a . . . political vacuum" while there. See Carroll, *Odyssey of the Abraham Lincoln Brigade*, 239.

60. Fond 545, op. 6, d. 215, l. 30, Moscow. An apparently closer relationship between the British and the Spaniards had been established by the time Jack Jones, the Liverpool docker and councilor, joined the battalion on the eve of the battle of the Ebro in the summer of 1938. He found the "relations with the Spaniards in the Battalion were close and friendly." Bob Cooney, the battalion commissar, shared this opinion. Moreover, Jones found "the use of basic Spanish" to have become "second nature in communications between all of us." Jones, *Union Man*, 68. Also see interview with Bob Cooney, August 1, 1976, Manchester, 10. *Hugo's Spanish* was a popular primer. See George Brown to Mick Jenkins, June 27, 1937 in Jenkins, *Brown*, 24.

61. Interview with Leonard Lamb, March 19, 1980, Brandeis, 34, 33.

62. W. K. MacGregor to Peter Kerrigan, November 19, 1937, MML.

63. On the other hand, what of that "fraction" of anarchosyndicalists in the British Battalion, whose existence was verified by Charles Bloom? Perhaps they managed to find copies of the special edition of the *Bulletin of Information, International Workingmen's Association*, June 1, 1937, which reported accurately that Largo Caballero fell because "he would not permit the introduction of Moscow methods into the internal policy of Spain."

64. "POUM UNMASKED," *Spanish News Bulletin*, June 1937, 2.

65. "Further Explanations of the Recent Disorders in Barcelona," *Spanish News Bulletin*, No. 11, n.d., 1.

66. See U.H.P., "Spain and the People's Front," *Labour Monthly* 3, March 1937, 169–78, especially 177.

67. Another volunteer who played a prominent role at Invergordon was Albert Cole. See O'Toole and Nettleton, "Jack Coward, Merseyside, and the International Brigades," in Coward, *Back from the Dead*.

68. In addition, Marty's father was condemned to death in absentia for the part he played in the Paris Commune. See Thomas, *The Spanish Civil War*, 457.

69. Gurney, *Crusade in Spain*, 70–71.

70. Copeman, *Reason in Revolt*, 52.

71. Ereira, *The Invergordon Mutiny*, 71, 165–66; Carew, *The Lower Deck*, 167.

72. Copeman, *Reason in Revolt*, 53.

73. Carew, *The Lower Deck*, 169.

74. Lee, *A Moment of War*, 74–75.

75. Ibid.

76. Interview with Fred Copeman, August 2, 1976, Manchester, 19.

77. Haldane, *Truth Will Out*, 98, 131.

78. Gurney, *Crusade in Spain*, 70.

79. Ibid., 88.

80. Interview with Fred Copeman, August 2, 1976, Manchester, 37.

81. Rust, *Spain Fights for Victory*, 14.

82. Interview with Fred Copeman, 1976, SRC, 794/13, 26.

83. Gregory, *The Shallow Grave*, 108.

84. Sam Wild, "Commissars," *Volunteer for Liberty* 4, April 1940, 4.

85. Haldane, *Truth Will Out*, 131.

86. Wintringham, *English Captain*, 85.

87. Fond 545, op. 6, d. 118, ll. 58, 62, Moscow.

88. Interview with Fred Copeman, 1976, SRC, 794/13, 61, 65.

89. Copeman, *Reason in Revolt*, 102–3. Copeman's reaction was typical. A female contemporary wrote, "It was said that [the milicianas] caused more discharges among the milicianos than the bullets of the Nationalist soldiers." The reasons for this were twofold: venereal disease was "rampant" and there was needless loss of life when Republican soldiers, encoded in their Spanish male gender roles, sacrificed themselves when their women comrades were in danger. See Mangini's *Memories of Resistance: Women's Voices from the Spanish Civil War*, 80–81.

90. Interview with Syd Quinn, 1976, SRC, 801/3, Reel 1.

91. Gregory, *The Shallow Grave*, 73.

92. MML, Box C 8/5.

93. MacDougall, ed., *Voices from the Spanish Civil War*, 62.

94. Interview with Fred Copeman, 1976, SRC, 794/13, 28.

95. Gurney, *Crusade in Spain*, 77.

96. Gregory, *The Shallow Grave*, 58.

97. Cited in Beevor, *The Spanish Civil War*, 128.

98. Interview with Fred Copeman, August 2, 1976, Manchester, 20.

99. Ibid., 42; an interview with Syd Quinn confirms this, SRC, 801/3, Reel 3.

100. Interview with Fred Copeman, August 2, 1976, Manchester, 7.

101. Copeman, *Reason in Revolt*, 94.

102. Fond 545, op. 6, d. 116, ll. 69–69v, Moscow.

103. Interview with Fred Copeman, 1976, SRC, 794/13, 96, 47.

104. Fond 545, op. 6, d. 118, ll. 58, 62, Moscow.

105. Holmes, *Acts of War*, 340.

106. Wintringham, *English Captain*, 73–74.

107. Interview with Fred Copeman, August 2, 1976, Manchester, 18, 61.

108. Interview with Jim Brewer, November 29, 1969, Swansea, 20.

109. Militiaman, "From the I.B. to the British Army," in *Volunteer for Liberty*, May 1940.

110. Interview with Fred Copeman, 1976, SRC, 794/13, 67.

111. Interview with Tommy Fanning, July–August 1976, Manchester, 8, 28.

112. Interview with Fred Copeman, 1976, SRC, 794/13, 86–87; See Fred Thomas, *To Tilt at Windmills*, 54.

113. Fond 545, op. 6, d. 126, l. 37, Moscow.

114. Ibid., Fond 545, op. 3, d. 478, l. 8.

115. Sheean, *Not Peace But a Sword*, 49.

116. Fond 545, op. 6, d. 126, l. 38, Moscow.

117. Ibid.

118. Jones, *Union Man*, 78.

119. Interview with Leonard Lamb, March 19, 1980, Brandeis, 15.

120. Interview with Frank Graham, January 28, 1977, Manchester, 67.

121. Interview with Sam Wild, BBC Tapes, 1974, Manchester, 72.

122. *The Heretics* was his most successful novel.

123. Interview with Fred Copeman, August 2, 1976, Manchester, 86–87. For the description of Slater see Brenan, *Personal Record*, 315.

124. For his part, Arthur Nicoll, who became political commissar of the Anti-Tank Battery, believed that Slater was extremely selfish. Nor could he have been pleased when Slater called him "an uncouth Scot." See interview with Arthur Nicoll, 1976, SRC, 817/3, Reel 3. The fact that Slater was English in a unit that was increasingly dominated by Scots undoubtedly had something to do with his unpopularity. Interview with John Dunlop, 1990, SRC, 11355/13, Reel 4. The eight or nine public-school- and/or university-educated members of the unit found the working-class Scots who had participated in strikes, demonstrations, and battles with Mosley's Blackshirts a formidable group of comrades. The Scots considered themselves working-class "revolutionaries" and were "snobbish" in the presence of an English accent. Interview with Chris Smith, 1991, SRC, 12290/9, Reel 4.

125. Roberts, *The Classic Slum*, 55. George Orwell's condemnation of the "nancy" poets is hardly more enlightened. Nor were the attitudes of the Americans. Bill Aalto of the Lincolns successfully kept his homosexuality a secret in Spain. While serving in the OSS during World War II, however, his friend and comrade from Spain, Vince Lossowski, discovered the truth. "I acted like everybody else at that period. . . . When I found out he was a homosexual, to me he was a pariah." Alto subsequently committed suicide. Lossowski adds, "He was a decent person, he was a good person, and since then I have learned better, too late." See Interview with Vince Lossowski, June 1, 1980, Brandeis, 63.

126. Interview with John Murra, June 26, 1981, Brandeis, 25.

127. Fond 545, op. 6, d. 120, l. 10, Moscow.

128. Interview with Jim Brewer, November 29, 1969, Swansea, 4.

129. Fond 545, op. 6, d. 201, ll. 13–14, Moscow.

130. O'Toole and Nettleton, "Jack Coward, Merseyside, and the International Brigades," Introduction to Coward, *Back from the Dead*.

131. Stratton, *To Anti-Fascism by Taxi*, 7.

132. Jim Brewer to Bill Alexander, December 3, 1979, MML, Box A-12 Br.

133. Interview with Fred Copeman, 1976, SRC, 794/13, 87; "United Front Song," *Songs of the Spanish Civil War: The Oldham Men Who Fought in*

Spain: 1936–1938. This was a program presented on February 15, 1986, which can be found in the Salford collection.

134. Interview with Fred Copeman, 1976, SRC, 794/13, 88–89.

135. Gregory, *The Shallow Grave*, 169.

136. For a married man to volunteer for Spain could have considerable domestic repercussions. The Dependents' Aid Fund distributed available monies, but John Murra, who worked in IB Headquarters, remembers that "you'd constantly get letters from the abandoned wife with four children, the man on the dole. And the wife and the kids would be complaining and weeping." Interview with John Murra, June 26, 1981, Brandeis, 31.

137. Orwell, *Down and Out in Paris and London*, 202.

138. Interview with Benny Goodman, February 23, 1977, Manchester, 38.

139. Interview with David Goodman, n.d., ibid.; 27.

140. Monks, *With the Reds in Andalusia*, 13.

141. Interview with Fred Copeman, August 2, 1976, Manchester, 46.

142. Kiernan, "Labour and the War in Spain," *Scottish Labour History Society Journal* 11, May 1977, 7.

143. Interview with Fred Copeman, 1976, SRC, 794/13, 47, 109.

144. "Ralph Cantor" [loose sheet], Salford.

145. Ibid., diary of Ralph Cantor, entries for April 11, 12, 13, 1937.

146. Other worker-poets included Hugh Sloan, Tony Hyndman, and Jack Roberts or Jack "Russia."

147. Diary of Ralph Cantor, entries for May 2, 3, 1937, Salford.

148. Billy Griffiths memoir, March 15, 1964, Swansea, 41.

149. International Brigade Souvenir Program, MML, 21.

150. Interview with Fred Copeman, August 2, 1976, Manchester, 49.

151. Gurney, *Crusade in Spain*, 46.

Chapter Eleven

1. Interview with Maurice Levine, February 10, 1977, Manchester, 25.

2. *London Forward*, October 17, 1938, 3.

3. Jones, *Union Man*, 70–72.

4. David Guest, "Reasons for My Decision, 1938," in Carmel Haden Guest, *David Guest*, 174.

5. *British Battalion: XV International Brigade Roll of Honour*, 40–41, 43.

6. Interview with Jim Brewer, November 29, 1969, Swansea, 20.

7. J. R. Jump, "International Brigader I," in Toynbee, ed., *Distant Drum*, 112.

8. Gregory, *The Shallow Grave*, 178.

9. Pitcairn, Introduction by Ralph Bates, *Reporter in Spain*, 7.

10. Quoted in Carroll, *Odyssey of the Abraham Lincoln Brigade*, 78.

11. Orwell, *Homage to Catalonia*, 171.

12. Author's interview in New York City, April 11, 1991. See *Homage to Catalonia*, 170. Although Orwell read of the accusation in the *New Republic*, Bates also made the charge in *En La España Leal Ha Nacido Un Ejército*, 16, which can be found in the Herbert Southworth Collection, San Diego. He

wrote it in New York a few weeks after leaving Spain to embark on a speaking tour.

13. Author's interview at University College, Oxford, July 26, 1989.

14. N. A., *In Spain with the International Brigade*, 11.

15. Spender, *World within World*, 243. After hearing Spender make this observation in Oxford, I sought out Bates with the help of the office of the Veterans of the Abraham Lincoln Brigade. He agreed to an interview in New York, where he held Professor Emeritus rank at New York University and has lived for many years. After four hours of conversation, I repeated Spender's remark. He answered that having discussed the war and his role in it with me at length, as well as the values that led to his active and significant participation in the war, he would leave me to make my own decision about the accuracy of Spender's comment. For what it is worth, the man I talked to could not have been the paradox—personally attractive, gifted, yet, morally execrable—that Spender believed him to be. As any reader of Bates's books would conclude, his politics were, if anything, extremely sympathetic to the anarchists of Catalonia, although he deplored their indiscipline. There is no question, however, concerning his intimate association with the communists and his condemnation of the POUM, even though he energetically denies ever having joined the Communist party. In fact, according to Bates, the *Manifesto* was the only work of Marx he took the time to read. His interest, he insisted, was exclusively in defending the Republic and defeating Franco.

16. Addendum, n.d., to a letter to Harry Pollitt, MML, Box C 8/3, f. 3.

17. Ms. diary of Ralph Cantor, entries for May 14, 21, 1937, Salford.

18. David Crook read Bates' *The Olive Field* while recovering from his wound at the Jarama, and waiting to return to the front. He wrote in his diary for April 3, 1937, "The poetic prose seems at times a trifle overdone." But he applauded Bates' "understanding of both extremes of the social scale." All in all, the Columbia University-educated Englishman found the novel "impressive." See MML, Box D4 Cr.

19. Edwin Rolfe to "Dearest," August 17, 1937, in Nelson and Hendricks, eds., *Madrid 1937*, 293.

20. Quoted in Pitcairn, *Reporter in Spain*, 9–10.

21. The physical description of Bates derives both from my meeting with him and Stanley Weintraub's *The Last Great Cause*, 291.

22. Leo Gordon [Leo Mendelowitz] to Gussy Moskowitz, August 26, 1937, "Volunteers for Liberty: Letters from Joe and Leo Gordon," Foreword by Daniel Czitrom, in *Massachusetts Review* 25, Autumn 1984, 349, 352, 356.

23. To the American ear, Bates has a middle-class accent.

24. Scott Watson, *Single to Spain*.

25. Ibid., 82–83, 94.

26. Fred Copeman once observed that the Lincolns "yap too much and they've got too much money." See interview with Fred Copeman, SRC 794/13, 90. The American Sandor Voros worked well with the British commissar, Bob Cooney. But this was an exception. Voros remembers that

Cooney "was about as friendly to me as the British were capable of being to any American." See Voros, *American Commissar*, 379. The British at first looked upon the Americans as soft, inexperienced schoolboys. Subsequently, they resented the ascension of Dave Doran, Robert Merriman, and John Gates to brigade-level responsibilities. Lieutenant Edward Bee, a veteran of the General Strike, Cable Street, and the Hunger Marches, and an accomplished topographer, proved himself to be relentlessly, irrepressibly, and damagingly anti-American (particularly as more Americans assumed prominent positions). Finally, Bee was relieved of his duties and sent to a detention squad. See Fond 545, op. 6, d. 105, ll. 27, 38–39, 40, 42, Moscow.

27. "A Letter from the Front," November 11, 1937, DMWC, 1–4. This is a letter from D. M. Miller, apparently written at the American broadcasting station in Madrid.

28. Ibid.

29. Ibid., 3–4.

30. Forster, *Howards End*, 27.

31. Edwin Rolfe to "Dearest," August 17, 1937, in Nelson and Hendricks, eds., *Madrid 1937*, 293.

32. Bates, *Sirocco and Other Stories*, 245.

33. Ibid., 246, 248. Not that such an act is unusual in wartime. Frank Pitcairn records a similar incident. See *Reporter in Spain*, 137. Bates tells of a Spanish guerrilla in the Pyrenees who felt compelled to kill a badly wounded enemy soldier whose unconscious cries of pain were endangering his position. *Sirocco*, 371–72.

34. Ibid., 249–51.

35. Bates, *Lean Men*, 464.

36. Carroll, *Odyssey of the Abraham Lincoln Brigade*, 146.

37. Fond 545, op. 6, d. 118, l. 58, Moscow.

38. Interview with Fred Copeman, August 2, 1976, Manchester, 32.

39. Sydney Quinn to Maurice Levine, February 24, 1975, MML, Box A-12, Qu.

40. Interview with Syd Quinn, 1976, SRC, 801/3, Reel 3.

41. PRO, FO 371/22645 XC152896, 256. Considering the possibility of his arrest for violating the Foreign Enlistment Act, there may have been some dissimulation in Copeman's response as well. If the constable believed he was not returning to Spain, there would probably be little likelihood of a prosecution. Special Branch detectives questioned another returning volunteer, Bernie McCormick, as to why he had been in Spain, and he walked past them, saying, "I was picking blood oranges." See O'Toole and Nettleton,"Jack Coward, Merseyside, and the International Brigades," Introduction, Coward, *Back from the Dead*.

42. Cited by Beevor, *The Spanish Civil War*, 213.

43. Interview with Fred Copeman, SRC, 794/13, 1976, 10.

44. PRO, FO 371/22645 XC152896, 260–62. These were the only comments made by Copeman that were taken down in shorthand by a Special Branch detective. The other reports consisted of paraphrases of this exchange.

See Will Paynter's similar account of the scene in Cook's *Apprentices of Freedom*, 57–58.

45. Ibid., FO 371/22645 XC152896, 252. Minikin's was one of nine statements collected by Special Branch, eight by their own personnel and one by an ex-member of the battalion, for a possible prosecution of Copeman for violating the Foreign Enlistment Act. Special Branch compiled an elaborate file on Copeman's activities both when he was in the country and upon his departure for and return from Spain.

46. [N.N.] to Peter Kerrigan, December 5 [1937], MML.

47. To Peter Kerrigan, October 2, 1937, MML.

48. Thomas McWhirter to Peter Kerrigan, November 2 [1937], MML.

49. Bob [?] to Peter Kerrigan, December 30, 1937, MML.

50. Interview with Syd Booth, December 10, 1976, Manchester, 16.

51. Henry Buckley, "Teruel," in Payne, *The Civil War in Spain*, 248. Buckley was one of the best correspondents of the war and observed the battle at great personal risk. I am grateful to his son, Ramón, a distinguished literary critic, for playing cicerone with unflagging good cheer and enthusiasm for my travels to civil war sites.

52. Sam Wild, "Four Years Ago: The Formation of the Brigades," in *Volunteer for Liberty* 9, December 8, 1940, 8.

53. Interview with Jim Brewer, November 29, 1969, Swansea, 20.

54. Interview with Sam Wild, BBC Tapes, 1974, Manchester, 44.

55. Ibid., 3–4, 44.

56. Interview with Jim Brewer, Swansea, 20.

57. A soldier's irrepressible companion of whom Orwell wrote so memorably in *Homage to Catalonia*, 76.

58. J. R. Jump, "International Brigader I," in Toynbee, ed., *Distant Drum*, 116.

59. Fond 545, op. 3, d. 444, ll. 15–15v, Moscow. These figures appear on a handwritten note, dated August 28, 1937. The recommendation was also made that a course in Spanish for foreigners be started. By this time, the number of Spanish effectives exceeded the number of British in the battalion.

60. Bob Cooney, "Proud Journey," MML, Box A-15/3, 137.

61. Ibid., Box A-15/7, quoted in David Heywood, "British Combatant Writers of the Spanish Civil War," M.A. thesis, McGill University, July 1988, 104.

62. Fond 545, op. 6, d. 155, l. 62, Moscow; Buchanan, *The Spanish Civil War and the British Labour Movement*. See chapter 5.

63. Ibid., op. 6, d. 155, l. 62.

64. Ibid.

65. Ibid., l. 63.

66. Jones, *Union Man*, 56. See also O'Toole and Nettleton, "Jack Coward, Merseyside, and the International Brigades," Introduction to Coward, *Back from the Dead*.

67. Interview with Jack Jones, August 25, 1978, Manchester, 12.

68. Jones, *Union Man*, 61–62.

69. Interview with Jack Jones, August 25, 1978, Manchester, 17, 5.

70. Ibid., 11, 17–18.

71. Fond 545, op. 6, d. 155, ll. 62–63, 48, 52, Moscow.

72. Quoted in John Jenks, M.Sc. thesis [no university], "The British Government and Communism: The Case of the International Brigades: 1936–37," 1991, MML, 18–19.

73. Fond 545, op. 6, d. 176, l. 121, Moscow.

74. "Notes relative to proposal re International Brigade 3-2-38," Edinburgh. This is a discussion of whether Murray should go to Spain.

75. Ibid.

76. Fond 545, op. 6, d. 176, l. 121, Moscow.

77. A form letter, March 22, 1938, Edinburgh.

78. Ibid., a letter to be generally circulated, April 10, 1938.

79. Fond 545, op. 6, d. 176, l. 126, Moscow.

80. Pimlott, *Labour and the Left in the 1930s*, 91.

81. Interview with Fred Copeman, August 2, 1976, Manchester, 49.

82. Frank Owen to his wife and children in Sydenham, "Did They Die in Vain: The International Brigade—A Compilation of Facts," typescript, Swansea, 10.

83. George Brown to Mick Jenkins, June 27, 1937, in Jenkins, *George Brown*, 24.

84. Fond 545, op. 6, d. 159, l. 13, Moscow.

85. Many of the interviews with Spanish veterans conducted by the staff of the Imperial War Museum took place at a reunion of the International Brigade Association at Loughbrough in 1976. Interviews could be conducted only with veterans who attended the event. Some volunteers did not learn of the reunion or were too ill to attend. Others had broken with the party while in Spain, or later, and may have decided the occasion would be painfully exclusive. In one case, a veteran believed he had been purposefully kept ignorant of the reunion because he had not joined the party in Spain (author's interview, anonymous, December 1, 1981, London). Therefore, the interviews that Hywel Francis and others undertook in the Rhondda, which are deposited in the South Wales Miners' Library in Swansea, are of particular interest because the collection exists independently of the International Brigade Association in London. Although only Welsh veterans were interviewed, the records were kept under the stewardship of a fine historian and University College, Swansea. Consequently, there is a greater range of political opinion and accessibility to materials.

86. Fond 545, op. 6, d. 145, ll. 29–31, Moscow. There is no indication of what happened to Hall. In another instance, however, a local secretary of the CPGB wrote to the battalion that a volunteer had once been "a member of the Fascist movement." But, the letter emphasized, this had been several years in the past. Now, "I'm convinced that he is anti-fascist." See Fond 545, op. 6, d. 145, l. 27.

87. Ibid., Fond 545, op. 6, d. 118, ll. 21, 34.

88. Interview with Bob Cooney, August 1, 1976, Manchester, 5, 7. There can be some legitimate doubts about this assertion. The Comintern archives are replete with references to volunteers who deserted, who had a "general bad record," or as in the case of one, "a lumpen element, [a] drunkard,

absolutely rotten," as well as a deserter. See, for example, Fond 545, op. 6, d. 108, Moscow.

89. The Moscow archives of the British Battalion conclusively support this.

90. Interview with Jim Brewer, November 29, 1969, Swansea, 28.

91. Alexander, *British Volunteers for Liberty*, 298.

92. Fond 545, op. 6, d. 99, ll. 1, 10, 12–19, Moscow. One of the "spies" is named Robert G. Colodny, undoubtedly the author of the classic, *The Struggle for Madrid*. He was badly wounded in Spain and subsequently pursued a long academic career at the University of Pittsburgh. In the 1950s he fought robustly and successfully against McCarthy and his zealots. A telephone conversation with Professor Colodny and correspondence have done nothing to clear up this baffling issue. The most obvious explanation is that it was a characteristically paranoid mistake. He is listed among the English, l. 15.

93. Ibid., Fond 545, op. 6, d. 140, l. 16. This is dated January 21, 1937.

94. Ibid., Fond 545, op. 6, d. 217, l. 28.

95. To HP, June 9, 1937, MML, Box C 14/5.

96. Ibid.

97. Ibid.

98. Ibid., to Harry Pollitt, July 20, 1937, Box C 15/3, f. 2.

99. Ibid. The origin of this report on battalion losses at Brunete is unknown. Wally Tapsell defended himself vigorously. See his statement in Box C 15/1. He severely criticizes George Aitken and Jock Cunningham, believing that both had lost contact with the battalion in pursuit of their own ambitions. On August 9, he wrote to Will Paynter saying that he was being railroaded. Paynter, however, agreed that Tapsell should be brought home. Aitken, Tapsell, Cunningham, and Copeman, the battalion's most experienced leaders, were called back to England and forced to justify their actions. See Box C 16/2, 16/3, 17/1. Aitken made a long, formal statement in which he, like Tapsell, vehemently defended himself in detail. See Box C, 17/7.

100. Ibid., Box C 15/5, July 21, 1937.

Chapter Twelve

1. "Theirs To Reason Why!" *Volunteer for Liberty* 10, February 3, 1941, 17.

2. This excludes those who went to the newspapers on their return from Spain.

3. Fond 545, op. 6, d. 39, ll. 156–57, Moscow.

4. Ibid., Fond 545, op. 6, d. 168, l. 15.

5. Interview with Alec Marcovitch, September 20, 1977, Manchester, 3.

6. Ibid., 11; see Fond 545, op. 6, d. 168, l. 6, Moscow.

7. Interview with Marcovitch, Manchester, 38–39. In his interview, Marcovitch refers specifically to the "trials" of Jewish doctors "in 32 or 33." Although Stalin was responsible for the deaths of five to ten million people from 1929 to 1932, the so-called "Doctors' Plot," the majority in the dock

being Jews, took place in 1953. They were charged with the deaths of two of Stalin's closest henchmen in 1945 and 1948. Since Marcovitch refers to himself as being a "boy" at the time, he apparently did not confuse the dates. On the morning of November 8, 1932, however, Stalin's second wife, Nadezhda Alliluyeva, was found dead, either a suicide or a homicide victim. She and Stalin had engaged in a furious argument the night before. After returning to the Kremlin, she predicted she would be killed. The doctors who signed the autopsy report were "destroyed" by Stalin. But there is no indication that there were "trials" of the doctors in 1932 or 1933. Of course, the attraction of Soviet communism to many Jews was its avowed rejection of antisemitism. The reality proved quite different, and it may be suspicion of a more generalized persecution to which Marcovitch refers that alarmed the Jewish community in Glasgow in the early thirties. Antisemitism was deeply embedded in Russian culture, and Soviet practice, as opposed to theory, demonstrated its continuing consequences (particularly after 1948). See Rapoport, *Stalin's War against the Jews*, xi, 39, 41–42.

8. Fond 545, op. 6, d. 168, l. 14, Moscow.

9. Interview with Alec Marcovitch, September 20, 1977, Manchester, 24.

10. Fond 545, op. 6, d. 168, l. 12, Moscow.

11. Box A-15/3, Bob Cooney, "Proud Journey," MML, 7–8.

12. Ironically, in an unsigned letter to Harry Pollitt on the eve of Teruel, Bob Cooney and Marcovitch are both singled out for "doing very good work." See Box C-19/1, MML, f. 3.

13. Fond 545, op. 6, d. 168, l. 13, 7–8, 10, 12, 13v; d. 173, l. 18, Moscow.

14. Interview with Alec Marcovitch, September 20, 1977, Manchester, 25.

15. Hyndman, "International Brigader 2," in Toynbee, ed., *Distant Drum*, 127.

16. N.A., *In Spain with the International Brigade*, 19.

17. Fond 545, op. 6, d. 162, l. 141, Moscow.

18. Angus, *International Brigade in Spain*, 6–8. Angus believed that the story of Camp Lucas "reflects very little credit on those involved and responsible, but one which ought to be recorded in the interest of historical accuracy and, perhaps, as a warning for the future."

19. Interview with Alec Marcovitch, September 20, 1977, Manchester, 26.

20. Ibid., 27.

21. Fond 545, op. 6, d. 99, l. 11, Moscow.

22. Interview with Alec Marcovitch, September 20, 1977, Manchester, 27, 38.

23. For numerous examples of such volunteers, see Moscow, Fond 545, op. 6, d. 100–218. This part of the huge archive focuses on cadre evaluations and includes biographical statements about hundreds of volunteers. They serve, among other things, to give Marcovitch's account veracity.

24. Fond 545, op. 6, d. 113, ll. 45, 73. Moscow.

25. McGovern, *Terror in Spain*, 15.

26. Fond 545, op. 6, d. 212, ll. 63–66, Moscow. In this letter Scott Watson writes that he has been told by a press official that he is in personal danger because of his perceived heterodoxy. He appealed to both Negrín and Prieto

with no success. They told him, "It is a matter for the Party." The young journalist wrote there is "no doubt as to who controls Valencia."

27. Jack Carson to Harry Pollitt, August 30 [1938], Fond 545, op. 6, d. 113, ll. 116, 119, 102, 104–6, 110, 120v, Moscow.

28. Ibid., Fond 545, op. 6, d. 114, l. 57; d. 200, l. 29; d. 207, l. 71.

29. Ibid., Fond 545, op. 6, d. 131, ll. 35, 40, 42–42v.

30. This information is in Stephen Spender's file, dated October 5, 1938. See Fond 545, op. 6, d.151, l. 4, Moscow.

31. Ibid., Fond 545, op. 6, d.162, l. 67; l. 4.

32. Billy Griffiths memoir, March 15, 1964, Swansea, 49. Those going to their executions were instead ordered to serve in a labor battalion, which may or may not have had the same effect as carrying out their sentences.

33. MacDougall, ed., *Voices from the Spanish Civil War*, 324.

34. Keene, *The Last Mile to Huesca*, 172.

35. Interview with Fred Copeman, August 2, 1976, Manchester, 49. For corroboration of Copeman's story, see interview with Jim Brewer, November 29, 1969, Swansea, 22. Brewer remembers an instance in which an Irish member of the battalion was accused of "sabotaging" his machine gun. "This chap was subsequently shot." But, Brewer says, "he was one of the very few people who were actually shot there for an offence."

36. Gurney, *Crusade in Spain*, 96.

37. Merriman and Lerude, *American Commander*, 106–10.

38. Tom McWhirter to Peter Kerrigan, January 31, 1938, MML.

39. Interview with Fred Copeman, 1976, SRC, 794/13, 123–24. Copeman was suprisingly sympathetic to those who became disaffected. "This is a volunteer army; these are lads that have come straight from their home or the factory or the college and of their own will have gone to Spain to fight." According to Copeman, "the same fellow can say . . . 'I want to go back.'" He said, "My attitude was, whatever they did, if they did anything at all that was more than anybody else did."

40. Haldane, *Truth Will Out*, 126–27.

41. Alexander, *British Volunteers for Liberty*, 107. The estimable brigade political commissar, George Aitken, remembers that Overton was "put on trial before the Battalion" because "he lost his head" at the Jarama. After Brunete he was "never seen again." Interview, 1984, SRC, 10357/3, Reel 2.

42. Fond 545, op. 6, d. 140, l. 5, 5v., 6v, Moscow. For Bob Cooney's version of the events that led to Glacken's death, see Corkill and Rawnsley, *The Road to Spain*, 120 – 21.

43. Fond 545, op. 6, d. 172, l. 6, Moscow.

44. Ibid., Fond 545, op. 3, d. 449, l. 34.

45. Ibid., Fond 545, op. 6, d. 119, l. 75.

46. Ibid., Fond 545, op. 6, d. 142, ll. 76, 74.

47. J. R. Jump, "International Brigader I," in Toynbee, ed., *Distant Drum*, 117–18.

48. MacDougall, ed., *Voices of the Spanish Civil War*, 309.

49. Bolloten, *The Spanish Revolution*, 469.

50. D. F. Springhall, "The International Brigade in the Unified Army," *Discussion* 1, June 1937, 4. This is an extract from a speech made by Springhall at the London District Congress. Jack Jones, a company commissar but a Labour party member, insisted, however, that "politics were not that much talked of and yet they all knew why they were there." See Jones, *Union Man*, 68.

51. Jim Brewer to Ben Bowen Thomas, June 20, 1937, Swansea.

52. Fond 545, op. 6, d. 102, l. 37; d. 103, l. 68, Moscow.

53. Carroll, *Odyssey of the Abraham Lincoln Brigade*, 108.

54. Fond 545, op. 6, d. 22, ll. 49–50; d. 102, l. 34; d. 138, l. 3, Moscow.

55. Ibid., Fond 545, op. 6, d. 103, l. 11.

56. Peter Kerrigan to Harry Pollitt, August 13–16, 1938, MML, Box C 24/6.

57. Fond 545, op. 6, d. 178, ll. 52–53; d. 105, l. 11; d. 215, l. 51; d. 141, ll. 69v.–70; d. 173, ll. 140–140v, Moscow.

58. Ibid., Fond 545, op. 6, d. 104, ll. 33, 37.

59. Ibid., Fond 545, op. 6, d. 181, ll. 73–73v.

60. N.A., *In Spain with the International Brigade*, 26.

61. Jones, *Union Man*, 69.

62. Esenwein and Shubert, *Spain at War*, 153.

63. In the spring of 1938, Vincent Sheean found Wattis and Malcolm Dunbar on the banks of the Ebro in conference with the commander of the XVth Brigade, Lt. Col. Copic. Dunbar's youthful appearance contrasted sharply with both that of Copic, whom Sheean estimated was about forty-two or forty-three, and the gray-haired Wattis of the same middle years. They were "the only ones I can remember in the XVth Brigade who appeared to have reached such an advanced age." See *Not Peace but a Sword*, 49.

64. Quoted in Merriman and Lerude, *American Commander in Spain*, 100.

65. Eby, *Between the Bullet and the Lie*, 63. In his memoir, Jason Gurney calls him "Watters" (presumably not referring to George Watters, the Scottish volunteer who had been a miner and general laborer and who was captured at the Jarama), writing that "everybody treated him with great deference and one was given to understand that he was some kind of military genius." In a typical mangling of fact, Gurney writes that after Merriman was wounded, Wattis threw the Americans into fruitless and decimating attacks before beating "a fast retreat," and disappearing. To the South African, who abhorred Wattis' British army style, he was another "mystery man." But the former officer did not "disappear," as Gurney believed, and was to lead and fight valiantly until he left Spain in 1938. See *Crusade in Spain*, 127–28.

66. Quoted in Carroll, *Odyssey of the Abraham Lincoln Brigade*, 101.

67. Contemporary accounts, MML, Box D-7, E/1.

68. Fond 545, op. 2, d. 200, l. 67, Moscow.

69. Eby, *Between the Bullet and the Lie*, 69; Landis, *Death in the Olive Groves*, 22; Carroll, *Odyssey of the Abraham Lincoln Brigade*, 101, 114. Other Lincolns beside Jason Gurney (who left the British Battalion to serve with them) believed that Wattis had unnecessarily sacrificed American lives.

Wattis, however, was formally cleared of the charge of forcing men from the trenches at gunpoint, considering the circumstances. It must be remembered, too, there was always considerable tension between the Americans and the British, and charges of one against the other were not infrequent; see Merriman and Lerude, *American Commander in Spain*, 100, 107–9.

70. Voros, *American Commissar*, 368–69. Voros, who wrote the narrative, confessed that the combination of "press agent stuff" and the "actual history" of the brigade resulted in "a sorry job." He conceded, however, that the men "liked it," particularly those whose pictures or names appeared.

71. D. R. Davies, "Comrade Wattis Scores," in Frank Ryan, ed., *Book of the XV Brigade*, 93–94.

72. *Pollitt Visits Spain*, 19.

73. Interview with Syd Quinn, SRC, 801/3, Reel 2. Quinn refers to him as "Clifford" Wattis but it seems certain that he is the same man.

74. Author's interview with Steve Nelson, May 13, 1991, Truro, Mass.

75. See Fond 545, op. 3, d. 497, ll. 17–20, Moscow, for Bob Cooney's report on the debacle. Wild confirms this in his own detailed account, l. 24.

76. D. F. Springhall, "The International Brigade in the Unified Army," *Discussion* 1, June 1937, 4.

77. Bill Rust to Harry Pollitt, n.d., MML, Box C 22/1, f. 2.

78. Ibid., Box C 22/3.

79. Fond 545, op. 6, d. 212, ll., 86, 93, Moscow.

80. Ibid., Fond 545, op. 6, d. 22; also see d. 21, l. 11.

81. Wood, *Communism and British Intellectuals*, 54.

82. PRO, FO 371/22624 152833.

83. Ibid.

84. Copeman, *Reason in Revolt*, 85.

85. Fred Copeman to Sam Wild, n.d., MML. Their relationship would not always remain so cordial. Copeman broke from the party and wrote his autobiography, *Reason in Revolt*, which Wild reviewed. He read the book's section on Spain "with my fist in my pocket," in part because of the factual errors, in part because of Copeman's self-glorification of his role. He was also obviously rankled that Copeman agreed to accept an OBE from the king for his work during World War II. Wild concluded, "Copeman's book will cut no ice because the people he slanders are not giving lessons to the Royal Family, not hobnobbing with prelates and peers, but working and fighting with their class to achieve what the 500 dead of the British Battalion gave their lives for: liberty, equality, and freedom from fear, superstition and want." See *Spain Today* 3, March 1949, 14.

86. Fond 545, op. 6, d. 87, l. 15, Moscow.

87. Bill Rust, "The Spanish People's Army," in *Labour Monthly* 8, August 1938, 513.

88. See *Spain Fights for Victory*, 4, in which Rust explains the reasons for the setbacks of the Republican army, including "treachery by Fascist agents and, in some places, the opening of the front by the Trotskyists."

89. Interview with Fred Copeman, 1976, SRC, 794/13, 44.

90. See Thomas, *Spanish Civil War*, 491–92, n. 4; Johnston, *Legions of Babel*, 68. Pat Murphy, one of the early leaders of the British volunteers, recovered two of LaSalle's suitcases, one of which contained money that should not have been in his possession, and the second, Murphy claimed, held correspondence from fascist leaders in Paris and Rome. See Rob Macmillan, "Pat Murphy, 1898–1974," 19–20. To my knowledge this is the first concrete evidence that has ever been presented to justify the French officer's execution. Also see Francis, *Miners against Fascism*, 224. As for the general issue of spies in the brigades, see Jackson, *Fallen Sparrows*, 108.

91. Elliott is clearly identified in Ralph Cantor's diary but the second is called "Pete," probably Peter Kerrigan. Kerrigan was on the Córdoba front and learned of LaSalle's arrest but denies having been at the trial. See interview with Peter Kerrigan, SRC, 810/6, Reel 2.

92. Diary of Ralph Cantor, January 3, 1937, Salford.

93. Interview with Maurice Levine, February 10, 1977, Manchester, 36. See Levine, *Cheetham to Cordova*, 36. Levine had no doubt about LaSalle's guilt. The Dutch interpreter at the trial told him that LaSalle had confessed to spying against the Russians when he had been an attaché at Bucharest.

94. Interview with Fred Copeman, 1976, SRC, 794/13, 123.

95. Carr, *The Spanish Tragedy*, 143.

96. For an explanation of the origins of the GPU, OGPU, and the NKVD, as well as the eventual merging of the latter two in 1934, see Bolloten, *Spanish Revolution*, 529, n. 26.

97. See Carroll, *Odyssey of the Abraham Lincoln Brigade*, 196. Joe Garber, a volunteer from the East End, served with the SIM for two years, working undercover, performing interrogations, examining correspondence, and picking up deserters. Interview with Joe Garber, 1991, SRC, 12291/10, Reel 10.

98. Fond 545, op. 6, d. 175, l. 42, Moscow.

99. Carroll, *Odyssey of the Abraham Lincoln Brigade*, 186–87, 233. Bob Gladnick's judgment of De Maio was unsparing. "He became the GPU man. . . . He would have the job of picking up stragglers all over Spain, and bring them here, and shooting them. And he used to brag and tell me how he used to shoot the sons of bitches." See Brandeis, Interview with Robert Gladnick, January 21–22, 1980, 258.

100. Fond 545, d. 168, ll. 29–29v., 30, Moscow.

101. Costello and Tsarev, *Deadly Illusions*, 258, 268, 275–76, 279, 269. This is a study of General Alexander Orlov, which is rooted in the Russian archives.

102. Krivitsky, *I Was Stalin's Agent*, 121.

103. James Griffiths Papers, January 25, 1938, typescript, Swansea, 80.

104. Interview with Tom Murray, *Scottish Labour History Society Journal* 11, May 1977, 36.

105. Fond 545, op. 6, d. 110, ll. 49–50, Moscow.

106. Green, *Spain against Fascism*, 22.

107. Fond 545, op. 6, d. 142, l. 92, Moscow.

108. Ibid., Fond 545, op. 6, d. 142, ll. 92, 95.

109. Typescript, "A Chronicle of Small Beer," MML, Box A-15, 13, 59–62, 66–67.

110. Ibid.

111. Ibid., 67.

112. Fond 545, op. 6, d. 88, l. 13, Moscow.

113. While Nan and George Green were in Spain, Wogan Philips paid for the education of their children at Summerhill.

114. Alexander, *British Volunteers for Liberty*, 248.

115. Not far from the frontier, the German writer and volunteer, Gustav Regler, came upon Marty and several of his henchmen who appeared to be preparing to massacre a group of brigaders. Regler speculated that they knew too much about Marty and the Communist party's behavior in Spain. Fortunately, as Regler records in *Owl of Minerva*, 324–25, he was able to prevent the atrocity.

116. This may conceivably be the Bulgarian communist, "Stepanov," who worked with Orlov. His real name was S. Mineff but he used many aliases. See Thomas, *Spanish Civil War*, 123, n. 2, and Costello and Tsarev, *Deadly Illusions*, 280.

117. PRO, FO 371/22625 152833, George Wattis to Sir Smedley Crooke.

118. Ibid.,,, FO 371/22624 152833. If the foreign office minute is to be believed, Wattis claimed he was "the commander of the 15th International Brigade." This, of course, was not the case. He *had* been briefly the commander of the British Battalion during the Retreats, but only because of highly unusual circumstances. Upon his return from hospital, the battalion reverted to Sam Wild's command with the Ebro offensive ahead of them. Copic still commanded the brigade until he turned over his duties to the Spaniard, Major Valledor, who led the XVth Brigade across the Ebro in July. If, indeed, Wattis so misidentified himself, it may have been for the purpose of getting the government's attention so that preparations for the battalion's evacuation might begin.

119. Ibid.,,, FO 371/21296 W12911/1/41.

120. Interview with Fred Copeman, 1976, SRC, 794/13, 109–10. There is absolutely no evidence that this was the case. Tapsell died at Calaceite when the battalion was ambushed by the Italians. Merriman apparently died somewhere outside Corbera during the Retreats. See Merriman and Lerude, *American Commander in Spain*, 219–33.

121. Quoted in Blaazer, *The Popular Front and the Progressive Tradition*, 165.

122. Morgan, *Pollitt*, 96.

123. Interview with Fred Copeman, August 2, 1976, Manchester, 38, 113.

124. Francis, *Miners against Fascism*, 230.

125. Aron, *The Opium of the Intellectuals*, 211–12.

126. M., "This Is a Democratic War!" *London Forward* 8, March 4, 1939, 15.

127. One of these was the well-connected ambulance driver, Wogan Philips, who left Spain at such an early date that his preconceptions remained intact. Married to Rosamond Lehmann, the novelist and sister of John, he

was the scion of a privileged family. He was wounded while attached to the Franco-Belge battalion taking part in a Republican offensive in the Guadar-ramas. In his memoir, Wogan Phillips said the commissars "were there to hear even the smallest complaint, discuss it, and try to put it right. Every-thing was to be explained. There were no orders that could not be discussed. . . . Their job was to be the friend of every single soldier, and always accessible." See "An Ambulance Man in Spain," in *New Writing*, New Series, Autumn 1938, in Cunningham, ed., *Spanish Front*, 46–47. After his evacu-ation, the commissar of his battalion accused its commander, Lt. Col. LaSalle, of being a spy for Franco. LaSalle was executed, perhaps as part of an André Marty– inspired intrigue.

128. Fond 545, op. 6, d. 87, l. 20, Moscow.
129. Ibid.
130. I am not suggesting that if the Republic had won the war, Spain would inevitably have become another communist satellite. My remarks are con-fined to what occurred in the British Battalion.

Chapter Thirteen

1. Peet, "Spain—Some of the Nuts and Bolts," MML, 17, 33–34.
2. Fond 545, op. 6, d. 21, ll. 3, 7, Moscow. This document is an analysis of the brigade after it put down its arms. In some units of the XVth Brigade, such as the Canadian MacKenzie-Papineaus, the party did not begin to function as "an organized force" until the actual withdrawal of the Interna-tional Brigades.
3. Ibid., Fond 545, op. 6, d. 21, l. 4.
4. Francis, *Miners against Fascism*, 236. Francis effectively utilizes the memoir that Griffiths wrote in 1964 for an adult education class. Although I rely on the same source, I see Griffiths' story as more central, illustrating the lengths to which the party was willing to go in order to maintain internal control of the battalion. Bill Alexander refers to Griffiths as a building worker, perhaps referring to his career either before or after he was a miner. See his *British Volunteers for Liberty*, 202.
5. Billy Griffiths memoir, March 15, 1964, Swansea, 1.
6. Ibid., 2.   7. Ibid., 5, 7.
8. Ibid., 8.   9. Ibid., 9.
10. Ibid., 8–9.   11. Ibid., 11.
12. For a discussion of the relationship between the individual soldier and his unit in wartime see Holmes, *Acts of War*, 25–27.
13. Peet, "Spain—Some of the Nuts and Bolts," MML, 14.
14. PRO, FO 371/22645 XC152896, 267. Lambert swore he was a former front-line soldier and officer who had been wounded at the Jarama. Though he suffered subsequent serious health problems, he served until April 17, 1938, when he was ordered back into the front lines, despite the fact that his health remained poor. As a result, he left Spain. His deposition found a place in the Special Branch file prepared for a possible prosecution of Fred Copeman.

15. Fond 545, op. 6, d. 143, Moscow.

16. Billy Griffiths memoir, Swansea, 16.

17. Ibid., 20.

18. Ibid., 25, 29.

19. Ibid., 30.

20. Gregory, *The Shallow Grave*, 89.

21. Guest, "Reasons for My Decision. 1938," in Carmel Haden Guest, ed., *David Guest*, 140.

22. Ibid., 145.

23. Gregory, *The Shallow Grave*, 93.

24. Billy Griffiths memoir, Swansea, 30.

25. Fond 545, op. 6, d. 143, ll., 11, 14, 18, 22, Moscow.

26. See, however, Gregory's views on Copic in *The Shallow Grave*, 59. According to Gregory, he was "never the subject of criticism."

27. Billy Griffiths memoir, 31, Swansea.

28. In his memoir, Griffiths calls his company commander, "MacNulty," but this is presumably a mistake.

29. Ibid., 31–32.

30. Interview with Benny Goodman, February 23, 1977, Manchester, 33. Goodman said of Wild, "He wasn't a Communist, nothing at all; I don't think he was nothing at the time. But . . . I've never seen a man with guts and nerves like this kid, never."

31. Billy Griffiths memoir, Swansea, 33.

32. Ibid.

33. Ibid., 36; interview with Frederick Arthur Thomas, 1986, SRC, 9396/8, Reel 8.

34. Billy Griffiths memoir, Swansea, 38–39.

35. Jackson, *The Spanish Republic and the Civil War*, 404–6; Bolloten, *The Spanish Revolution*, 574, n. 73.

36. MacDougall, ed., *Voices from the Spanish Civil War*, 102–3. According to Murray he was in the Anti-Tank Battery on the Jarama Front when he was wounded. Apparently, he returned to the battery after his recovery because Bill Alexander places him there at the time of the Ebro offensive. If this was true, then it appears he was acting secretly as a counterespionage agent at the same time he was serving in the Anti-Tanks. See Alexander, *British Volunteers for Liberty*, 204.

37. Interview with Lillian Buckoke, February 28, 1978, Manchester, 2, 15.

38. Ibid., 28, 15, 2, 28, 25, 47, 46. On the other hand, Winifred Sandford, the wife of Ralph Bates, who helped coordinate the activities of volunteer nurses, claims that few were politically motivated. According to her, their reasons for going to Spain were humanitarian. (See interview with Sandford, August 1, 1976, Manchester.) Nevertheless, Buckoke refused to join the Communist party, which made her feel politically suspect, a view she staunchly held to when interviewed by the author in November 1981.

39. Billy Griffiths memoir, Swansea, 43.

40. Ibid., 44.

41. Ibid., 47.

42. Ibid, 45. See interview with Benny Goodman, February 23, 1977, Manchester, 33. For Wild's illness there is corroborating evidence in his final evaluation before repatriation. Fond 545, op. 6, d. 215, 30, Moscow.

43. Ibid., 40.

44. Ibid., 49.

45. Ibid., 50.

46. Vivian Cadden, "Reunion of the Spanish Brigades," in *The Nation* 19, December 4, 1976, 594.

47. Interview with Sam Wild, BBC Tapes, 1974, Manchester, 85.

48. Gregory, *The Shallow Grave*, 120.

49. Ibid., 120–23, 88.

50. Billy Griffiths memoir, Swansea, 56–57.

51. Ibid., 65–66.

52. Quoted in *International Brigade Memorial Souvenir*, MML, 25.

53. Interview with Bill Bailey, August 8, 1980, Brandeis, 132–33.

54. *International Brigade Memorial Souvenir*, 57.

55. Billy Griffiths memoir, Swansea, 58.

56. See Bessie's *Men in Battle*, 270 – 95.

57. Billy Griffiths memoir, Swansea, 61.

58. Interview with Jim Brewer, November 29, 1969, Swansea, 21.

59. Billy Griffiths memoir, Swansea, 74.

60. Ibid., 81.

61. Ibid., 82–83.

62. Fond 545, op. 6, d. 139, l. 61, Moscow.

63. Ibid., d. 22, l. 51.

64. Gregory, *The Shallow Grave*, 177.

65. Quoted in *The Voice of Spain*, December 28, 1940, 361.

66. Fred Copeman to Sam Wild, n.d., MML.

67. Ibid.

68. PRO, FO 371/22698 XC152896. This is a letter from the British Consul in Paris making arrangements for the return of the British Battalion.

69. December 8, 1938, quoted in Watkins, *Britain Divided*, 171.

70. Symons, *The Thirties*, 165.

71. Quoted in Baldwin, *Bill Feeley*, 5.

72. Stedman Jones, *Languages of Class*, 238.

Chapter Fourteen

1. A telegram from J. Pilchik and N. Weiner to the International Brigade Dependents' Aid Committee, 1938, MML.

2. Williams, Alexander, and Gorman, *Memorials of the Spanish Civil War*, 68.

3. Vivian Cadden, "Reunion of the Spanish Brigades," *The Nation* 19, December 4, 1976, 596.

4. Foot, Preface, *No Pasaran!* 5.

5. Hobsbawm, *The Age of Extremes*, 160.

6. Fond 545, op. 6, d. 101, ll. 66, 69, 71, Moscow.

7. Unpublished ms., May 22, 1941, in David Fernbach's entry on Tom Wintringham in Bellamy and Saville, eds., *Dictionary of Labour Biography* 7: 258.

8. April 11, 1940, in Orwell, *The Collected Essays, Journalism and Letters*, 1: 531.

9. Wood, *Communism and British Intellectuals*, 197.

10. Macmillan, "Pat Murphy, 1898–1974," 1, 26.

11. Megan Laird, "A Diary of Revolution: Day by Day in Barcelona," in *Atlantic Monthly* 5, November 1936, 513.

12. Of course, these views were those of foreigners who created a myth about the Catalán city. See Michael Seidman's essay, "The UnOrwellian Barcelona," in *European History Quarterly* 2, April 1990, 163–80. Seidman argues that Orwell imposed his socialist ideals on the city and he, as did others, saw what he wanted to see.

13. Borkenau, *The Spanish Cockpit*, 69.

14. Orwell, *Homage to Catalonia*, 4–5.

15. To Cyril Connolly, June 8, 1937, in *Collected Essays, Journalism and Letters of George Orwell*, 1: 269.

16. Gurney, *Crusade in Spain*, 49.

17. His name was sometimes spelled Cook.

18. Acier, ed., *From Spanish Trenches*, 98.

19. Worsley, *Fellow Travellers*, 208.

20. Interview with Donald Renton in *Scottish Labour History Society Journal* 11, May 1977, 19.

21. See Blaazer's *The Popular Front and the Progressive Tradition*.

22. Pollitt, *Labour and Spain*, 488–89.

23. Gorman, *To Build Jerusalem*, 167.

24. Interview with Jack Edwards, August 3, 1976, Manchester, 14.

25. *Volunteer for Liberty* 6, March 1942, 10.

26. Diary of Ralph Cantor, n. 4, Salford.

27. *British Battalion: XV Brigade Roll of Honour*, 39.

28. Frank Owen to his wife and children, May 24, 1937, in Sydenham, "Did They Die in Vain: The International Brigade—A Compilation of Facts," typescript, Swansea, 10.

29. Rust, *Britons in Spain*, 131.

30. George Leeson makes this point as well in "There's a Valley in Spain," *Spain Today*, February 1947, 5.

31. Interview with Bill Bailey, August 8, 1980, Brandeis, 119.

32. Frank Owen to his wife and children, May 24, 1937, in Sydenham, "Did They Die in Vain," typescript, Swansea, 9–10.

33. Bob Cooney, "Proud Journey," MML, Box A-15/3, 155.

34. Corkill and Rawnsley, *The Road to Spain*, 20–21.

35. Barke, *Land of the Leal*, 608–9.

36. Tom McWhirter to Peter Kerrigan, February 7, 1938, MML.

37. "Leaders All," *Volunteer for Liberty* 8, May 8, 1940, 24–25.

38. Judith Cook, "For Freedom's Sake . . . ," *Western Mail*, March 3, 1979.

39. Ms. "Citations: British Battalion—International Brigades," MML.

40. Cook, *Apprentices of Freedom*, 145.

41. *The Volunteer* 1, Winter 1993, 7.

42. Ibid.; see Fyrth, *The Signal Was Spain*, 123.

43. *The Volunteer*, 7. For the exceptional career of the volunteer, David Mackenzie, see *Scottish Labour History Journal* 11, May 1977, 41.

44. For an example, see John Saville's entry on Donald Renton in Bellamy and Saville, eds., *Dictionary of Labour Biography*, 9: 246.

45. Buchanan, "Britain's Popular Front?" 64; Fyrth, *The Signal*, 21.

46. Quoted in Salter and Stevenson, *The Working Class and Politics in Europe and America*, 147.

47. Quoted in Watkins, *Britain Divided*, 84.

48. Pollitt, *Spain and the T.U.C.*, 6.

49. "Reply to Winston Churchill," *Spanish News*, January 15, 1937.

50. *Evening Standard*, August 10, 1936, quoted in Pollitt, *Arms for Spain*, 11–12.

51. Taylor, *From the Boer War to the Cold War*, 423.

52. Churchill, *The Gathering Storm*, 167.

53. Watkins, *Britain Divided*, 251. Also see Gilbert, *Churchill's Political Philosophy*, 98. Dorothy Boyd Rush discusses the shifts in Churchill's position in her "Winston Churchill and the Spanish Civil War," *Social Science* 2, 1979, 86–92.

54. Pollitt, *Arms for Spain*, 11.

55. Sam Wild, "Four Years Ago: The Formation of the Brigades," *Volunteer for Liberty* 9, December 8, 1940, 11.

56. Rust, *Spain Fights for Victory*, 14; quoted in Thomas, *Spanish Civil War*, 792–93, n. 2.

57. Fyrth, ed., *Labour's High Noon*, 271. Baldwin, *Bill Feeley*, 2.

58. Quoted in Laqueur, *Europe since Hitler*, 41.

59. Pollitt, *Spain and the T.U.C.*, 7.

60. Nan Green to Aileen Palmer, March 26, 1946, MML.

61. Quoted in Baldwin, *Bill Feeley*, 2.

62. As Arthur Marwick points out, despite the quotations that Greenwood chose to emphasize class struggle, his novel is an essay in resignation. See "Images of the Working Class since 1930," in Winter, ed., *The Working Class in Modern British History*, 222–24.

63. Norman Jackson, "The Men Who Fought for Peace," *Manchester Evening News*, February 14, 1975, 8.

64. Typescript, remarks at the memorial service for Sam Wild, Salford, 5–7.

65. Ibid.

66. Box A-12 Wi, MML.

67. Ibid., William Scott, a letter dated October 18, 1975, attached to an article, "Yesterday's Horrors Today's Memories," *Grimsby Evening Telegraph*, November 21, 1975.

68. Spender, *World within World*, 249.

69. Pollitt, *Arms for Spain*, 24.

70. N.A., *In Spain with the International Brigade*, 39.

71. Scherf, ed., *Collected Poetry of Malcolm Lowry*, 93–94.

72. Breit and Lowry, *Malcolm Lowry*, 63. There is an existing copy of Sommerfield's book that apparently once belonged to Lowry, or at least he felt free enough to write a poem in it.

73. Ibid., 182, 134.

74. To Jonathan Cape [January 2, 1946], in Grace, ed., *Sursum Corda!* 1: 515.

75. Bowker in Vice, ed., *Malcom Lowry Eighty Years On*, 152.

76. Bowker, *Pursued by Furies*, 130, 168, 185, 194–95, 200, 216, 228.

77. Ibid., xvii.

78. Lowry, *Under the Volcano*, 35.

79. Ibid., 267, 306, 340, 404.

80. The account of Clem Beckett is taken from Edmund and Ruth Frow's *Clem Beckett*. Also see *Clem Beckett: Hero and Sportsman* (Manchester: Manchester Dependents' Aid Committee, 1937), as well as an interview with Mary Whitehead (Beckett's sister), March 15, 1978, Manchester. In addition to other interesting information, she says that Beckett spoke Spanish.

81. Interview with Joe Norman [1976], Manchester, 3.

82. Leda Beckett, "My Clem," Salford.

83. Edmund and Ruth Frow, "Clem Beckett and the Oldham Men Who Fought in Spain, 1936–1938," typescript, n.p.

84. Interview with Maurice Levine, 1987, SRC, 9722/6, Reel 4.

85. Interview with Frank Graham, January 28, 1977, Manchester, 34.

86. Frow, "Clem Beckett,", n.p.

87. Ibid.

88. Fond 545, op. 6, d. 105, l. 14, Moscow.

89. MML, Box C 9/8, January 19, 1936.

90. To Theo, December 9, 17, 1936, Texas.

91. Ibid., to T. Stanhope Sprigg, n.d., 1935.

92. Ibid., Stuart Samuels to Theo, December 14, 1966. Samuels conducted research in the Communist party archives, where he found a letter from Caudwell to the party outlining his reasons for remaining in Spain, thus clearing up the mystery of why the writer didn't return to England after delivering his ambulance.

93. Ibid., to Bottle, January 24, 1937.

94. Ibid.

95. Ibid., to Nick [Cox], January 7, 1937.

96. Ibid., to John Larmour, January 6 [or 7], 1937.

97. Ibid., to Theo and Vida, January 14, 1937.

98. Ibid.

99. Ibid., to Peggy, January 24, 1937.

100. Ibid., to the Poplar Branch, January 24.

101. Ibid., to Hart, January 30, 1937.

102. Ibid., to Theo and Vida, January 30, 1937.

103. Ibid., to Peg, January 30, 1937.

104. Graham, *Battle of Jarama*, 67; interview with Frank Graham, 1991, SRC, 11877/6, Reel 2.

105. Len Cockran to Peggy, March 10, 1937, Texas.

106. Ibid., Len Cockran to T. Stanhope Sprigg, May 24, 1937.

107. Ibid., Fred Copeman to Theo, n.d. See Phil Gillan, *The Defence of Madrid*. Gillan fought in the battles of Madrid in the early months of the war before being wounded. He reserved his greatest admiration for the Poles who always kept their heads "and on the single occasion we had to retreat, they did some heroic work bringing back every single machine gun and piece of ammunition." See Gillan, *Madrid*, 4. It is hard to imagine either St. John Sprigg or Beckett forgetting the lock in his machine gun. Each was in his own way something of a mechanical genius. Certainly, no one can judge either of them in such a situation. But, St. John Sprigg aside, it is extremely difficult to think of the fearless Beckett, who had faced death innumerable times on the race track, "panicking" and abandoning the gun without retrieving the lock.

108. C. B. Gray to Theo, March 10, 1937, Texas.

109. Ibid., Maurice Cornforth to Theo, February 28, 1966.

110. Ibid., Fred Copeman to Theo, n.d.

111. Christopher Caudwell, "To Aldous Huxley," *Left Review*, 11, December 1937, 657–60.

112. "Far from their Homeland," *In Memoriam*, September 16, 1938, Birmingham Town Hall.

113. Cook, *Apprentices of Freedom*, 147, 144.

114. Interviews with Donald Renton and Tommy Bloomfield, *Scottish Labour History Society* 11, May 1977, 22, 33.

115. Cook, *Apprentices of Freedom*, 146.

116. Jim Brewer to Ben Bowen Thomas, Warden of Coleg Harlech, June 20, 1937, Swansea.

117. Fond 545, op. 3, d. 480, l. 158, Moscow. This is part of a long handwritten account about the Jarama battle by Tom Wintringham.

118. Edinburgh, Box 1 (6).

119. R. F. Willets, *Envoi*, no. 15, 1962, quoted in E. P. Thompson, "Caudwell," in *The Socialist Register* 1977, 272.

Chapter Fifteen

1. Hynes, *A War Imagined*, 467–68.

2. Bob Cooney, "Proud Journey," MML, Box A 15/3, 127.

3. Gathorne-Hardy, *Gerald Brenan*, 307–10.

4. Ibid., 305, 314–15. The Liverpool novelist and pacifist, Olaf Stapledon, deserves an honorable place among those who refused to succumb to political didacticism. Although Stapledon supported the Republic in significant public and private ways, he wrote a distinctly unsentimental review of Caudwell's *Studies in a Dying Culture*. Stung by the author's contempt for pacifism, Stapledon charged him with "the blindness and ruthlessness of the

young man who is so dazzled by one truth that he neglects all others." See Crossley, *Stapledon*, 239.

5. Ibid., 315–16; Brenan, *Personal Record*, 335.

6. Shelden, *Friends of Promise*, 163, 37, 45.

7. Rowse, *The Poet Auden*, 85.

8. Ian Hamilton, "Spender's Lives," *New Yorker* 2, February 28, 1994, 72, 80, 84. The fiftieth anniversary of the Spanish Civil War was the occasion of a heated exchange in the United States between Ronald Radosh, whose uncle died in Spain, and Irving Howe concerning what posterity should conclude from the attitude of intellectuals toward Spain. Radosh shows little but contempt for those who believed that the defense of the Republic was a just cause. Among others who took part were Alfred Kazin and Bernard Knox. See Alfred Kazin, "The Wound That Will Not Heal: Writers and the Spanish Civil War," in *New Republic* 195, August 25, 1986, 39–41. Also, Bernard Knox "The Spanish Civil War," in *New York Review of Books* 24, March 26, 1987, 21–28; and Ronald Radosh and Bernard Knox, "'The Spanish Tragedy': An Exchange," also in *New York Review of Books* 34, June 23, 1987, 52–53, 84.

9. Inglis, *Radical Earnestness*, 202.

10. Orwell, *Keep the Aspidistra Flying*, 202. The title was taken from a reference to the plant in *The Ragged Trousered Philanthropists*, a book that moved Comstock to "make friends with the lower classes." Kubal believes the novel "clearly marks Orwell's transition from protest to commitment." See *Outside the Whale*, 89.

11. Thompson would not be pleased with this juxtaposition. He attacked Orwell for his admiration of Henry Miller's pacifism, arguing that his "Inside the Whale" had done more than any work of the forties to create a generation of resigned and despairing "Jimmy Porters." Orwell's appreciation of Miller was nothing less than "an apology for quietism." For a discussion of Orwell's reputation on the left see Norris, ed., *Inside the Myth*, and Rodden, *The Politics of Literary Reputation*, 192–95.

12. Inglis, *Radical Earnestness*, 203.

13. Shelden, *Friends of Promise*, 88, 66.

14. Kermode, *History and Value*, 79–80.

15. Spender, *World within World*, 204.

16. Caute, *The Fellow-Travellers*, 111.

17. "The Ancient Warrior and his Battles of the Past and Present", *Health and Social Service Journal*, 1337, MML.

18. A. L. Cochrane, "Forty Years Back: A Retrospective Survey," *British Medical Journal*, December 22–29, 1979, 1662–63.

19. Ibid. Also see *Health and Social Service Journal*, November 24, 1978, 1336–37.

20. *Health and Social Service Journal*, 1340.

21. Said, *Representations of the Intellectual*, 120–21.

22. Ibid., x–xi.

23. Timothy Garton Ash, "Intellectuals & Politicians in Prague," *New York Review of Books* 1, January 12, 1995, 36–38.

24. Stephen Spender, "Looking Back in 1994: A New Introduction to World within World," in *World within World* (New York: St. Martin's Press, 1994), xiii. In his valediction to Spain, he wrote, "If the Republic had won, and Fascism been defeated on Spanish earth, the course of history would have been altered and the Second World War averted": xvi.

25. Garton Ash, *The File*, 149.

26. Quoted in Erik Nakjavani, "Intellectuals as Militants: Hemingway's *For Whom the Bell Tolls* and Malraux's *L'Espoir*: A Comparative Study," in Brown, ed., *Rewriting the Good Fight*, 202.

27. Havel, "The Responsibility of Intellectuals," *New York Review of Books*, June 22, 1995, 36–37.

28. Fond 545, op. 6, d. 208, ll. 47, 52, Moscow.

29. Ibid., Fond 545, op. 6, d. 109, l. 16.

30. Ibid., Fond 545, op. 6, d. 109, l. 63.

31. The Lanarkshire Roll of Honour (with quotations from veterans killed in Spain), Swansea.

32. MacDougall, ed., *Voices from the Spanish Civil War*, 317.

33. Ibid., 318, 317.

34. Jim Brewer to Ben Thomas, Warden of Coleg Harlech, June 20, 1937, Swansea.

35. Miles Tomalin, "Memories of the Spanish War," in *New Statesman*, October 31, 1975, 541.

36. Sam Lesser, "Madrid Showed the Way," *Volunteer for Liberty*, November–December, 1943.

37. *London Forward*, October 17, 1938, 3.

38. Interview with Huw Alun Williams, 1988, SRC, 10181/5, Reel 5.

39. Fond 545, op. 6, d. 125, l. 80, Moscow.

40. To Jimmy, April 22, 1937, in Acier, ed., *From Spanish Trenches*, 102.

41. Quoted in Blaazer, *The Popular Front and the Progressive Tradition*, 162.

42. Campbell, *The Hero with a Thousand Faces*, 11.

43. Jack Lindsay, "Requiem Mass (for the Englishmen fallen in the International Brigade)," in Cunningham, ed., *The Penguin Book of Spanish Civil War Verse*, 179, 182.

44. *In Proud Memory of the St. Pancras Men Who Died Fighting in the British Battalion of the International Brigade in Spain* (London: International Brigade Dependents' Aid Committee, n.d.). This is a souvenir program.

45. Jack Lindsay, "On Guard for Spain! A Poem for Mass Recitation," in Cunningham, ed., *The Penguin Book of Spanish Civil War Verse*, 262. Lindsay delineates the public and private issues that led to his espousal of Marxism in his autobiography, *Fanfrolico and After*, 252–68. He wrote, "The Civil War had itself affected me as no other event in my whole life," confessing that he was conscience-stricken that he had not joined the British volunteers in Spain.

46. Anon., loose sheets, Salford.

47. Fond 545, op. 6, d. 473, l. 5, Moscow.

Bibliography

Archives

Berg: Berg Collection, New York Public Library.
Brandeis: Abraham Lincoln Brigade Archive, Brandeis University, Waltham, Massachusetts.
Columbia: Special Manuscript Collection, Spanish Refugees, Columbia University.
DMWC: David McKelvie White Collection, New York Public Library.
Edinburgh: Thomas Murray Papers, National Library of Edinburgh.
Manchester: International Brigade Archive, Manchester Metropolitan University.
MML: International Brigade Collection, Marx Memorial Library, London.
Moscow: International Brigade Collection, Russian Center for the Preservation and Study of Recent Historical Documents, Moscow.
PRO: Public Record Office, Kew.
Salford: Spanish Civil War Collection, Working Class Movement Library, Salford.
San Diego: Herbert Southworth Collection, University of California at San Diego.
SRC: Sound Record Collection, Imperial War Museum, London.
Swansea: Spanish Civil War Collection, South Wales Miners' Library, Swansea.
Texas, Christopher Caudwell Collection, Humanities Research Center, University of Texas at Austin.

Secondary Sources

A. "Britons in Spain," *Labour Monthly* 21 (1939).
Abel, Lionel. *The Intellectual Follies: A Memoir of the Literary Venture in New York and Paris.* New York: Norton, 1984.

Academy of Sciences of the USSR. *International Solidarity with the Spanish Republic: 1936–1939.* Moscow: Progress Publishers, 1974.

Acier, Marcel, ed. *From Spanish Trenches: Recent Letters from Spain.* New York: AMS Press, 1983 [orig. ed. 1937].

Ackerley, Chris. *A Companion to "Under the Volcano."* Vancouver: University of British Columbia Press, 1984.

Addison, Paul. *The Road to 1945: British Politics and the Second World War.* London: Pimlico, 1994.

Aldgate, Anthony. *Cinema and History: British Newsreels and the Spanish Civil War.* London: Scolar Press, 1979.

Alexander, Bill. *British Volunteers for Liberty: Spain—1936–39.* London: Lawrence and Wishart, 1986.

Alpert, Michael. "Humanitarianism and Politics in the British Response to the Spanish Civil War, 1936–39," *European History Quarterly* 4, October 1984.

———. *A New International History of the Spanish Civil War.* London: Macmillan, 1994.

Anderson, Perry. "Origins of the Present Crisis," *New Left Review* 23, January–February 1964.

Angus, John. *With the International Brigade in Spain.* Loughborough: Department of Economics, Loughborough University, 1983.

An Anthology of Chartist Literature. Moscow: Publishing House of Literature in Foreign Languages, 1956.

Annan, Noel. "The Intellectual Aristocracy, " in J. H. Plumb, ed. *Studies in Social History: A Tribute to G. M. Trevelyan.* New York: Longmans, Green, 1955.

———. *Our Age: English Intellectuals between the World Wars—A Group Portrait.* New York: Random House, 1990.

Aron, Raymond. *The Opium of the Intellectuals.* Garden City, New York: Doubleday, 1957.

Atholl, Katherine, Duchess of Atholl. *Searchlight on Spain.* Harmondsworth, Middlesex: Penguin, 1938.

Attlee, C. R. *As It Happened.* New York: Viking Press, 1954.

Baldwin, John. *Bill Feeley: Singer, Steel Erector, International Brigader.* St. Helens: The Constructional Division of the AUEW and the Greater Manchester Trade Union Spanish Solidarity Committee, 1987.

Banville, John. *The Untouchable.* New York: Alfred A. Knopf, 1997.

Baring, Maurice. *The Puppet Show of Memory.* London: Cassell, 1987.

Barke, James. *The Land of the Leal.* Introduction by John Burns. Edinburgh: Canongate Classic, 1987.

Bartlett, Lee, ed. *Letters to Christopher: Stephen Spender's Letters to Christopher Isherwood, 1929–1939.* Santa Barbara: Black Sparrow Press, 1980.

Bates, Ralph. *Lean Men: An Episode in a Life.* London: Peter Davies, 1934.

———. *The Olive Field.* London: Hogarth Press, 1986.

———. *Sirocco and Other Stories.* New York: Random House, 1939.

Beeching, William C. *Canadian Volunteers: Spain, 1936–1939.* Regina, Sask.: University of Regina, 1989.

Beevor, Antony. *The Spanish Civil War.* New York: Peter Bedrick Books, 1983.

Beilharz, Peter. *Labour's Utopias: Bolshevism, Fabianism, Social Democracy.* London and New York: Routledge, 1992.

Bell, Anne Olivier, ed. *A Moment's Liberty: The Shorter Diary—Virginia Woolf.* Toronto: Lester and Orpen Dennys, 1990.

Bell, Quentin, ed. *Julian Bell: Essays, Poems and Letters.* London: Hogarth Press, 1938.

Bellah, Robert N., et al. *The Good Society.* New York: Alfred A. Knopf, 1991.

Bellamy, Joyce M. and John Saville, eds. *Dictionary of Labour Biography.* Clifton, New Jersey: A. M. Kelley, 1972—.

Benda, Julien. *The Betrayal of the Intellectuals.* Introduction by Herbert Read. Translated by Richard Aldington. Boston: Beacon Press, 1955 [orig. ed. 1930].

Benson, Frederick. *Writers in Arms: The Literary Impact of the Spanish Civil War.* New York: New York University Press, 1967.

Benson, John. *The Working-Class in Britain, 1850–1939.* London and New York: Longman, 1989.

Bertrand de Muñoz, Maryse. *La Guerra Civil Española en la Novela: Bibliografía Comentada.* Madrid: J. Porrua Turanzas, 1982.

Bessie, Alvah. *Men in Battle.* New York: Veterans of the Abraham Lincoln Brigade, 1954.

——— and Albert Prago, eds. *Our Fight: Writings by Veterans of the Abraham Lincoln Brigade: Spain, 1936–1939.* New York: Monthly Review Press, 1987.

Biagini, Eugenio F. and Alastair J. Reid. *Currents of Radicalism: Popular Radicalism, Organised Labour and Party Politics in Britain, 1850–1914.* New York: Cambridge University Press, 1991.

Blaazer, David. *The Popular Front and the Progressive Tradition: Socialists, Liberals, and the Quest for Unity, 1884–1939.* New York: Cambridge University Press, 1992.

Blythe, Ronald. *The Age of Illusion.* Boston: Houghton Mifflin, 1964.

Bolloten, Burnett. *The Spanish Civil War: Revolution and Counterrevolution.* Chapel Hill and London: University of North Carolina Press, 1991.

———. *The Spanish Revolution: The Left and the Struggle for Power during the Civil War.* Chapel Hill: University of North Carolina Press, 1979.

Borkenau, Franz. *The Spanish Cockpit: An Eye-witness Account of the Political and Social Conflicts of the Spanish Civil War.* London: Faber and Faber, 1937.

Bowker, Gordon. *Pursued by Furies: A Life of Malcolm Lowry.* London: Harper Collins, 1993.

———, ed. *Malcolm Lowry Remembered.* London: BBC, 1985.

Bradbrook, M. C. *Malcolm Lowry: His Art and Early Life, A Study in Transformation.* Cambridge: Cambridge University Press, 1974.

Brailsford, Henry N. *Socialism for Today*. London: New Leader, 1927.

Branson, Noreen. *Britain in the Nineteen Twenties*. Minneapolis: University of Minnesota Press, 1976.

———. *History of the Communist Party of Great Britain, 1927–1941*. London: Lawrence and Wishart, 1985.

Branson, Noreen, and Margot Heinemann. *Britain in the Nineteen Thirties*. London: Weidenfeld and Nicolson, 1971.

Breit, Harvey, and Margerie Bonner Lowry. *Malcolm Lowry: Selected Letters*. Harmondsworth: Penguin Books, 1985.

Brenan, Gerald. *Personal Record: 1920 –1972*. New York: Knopf, 1975.

———. *South from Granada*. Baltimore: Penguin Books, 1963.

———. *The Spanish Labyrinth: An Account of the Social and Political Background of the Civil War*. Cambridge: Cambridge University Press, 1978 [orig. pub. 1943].

Briggs, Asa, and John Saville, eds. *Essays in Labour History: In Memory of G. D. H. Cole*. London: Macmillan and Co., 1960.

Brockway, Fenner. *A Lead to World Socialism on Spain, War, Fascism, Imperialism: Report of Revolutionary Socialist Congress*. Brussels, October 31–November 2, 1936.

Brome, Vincent. *The International Brigades*. London: Heinemann, 1965.

Broué, Pierre, and Émile Témime. *The Revolution and Civil War in Spain*. London: Faber and Faber, 1970.

Brown, Frieda, et al. *Rewriting the Good Fight: Critical Essays on the Literature of the Spanish Civil War*. East Lansing: Michigan State University Press, 1989.

Brown, Kenneth D. *The English Labour Movement: 1700 –1951*. New York: St. Martin's Press, 1982.

———, ed. *Essays in Anti-Labour History: Responses to the Rise of Labour in Britain*. London: Macmillan, 1974.

Browne, Harry. *Spain's Civil War*. Harlowe, Essex: Longman, 1983.

Buchanan, Tom. *Britain and the Spanish Civil War*. Cambridge: Cambridge University Press, 1997.

———. "Britain's Popular Front? Aid Spain and the British Labour Movement," *History Workshop* 31, Spring 1991, 60 –73.

———. "The Death of Bob Smillie, the Spanish Civil War, and the Eclipse of the Independent Labour Party," *The Historical Journal* 2, June 1997, 435–61.

———. "'A Far Away Country of Which We Know Nothing'?: Perceptions of Spain and its Civil War in Britain, 1931–1939." *Twentieth Century British History* 1 (1993), 1–24.

———. *The Spanish Civil War and the British Labour Movement*. Cambridge: Cambridge University Press, 1991.

Buckley, Henry. *The Life and Death of the Spanish Republic*. London: Hamish Hamilton, 1940.

Bucknell, Katherine, and Nicholas Jenkins, eds. *W. H. Auden: "The Map of All My Youth."* Oxford: Clarendon Press, 1990.

Campbell, John. *Edward Heath: A Biography*. London: Pimlico, 1993.

Campbell, Joseph. *The Hero with a Thousand Faces*. New York: Pantheon, 1949.

Campbell, J. R. *Spain's Left Critics*. London: CPGB, 1937.

Carew, Anthony. *The Lower Deck of the Royal Navy, 1900–1939: The Invergordon Mutiny in Perspective*. Manchester: Manchester University Press, 1981.

Carey, John. *The Intellectuals and the Masses: Pride and Prejudice among the Literary Intelligentsia, 1880–1939*. London: Faber and Faber, 1992.

Carpenter, Humphrey. *A Serious Character: The Life of Ezra Pound*. Boston: Houghton Mifflin, 1988.

———. *The Brideshead Generation: Evelyn Waugh and His Friends*. Boston: Houghton Mifflin, 1990.

Carr, E. H. *The Comintern and the Spanish Civil War*. New York: Pantheon, 1984.

———. *Socialism in One Country, 1924–1926*. Vol. 3. London: Macmillan, 1964.

Carr, Raymond. "Heroes and Guerrilleros: Spanish Communists in Moscow, France, and the Death Camps." *Times Literary Supplement*, December 17, 1993.

———. *Modern Spain: 1808–1975*. 2d ed. Oxford: Clarendon Press, 1982.

———. *The Spanish Tragedy: The Civil War in Perspective*. London: Weidenfeld and Nicolson, 1977.

Carroll, Peter N. *The Odyssey of the Abraham Lincoln Brigade: Americans in the Spanish Civil War*. Stanford: Stanford University Press, 1994.

Carson, Tom. "With the International Brigades in Nicaragua: Beside the Sandinistas." *Village Voice* 20, May 19, 1987.

Castells, Andreu. *Las Brigadas Internacionales de la Guerra de España*. Barcelona: Ariel, 1974.

Cattell, David. *Communism and the Spanish Civil War*. Berkeley: University of California Press, 1955.

Caudwell, Christopher. *Collected Poems, 1924–1936*. Introduction by Alan Young. Manchester: Carcanet, 1986.

———. *Illusion and Reality: A Study of the Sources of Poetry*. London: Lawrence and Wishart, 1946.

———. *Romance and Realism: A Study in English Bourgeois Literature*. Introduction by Samuel Hynes. Princeton: Princeton University Press, 1970.

———. *Studies in a Dying Culture*. Introduction by John Strachey. Westport, Conn.: Greenwood Press, 1973 [orig. ed. 1938].

———. *This My Hand*. London: Hamish Hamilton, 1936.

Caute, David. *The Fellow-Travellers*. Rev. ed. New Haven: Yale University Press, 1988.

Chalmers Mitchell, Sir Peter. *My House in Málaga*. London: Faber and Faber, 1938.

Chomsky, Noam. "Objectivity and Liberal Scholarship," *The Chomsky Reader*. Edited by James Peck. New York: Pantheon, 1987.

Churchill, Winston. *The Gathering Storm*. Boston: Houghton Mifflin, 1948.

Citrine, Sir Walter. *I Search for Truth in Soviet Russia*. London: George Routledge and Sons, 1936.

———. *Men and Work*. London: Hutchinson, 1964.

Clark, Bob. *No Boots To My Feet*. Stoke on Trent: Student Bookshops Ltd., 1984.

Clark, Jon, Margot Heinemann, et al., eds. *Culture and Crisis in Britain in the Thirties*. London: Lawrence and Wishart, 1979.

Clark, Ronald. *J. B. S. Haldane: The Life and Work of J. B. S. Haldane*. London: Hodder and Stoughton, 1968.

Clarke, J., C. Critcher, and R. Johnson. *Working-Class Culture: Studies in History and Theory*. New York: St. Martin's Press, 1979.

Cloud, Stanley, and Lynne Olson. *The Murrow Boys: Pioneers on the Front Lines of Broadcast Journalism*. Boston: Houghton Mifflin, 1996.

Cockburn, Claud. *Cockburn in Spain: Despatches from the Spanish Civil War*. Edited by James Pettifer. London: Lawrence and Wishart, 1986 [orig. ed. 1936].

———. *In Time of Trouble: An Autobiography*. London: Rupert Hart-Davis, 1956.

Collum, Danny Duncan, ed. *African Americans in the Spanish Civil War: "This Ain't Ethiopia, But It'll Do."* New York: G. K. Hall, 1992.

Colodny, Robert. *The Struggle for Madrid: The Central Epic of the Spanish Conflict*. New York: Paine-Whitman, 1958.

Connolly, Cyril. *Enemies of Promise*. Boston: Little, Brown and Company, 1939.

Constantine, Stephen. *Social Conditions in Britain, 1918–1939*. London and New York: Methuen, 1983.

Cook, Judith. *Apprentices of Freedom*. London: Quartet Books, 1979.

Coombes, John E. *Writing from the Left: Socialism, Liberalism and the Popular Front*. New York: Harvester Wheatsheaf, 1989.

Copeman, Fred. *Reason in Revolt*. London: Blandford Press, 1948.

Corkill, David, and Stuart Rawnsley. *The Road to Spain: Anti-Fascists at War, 1936–1939*. Dunfermline, Fife: Borderline Press, 1981.

Coser, Lewis A. *Men of Ideas: A Sociologist's View*. New York: Free Press, 1965.

Costello, John, and Oleg Tsarev, *Deadly Illusions*. New York: Crown, 1993.

Coward, Jack. *Back from the Dead*. Introduction by Alan O'Toole and John Nettleton. Preface by R. Gordon Patterson. Liverpool: Merseyside Writers, n.d. [orig. ed. 1939].

Cox, Geoffrey. *Defence of Madrid*. London: Victor Gollancz, 1937.

Crick, Bernard. *George Orwell: A Life*. Boston: Little, Brown, 1980.

Cronin, James E. *Labour and Society in Britain: 1918–1979*. London: Batsford, 1984.

————, and Jonathan Schneer, eds. *Social Conflict and the Political Order in Modern Britain*. New Brunswick: Rutgers University Press, 1982.

Crossley, Robert. *Olaf Stapledon: Speaking for the Future*. Liverpool. Liverpool University Press, 1994.

Crossman, Richard, ed. *The God That Failed*. Foreword by Norman Podhoretz. Chicago: Regnery Gateway, 1983 [orig. ed. 1963].

Croucher, Richard. *We Refuse to Starve in Silence*. London: Lawrence and Wishart, 1987.

Cunningham, Valentine. *British Writers of the Thirties*. Oxford: Oxford University Press, 1988.

————. "Marooned in the 30s." *Times Literary Supplement*. 4768, August 19, 1994.

————, ed. *The Penguin Book of Spanish Civil War Verse*. Harmondsworth: Penguin Books, 1980.

————, ed. *Spanish Front: Writers on the Civil War*. New York: Oxford University Press, 1986.

Davenport-Hines, Richard. *Auden*. New York: Pantheon Books, 1995.

David, Hugh. *Stephen Spender: A Portrait with Background*. London: William Heinemann, 1992.

Day Lewis, C. *The Buried Day*. New York: Harper and Brothers, 1960.

————. "English Writers & A People's Front," *Left Review* 13, October, 1936.

Day, Douglas. *Malcolm Lowry: A Biography*. New York: Oxford University Press, 1973 [with corrections, 1984].

Delmer, Sefton. *Trail Sinister*. London: Secker and Warburg, 1961.

Drake, Peter, "Labour and Spain: British Labour's Response to the Spanish Civil War with Particular Reference to the Labour Movement in Birmingham," M.Litt. thesis, School of History, University of Birmingham, 1978.

Duparc, Jean, and David Margolies, eds. *Scenes and Actions: Unpublished Manuscripts, Christopher Caudwell*. London and New York: Routledge and Kegan Paul, 1986.

Durán García, Juan. *La Guerra Civil Española, Fuentes: Archivos, Bibliografía y Filmografía*. Prólogo de Gabriel Jackson. Barcelona: Editorial Crítica, 1985.

Dyck, Ian. "Local Attachments, National Identities and World Citizenship in the Thought of Thomas Paine," *History Workshop Journal* 35, Spring 1993.

Eaton, George. *Neath and the Spanish Civil War, 1936–39: Catalyst of the Angry Thirties*. Neath, West Glamorgan: privately published, 1980.

Eby, Cecil. *Between the Bullet and the Lie*. New York: Holt, Rinehart and Winston, 1969.

Edwards, Jill. *The British Government and the Spanish Civil War*. London: Macmillan, 1979.

Ellwood, Sheelagh M. *The Spanish Civil War*. Oxford: Blackwell, 1991.

Ereira, Alan. *The Invergordon Mutiny*. Boston: Routledge and Kegan Paul, 1981.

Esenwein, George, and Adrian Shubert. *Spain at War: The Spanish Civil War in Context, 1931–1939*. London: Longman, 1995.

Falcoff, Mark, and Frederick B. Pike, eds. *The Spanish Civil War, 1936–39: American Hemispheric Perspectives.* Lincoln: University of Nebraska Press, 1982.

Felsen, Milt. *The Anti-Warrior: A Memoir.* Iowa City: University of Iowa, 1989.

Felstead, Richard. *No Other Way: Jack Russia and the Spanish Civil War: A Biography.* Port Talbot, West Glamorgan: Alun Books, 1981.

Femia, Joseph V. *Gramsci's Political Thought: Hegemony, Consciousness, and the Revolutionary Process.* Oxford: Clarendon Press, 1981.

Fiedler, Leslie. "The Two Memories: Reflections on Writers and Writing in the Thirties." In David Madden, ed. *Proletarian Writers of the Thirties.* Carbondale: Southern Illinois University Press, 1968.

Fink, Leon, Stephen T. Leonard, and Donald M. Reid, eds. *Intellectuals and Public Life.* Ithaca: Cornell University Press, 1996.

Fischer, Louis. *Men and Politics: Europe between the Two World Wars.* New York: Harper and Row, 1966 [orig. ed. 1941].

Fisher, Clive. *Cyril Connolly: The Life and Times of England's Most Controversial Literary Critic.* New York: St. Martin's Press, 1996.

Fishman, Nina. *The British Communist Party and the Trade Unions: 1933–45.* Aldershot: Scolar Press, 1995.

Fitzpatrick, Sheila. *The Cultural Front: Power and Culture in Revolutionary Russia.* Ithaca: Cornell University Press, 1992.

Foot, Michael. "Preface" to *No Pasaran! Photographs and Posters of the Spanish Civil War.* Bristol: Arnolfini, 1986.

Foote, Geoffrey. *The Labour Party's Political Thought: A History.* London: Croom Helm, 1986.

Ford, Hugh D. *A Poets' War: British Poets and the Spanish Civil War.* Philadelphia: University of Pennsylvania Press, 1965.

Forster, E. M. *Howards End.* London: Edward Arnold, 1973 [orig. ed. 1921].

Fox, Ralph. "Lawrence the 20th Century Hero," *Left Review* 10, July 1935, 391–96.

———. *A Writer in Arms.* London: Lawrence and Wishart, 1937.

Francis, Hywel. "The Background and Motives of Welsh Volunteers in the International Brigades," *Journal of Oral History* 2, 1981.

———. *Miners against Fascism.* London: Lawrence and Wishart, 1984.

———. "'Say Nothing and Leave in the Middle of the Night': The Spanish Civil War Revisited," *History Workshop* 32, Autumn 1991, 69–76.

———, and David Smith. *The Fed: A History of the South Wales Miners in the Twentieth Century.* London: Lawrence and Wishart, 1980.

Fraser, Ronald. *Blood of Spain: An Oral History of the Spanish Civil War.* New York: Penguin Books, 1981.

Frow, Edmund and Ruth. *Clem Beckett and the Oldham Men Who Fought in Spain.* Salford: Working Class Movement Library, n.d.

Furbank, P. N. *E. M. Forster: A Life.* New York: Harcourt Brace, Jovanovich, 1978.

Fussell, Paul. *Abroad: British Literary Traveling between the Wars*. New York: Oxford University Press, 1980.

———. *The Great War and Modern Memory*. New York: Oxford University Press, 1975.

Fyrth, Jim. *The Signal Was Spain: The Spanish Aid Movement in Britain, 1936–39*. London: Lawrence and Wishart, 1986.

———, ed. *Britain, Fascism, and the Popular Front*. London: Lawrence and Wishart, 1985.

———, ed. Introduction by John Saville. *Labour's High Noon: The Government and the Economy, 1945–1951*. London: Lawrence and Wishart, 1993.

Fyrth, Jim, and Sally Alexander, eds. *Women's Voices from the Spanish Civil War*. London: Lawrence and Wishart, 1991.

Fyvel, Penelope. *English Penny*. Ilfracombe, Devon: Arthur H. Stockwell, 1992.

Galassi, Jonathan, ed. *Understand the Weapon, Understand the Wound: Selected Writings of John Cornford*. Manchester: Carcanet, 1986.

Gallacher, William. *The Last Memoirs*. London: Lawrence and Wishart, 1966.

Gannes, Harry, and Theodore Repard. *Spain in Revolt: A History of the Civil War in Spain in 1936 and a Study of its Social, Political, and Economic Causes*. London: Victor Gollancz, 1936.

Garton Ash, Timothy. *The File: A Personal History*. New York: Random House, 1997.

Gathorne-Hardy, Jonathan. *Gerald Brenan: The Interior Castle*. New York: W. W. Norton and Co., 1993.

Gella, Aleksander, ed. *The Intelligentsia and the Intellectuals: Theory, Method and Case Study*. London: Sage Publications, 1976.

Gellhorn, Martha. *The Face of War*. New York: Atlantic Monthly Press, 1988.

Gibson, Charles, comp. *The Black Legend: Anti-Spanish Attitudes in the Old World and the New*. New York: Alfred A. Knopf, 1971.

Gilbert, Martin. *Churchill's Political Philosophy*. Oxford: Oxford University Press, 1981.

Gillan, Phil. *The Defence of Madrid*. London: CPGB, 1937.

Gloversmith, Frank, ed. *Class, Culture and Social Change: A New View of the 1930s*. Brighton: Harvester Press, 1980.

Gollancz, Victor. *The Betrayal of the Left*. London: Victor Gollancz, 1941.

Goodman, David. "From the Tees to the Ebro: My Road to Spain," typescript, n.d. Working Class Movement Library, Salford.

Goodway, David. *London Chartism: 1838–48*. Cambridge: Cambridge University Press, 1982.

Gorman, John. *To Build Jerusalem: A Photographic Remembrance of British Working Class Life, 1875–1950*. Foreword by Len Murray. London: Scorpion Publications, 1980.

Grace, Sherrill, ed. *Sursum Corda! The Collected Letters of Malcolm Lowry. Volume I: 1921–1946*. Toronto: University of Toronto Press, 1995.

———, ed. *Swinging the Maelstrom: New Perspectives on Malcolm Lowry*. London: McGill–Queen's University, 1992.

Graham, Frank. *Battle of Jarama, 1937: The Story of the British Battalion of the International Brigade in Spain*. Newcastle: Frank Graham, 1987.

Gramsci, Antonio. *Selections from the Prison Notebooks of Antonio Gramsci*. Edited and Translated by Quintin Hoare and Geoffrey Nowell-Smith. New York: International Publishers, 1971.

———. *Letters from Prison*. Introduction and Translation by Lynne Lawner. New York: Harper and Row, 1973.

Graves, Pamela M. *Labour Women: Women in British Working-Class Politics, 1918–1939*. Cambridge: Cambridge University Press, 1994.

Graves, Robert, and Alan Hodge. *The Long Week-End: A Social History of Great Britain, 1918–1939*. New York: W. W. Norton and Company, 1963 [orig. ed. 1940].

Green, Martin. *Children of the Sun: A Narrative of "Decadence" in England after 1918*. New York: Basic Books, 1976.

Green, Nan, and A. M. Elliott, "Spain against Fascism, 1936–39," *Our History*, 67.

Greene, Graham. *A Sort of Life*. New York: Simon and Schuster, 1971.

———. *Ways of Escape*. New York: Simon and Schuster, 1980.

Gregory, Walter. *The Shallow Grave: A Memoir of the Spanish Civil War*. London: Victor Gollancz, 1986.

Griffiths, Richard. *Fellow Travellers of the Right: British Enthusiasts for Nazi Germany, 1933–39*. Oxford: Oxford University Press, 1983.

Gurney, Jason. *Crusade in Spain*. Newton Abbot: Readers Union, 1974.

Guttman, Allen. *The Wound in the Heart: America and the Spanish Civil War*. New York: Free Press of Glencoe, 1962.

Haden Guest, Carmel, ed. *David Guest: A Scientist Fights for Freedom, 1911–1938*. London: Lawrence and Wishart, 1939.

Haldane, Charlotte. *Truth Will Out*. London: G. Weidenfeld and Nicolson, 1949.

Haldane, J. B. S. "International Column," *Spain Illustrated: A Year's Defence of Democracy*. London: Lawrence and Wishart, 1937.

———. *On Being the Right Size and Other Essays*. John Maynard Smith, ed. New York: Oxford University Press, 1985.

Hanley, James. *Grey Children: A Study in Humbug and Misery*. London: Methuen, 1937.

Harman, Claire. *Sylvia Townsend Warner: A Biography*. London: Minerva, 1991.

Harris, Kenneth. *Attlee*. Rev. ed. London: Weidenfeld and Nicolson, 1995.

Harrison, J. F. C. *The Common People of Great Britain. A History from the Norman Conquest to the Present*. Bloomington: Indiana University Press, 1985.

Harrison, Royden, comp. *The English Defence of the Commune, 1871*. London: Merlin Press, 1971.

Havel, Václav. "The Responsibility of Intellectuals," *New York Review of Books* 42, June 22, 1995.

Heaton, P. M. *Welsh Blockade Runners in the Spanish Civil War.* Pontypool, Gwent: The Starling Press, 1985.

Heinemann, Margot. "The People's Front and the Intellectuals." In Jim Fyrth, ed., *Britain, Fascism, and the Popular Front.* London: Lawrence and Wishart, 1985.

Herrick, William. *¡Hermanos!* New York: Simon and Schuster, 1969.

Hewison, Robert. *Under Siege: Literary Life in London: 1939–1945.* London: Weidenfeld and Nicolson, 1977.

Heyck, T. W. "From Men of Letters to Intellectuals: The Transformation of Intellectual Life in Nineteenth-Century Engand," *Journal of British Studies* XX 1, Fall 1980.

Hinton, James. *Labour and Socialism: A History of the British Labour Movement: 1867–1974.* Amherst: University of Massachusetts Press, 1983.

———. *Protests & Visions: Peace Politics in Twentieth Century Britain.* London: Hutchinson Radius, 1989.

Hobsbawm, Eric. *The Age of Extremes: A History of the World, 1914–1991.* New York: Pantheon Books, 1994.

———. *Workers: Worlds of Labor.* New York: Pantheon Books, 1984.

Hogenkamp, Bert. *Deadly Parallels: Film and the Left in Great Britain.* London: Lawrence and Wishart, 1986.

———. "Film and the Workers' Movement in Britain, 1929–39," *Sight and Sound* 45, Spring 1976.

Hoggart, Richard. *The Uses of Literacy: Changing Patterns in English Mass Culture.* Fair Lawn, New Jersey: Essential Books, 1957.

Holmes, Richard. *Acts of War: The Behavior of Men in Battle.* New York: Free Press, 1986.

Hopkins, Eric. *The Rise and Decline of the English Working Classes, 1918–1990: A Social History.* New York: St. Martin's Press, 1991.

Hoskins, Katharine Bail. *Today the Struggle: Literature and Politics in England during the Spanish Civil War.* Austin: University of Texas Press, 1969.

Hutt, Allen. *The Post-War History of the British Working Class.* New York: Barnes and Noble, 1972 [orig. ed. 1937].

Hynes, Samuel. *The Auden Generation: Literature and Politics in the 1930s.* London: The Bodley Head, 1976.

———. "Introduction" to *Christopher Caudwell. Romance and Realism: A Study in English Bourgeois Literature.* Princeton: Princeton University Press, 1970.

———. *A War Imagined: The First World War and English Culture.* New York: Atheneum, 1991.

Ibarruri, Dolores. *They Shall Not Pass: The Autobiography of La Pasionaria.* New York: International Publishers, 1966.

Inglis, Amirah. *Australians in the Spanish Civil War*. London: Allen and Unwin, 1987.

Inglis, Fred. *Radical Earnestness: English Social Theory 1880–1980*. Oxford: Martin Robertson, 1982.

Ingram, Kevin. *Rebel: The Short Life of Esmond Romilly*. London: Weidenfeld and Nicolson, 1985.

Isherwood, Christopher. *Christopher & His Kind: 1929–1939*. New York: Farrar, Straus and Giroux, 1976.

Jackson, Gabriel. *The Spanish Republic and the Civil War, 1931–1939*. Princeton: Princeton University Press, 1965.

Jackson, Michael. *Fallen Sparrows: The International Brigades in the Spanish Civil War*. Philadelphia: American Philosophical Society, 1994.

Jenkins, Mick. *George Brown*. Manchester: North West Communist Party, n.d.

Jennings, Humphrey, and Charles Madge, eds. *May the Twelfth: Mass-Observation Day-Surveys, 1937*. London: Faber and Faber, 1987 [orig. ed. 1937].

Johnson, Hewlett. *The Socialist Sixth of the World*. London: Victor Gollancz, 1940.

Johnson, Paul. *Intellectuals*. New York: Harper and Row, 1988.

———. *Modern Times: The World from the Twenties to the Eighties*. New York: Harper and Row, 1983.

Johnston, Verle B. *Legions of Babel: The International Brigades in the Spanish Civil War*. University Park and London: Pennsylvania State University Press, 1967.

Jones, Jack. *Union Man: The Autobiography of Jack Jones*. London: Collins, 1986.

Jones, Jeff, ed. *Brigadista: Harvest and War in Nicaragua*. New York: Praeger, 1986.

Jones, Lewis. *Cwmardy: The Story of a Welsh Mining Village*. Introduction by David Smith. London: Lawrence and Wishart, 1978 [orig. ed. 1937].

———. *We Live: The Story of a Welsh Mining Valley*. London: Lawrence and Wishart, 1978 [orig. ed. 1939].

Joyce, Patrick. *Visions of the People: Industrial England and the Question of Class, 1848–1914*. Cambridge: Cambridge University Press, 1991.

Judt, Tony. *Past Imperfect: French Intellectuals, 1944–1956*. Berkeley: University of California Press, 1992.

Jupp, James. *The Radical Left in Britain: 1931–1941*. London: Frank Cass, 1982.

Kaye, Harvey J., and Keith McClelland, eds. *E. P. Thompson: Critical Perspectives*. Oxford: Polity Press, 1990.

Keegan, John. *A History of Warfare*. New York: Vintage Books, 1994.

Keene, Judith. *The Last Mile to Huesca: An Australian Nurse in the Spanish Civil War*. Kensington: New South Wales University Press, 1988.

Kemp, Peter. *Mine Were of Trouble*. London: Cassell, 1957.

Kenwood, Alun, ed. *The Spanish Civil War: A Cultural and Historical Reader*. Providence: Berg, 1993.

Kermode, Frank. *History and Value*. New York: Clarendon Press, 1988.

Kiernan, Victor. "Labour and the War in Spain." *Scottish Labour History Society Journal*, 11, 1977.

King, James. *The Last Modern: A Life of Herbert Read*. New York: St. Martin's Press, 1990.

Kingsford, Peter. *The Hunger Marchers in Britain: 1920–1939*. London: Lawrence and Wishart, 1982.

Kitchen, Martin. *Europe between the Wars*. London and New York: Longman, 1988.

Klaus, Gustav H. "Socialist Fiction in the 1930s: Some Preliminary Observations." In John Lucas, ed., *The 1930s: A Challenge to Orthodoxy*. Sussex: Harvester Press, 1978.

Knight, Patricia. *The Spanish Civil War: Documents and Debates*. London: Macmillan, 1991.

Knightley, Phillip. *The First Casualty: From the Crimea to Vietnam—The War Correspondent As Hero, Propagandist, and Myth Maker*. London: Quartet Books, 1982.

———. *The Master Spy: The Story of Kim Philby*. New York: Vintage, 1990.

Knox, Bernard. *Essays: Ancient and Modern*. Baltimore: Johns Hopkins University Press, 1989.

Knox, William, ed. *Scottish Labour Leaders 1918–1939: A Biographical Dictionary*. Edinburgh: Mainstream Publishing, 1984.

Koch, Stephen. *Double Lives: Spies and Writers in the Secret Soviet War of Ideas against the West*. New York: Free Press, 1994.

Koestler, Arthur. *Arrow in the Blue: An Autobiography*. London: Collins, 1952.

———. *The Invisible Writing*. New York: Stein and Day, 1984.

———. *Spanish Testament*. London: Victor Gollancz, 1937.

Kramnick, Isaac, and Barry Sheerman. *Harold Laski: A Life on the Left*. New York: Allen Lane, 1993.

Krivitsky, Walter G. *I Was Stalin's Agent*. London: Hamish Hamilton, 1939.

Kubal, David Lawrence. *Outside the Whale: George Orwell's Art & Politics*. London: University of Notre Dame Press, 1972.

Kurzman, Dan. *Miracle of November: Madrid's Epic Stand, 1936*. New York: Putnam, 1980.

Kurzweil, Edith, and William Phillips, eds. *Writers and Politics: A Partisan Review Reader*. Boston: Routledge and Kegan Paul, 1983.

Landis, Arthur. *Death in the Olive Groves: American Volunteers in the Spanish Civil War, 1936–1939*. New York: Paragon House, 1989.

Laqueur, Walter. *Europe since Hitler: The Rebirth of Europe*. Rev. ed. New York: Penguin, 1982.

Lawther, Will. *Spain and Ourselves*. London: Mineworkers Federation of Great Britain, [1938].

Laybourn, Keith. *The General Strike of 1926*. Manchester: Manchester University Press, 1993.

Leavitt, David. *While England Sleeps*. New York: Viking, 1993.

Lee, Laurie. *A Moment of War*. London: Penguin Books, 1991.

Lee, Stephen J. *Aspects of British Political History, 1914–1995*. London and New York: Routledge, 1996.

Le Goff, Jacques. *History and Memory*. Translated by Steven Rendall and Elizabeth Claman. New York: Columbia University Press, 1992.

Lehmann, John. *I Am My Brother, Autobiography II*. London: Longmans, Green, 1960.

———. "Should Writers Keep to Their Art." *Left Review* 16, January 1937.

———. *Thrown to the Woolfs*. New York: Holt, Rinehart, and Winston, 1979.

———. *The Whispering Gallery, Autobiography I*. New York: Harcourt, Brace, 1955.

Lemert, Charles, ed. *Intellectuals and Politics: Social Theory in a Changing World*. Newbury Park: Sage Publications, 1991.

Lenin, V. I. *What Is To Be Done?* Translated by S. V. and Patricia Utechin. Edited by S. V. Utechin. Oxford: The Clarendon Press, 1963 [orig. ed. 1903].

Leventhal, F. M. *The Last Dissenter: H. N. Brailsford and His World*. Oxford: Calrendon Press, 1985.

Levine, Maurice. *Cheetham to Cordova: A Manchester Man of the Thirties*. Manchester: N. Richardson, 1984.

Levy, Carl, ed. *Socialism and the Intelligentsia: 1880–1914*. London and New York: Routledge and Kegan Paul, 1987.

Lewis, J. *The Left Book Club: An Historical Record*. London: Gollancz, 1970.

Lewis, John. "Christopher Caudwell and the Problem of Freedom," *Spain Today* 11, June 1947.

Lindsay, Jack. *Fanfrolico and After*. London: The Bodley Head, 1962.

London, Jack. *The People of the Abyss*. Edited and Introduced by I. O. Evans. New York: Archer House, 1963 [orig. ed. 1903].

———. *The Iron Heel*. Introduced by H. Bruce Franklin. Chicago: Lawrence Hill Books, 1980 [orig. ed. 1907].

Low, Robert. *La Pasionaria: The Spanish Firebrand*. London: Hutchinson, 1992.

Lowry, Malcolm. Introduced by Stephen Spender. *Under the Volcano*. New York: NAL, 1966 [orig. ed. 1947].

Lucas, James. *Experiences of War: The British Soldier*. London: Arms and Armour Press, 1989.

Lucas, John, ed. *The 1930s: A Challenge to Orthodoxy*. New York: Barnes and Noble, 1978.

Lyons, F. S. L. *Ireland since the Famine*. London: Weidenfeld and Nicolson, 1971.

Macartney, Wilfred. *The Walls Have Mouths: A Record of Ten Years' Penal Servitude*. London: Gollancz, 1936.

MacDougall, Ian, ed. *Voices from the Hunger Marches: Personal Recollections by Scottish Hunger Marchers of the 1920s and 1930s.* 2 vols. Edinburgh: Polygon, 1990.

——, ed. *Voices from the Spanish Civil War: Personal Recollections of Scottish Volunteers in Republican Spain, 1936–39.* Edinburgh: Polygon, 1986.

MacFarquhar, Roderick. "In Spain," *The Railway Service Journal*, March 1939.

MacIntyre, Stuart. *Little Moscows: Communism and Working-Class Militancy in Inter-war Britain.* London: Croom Helm, 1980.

——. *A Proletarian Science: Marxism in Britain, 1917–1933.* London: Lawrence and Wishart, 1986.

Maclean, Ian, Alan Montefiore, and Peter Winch, eds. *The Political Responsibility of Intellectuals.* Cambridge: Cambridge University Press, 1990.

Macmillan, Rob. "Pat Murphy, 1898–1974." typescript, n.d. Working Class Movement Library, Salford.

MacNeice, Louis. *The Strings Are False: An Unfinished Autobiography.* New York: Oxford University Press, 1966.

McCarthy, Margaret. *Generation in Revolt.* London: William Heinemann, 1953.

McGann, Thomas. *Portrait of Spain: British and American Accounts of Spain in the Nineteenth and Twentieth Centuries.* New York: Alfred A. Knopf, 1963.

McGovern, John. *Terror in Spain: How the Communist International Has Destroyed Working Class Unity, Undermined the Fight against Franco, and Suppressed the Social Revolution.* London: ILP, 1938.

McKibbin, Ross. *The Ideologies of Class: Social Relations in Britain, 1880–1950.* Oxford: Oxford University Press, 1991.

——. "Why Was There No Marxism in Great Britain," *English Historical Review* 391, April 1984.

McPherson, James M. *For Cause & Comrades: Why Men Fought in the Civil War.* New York: Oxford University Press, 1997.

Madden, David, ed. *Proletarian Writers of the Thirties.* Carbondale: Southern Illinois University Press, 1968.

Malia, Martin. *The Soviet Tragedy: A History of Socialism in Russia, 1917–1991.* New York: Free Press, 1994.

Malraux, André. *Man's Hope.* Translated by Stuart Gilbert and Alastair Macdonald. New York: Grove Press, 1979 [orig. ed. 1938].

Maltby, William S. *The Black Legend in England: The Development of Anti-Spanish Sentiment, 1558–1660.* Durham: Duke University Press, 1971.

Mangini, Shirley. *Memories of Resistance: Women's Voices from the Spanish Civil War.* New Haven and London: Yale University Press, 1995.

Mannheim, Karl. *Ideology and Utopia: An Introduction to the Sociology of Knowledge.* New York: Harcourt, Brace and Company, 1936.

Manning, Olivia. *The Levant Trilogy.* New York: Penguin Books, 1982.

MARHO. *Visions of History*. Manchester: Manchester University Press, 1983.

Martin, David E., and David Rubinstein, eds. *Ideology and the Labour Movement: Essays Presented to John Saville*. Totowa, N.J.: Rowman and Littlefield, 1979.

Matthews, Herbert. *The Education of a Correspondent*. Westport, Connecticut: Greenwood Press, 1970.

———. *Two Wars and More To Come*. New York: Carrick and Evans, 1938.

———. *The Yoke and the Arrows: A Report on Spain*. Rev. ed. New York: George Braziller, 1961.

Mayne, Brian. "The Ragged Trousered Philanthropists: An Appraisal of an Edwardian Novel of Social Protest." *Twentieth Century Literature*, XIII (1967).

Meacham, Standish. *A Life Apart: The English Working Class, 1890–1914*. Cambridge: Harvard University Press, 1977.

Mendelson, Edward. *Early Auden*. New York: The Viking Press, 1981.

Merriman, Marion, and Warren Lerude. *American Commander in Spain: Robert Hale Merriman and the Abraham Lincoln Brigade*. Reno: University of Nevada Press, 1986.

Milibrand, Ralph, and John Saville, eds. *The Socialist Register 1977*. London: The Merlin Press, 1977.

———. *The Socialist Register 1981*. The Merlin Press, 1981.

Mill, Samuel. "The Rebellious Needleman: Tom Paine," *Left Review* 4, May 1937.

Miller, John, ed. *Voices against Tyranny: Writing of the Spanish Civil War*. Introduction by Stephen Spender. New York: Charles Scribner's Sons, 1986.

Mitford, Jessica. *Daughters and Rebels: An Autobiography*. New York: Holt, Rinehart, and Winston, 1960.

Monks, Joe. *With the Reds in Andalusia*. London: The John Cornford Poetry Group, 1985.

Monteath, Peter. *Writing the Good Fight: Political Commitment in the International Literature of the Spanish Civil War*. Westport, Connecticut: Greenwood Press, 1994.

Morgan, Kenneth O. *The People's Peace: British History, 1945–90*. Oxford: Oxford University Press, 1992.

———, ed. *The Oxford History of Britain*. Oxford: Oxford University Press, 1993.

Morgan, Kevin. *Against Fascism and War: Ruptures and Continuities in British Communist Politics, 1935–41*. Manchester and New York: Manchester University Press, 1989.

———. *Harry Pollitt*. Manchester and New York: Manchester University Press, 1993.

Morris, Lynda, and Robert Radford. *AIA, The Story of the Artists International Association, 1933–1953*. Oxford: The Museum of Modern Art, 1983.

Mowat, Charles Loch. *Britain between the Wars: 1918–1940.* London: Methuen, 1968 [orig. ed. 1955].

Muggeridge, Malcolm. *Chronicles of Wasted Time.* New York: William Morrow and Company, 1973.

———. *The Thirties: 1930–1940 in Great Britain.* London: Weidenfeld and Nicolson, 1989 [orig. ed. 1940].

Mulford, Wendy. *This Narrow Place: Sylvia Townsend Warner and Valentine Ackland: Life, Letters and Politics, 1930–1951.* London: Pandora, 1988.

Muste, John M. *Say That We Saw Spain Die: Literary Consequences of the Spanish Civil War.* Seattle: University of Washington Press, 1966.

N.A. *In Spain with the International Brigade: A Personal Narrative.* London: Burns Oates and Washbourne, 1938.

Nairn, Tom. *The Break-Up of Britain.* London: Verso, 1981.

Nelson, Cary, and Jefferson Hendricks, eds. *Madrid 1937: Letters of the Abraham Lincoln Brigade from the Spanish Civil War.* New York and London: Routledge, 1996.

Nelson, Steve, James R. Barrett, and Rob Ruck. *Steve Nelson: American Radical.* Pittsburgh: University of Pittsburgh Press, 1981.

Newman, Michael. *John Strachey.* Manchester: Manchester University Press, 1989.

Nichols, Ray. *Treason, Tradition, and the Intellectual: Julien Benda and Political Discourse.* Lawrence: The Regents Press of Kansas, 1978.

Norman, James. *The Fell of Dark.* London: Michael Joseph, 1960.

Norris, Christopher, ed. *Inside the Myth: Orwell—Views from the Left.* London: Lawrence and Wishart, 1984.

O'Brien, Kate. *Farewell Spain.* London: W. Heinemann, 1937.

O'Riordan, Michael. *Connolly Column: The Story of the Irishmen Who Fought for the Spanish Republic: 1936–1939.* Dublin: New Books, 1979.

Orwell, George. *The Collected Essays, Journalism and Letters of George Orwell.* Edited by Sonia Orwell and Ian Angus. 4 vols. New York: Harcourt, Brace, Jovanovich, 1968.

———. *A Collection of Essays.* New York: Harcourt, Brace, and World, 1946.

———. *Down and Out in Paris and London, A Novel.* New York: Harcourt, Brace, 1958 [orig. ed. 1933].

———. *Homage to Catalonia.* New York: Harvest/HBJ Book, 1980 [orig. ed. 1938]

———. *Keep the Aspidistra Flying.* New York: Harcourt, Brace, Jovanovich, 1956 [orig. ed. 1936].

———. *The Road to Wigan Pier.* Foreword by Victor Gollancz. New York and London: Harcourt, Brace, 1958 [orig. ed. 1937].

Osborne, John. *Look Back in Anger.* New York: Penguin Books, 1982.

Page, Norman. *The Thirties in Britain.* London: Macmillan, 1990.

Palmer, Bryan D. *E. P. Thompson: Objections and Oppositions.* London: Verso, 1994.

Parker, Peter, ed., and Frank Kermode, consultant ed. *A Reader's Guide to the Twentieth Century Novel*. New York: Oxford University Press, 1995.

Pawling, Christopher. *Christopher Caudwell: Towards a Dialectical Theory of Literature*. London: Macmillan, 1989.

Payne, Robert, ed. *The Civil War in Spain, 1936–39*. New York: Putnam, 1962.

Payne, Stanley. *The Spanish Revolution*. London: Weidenfeld and Nicolson, 1970.

Paynter, Will. *My Generation*. London: Allen and Unwin, 1972.

Pelling, Henry. *The British Communist Party: A Historical Profile*. London: Adam and Charles Black, 1975 [orig. ed. 1958].

Pérez, Janet, and Wendell Aycock. *The Spanish Civil War in Literature*. Lubbock: Texas Tech University Press, 1990.

Peters, Anthony, ed. *The Guardian Book of the Spanish Civil War*. Aldershot: Wildwood House, 1987.

Pierson, Stanley. *British Socialists: The Journey from Fantasy to Politics*. Cambridge and London: Harvard University Press, 1979.

Pimlott, Ben. *Labour and the Left in the 1930s*. Cambridge: Cambridge University Press, 1977.

Pitcairn, Frank [Claud Cockburn]. *Reporter in Spain*. Introduction by Ralph Bates. London: Lawrence and Wishart, 1936.

Plumb, J. H. *Studies in Social History: A Tribute to G. M. Trevelyan*. New York: Longmans, Green, 1955.

Pollitt, Harry. *Arms for Spain*. London: CPGB, 1936.

———. *Labour and Spain*. London: Labour Spain Committee, 1938.

———. *Pollitt Visits Spain: Harry Pollitt's Story of His Visit to Spain in December 1937*. Foreword by J. B. S. Haldane. London: International Brigade Dependents' Aid Fund, 1938.

———. *Save Spain from Fascism*. London: CPGB, 1936.

———. *Spain and the T.U.C.* London: CPGB, 1936.

———. *Spain: What Next?* London: CPGB, 1939.

Powell, Anthony. *Messengers of Day: The Memoirs of Anthony Powell*. London: Heinemann, 1978.

Powell, David. *British Politics and the Labour Question, 1868–1990*. London: Macmillan, 1992.

Preston, Paul. *Franco: A Biography*. New York: BasicBooks, 1994.

———. *The Spanish Civil War, 1936–39*. London: Weidenfeld and Nicolson, 1986.

———, ed. *Revolution and War in Spain: 1931–1939*. New York: Methuen, 1984.

Priestley, J. B. *English Journey*. New York: Harper and Brothers, 1934.

Pritchett, V. S. *Marching Spain*. London: Ernest Benn, 1928.

———. *The Spanish Temper: Travels in Spain*. New York: Ecco Press, 1989 [orig. ed. 1954].

Pugh, Jane. *A Most Expensive Prisoner: Tom Jones, Rhosllannerchrugog's Biography*. Llanrwst, Wales: Gwasg Carreg Gwalch, 1988.

Quennell, Peter. *The Marble Foot: An Autobiography.* New York: Viking Press, 1977.

Radice, Lisanne. *Beatrice and Sidney Webb: Fabian Socialists.* New York: St. Martin's Press, 1984.

Rapoport, Louis. *Stalin's War against the Jews: The Doctors' Plot and the Soviet Solution.* New York: Free Press, 1990.

Rée, Jonathan. *Proletarian Philosophers: Problems in Socialist Culture in Britain, 1900–1940.* Oxford: Clarendon Press, 1984.

Regler, Gustav. *The Owl of Minerva: The Autobiography of Gustav Regler.* Translated by Norman Denny. London: Rupert Hart-Davis, 1959.

Richardson, Dick, and Glyn Stone, eds. *Decisions and Diplomacy: Essays in Twentieth-Century International History.* London and New York: Routledge, 1995.

Richardson, R. Dan. *Comintern Army.* Lexington: University Press of Kentucky, 1982.

Roberts, Robert. *The Classic Slum: Salford Life in the First Quarter of the Century.* Manchester: Manchester University Press, 1971.

Rodden, John. *The Politics of Literary Reputation: The Making and Claiming of 'St. George' Orwell.* New York: Oxford University Press, 1989.

Romilly, Esmond. *Boadilla.* Introduction by Hugh Thomas. London: Macdonald, 1971 [orig. ed. 1937].

Rosenberg, Suzanne. *A Soviet Odyssey.* Toronto: Penguin Books, 1991.

Rosenstone, Robert. *Crusade of the Left: The Lincoln Battalion in the Spanish Civil War.* Landham, MD: University Press of America, 1980.

Rowse, A. L. *The Poet Auden: A Personal Memoir.* New York: Weidenfeld and Nicolson, 1988.

Rubinstein, David, ed. *People for the People: Radical Ideas & Personalities in British History.* Introduction by Michael Foot. New York: Humanities Press, 1973.

Rust, William. *Britons in Spain: The History of the British Battalion of the XVth International Brigade.* London: Lawrence and Wishart, 1939.

———. *Spain Fights for Victory.* London: CPGB, 1938.

Ryan, Frank, ed. *The Book of the XV Brigade.* Madrid: Commissariat of War, XV Brigade, 1938.

Said, Edward. *Orientalism.* New York: Pantheon Books, 1978.

———. *Representations of the Intellectual: The 1993 Reith Lectures.* New York: Pantheon Books, 1994.

Salaun, Serge, comp. *Romancero de la Defensa de Madrid.* Barcelona: Ruedo Ibérico, 1982.

Salter, Stephen, and John Stevenson, eds. *The Working Class and Politics in Europe and America, 1929–1945.* London and New York: Longman, 1990.

Samuel, Raphael. "The Lost World of British Communism, Part One." *New Left Review* 85, 1974.

Savage, Michael, and Andrew Miles. *The Remaking of the British Working Class, 1840–1940.* London: Routledge, 1994.

Save Peace! Aid Spain. London: CPGB, 1937.

Saville, John. *The Labour Movement in Britain: A Commentary*. London: Faber and Faber, 1988.

———. *Socialist Register*, London: Merlin Press, 1981.

Schalk, David L. *War and the Ivory Tower: Algeria and Vietnam*. New York: Oxford University Press, 1991.

Scherf, Kathleen, ed. *The Collected Poetry of Malcolm Lowry*. Vancouver: University of British Columbia Press, 1992.

Scott Watson, Keith. *Single to Spain*. New York: E. P. Dutton, 1937.

Seaman, L. C. B. *Life in Britain between the Wars*. London: Batsford, 1970.

Seldes, George. *Witness to a Century: Encounters with the Noted, the Notorious, and the Three SOBS*. New York: Ballantine Books, 1987.

Sheean, Vincent. *Not Peace but a Sword*. New York: Doubleday, Doran, and Company, 1939.

Shelden, Michael. *Friends of Promise: Cyril Connolly and the World of Horizon*. London: Hamilton, 1989.

———. *Orwell: The Authorized Biography*. New York: HarperCollins, 1991.

Shelley, Ronald G. *The British Legion in Spain during the First Carlist War: 1832–1839*. Brighton: Spanish Philatelic Society, 1975.

Sherry, Norman. *The Life of Graham Greene, 1904–1939*. New York: Viking Penguin, 1989.

Simon, Roger. *Gramsci's Political Thought: An Introduction*. London: Lawrence and Wishart, 1982.

Sked, Alan and Chris Cook, eds. *Crisis and Controversy. Essays in Honour of A. J. P. Taylor*. New York: St. Martin's Press, 1976.

Skelton, Robin, ed. *Poetry of the Thirties*. Harmondsworth: Penguin Books, 1964.

Skidelsky, Robert. *John Maynard Keynes: The Economist as Saviour, 1920–1937*. New York: Viking Penguin, 1994.

Slater, Humphrey, *The Heretics*. [London]: Secker and Warburg, 1946.

Sloan, Pat. *John Cornford: A Memoir*. London: Jonathan Cape, 1938.

Sommerfield, John. *Volunteer in Spain*. New York: Knopf, 1937.

Spain Assailed: Student Delegates to Spain Report. London: Student Delegation to Spain, 1937.

The Spanish Civil War Collection. London: Trustees of the Imperial War Museum, 1996.

Spender, Stephen. *The Destructive Element: A Study of Modern Writers and Beliefs*. Philadelphia: Albert Saifer, 1953 [orig. ed. 1935].

———. *T. S. Eliot*. New York: Viking Press, 1975.

———. *Forward from Liberalism*. New York: Random House, 1937.

———. *Journals, 1939–1983*. Edited by John Goldsmith. New York: Random House, 1986.

———. *Letters to Christopher: Stephen Spender's Letters to Christopher Isherwood, 1929–1939*. Edited by Lee Bartlett. Santa Barbara, California: Black Sparrow Press, 1980.

———. *The Temple*. Restored version. London: Faber and Faber, 1988.

———. *The Thirties and After: Poetry, Politics, People, 1933–1970.* New York: Vintage, 1979.

———. *World within World: The Autobiography of Stephen Spender.* London: Hamish Hamilton, 1951.

———, ed. *Poems for Spain.* With John Lehmann. Introduction by Stephen Spender. London: Hogarth Press, 1939.

Sperber, Murray A., comp. *And I Remember Spain: A Spanish Civil War Anthology.* New York: Collier Books, 1974.

Srebrnik, Henry. "Jewish Communist Activity in London on Behalf of the Spanish Republic," *Michigan Academician* XVI, 2, Winter 1984.

Stallworthy, Jon. *Louis MacNeice.* New York and London: W. W. Norton, 1995.

Stansky, Peter, and William Abrahams. *Journey to the Frontier: Two Roads to the Spanish Civil War.* New York: Norton, 1970.

———. *Orwell: The Transformation.* London: Granada, 1981.

Stedman Jones, Gareth. *Languages of Class: Studies in English Working Class History, 1832–1982.* Cambridge: Cambridge University Press, 1983.

Sternlicht, Sanford. *Stephen Spender.* New York: Twayne Publishers, 1992.

Stevenson, John, and Chris Cook. *Britain in the Depression: Society and Politics, 1929–1939.* 2d. ed., rev. London and New York: Longmans, 1994.

Strachey, John. *The Coming Struggle for Power.* New York: Covici, Friede, 1932.

———. "The Education of a Communist." *Left Review* 3, December 1934.

———. *The Menace of Fascism.* New York: Covici, Friede, 1933.

———. *The Nature of Capitalist Crisis.* New York: Covici, Friede, 1935.

Strachey, Lytton. *Eminent Victorians.* London: Penguin Books, 1986.

Straight, Michael. *After Long Silence.* New York: W. W. Norton, 1983.

Stratton, Harry. *To Anti-Fascism by Taxi.* Port Talbot, West Glamorgan: Alun Books, 1984.

Stromberg, Roland. *Europe in the Twentieth Century.* 3rd edition. Englewood Cliffs, N.J.: Prentice Hall, 1992.

Sullivan, Robert. *Christopher Caudwell.* New York: Croom Helm, 1987.

Swingewood, Alan. *The Myth of Mass Culture.* Atlantic Highlands, N.J.: Humanities Press, 1977.

Symons, Julian. "The Betrayed Idealists." *Sunday Times Magazine,* July 23, 1961.

———. *Between the Wars: Britain in Photographs.* London: Batsford, 1972.

———. *The General Strike: A Historical Portrait.* London: Cresset Library, 1987 [orig. ed. 1957].

———. *The Thirties: A Dream Revolved.* London: Cresset Press, 1960.

Tamames, Ramón, ed. *La Guerra Civil Española: 50 Años Después.* Barcelona: Editorial Planeta, 1986.

The Tasks and Duties of Commissars [by Crescenciano Bilbao]. Barcelona: Comisariat of War of the International Brigades, 1937.

Taylor, A. J. P. *English History: 1914–1945.* New York and London: Oxford University Press, 1965.

————. *From the Boer War to the Cold War: Essays on Twentieth-Century Europe*. New York: Penguin, 1996.

These Men Have Died. Madrid: U.G.T., 1937.

Thomas, Fred. *To Tilt at Windmills: A Memoir of the Spanish Civil War*. East Lansing: Michigan State University Press, 1996.

Thomas, Hugh. *John Strachey*. New York: Harper and Row, 1973.

————. *The Spanish Civil War*. New York: Harper and Row, 1977.

Thompson, Dorothy. *The Chartists: Popular Politics in the Industrial Revolution*. New York: Pantheon, 1984.

Thompson, E. P. *The Making of the English Working Class*. New York. Vintage Books, 1963.

Thompson, Noel. *John Strachey: An Intellectual Biography*. London: Macmillan, 1993.

Thompson, Paul. *The Voice of the Past: Oral History*. Oxford: Oxford University Press, 1978.

Thompson, Willie. *The Good Old Cause: British Communism, 1920–1991*. London: Pluto Press, 1992.

Thorpe, Andrew. *Britain in the Era of the Two World Wars, 1914–45*. London and New York: Longman, 1994.

————. *Britain in the 1930s: The Deceptive Decade*. Cambridge, Massachusetts: Blackwell, 1992.

————, ed. *The Failure of Political Extremism*. Exeter: University of Exeter, 1989.

Thurlow, Richard. *Fascism in Britain: A History, 1918–1985*. Oxford: Blackwell, 1987.

Thwaites, Peter. "The Independent Labour Party Contingent in the Spanish Civil War." *Imperial War Museum Review* 2, 1987, 50–61.

Tisa, John. *Recalling the Good Fight: An Autobiography of the Spanish Civil War*. South Hadley, Massachusetts: Bergin and Garvey, 1985.

Toynbee, Philip. *Friends Apart: A Memoir of Esmond Romilly & Jaspar Ridley in the Thirties*. London: MacGibbon and Kee, 1954.

————, ed. *The Distant Drum: Reflections on the Spanish Civil War*. London: Sidgwick and Jackson, 1976.

Tressell, Robert. *The Ragged Trousered Philanthropists*. London: Grant Richards, 1918.

————. *The Ragged Trousered Philanthropists*. [Restored] London: Lawrence and Wishart, 1955.

Tsuzuki, Chushichi. *Tom Mann, 1856–1941: The Challenges of Labour*. Oxford: Clarendon Press, 1991.

Tucker, Robert. *Stalin in Power: The Revolution from Above, 1928–1941*. New York: W. W. Norton, 1992.

————, ed. *The Marx-Engels Reader*. New York: W. W. Norton, 1972.

Tuñon de Lara, Manuel. *La Guerra Civil Española: 50 Años Después*. Barcelona: Editorial Labor, 1985.

Tuominen, Arvo. *The Bells of the Kremlin: An Experience in Communism*. Edited by Piltti Heiskanen. Translated by Lily Leino. Introduction by

Harrison E. Salisbury. Hanover, N.H.: University Press of New England, 1983.

Upward, Edward. *In the Thirties*. London: Quartet Books, 1978.

Valleau, Marjorie A. *The Spanish Civil War in American and European Films*. Ann Arbor: UMI Research Press, 1982.

Van Holthoon, Fritz, and Marcel Van der Linden, eds. *Internationalism in the Labour Movement, 1830 –1940*. 2 vols. New York: E. J. Brill, 1988.

Vernon, Betty. *Ellen Wilkinson, 1891–1947*. London: Croom Helm, 1982.

Vice, Sue, ed. *Malcolm Lowry Eighty Years On*. London: Macmillan, 1989.

Vilar, Pierre. *La Guerra Civil Española*. Barcelona: Editorial Crítica, 1986.

Vincent, David. *Literacy and Popular Culture: England 1750–1914*. Cambridge: Cambridge University Press, 1989.

Voros, Sandor. *American Commissar*. Philadelphia: Chilton, 1961.

Watkins, K. W. *Britain Divided: The Effect of the Spanish Civil War on British Political Opinion*. London: Thomas Nelson and Sons, 1963.

Webb, Beatrice. *The Diary of Beatrice Webb: "The Wheel of Life": 1924–1943*. Vol. 4. Edited by Norman and Jeanne Mackenzie. Cambridge: Belknap Press of Harvard University, 1985.

Weintraub, Stanley. *The Last Great Cause: The Intellectuals and the Spanish Civil War*. New York: Weybright and Talley, 1968.

Weisser, Henry. *British Working-Class Movements and Europe, 1815–1848*. Manchester: Manchester University Press, 1975.

West, W. J., ed., *Orwell: The Lost Writings*. New York: Arbor House, 1985.

Wiener, Martin. *English Culture and the Decline of the Industrial Spirit: 1850 –1980*. Cambridge: Cambridge University Press, 1981.

Wilkinson, James. "Truth & Delusion," *Salmagundi* 76–77, Fall 1987–Winter 1988.

Williams, Colin, Bill Alexander, and John Gorman. *Memorials of the Spanish Civil War*. Far Thrupp, Stroud: Alan Sutton, 1996.

Williams, Raymond, ed. *George Orwell: A Collection of Critical Essays*. Englewood Cliffs, N.J.: Prentice-Hall, 1974.

Wilson, Edmund. *Letters on Literature and Politics: 1912–1972*. New York: Farrar, Strauss and Giroux, 1977.

Winter, Jay, ed. *The Working Class in Modern British History: Essays in Honour of Henry Pelling*. Cambridge: Cambridge University Press, 1983.

Wintringham, Tom. *English Captain*. Harmondsworth: Penguin Books, 1941.

Wolff, Milton. *Another Hill*. Urbana and Chicago: University of Illinois Press, 1994.

Wood, Ian S. "Homage to the Fifteenth Brigade," *Weekend Scotsman*, June 30, 1979.

———. "Scotland and the Spanish Civil War," *Cencrastus* 18, Autumn 1984.

Wood, Neal. *Communism and British Intellectuals*. New York: Columbia University Press, 1959.

Woodcock, George. *The Crystal Spirit: A Study of George Orwell*. Boston: Little Brown, 1966.

———. *Orwell's Message: 1984 and the Present*. Madeira Park, British Columbia: Harbour, 1984.

Woolf, Virginia. *Collected Essays*. Vol. 2. London: Hogarth Press, 1966.

Worsley, T. C. *Behind the Battle*. London. Robert Hale Ltd., 1939.

———. *The Fellow Travellers*. London: Gay Modern Classics, 1984 [orig. ed. 1971].

Wyden, Peter. *The Passionate War: The Narrative History of the Spanish Civil War, 1936–1939*. New York: Simon and Schuster, 1983.

Young, James D. *Socialism and the English Working Class: A History of English Labour, 1883–1939*. Hemel Hempstead: Harvester Wheatsheaf, 1989.

Zwerdling, Alex. *Orwell and the Left*. New Haven and London: Yale University Press, 1974.

Index

Aalto, Bill, 410–11
Aberdeen Labour College, 102
Ablett, Noah, 77
Abraham Lincoln Brigade, 11, 150, 215, 273, 412; African-Americans in, 172, 399; commander blamed, 267; commissars' role in, 164; and language barrier, 115; leadership of, 399; Merriman wounded, 419; officers contrasted, 230; political understanding, 397
Ackland, Valentine, 119, 200
"Activist" movement, 291
Addley, Harry, 133
Agrarian reform, 121–22, 124–25
Aid Spain movement, 92, 243
Aiken, Conrad, 334
Aitken, George, 161, 165, 169, 185, 190, 195, 242, 416, 418; leftist publications, 54
Alcohol use, 248, 304
Alexander, Bill, x–xi, 141, 156, 170, 171, 223, 245–46, 254, 324, 325, 326, 370, 403, 424
Alfonso XIII, 122
American Civil War, 397
Anarchism, 284, 298
Anarchists, 121, 140; Bates and, 236; warning of dictatorship, 151
Anarchosyndicalists, 140, 408; and CNT-FAI, 203; rank and privilege, 17
Anderson, David, 160
Angell, Norman, 313
Angus, John, 263, 318–19, 417

Annan, Noel, 13, 20
Anti-Americanism, 412–13
Anticommunism, and Labour party leaders, 98
Antifascism, 3, 327; at home, 325; Churchill's position on, 327; Communist party treachery versus, 216; in film, 145–46; and Heath, 202; leaflets on, 145–46; movement, 63–64; opposition to Churchill, 327; volunteers, 141
Antisemitism: in British Battalion, 171–72; and Jewish workers, 144; Mosley's, 144; of Spanish fascists, 383; and USSR, 416–17
Anti-Tank Battery, 224–28, 302, 359, 425; composition of, 359
Aragón offensive, 244
Armstrong, Alex, 145
Army of Catalonia, Ebro offensive, 306
Arthur, James, 270
Artists, bourgeois concerns, 51; Caudwell on, 50–51
Association of Writers for the Defense of Culture, 349
Asturian miners' revolt (1934), 116–17, 122–23
Atrocities, Franquist, 243
Attlee, Clement, 196, 313, 326, 328
Auden, W. H., 155, 197, 367, 375; and General Strike of 1926, 404; political action of, 335; postwar political commitment of, 350, 351; *Spain* (poem), 353
Austria, 154

Federación Anarquista Ibérica
(CNT-FAI), 203–4
Conical Hill, 189
Connolly, Cyril, 19, 20, 21, 197, 209,
350, 353; intellectuals' role, 38–39
Contra war, vii–viii
Conway, Kit, 175
Cook, Judith, 75
Cooney, Bob, 89, 161, 173, 175–76, 247,
248, 254, 261, 299, 300, 301, 304,
309, 323, 349, 392, 408, 412–13, 415,
417; Lenin School, 101–3
Copeman, Fred, x, xv, 111, 140, 148,
156, 162, 170, 172, 177, 180, 184,
189, 201, 217–22, 230, 235, 246, 253,
256, 278, 279, 281, 301, 304, 311–12,
322, 344, 357, 359, 396, 414, 416,
418; Anti-Tank Battery, 224–28; appendicitis, 245; autobiography, 420;
battle of Brunete, 224; class prejudice, 233, 234; as commander, 217–
22, 223; disaffected volunteers, 418;
end of service, 241–42; on executions, 267; identification with rank
and file, 229–30; Invergordon mutiny, 217–18; knowledge of Spain,
115; LaSalle execution, 280; on Lincolns, 412–13; OBE, 420; oratorical
skills, 243–44; Pollitt relationship,
279; return to Britain, 243; return to
Spain, 244–45; Soviet action, 287–
88; Wintringham's status, 402; on
women, 409; young intellectuals,
229
Copic, Vladimir, 267, 299, 419, 422
Cornford, Christopher, 36
Cornford, John, xv, 8, 20–21, 22, 31,
129, 141, 156, 233, 275, 333, 371,
374, 394; Chartism, 109; early war
experiences, 131–32; on noncommunist intellectuals, 56–57; poetry,
278; Pollitt and, 48; POUM militia,
129; recruiting others, 129–30, 132
Cornforth, Maurice, 31
Correction camps, 262–63
Cottman, Stafford, 205, 207
Coward, Jack, 212–13, 382
Cox, Raymond, 134
Coyle, George, 268
CPGB. *See* British Communist Party
(Communist Party of Great Britain)

Crick, Bernard, 406
Cripps, Sir Stafford, 113, 313, 360
Crook (also Cook), David, 182, 184–86,
189, 193, 209–10, 321, 360, 406, 412,
426
Crossman, Richard, 22, 43–44
Cummings, Alec, 106
Cunard, Nancy, 12–13, 209
Cunningham, Jock, 140, 176–77, 191,
221, 223, 230, 231, 242, 245, 280,
281, 416; as leader, 229–30
Cunningham, Miriam, 145

Daily Worker, books on, 212; false sto-
ries planted, 212; version of history,
212–13; among volunteers, 211
Dalton, Hugh, attitudes toward work-
ers, 43
Daly, Peter, 175, 222
Darke, Bob, 48
*Daughters and Rebels: An Autobiogra-
phy* (Mitford), 391
Davies, D. R., 274
Davies, Harold, 142
Davison, Bill, 298
Death theme, 335; Bates on, 240; Ebro
offensive, 306; memorial services,
361–63; Spain as killing ground, 245
De Brouckère, Louis, 124
Deegan, Frank, 326
Deegan, William, 138
Delmer, Sefton, 132, 238
De Maio, Anthony, 281, 421
Democracy, British, idealism, 136; par-
liamentary, 137; social contract, 137
Demonstrations, 8
De Palencia, Isobel, 148
Dependents' Aid Committee. *See* In-
ternational Brigade Dependents' As-
sociation
Dependents' Aid Fund, 411
Depression, middle-class conditions, 1;
working-class conditions, 2
Desertions, 254–56, 268; dissenters
and, xiv; executions, 266–68; Hynd-
man and Lepper, 266; reasons given,
269–71; Retreats, 295; Rust explain-
ing, 8; typical punishments, 222;
Wattis, 277
Detention camps, 417
Dickens, Charles, 80

Dirt Track Riders' Association, 337

Discipline, 221, 247; bourgeois discipline attacked, 305; Wild, 303–4

Discussion groups, 96–97

Dissidents, anti-party sentiment, 299, 300; desertions, xiv; detention camps, 262–63; Marcovitch, 260–64

Dobb, Maurice, 31, 37

Dobson, Harry, 102, 173, 295, 300, 302, 304–5

Donaldson, Alex, 139, 311, 319

Donnelly, Charles, 372

Donnelly, Tom, 360

Dos Passos, John, 208

Doyle, Gerrard, 146–47

Dress, 305–6; uniforms, 341

Drever, George, 137, 171

Dunbar, Malcolm, 176, 178, 225–26, 227, 235, 296, 311, 346, 358, 359, 419

Duncan, Thomas, 100–1, 384

Dunlop, John, 410

Durán, Gustavo, 374

Dutt, R. Palme, 44, 91, 383

Ebro offensive, 305–8, 310; citations given, 324–25

Economic democracy, Spender on, 27

Economides, Mike, 167, 294

Eden, Anthony, 401

Education Act of 1870, 5

Edwards, Bob, 204, 205

Edwards, Jack, 322

Egalitarianism, viii, 323–24, 341, 360

Eliot, T. S., 20–21

Elite culture, politics and war, xiii

Elites, internationalism, 108

Elliott, Alonzo, 139, 151, 215, 265, 270, 277, 283, 286, 311, 408

Elliott, Bob, 279, 322, 421

Emergency National Conference, 321

Emotional adjustment to the reality of war, 194

Ends and Means (Huxley), 345–46

Engels, Friedrich, 101

Espionage, 161

Executions, 236, 266–68, 422; for disciplinary reasons, 221–22; French commander LaSalle, 279, 422. *See also* Desertions

Fabians, 55, 57

Fanning, Tommy, 138, 225

Farr, Frank, 265–66

Fascism: appeal in England, 3; effects of European, 111; internationalism, 111; Manchester workers' understanding, 144–46; Spanish right wing, 120; and Spanish Second Republic, 122. *See also* British Union of Fascists; Franco, Francisco; Mosley, Sir Oswald

Feeley, Bill, 2, 346

Fellow travelers, 51

Fellow Travelers (Worsley), 48–49

Ferguson, Alec, 89, 215

Fernsworth, Lawrence, 311

Fiedler, Leslie, 14

Fifth Column, 294

Films, "The Defence of Madrid," 145; "Land and Freedom," 405; Manchester showings, 145; popularity, 388; Russian, 193; Spain in, 115; on Spanish Civil War, 388; "The Sailors of Kronstadt," 193; "The Spanish Earth," 388

Fletcher, George, 235, 276, 301, 393

Food, 293–94

Foot, Michael, 318

Foreign Enlistment Act (1870), 179, 401, 414

Formal courses of instruction, Lenin School, 99–103

Formal instruction, 95–96

Forster, E. M., 32, 240

Forward from Liberalism (Spender), 25–27, 47, 52, 197; Pollitt on, 47; Webbs influencing, 56

Foulkes, Taffy, 272

Fox, Ralph, 8, 154, 275, 377, 380, 385; Chartism, 109; Lenin School, 102; memorial committee, 352; Pollitt and, 48

France, 154, 165, 395, 421; battalions, 132–33; frontier crossings, 398; travel through, 339

Francis, Hywel, 415

Franco-Belgian battalion, 154, 189

Franco, Francisco: British volunteers with, 267, 369; Churchill's support, 328; international fascist support, ix; Jarama offensive, 185–86, 187; Madrid offensive, 203; symbol, 99

Lawther, Clifford, 141
Lawther, Will, 111, 141, 313
Leadership, 219–23, 224, 245; defined, 222–23; military, 150
Leaflets, antifascist, 145–46
Lean Men (Bates), 70–71, 241
Leave to England, 255–56
Lee, Laurie, ix, xv, 10, 140, 156, 157, 158, 218, 396
Lees, Joe, 77
Leeson, George, 77, 312
Left Book Club, Brewer, 80; discussion groups, 53; founding, 52–54; influence, 25; Marcovitch, 260; positions, 53; *The Road to Wigan Pier*, 60; South Wales miners, 147; *Spain in Revolt* (1936), 119; Spanish Republic, 53–54; Spanish topics, 125; among volunteers, 211; working class, 53
Left Review, 51
Left wing, Spain, 120–23
Lehmann, John, 31, 38, 59, 375
Lehmann, Rosamond, 422
Lenin School (International Lenin University), 76, 99–103, 384; and African-Americans, 173; and South Wales, 147
Lenin, V. I., 43
Lepper, John, 266
Lesser, Sam, 359, 406
Letters in Red (Lewis), 110–11
Levine, Maurice, 233, 279, 280, 395, 421; idealism, 136, 141, 143, 149, 233
Lewis, Cecil Day, 19–20; communism, 62; on communism, 34; internationalism, 110; middle-class intellectuals, 45; Popular Front, 4, 38; working class, 48
Lewis, John, workers as philosophers, 96
Lewis, Reuben, 263
Lewis, Wyndham, 113
Liberalism, Spender on, 25, 199–200
Lindsay, A. D., 202
Lindsay, Jack, 173, 361, 431
Lister, Enrique, 276
Literacy, British mass, 5–6; growth of, 78; oral culture, 86; rates in Spain, 120; among Spanish volunteers, 247; views of homosexuality and, 226–27

Literature, books on Spain before 1936, 118–25
Liverpool Trades Council, 249
Loban, John, 325
Lochore, John, 338–39
Lolly Willowes: or the Loving Huntsman (Warner), 200
London (England), East End slums, 80–81
London, Jack, 7, 79, 80–81, 86
Longo, Luigi, 286
Loss of faith, 35–36
Lossowski, Vince, 411
Lowry, Malcolm, 332–36, 428

McCaig, Cheeky, 142
McCarthyism, 416
McCarthy, Margaret, 99, 157, 158; conditions for workers, 101; early influences, 104–5; effective communication, 91; Lenin School, 103; postwar political commitments, 352; YCL meetings, 97
Macartney, Wilfred, 168–71, 223
McCartney, Garry, 89
McCormick, Bernie, 413
McCusker, Frank, 29
McDade, Alex, 155, 224
MacDonald, Ramsay, 204
MacDougall, William, 175
McGovern, John, 117, 208, 264
MacFarquhar, Roderick, 325–26, 377
MacGregor, W. K., 216
McGregor, Liam, 325
McIntyre, Geordie, 14
MacKenzie-Papineau (Canadian Battalion), 160, 299, 306
McLanders, Alexander, 141
Maclean, John, 91
McLeod, Charlie, 358
McNair, John, 206
McNally, Eddie, 259
MacNeice, Louis, 21, 40, 374, 376; on armchair revolutionaries, 37
McWhirter, Tom, 244, 324
Madge, Charles, 7, 29–30
Mail, censorship, 213–14, 272; party criticized, 270–71; "political unreliables," 265
Mail delivery, 160, 161
Maley, James, 142

Library of Congress Cataloging-in-Publication Data

Hopkins, James K.
  Into the Heart of the Fire: the British in the Spanish Civil War / James K. Hopkins
    p.   cm.
  Includes bibliographical references and index.
  ISBN 0-8047-3126-8 (cloth: alk. paper). —ISBN 0-8047-3127-6 (pbk.: alk. paper)
    1. Spain—History—Civil War, 1936–1939—Participation, British. 2. Spain. Ejér-
  cito Popular de la República. British Batallion. 3. British—Spain—History—20th
  century. I. Title.
  DP269.47.B7H66 1998
  946.081′4′09222—dc21   98-7835